Lecture Notes in Computer Science 2347
Edited by G. Goos, J. Hartmanis, and J. van Leeuwen

Springer
*Berlin
Heidelberg
New York
Barcelona
Hong Kong
London
Milan
Paris
Tokyo*

Paul De Bra   Peter Brusilovsky
Ricardo Conejo (Eds.)

Adaptive Hypermedia and Adaptive Web-Based Systems

Second International Conference, AH 2002
Málaga, Spain, May 29-31, 2002
Proceedings

Springer

Series Editors

Gerhard Goos, Karlsruhe University, Germany
Juris Hartmanis, Cornell University, NY, USA
Jan van Leeuwen, Utrecht University, The Netherlands

Volume Editors

Paul De Bra
Eindhoven University of Technology
Department of Computer Science
P.O. Box 513, 5600 MB Einhoven, The Netherlands
E-mail: debra@win.tue.nl

Peter Brusilovsky
University of Pittsburgh, School of Information Sciences
Department of Information Science and Telecommunications
135 North Bellefield Avenue, Pittsburgh, PA 15260, USA
E-mail: peterb@mail.sis.pitt.edu

Ricardo Conejo
Universidad de Málaga, Escuela Tecnica Superior de Ingenieros en Informatica
Departamento de Lenguajes y Ciencias de la Computacion
Boulevard Luis Pasteur, 35, Málaga, Spain
E-mail: conejo@lcc.uma.es

Cataloging-in-Publication Data applied for

Die Deutsche Bibliothek - CIP-Einheitsaufnahme

Adaptive hypermedia and adaptive Web based systems : second international
conference ; proceedings / AH 2002, Malaga, Spain, May 29 - 31, 2002. Paul
de Bra ... (ed.). - Berlin ; Heidelberg ; New York ; Barcelona ; Hong Kong ;
London ; Milan ; Paris ; Tokyo : Springer, 2002
 (Lecture notes in computer science ; Vol. 2347)
 ISBN 3-540-43737-1
CR Subject Classification (1998): H.5.4, H.4, H.5, H.3

ISSN 0302-9743
ISBN 3-540-43737-1 Springer-Verlag Berlin Heidelberg New York

This work is subject to copyright. All rights are reserved, whether the whole or part of the material is
concerned, specifically the rights of translation, reprinting, re-use of illustrations, recitation, broadcasting,
reproduction on microfilms or in any other way, and storage in data banks. Duplication of this publication
or parts thereof is permitted only under the provisions of the German Copyright Law of September 9, 1965,
in its current version, and permission for use must always be obtained from Springer-Verlag. Violations are
liable for prosecution under the German Copyright Law.

Springer-Verlag Berlin Heidelberg New York
a member of BertelsmannSpringer Science+Business Media GmbH

http://www.springer.de

© Springer-Verlag Berlin Heidelberg 2002
Printed in Germany

Typesetting: Camera-ready by author, data conversion by Steingräber Satztechnik GmbH, Heidelberg
Printed on acid-free paper   SPIN 10869993   06/3142   5 4 3 2 1 0

Preface

Hypermedia as a means for accessing information was first proposed by Vannevar Bush, in 1945, in his memorable article "As We May Think". The first research that resembles what we consider as hypermedia (i.e. at least using computers with textual or graphical displays) was started much later, by great minds including Doug Engelbart (known for many inventions including the mouse) and Ted Nelson (known for inventing Xanadu, an architecture similar but superior to that of the World Wide Web). After 20 years of hypermedia research the Web started and really changed hypermedia from a small research community and mostly small stand-alone applications to a world-wide network of interconnected information sources. Hypermedia applications serving a large audience suffer greatly from the traditional "one-size-fits-all" approach of static websites. Starting in the 1990s, and essentially in parallel with the development of the Web, many research teams began to investigate ways of modeling features of the users of hypermedia systems. This has led to a number of interesting adaptation techniques and adaptive hypermedia systems. Nowadays adaptive hypermedia and the Web have really come together. Virtually all adaptive systems use the Web for both the (browser) front end and the server back end.

Following a number of successful workshops on adaptive hypermedia, the first conference on Adaptive Hypermedia and Adaptive Web-Based Systems (AH 2000) was held in Trento, Italy, in August 2000. (See Springer Lecture Notes in Computer Science, vol. 1892.) The research community has continued to grow. The Second International Conference on Adaptive Hypermedia and Adaptive Web-Based Systems (AH 2002) attracted twice as many full paper submissions, and also a large number of short papers describing ongoing research.

AH 2002 continued the tradition of earlier workshops, and the AH 2000 conference, in being a meeting place for researchers with very different backgrounds such as hypertext, user modeling, machine learning, natural language generation, information retrieval, intelligent tutoring systems, cognitive science, and Web-based education. In 2001 the community gathered at the User Modeling Conference in Sonthofen, Germany and at the ACM Hypertext Conference in Århus, Denmark for a two-session workshop on adaptive hypermedia, reported on in LNCS vol. 2266. A lot of research that was ongoing in 2001 can now be found in the full papers of the AH 2002 conference proceedings. A lot of new research is presented in short papers and posters.

The success of the conference generated a tremendous amount of work for the Program Committee members and the External Reviewers. We are immensely greatful for the effort they put into the process of selecting the very best papers. This has resulted in 33 full-paper presentations (selected from 109 submitted), 23 short-paper presentations, 30 posters, and 5 presentations at the Doctoral Consortium. All presentations can be found in this volume (except for two keynote talks, where we only have an abstract).

The success also generated an incredible amount of work for the program chair's team in Eindhoven (The Netherlands). The timely production of these proceedings from 94 contributions would not have been possible without the help of Lora Aroyo and Alexandra Cristea who worked almost round the clock to fix formatting and English language problems.

We gratefully acknowledge the help from AH 2002 cooperative societies, institutes, and sponsors. First of all we thank the University of Málaga, and especially the School of Informatics, that kindly hosted the conference. Thanks also for the economic contribution of Unicaja, and the support of the city institutions, the Excm. Ayuntamiento de Málaga, and the Exma. Diputacion Provincial de Málaga. Their sponsorship was very important. We thank doctor Chen's family, Springer-Verlag, and Kluwer for the best paper awards they supported. We also thank the Organizing Committee in Málaga for their support with web pages, scheduling, and all the arrangement they made. We would also like to thank to the cooperative societies: the Association for Computing Machinery (ACM) and the Special Interest Groups SIGART, SIGCHI, SIGIR, SIGWEB, SIGECOM; the Asociación Española Para la Inteligencia Artificial (AEPIA), the European Coordinating Committee for Artificial Intelligence (ECCAI), the EUropean Network on Intelligent TEchnologies for Smart Adaptive Systems (EUNITE), the International Artificial Intelligence in Education Society (IAED), User Modeling Inc. (UMInc.), and the International World Wide Web Conference Committee, that endorsed this conference.

The University of Málaga also provided an excellent local organization committee, which handled mailings, registrations, and all local arrangements.

Last but not least, we would like to thank the more than 200 authors from over 30 different countries who contributed to this book and conference. We thank them, not only for their valuable contribution to this research field, but also for their effort in supplying us with all the necessary information in a timely fashion.

May 2002

Paul De Bra
Peter Brusilovsky
Ricardo Conejo

Organization

AH 2002 was organized by the University of Málaga, Spain.

General Chairs

Peter Brusilovsky (University of Pittsburgh)
Francisco Triguero (Universidad de Málaga)

Program Chair

Paul De Bra (Technische Universiteit Eindhoven)

Local Organization Chair

Ricardo Conejo (Universidad de Málaga)

Doctoral Consortium Chairs

José-Luís Pérez de la Cruz (Universidad de Málaga)
Wolfgang Nejdl (Universität Hannover)

Workshops/Tutorials Chair

Carlo Strapparava (ITC-IRST, Trento)

Industry Chair

Barry Smyth (Changingworlds, and University College Dublin)

Program Committee

Elisabeth André, DFKI GmbH
Liliana Ardissono, Università degli Studi di Torino
Alexandra Cristea, Technische Universiteit Eindhoven
Fiorella De Rosis, Università di Bari
Franca Garzotto, Politecnico di Milano
Wendy Hall, University of Southampton
Lynda Hardman, CWI, Amsterdam

Nicola Henze, Institut für Technische Informatik, Hannover
Kristina Höök, Swedish Institute for Computer Science
Lewis Johnson, University of Southern California
Judy Kay, University of Sydney
Alfred Kobsa, University of California at Irvine
Paul Maglio, IBM Almaden Research Center
Mark Maybury, The MITRE Corporation
Alessandro Micarelli, Università di Roma 3
Eva Millán, Universidad de Málaga
Maria Milosavljevich, Dynamic Multimedia Pty. Ltd.
Tanja Mitrovic, University of Canterbury, New Zealand
Dunja Mladenic, J. Stefan Institute, Slovenia
Marc Nanard, LIRMM
Vittorio Scarano, Università degli Studi di Salerno
Daniel Schwabe, Universidade Católica do Rio de Janeiro
Jude Shavlik, University of Wisconsin
Marcus Specht, GMD
Myra Spliopoulou, Handelshochschule Leipzig
Oliviero Stock, ITC-IRST, Trento
Carlo Tasso, Università degli Studi di Udine
Julita Vassileva, University of Saskatchewan
Gerhard Weber, Pedagogical University Freiburg
Massimo Zancanaro, ITC-IRST, Trento

External Reviewers

Rogelio Adobbati
Demosthenes
Akoumianakis
Rudström Åsa
Janez Brank
Susan Bull
Giovanna Castellano
Ricardo Conejo
Berardina De Carolis

Ralph Deters
Josef Fink
Milos Kravcik
Donato Malerba
Lawrence Mandow
Martin Müller
Leonid Pessine
Francesco Ricci
Thomas Rist

Paola Rizzo
Ralph Schaefer
Erin Shaw
Maja Skrjanc
Carlo Strapparava
Martin Svensson
Stephan Weibelzahl

Local Organization Committee

María Victoria Belmonte
David Bueno
Eduardo Guzmán
Eva Millán
Rafael Morales
José Luís Pérez de la Cruz
Mónica Trella

Table of Contents

Invited Papers

Is Personalization All About Technology? 1
    J. Aaronson

Adaptive Linking between Text and Photos Using Common Sense Reasoning   2
    H. Lieberman, H. Liu

Resource-Adaptive Interfaces to Hybrid Navigation Systems 12
    W. Wahlster

Full Papers

Ubiquitous User Assistance in a Tourist Information Server 14
    L. Ardissono, A. Goy, G. Petrone, M. Segnan, P. Torasso

Automatic Extraction of Semantically-Meaningful Information
from the Web. 24
    J.L. Arjona, R. Corchuelo, A. Ruiz, M. Toro

Towards Open Adaptive Hypermedia 36
    C. Bailey, W. Hall, D.E. Millard, M.J. Weal

GAS: Group Adaptive System 47
    M. Barra, P. Maglio, A. Negro, V. Scarano

TV Scout: Lowering the Entry Barrier
to Personalized TV Program Recommendation 58
    P. Baudisch, L. Brueckner

Adaptivity, Adaptability, and Reading Behaviour:
Some Results from the Evaluation of a Dynamic Hypertext System 69
    K. Bontcheva

Towards Generic Adaptive Systems: Analysis of a Case Study 79
    L. Calvi, A. Cristea

A Methodology for Developing Adaptive Educational-Game Environments   90
    R.M. Carro, A.M. Breda, G. Castillo, A.L. Bajuelos

Multi-model, Metadata Driven Approach to Adaptive Hypermedia Services
for Personalized eLearning 100
    O. Conlan, V. Wade, C. Bruen, M. Gargan

Adaptation and Personalization on Board Cars:
A Framework and Its Application to Tourist Services 112
   L. Console, S. Gioria, I. Lombardi, V. Surano, I. Torre

Adaptive Authoring of Adaptive Educational Hypermedia 122
   A. Cristea, L. Aroyo

Hypermedia Presentation Adaptation on the Semantic Web 133
   F. Frasincar, G.-J. Houben

User Data Management and Usage Model Acquisition
in an Adaptive Educational Collaborative Environment 143
   E. Gaudioso, J.G. Boticario

Personalizing Assessment in Adaptive Educational Hypermedia Systems .. 153
   E. Gouli, K. Papanikolaou, M. Grigoriadou

Visual Based Content Understanding towards Web Adaptation 164
   X.-D. Gu, J. Chen, W.-Y. Ma, G.-L. Chen

Knowledge Modeling for Open Adaptive Hypermedia 174
   N. Henze, W. Nejdl

Adaptive Navigation for Learners in Hypermedia Is Scaffolded Navigation . 184
   R. Hübscher, S. Puntambekar

Pros and Cons of Controllability: An Empirical Study 193
   A. Jameson, E. Schwarzkopf

Personis: A Server for User Models 203
   J. Kay, B. Kummerfeld, P. Lauder

The Munich Reference Model for Adaptive Hypermedia Applications 213
   N. Koch, M. Wirsing

Tracking Changing User Interests through Prior-Learning of Context 223
   I. Koychev

Prediction of Navigation Profiles in a Distributed Internet Environment
through Learning of Graph Distributions 233
   D. Kukulenz

EDUCO – A Collaborative Learning Environment
Based on Social Navigation 242
   J. Kurhila, M. Miettinen, P. Nokelainen, H. Tirri

GOOSE: A Goal-Oriented Search Engine with Commonsense 253
   H. Liu, H. Lieberman, T. Selker

On Adaptability of Web Sites for Visually Handicapped People 264
    M. Macías, J. González, F. Sánchez

A Framework for Filtering and Packaging Hypermedia Documents 274
    *L.C. Martins, T.A.S. Coelho, S.D.J. Barbosa, M.A. Casanova,
    C.J.P. de Lucena*

Adaptation in an Evolutionary Hypermedia System:
Using Semantic and Petri Nets 284
    *N. Medina-Medina, L. García-Cabrera, M.J. Rodríguez-Fortiz,
    J. Parets-Llorca*

Evaluating the Effects of Open Student Models on Learning 296
    A. Mitrovic, B. Martin

Ephemeral and Persistent Personalization in Adaptive Information Access
to Scholarly Publications on the Web 306
    S. Mizzaro, C. Tasso

Fuzzy Linguistic Summaries in Rule-Based Adaptive Hypermedia Systems 317
    M.-Á. Sicilia, P. Díaz, I. Aedo, E. García

The Plight of the Navigator:
Solving the Navigation Problem for Wireless Portals................... 328
    B. Smyth, P. Cotter

Towards an Adaptive Web Training Environment
Based on Cognitive Style of Learning: An Empirical Approach 338
    *M.A.M. Souto, R. Verdin, R. Wainer, M. Madeira, M. Warpechowski,
    K. Beschoren, R. Zanella, J.S. Correa, R.M. Vicari, J.P.M. de Oliveira*

Automated Personalization of Internet News 348
    A.V. Sunderam

Short Papers

Conceptual Modeling of Personalized Web Applications 358
    S. Abrahão, J. Fons, M. González, O. Pastor

On Evaluating Adaptive Systems for Education 363
    *R. Arruabarrena, T.A. Pérez, J. López-Cuadrado, J. Gutiérrez,
    J.A. Vadillo*

Recommending Internet-Domains Using Trails and Neural Networks 368
    T. Berka, W. Behrendt, E. Gams, S. Reich

Learning Grammar with Adaptive Hypertexts: Reading or Searching? 372
    A. Brunstein, J. Waniek, A. Naumann, J.F. Krems

SIGUE: Making Web Courses Adaptive 376
  C. Carmona, D. Bueno, E. Guzman, R. Conejo

An Ontology-Guided Approach to Content Adaptation in LEO:
A Learning Environment Organizer 380
  J.W. Coffey

A Scrutable Adaptive Hypertext 384
  M. Czarkowski, J. Kay

AHA! Meets AHAM 388
  P. De Bra, A. Aerts, D. Smits, N. Stash

Adaptive Real Time Comment Generation for Sail Racing Scenarios 392
  A. Esuli, A. Cisternino, G. Pacini, M. Simi

A Web-Based Selling Agent That Maintains Customer Loyalty
through Integrative Negotiation 397
  M. Grimsley, A. Meehan

Adaptive Content
for Device Independent Multi-modal Browser Applications 401
  J. Healey, R. Hosn, S.H. Maes

Behavioral Sequences: A New Log-Coding Scheme
for Effective Prediction of Web User Accesses 406
  R. Kanawati, M. Malek

A Fuzzy-Based Approach to User Model Refinement
in Adaptive Hypermedia Systems 411
  C. Martinovska

Towards an Authoring Coach for Adaptive Web-Based Instruction 415
  J. Masthoff

Generation of Personalized Web Courses Using RBAC 419
  S. Montero, I. Aedo, P. Díaz

An Automatic Rating Technique Based on XML Document 424
  H. Mun, S. Ok, Y. Woo

Using Effective Reading Speed
to Integrate Adaptivity into Web-Based Learning 428
  M.H. Ng, W. Hall, P. Maier, R. Armstrong

A Non-invasive Cooperative Student Model 432
  T. Roselli, E. Gentile, P. Plantamura, V. Rossano, V. Saponaro

Category-Based Filtering in Recommender Systems
for Improved Performance in Dynamic Domains 436
    M. Sollenborn, P. Funk

Protecting the User from the Data:
Security and Privacy Aspects of Public Web Access 440
    A. Spalka, H. Langweg

Exploiting a Progressive Access Model to Information 444
    M. Villanova-Oliver, J. Gensel, H. Martin

Adapting to Prior Knowledge of Learners 448
    S. Weibelzahl, G. Weber

Monitoring Partial Updates in Web Pages Using Relational Learning 452
    S. Yamada, Y. Nakai

Posters

Adaptation in the Web-Based Logic-ITA 456
    D. Abraham, K. Yacef

Collaborative Radio Community 462
    P. Avesani, P. Massa, M. Nori, A. Susi

Improving Interactivity in e-Learning Systems
with Multi-agent Architecture 466
    R.A. Silveira, R.M. Vicari

Adaptive Hypermedia Made Simple
with HTML/XML Style Sheet Selectors............................... 472
    F. Bry, M. Kraus

A Framework for Educational Adaptive Hypermedia Applications 476
    F. Buendía, P. Díaz

METIORE: A Publications Reference
for the Adaptive Hypermedia Community 480
    D. Bueno, R. Conejo, C. Carmona, A.A. David

User-Driven Adaptation of e-Documents 484
    P. Carrara, D. Fogli, G. Fresta, P. Mussio

Server Independent Personalization for Effective Searching
in the World Wide Web 488
    L.N. Cassel, U. Wolz, R.E. Beck

Preventing Misleading Presentations of XML Documents:
Some Initial Proposals 492
  *A. Cawsey, E. Dempster, D. Bental, D. Pacey, H. Williams,
  L. MacKinnon, D. Marwick*

Adaptivity Conditions Evaluation for the User of Hypermedia Presentations
Built with AHA! 497
  A. Cini, J. Valdeni de Lima

Development of Adaptive Web Sites
with Usability and Accessibility Features 501
  M. Fernández de Arriba, J.A. López Brugos

An Adaptive e-Commerce System Definition 505
  F.J. García, F. Paternò, A.B. Gil

Web Site Personalization Using User Profile Information 510
  M. Goel, S. Sarkar

Who Do You Want to Be Today?
Web Personae for Personalised Information Access 514
  J.P. McGowan, N. Kushmerick, B. Smyth

Adaptive Navigation Path Previewing for Learning on the Web 518
  A. Kashihara, S. Hasegawa, J. Toyoda

A Case-Based Recommender System Using Implicit Rating Techniques ... 522
  Y. Kim, S. Ok, Y. Woo

IMAP - Intelligent Multimedia Authoring Tools for Electronic Publishing   527
  S. Kraus, A. Kröner, L. Tsaban

A Hybrid Recommender System
Combining Collaborative Filtering with Neural Network 531
  M. Lee, P. Choi, Y. Woo

An Adaptive Cooperative Web Authoring Environment 535
  A.M. Martínez-Enríquez, D. Decouchant, A.L. Morán, J. Favela

Adapting Learner Evaluation by Plans 539
  A. Martens, A.M. Uhrmacher

WETAS: A Web-Based Authoring System for Constraint-Based ITS 543
  B. Martin, A. Mitrovic

Open-Ended Adaptive System for Facilitating Knowledge Construction
in Web-Based Exploratory Learning 547
  H. Mitsuhara, Y. Ochi, Y. Yano

Adapting Web Interfaces By WHAT 551
  W. Ng, J. Yau

Considering Sensing-Intuitive Dimension to Exposition-Exemplification
in Adaptive Sequencing 556
  P. Paredes, P. Rodriguez

PlanEdit: An Adaptive Problem Solving Tool for Design 560
  M.A. Redondo, C. Bravo, M. Ortega, M.F. Verdejo

Dynamic Generation of Interactive Dialogs Based on Intelligent Agents ... 564
  M. González Rodríguez, B. López Pérez, M.P. Paule Ruíz,
  J.R. Pérez Pérez

A Simple Architecture for Adaptive Hypertext 568
  O. Signore

Adaptive Learning Environment for Teaching and Learning in WINDS 572
  M. Specht, M. Kravcik, R. Klemke, L. Pesin, R. Hüttenhain

Adaptation through Interaction Modelling in Educational Hypermedia 576
  E. Toppano

The Hybrid Model for Adaptive Educational Hypermedia 580
  M.R. Zakaria, A. Moore, H. Ashman, C. Stewart, T. Brailsford

Doctoral Consortium

Navigation Modelling in Adaptive Hypermedia 586
  P. Dolog, M. Bieliková

An Adaptive Agent Model for e-Commerce Architecture 592
  A.B. Gil, F. García, Z. Guessoum

Personalized Adaptation to Device Characteristics 598
  E. Herder, B. van Dijk

Users Modeling for Adaptive Call Centers 603
  I. Torre

The Exploratory of Personal Assistants 608
  L.T. Yong, T.E. Kong

Author Index 613

Is Personalization All About Technology?
(Keynote Talk)

Jack Aaronson

Jack Aaronson Consulting
666 Greenwich Street, Suite 409
New York, New York 10014
Jack@JackAaronson.com

Abstract. A lot of research and development has pushed the limits of personalization far beyond where they were just a few years ago. Yet the major goals of personalization continue to elude us: serving customers what they want, when they want it. Is all this research being developed with pure science in mind, or do the new technologies actually solve real business needs? In this lecture, we will discuss the business needs around personalization. We will explore which technologies have been effective, and which haven't been. We will discuss the importance of mixing technology with smart design to ensure that personalized features are intuitive and easy-to-use. We will also talk about personalization that doesn't require technology.

Adaptive Linking between Text and Photos Using Common Sense Reasoning
(Keynote Talk)

Henry Lieberman and Hugo Liu

MIT Media Laboratory
20 Ames St., E15-320G
Cambridge, MA 02139, USA
{lieber,hugo}@media.mit.edu

Abstract. In a hypermedia authoring task, an author often wants to set up meaningful connections between different media, such as text and photographs. To facilitate this task, it is helpful to have a software agent dynamically adapt the presentation of a media database to the user's authoring activities, and look for opportunities for annotation and retrieval. However, potential connections are often missed because of differences in vocabulary or semantic connections that are "obvious" to people but that might not be explicit.

ARIA (Annotation and Retrieval Integration Agent) is a software agent that acts an assistant to a user writing e-mail or Web pages. As the user types a story, it does continuous retrieval and ranking on a photo database. It can use descriptions in the story to semi-automatically annotate pictures. To improve the associations beyond simple keyword matching, we use natural language parsing techniques to extract important roles played by text, such as "who, what, where, when". Since many of the photos depict common everyday situations such as weddings or recitals, we use a common sense knowledge base, Open Mind, to fill in semantic gaps that might otherwise prevent successful associations.

1 Introduction

As digital photography becomes more popular, consumers will need better ways to organize and search their large collections of images, perhaps collected over a lifetime. Just as people compile ordinary photos into albums and scrapbooks in order to share stories with friends and family, people will want to share stories online. It is popular for users to engage in the hypermedia authoring task of sharing stories both by email and through a web page. However, there are few tools available which assist the user in their task of selecting the pictures to use to tell stories with.

ARIA [6], the software agent presented in this paper, aims to facilitate the user's storytelling task by observing the user as she tells a story, and opportunistically suggesting photos which may be relevant to what the user is typing. When a user incorporates one of the system's photo suggestions by dragging the photo into the story, our system will automatically associate with the photo any relevant keywords and phrases from the story context.

1.1 ARIA

The ARIA Photo Agent combines an email client or web page editor with a database of the user's photos, as shown in Fig. 1.

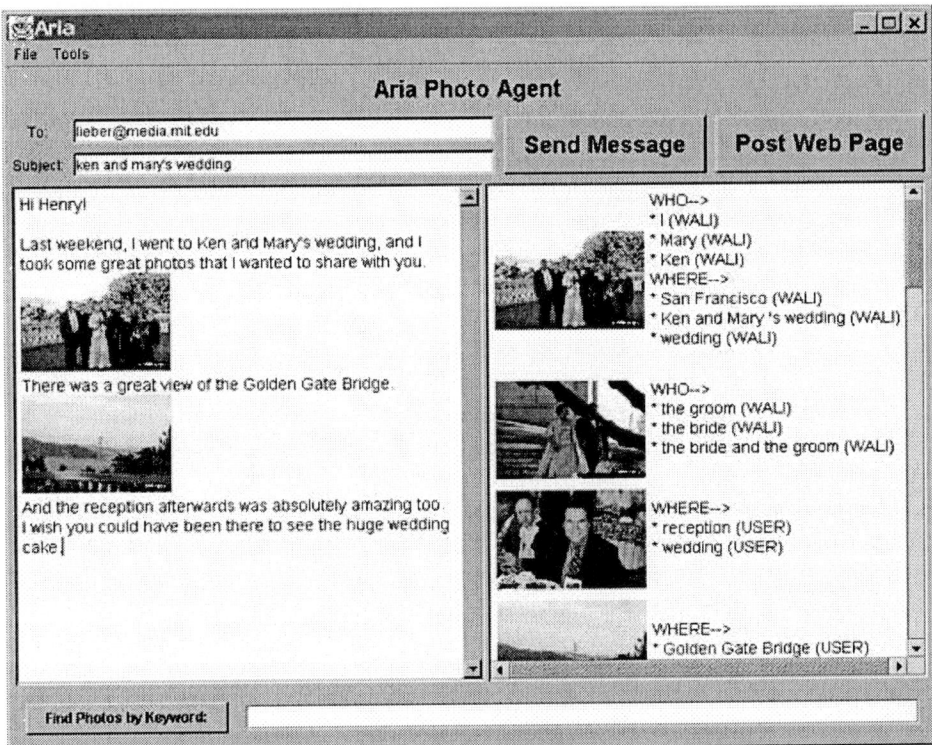

Fig. 1. A screenshot of ARIA which combines an email panel (left) with a photo database (right) that dynamically reorders itself in real-time, as the user types

Photos are automatically imported into ARIA when a digital camera flash card is inserted into the computer. Rather than requiring the user to organize photos into a directory or album structure, our system tags photos with text annotations, organized into "who, what, where, when" for each picture. The user composes an email or web page in the text client on the left. Whenever a photo is dragged from the photo pane into the text pane, new annotations are automatically associated with the photo. These annotations consist of people, places, things, and events, and are extracted from the story text adjacent to the photo in the text. Users can also edit and add to the annotations associated with a photo by double-clicking on that photo.

As the user goes about his authoring task, the photo agent monitors what he types, and in real-time, the agent reorders the annotated photos in the photo pane to suggest photos that might be relevant to the user. A photo is deemed relevant if any of its annotations can be potentially linked with the current focus of the text, either through explicit keywords, or through a variety of semantic connections.

1.2 Our Approach

ARIA goes beyond the naïve approach of suggesting photos by a simple match between keywords in a photo's annotations with keywords in the story. Such an approach often misses potential connections between keywords with different vocabulary, or keywords that exhibit *implicit semantic connectedness*. By this, we mean that it may be obvious to a person that two different keywords are conceptually related, such as "bride" and "wedding;" however, computer programs cannot usually understand such connections. Our approach remedies the problems associated with naïve keyword matching by applying natural language parsing techniques to the annotation process, and commonsense reasoning to the retrieval of pictures.

To address the issue of different vocabulary, we apply natural language techniques to the annotation process such that we extract concepts rather than keywords from the text. Unlike keywords, concepts are not sensitive to morphological variation, such as "bridesmaids" versus "bridesmaid," or abbreviations or near synonyms, such as "LA" versus "Los Angeles." We map keywords into concepts using a morphological tool and abbreviation and near synonym dictionary.

In cases where potential connections are missed due to keywords that are related semantically rather than explicitly, "common sense" can help. Consider a photo annotated with "bride." Knowing some everyday knowledge about the world, ARIA can infer concepts closely related to "bride" such as "groom," "wedding," "flower girl," and "wife." These concepts are related socially, spatially, and temporally to the original concept. Expanding the original annotation with semantically related concepts gives the software agent more opportunities to recommend relevant photos to the user.

1.3 Shaping Authoring Behavior

ARIA assists the user in her authoring task by annotating photos with descriptions from the story, and dynamically adapting the presentation of the photos while the user writes the story.

Our preliminary experience with ARIA shows that the opportunistic presentation of photos can even shape the user's authoring behavior. While a user may begin the authoring task with a predisposition to tell the story a certain way, she may change her mind if the agent suggests an interesting photo at an unexpected moment. This might cause her to recall a memory, think differently, and tell the story differently. As the story unfolds, the presentation of photos will adapt accordingly, and if the agent suggests another interesting photo, the user may again revise her authoring behavior, and so on. The interaction between ARIA and the user may be able to stimulate interesting changes in the user's authoring behavior.

This paper is structured as follows: First, we discuss the source and nature of the corpus of common sense knowledge used by ARIA. Second, we present how natural language processing can incorporate commonsense knowledge in the automated annotation mechanism. Third, we discuss how commonsense can be used with shallow inference in the adaptive retrieval mechanism. Fourth, we compare our approach to related work. The paper concludes with a discussion of the benefits and limitations of our approach, and the application of commonsense to other domains.

2 Open Mind: A Source of Common Sense

The source of the commonsense knowledge used by ARIA is the Open Mind Commonsense Knowledge Base (OMCS) [11] – an endeavor at the MIT Media Laboratory that allows a web-community of teachers to collaboratively contribute to a knowledge base of "common sense." OMCS contains over 400,000 semi-structured English sentences, each of which represents a simple fact about the everyday world. Some examples of entries in the knowledge base are as follows:
1. Something you may find in a restaurant is a waiter.
2. Something that might come after a wedding is a wedding reception.
3. People get married at weddings.

OMCS is often compared with its more famous counterpart, the CYC Knowledge Base [5]. CYC contains over 1,000,000 hand-entered rules of common sense. The difference between OMCS and CYC is that CYC is meant for a more formal type of reasoning using logic, while OMCS's English sentence representation may not be constrained enough for formal logic. Even though OMCS is noisier than CYC and inherits the ambiguities associated with its natural language representation, it is still suitable to our task because we only need binary semantic relations to make adaptive linking work. This can be achieved through shallow techniques.

3 Common Sense for Parsing

When a user drags and drops a photo into the story, the description of the photo given in the story is used to automatically annotate the photo. The annotations extracted from the text are the semantically important concepts of person, place, thing, and event, which can be used to answer the "who, what, and where" questions about a photo. For the natural language parser to correctly identify these semantic types, it needs dictionaries of concepts falling under each type.

To recognize people's names, we obtain a dictionary of first names from the Web, and combine that with regular expressions to recognize full names. Geographical places are also mined from databases on the Web and added to the parser's semantic lexicon. As for everyday places, thing, and events, we extract dictionaries from Open

Mind. The extraction is fairly straightforward, because many of the sentence patterns, or ontological relations, found in Open Mind sufficiently constrain the semantic types of the slots.

The result is a lexicon of words and phrases with their associated semantic type. The natural language parser uses this to enhance a syntactic parse tree with semantic and thematic phrasal tags. The resulting tree represents an event structure using an ontology based on the work of Jackendoff [3]. Below is an example of a sentence and its parse.

Sentence:
> Last weekend, I went to Ken and Mary's wedding in San Francisco, and I took gorgeous pictures of the Golden Gate Bridge.

Event Structure Parse:
```
(ROOT   (ASSERTION   (TIME   ARIA_DATESPAN{03m09d2002y-
03m10d2002y}  )  ,  (ASSERTION  (PERSON  I  )  (ACTION
went  (PROPERTY  to  (EVENT  (THING  (PERSON  Ken  and  )
(PERSON  Mary  's  )  )  wedding  )  )  (PROPERTY  in  (PLACE
San  Francisco  )  )  )  ,  and  (ASSERTION  (PERSON  I  )
(ACTION  took  (THING  (THING  gorgeous  pictures  )
(PROPERTY  of  (PLACE  the  Golden  Gate  Bridge  )  )  )  )
) ) . ) )
```

As shown in this example, knowledge mined from Open Mind and the Web allows a semantically meaningful parse to be produced. ARIA uses heuristics to decide which people, places, things, and events are relevant to the photo and should be used to annotate the photo placed adjacent to this sentence in the story.

4 Commonsense Inference for Adaptive Retrieval

ARIA uses commonsense relations mined out of Open Mind to expand annotations with semantically connected concepts that make adaptive retrieval of photos possible. To do this, a resource was automatically constructed from Open Mind by applying sentence patterns to the corpus, and extracting simple predicate argument structures (usually a binary relation). Arguments are normalized into syntactically neat concepts, and these concepts, together with the predicate relations, are used to construct a spreading activation network of nodes and directed edges. The edges between the concept nodes in the network represent the notion of semantic connectedness. The task of expanding an annotation with its related concepts is modeled as spreading activation over the network. Another way to think about spreading activation is as inference directed by the strength of relations between concepts (edge weight).

In this section, we describe how a subset of the knowledge in OMCS is extracted and structured to be useful to annotation expansion, and how spreading activation can return semantically connected concepts. Examples of actual runs of the concept expansion are given.

4.1 Extracting Concepts and Relations from OMCS

The first step of extracting predicate argument structures from OMCS is to apply a fixed set of mapping rules to the sentences in Open Mind. Each mapping rule captures a different commonsense relation that may be valuable to facilitating the retrieval task in our problem domain. The relations of interest fall under the following general categories of knowledge:

1. Classification: A dog is a pet
2. Spatial: San Francisco is part of California
3. Scene: Things often found together are: restaurant, food, waiters, tables, seats
4. Purpose: A vacation is for relaxation; Pets are for companionship
5. Causality: After the wedding ceremony comes the wedding reception.
6. Emotion: A pet makes you feel happy; Rollercoasters make you feel excited and scared.

In our extraction system, mapping rules can be found under all of these categories. To explain mapping rules, we give an example of knowledge from the aforementioned Scene category:

```
somewhere THING1 can be is PLACE1
somewherecanbe
THING1, PLACE1
0.5, 0.1
```

This rule contains a sentence pattern with the variables THING1 and PLACE1 binding to some text blob, and the name of the predicate that this relation should map to. Text blobs are normalized into concepts using a sieve-like grammar. The pair of numbers on the last line represents the confidence weights given to forward relation (left to right), and backward relation (right to left), respectively, for this predicate relation. This also corresponds to the weights associated with the directed edges between the nodes, THING1 and PLACE1 in the spreading activation network representation.

It is important to distinguish the value of the forward relation on a particular rule, as compared to a backward relation. For example, let us consider the fact, "somewhere a bride can be is at a wedding." Given the annotation "bride," it may be very useful to return "wedding." However, given the annotation "wedding," it is arguably not as useful to return all the things found at a wedding such as "bride," "groom," "wedding cake," "priest," etc. For our problem domain, we will generally penalize the direction in a relation that returns hyponymic (taxonomic child) concepts as opposed to hypernymic ones (taxonomic parent).

Approximately 20 mapping rules are applied to all the sentences (400,000+) in the OMCS corpus, and a set of 50,000 predicate argument relations is extracted. These structures are compiled into a spreading activation network consisting of 30,000 concept nodes and 160,000 direct edges. The average branching factor is 5.

4.2 Expansion as Spreading Activation

In spreading activation, the origin node is the annotation or concept we wish to expand and it is the first node to be activated. Next, the nodes one hop away from the origin node are activated, then two levels away, and so on. Nodes will continue to be activated so long as their activation score meets the activation threshold, which is a number between 0 and 1.0. Given nodes A and B, where A has one edge pointing to B, the activation score (AS) of B can be constructed:

$$AS(B) = AS(A) * weight(edge(A,B))$$

When no more nodes are activated, we have found all the relevant concepts that expand the input concept. One problem that can arise with spreading activation is that nodes that are activated two or more hops away from the origin node may quickly lose relevance, causing the search to lose focus. This can be due to noise. Because concept nodes do not make distinctions between different word senses, it is possible that a node represents many different word senses. Therefore, activating more than one hop away risks exposure to noise. Although associating weights with the edges provides some measure of relevance, these weights form a homogenous class for all edges of a common predicate (recall that the weights came from mapping rules).

We identify two opportunities to re-weight the graph to improve relevance: reinforcement and popularity. Both are relatively common techniques associated with spreading activation, but we motivate their explanations in the context of common sense.

Reinforcement
We make the observation that if the concept "bride" is connected to "groom," both directly, and through "wedding," then "groom" is more semantically relevant to "bride" because two paths connect them. This is the idea of *reinforcement*. Looking at this another way, if three or more concepts are mutually connected, as all the concepts about a wedding might be, they form a cluster, and any two concepts in the cluster have enhanced relevance because the other concepts provide additional paths for reinforcement. Applying this, we re-weight the graph by detecting clusters and increasing the weight on edges within the cluster.

Popularity
The second observation we make is that if an origin node A has a path through node B, and node B has 100 children, then each of node B's children are less likely to be relevant to node A than if node B had had 10 children. This is a common notion used in spreading activation, often referred to as "fan-out" [10].

We refer to nodes with a large branching factor as being popular. It so happens that popular nodes in our graph tend to be very common concepts in commonsense, or tend to have many different word senses, or word contexts. This causes its children to be in general, less relevant.

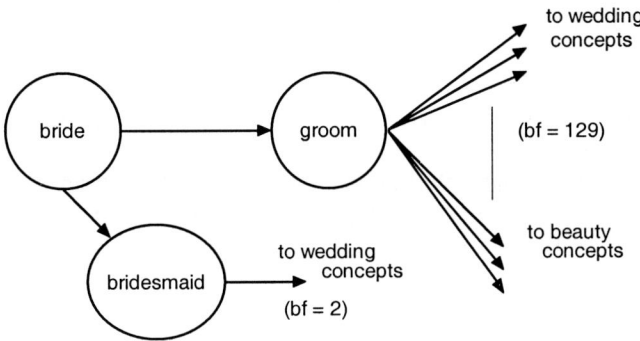

Fig. 2. Illustrating the negative effects of popularity

As illustrated in Figure 2, the concept *bride* may lead to *bridesmaid* and *groom*. Whereas *bridesmaid* is a more specific concept, not appearing in many contexts, *groom* is a less specific concept. In fact, different senses and contexts of the word can mean "the groom at a wedding," or "grooming a horse," or "he is well-groomed." This causes *groom* to have a much larger branching factor.

Despite being a knowledge base of common sense, there seems to be more value associated with more specific concepts than general ones. To apply this principle, we visit each node and discount the weights on each of its edges based on the following heuristic (• and • are constants):

$$newWeight = oldWeight * discount$$

$$discount = \frac{1}{\log(\alpha * branchingFactor + \beta)}$$

4.3 Example

Below is actual output of the concept expansion program using an activation threshold of 0.1.

```
>>> expand("bride")
('wedding', '0.3662') ('woman', '0.2023')
('ball', '0.1517') ('tree', '0.1517')
('snow covered mountain', '0.1517')
('flower', '0.1517') ('lake', '0.1517')
('cake decoration', '0.1517') ('grass', '0.1517')
('groom', '0.1517') ('tender moment', '0.1517')
('veil', '0.1517') ('tuxedo', '0.1517')
('wedding dress', '0.1517') ('sky', '0.1517')
('hair', '0.1517') ('wedding boquet', '0.1517')
```

5 Related Work

The state-of-the-art in image annotation for consumer photography is probably best represented by Kuchinsky et. al. [4]. Kuchinsky does not observationally learn annotations from text descriptions, but it does use some image analysis to propose annotations. Budzik and Hammond's Watson [1] is an agent that observes user actions and automates retrieval, but does not consider annotation. Neither of the aforementioned programs provides real-time recommendations of images or adaptively links text with images through semantic connectedness.

The concept expansion mechanism proposed here is not necessarily a new approach, but performing concept expansion with commonsense relations *is* new. In the past, other dictionary-like resources such as lexical semantic relations [12], and keyword co-occurrence statistics [9] have been used. The limitations of these resources have been that for the most part, they operate on a word, rather that concept level. In addition, the size and variety of their relational ontologies have been a limiting factor. For example, OMCS gives us numerous relations including temporal, social, and emotion but a resource like WordNet [2] can only give us a small set of nymic relations. Represented as semi-structured English sentences, it is also relatively easy to augment the relational ontology, and easy to update.

6 Conclusion

In this paper, we presented ARIA, a software agent that facilitates a hypermedia authoring task. While the user tells a story in an email client, the agent observes the text pane and continuously presents suggestions of photos that may be relevant to the context of the developing story. By using a semantically enriched parsing technique on description text, the agent is able to automatically annotate photos used in the story with semantically important concepts like the "who, what, and where" of the photo. Then using concepts and relations extracted from Open Mind, the photo recommendation mechanism is able to adaptively present not only photos whose annotations explicitly match the text, but also photos whose annotations exhibit implicit semantic connectedness to the text.

In user testing [6], we saw not only that ARIA adapts to the user, but that the user adapts to ARIA. Often a user's typing will bring up some photos relevant to the user's current text, but that also trigger the user's memory, encouraging him or her to explain related pictures in subsequent text, triggering new picture retrieval. This *mutual adaptation* is an important characteristic of adaptive systems, and our users particularly liked the continual interplay between their story and ARIA's suggestions.

Another example of a system that successfully integrates common sense knowledge into an interactive application is Erik Mueller's Common Sense Calendar [8]. It makes "sanity checks" such as helping you avoid situations like inviting a vegetarian friend to a steak house for dinner. We think applications like this, and ARIA, show that it is not necessary to find complete solutions to the common sense reasoning problem in order to make common sense knowledge useful in an interactive application. All you have to do is use a little common sense.

References

1. Budzik, J. and Hammond, K. J.: User Interactions with Everyday Applications as Context for Just-in-Time Information Access, ACM Conf. Intelligent User Interfaces (IUI 2000), ACM Press, New York, (Jan. 2000), pp.44-51.
2. Fellbaum, C. (Ed.): WordNet: An Electronic Lexical Database. MIT Press, Cambridge, MA. (1998).
3. Jackendoff, R.: Semantic structures. Cambridge, MA: MIT Press, (1990).
4. Kuchinsky, A., Pering, C., Creech, M. L., Freeze, D., Serra, B., and Gwizdka, J.: FotoFile: a consumer multimedia organization and retrieval system, ACM Conference on Human-Computer Interface, (CHI-99) Pages 496 – 503, Pittsburgh, (May 1999).
5. Lenat, D.: The dimensions of context-space, Cycorp technical report, (1998), www.cyc.com.
6. Lieberman, H., Rosenzweig, E., and Singh, P.: Aria: An Agent For Annotating And Retrieing Images. IEEE Computer, (July 2001), pp. 57-61.
7. Minsky, M.: Commonsense-Based Interfaces. Communications of the ACM. Vol. 43, No. 8 (August, 2000), Pages 66-73
8. Mueller, E. T.: A calendar with common sense. In Proceedings of the 2000 International Conference on Intelligent User Interfaces, 198-201. New York: Association for Computing Machinery. (2000).
9. Peat, H. J. and Willett, P.: The limitations of term co-occurrence data for query expansion in document retrieval systems. Journal of the ASIS, 42(5), (1991), 378--383.
10. Salton G. and Buckley C.: On the Use of Spreading Activation Methods in Automatic Information Retrieval, In Proc. 11th Ann. Int. ACM SIGIR Conf. on R&D in Information Retrieval (ACM), (1988), 147-160.
11. Singh, P.: The Public Acquisition of Commonsense Knowledge. AAAI Spring Symposium, Stanford University, Palo Alto, CA, (2002).
12. Voorhees, E.: Query expansion using lexical-semantic relations. In Proceedings of ACM SIGIR Intl. Conf. on Research and Development in Information Retrieval. (1994) 61-69.

Resource-Adaptive Interfaces to Hybrid Navigation Systems
(Keynote Talk)

Wolfgang Wahlster

DFKI - German Research Center for Artificial Intelligence
Stuhlsatzenhausweg 3
D-66123 Saarbrücken, Germany
wahlster@dfki.de
www.dfki.de/~wahlster/

We present the hybrid navigation systems REAL [1] and SmartKom [2] that combine various positioning technologies to determine the user's location in outdoor and indoor situations and that adapt the multimodal presentation of spatial information to the limited technical resources of various output devices and to the limited cognitive resources of the user.

We distinguish three different classes of resource sensitive processes: (a) resource adapted processes, (b) resource adaptive processes and (c) resource adapting processes [1]. Resource adapted processes have been optimized in advance for restricted resources that are well-known and follow regular patterns. The quality of their results remains constant for a given input. In contrast, resource adaptive and resource adapting processes can handle varying resource restrictions. Therefore, their results depend on the available resources during runtime. Resource adaptive processes rely on a single strategy to react to varying resources, whereas resource adapting processes select among a number of strategies on a meta-cognitive level to comply with different resource situations. REAL uses both resource adaptive and resource adapting processes to generate multimodal space descriptions.

Personal navigation systems that extend beyond today's use in cars will play a major role in the future. Especially pedestrians will benefit from getting localized information on mobile devices anywhere at any time. One essential issue in this context is the switch between various positioning technologies, e. g., from outdoor systems based on GPS or cell-based positioning based on GSM or UMTS to indoor systems based on infrared or Bluetooth and vice versa. Ideally, a system should conceal the switching between these technologies from the user entirely. In addition, the presentation of spatial information has to be adapted to the specific output devices that may be used. This includes adaptations to the screen size, resolution, and color.

In terms of cognitive resources we take into account the user's actual travelling speed, his familiarity with the environment, and the time pressure in the current situation. Special adaptation services are provided when navigation is not the primary goal of the user. Additional tasks that have to be performed in parallel such as carrying heavy luggage or answering a telephone call while walking generate additional stress that has to be compensated by the system. Our system already attempts to achieve this during the process of way finding. Instead of choosing the shortest route, it tries to avoid complex instructions at the cost of a slightly longer route, thus minimizing the additional cognitive load on the user.

SmartKom is a multimodal dialogue system that combines speech, gesture, and facial expressions for input and output. SmartKom-Mobile uses a PDA as a front end. Currently, the iPAQ Pocket PC with a dual-slot PC card expansion pack is used as a hardware platform. It can be added to a car navigation system or carried by a pedestrian. SmartKom-Mobile provides personalized mobile services. Examples of value-added services include route planning and interactive navigation through a city.

SmartKom provides an anthropomorphic and affective user interface through its personification of an interface agent. Understanding of spontaneous speech is combined with recognition of natural gestures and facial expressions. One of the major scientific goals of SmartKom is to design new computational methods for the seamless integration and mutual disambiguation of multimodal input and output on a semantic and pragmatic level. SmartKom is based on the situated delegation-oriented dialogue paradigm, in which the user delegates a task to a virtual communication assistant, visualized as a life-like character on a graphical display. The life-like character designed for the SmartKom system is called "Smartakus". The "i"- shape of Smartakus reminds one of the "i" often used as a sign that directs people to information kiosks. The display of the 3D character Smartakus is adapted to the user's viewing angle.

SmartKom's interaction style breaks radically with the traditional desktop metaphor. SmartKom is based on the situated delegation-oriented dialogue paradigm (SDDP):The user delegates a task to a virtual communication assistant, visible on the graphical display. Since for more complex tasks this cannot be done in a simple command-and-control style, a collaborative dialogue between the user and the agent, visualized as a life-like character, elaborates the specification of the delegated task and possible plans of the agent to achieve the user's intentional goal. In contrast to task-oriented dialogues, in which the user carries out a task with the help of the system, with SDDP the user delegates a task to an agent and helps the agent, where necessary, in the execution of the task. The interaction agent accesses various web and navigation services on behalf of the user, collates the results, and presents them to the user.

REAL and SmartKom represent, reason about, and exploit models of the user, his current cognitive state, his task, the situational context, and the available technical resources and media in order to generate situation- and user-adaptive multimodal route descriptions.

References

1. Baus, J., Krüger, A., Wahlster, W.(2002): A Resource-Adaptive Mobile Navigation System. In: Proceedings of the 2002 International Conference on Intelligent User Interfaces (IUI'02), ACM Press, pp. 15- 22, ISBN 1-58113-459-2
2. Wahlster, W.,Reithinger N., Blocher, A. (2001): SmartKom: Multimodal Communication with a Life-Like Character. In: Proceedings of Eurospeech 2001, 7th European Conference on Speech Communication and Technology, Aalborg, Denmark, September 2001, Vol. 3, pp. 1547 – 1550.

Ubiquitous User Assistance in a Tourist Information Server

Liliana Ardissono, Anna Goy, Giovanna Petrone,
Marino Segnan, and Pietro Torasso

Dip. Informatica, Università di Torino, Corso Svizzera 185, I-10149 Torino, Italy
{liliana, goy, giovanna, marino, torasso}@di.unito.it
http://www.di.unito.it/~seta

Abstract. This paper discusses the provision of ubiquitous services for desktop and handheld interfaces. The focus of the paper is on the interactive agenda offered by INTRIGUE, a tourist information server which assists the user in the organization of a tour by providing personalized recommendations of tourist attractions and helping the user to schedule her itinerary. The interactive agenda can be accessed both remotely, by interacting with the central server, and locally to the user's device.

1 Background

With the current expansion of wireless communications, several Web-based services have been extended to the mobile phone market, with special attention to context-awareness and to the adaptation of the user interface to the peculiarities of the various handset devices. However, only very basic, "real-time" services, such as the consultation of stock quotes, are accessed by mobile phone users, because wireless connections are extremely expensive. In contrast, the applications that can be executed locally to the device, such as music and games, are appreciated by a broader customer base. Although the situation might change in the future, at the current stage applications should rely on wireless network connections for the tasks that really need a remote connection [1].

In our recent research, we have addressed the design of system architectures for the development of services accessible both from desktop environments and handset devices, via remote connections to central servers, or local execution of tasks within the devices themselves. In these applications, persistent interaction contexts have to be managed to support the synchronization of the user's activities when switching from one device to the other [2]. We experimented our ideas with INTRIGUE (INteractive TouRist Information GUidE), a prototype information service presenting tourist information on Web browsers and WAP phones. This paper describes INTRIGUE's interactive agenda, which supports the tour scheduling by generating optimized itineraries on the basis of the user's temporal constraints, the attractions' opening times and their location. In this application, the persistent interaction context is represented by the user's itinerary, which can be consulted and modified during different sessions. The

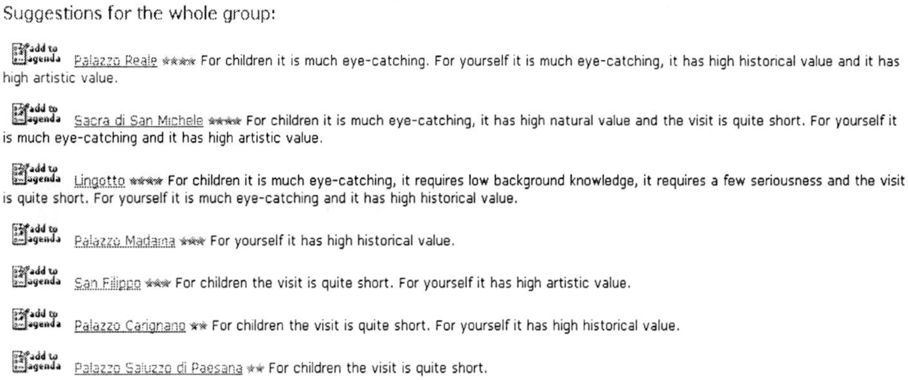

Suggestions for the whole group:

[add to agenda] Palazzo Reale ★★★★ For children it is much eye-catching. For yourself it is much eye-catching, it has high historical value and it has high artistic value.

[add to agenda] Sacra di San Michele ★★★★ For children it is much eye-catching, it has high natural value and the visit is quite short. For yourself it is much eye-catching and it has high artistic value.

[add to agenda] Lingotto ★★★★ For children it is much eye-catching, it requires low background knowledge, it requires a few seriousness and the visit is quite short. For yourself it is much eye-catching and it has high historical value.

[add to agenda] Palazzo Madama ★★★ For yourself it has high historical value.

[add to agenda] San Filippo ★★★ For children the visit is quite short. For yourself it has high artistic value.

[add to agenda] Palazzo Carignano ★★ For children the visit is quite short. For yourself it has high historical value.

[add to agenda] Palazzo Saluzzo di Paesana ★★ For children the visit is quite short.

Fig. 1. Recommendation of attractions generated by INTRIGUE for a Web browser.

interactive agenda is downloadable and can run both in remote modality, by interacting with the tourist information server, and local modality, where the user can re-schedule her itinerary, without connecting to the server. This facility supports a quick revision of itineraries during the tour, therefore extending the role of our system, from tourist information service to interactive tourist guide, supporting the user during the visit of the attractions.

The paper is organized as follows: Section 2 provides an overview of IN-TRIGUE. Sections 3 and 4 describe the interactive agenda service and the ubiquitous access facilities offered by our system. Section 5 sketches the system architecture and the dynamic generation techniques exploited to manage the user interface. Finally, Section 6 discusses some related work and concludes the paper.

2 Overview of the System

INTRIGUE provides multilingual information about tourist attractions and services, such as accommodation and food, in a geographical area. The main goal is assisting the user in the organization of a tour, by taking into account the possibly conflicting preferences of a group of people traveling together; for instance, a family with adults and children. Our current prototype presents information about the city of Torino and the surrounding Piedmont area, in Italian and in English [5]. The system supports the search for tourist attractions by offering orthogonal criteria, such as category-based and geographical search: e.g., the user can look for churches in Torino city, buildings in the area around Torino, and so forth. The search queries are created by exploiting a graphical interface hiding the details of the query specification language: the user browses a taxonomy of categories and selects the desired geographical area by clicking on a map, or by following suitable hypertextual links, depending on the device she is using.

Personalization strategies are applied to recommend the attractions best suiting the preferences of the tourist group. For instance, Fig. 1 shows a recommendation list generated by our system: each item is a hypertextual link, which the

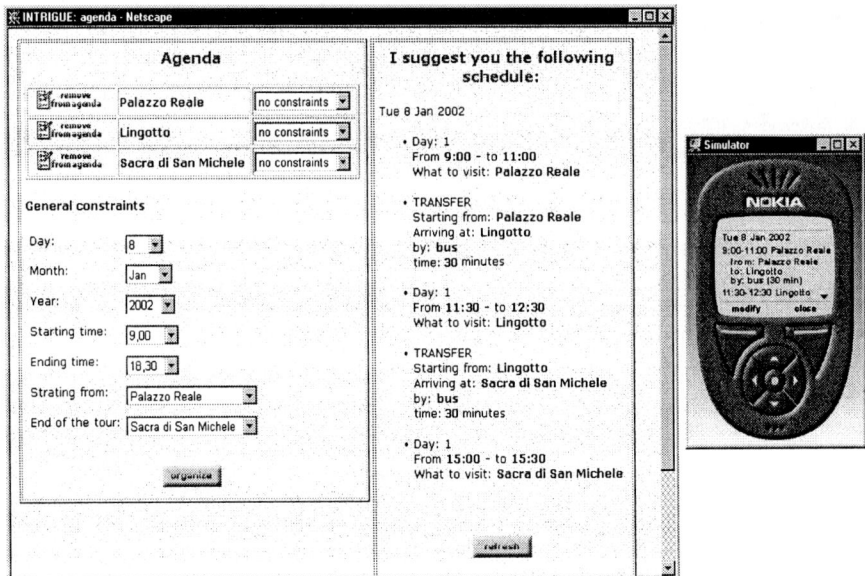

Fig. 2. Specification of constraints and itinerary presentation in the interactive agenda: (a) desktop and (b) handheld interfaces.

user can follow to view a page presenting the most relevant information about the attraction. Moreover, each item is associated with a pictorial representation of its recommendation degree (stars) and, if relevant, with an explanation of the system's suggestion. Finally, an "add to agenda" button enables the user to include the item in the list of attractions to be scheduled in her itinerary.

3 The Interactive Agenda

The interactive agenda can be accessed by clicking a "View Agenda" button available in the recommendation pages. Given the set of attractions selected by the user, the agenda supports the specification of various types of constraints: e.g., day of visit, arrival/departure time and location, preferred time of visit. On the basis of the user's choices, the system tries to generate an itinerary that includes as many selected attractions as possible, complies with the attractions' opening times and the user preferences, and minimizes the overall transfer time.[1] The presentation of an itinerary specifies, for each attraction, the estimated transfer time to reach it, the time of the visit and its expected duration.

---

[1] The system applies constraint-solving techniques for the generation of candidate solutions, which are then compared for the selection of the one to be suggested on the basis of their total transfer times. The straight application of "shortest path" algorithms, such as the sales traveler one, is not possible, as they do not guarantee that the generated permutations of attractions satisfy temporal constraints like those concerning the opening time of attractions.

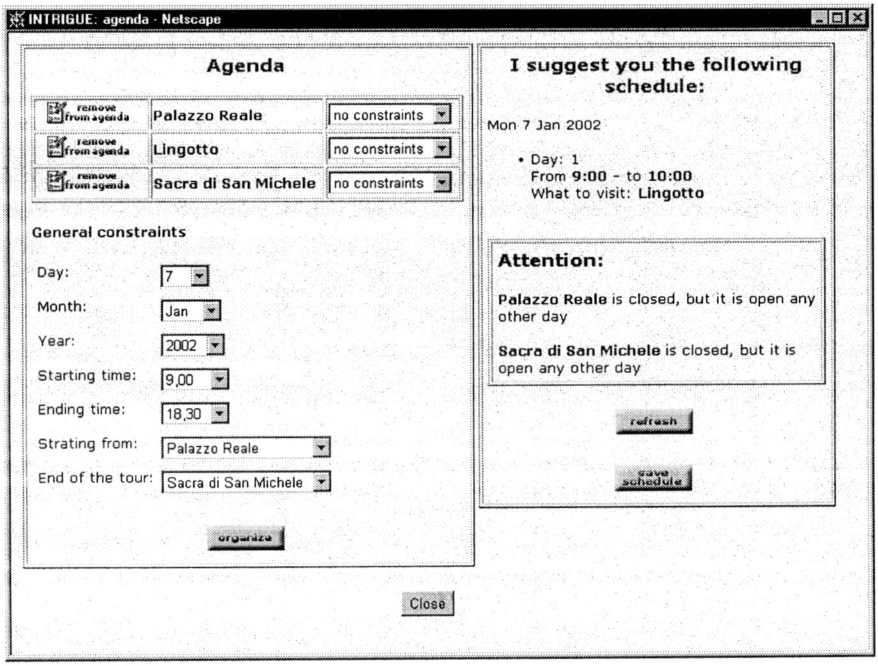

Fig. 3. Failure in the organization of an itinerary.

Figures 2.(a) and 2.(b) present an itinerary for visiting Palazzo Reale, the Lingotto building and the Sacra di San Michele, in a situation where the user asked to start the visit from the Royal Palace and to end it at the Sacra. The presentation is different for desktop and handheld interfaces: in the former case, the system shows the user's constraints and the itinerary in the same page. In the latter, for space limitations, this information is compactly presented, in separate pages.

If the system fails in scheduling some of the selected attractions, it explains the problem and provides useful information to re-schedule the itinerary. For instance, the failure shown in Fig. 3 is due to the fact that most tourist attractions are closed on Mondays. The user can solve the conflict by changing her selections. For example, she could try to visit other attractions, such as the parks, or she could modify her constraints, e.g., by changing the day of the tour. The interactive agenda enables the user to save an itinerary for further consideration ("save schedule" button in Fig. 3).

4 Ubiquitous Interaction with INTRIGUE

As our system can be accessed by exploiting desktop computers and mobile phones, the user can use it during the organization of a tour and during the tour itself, in order to view the tourist catalog and generate itineraries for the visit of

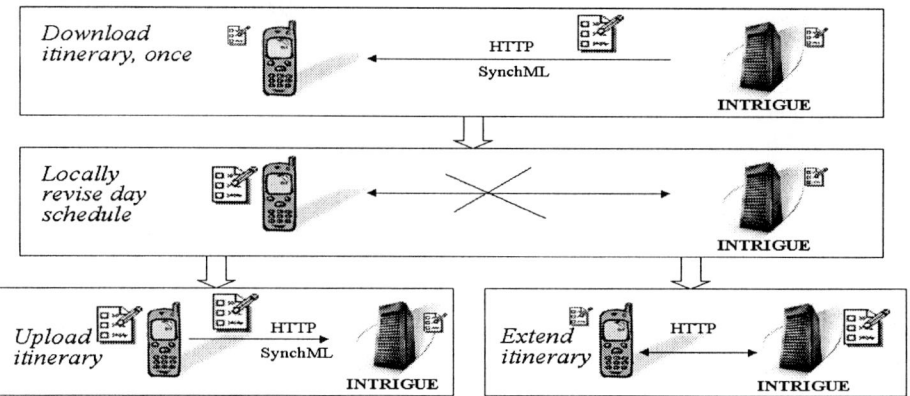

Fig. 4. Local interaction with INTRIGUE.

attractions. Moreover, the possibility to store the user's itinerary supports the any time revision of previously generated itineraries. However, the peculiarity of our system is the possibility to access some of its services locally to the user's device, which enables the access to the interactive agenda without a continuous connection to the central server. In this way, the user can consult her itinerary and possibly re-schedule it, by exploiting the mobile phone in a similar fashion to the way people use to run games on such devices.

The remote interaction with INTRIGUE is similar for desktop and handset devices: the user browses the catalog, selects tourist attractions to be visited and schedules itineraries. The central server stores the interaction context, which can include the user's itinerary, her last search query and maintains the information about the list of attractions satisfying the query (e.g., buildings around Torino, corresponding to the recommendation list shown in Fig. 1). Moreover, the connection to the tourist information database supports the execution of further queries to retrieve new items that can be added to the agenda.

The local access to the services deserves further discussion. A possible scenario of a local use of the agenda is shown in Fig. 4: the user connects to the remote server, downloads a previously generated itinerary on her handset and closes the interaction. Then, she opens the agenda to view and possibly reschedule her itinerary on the handset, in local modality. When the user later on connects again to the server, local changes to the itinerary are sent back to the networked data repository for permanent storage.[2] In local access modality, the interactive agenda exploits its own information resources: the itinerary generation and scheduling capabilities are offered, but the user cannot add new items to the agenda, as only the information about the previous selections is available on the device. Therefore, if the user wants to consider new tourist attractions, she

---

[2] In the figure, the currently used agenda is shown by a medium size icon; the possibly out of date one is shown as a small icon.

has to connect to the central server, by clicking a "modify → extend itinerary" link available in the interface of the handheld interactive agenda.

The support of local and remote connections to the interactive agenda relies on the storage of an interaction context aimed at managing subsequent accesses to the system as portions of the same session.

- On the one hand, when saving an itinerary, the system also saves the information about the attractions selected by the user for further consultation. Moreover, the user's search query, representing the last focus of attention during the interaction, is saved. This information enables the user to connect to the central server for retrieving new items without browsing the catalog from the beginning. For instance, if the user initially searched for the buildings around Torino and wants to visit more places than those available in the agenda, she can directly access the recommendation page where the items are available; see Fig. 1.
- On the other hand, when the user downloads an itinerary, the network connection is needed to download the itinerary and the information about the selected tourist attractions, which permanently reside in the database of the INTRIGUE server. After this synchronization phase, the agenda runs locally, without requiring further connections to the central server.

5 Technical Aspects

5.1 Architecture

INTRIGUE is based on the architecture described in [4], which has been extended to manage the interaction with mobile phones by exploiting the WAP protocol: we used the Nokia mobile phone simulator for our experiments. The generation of the device-dependent user interface relies on the exploitation of standard XML-based techniques; the local execution of the interactive agenda on handset devices is based on the exploitation of Java Micro Edition and of the synchronization facilities offered by such environment (SynchML [14]).

5.2 Generation of the User Interface

The User Interface (UI) of INTRIGUE can be viewed as a sequence of dynamically generated pages. The generation of each page is performed according to four distinct steps, listed in the following. While the first three steps are independent of the device the UI is implemented on, the last one generates the appropriate UI on the basis of the user's device.

- *Selection of the information to be presented.* Different information is selected for the various page types generated by the system. In a recommendation page (see Fig. 1) the selected information consists of a list of attractions, sorted on the basis of the tourist group's preferences. In a page describing an attraction, such as the one in Fig. 5, this information includes one or

Fig. 5. Portion of a page prefenting a tourist attraction for desktop interface.

more sets of features describing the attraction from different points of view. Finally, the information selected for the agenda includes the list of attractions chosen by the user and the itinerary calculated by the system.

– *Generation of linguistic descriptions.* The internal representation of the selected information is translated to natural language by exploiting efficient template-based NLG techniques supporting the production of simple sentences in Italian and English [3].

– *Generation of the content structure of the page.* A DTD defines the logical structure of the various types of page the system can produce; navigation pages, presentation pages, agenda pages, and so forth. An XML object (i.e., an XML instance document) representing the personalized content of the page, independent of the actual UI, is produced.

– *Surface generation.* The UI is generated by transforming the XML object to a standard HTML, or WML page, depending on the user's device (desktop or mobile phone). In both cases, XSL stylesheets are exploited for the transformation. In contrast, when the user accesses the agenda in local modality, XSL stylesheets cannot be used, since the Java Micro Edition, running on mobiles, does not currently support standard tools for XSL processing such as Xalan. Taking also performance limitation of handset devices into account, we implemented a low-level WML generation module, based on light XML parsing (basically relying on SAX 1.0 APIs).

In the transformation from XML to HTML/WML, the surface generator performs two choices:

- It selects the subset of content stored in the XML object to presented, given the space constraints of the display. For instance, the page describing the tourist attraction in Fig. 5 is generated for a Web browser, where there are no serious space constraints: thus, all types of features are displayed. When generating the same type of page for a mobile, the surface generator omits the picture and selects only the most important types of features, leaving the rest available via "more info" links. For instance, both the "DESCRIPTION" paragraph (containing qualitative information about the item), and the "CHARACTERISTICS" section (reporting detailed information) are hidden, although they can be accessed via a link.
- It provides the layout information, deciding where and how, on the display, the various pieces of content should be placed.

6 Related Work and Discussion

The dynamic, context-aware organization of a tour was initially proposed in the GUIDE system to support users in the real-time organization of their visit to the Lancaster town [12]. However, the architecture of such system is based on the exploitation of specialized hardware, physically located in the place to be visited, and on the use of special handset devices. In contrast, INTRIGUE is based on standard wireless connections and on the use of (Java-enabled) mobile phones. Moreover, the interactive agenda maintains persistent itineraries that can be consulted and updated by exploiting wired and wireless connections. Therefore, our system offers an effective ubiquitous service accessible from any place.

Ubiquitous computing has been interpreted by several researchers as a way to offer, on wireless connections, the same services already developed for internet-based browsers. As discussed in [8], the user interfaces offered by desktops, televisions and handset devices differ in size, interaction tools (e.g., keyboard, mouse, etc.) and usage environment (e.g., desktop, handheld device). In order to face this heterogeneity, the Adaptive Hypermedia community has developed adaptation techniques to tailor the interaction to the specific devices. For instance, interesting examples of services that the user can access both from desktop and WAP phone are provided in [10, 11, 15, 17]. Although these examples deeply differ from one another in the offered functionalities and underlying technologies, all of them exploit the user's device as a lightweight client, continuously interacting with a remote server, where the logic of the application resides. Moreover, they mainly interpret context-awareness as taking the user's physical (or temporal) coordinates into account.

Our proposal differs from these approaches in the following two main aspects.

- In addition to the basic service provision, which has to rely on a server-based management of the interaction with the user, we offer an interactive agenda and other services that the user can access locally to the device.
- We interpret context awareness and ubiquitous computing as a persistence property of the interaction with the user. In particular, the interactive agenda is modeled as a persistent object, that the user can create, update and carry with herself at any time, and along different interactions with the system, regardless the device she is using.

The first aspect is particularly relevant to the exploitation of handset devices, which are subject to important limitations: first, at the current stage of technological development, wireless connections are not reliable; therefore, long-lasting interactions, typically performed in the wired case, are problematic. Similarly, bandwidth is limited, so that there are clear demands for traffic minimization. Finally, in most countries wireless communications are very expensive; therefore, in order for users to appreciate the service, such connections should be limited to the services that cannot be offered off-line: e.g., the search for continuously updated information, such as stock quotations, and the management of business interactions, such as reservations and payment transactions. Although the first two issues might be overcome in few years, it is not clear whether the third one will be solved in the medium term. In order to develop successful applications, such constraints should be taken into serious account.

We have performed an initial testing of our system with users who helped us to improve its interface and functionalities. The users were happy about the system's explanation facilities, both regarding group recommendations and failures in itinerary generation, because they clarify the system's behavior, therefore increasing the trust in the system's recommendations. Moreover, users appreciated the possibility of saving itineraries and retrieving (and modifying) them in subsequent interactions, as this facility would enable them to use the interactive agenda during the tour. In contrast, there was some negative feedback in the organization of the device-dependent interaction with the user. For instance, the registration form for the specification of heterogeneous tourist groups, which was well-accepted during the desktop interaction, was considered too time consuming for a minibrowser. To address this issue, we have extended the system to support logging without registering: if the user logs in this way, she receives non personalized recommendations, but she can access the other facilities offered by the system, such as category and geographical search, itinerary scheduling and presentation of tourist attractions. Moreover, we will investigate the application of unobtrusive user modeling techniques aimed at the identification of the user's preferences on the basis of the observation of her browsing behavior [6, 9].

Our future work will include further testing of the system, in order to collect more usage information and hopefully to try the system with real mobile phones: the mobile functionalities of our system are currently tested by exploiting a the WAP simulator. Moreover, we will exploit further contextual information to enhance the itinerary generation capabilities; e.g., to take location and temporal information into account, as done in other systems [2, 7, 13, 16].

References

1. Special issue: The mobile internet. *The Economist*, (October 11, 2001) 27–54
2. G.D. Abowd and E.D. Mynatt. Charting past, present and future research in ubiquitous computing. *ACM Transactions on Computer-Human Interaction, Special Issue on HCI in the new Millennium*, 7(1) (2000) 29–58
3. L. Ardissono and A. Goy. Dynamic generation of adaptive Web catalogs. In *Lecture Notes in Computer Science, Vol. 1892: Adaptive Hypermedia and Adaptive Web-Based Systems*. Springer-Verlag, Berlin (2000) 5–16
4. L. Ardissono, A. Goy, G. Petrone, and M. Segnan. A software architecture for dynamically generated adaptive Web stores. In *Proc. 17th IJCAI*, Seattle (2001) 1109–1114
5. L. Ardissono, A. Goy, G. Petrone, M. Segnan, and P. Torasso. Tailoring the recommendation of tourist information to heterogeneous user groups. In *Third Workshop on Adaptive Hypertext and Hypermedia*, Aarhus, Denmark (2001) 93–107
6. L. Ardissono and P. Torasso. Dynamic user modeling in a Web store shell. In *Proc. 14th Conf. ECAI*, Berlin (2000) 621–625
7. B.B. Bederson. Audio augmented reality: a prototype automated tour guide. In R. Mack J. Miller, I. Katz and L. Marks, editors, *Conf. companion for the ACM Conf. on Human Factors in Computing Systems*, Denver (1995) 210–211
8. E. Bergman, editor. *Information Appliances and Beyond. Interaction design for consumer products*. Morgan Kaufmann Publishers (1999)
9. D. Billsus and M. Pazzani. A personal news agent that talks, learns and explains. In *Proc. 3rd Int. Conf. on Autonomous Agents*, Seattle (1999) 268–275
10. D. Billsus, M. Pazzani, and J. Chen. A learning agent for wireless news access. In *Proc. 2000 Int. Conf. on Intelligent User Interfaces*, New Orleans (2000) 33–36
11. B. De Carolis, F. de Rosis, and S. Pizzutilo. Context-sensitive information presentation. In *Proc. UM'2001 Workshop on User Modelling in Context-Aware Applications*, Sonthofen, Germany (2001)
12. K. Cheverest, N. Davies, K. Mitchell, A. Friday, and C. Efstratiou. Developing a context-aware electronic tourist guide: some issues and experiences. In *Proc. CHI'2000: Human factors in computing systems*, The Hague, NL (2000) 17–24
13. A.K. Dey and D. Abowd. Towards a better understanding of context and context-awareness. In *Proc. CHI2000 Workshop on the What, Who, Where, When and How of Context-Awareness*, The Hague, NL (2000)
14. Y. Feng and J. Zhu. *Wireless Java Programming with J2ME*. SAMS (2001)
15. C. Paris, S. Wan, R. Wilkinson, and M. Wu. Generating personal travel guides - and who wants them? In *Proc. 8th Int. Conf. on User Modeling* Sonthofen, DE (2001) 251–253
16. D. Petrelli, A.De Angeli, and G. Convertino. A user centered approach to user modelling. In *Proc. 7th Int. Conf. on User Modeling*, Banff (1999) 255–264
17. D. Riecken, editor. *Special Issue on Personalization*, 43. Communications of the ACM (2000)

Automatic Extraction of Semantically-Meaningful Information from the Web.*

J.L. Arjona, R. Corchuelo, A. Ruiz, and M. Toro

Escuela Técnica Superior de Ingeniería Informática de la Universidad de Sevilla
Departamento de Lenguajes y Sistemas Informáticos
Avda. de la Reina Mercedes, s/n, Sevilla (SPAIN)
{arjona,corchu,aruiz,mtoro}@lsi.us.es

Abstract. The semantic Web will bring meaning to the Internet, making it possible for web agents to understand the information it contains. However, current trends seem to suggest that the semantic web is not likely to be adopted in the forthcoming years. In this sense, meaningful information extraction from the web becomes a handicap for web agents. In this article, we present a framework for automatic extraction of semantically-meaningful information from the current web. Separating the extraction process from the business logic of an agent enhances modularity, adaptability, and maintainability. Our approach is novel in that it combines different technologies to extract information, surf the web and automatically adapt to web changes.

Keywords: *Web agents, information extraction, wrappers, and ontologies.*

1 Introduction

In recent years, the web has consolidated as one of the most important knowledge repositories. Furthermore, the technology has evolved to a point in which sophisticated new generation web agents proliferate. They enable efficient, precise, and comprehensive retrieval and extraction of information from the vast web information repository. They can also circumvent some problems related to slow Internet access, and free up prohibitively expensive surf time by operating in the background. It is thus not surprising that web agents are becoming so popular.

A major challenge for web agents has become sifting through an unwieldy amount of data to extract meaningful information. Two important factors contribute to these difficulties: first, the information on the web is mostly available in human-readable forms that lack formalised semantics that would help agents

---

* The work reported in this article was supported by the Spanish Inter-ministerial Commission on Science and Technology under grant TIC2000-1106-C02-01

use it [3]; second, the information sources are likely to change their structure, which usually has an impact on their presentation but not on their semantics.

Thus, if we want to succeed in the development of web agents, we need a framework in which they can be separated from the information sources or the way to extract semantically-meaningful information from them. This way we enhance modularity, adaptability and maintainability, as well as agent interoperability. In this article, we present such a framework. It is organised as follows: Section 2 goes into details about our motivation and some related work; Section 3 presents our proposal and a case study; finally, Section 5 reports on our main conclusions and future research directions.

2 Motivation and Related Work

The incredible successfulness of the Internet world has paved the way for technologies whose goal is to enhance the way humans and computers interact on the web. Unfortunately, the information a human user can easy interpret is usually difficult to be extracted and interpreted by a web agent.

Figure 1 shows two views of a web page picked from Amazon.com. On the left, we present a shot of the page a human sees when he or she searches for information about a book; on the right, we present a portion of HTML that describes how to render this page. If we were interested in extracting the information automatically, the following issues would arise immediately:

– The implied meaning of the terms that appear in this page can be easily interpreted by humans, but there is not a reference to the ontology that describes them precisely, which complicates the communication interface between user and agent, and the interoperability amongst agents. For instance,

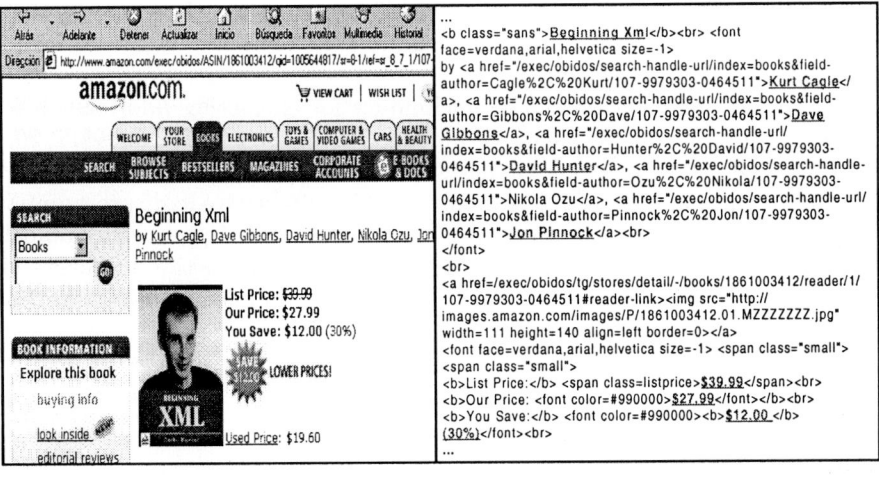

Fig. 1. A web page that shows information about a book.

if we do not consider semantics and we interpret prices as real numbers, a US librarian agent that deals with dollars would be likely to misinterpret a European one that deals with euros.
- The layout and the aspect of a web page may change unexpectedly. For instance, it is usual that web sites incorporate Christmas stuff in December, which does not affect the information they provide, but may invalidate the automatic extraction methods used so far.
- The access to the page that contains the information in which we are interested may involve navigating through a series of intermediate pages, such as login or index pages. Furthermore, this information may spread over a set of pages.

On sight of these issues, several researchers began working on proposals whose goal is to achieve a clear separation between presentation concerns and data themselves. XML [12] is one of the most popular languages aimed at representing structured data, but, unfortunately, it lacks a standardised way to link them with an abstract description of their semantics. There are many proposals that aim at solving this problem. They usually rely on annotating web pages with instances of ontologies that is usually written in a language such as DAML [1] or SHOE [19].

Most authors agree in that it would be desirable for a web in which pages are annotated with semantics to exist, because this would help web agents understand their contents, and would enhance semantic interoperability. Unfortunately, there are very little annotated pages if we compare them with non-annotated pages. As of the time of writing this article, the DAML crawler (www.daml.org/crawler) reports 17,019 annotated web pages, which is a negligible figure if we compare it with 2,110 millions, which is the estimated number of web pages (Cyveillance.com). Current trends seem to suggest that the semantic web is not likely to be adopted in the forthcoming years [14]. This argues for an automatic solution to extract semantically-meaningful information from the web that is clearly separated from the business logic so as to enhance modularity, adaptability, and maintainability.

Several authors have worked on techniques for extracting information from the web, and inductive wrappers are amongst the most popular ones [17, 23, 15, 4, 21, 2]. They are components that use a number of extraction rules generated by means of automated learning techniques such as inductive logic programming, statistical methods, and inductive grammars. These techniques use a number of web pages as samples that feed an algorithm that uses induction to generalise a set of rules that allows to extract information from similar pages automatically. Recently, researchers have put a great deal of effort to deal with changes, so that extraction rules can be regenerated on the fly if the layout of the web page changes [18, 16]. Although induction wrappers are suited to extract information from the web, they do not associate semantics with the extracted data, This being their major drawback.

There are also some related proposals in the field of databases, e.g., TSIM-MIS [11] and ARANEUS [20]. Their goal is to integrate heterogeneous information sources such as traditional databases and web pages so that the user can work on them as if they were a homogeneous information source. However, these proposals lack a systematic way to extract information from the web because extraction rules need to be implemented manually, which makes them not scalable and unable to recover from unexpected changes on the web.

3 Our Proposal

Our proposal aims at providing agent developers with a framework in which they can have access to semantically-meaningful data that resides on web pages not annotated with semantics. It relies on using a number of agents that we call information channels or IC for short. They allow to separate the extraction of information from the logic of an agent, and offer agent developers a good degree of flexibility. In order to allow for semantic interoperability, the information they extract references a number of concepts in a given application domain that are described by means of ontologies.

Before going into details, it is important to say that our notion of agent was drawn from [24]: *"Agents have their own will (autonomy), they are able to interact with each other (social ability), they respond to stimulus (reactivity), and they take initiative (pro-activity)."* In our proposal, web agents are software agents that interact with the web to retrieve, extract or manage information.

3.1 The Architecture

Figure 2 sketches the architecture of our proposal. As we mentioned above, information channels are at its core agents because they specialise in extracting information from different sources, and are able to react to information inquiries (reactivity) from other agents (social ability). They act in the background proactively according to a predefined schedule to extract information and to maintain the extraction rules updated.

Each information channel uses several inductive wrappers to extract information so that they can detect inconsistencies amongst the data each one extracts. If such inconsistencies are found, they then use a voting algorithm to decide whether to use the data extracted by most wrappers or regenerate the set of extraction rules on the fly. This may happen because of an unexpected change to the structure of the web page that invalidates the extraction rules used so far.

There is also an agent broker for information extraction that acts as a trader between the agents that need information from the web and the set of available information channels. When an agent needs some information, it contacts the broker, which redirects the request to the appropriate information channel, if possible. This way, agents need not be aware of the existence of different ICs, which can thus be adapted, created or removed from the system transparently. However, every time an IC is created or destroyed, it must be registered or unregistered so that the broker knows it. It therefore has a catalogue with the description of every IC in the system (yellow pages).

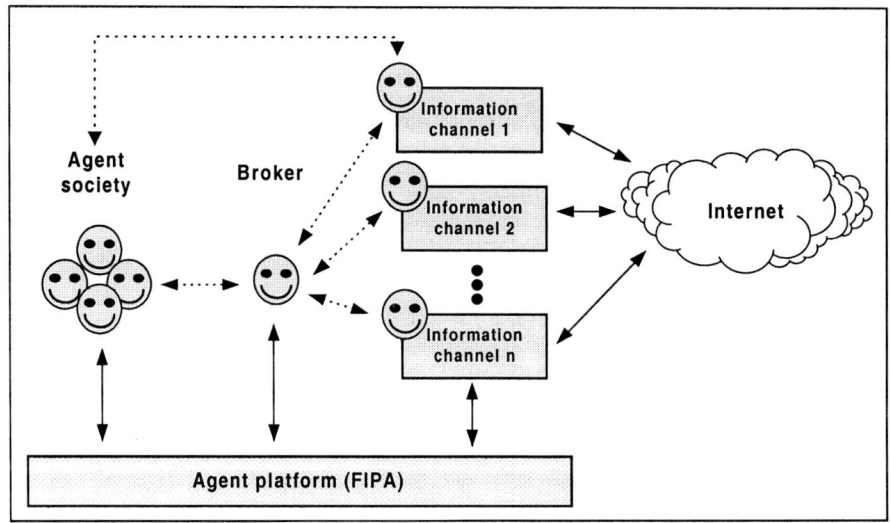

Fig. 2. Proposed architecture.

We use ACL [10] as a transport language to send messages from an agent to another. The content of the messages describes how an agent wants to interact with another, and it is written in DAML. Figure3 shows the brokering protocol [9] to communicate user agents with the ICs using the notation AUML [13, 22]. When an initiator agent sends a message with the performative *proxy* to the broker, it then replies with one of the following standard messages: *not-understood*, *refuse* or *agree*. If the broker agrees on the inquiry, it then searches for an adequate IC to serve it. If not found, it then sends a *failure-no-match* message to the initiator; otherwise, it tries to contact the IC and passes the inquiry onto it. If the broker succeeds in communicating with the IC, this will later send the requested information to the initiator; otherwise, a *failure-com-IC message* is sent back to the initiator, which indicates that an appropriate IC exists, but cannot respond.

3.2 A Case Study

We illustrate our proposal by means of a simple example in which we are interested in extracting information about books from Amazon.com. We first need to define an information channel, i.e., we need to construct an expert system whose goal is to extract information about books from the web. Such a channel is characterised by the following features: a set of ontologies, a set of extraction rules, and a navigational document.

The Ontologies. The ontologies [6] associated with an IC describes the concepts that define the semantics associated with the information we are going

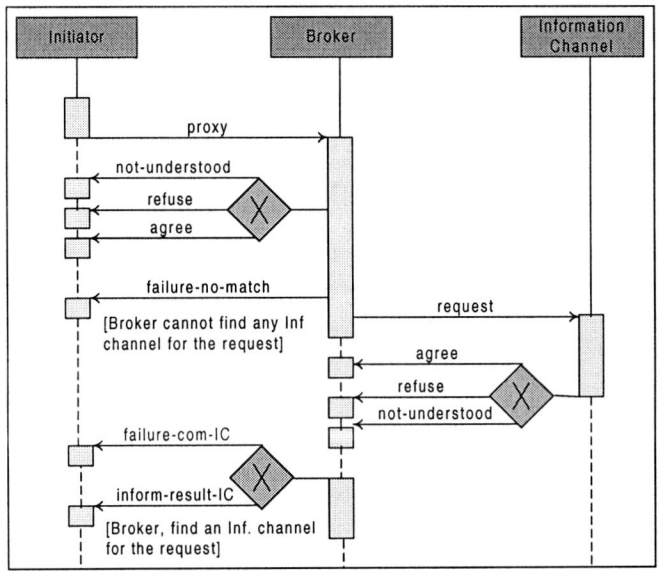

Fig. 3. Broker Interaction Protocol in AUML.

to extract from a high-level, abstract point of view. An ontology allows to define a common vocabulary by means of which different agents may interoperate semantically.

Figure 4 shows a part of the ontology that describes books using DAML. We selected this language because it is one of the most important contributions to the semantic web, it is being supported by many researchers, and the repository of available tools is quite rich, c.f. http://www.daml.org/tools.

The Extraction Rules. The extraction rules allow to define how to have access to the information in which we are interested. To generate them, we need a set of sample pages containing test data on which we use inductive techniques. To endow the sample pages with semantics, we also need to annotate them with DAML tags that allow to associate the concepts they contains with their corresponding ontologies. Figure 5 shows a piece of DAML code that we can use to annotate the web page in Fig. 1.

Once the sample pages have been annotated, we can generate the extraction rules. The input to the wrapper generator is a tuple of the following form:

$$(\{O_1, O_2, ..., O_n\}, \{(P_1, D_1), (P_2, D_2), ..., (P_k, D_k)\}); n \geq 1, k \geq 1$$

The first element of the tuple denotes the set of ontologies under consideration, and the second element is a set of pairs of the form (P, D), where P denotes a web page containing sample data, and D its corresponding annotation. With this information, we apply several induction algorithms [17, 23, 15, 4] to generate

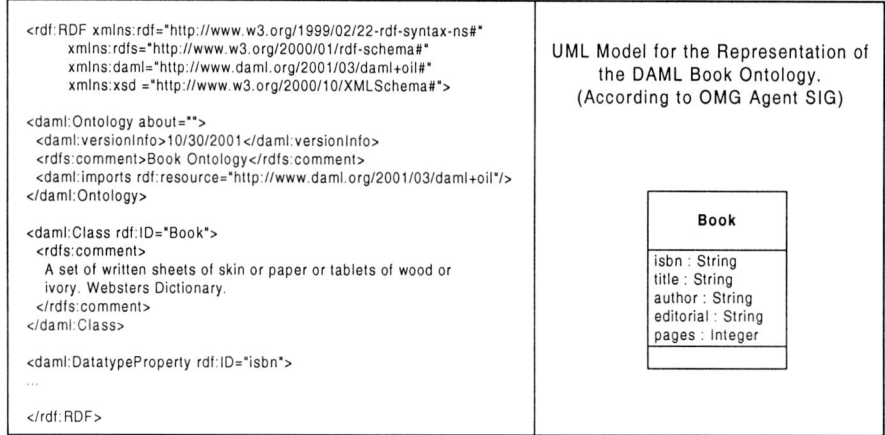

Fig. 4. An ontology that describes books from an abstract point of view.

```
<Book rdf:ID="A book">
  <rdfs:label>A book</rdfs:label>
  <rdfs:comment>Instance of Book.</rdfs:comment>
  <title>Beginning Xml</title>
  <isbn>1861003412</isbn>
  <editorial>Wrox Press, Inc</editorial>
  <author>Kurt Cagle</author>
  <author>Dave Gibbons</author>
  <author>David Hunter</author>
  <author>Nikola Ozu</author>
  <author>Jon Pinnock</author>
  <pages>823</pages>
</Book>
```

Fig. 5. Annotations to a web page with information about a book.

a set of extraction rules $R1, R2, ..., Rm$. Their exact form depend on the algorithm used to produce them, and may range from simple regular expressions to search procedures over a DOM Tree [5] or even XPointers [8]. hereafter, we refer to this set of rules as *BookRules*.

The Navigational Document. A navigational document defines the path of intermediate pages, such as login or index, we need to visit in order to have access to the page that contains the information in which we are interested.

Figure 6 shows a navigational document that describes how to have access to the web page that contains information about a book with a given ISBN. This document indicates that there exists a web page at www.amazon.com called d1. This page has quite a complex structure, but it contains a form called *searchform* with two fields a human user may use to select the kind of product he or she is searching for (*index*) and some key words that describe it (*field-keywords*).

Thus, d2 denotes the web page that we obtain when the server processes this form using *"index" := "Books"* and *"field-keywords" := ":Book#isbn"*. Books is the value that indicates the server that we are looking for books, and *:Book#isbn* denotes the ISBN code associated with the book for which we are searching.

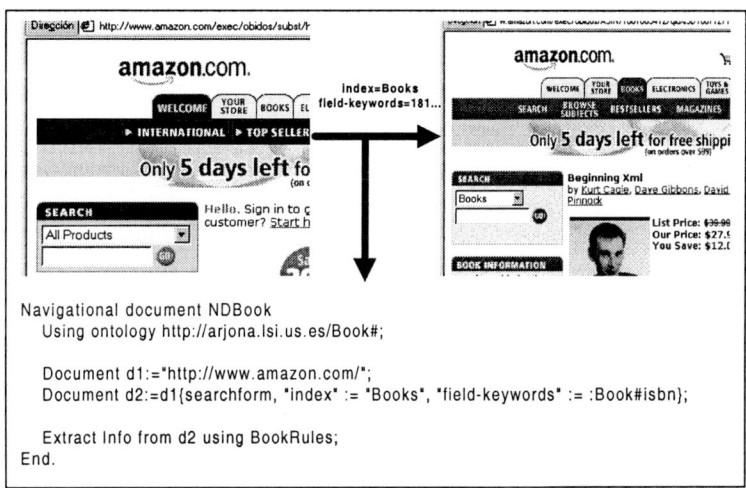

Fig. 6. A sample navigational document.

Roughly speaking, a navigational document may be viewed as a state machine in which each state is a web page, and the transitions between states may be viewed as the navigation from the page associated with the initial state to the page associated with the destination state.

3.3 Dealing with Pagers and Indexers

In this section, we present a slightly modified version of the previous case study in which we are interested in extracting information about the set of books written by a given author. If we write the name of an author in the above-mentioned search form, we can get a result page similar to the one presented in Fig. 1. In this case, the initial page does not lead directly to the requested information. Instead, it leads to an index page in which we can find some links that point to pages that describe books written by that author, and a pager that allows to search for more results. Although the wrapper we generated previously keeps working well, the way to have access to the information has changed substantially.

The new navigational document we need is presented in Fig. 7. There, we define a new document called $d3$ that represents the web page to which the initial search form leads. $d4[]$ references the set of web pages that we can get if we dereference the link labelled with *"More results"* by means of a sequential pager. This is an artefact that allows to navigate through the complete set of

```
Navigational document NDBook
  Using ontology http://arjona.lsi.us.es/Book#;

  Document d1 := "http://www.amazon.com/*";
  Document d2 := d1{"searchform", "index" := "Books", "field-keywords" := :Book#isbn};
  Document d3 := d1{"searchform", "index" := "Books", "field-keywords" := :Book#author};
  Document d4[] := SequentialPager(d3, "More Results");
  Document d5[] := Indexer(d4[], AmazonIndexer);

  Extract Info from d2, d5[] using BookRules;
End.
```

Fig. 7. Modified version of the navigational document.

pages that contain the information about the books written by an author. *d5[]* references the set of web pages we obtain by dereferencing the links on books that appear in the set of pages *d4[]*. This set is obtained by means of an indexer, which is an artefact that analyses a set of pages and extracts the links to the pages in which we are interested. In this case, we use an inductive wrapper called *AmazonIndexer*, but new indexers can be easily generated.

3.4 Using the Information Channel

Once we have set up an abstract channel, we can send messages to it in order to retrieve information about a given book by means of the broker. The content of the messages in DAML is based on an ontology that defines the communication [7]. This ontology is illustrated in Fig. 8.

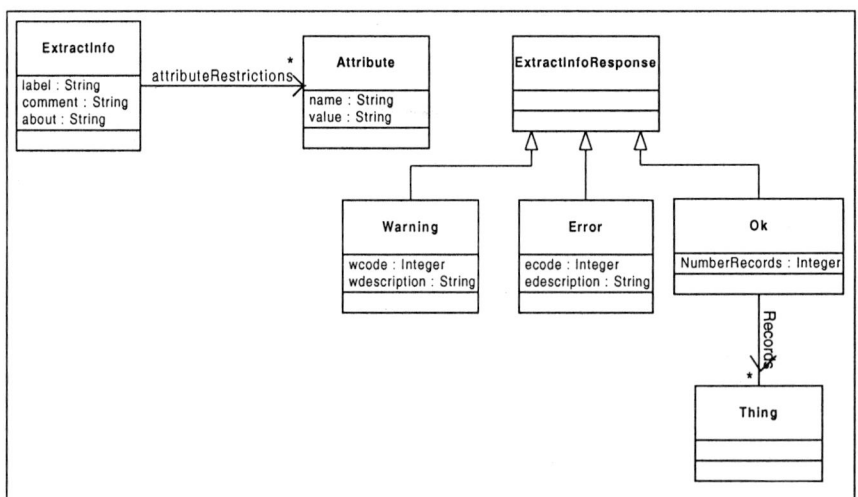

Fig. 8. Ontology for the content language.

Information requests are expressed as instances of class *ExtractInfo*. The reply from the abstract channel is an instance of *ExtractInfoResponse*, an error message (for instance, the channel can not have access the web page that contains the information), a warning message (for instance, 0 records have been found) or the information requested by the agent (as instances of the ontology class that defines the channel).

Figure 9 shows two example messages, the first one relative to an information request from an agent called *Agent-1* to the broker agent; the second one is the reply from the IC to *Agent-1*. In this case a book instance is returned.

```
(request :sender Agent-1
 :receiver broker
 :content (
    <rdf:RDF xmlns:rdf="http://www.w3.org/1999/02/22-rdf-syntax-ns#"
        xmlns:rdfs="http://www.w3.org/2000/01/rdf-schema#"
        xmlns:daml="http://www.daml.org/2001/03/daml+oil#"
        xmlns:xsd="http://www.w3.org/2000/10/XMLSchema#"
        xmlns:libro="http://arjona.lsi.us.es/Book#"
        xmlns="http://arjona.lsi.us.es/ie#">
    <ExtractInfo rdf:ID="El1">
        <rdfs:label>El1</rdfs:label>
        <about>http://arjona.lsi.us.es/Book#Book</about>
        <attributeRestrictions>
            <attribute>
                <name>http://arjona.lsi.us.es/Book#isbn</name>
                <value>1861003412</value>
            </attribute>
        </attributeRestrictions>
    </ExtractInfo>
    </rdf:RDF>
)
:language daml)
```

```
(inform :sender BookChannel
 :receiver Agent-1
 :content (
    <rdf:RDF xmlns:rdf="http://www.w3.org/1999/02/22-rdf-syntax-ns#"
        xmlns:rdfs="http://www.w3.org/2000/01/rdf-schema#"
        xmlns:daml="http://www.daml.org/2001/03/daml+oil#"
        xmlns:xsd="http://www.w3.org/2000/10/XMLSchema#"
        xmlns:ie="http://arjona.lsi.us.es/ie#">
        xmlns="http://arjona.lsi.us.es/Book#">
    <ie:Ok rdf:ID="Request 123332">
        <ie:numberRecords>1</ie:numberRecords>
        <ie:records>
            <Book rdf:ID="A-Book">
                <title>Beginning Xml</title>
                <isbn>1861003412</isbn>
                <editorial>Wrox Press Inc</editorial>
                <author>Kurt Cagle</author>
                <author>Dave Gibbons</author>
                <author>David Hunter</author>
                <author>Nikola Ozu</author>
                <author>Jon Pinnock</author>
                <pages>823</pages>
            </Book>
        </ie:records>
    </ie:Ok>
)
:language daml)
```

Fig. 9. Example of messages.

4 Benefits of the Framework for the Adaptative Hypermedia Community

The Adaptative Hypermedia Community can use the framework presented in this paper to personalise web sites based on users' profiles. In this respect, the information from the web that is interesting to a user can be extracted automatically and displayed in a suitable form.

We illustrate this idea with a fictitious case study whose aim is the personalisation of an e-commerce portal that sells VHS, DVDs, and so on. Using the information infered from the buys by some customers, we can identify who the the preferred actors are. Once the actors have been indentified, we can develop an agent that uses the proposed framework. It queries an abstract channel that is able to extract relevant information about this actor (birth name, location, filmography, ...) from several web sites, for example The Internet Movie Database (IMDb)[1].

---

[1] http://www.imdb.com/

5 Conclusions and Future Work

In this article, we have shown that the process of extracting information from the Internet can be separated from the business logic of a web agent by means of abstract channels. They rely on inductive wrappers and can analyse web pages to get information with its associated semantics automatically.

Our proposal shows that there is no need to annotate every web page, to extract information with associated semantics. In this sense we are contributing to bring together the community of agents programmers and the semantic web.

In the future, we are going to work on an implementation of our framework in which data sources can be more heterogeneous (databases, news servers, mail servers, and so on). Extraction of information from multimedia sources such as videos, images, or sound files will be also paid much attention.

References

1. DARPA (Defense Advanced Research Projects Agency). The darpa agent mark up language (daml). http://www.daml.org, 2000.
2. R. Baumgartner, S. Flesca, and G. Gottlob. Visual web information extraction with lixto. In *27th VLDB Conference*, 2001.
3. T. Berners-Lee, J. Hendler, and O. Lassila. The semantic web. *Scientific American*, May 2001.
4. W. W. Cohen and L. S. Jensen. A structured wrapper induction system for extracting information from semi-structured documents. In *Workshop on Adaptive Text Extraction and Mining (IJCAI-2001)*, 2001.
5. W3C (The World Wide Web Consortium). Document object model. http://www.w3.org/DOM/, 2000.
6. O. Corcho and A. Gómez-Pérez. A road map on ontology specification languages. In *Workshop on Applications of Ontologies and Problem solving methods. 14th European Conference on Artificial Intelligence (ECAI'00)*, 2000.
7. S. Cranefield and M. Purvis. Generating ontology-specific content languages. In *Proceedings of Ontologies in Agent Systems Workshop (Agents 2001),*, pages 29–35, 2000.
8. S.J. DeRose. Xml linking. *ACM Computing Surveys*, 1999.
9. Finin, T. Labrou, and Y. Mayfield. Kqml as an agent communication language. *Software Agents, MIT Press*, 1997.
10. FIPA (The Fundation for Intelligent Physical Agents). Fipa specifications. http://www.fipa.org/specifications/index.html.
11. H. García-Molina, J. Hammer, K. Ireland, Y. Papakonstantinou, J. Ullman, and J. Widom. Integrating and accessing heterogeneous information sources in tsimmis. In *The AAAI Symposium on Information Gathering*, pages 61–64, March 1995.
12. C.F. Goldfarb and P. Prescod. *The XML Handbook*. Prentice-Hall, 2nd edition, 2000.
13. OMG (Object Management Group). Unified modelling language version 2.0. http://www.omg.org/uml/, 2001.
14. J. Hendler. Agents and the semantic web. *IEEE Intelligent Systems Journal*, 2001.
15. C. A. Knoblock. Accurately and reliably extracting data from the web: A machine learning approach. *Bulletin of the IEEE Computer Society Technical Com-mittee on Data Engineering*, 2000.

16. N. Kushmerick. Regression testing for wrapper maintenance. In *Proceedings of the 16th National Conference on Artificial Intelligence (AAAI-1999)*, pages 74–79, 1999.
17. N. Kushmerick. Wrapper induction: Efficiency and expressiveness. *Artificial Intelligence*, 118(2000):15–68, 1999.
18. N. Kushmerick. Wrapper verification. *World Wide Web Journal*, 2000.
19. S. Luke, L. Spector, D. Rager, and J. Hendler. Ontology-based web agents. In *First International Conference on Autonomous Agents*, 1997.
20. G. Mecca, P. Merialdo, and P. Atzeni. Araneus in the era of xml. *Data Engineering Bullettin, Special Issue on XML*, September 1999.
21. I. Muslea, S. Minton, and C. Knoblock. Wrapper induction for semistructured, web-based information sources. In *Proceedings of the Conference on Automated Learning and Discovery (CONALD)*, 1998.
22. J. Odell, H. Van Dyke, and B. Bauer. Extending uml for agents. In *AOIS Worshop (AAAI)*, pages 3–17, 2000.
23. S. Soderland. Learning information extraction rules for semi-structured and free text. *Machine Learning*, pages 1–44, 1999.
24. M. J. Wooldridge and M. R. Jennings. Intelligent agents: Theory and practice. *The Knowledge Engineering Review*, 10(2):115–152, 1995.

Towards Open Adaptive Hypermedia

Christopher Bailey, Wendy Hall, David E. Millard, and Mark J. Weal

IAM Group, ECS, University of Southampton, UK
{cpb99r,wh,dem,mjw}@ecs.soton.ac.uk

Abstract. Research at the University of Southampton has extended generalised Open Hypermedia (OH) models to include concepts of context and behaviour, both traditionally very important to the Adaptive Hypermedia (AH) domain. In this paper we re-evaluate Brusilovsky's pragmatic taxonomy of AH techniques from a structural perspective. A variety of OH structures are discussed that can be used to implement the techniques found in the taxonomy. By identifying common structures we gain a new perspective on the relationship between different AH techniques.

Keywords. Open Hypermedia, Adaptive Techniques, Hypermedia Structure, FOHM, taxonomy

1 Introduction

In the late 1980's, the hypermedia research community developed, amongst others, two separate research threads; one focusing on Open Hypermedia systems (OH) and one on Adaptive Hypermedia systems (AH). The AH community arose partly from the extensive work that had already been conducted into artificial intelligence and partly from Intelligent Tutoring Systems (ITS). AH researchers are primarily concerned with using pre-existing methods and techniques found in the fields of AI, ITS and User Modelling, and extending, combining and merging these ideas to create complete systems that understand and aid the user in knowledge acquisition.

ITS promoted the development of educational server-side adaptive web-based systems such as MANIC [19], INTERBOOK [5] and more recently AHA [8]. Other such server-side systems index web sites [18] or provide personalized interfaces to large hypermedia systems [9].

AH has also seen the development of client-side adaptive systems that follow users as they browse the WWW. Examples of these systems include WebMate [6], Letizia [14] and LiveInfo [15].

A second thread of hypermedia research focused on the Open Hypermedia (OH) field. Open Hypermedia Systems (OHSs) such as Microcosm [10], Chimera [1] and DHM [11] separate links from documents, allowing hyperstructure to be processed separately from the media it relates to.

In recent years the OH community have tackled the issue of interoperability between different OHSs, in particular the development of the Open Hypermedia Protocol (OHP) [7]. The scope of the OHP project evolved into an attempt to create a reference model and architecture for Open Hypermedia Systems in general.

This change has focused the OH community on the fundamental structures that such systems deal with, which has resulted in the promotion of structure to a first-class status and the consideration of how context might affect that structure. In particular the development of the Fundamental Open Hypermedia Model (FOHM) [17] deals directly with issues of context, and behaviour that can modify context.

The most recent OHS developed at Southampton, Auld Linky [16], is a contextual structure server that stores and serves structures expressed in FOHM.

1.1 Motivation

Our involvement in OH began with the Microcosm system in 1989 [12]. Although it was not designed as an AH system, Microcosm did provide a framework for building adaptive hypermedia systems. We first reported the use of Microcosm to develop an educational adaptive hypermedia application in [13]. More recently we have developed an adaptive hypermedia system that uses a collection of agents to process the contents of pages visited by the user and augment the current page with contextual links to related information [2].

It is our early experiments with using Linky to support AH [16] that have led us to the observation that many of the current AH techniques can be described and supported with a simple set of contextual structures.

The purpose of this paper is to produce an alternative view of the AH domain from a contextually aware OH perspective, to this end we will be using Brusilovsky's taxonomy of adaptive techniques [4]. We will show that many of the techniques in the taxonomy can be implemented with a small key group of hypermedia structures. This structural perspective is used to analyse and critique the taxonomy and inform the continued development of our contextual link server.

2 Techniques of Adaptive Hypermedia

Figure 1 shows Brusilovsky's taxonomy [4], updated from [3]. This diagram will be used as a basis for a structural comparison of OH and AH techniques.

The taxonomy focuses on the interface and user interaction, and has been divided into two distinct areas: 'Adaptive presentation' and 'Adaptive navigation support'.

Adaptive navigation support focuses on aspects of navigational hyperlinks such as generation, appearance, spatial placement and functionality.

Adaptive presentation systems rely on information chunks (or fragments) that can be processed and rendered in a variety of ways depending on the user preferences. In broad terms, Adaptive navigation support is about links and Adaptive presentation about content.

While the distinctions of the taxonomy are important for identification and classification of adaptive systems, the implementation of these techniques can be achieved using a small selection of fundamental data structures that can be combined to create powerful AH systems.

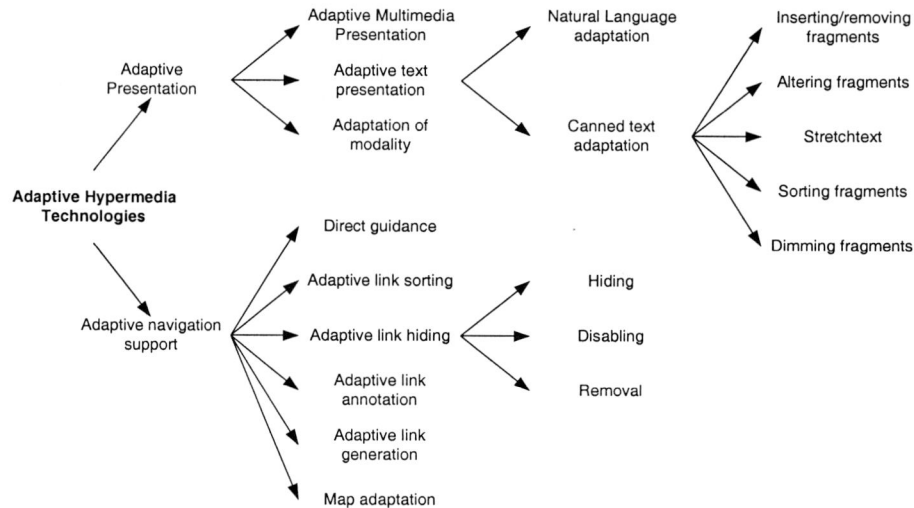

Fig. 1. Updated taxonomy of adaptive hypermedia technologies [4]

3 Structures for Adaptive Hypermedia

In this section we present a selection of hypermedia structures that could be used to represent the underlying information within an adaptive system. It is not our intention that these structures be exhaustive, more that they provide enough richness to support Brusilovsky's taxonomy. The structures are represented using the Fundamental Open Hypermedia Model (FOHM).

3.1 Data

The *Data* object (shown in Fig. 2) is the basic building block of FOHM, it can represent any piece of media (text, graphic, video stream, etc.). A *Context* object can be attached to the data and describes the context in which the data item is visible (the precise format of a context object is not specified in FOHM although one might imagine a set of key/value pairs as a basic format). When used in an AH system, the context of the data item would be matched against a user's profile to see whether the data item should be hidden from the user.

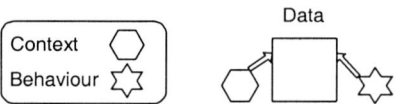

Fig. 2. FOHM Data structure

In addition to context, *Behaviour* objects can be attached to a Data object. These describe an action that occurs as a result of an event associated with the object they are attached to. In an AH system this can be used to modify the user profile, for example, in the case of data, the behaviour event might be 'on display' with an action of setting a flag in the user profile stating that the information in that data item has been read. Any technique from Brusilovsky's taxonomy that manipulates content might utilise data objects, while context and behaviour can be used for modelling prerequisite information in the system.

3.2 Link

Navigational link structures are represented in FOHM as A*ssociations*, bound to these are *Reference* objects that are used to address Data objects or other Associations. Figure 3 shows a Link with three Data members, the first is bound as a source and the other two as destinations.

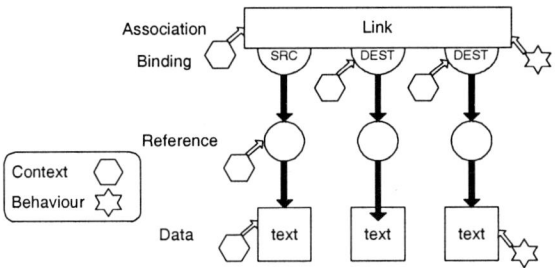

Fig. 3. FOHM Navigational Link

Context objects can be placed on Associations in a number of positions. When attached to the link, it can be used to scope the link (i.e. the link is only visible to the user if their profile matches the link's context). If the context is placed on the destination bindings instead, then while the link will always be visible, the destinations will change depending on the profile.

Behaviour objects can also be attached to Associations. For example, if we attach a behaviour with the event 'on traversal' then, when the user follows the link, the action specified in the behaviour object would be enacted by the system.

Contextual link structures could be used to implement any of the 'Adaptive Link Hiding' techniques described by Brusilovsky. For example a link could be authored with a context object attached that specified that it was only visible to an expert. When a novice queries the system for links, their user profile does not match against the link's context and the link is effectively hidden.

3.3 Tour

A *Tour* is an association that represents a set of objects designed to be viewed in sequence. These objects might be data items representing a sequence of pages, association objects representing a sequence of sub structures or a mixture of both.

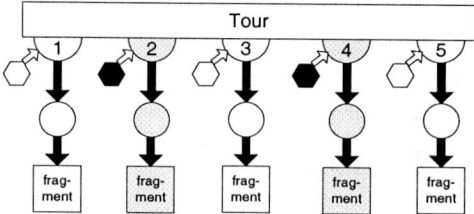

Fig. 4. Pruning the hyperstructure using context. The black contexts have failed to match leading to the pruning of the grey sub-structures.

A tour of data objects could be used to implement Brusilovsky's 'Inserting/Removing Fragments'. The client would query the link server to extract the structure shown in Fig. 4. Before being returned by the link server, it is pruned to remove sub-structures whose context does not match the user profile. The client inserts the remaining sub-structures, in the order they appear in the tour, into the document.

3.4 Concept

A *Concept* association can be used to collect together multiple objects that represent the same conceptual entity (for example the same piece of text in different languages). Brusilovsky's 'Adaptation of Modality' could be implemented with such a structure. Different media representations of the same information (e.g. video, audio, text) could be gathered together in a concept and then selected via querying with a particular user profile. When the concept structure is returned it will contain only those members that fit the query profile. The concept might be structured to be mutually exclusive, or to allow for multiple representations to be applicable at any given time.

3.5 Level Of Detail (LoD)

Like the concept, the LoD structure associates multiple representations of the same object. Unlike the concept structure, these representations are ordered within the association, from the simplest representation to the most complex. When queried in context the members of the LoD will be filtered. The application can then choose which of the remaining bindings to display according to what level of detail the current user would prefer.

For example, a system could support 'Stretchtext' from the taxonomy by storing a LoD structure containing data objects representing text at increasingly advanced levels. Initially the lowest positioned data object in the LoD would be displayed. When the user selects the text it could be replaced with the next available data object in the LoD.

3.6 Equator "City" Example

It is possible to combine these structures to produce more advanced effects (for example a tour of concepts). Before we go any further it is useful to see how they have been used in a real-world application.

City is a museum-based sub-project of the Equator Interdisciplinary Research Collaboration (IRC). The premise of the City project is that data objects represent real world locations so that adaptive structure can be authored about them. These structures can then be queried contextually to obtain personal views of the physical space (interpreted for the user via a device such as a PDA). Figure 5 shows the structures that we are using.

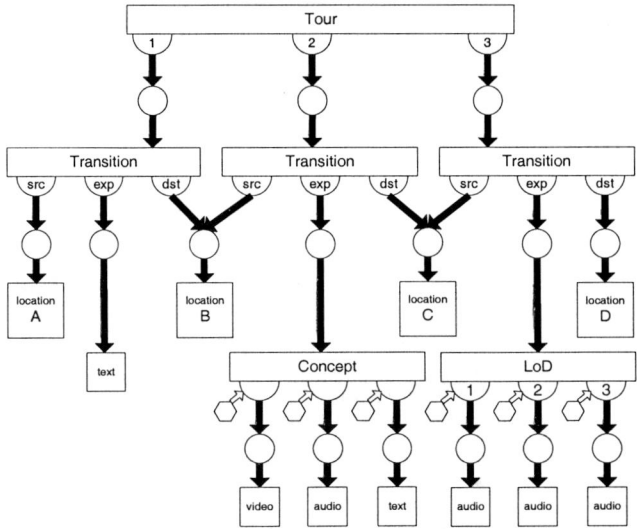

Fig. 5. FOHM Tour, Concept, LoD and Transition structures

The fundamental structure used in City is a *Transition*. This is very similar to a link in that it indicates a navigational move from one Data object (*src*) to another (*dst*). Unlike a link it also includes an explanation (*exp*) member that explains why that move is relevant. For example, when moving from A to B, the explanation might describe in what ways the objects at location B are related to those at location A.

We have used the structures previously described along with these transitions to provide AH functionality. Curators of the museum space can organise sets of these transitions into *tours* that describe a number of steps that a visitor might like to take around the museum space. At any particular location the visitors' PDAs would present the available transitions that are available given the users current context, including any tours that progress from that point.

We can also use the *concept* and *LoD* structures to tailor the explanations of transitions. For example on the B to C transition there are explanations available in several formats, while on the C to D transition there are several audio explanations of different lengths and complexity. When retrieving these structures, the users context will determine which explanation they will actually see.

42 C. Bailey et al.

4 Revisiting the Taxonomy

Having discussed the fundamental structures that can be used to provide adaptivity and seen how they can be used in a novel AH application, Fig. 6 illustrates how these structures could be used to implement the various adaptive techniques described in Brusilovsky's taxonomy.

The legend in Fig. 6 is divided up between the two fundamental objects (data and links) and the extended FOHM structures. In addition, some of the techniques in the taxonomy require extra resources such as System Information (e.g. user access logs), or a Weight Metric that describes not only which parts of the structure match in a particular context but also *how well they match*.

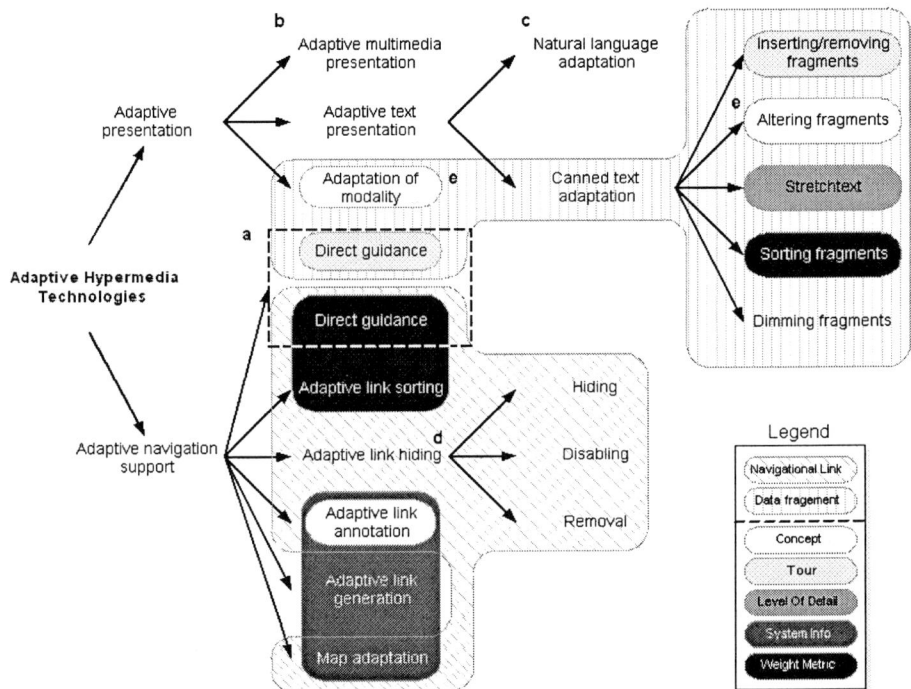

Fig. 6. A structural view of Brusilovsky's taxonomy that shows how FOHM structures can be combined to implement a range of adaptive hypermedia techniques.

Each technique in the taxonomy is built up using the structures or resources required to implement that technique. For example, 'Adaptive link annotation' would require explicit *link structures* to store each hyperlink and collections of alternative annotations for each link would be stored in a *concept structure*. Finally the adaptive system would analyse the *system information* (in the form of user history) when choosing which annotation to present to the user.

The only visual change to the taxonomy that was required, involves duplicating 'Direct Guidance' (labelled *a* on Fig. 6) as it was felt that this technique has two possible implementations.

The first approach could use a tour of the information domain; the adaptive 'next' button would therefore point to the next appropriate destination on the tour. An alternative approach would be to apply a link sorting routine (requiring a weight on each link) and then automatically select the link with the highest weight as the next destination.

One of the philosophies behind OHSs is that there is a general view of data that covers all media types. From this point of view, it can be seen that any of the 'Adaptive text presentation' techniques described in the taxonomy can also be applied equally well to 'Adaptive multimedia presentation'. To improve clarity, both techniques could be combined and re-labelled *'Adaptive Media Presentation'*. This issue is highlighted as *b* in Fig. 6.

The same perspective leads us to question the way that Natural Language (NL) Adaptation (*c* in Fig. 6) is placed under text adaptation. Because the same techniques can be used with any media type, we believe that NL adaptation falls under a larger umbrella of *'Adaptive Sequencing'*, which might use canned or constructed information fragments. Moreover, NL adaptation influences nearly every single technique in the taxonomy. Whenever information fragments (or pages) are sequenced together, there is a need to conserve the progression of the narrative flow. In these situations, NL techniques, and wider sequencing methods in general, can be used as the glue to join fragments together.

Another consideration is that the various subcategories of 'Adaptive link hiding' (hiding, disabling and removal, labelled *d*) are all structurally equivalent. This means that in a system that uses navigational link objects to implement a particular technology, for example link hiding, it has in place all the requirements needed to implement any of the other adaptive link techniques.

The diagram also shows the apparent similarity between 'Adaptation of modality' and 'Altering fragments' labelled *e* in Fig. 6. These two techniques are functionally identical if one considers that fragments can contain multiple media representations of the same data objects. In such cases, choosing the best media type to display (adaptation of modality) is a process of selecting one fragment from a set of fragments (altering fragments).

4.1 Reflections on Brusilovsky's Taxonomy

Brusilovsky's taxonomy originally provided a mechanism for classifying the various AH systems at the time. Since then, more systems have been developed, some of which fit in to the existing taxonomy, and others that have forced extensions to the taxonomy making it more lengthy and complex.

With our focus on structure we propose that many techniques described by the taxonomy as textual are in fact applicable to a wide range of media.

It initially seems clear that the taxonomy divides structurally into two halves. The upper half is concerned with content, and requires a contextual data representation; the lower is concerned with navigation, and requires links with contextual membership. However, we have argued that Natural Language Adaptation impacts on both halves of the taxonomy and therefore blurs the division of the taxonomy into presentation and navigation. In our opinion both adaptive presentation and adaptive navigation are about adaptive sequencing. The first is concerned with *intra*-document adaptive sequencing, the second in *inter*-document adaptive sequencing. The difference concerns the presentation of the sequence i.e. as a linearisation or as a hyperstructure.

Other aspects of the taxonomy can also become blurred when viewed with a structural eye. In particular Map Adaptation seems a vague term that is concerned with the visualisation of many other aspects of the taxonomy (such as link hiding, altering fragments etc.) rather than being a category in its own right.

4.2 Reflections on Auld Linky

Auld Linky was designed as a contextual link server to deal with all the structures discussed in this paper. However, it is unable to totally support the taxonomy of techniques.

Linky is designed only to store and serve structure and for any particular problem clients need to be written that interpret the structures served by Linky and present them to the user. On its own Linky supports the first five criteria in the legend of Fig. 6 (the contextual structures). If a client were written that maintains a basic user history then it would also be able to support the sixth criteria, System Information. We feel that this division of responsibility is correct.

The reason Linky cannot support the entire taxonomy of techniques is because it lacks support for the seventh criteria, Weight Metrics. Currently Linky's matching process is binary (if a structural element does not match the users current context then it is culled from the context) and therefore provides no feedback on the quality of the match. The client is left unable to sort the resulting structure; a process needed to implement two of the techniques in the taxonomy, 'Adaptive Link Sorting' and 'Sorting Fragments'.

5 Conclusions

While both the OH and AH communities exist largely independently of each other, there are many areas where crossover could yield new research directions and offer solutions to shared problems. In this paper we have used Brusilovsky's taxonomy as a means to show how the structural OH approach could inform AH research, but also to explore what our own OH research, particularly the development of our contextual structure server, Auld Linky, could learn from established AH techniques.

OH's emphasis on structure provides the means to implement a wide range of adaptive technologies and helps clarify the taxonomy. However it neither completely covers the taxonomy, nor provides the best programming solution in every situation. As we have shown, to implement every AH feature would require additional information such as system information and weight metric's.

We believe that AH systems that acknowledge the structural equivalence of many AH techniques have an advantage in that they may handle adaptation consistently across different techniques and media.

We also believe that any contextual OH server needs to provide for the problem domains being explored in AH research. To this end we are exploring the possibility of adding contextual weight metrics to the structures served by Auld Linky to allow it to support all the techniques described by Brusilovsky.

Acknowledgements

This research is funded in part by EPSRC Interdisciplinary Research Collaboration (IRC) project "EQUATOR" GR/N15986/01. Thanks to the Equator City Project, particularly Matthew Chalmers and Ian McColl of the University of Glasgow.

References

1. Anderson, K.M., Taylor, R.N. and Whitehead, E.J. (1994). "Chimera: Hypertext for Heterogeneous Software Environments". In ECHT '94. Proceedings of the ACM European conference on Hypermedia technology, Sept. 18-23, Edinburgh, Scotland, UK, pp 94-197, 1994.
2. Bailey C., El-Beltagy, S.R. and Hall, W. (2001). "Link Augmentation: A Context-Based Approach to Support Adaptive Hypermedia". In Proceedings of the 3rd Workshop on Adaptive Hypertext and Hypermedia, August 14-18, Århus, Denmark, LNCS 2266, pp. 239-251.
3. Brusilovsky, P. (1996). "Methods and Techniques of Adaptive Hypermedia". Journal of User Modelling and User-Adaptive Interaction 6, n 2-3, pp 87-129.
4. Brusilovsky, P. (2001). "Adaptive hypermedia". User Modeling and User-Adapted Interaction, Ten Year Anniversary Issue 11 (Alfred Kobsa, ed.), pp 87-110.
5. Brusilovsky, P., Eklund, J. and Schwarz, E. (1998). "Web-based education for all: A tool for developing adaptive courseware". Computer Networks and ISDN Systems. Proceedings of 7th International World Wide Web Conference, April 14-18, 30 (1-7), pp 291-300, 1998.
6. Chen, L. and Sycara, K. (1998). "WebMate: Personal Agent for Browsing and Searching". In Proceedings of the 2nd International Conference on Autonomous Agents, St. Paul, MN, May. ACM Press, New York, NY. pp. 132-139.
7. Davis, H.C., Rizk A. and Lewis A.J. (1996). "OHP: A Draft Proposal for a Standard Open Hypermedia Protocol". In Uffe Kock Wiil and Serge Demeyer, editors, Proceedings of the 2nd Workshop on Open Hypermedia Systems, ACM Hypertext '96, Washington, D.C., March 16-20, 1996.
8. De Bra, P. and Calvi, L. (1998). *"AHA! An open Adaptive Hypermedia Architecture"*. The New Review of Hypertext and Multimedia 4, 115-139.
9. Espinoza, F. and Höök, K. (1997). "A WWW Interface to an Adaptive Hypermedia System". Presented at PAAM'96, London, UK, April 1996.
10. Fountain, A.M., Hall, W., Heath, I. and Davis, H.C. (1990). "MICROCOSM: An Open Model for Hypermedia With Dynamic Linking". In A. Rizk, N. Streitz, and J. Andre, editors, Hypertext: Concepts, Systems and Applications (Proceedings of ECHT'90), pp 298-311. Cambridge University Press, 1990.
11. Grønbæk, K. and Trigg, R.H. (1994). "Design issues for a Dexter-based hypermedia system". Communications of the ACM, 37(3) pp 40-49, Feb. 1994.

12. Hall, W., Davis, H., Hutchings, G. (1996). "Rethinking Hypermedia: The Microcosm Approach" Electronic Publishing Series, No 4. Kluwer Academic Pub; ISBN: 0792396790.
13. Hothi, J. & Hall, W. (1998). "An Evaluation of Adapted Hypermedia Techniques using Static User Modelling". In Proceedings of the 2nd Workshop on Adaptive Hypertext and Hypermedia, Pittsburgh, USA, June 20-24, pp 45-50, 1998.
14. Lieberman, H. (1995). "Letizia: An Agent That Assists Web Browsing". In Proceedings of the International Joint Conference on Artificial Intelligence, Montreal, August 1995.
15. Maglio, P.P. and Farrell, S. (2000). "LiveInfo: Adapting web experience by customization and annotation". In Proceedings of the 1st International Conference on Adaptive Hypermedia and Adaptive Web-based Systems. AH2000, Trento, Italy, August 2000.
16. Michaelides, D.T., Millard, D.E., Weal, M.J. and De Roure, D., C. (2001). "Auld Leaky: A Contextual Open Hypermedia Link Server". In Proceedings of the 7th Workshop on Open Hypermedia Systems, ACM Hypertext 2001 Conference. Aarhus, Denmark 2001.
17. Millard, D.E., Moreau, L, Davis, H.C. and Reich, S. (2000). "FOHM: A Fundamental Open Hypertext Model for Investigating Interoperability Between Hypertext Domains". In Proceedings of the '00 ACM Conference on Hypertext, May 30 - June 3, San Antonio, TX, pp 93-102, 2000.
18. Perkowitz, M. and Etzioni, O. (1999). "Towards adaptive web sites: Conceptual cluster mining". In Proceedings of the 17th International Joint Conference on Artificial Intelligence, 1999.
19. Stern, M.K. & Woolf, B.P. (1998). "Curriculum Sequencing in a Web-Based Tutor". In the Proceedings of Intelligent Tutoring Systems, 1998.

GAS: Group Adaptive System

Maria Barra[1], Paul Maglio[2], Alberto Negro[1], and Vittorio Scarano[1]

[1] Dipartimento di Informatica ed Applicazioni
Università di Salerno
Baronissi (Salerno), 84081, Italy
{marbar,alberto,vitsca}@dia.unisa.it
[2] IBM Almaden Research Center
San Jose, California, USA
pmaglio@almaden.ibm.com

Abstract. This paper describes an ongoing research project to design a Group Adaptive System (GAS) for collaborative navigation on the web. Our objective is to provide information that adapts to web users based on automatically determined, dynamic user groups. To do this, our approach takes into account the structure of the web (using the CLEVER algorithm [16]) and user interactions when navigating the web (gathered by our collaborative environment) to offer users in a consistent information space determined by their interests and activities. In the end, our system, GAS, enables users to perform asynchronous collaborative navigation by combining resources discovered by a group of users and suggestions discovered by the CLEVER algorithm to provide recommendations to the group.

1 Introduction

Collaborative navigation on the web can improve information-finding by making users aware of others' information activities. Collaborative navigation can be used, for example, to provide users with relevant resources others have found automatically, and to enable users to share information deliberately.

We all know that finding information on the web can be time consuming and frustrating given the vast number of resources available. Though people use the web to find information all the time, their experiences are rarely captured and used to guide or inform others. Of course, in most other information-finding contexts, people routinely rely on the experiences of others to help make choices and find desired information. For instance, librarians guide library users and friends ask one another what books to read. Relying on the experience of others is commonplace. Put simply, the world is a social place and people often rely on social interactions to find information.

Making the web more of a social place enables users to (1) take advantage of the other people's activity, (2) save the time they spent searching for relevant information on the web (using others people navigation and judgments), (3) become aware of others' interests and knowledge, (4) get recommendations of relevant information based on others' opinions, (5) use web navigation as a kind of communication channel. Social navigation can be *direct* (people give recommendations or guide each other) or it can be *indirect* (the system creates a feeling of awareness for other people's activities in an information space [12]). Information on preferences and judgments aggregated over a community of users, is a valuable tool to make navigation decisions for users who have shared interests (e.g., discovering new resources is a useful group activity to share and to learn from). Thus, collaborative navigation can promote knowledge and information exchange among users as well as creating awareness of others on the web.

Recommendation systems on the web often suggest products to customers based on their explicit and implicit preferences, similarity of user interests, and consumer and product attributes (e.g., user skills preferences, titles, authors, brands). These systems have been widely studied and constitute a large number of web-based applications, including on-line stores that sell books, movies, or music, and on-line newspapers, newsgroups, or scientific articles services that tailor content to individual users. Though such domains are huge, the space of elements are enumerable, and therefore can easily be classified to provide reasonable customization. Applying the approach of such specialized recommendation systems to the more general problem of web browsing or searching (i.e., recommending web pages based on many users' histories of web page navigation) is not straightforward. One major obstacle is that the information on the web is not fixed or under the control of a system designer, which makes it difficult to classify items into domains of interest. In addition, users navigate the web in many different contexts and for many different reasons, making it difficult even to know what content area might be of interest.

1.1 Group Adaptive System

Our Group Adaptive System offers users a collaborative navigation environment on the web, enabling group- and web-resource adaptation to users based on their interactions and behavior. Rather than classify documents and rely on static or manually developed profiles for users and groups, we chose to rely on (1) user interactions with pages and with other users, and (2) the underlying structure of the portions of the web that users interact with. This choice was motivated by the fact that reasons for web navigation can be as different as documents on the web itself, making stereotypes limited relative to users' interests.

In our system, users navigate independently on the web but belong to groups joined by common interests, which are determined through resource access and other interactions. Group membership depends on (1) resources accessed and the information clusters these resources belong to, (2) the group related to these information clusters, (3) the interactions among users in each group, and (4) the group the user currently belongs to. To make such a system work, we are studying users' interactions with web resources to measure user interest in the information they see. We intend to correlate user interest with group interest and use this correlation to determine group membership.

In this paper, we report on the status of our project. Our prototype Group Adaptive System (GAS) has been tested with a group of users. The system allows users to interact through web resources (message exchanges, rating, providing shortcuts, etc.) and presents a common information space or "Collaborative View" that is, determined by a rough classification on the number of interactions. In the end, the GAS is meant to provide users (1) awareness of others and (2) authoritative recommendations focused on group interest.

In the rest of this section, we describe the model we are currently testing to provide recommendations. In Sect. 2, we describe related work. In Sect. 3, we briefly describe the prototype architecture and its implementation. In Sect. 4, we report on a first validation study of the model based on data collected during a usability test. Finally, future work is outlined in Sect. 5.

1.2 CLEVER-Based Model

Our model for determining group adaption of web resources with respect to group interest is based heavily on Kleinberg's HITS [16] and CLEVER [10] algorithms for discovering authoritative sources of information (authorities and hubs) leveraging on the linked structure of the web. In this algorithm, a query (standard result by text-based search engines) is a subgraph of nodes (HTML pages) and edges (HTML links) augmented with several "close" nodes. In particular, the algorithm evaluates a starting set of a few (200) pages (called *"core"*) by submitting a text query to a standard search engine, enlarging the core by adding pages that point to or are pointed to by pages into the core.

Initial authority and hub weights are set to 1 for each node. Then an iterative algorithm is run on the graph, alternatively evaluating authority and hub weights depending on neighbors' weights. The algorithm is shown to converge in identifying *good authorities* (nodes well recognized as good sources) and *good hubs* (nodes well recognized as repository of links to good authorities). This algorithm takes into account the structure of the underlying portion of the web, relying on the authors of the pages or nodes to help determine "good pages" on a topic. The key point is to leverage the hundreds of authors of pages that know about the topic: placing a link from a page toward another infers authority on a resource that is believed (by the author) to be relevant.

Recommender and adaptive models usually do not take such things into account to provide users with suggestions or to cut down the amount of information available on a topic (filtering). Thus, our approach adds this dimension to the common information space created by the group participants' navigation. We consider documents navigated by the group as the result of a *broad-topic* query by the users to the search engine, and apply the CLEVER algorithm to these, obtaining recommendations that are based not only on interactions of the group with pages but also on the pages own structure. In fact, a link $X \Rightarrow Y$ is meant as "inferring authority from X on Y" and is explicitely chosen (suggested) by X's author that knows both resources. In this way, if user U_1 and user U_2 access page P_1 and page P_2, (authored, respectively, by A_1 and A_2) and both pages point to a page P_3 (which was not actually visited by either user) the algorithm can "discover" P_3 and propose it as a possibly useful resource to U_1 and U_2 (or to any other similar user). Since this suggestion derives, in a certain way, both from

U_1 and U_2 accesses and from A_1 and A_2 choices, it is widely supported by an authoritative chain that begins at users, passes through page authors and identifies a useful resource. Put another way, we consider the HTML pages accessed by the group (representing group experience and current interests) as the core (i.e., the results of the standard text-based query in CLEVER), enlarge it with the pages that point to the set itself and those that are pointed to by it (using authors' "experience" in terms of links established), and then run the algorithm. This can help to identify authoritative resources that might be relevant for the group.

Now, the cooperation among the group members steps in. In fact, in everyday life, people rely on recommendations from others, such as movie and book reviews printed in newspapers, or general surveys such as restaurant guides [22]. The Group Adaptive System's goal is to use the structure of users' behavior to present group members with a shared space relevant to the group. The common information space is a view of group knowledge adapted to participants' behavior (i.e. the authorities and hubs previously discovered), enhancing the awareness of the community's activity and providing participants a place for interaction by allowing them to create new relationships among people and resources. Users' interactions, such as adding links, exchanging messages or explicitly ranking a resource (or even the simple navigation of a suggested page), add information to the model and provide feedback that is, then, taken into account in the next evaluation of authorities and hubs. The initial authority and hub weights, that in CLEVER algorithm are set to 1, can, in fact, be changed according to a weighted measure of all the interactions taken.

As described in Sect. 4, we tested the first part of the model (i.e., running CLEVER by using as core a set of pages navigated by the group) and the results are encouraging. The next step will be to further refine the already significant suggestions by determining an initial weighted measure of interactions for authority and hub weights. Finally, the model will be tested in a real case study.

2 Related Work

Social navigation in information space is a relatively new research direction that examines user behavior and user interaction in information-seeking. The objective of social navigation work is to use information about other people's behavior and suggestions to decide what to do. In short, the hope is to support people taking advantage of the navigation of others who have similar tastes or interests.

Recommender systems are a branch of social navigation systems [12, 18, 22]. In a typical system, people provide recommendations as inputs, which the system then aggregates and directs to appropriate recipients. In this case, the main step is in the aggregation. User evaluations may be expressed by a single bit (good or bad) or by unstructured textual annotations. Recommendations may be entered explicitly or may be gathered by implicit evaluations, and even may be anonymous. Evaluations can be aggregated through content analysis and weighted voting. Aggregated evaluations may be used to select items, or to filter out negative recommendations, or may accompany items in a display. In collaborative filtering, the goal is to predict the preferences of one user based on the preferences of a group of users. Here, the main problem is the ability to make good matches between those who recommend and those seeking recommendations.

GroupLens [15] is a collaborative filtering system for net news that gathers, disseminates, and uses ratings from some users to predict other users' interest in articles. It is based on the simple idea that people who agreed in their subjective evaluation of past articles are likely to agree again in the future. GroupLens asks its users to rate the articles they read, and uses ratings in two different ways: (1) correlates them to determine which users' ratings are most similar to each other, and (2) predicts how well a user will like new articles based on rating from similar users. Another system, Fab [1, 2], combines collaborative and content-based filtering by maintaining users profiles based on content analysis and directly comparing these profiles to determine similar users. With Fab, users receive items both that score highly against their own profile and that are rated highly by a user with a similar profile.

Mathe and Chen [17] propose a method to adapt information access to individual user profiles based on contextual information relevance. They rely on a descriptive user model containing tasks and user names to describe profiles, and on an information relevance network incrementally built from user feedback. The model records the relevance of references based on user feedback for specific queries and profiles, and derives relevant references for similar queries and profiles.

Swiki [14] is a collaborative web server in which every user can easily modify and extend pages by simply clicking on a link labelled "Edit this page" and then modifying the page in a web form. Swiki maintains a list of recently modified pages accessible by authorized users. This server has also been modified to add functionality to enhance the awareness of the community's activities through annotations posted on the documents list. These annotations are interpreted as footprints pointing out links the lead to pages that have been used recently and that give the feeling of the activity of a virtual community. These tools have been shown to be most useful within a small close group of users, such as a work group, where people are already know of each other's interests.

Plastic [21] is a new web site in the Automatic Media Network. It is a live collaboration between the web readers and editors. Operating somewhere between anarchy and hierarchy, it is a place to suggest and discuss news, opinions, rumors, humor, and anecdotes online. Drawing from the best material posted to Plastic's sections by editors, the Plastic homepage gives a summary view of what people at Plastic are talking about at any given moment. The goal is to allow people to share information, with the hope that the stories and reader comments will engage people in conversation with readers and editors.

3 Group Adaptive System: Prototype

This section describes GAS, the prototype for the Group Adaptive System, as it was developed to support our user study (described in the next section) to validate its interface and, later, the model described in Sect. 1.1. It must be also noted that the prototype tested (and described here) did not include a sophisticated model for automatically determining suggestions.

The prototype is a proxy server infrastructure that lies between user clients and web servers. GAS offers collaborative and adaptive web navigation to users through a collaborative interface added to pages (viewed in the browser). The collaborative interface enables information exchange in the form of documents and comments among participants through (*1*) a "common information space" adapted and created based on participants' interactions (annotations) and (*2*) a "communication channel" obtained by annotating the resources navigated to.

In particular, GAS allows group participants to navigate the web independently, using the interaction tools to augment the page contents with shortcuts to other resources, comments (ideas, opinions, clues), scores, messages, as well as to observe other people's behavior by accessing trails left on the pages. Because the number of resources involved in navigation is incremental, these are dynamically filtered and tailored to represent the state of the group navigation (new resources, new users, new annotations). When users access to web, the "data collector" stores their interactions, the "adaptive engine" uses these to determine those resources that are "relevant" for the group, and the "presentation module" builds the common information space to be delivered to participants.

GAS is intended to make participants aware of each other and also to suggest relevant information and provide an access point for future navigation. In particular, the common information space or Collaborative View is a source of information based on group interests and, it is a place from which participants can gather others' ideas and knowledge. The accessed documents provide awareness of others through footprints[1] that GAS embeds into pages.

In order to determine group relevant resources, and elaborate the common information space, GAS (in this preliminary version we are describing) considers only the number of interactions group members taken on the resource: the higher the number of these interactions, the more relevant the resource, and once the number crosses some threshold, the resource becomes eligible to be part of the common space.

GAS Architecture. GAS' s distributed architecture is dictated by its characteristics (see also [4]). People must be able to access different servers (we provide group adaptation of web resources) with different clients (laptop, as phone, as pc). To achieve this, the system exhibits a three level architecture and uses a programmable proxy as its middle layer. The proxy knows the client-server protocol and can manipulate information during transactions. The proxy is not

---

[1] Footprints signal the presence of the group interactions and allow users to access the contents.

constrained to run at a specified location, but can be placed anywhere [6] along the information stream. GAS consists of three parts: a *data collector*, an *adaptive engine*, and a *data presentation module*. Using GAS is easy: First, the user sets the browser's HTTP proxy, registers with the system, and logs in. Once logged in, the user can access any web page, but the pages will have additional information embedded into them, namely, the GAS interface and the footprints of other users.

GAS User Interface. The access point to the system is the GAS registration and log-in page. Once the user is logged in, he or she can choose to access any web site (the login phase is required only when the user accesses from a new browser instance). The GAS user interface consists of the 3 elements a *Tools bar*, an *Annotations bar*, and a *Collaborative View*. Tools and Annotations bars are embedded in the pages by including HTML and JavaScript into the sources without modifying the "original" page display. These consist of a set of links to the tools to annotate pages and the group footprints (annotations posted by the participants). The *Collaborative View* consists of an HTML page (shown on a separate window) with links to resources that are considered relevant for the group by the adaptive engine that uses the modified CLEVER algorithm.

GAS Implementation. GAS is implemented using the Web Intermediaries (WBI) framework [6, 7]. WBI is an HTTP request processor that receives the user's requests and produces or filters the responses to these requests. More simply, WBI is a programmable HTTP proxy. The basic programmable unit in WBI is the MEG (request editor, generator, monitor end document editor), which are combined together into applications called plugins. GAS is implemented by a set of WBI plugins: (1) the web server/proxy plugin provides the access to the system, (2) the authorization plugin provides the users registration and their identification, and (3) the GAS plugin that provides the collaborative environment.

The GAS MEGS are triggered when users interact with a web page: collecting and analyzing data, and generating of dynamic contents are their main functionalities. Users interactions, on documents accessed, are stored in a persistent store mechanism provided by WBI, a hierarchical database much like a file-system, which contains arbitrary key/value pairs. Pages accessed are stored in the filesystem by URL. A GAS MEG chain constructs the user interface by embedding HTML and JavaScript in the pages loaded by the browser. When the footprints contents are requested by a user, the presentation module MEGs are triggered, displaying the interface for that query. Different HTML and JavaScript implement the user interface properly in different browsers (e.g., Netscape and Internet Explorer).

4 Preliminary Results

During the development of the prototype GAS user interface, we tested usability with a group of 10 users (faculties, Ph.D and Master degree students) at the

University of Salerno, all conducting research in our research lab. This usability test allowed us to improve the system and better define the user interface based on feedback and user requirements.

To preliminarily validate the model used to provide suggestions to the users, we decided to use the data collected during the Salerno students' navigation (model validation test). It must be said that almost 5 months passed between the usability test of the system and our testing of the model with these data. At the time of the usability test, none of the users knew of the existence of the model to be used.

Data were collected during the usability test and users navigated for about a month. First, we examined data subdivided by week. From the results, it appears that the authorities and hubs the algorithm determines for each week are different (new resources can always be added as suggestions with the time), and also that many of the authorities and hubs are not from the core (the pages determined are unknown, i.e. not visited, to users).

During the week that users navigated most[2], 498 URLs were accessed. A manual screening of the results showed that many of the hubs and authorities with higher scores were rather heterogeneous (as well as the pages navigated by the group), making it difficult to fully establish their validity as suggestions for the group. Nevertheless, some of the resources suggested (but which were not navigated by the users) were both meaningful and useful . For example, the first authority was a site for nVidia Developers about an OpenGL demo on Fluid Visualization[3], as a group of students was actually working on a project about OpenGL. The second authority was a soccer site from an Italian provider[4], many students accessed resources (on other sites) about Italian soccer league results. Hubs were also rather significant. Although the first hub was a project site in the Gnome Developer's site (and almost all of the students were developing under Linux though none were directly involved with Gnome), the second was the URL of the FAQ for the newsgroup comp.graphics.algorithms[5], a relevant resource, for the group that had the graphics project. Other hubs included a description of Enterprise JavaBeans at CalTech, a very good resource of information about the web (a personal home page at the CS Dept. in University of Milan, Italy) and a very good Italian hub for resources about thesis writing (including style manuals and software manuals on text- and word-processors).

To get a more precise estimation of the validity of suggestions, we decided to select the two group members who showed the highest level of activity in the system (number of pages navigated and interactions with GAS), and re-run the algorithm on only the resources accessed by them during the entire month. The two users accessed a total of 761 URLs. From the manual analysis of the results, we were able to determine that many of the hubs and authorities were

---

[2] Note that the system was down intermittently for modifications to improve the visualization of bars on particularly intricate pages.
[3] http://developer.nvidia.com/view.asp?IO=ogl_fluid_viz.
[4] http://calcio.iol.it
[5] http://www.faqs.org/faqs/graphics/algorithms-faq/.

indeed fully meaningful, and therefore useful as suggestions given by the system. For example, analyzing the core of pages navigated, it was clear the two users were mainly looking for conferences on Cooperative and Adaptive systems, Latex manuals (one of the two was writing a thesis), a specific conference to be held in Finland (and consequent search of travel information and accommodation). Among the highest ranked hubs and authorities obtained were links to conference lists and conferences sites on the same topics or related topics, links to previously unvisited resources to Latex manuals, and a link to an interesting and particularly useful resource about Finland: a student hostel in Helsinki.

A final comment is necessary: The dynamic nature of some sites (news, advertisements, etc.), makes some of the suggestions useless after a while. This was one of the facts that limited the effectiveness of the validation test for the whole group of users, many of whom accessed news sites (e.g., newspapers) whose outgoing links and backlinks dramatically changed over time and were often broken. Of course, in a real setting, this is not going to be a problem, as backlinks and outgoing links can be computed immediately after the resource is accessed .

In the next experiment, we plan to plug users' interactions and explicit ranking into the CLEVER model. For example, the initial authority weight given to a node can be incremented proportionally to the number of interactions by different users and to the ranking given by the users. Moreover, by evaluating the interactions of users with the resources suggested, we can further provide refined suggestions. Though we believe that the validation of the model provided us with positive feedback, we also believe that these refinements can improve the quality of the system's suggestions.

5 Conclusions and Future Work

In this paper we presented the status of the GAS project. We described the model and prototype, and reported encouraging results from an initial validation test. We plan to conduct more complete tests to determine the best way to combine user interactions and the explicit ranking of the resources with a CLEVER-like model. In addition, we would like to study how best to determine subgroups of users with more closely related interestes. Known methods of coclustering information in bipartite graphs (users and resources) can probably be helpful in this. Subgroup identification will be very useful, as we then can (1) further refine the suggestions given (e.g., by re-running the CLEVER-based algorithm on the resources navigated by the subgroup and subgroup member's interactions), and (2) allow multiple membership for each user in such a way that suggestions will relate to the "current" interests of the user as shown by his or her current navigation pattern.

We are well aware of the implications that a widely used GAS can have on performance, and thus the need for distributing the load of such a system among different machines, either on a cluster that team up to provide the service or on a truly distributed architecture that incorporates several cooperating GASs. One intriguing scenario is a distributed hierarchy of GASs that act as a proxy chain, each providing suggestions to a larger group of users (in subgroups) before finally gathering the resources requested by a single user.

References

1. Balabanovic M., Shoham Y.: *"Fab: Content-Based, Collaborative Recommendation"*. In Communications of the ACM. Vol. 40, N. 3. March 1997.
2. Balabanovic M.: *"An Adaptive Web Page Recommendation Service"*. In The First International Conference on Autonomous Agents. Marina del Rey, California. February 1997.
3. Barra M., Cattaneo G., Negro A., Scarano V.: *"Symmetric Adaptive Customer Modeling in a Electronic Store"*. In Proc. of 3th IEEE Symposium on Computers and Communications (ISCC). Greece 1998.
4. Barra M.: *"Distributed Systems for Group Adaptivity on the Web"*. In the Proc. of AH2000 Inter. Conf. on Adaptive Hypermedia and Adaptive Web-based Systems. ITC/IRST Trento, Italy. August 2000.
5. Barra M.: *"Group Adaptation and Collaboration on the Web"*. In Proc. of Inter. Conference of Computer Supported Cooperative Work (CSCW2000). Philadelphia, PA. December 2000.
6. Barrett R., Maglio P.: *"Intermediaries: New Places for Producing and Manipulating Web Content"*. In Proc. of 7th International WWW Conference. 1998.
7. Maglio P., Barrett R.: *"WebPlaces: Adding people to the Web"*. In Poster Proc. of 8th International WWW Conference. Canada 1999.
8. Breese J., Heckerman D, Kadie C.: *"Empirical Analysis of Predictive Algorithms for Collaborative Filtering"*. In Proc. of the 14th Conference on Uncertainty in Artificial Intelligence, Madison, WI, July, 1998.
9. Brusilovsky P.: *"Methods and techniques of adaptive hypermedia"*. User Modeling and User-Adapted Interaction, 6 (2-3), 87-129, 1996.
10. Chakrabarti, S. Dom, B., Gibson, D., Kleinberg, J., Raghavan R., and Rajagopalan S.: *"Automatic Resource Compilation by Analyzing Hyperlink Structure and Associated Text."* Proceedings of the 7th World-Wide Web Conference, 1998.
11. Dieberger A.: *"Where did all the people go? A collaborative Web space with social navigation information"*, Poster at WWW9, Amsterdam, The Netherlands, May 2000.
12. Dieberger, A., Höök K.: *"Applying principles of social navigation to the design of shared virtual spaces"*, presented at WebNet'99, Honolulu, Hawaii, 1999.
13. Erickson T., Laff M. R.: *"The Design of the 'Babble' Timeline: A Social Proxy for Visualizing Group Activity over Time"*. In Proc. of CHI2001. Conference on Human Factors in Computing Systems. Seattle, Washington, 31 March-5 April 2001.
14. Guzdial M.: *"Swiki"* Georgia Tech.
http://www.cc.gatech.edu/mark.guzdial/squeak/
15. Konstan J. A., Miller B. N., Maltz D., Herlocker J. L., Gordon L. R., Riedl J.: *"GroupLens: Applying Collaborative Filtering to Usenet News"*. In Communications of the ACM. March 1997.
16. Kleinberg J.: *"Authoritative sources in a hyperlinked environment"*. In Proc. of 9th ACM-SIAM Symposium on Discrete Algorithms. San Francisco, California January 25-27, 1998. Extended version in Journal of the ACM 46(1999).

17. Mathe N., Chen J.: *"A User-Centered Approach to Adaptive Hypertext based on a Information Relevance Model"*. In the Proc. of 4th International Conference on User Modeling, UM94. Hyannis, MA 1994.
18. Murno A. J., Hook K., Benyon D.: *"Computer Supported Cooperative Work. Social Navigation of Information Space"*. Springer-Verlag. G. Britain 1999.
19. O' Connor M., Herlocker J.: *"Clustering Items for Collaborative Filtering"*. In Proc. of the ACM SIGIR '99 Workshop on Recommender Systems: Algorithms and Evaluation. Berkeley. August 1999.
20. Billsus D., Pazzani M.: *"A Hybrid User Model for News Story Classification"*. In Proc of the Seventh International Conference on User Modeling (UM '99), Banff, Canada 1999.
21. Plastic: http://www.plastic.com.
22. Resnick P., Varian H.R.: *"Recommender Systems"*. In Communications of the ACM,40,3. March 1997.
23. Ungar L. H., Foster D. P.: *"Clustering Methods for Collaborative Filtering"*. In AAAI Workshop on Recommendation Systems, 1998.

TV Scout: Lowering the Entry Barrier to Personalized TV Program Recommendation

Patrick Baudisch[1,*] and Lars Brueckner[2,*]

[1] Inf. Sciences and Technologies Lab.
Xerox Palo Alto Research Center
Palo Alto, CA 94304, U.S.A.
+1 (650) 812 4656
patrick.baudisch@acm.org
[2] IT Transfer Office (ITO)
Darmstadt University of Technology
64283 Darmstadt, Germany
+49 (6151) 16-6217
brueckner@ito.tu-darmstadt.de

Abstract. In this paper, we present *TV Scout,* a recommendation system providing users with personalized TV schedules. The TV Scout architecture addresses the "cold-start" problem of information filtering systems, i.e. that filtering systems have to gather information about the user's interests before they can compute personalized recommendations. Traditionally, gathering this information involves upfront user effort, resulting in a substantial entry barrier. TV Scout is designed to avoid this problem by presenting itself to new users not as a filtering system, but as a retrieval system where all user effort leads to an immediate result. While users are dealing with this retrieval functionality, the system continuously and unobtrusively gathers information about the user's interests from implicit feedback and gradually evolves into a filtering system. An analysis of log file data gathered with over 10,000 registered online users shows that over 85% of all first-time users logged in again, suggesting that the described architecture is successful in lowering the entry barrier.

1 Introduction

Information filtering systems [7] suffer from a bootstrapping problem. Before they can give personalized recommendations to a user, they have to find out what the user's interests are. Only then can filtering systems build user profiles and compute personalize recommendations. The problems resulting from this undesirable order of required user effort and delayed benefit is a well-known phenomenon in collaborative filtering, the so-called *cold start* problem [17]. Users are reluctant to invest effort, especially if they don't know whether the offered service will be worth the effort. This approach bears the risk that users will avoid the gamble and stick with a system offering more immediate benefit, such as a retrieval-oriented system. Users making this decision, however, will never come to discover the long-term benefits the filter-

---

[*] The work presented in this paper was carried out during the authors' affiliation at GMD-IPSI.

ing system would have offered. For additional studies on incentive structures and the results of the lack of incentives see [11].

In this paper, we describe an architecture designed to address this incentive problem and we will demonstrate this architecture at the example of our TV program recommendation system TV Scout. We will begin by briefly introducing the field of TV recommendation. We will then discuss TV Scout and its user interface and discuss the underlying filtering architecture. Finally, we will report results of an analysis of TV Scout online usage data, discuss our findings, and present conclusions and future work.

2 Recommending TV Programs

In 1992, Belkin and Croft wrote "In particular, applications such as the recreational use of television programming pose special problems and opportunities for research in filtering" [7, p.37]. Several current trends make TV an interesting application area for information filtering. TV viewers are facing an information overload situation [10]. A number of technical improvements, such as cable, satellite, and digital TV technology have resulted in an increasing number of available TV channels. Today, hundreds of channels broadcast thousands of programs every day. Since the amount of content that is of interest for a given viewer has not increased proportionally, *planning* ones TV consumption has become a challenge. The amount of TV programs will soon exceed the limits of what can reasonably be printed and channel surfing is no longer fast enough to allow getting an overview of all channels [11]. Attempting to meet the changing requirements, web-based TV program guides (e.g. TV Guide, http://www.tvguide.com), set-top boxes with electronic program guides (EPGs, [20]), and digital VCRs (e.g. *Tivo* http://www.tivo.com) have emerged in the past few years.

There have been several research projects around TV recommendation in the past [11, 9], but most of them focused on set-top boxes and on the technical possibilities for monitoring user behavior rather then on web-based systems and usability. Current research in personalized TV evolves still around personalized EPGs [1], but also around new concepts, such as multi-agent recommender systems [14]. A more thorough overview of current research in the field of personalized TV recommendation can be found in [18].

3 TV Scout

TV Scout [3, 4] is a web-based TV recommendation system. Its goal is to support users in planning their personal TV consumption.

In order to understand the design requirements for such a system, we began our research with an informal survey among students [3]. The survey indicated that expectations about the functionality of an ideal TV recommendation system were dominated by experiences with printed TV program guides. While our goal was to eventually provide users with a personalized TV program at a single mouse click, our survey indicated that only a minority of the users we had interviewed would be willing to invest the required effort. We concluded that in order to attract users, a successful TV recommendation system would first have to emulate the expected print-like functionality, as well as the straightforward usage of printed guides: pick up the TV guide, find today's listing, pick a program, and watch TV. The challenge was to provide a seamless transition from this scenario to the filtering functionality we had in mind. To prevent the filtering functionality from conflicting with the user expectations and system learnability, we decided to create a system that would progressively disclose its filtering features to users.

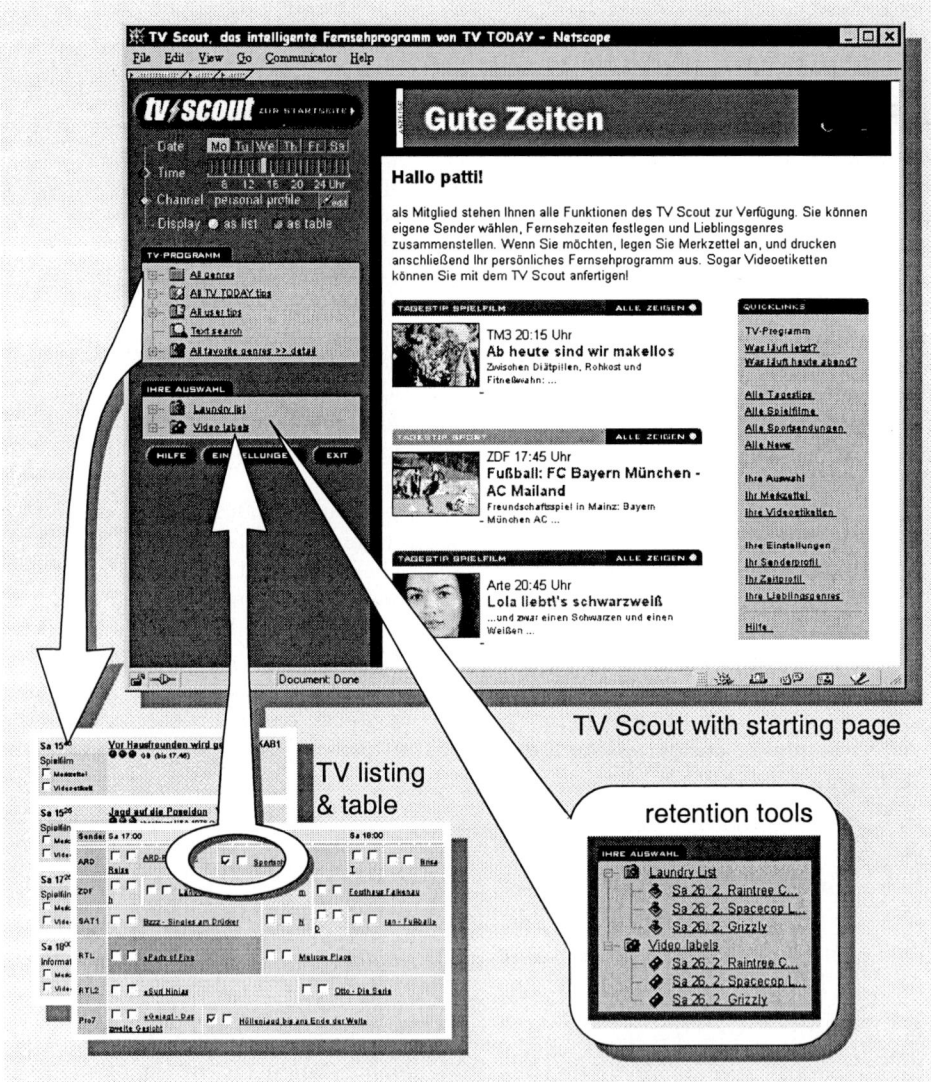

Fig. 1. How TV Scout presents itself to first-time users (screenshots partially translated from German)

3.1 Implementation

The TV Scout project was conducted in cooperation with the TV program guide publisher TV TODAY. While this resulted in TV Scout getting implemented as a web-based system, we see no architectural problems in porting the resulting architecture to a set-top box. To allow maintaining personal user profile data, first-time users have to create an account, which they access using a self-selected login name and password. The web-based TV Scout front end is implemented in HTML, Java, and JavaScript.

3.2 Retrieving Program Descriptions

To users entering TV Scout for the first time, the system presents itself as a retrieval system. Its functionality at this stage restricts itself to the functionality of a printed TV program guide, with a graphical user interface. Users specify a query (or simply hit a button for the default "what's on now"), sort through the resulting list and select programs to watch. Users can also print the list of selected programs for later use.

Fig. 1 shows how users accomplish that using the TV Scout user interface. The interface consists of the menu frame on the left and the content frame on the right. The menu frame provides users with access to all retrieval and filtering functions and is permanently visible. The content frame is used to display various types of TV listings and all profile editing tools.

The system is used as follows. Users execute a query by picking a query from the query menu. Fig.2 shows several close-ups of this menu. In its current version, TV Scout offers four query groups: *text search*, *genres*, *user tips*, and *TV TODAY tips*, plus a *favorites* group that we will explain later. Text search allows users to search for keywords using optional Boolean syntax. The other three submenus are executed by picking the corresponding menu entry. To provide more precise queries, theses query

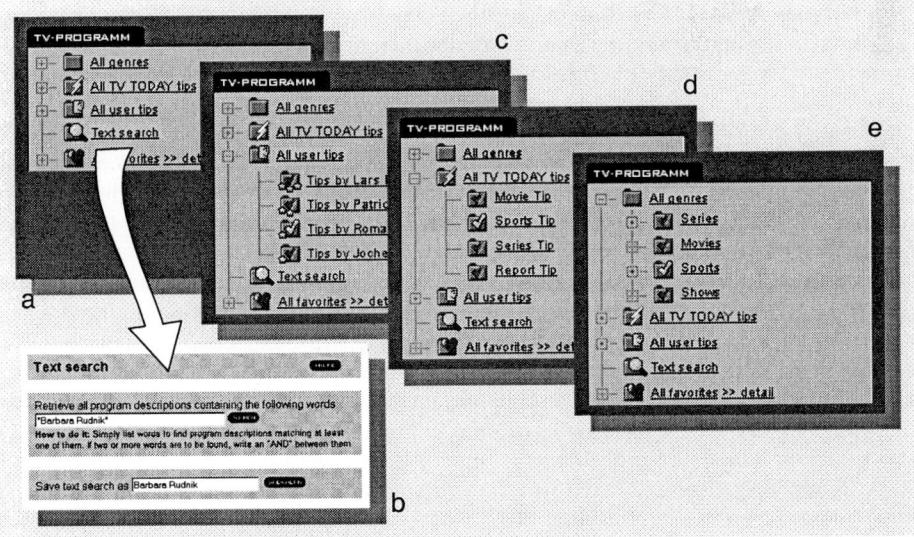

Fig. 2. The query menu offers four groups of queries

groups contain hierarchies of submenus that can be browsed in a file system explorer-like fashion. *Genres* contains a historically grown genre classification of TV programs, such as *sports*, *comedy*, and *series* [14]. *User tips* contains recommendations volunteered by users who serve as self-proclaimed editors, so-called *opinion leaders* [4]. Finally, *TV TODAY tips*, are recommendations provided by the editors of TV Scout's printed counter part.

By default, all queries are restricted to the programs starting within the current hour, but TV Scout provides customized controls that allow specifying arbitrary time and date intervals using mouse drag interactions (Fig. 4a). Channels can be selected from two predefined sets or can be selected in detail using a paintable interface (Fig. 4b) [6].

When a query is executed, the resulting set of TV program descriptions (Fig. 1 bottom left) is displayed in the content area. Descriptions consist of the program title, a rating describing how well the program matches the query, an extract of the program description, and links to a more detailed description. Users can choose between the display styles *ranked list* and *table*.

Two toggle switches per program description allow users to retain programs they plan to watch in the so-called *retention tool* (Fig. 1 bottom left, circled). The retention tool *laundry list* can be used to print a list of programs; *video labels* are designed to retain and print programs to be videotaped. The retention menu allows users to display the content of their retention tools for reviewing or printing. The printed list can be used to remind users of the programs that they plan to watch.

3.3 Filtering Functionality: Creating "Bookmarks"

Using the functionality described so far, the effort for repeated usage is the same each time the service is used. The next step therefore is for the system to reduce the effort required of the user when querying, since the primary purpose of IF systems is to be "time-saving devices" [2].

When a user enters a query that is broader than necessary, the user is forced to sort through an unnecessarily long listing when trying to find desired programs. When the system detects that the user has used such a sub-optimal query repeatedly while another query with better precision exists, it makes a suggestion. Fig. 3 shows an example. Let's assume that the user has repeatedly used the query "movies" to exclusively find and retain comedies and horror movies. By computing the overlap between the retained programs and all available queries [3], the system detects that the retained programs can also be covered by the more specific queries "horror movies" and "comedies". A dialog box opens and suggests using these queries instead. The user can execute the suggested queries like any other query, i.e. by clicking their names.

The more important function of the dialog box, with respect to our filtering concept, is that it also suggests retaining these queries as *bookmarks*. Users can do this by clicking the toggle switch that accompanies each query (a folder symbol with a check mark, see Fig. 3a). Retained queries pop up in the user's *favorites* (Fig. 3b). The *favorites* folder is collocated with the other query groups and can be executed the same way. Retained queries are listed in a flat hierarchy, thereby providing the users with convenient access to queries that would otherwise be hidden in multiple different submenus. This functionality corresponds to the bookmark folder in a web browser.

Unlike web bookmarks these bookmarks are stored on the TV Scout server, allowing TV Scout to use them as input for additional computation.

Retention check boxes accompany all queries in the system (see Fig. 3b), so users can bookmark queries anytime, independent of suggestions. The primary purpose of query suggestions is to inform users about the bookmaking concept and to encourage its usage.

Note the special importance of the retention tools. Although the declared purpose of the retention tools is to allow users to memorize programs and print schedules, their primary purpose from the system's point of view is to serve as an information source about the user's interests. The content of the retention tools is considered an implicit positive rating for the retained programs, making the retention tools serve as a source of implicit retention feedback [16]. Although implicit feedback is commonly agreed to be a less reliable source of rating information than explicit feedback, it has the benefit of being unobtrusive, which we considered essential for this type of filtering system. See [3, 4] for how TV Scout uses the same implicit input for various types of filtering functionality based on collaborative filtering.

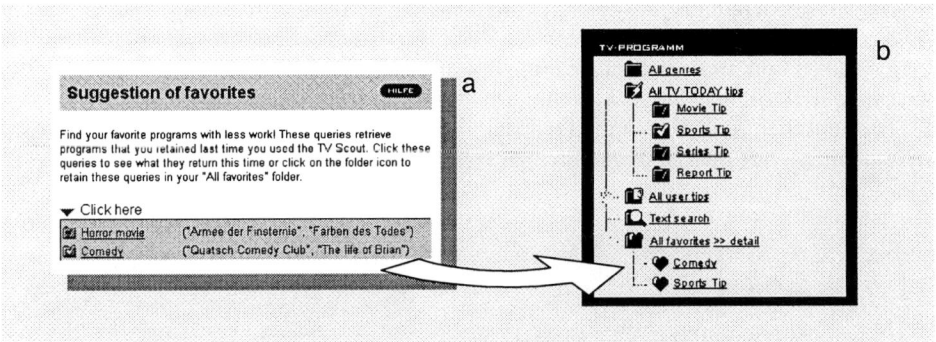

Fig. 3. By clicking a checkmark-shaped button, queries can be retained in *All favorites*.

3.4 Filtering Functionality: One-Click Personalized TV Schedules

To provide a container for bookmarked queries is not the only purpose of the *favorites* folder. The real value of this folder lies in the fact that users can execute it as a whole by clicking the top menu entry labeled *all favorites*. This executes all retained queries at once. The result listings of the individual queries, however, are not appended to each other—they are merged into a single relevance-ordered result list. This is the most powerful function of the TV Scout system—it fulfills the initial goal of generating personalized TV schedule with a single mouse click.

How are the individual query results merged in order to obtain a useful result? When the query profile *all favorites* is executed, a script running inside the TV Scout server executes all contained queries. This is done by delegating each query to the corresponding subsystem; text search, for example, is executed by FreeWAIS, while genre queries are executed by a relational database. As a result, the subsystems deliver sets of pairs (program, rating). The task of the query profile script is to merge all these results into a single ranked list. This requires transforming the individual ratings such that they include the user's perceived importance of the interest represented by the query. In order to express this perceived importance, the query profile stores a linear function (i.e. a factor and an offset) for each retained query. The resulting ratings are computed by transforming the ratings returned by the subsystem using this function. If a TV program is returned by multiple queries its ratings are summed up. Finally, programs are sorted by their result rating and returned to the user.

The critical factor is the parameters of the linear transformation. The system acquires these parameters through initialization, learning, and manual updating. When queries are bookmarked, their functions are initialized using Zipf's law [19, p. 60]. This means that more specific queries are given positive offsets, propagating the results of these queries towards the top ranks of the resulting listings, thus preventing them from being buried inside the large result sets of less specific queries.

After initialization, the parameters of the rating transformations can be improved by two means. First, TV Scout continuously optimizes the query profile based on the same implicit retention feedback that was already used for suggesting queries. See [3] for a description of the algorithm. Second, interested users are allowed to manually inspect and update their profile. Clicking the ">>details" link in the *all favorites* menu invokes a profile editor. The simplest version of this editor provides users with a single pull-down menu per query (Fig. 4c), allowing users to assign a symbolic rating to each query, such as "*Action movies* are [very important] to me" [3, 5].

Through the use of relevance feedback the query profile improves continuously, so that the quality of the rankings obtained by clicking *all favorites* increases over time.

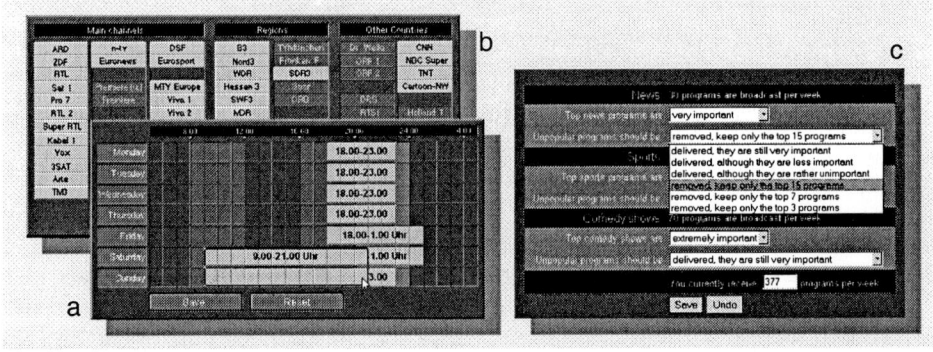

Fig. 4. The TV Scout profile editing tools (a) viewing time profile editor, (b) channel profile editor, and (c) query profile editor.

3.5 Summary

Fig. 5 summarizes how the usage of TV Scout by a given user can evolve over time. Each transition to a more personalized phase can be suggested by the system (T1-T3) or initiated by the user (U1-U3). However, users are not forced through these phases and may equally well settle with the functionality of one of the earlier phases.

1. **Query phase (S1):** Users can pick predefined queries (T1) or can formulate queries, such as text searches, manually (U1).
2. **Bookmark/reuse phase (S2):** If the system detects reoccurring or sub-optimal queries it proposes better-suited queries and suggests retaining them as *favorites* (U2). Independent of suggestion, users can bookmark queries anytime (T2).
   Profile creation (T*): The user's query profile is created automatically when the first query is bookmarked.
3. **Profile phase (S3):** Initially, the query profile provides users with a convenient way of executing all their bookmarks with a single click. Continuous supply of relevance feedback (T3) or manual profile manipulation (U3) improves the profile.

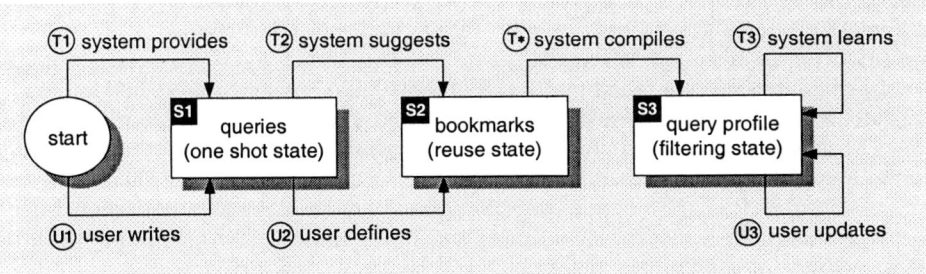

Fig. 5. Evolving usage of a proposed filtering architecture

4 TV Scout Usage Data

The purpose of the TV Scout design is to reduce the entry barrier for new users by using a progressive disclosure of the filtering functionality. How can we verify the success of our interaction design? A controlled experimental comparison with a competing system would be problematic because of the vast amount of interface variables that would be difficult to control. In addition, modeling a realistic web-usage scenario in a lab setting is challenging. Alternatively, a naturalistic study of web use would provide more realistic data, but we would be unable to measure factors such as subjective satisfaction. Ultimately, we decided to conduct an informal analysis of log file data from actual web usage.

When we conducted our data analysis April 20, 2000, TV Scout had been publicly available at for 18 months. The entire 18 months of log file data are included in this study. All usage data was extracted from the web server log files and the system's database. With respect to the filtering functionality, this data was slightly biased, in that the suggestion feature became available later. Because of this, we expected that the usage of bookmarking would be underrepresented.

The main purpose of the analysis was to verify whether our filtering system design fulfilled the primary goal, namely to provide a low entry barrier. If our design was appropriate, then TV Scout would meet the expectations of first-time users and would not overwhelm them. Repeated usage would indicate that users had taken the entry hurdle; one-shot users would suggest the opposite.

We were also interested in learning more about the users' demand for the offered filtering functionality. How many users would adopt bookmarking functionality; how many would make use of their personal query profiles? Based on our informal survey, we expected the majority to be satisfied with the initial retrieval functionality, but we had no clear expectations about the percentages. Finally, we were interested in seeing how useful users would find the query profile. Once they had created one, would they continue to use it or would they abandon it rapidly?

4.1 Results

At the day we examined the log data, TV Scout had 10,676 registered users. In total, users had executed 48,956 queries. 53% of all queries (25,736 queries) were specific queries different from the default query.

Repeated log-ins: We found that 9,190 of the 10,676 registered users had logged in repeatedly, i.e. twice or more. This corresponds to a percentage or 86% repeated users. The most active user with 580 logins had logged in almost daily.

Bookmarks: 1770 users had bookmarked one or more queries. Together, these users had bookmarked 4383 queries, mostly genres. The most frequently executed queries were the genres movies (736 times) and information (364 times), and TV TODAY Movie tips (369 times). Over 300 text searches were bookmarked.

Query profiles: Out of the 1770 users who had bookmarked at least one query, 270 users (about 15%) executed their query profile at least once to obtain personalized listings. These users executed their query profiles a total of 5851 times, which corresponds to an average of 21 times per user. These users manually fine-tune their profiles a total of 1213 times, with an average of 4.5 times per user. These results indicate that query profiles were highly appreciated by those who used them.

5 Conclusions

We interpret the measured percentage of repeated users as a confirmation of our design. 86% of all first time users logged in repeatedly; we consider this to be a very high percentage for a web-based system. This indicates that presenting first-time users with a retrieval setting is a successful approach to keeping the entry barrier for first-time users low.

Only 17% of users made use of the bookmark feature; out of these, only 15% made used of the query profile. These numbers seem low even taking into account that the suggestion feature was not available most of the logged time. Does this result indicate that the filtering functionality is inappropriate or difficult to learn? Why did the majority of the users not reach the "goal" of the system?

This is not how we interpret these results. In an earlier TV usage survey we conducted [3] we found TV users to plan their TV consumption for very different timeframes. Most of these users only planned a TV schedule for the following day or they did not plan at all. Many users only used a guide to determine what was currently on TV. Only 12% of the users planned a TV schedule for the entire week. Considering that the filtering functionality of TV Scout addresses the relatively small subgroup of users who plan their TV consumption, the observed results seem appropriate. The majority of users who only used the retrieval functionality may have found the retrieval functionality of TV Scout to be the appropriate support for *their* information seeking strategy. An online survey as well as an experimental study should help to verify this interpretation.

Acknowledgements

We would like to thank Dieter Böcker, Joe Konstan, Marcus Frühwein, Michael Brückner, Gerrit Voss, Andreas Brügelmann, Claudia Perlich, Tom Stölting, and Diane Kelly.

References

1. L. Ardissono, F. Portis, P. Torasso. F. Bellifemine, A. Chiarotto and A. Difino Architecture of a system for the generation of personalized Electronic Program Guides. In *Proceedings of the UM 2001 workshop "Personalization in Future TV"*, July 13 to July 17, 2001, Sonthofen, Germany.
2. P.E. Baclace. Information intake filtering. In *Proceedings of Bellcore Workshop on High-Performance Information Filtering*, Morristown, NJ, November 1991.
3. P. Baudisch. Dynamic Information Filtering. Ph.D. Thesis. GMD Research Series 2001, No. 16. GMD Forschungszentrum Informationstechnik GmbH, Sankt Augustin. ISSN 1435-2699, ISBN 3-88457-399-3. Also at http://www.patrickbaudisch.com/publications
4. P. Baudisch. Recommending TV Programs on the Web: how far can we get at zero user effort? In Recommender Systems, Papers from the 1998 Workshop, Technical Report WS-98-08, pages 16-18, Madison, WI. Menlo Park, CA: AAAI Press, 1998.
5. P. Baudisch. The Profile Editor: designing a direct manipulative tool for assembling profiles. In *Proceedings of Fifth DELOS Workshop on Filtering and Collaborative Filtering*, pages 11-17, Budapest, November 1997. ERCIM Report ERCIM-98-W001.
6. P. Baudisch. Using a painting metaphor to rate large numbers of objects. In Ergonomics and User Interfaces, Proceeding of the HCI '99 Conference, pages 266-270, Munich, Germany, August 1999. Mahwah: NJ: Erlbaum, 1999.
7. N.J. Belkin and W.B. Croft. Information filtering and information retrieval: two sides of the same coin? CACM, 35(12):29-37, Dec. 1992.
8. A. Borchers, J. Herlocker, J. Konstan, and J. Riedl. Ganging up on information overload. Computer, 31(4):106-108, April 1998.
9. D. Das and H. ter Horst. Recommender systems for TV. In Recommender Systems, Papers from the 1998 Workshop, Technical Report WS-98-08, pages 35-36, Madison, WI. Menlo Park, CA: AAAI Press, 1998.
10. P. Denning. Electronic junk. CACM, 23(3):163-165, March 1982.
11. M. Ehrmantraut, T. Härder, H. Wittig, and R. Steinmetz. The Personal Electronic Program Guide—towards the pre-selection of individual TV Programs. In Proc. of CIKM'96, pages 243-250, Rockville, MD, 1996.
12. L. Gravano and H. García-Molina. Merging ranks from heterogeneous Internet sources. In Proceedings of the 23rd VLDB Conference, pages 196-205, Athens, Greece, 1997.

13. J. Grudin. Social evaluation of the user interface: who does the work and who gets the BENEFIT? In *Proc. of INTERACT'87*: pages 805-811, 1987.
14. M. Kuhn. The New European Digital Video Broadcast (DVB) Standard. ftp://ftp.informatik.uni-erlangen.de/local/cip/mskuhn/tv-crypt/dvb.txt.
15. K. Kurapati, S. Gutta, D. Schaffer, J. Martino and J. Zimmerman. A multi-agent TV recommender. In *Proceedings of the UM 2001 workshop "Personalization in Future TV"*, July 13 to July 17, 2001.
16. D.M. Nichols. Implicit ratings and filtering. In *Proceedings of Fifth DELOS Workshop on Filtering and Collaborative Filtering*, pages 31-36, Budapest, November 1997. ERCIM Report ERCIM-98-W001. Le Chesnay Cedex, France, European Research Consortium for Informatics and Mathematics, 1998.
17. P. Resnick and H. Varian (Eds.). Special issue on Recommender Systems. Communications of the ACM, 40(3):56-89, March 1997.
18. Proceedings of the UM 2001 workshop "Personalization in Future TV", July 13 to July 17, 2001, Sonthofen, Germany. Online at http://www.di.unito.it/~liliana/UM01/TV.html
19. G. Salton and M.J. McGill. *Introduction to Modern Information Retrieval*. New York: McGraw-Hill, 1983.
20. H. Wittig and C. Griwodz. Intelligent media agents in interactive television systems. In *Proc. of the International Conference on Multimedia Computing and Systems '95*, pages 182-189, Boston, May 1995. Los Alamitos, CA: IEEE Computer Science Press, 1995.

Adaptivity, Adaptability, and Reading Behaviour: Some Results from the Evaluation of a Dynamic Hypertext System

Kalina Bontcheva

University of Sheffield,
Regent Court, 211 Portobello St., Sheffield S1 4DP, UK
kalina@dcs.shef.ac.uk

Abstract. This paper presents the evaluation of a dynamic hypertext system that generates personalised explanations. The main focus is on some of the results, which showed that future experiments need to control for users' reading behaviour, as well as other factors

1 Introduction

HYLITE+ [2, 3] is a dynamic hypertext system[1] that generates encyclopaedia-style explanations of terms in two specialised domains: chemistry and computers. The user interacts with the system in a Web browser by specifying a term she wants to look up. The system generates a hypertext explanation of the term; further information can be obtained by following hypertext links or specifying another query (see Fig. 1). The system is based on applied NLG techniques, a re-usable user modelling component (VIEWGEN), and a flexible architecture with module feedback. The adaptivity is implemented on the basis of a user and a discourse models which are used to determine, for example, which concepts are unknown, so clarifying information can be included for them. The user model is updated dynamically, based on the user's interaction with the system. When a user registers with the system for the first time, her model is initialised from a set of stereotypes. The system determines which stereotypes apply on the basis of information provided by the user herself. If no such information is provided, the system assumes a novice user.

In this paper we discuss the results of the system's task-based evaluation. In a nutshell, the participants found the system easy to use and the hypertext understandable and intuitive to navigate. The generation techniques were sufficiently fast, so users did not have to wait for the system response. Similar to other evaluated adaptive hypertext systems (e.g., [5, 6]), the majority of the users expressed a preference for the adaptive version.

More importantly, the evaluation results showed that future experiments which attempt to measure quantitatively the benefit or otherwise of the adaptivity techniques, need to control for users' reading behaviour, as well as other

---

[1] In *dynamic hypertext* page content and links are created on demand and are often adapted to the user and the previous interaction.

factors like users' domain knowledge and experience with the application. In addition, the users' feedback showed that preference for adaptivity can be improved, if users are allowed some control over the system's decisions, e.g., if they can disable some features they are not happy with. In other words, as argued previously in [8, 2], adaptability and adaptivity can benefit each other.

The paper is structured as follows. Section 2 describes the goals and the methodology of this evaluation. The results are discussed at length in Section 3. The paper concludes by summarising the results and outlining some future work.

2   HYLITE+ Evaluation Setup

The acceptability and utility of the adaptive features were evaluated by users who interacted with two versions of our system: a baseline one and the adaptive one. The two versions were, in fact, the same system with the user model and adaptivity features switched off to form the non-adaptive baseline. In this way, we ensured that the same information was available in both systems. Also, this approach minimises the potential influence of different systems' response times on the experiment results, because both versions generate hypertext on the fly and have similar performance.[2]

The initial system page, which was identical in the two versions, contained an alphabetical list of topics, relevant to the experimental tasks (see Fig. 1 left). The users requested an explanation on a given topic by selecting it and clicking **Explain**. After reading the generated page, the participants could obtain further information by following links, navigating back and forward with the browser buttons, or by selecting a new term in the topic list (see Fig. 1 right).

The explanations generated by the adaptive version were enriched with parenthetical definitions of unknown terms, examples, and links to other more general, specific, and related terms (see Fig. 1 right).

2.1   Main Goals

Hypermedia applications are often evaluated with respect to: *interface look and feel*, *representation of the information structure*, and *application-specific information* [9]. The information structure is concerned with the hypertext network (nodes and links) and navigation aids (e.g., site maps, links to related material, index). The application-specific information concerns the hypermedia content – text, images, etc. For our system there is no need to evaluate the interface, since HYLITE+ generates simple HTML and uses Web browsers as rendering tools. Therefore, the evaluation efforts were concentrated on the information content and navigational structure of the generated hypertext. In addition, observation, questionnaires and informal interviews were used to elicit problems and assess the acceptability of the implemented adaptivity techniques.

---

[2] ILEX, for example, used pre-generated static pages as a baseline and the study reported that the difference in the two systems' response times might have influenced some of the results [4].

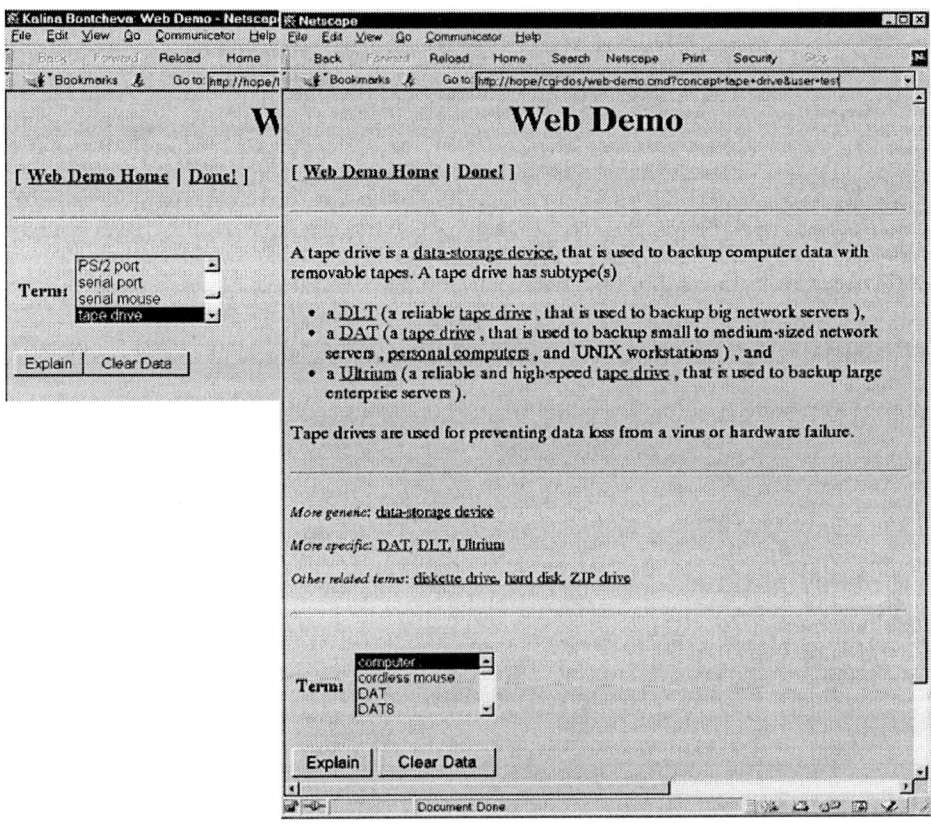

Fig. 1. The system home page (left) and a generated explanation by the adaptive system (right)

For the purpose of this experiment, **information content** was compared on the basis of:

- average *time to complete* each task;
- average number of *pages visited* per task;
- average number of *distinct pages* visited per task;
- percent of *correctly answered questions* per task;
- questionnaire results about *content* and *comprehension* of the generated pages;
- *user preference* for any of the systems.

The **navigational structure** was measured by the following metrics:

- average *time per page visited*;
- average *number of pages visited*;
- *total number of pages visited*;
- number of *links followed*;

- usage of the browser **Back** button;
- usage of the *system's topic list* to find information;
- observation and subjective *opinion on orientation*;
- subjective *opinion on navigation* and ease of finding information.

2.2 Methodology

The experiment has a *repeated measures, task-based* design (also called within-subjects design), i.e., the same users interacted with the two versions of the system, in order to complete a given set of tasks. Prior to the experiment, the participants were asked to provide some *background information* (e.g., computing experience, familiarity with Web browsers, and electronic encyclopaedia) and fill in a *multiple choice pre-test*, that diagnosed their domain knowledge.

After completing all the tasks, the participants were asked to fill in a *questionnaire* and participate in a *semi-structured interview* discussing their experience with the two systems.

2.3 Subjects

The tasks were completed by eight participants – three male and five female. They were assigned randomly to the system they used first: four started with the adaptive and four - with the non-adaptive system. After completing the first three tasks, the users swapped systems for the other three tasks. None of the users had any prior experience with the system, but they all had extensive experience with Web browsing and hypertext. All users had previously used on-line dictionaries and encyclopaedia, which are the types of systems most similar to ours. The participants also had similar computing background, i.e., they all had computer science degrees and were either postgraduate students or research staff at the Computer Science department.

With respect to knowledge of the computer hardware concepts, used in the evaluation tasks, the pre-test differentiated two groups of participants: *complete novices*, who scored between 2 and 4 out of the maximum 15 points on the test; and users with *basic knowledge*, who scored 7 to 8. The two types of users were split equally between the two groups: adaptive-first and non-adaptive first.

2.4 Tasks

Each of the participants was first given a set of three tasks – each set contained one browsing, one problem-solving, and one information location task[3]. The order was not randomised, because the browsing task was also intended as a task that would allow users to familiarise themselves with the system and the available information. The participants performed the first set of tasks with the non-adaptive/adaptive system and then swapped systems for the second set.

---
[3] The design of the tasks follows the design used in the evaluation of two other adaptive hypermedia applications – PUSH [6] and [9].

The participants were not given a specific time limit for performing these tasks because we wanted to provide an environment in which they would interact as they normally would with online reference systems.

2.5 User Recording and Logging

The system's user interaction logs provide a detailed record of: the *user query* in the list of topics, the *hypertext generated*, *links followed*, state of the *user model before and after* the explanation, and time stamps for *each page*. This information was used to derive the quantitative statistics needed for measuring the information content and the navigational structure of the hypertext.

In addition, all browser actions (e.g., use of the Back button) and viewed pages were logged using Astra Quick Test – a tool for testing Web applications with extensive recording facilities. These logs were needed, first, as a backup in case some data got lost in the system logs, and second, in order to derive statistics of the usage of the browser's Back, Forward and History buttons.[4]

3 Results

Due to the small sample size (8 subjects) and the differences in users' prior domain knowledge and browsing styles, the results obtained could not be used to derive a statistically reliable comparison between the measures obtained for the adaptive and the non-adaptive versions, but the quantitative results and user feedback are sufficiently encouraging to suggest that HYLITE+ adaptivity is of benefit to the user.

3.1 Importance of Users' Reading Behaviour: Skimmers vs Readers

As discussed in Sect.2.1, the information content provided in the two system versions was evaluated using quantitative measures, derived from the user interaction logs.

The **mean time per task** results showed that the users who completed the first three tasks with the non-adaptive system took longer on average, with the biggest differences for the browsing and information location tasks. Since the participants swapped systems for the next three tasks and were already familiar with the hyperspace, the average times with both the adaptive and non-adaptive versions are naturally lower.

Unfortunately the results for this particular element of the evaluation cannot be taken as an indication that, for example, the adaptive system might be more helpful when the user is not familiar with the hyperspace, because we discovered

---

[4] Their use cannot be logged by our application, since these actions do not generate requests to it; the browser uses a cached copy instead. Other adaptive systems, e.g., ILEX [4] used and logged their own navigation buttons. However, users expect to be able to use the browser's default buttons [7] and such non-conventional behaviour might influence their attitude to the system.

post-hoc that the experiment failed to control for an important user characteristic which influenced the task completion times. The problem is that even when asked to locate particular information, some users still read thoroughly the hypertext pages, instead of just skimming them to find only the facts relevant to the task.[5] Although we were aware that previous studies of people browsing hypertext (e.g.,[7]) have differentiated two types, *skimmers* and *readers*, we did not expect that this distinction would be important when the users perform information location tasks. Unfortunately, not only does the difference appear to remain, regardless of the task, but it also happened that when the participants were randomly assigned to the systems, all three 'readers' were assigned to the same systems, i.e., the non-adaptive for the first three tasks, then the adaptive one for the remaining three. This explains why the results obtained for the two groups are so different.

Consequently, the results for mean time per task need to be interpreted by taking into account this group effect. As can be seen in Fig. 2,[6] both groups were faster when they interacted with the second system (adaptive for the first group and non-adaptive for the second group), because they were familiar with the hyperspace. The group effect also explains why the mean times per task are consistently higher for the non-adaptive system in the first three tasks and higher for the adaptive system in the second set of three tasks. The readers group (non-adaptive first) was always much slower than the other group, which consisted only of skimmers.

This group effect will become apparent again in other measures discussed below. Its impact on the evaluation results show that it is very important to control for the differences in user characteristics and behaviour, which influence the subjects' task performance much more than the two different experimental conditions, i.e., adaptive versus non-adaptive system. In order to avoid this problem in future experiments, we intend to control for users' reading behaviour prior to the experiment, just as we did for domain knowledge.

3.2 Other Information Content Measures

On average subjects visited more *pages per task* in the non-adaptive, than in the adaptive system. In comparison, the average number of distinct pages visited per task is about the same for the two versions, i.e., in the non-adaptive version users tend to have more visits to the same pages.

We also computed the average **user score per information location task**[7] for the two system versions. On average the subjects had higher task success rate

---

[5] This readers/non-readers problem was discovered by comparing the mean time each participant spent per visited hypertext page.
[6] The rows of the table show the mean and standard deviation for each of the six tasks and the total. The rows called 'Browse...' are for the browsing tasks, 'Choose...' are the problem-solving tasks, and 'Locate...' are for the information location tasks.
[7] The experiment did not measure task score for the browsing tasks, because its role was to allow the participants to familiarise themselves with the system. Also, due to the unconstrained, goal-free nature of the task, task success would have been difficult

Report

Task		Seconds to complete non-adaptive	Seconds to complete adaptive
Browse ZIP drive	Mean	194.50	129.00
	Std. Deviation	86.87	59.67
Choose '10/1 GB tape drive'	Mean	214.50	193.75
	Std. Deviation	93.49	81.33
Locate mouse details 1	Mean	260.25	158.25
	Std. Deviation	78.93	75.74
Browse PCMCIA cards	Mean	113.75	133.75
	Std. Deviation	39.91	61.82
Choose 30/50 GB tape drive	Mean	102.75	135.50
	Std. Deviation	42.92	55.16
Locate mouse details 2	Mean	87.75	162.25
	Std. Deviation	42.46	78.13
Total	Mean	162.25	152.08
	Std. Deviation	89.08	65.52

Fig. 2. Mean and standard deviation of task completion time (in seconds)

with the adaptive system. The novice users exhibited a bigger difference between the task scores with the two systems: an average 86.8% correct with the non-adaptive and 94.3% correct with the adaptive system, while those in the medium group performed equally well with both systems, with an average of 95.8%. Here again the results might have been also influenced by the readers/skimmers group effect, because the skimmers (adaptive first) group did less well on the location task than the readers (non-adaptive first) group. In a larger-scale future experiment it will also be worthwhile checking whether there is a correlation between task success and time on task, because the skimmers group was always faster than the other one which might account for their lower location task success.

Finally, the questionnaire showed that the users did not have problems locating information, neither did they find the texts too long. The results also showed that most users (75%) found the additional information in the adaptive system useful, while the rest were neutral. Overall, the participants did not have problems understanding the generated explanations.

3.3 Navigation Measures

Apart from the statistics of *average time per page visited* and *mean number of pages visited* which were discussed above, the other measures related to navigation are the use of links, navigation browser buttons and the topics list (see Fig. 1). The statistics of the use of these navigation aids in the non-adaptive and adaptive versions are shown in Fig. 3.

---

to measure. The score for the other tasks was computed as percentage of correctly answered questions.

Task		Links used non-adaptive	Links used adaptive	Back button used non-adaptive	Back button used adaptive	Topics list used non-adaptive	Topics list used adaptive
Browse ZIP drive	Mean	3.25	4.25	3.25	3.25	.25	.00
	Std. Dev.	1.26	2.36	1.26	2.06	.50	.00
Choose '10/1 GB tape drive'	Mean	7.75	7.25	6.50	5.25	.00	.25
	Std. Dev.	5.68	2.99	3.32	1.50	.00	.50
Locate mouse details 1	Mean	5.67	6.00	4.67	2.33	2.33	1.00
	Std. Dev.	2.52	4.58	1.53	2.52	1.15	1.00
Browse PCMCIA cards	Mean	4.33	3.50	2.33	1.25	.33	.00
	Std. Dev.	.58	.58	2.31	1.89	.58	.00
Choose 30/50 GB tape drive	Mean	5.33	4.33	5.00	1.00	.00	.00
	Std. Dev.	.58	1.53	1.00	1.73	.00	.00
Locate mouse details 2	Mean	4.00	7.00	3.33	2.75	2.00	1.00
	Std. Dev.	3.46	5.35	3.21	2.75	1.73	1.41
Total	Mean	5.10	5.41	4.25	2.73	.75	.36
	Std. Dev.	3.14	3.28	2.47	2.35	1.21	.79

Fig. 3. Statistics of the use of navigation features by task

In both systems, the subjects used links as their primary way to navigate the hyperspace. The browser **Back** button and the topics list, however, were used much more frequently in the non-adaptive system, e.g., the topic list was used, on average, twice as often. The topic list was used mostly in the two 'locate mouse details' tasks to access directly information about particular types of mouse (e.g. wheel, optical) – see Fig. 3.

The difference in the use of the browser **Back** button between the two versions, seems to be due mostly to the different ways in which the participants navigated the hyperspace. In the non-adaptive version, they would often start from a topic, e.g., tape drive, then follow a link to the first subtype, e.g., DLT, then return to the previous page, explore the next subtype, etc. In other words, the most common navigation pattern was similar to a depth-first traversal of the domain taxonomy. On the other hand, the additional information and links provided by the adaptive system changed the subjects' navigation pattern. The interaction logs showed an increased use of 'horizontal' taxonomic links, i.e., users would often jump from one subtype straight to the next, without going back to the 'parent' node. This change of behaviour was observed for more than half of the participants and accounts for the reduced number of repeated visits to the same page, and hence the reduced number of pages visited per topic in the adaptive system.

If we look into those results in more detail, we see again the difference between the two groups: readers (non-adaptive first) and skimmers (adaptive first). The use of the button by the readers group changes substantially when they move to the adaptive system (e.g., from 3.25 for task 1 to 1.25 for task 4). Unlike them, the behaviour of the skimmers group hardly changes between the two systems (e.g., 5.25 for task 2 and 5.00 for task 5). Here again we suspect that the difference might be due to the readers/skimmers effect, rather than due to the different treatment they received, i.e., which system they interacted with first. The reason for this is that possibly the people who read the pages more carefully could remember better which of the other terms present on the previous page were worth exploring and jump straight to them, i.e., benefit from the extra links. Unlike them, the skimmers needed to go back to the previous page to remind themselves of the other terms, so they could choose where they want to go next. This conjecture is also supported by the difference in the total number of pages visited by the two types of users.

The questionnaire results showed that none of the users felt disoriented in any of the systems and the majority had no problems finding information. When deciding which links to follow in the non-adaptive system, some of the novice users reported problems with unfamiliar terminology (25% of all users). In addition, half of the participants responded that there were not enough links in the non-adaptive pages. 37.5% of the users also felt that they had to visit too many pages in the non-adaptive system in order to find the information needed. For the adaptive system this number was down to just one and all the other users disagreed with that statement. The majority of the users also felt that the extra information and links provided in the adaptive version were making it easier for them to choose which link to follow next.

3.4 Subjective Satisfaction

The remaining statements in the questionnaire and the topics in the interview were aimed at collecting feedback on user satisfaction and impression of the two systems, as well as collecting opinions on ways of improving the generated hypertext.

All participants found the system intuitive to use and had no problems interacting with it without any prior experience. They were also satisfied with the system response time, both for the adaptive and non-adaptive versions. The majority of users were also positive about their experience with the adaptive system and did not find it confusing. 75% agreed that working with the adaptive system was more enjoyable than with the non-adaptive one, while only 12.5% disagreed.

The evaluation also showed that the preference for the adaptive system could be improved if its interface provided users with a way of changing the default system behaviour. For example, only one of the users did not like the links to related information, included at the bottom of the page, while she liked the rest of the adaptivity features.

4 Conclusion

In this paper we discussed the evaluation of the dynamic hypertext generation system HYLITE+ and the lessons learned from it. Probably the most important outcome of this small-scale evaluation was that it showed the need to control not just for user's prior knowledge (e.g., novice, advanced), but also for hypertext reading style. Although previous studies of people browsing hypertext (e.g., [7]) have distinguished two types: *skimmers* and *readers*, in this experiment we did not control for that, because the tasks were concerned with locating information, not browsing. Still, the results obtained showed the need to control for this variable, regardless of the task type, because reading style influences some of the quantitative measures (e.g., task performance, mean time per task, number of visited pages, use of browser navigation buttons).

The other important outcome from this evaluation was that it showed that users' acceptance of adaptive hypertext systems could be improved if they are also made adaptable, i.e., allow users to control their behaviour, so unwanted features could be disabled (for further details see [1]). Since our earlier empirical studies [2] had already indicated that adaptability could be beneficial to the users, HYLITE+ was designed to allow user control of the personalisation. Our next step will be to evaluate an adaptable adaptive version of the system against the other two versions discussed here.

References

1. Kalina Bontcheva. *Generating Adaptive Hypertext Explanations with a Nested Agent Model*. PhD thesis, University of Sheffield, 2001.
2. Kalina Bontcheva. The impact of empirical studies on the design of an adaptive hypertext generation system. In S. Reich, M. Tzagarakis, and P. De Bra, editors, *Hypermedia: Openness, Structural Awareness, and Adaptivity*, volume 2266 of *Lecture Notes in Artificial Intelligence*. Springer Verlag, Berling Heidelberg, 2001.
3. Kalina Bontcheva. Tailoring the content of dynamically generated explanations. In M. Bauer, P. Gmytrasiewicz, and J. Vassileva, editors, *User Modelling 2001*, volume 2109 of *Lecture Notes in Artificial Intelligence*. Springer Verlag, Berling Heidelberg, 2001.
4. Richard Cox, Mick O'Donnell, and Jon Oberlander. Dynamic versus static hypermedia in museum education: an evaluation of ILEX, the intelligent labelling explorer. In S.P. Lajoie and M. Vivet, editors, *Artificial Intelligence in Education: Open Learning Environment: New Computational Technologies to Support Learning, Exploration and Collaboration*, pages 181–188. IOS Press, Amsterdam, 1999.
5. John Eklund and Peter Brusilovsky. The value of adaptivity in hypermedia learning environments: A short review of empirical evidence. In *Proceedings of the 2nd Workshop on Adaptive Hypertext and Hypermedia*, pages 13 – 20, Pittsburgh, PA, June 1998. A workshop held in conjunction with the Nineth ACM International Hypertext Conference (Hypertext'98), http://wwwis.win.tue.nl/ah98/Eklund.htm.
6. Kristina Höök. Evaluating the utility and usability of an adaptive hypermedia system. *Knowledge-Based Systems*, 10:311—319, 1998.
7. Jakob Nielsen. *Designing Web Usability: The Practice of Simplicity*. New Riders Publishing, 2000.
8. Reinhard Opperman. Adaptively supported adaptability. *International Journal of Human-Computer Studies*, 40:455 – 472, 1994.
9. G. B. Wills, I. Heath, R.M. Crowder, and W. Hall. User evaluation of an industrial hypermedia application. Technical report, M99/2, University of Southampton, 1999. http://www.bib.ecs.soton.ac.uk/data/1444/html/html/.

Towards Generic Adaptive Systems: Analysis of a Case Study

Licia Calvi and Alexandra Cristea

Information Systems Department
Eindhoven University of Technology
Eindhoven, The Netherlands
{a.i.cristea, l.calvi}@tue.nl
http://wwwis.win.tue.nl/~{calvi, alex}

Abstract. This paper analyses one of the most well-known general purpose adaptive hypermedia systems, AHA!, and, based on this analysis, make some general observations about adaptive hypermedia systems and some improvement suggestions for the AHA! system. We suggest here a concept-based approach to the structuring of adaptive hypermedia systems, as well as an extension of the well-known rule-based overlay method for user-adaptation. This approach is another step towards flexible generic-purpose adaptive hypermedia.

1 Introduction

Adaptation in hypermedia has been traditionally divided [3] into *adaptive navigation support* (link level adaptation) and *adaptive presentation* (content level adaptation). However, this division causes problems at a conceptual level, which can lead, from an authoring point of view, to difficulties in the definition of concept relationships.

Defining which links to show to users and which *concept granularity* to associate to those links presupposes a correlation between concepts and links that is not directly matched onto the simple link visibility function adopted by most adaptive systems. Learning is indeed always situated, it never occurs in the vacuum. In a situated learning scenario, concepts interact with one another to the extent that one concept may assume a meaning on the basis of the context it belongs to, i.e., of the concepts that surround it. The influence of contextualization on the learning process is more evident if we think of the adaptive system as a tool to enhance knowledge acquisition.,

In this view, concepts and links need to be intertwined in order to allow authors to distinguish between the events producing the knowledge (the actions, i.e., adding/deleting links or concept fragments, triggering the acquisition of knowledge, what Idinopulos [13] calls *causally mediated knowledge*) and the inferential process at its basis, i.e., how to construct the "new" evidence the information that is presented to the user may lead to once clicking on a link (*epistemic mediated knowledge* [13]).

From the adaptation engine point of view [24], indeed, it should not make any difference if the adaptation concerns what links to show to the user, or what text to show to the user: if the specific prerequisites are satisfied, the respective action (of adding links, or text/ multimedia content, etc.) is triggered. Actually, some systems (e.g., AHA! [8]) do not make this distinction in their adaptation model totally explicit.

We argue however that, for an adaptive hypermedia author, it is difficult to separate the two notions (links versus concepts; adaptive navigation versus adaptive presentation) and at the same time to carefully design the whole system so that adaptive navigation support actions, triggered directly by the adaptive engine, and adaptive presentation actions, triggered by in-page (or in-concept/ content) rules, are synchronous.

In the following, we propose a better way to look at the whole authoring problem in adaptive hypermedia. This approach consists of a combination of the concept mapping paradigm to construct the course narrative and of several new adaptation rules. We also show how the two formalisms may be integrated on an example version of AHA!.

2 The AHA! System

AHA! [1] is a well-known system, one of the pioneers of adaptive hypermedia (with its first version developed in 1996/97), which became almost a benchmark for the domain. One of the co-authors was involved in the research and development from the very beginning [7], while the other is involved in supervising the project towards new developments since the support received from the NL foundation.

The power and popularity of AHA! lies on the fact that it is very simple. However, this simplicity can have drawbacks, as shown in Fig. 1: if the system complexity is low, the authoring efficiency cannot be very high – unless the author puts a great effort into creative authoring. This is about the point where the AHA! system is now.

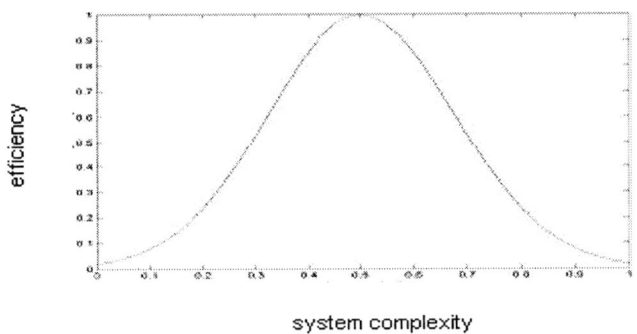

Fig. 1. Relation between system complexity and authoring efficiency

In its present form, AHA! offers the following adaptation methods:
1. each page is considered a concept, and is presented or not according to some conditions (on some variables) present in an XML file called "requirement list";

2. the variables changing rules are relatively simple, and are recorded in another XML file called "generate list";
3. AHA! uses an XML based AHA! tag language for conditional fragments within pages.

Items 1-2 permit adaptive navigation support at page level, and item 3 permits adaptive presentation. Recently, AHA! was extended with the following authoring tools:

1. an editor to connect requirements to pages;
2. an editor for the generate rules;
3. forms to make changes to the user model. The most important one is a form that allows the adaptive hypermedia user to modify knowledge attributes associated to page-concepts.

All these features unfortunately rely on an inadequate definition of knowledge and of knowledge acquisition because they do not seem to take into account the importance of context in concept meaning attribution (as discussed in Sect. 3). In particular, the possibility of altering knowledge attributes in the user model seems dangerous if this is not coupled with a redefinition of knowledge within the whole system, with the inevitable consequences that such an action has in determining concept presentation. AHA! now is moving towards database-base multiple-attribute concepts (while still trying to keep complete compatibility with the so fashionable XML format). Next, we will present some suggestions on the conceptual structure and on adaptation techniques, also pointing to possible problems that AHA! will have to face and deal with.

3 The Concept-Mapping Paradigm

A quite intuitive classification is to divide the source material into concepts [6], as derived from the concept mapping paradigm [18]. In such a structure, each piece has an independent semantics - in the sense of the semantic Web [21]: starting with low level, *atomic concepts*, to collections of concepts (*composite concepts*), that together form a *concept hierarchy*. Concepts can relate at any level of the hierarchy. The creation of these building bricks is the role of the adaptive hypermedia designer [6].

This hierarchy represents the primitive building blocks of the hypermedia. Putting these building blocks together with different sequences generates different presentations at a relatively high granularity level (concept level). At this level, indeed, we would be only speaking of adaptive navigation support. Normally, adaptive presentation is at a lower, concepts fractions level. A simple example is the construction of text introduction. This construct can be used together with other introductory fragments in an introductory chapter, or dropped at later browsing, etc. However, such a construct has usually no independent meaning. A common solution to this is to divide concepts into sub-concepts, without sometimes caring about the loss of semantics. Such sub-concepts cannot be easily further used (in the context of *collaborative authoring*), because they cannot be semantically annotated, and therefore will not be significant for searching mechanisms.

A more appropriate solution, introduced in [6], is to sub-divide the concept into its *attributes*. These can be a concept name, alternative contents, fragments, etc. By mapping the course content on a concept hierarchy, and describing the concepts with a set of attributes, the adaptation has only to deal with *concept-level adaptation* and *attribute adaptation*. The advantage is that it can all be performed (and viewed) from a high level, and does not need separate consideration of conditional fragments written within the text, which are more difficult to re-use by other authors. In this way, the content authoring and the adaptative engine rules authoring is clearly separated, making also automatic checks easier. Adaptation is here only a matter of combining concept attributes into pages (pieces of information that can be show at a time). Navigation, in this context, is dependent on the *presentation format* (Fig. 2). (e.g., a handheld device with shorter pages (than the regular browser) will display the "next" button more often within the same lesson(check SMIL [22], for presentation issues).

Such a model is compatible with the RDF [20] standard, where the RDF *resources* become concepts, the *properties* attributes and the *literals* attribute values. AHA! has partially implemented a similar structure, the main important difference being that concepts are at the granulation of pages, and can have a single attribute in the current implementation. Constructs within pages (such as conditional fragments) are not concept attributes in AHA!, and cannot be independently used with other concepts or concept attributes. New under development versions of AHA! consider multiple attributes, and a database structure, that will allow more flexibility – including hopefully dropping of the artificial separation of conditional fragments (such as in adaptive presentation) and concept linking (such as in adaptive navigation support).

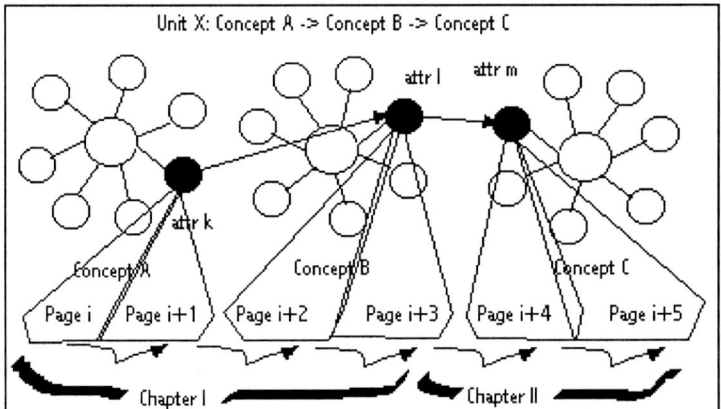

Fig. 2. A unit X is composed of, e.g., parts of 3 concepts (A, B and C) which have some attributes (attr-k, attr-l, attr-m). The presentation order is represented by directed connections between concept attributes. The unit is formed of 2 chapters that contain (parts of) the concepts. The information in a chapter is presented (by a browser) in pages (which may be shorter than a chapter). "Next" buttons at page level are navigation support of presentation nature, and have nothing to do with the user-model related adaptation.

Figure 2 shows how connections are done at concept attribute level. Concept attributes can appear more than once, within one or more unit(s), and there is no restriction for attribute contents: text, video, audio, flash technology, etc. Next, we will explain the benefits of this simplification by presenting new adaptation types based on it.

4 New Adaptation Rules: How to Augment the Adaptation Engine

Different rules can be conceived to augment the functionality of the adaptation engine. As they trigger when some quality measurement is reached, these rules, although apparently retraceable to standard commands in traditional programming languages, can be also viewed as deriving from the Genetic Graph modeled by Goldstein [14]: both paradigms indeed explain how the user's knowledge can evolve during learning.

Most adaptive systems are rule-based. Adaptation is mainly triggered by *conditional* rules, which take the form:

                           IF <PREREQUISITE> THEN <ACTION>

We propose some alternative forms of conditional rules that allow more freedom, both in authoring as well as in studying with this type of environment.

1. A *level* rule [6]:
                    IF ENOUGH (<PREREQUISITES>) THEN <ACTION>
   where ENOUGH = function of number and quality of prerequisites; true when, e.g., a given number of prerequisites from a PREREQUISITES set is fulfilled. This type of relaxation of the prerequisites is intuitive, in the sense that it allows the author to write simplified rules, instead of writing a great number of complex ones; the idea is derived from game levels.
   Example: **PREREQUISITES** = *time_spent;* **ACTION** = *"go to next level"*
   The rule becomes:
      IF ENOUGH (time_was spent on current level) **THEN** "go to next level"
   Where ENOUGH is defined, e.g., as follows:
   ENOUGH (time) = 30 time units;
   time (advanced topic) = 10 (time units per topic);
   ENOUGH (medium topic) = 5 (time units per topic);
   ENOUGH (beginner topic) = 2 (time units per topic);
2. A *temporal* rule: a certain action is repeated as long as one or more conditions hold. To capture unbound minimization, we add therefore the WHILE construct:
                      WHILE <CONDITION> DO <ACTION>
   According to the concept mapping paradigm, concepts are not canned but are assembled depending on the user model based on their attributes (see Sect. 3). Therefore this operation requires more than the mere addition/deletion of links.
3. A *repetition* rule: a certain action (simple / composed) is repeated for a number of times that is predefined by the author. This rule forces the user to reread a concept

(as described in [15]) that is presented to her invariably. In non-educational contexts, this rule might have a lyrical effect[1] – such as a refrain in a song.
The temporal rule could be expressed as:
    FOR <i=1...n> DO <ACTION>
This rule therefore describes the time this action has to last before the reader can move on to another one.

4. An *interruption* command: the action the user is performing is interrupted (broken) and she is forced to undertake a different one abruptly.
    BREAK <ACTION>
The adoption of this rule might be due to lyrical reasons. This is the case in *A life set for two* [11], where the reader is forced to reach the end of the fiction once she has read a predefined percentage of it In educational contexts, this rule might be used by the author to constraint the user's explorative behavior within predefined boundaries, i.e., those corresponding to the pedagogical rules implemented in the system. In this sense, the implementation of this rule represents an exacerbation of the traditional behavior of AH systems: here, indeed, the user is "punished" if she does not stick to the learning pathways provided by the system.

5. A *generalization* command: the new concept the reader has come across is compared with the more general ones it refers to. As a result of this inductive action, the reader is pointed to the related concepts she may be interested in reading. So, the reader has selected a node that describes a certain concept in specific, individual terms. The system "interprets" this behavior as an interest from the reader about that particular notion and therefore performs an inductive action to point her to the more general ones it refers to.
    GENERALIZE (COND, COND$_1$, ..., COND$_n$)

6. A *specialization* command: conversely, if the concept is general, the system deductively points the reader to its more specific instantiations.
    SPECIALIZE (COND, COND$_1$, ..., COND$_n$)
So, for instance, if a student is reading a page about the concept of the "Model Reader" in a course about postmodern literature, she could be further pointed to an extract from Calvino's novel 'Se una notte', where this notion is exemplified, or to a further theoretical elaboration on the same topic (by, for example, Genette), or, again, to a description of how this idea is realized in hyperfiction (see [4]).

Other commands that could appear are *comparison* (concept analogy search) and *difference* – both instances of generalization; or *duration* – a rule related to repetition.

The appropriateness of these rules directly depends on the context and on the concepts to be modeled. Certainly, educational material may be simpler and more straightforward to model than a less formal one, like, for instance literary material. In an educational setting, Indeed, the assumption is often to guide the student to evolve from novice to expert in the content domain [5]: this is why the content structure has to be well defined and normally hierarchically organized. Literature, however, exemplifies a case where not only the reader's goal is not clear (contrary to the learning

---

[1] The lyrical use of repetitions in hyperfiction has given rise to a particular design pattern as described in [2].

goal of educational systems[2]) and, as a consequence, the way readers use information to construct meaning [12], but, also, it enacts a different approach: not a "guided pulling" approach [19] like in educational systems, but one based on a "suspension of disbelieving" [9], on the importance of rereading in constructing meaning [15], on suspense, on playing with the reader[3].

Some of these principles would however be effective also in educational systems: we think, for instance, of the notion of rereading (the old say "repetita iuvant"); of suspension, of disbelieving as a way of addressing the question of authority and authenticity by assigning it to the author of the content; of a sort of suspense in the way information is presented to readers as to encourage and to motivate them to read further. Moreover, the possibility of expressing these sorts of rules is precisely what guarantees the general-purpose character of the underlying formalism.

5 Implementing New Rules in the Current AHA!

Following the present syntax used by AHA! to express rules, we could extend it to represent the above mentioned functions in the following way :

1. the level rule:	2. the temporal rule:

<if expr="enough">
<enough>
    Here definition of enough
</enough>
<block>
    Here a conditional fragment
</block>
<block>
    Here an optional alternative fragment
</block>
	<while expr="wrong_search>50">
	<block>
	    Here a conditional fragment
	</block>
	</while>
	
	In this case, a certain action is repeated as long as a certain condition holds. For instance, a warning is repeated that the search performed by the user is in the wrong direction, while the system is still performing the search. Another condition then could trigger a service denial response if the above threshold would be passed.

---

[2] For an overview of the possible goals and their related reading strategies adopted by readers in hyperfiction see, for instance, [4].
[3] We refer again to the illuminating paper in [12], where they describe one of the first systems developed to deal with adaptivity in literature.

	Another example is:
	<while expr="art>70 and
	                           not culture>80">
	    <block>
	        Here a predefined
	        sequence of events
	    </block>
	    <block>
	        Here an alternative event (action)
	    </block>
	</while>

3. the repetition rule:	**4. the interruption command:**

<for expr="question&sm;5">
 	
<block>
 	
   Here a conditional fragment
</block>
</for>
 	
In a particular context, this action may make sense. For the example above, some explanation is given as long as the number of questions is not larger than 5. After that, a different strategy has to be taken into consideration – such as the suggestion of consulting different material, etc.
	<break>
	
	<block>
	
	   Here a conditional fragment
	</block>
	</break>

5. the generalization command:	**6. the specialization command:**

<generalize concept="myconcept">
   Here details of generalization (levels, etc.)
</generalize>
 	
Example:
<generalize concept= "double_code_theory">
   Here details of generalization (levels, etc.)
</generalize>
 	
Such a rule can be used to jump 1 or more levels in the hierarchy of concepts. Extra processing can be done in the body of the above command, such as giving comments on the level to be visited and the reason why.
	<specialize concept="myconcept">
	   Here details of specialization (levels, etc.)
	</specialize>
	
	Example:
	<specialize concept="Model Reader">
	   Here details of specialization (levels, etc.)
	</specialize>
	
	The application is similar as the above command, with the difference that the direction of the processing in the concept hierarchy is *top-down* instead of *bottom-up*.

6 Problems and the Need of Checking Mechanisms

As shown in Fig. 1, by increasing the system complexity, the authoring efficiency grows for a while, and then drops. The problem with the current AHA! system is that is it somewhere at the beginning of the slope. Adding to many more features and

flexibilities can increase the authoring efficiency for a while, but it is necessary to stop before the down-curve. When authors have to deal with complex unit graphs with many concepts and many concept attributes, it is easy to leave something out by mistake. AHAM [24] tries to deal with such problems as:
- *termination* (avoiding of loops) and
- *confluence* (equivalence of order of rule execution - for rule-based adaptation engines).

Their suggestion is to use *activation graphs* (from the static analysis of active database rules), therefore constructing the whole graph of possible states that is determined by the concepts, their links, the attributes, their values (especially, initial values and possible ranges – to eliminate unnecessary branches and optimize the search tree with the help of constrains) and the rule sets. If such a graph has no loops, the system will always terminate. For confluence, a difficult procedure of checking the possibility of *commutation* between each rule pair (so their order equivalence) is proposed. AHA! at the moment ensures termination by allowing only monotonic increases of the attributes (per concept), which will be more difficult for the following version with multiple attributes. As for confluence, AHA! doesn't deal with it at all.

Other problems that can appear are:
- concepts (or concept fragments) *never reached*;
- rules (or other adaptation mechanisms) that generate attributes with *out of range (or domain) values*.

The good news is that the added rules that we have proposed don't require extra checking mechanisms than the ones studied previously in the AHAM context [24]. Basically, loops existing in the regular rules will also be present (and noticeable) in level rules, temporal rules or repetition rules. (and vice-versa). Non-equivalent rules that can be executed at a given time but are not commutable will pose the same problems on regular rules as on the extended set. The extended commands of generalization and specialization can be treated the same as regular links (or rules). The interruption command can actually help in breaking infinite loops, or signaling problems, similar to the *catch-throw* mechanism of exception handling in Java.

The bad news is that such a mechanism can be rather *time* - and *space* - consuming.

A better way of dealing with this problem is by means of various simplifications and complexity decreasing assumptions. One such simplification could be by means of a belief revision technique to check inconsistencies among knowledge attributes to concepts and the consequent knowledge acquisition problem. Belief revision consists in the introduction of a sort of case-based heuristics that:
1. recalls a previous concept with the same features and its associated attributes;
2. adapts, via some rule-based formalism, the course structure (the narrative) to the current learning scenario;
3. resolves the emerging inconsistencies to make sure that changes of state are epistemologically conservative (so that the resulting narrative is not subverted).

7 Future Directions

With the standardization of the building bricks of adaptive systems (such as LOM [17], Learner model [16]– IEEE, LTSC for education, RDF [20], etc.) it becomes more and more feasible to collaborate and share adaptive techniques, technologies but also, system parts, developed adaptive hypermedia presentations, etc. Adaptive and adaptable systems are necessary in education, where learners come with different cultural and knowledge backgrounds, different learning styles, genders, ages, especially in the new context of life-long learning. Such systems are definitely necessary in commerce (and are having a tremendous success in e-commerce, even with extremely simple adaptation techniques – such as the well-known Amazon.com technique of suggesting "buyers who bought this book also bought..."). But they can have, as we have shown also some other, surprising applications, such as adaptive literature and adaptive art.

It is extremely important to find the right balance between system complexity and authoring efficiency, as shown in Fig. 1. Extending adaptive systems with extra adaptation rules can be beneficial, especially if these rules can express situations that were not possible (or difficult) to express with the given set of tools/ rules. Moreover, this enhancement makes sense if it does not impose on the checking mechanisms, by increasing dramatically the types of tests an adaptive hypermedia author has to perform in order to verify his/her output.

As a direction we predict to be rewarding for such checking mechanisms we see the replacement of large state trees with all possible situations to be reached from the existing rule base (or, generally speaking, adaptation procedure) with a visual, dynamical representation of the processes involved. For example, the effect of a new rule on the rest can be shown on the static (and much smaller) unit link graph, as the propagation of some colored fluid through the graph, etc.

8 Conclusion

The paper has started with a criticism on the widespread practice to distinguish adaptation in hypermedia between an adaptive navigation support and an adaptive presentation. This criticism is based on the claim that, in this way, authors of adaptive courseware have to artificially separate links from concepts but still to coordinate and tune them in order to provide an adaptation that is conceptually valid and that contributes to a significant knowledge acquisition.

We have suggested a better way to look at the whole authoring problem in adaptive hypermedia. This approach consists in the combination of the concept mapping paradigm to construct the course narrative and of several new adaptation rules. We have highlighted a few new rules that should be integrated into an adaptive authoring shell or toolkit.

We have shown how these two formalisms may be integrated in an example version of AHA!. Moreover, we have augmented the present rule behavior performed by

AHA! to allow it more adaptivity. We claim that this approach is another step towards flexible generic-purpose adaptive hypermedia.

References

1. AHA, Adaptive Hypermedia for All; http://aha.win.tue.nl/
2. Bernstein, M.: Patterns of Hypertext. Ninth ACM Conference on Hypertext (1998) 21-29
3. Brusilovsky, P.: Methods and Techniques of Adaptive Hypermedia. User Modeling and User-Adapted Interaction 6 (1996) 87-129
4. Calvi, L.: 'Lector in rebus': the Role of the Reader and the Characteristics of Hyperreading. Tenth ACM Conference on Hypertext '99. ACM Press (1999) 101-109
5. Calvi, L., De Bra, P.: Using Dynamic Hypertext to Create Multi-Purpose Textbooks. In T. Müldner and T.C. Reeves (eds.), ED-MEDIA'97, AACE Press (1997), 130-135
6. Cristea, A., Okamoto, T.: MyEnglishTeacher – A WWW System for Academic English Teaching ICCE 2000, Taipei, Taiwan (2000)
7. De Bra, P., Calvi, L.: AHA! An open Adaptive Hypermedia Architecture. The New Review of Hypermedia and Multimedia (1998) 115-139
8. De Bra, P., Ruiter, J.P.: AHA! Adaptive Hypermedia for All. WebNet (2001) 262-268
9. Eco, U.: Six Walks in the Fictional Woods. Harvard University Press (1994)
10. Goldman, A.: Telerobotic Knowledge: A Reliabilist Approach. In K. Goldberg (ed.). The Robot in the Garden. Telerobotics and Telepistemology in the Age of the Internet. MIT Press (2000) 126-142
11. Kendall, R.: A Life Set For Two. Eastgate Systems, Watertown, MA (1996)
12. Kendall, R., Réty, JH.: Toward an Organic Hypertext. Hypertext '00. (2000) 161-170
13. Idinopulos, M.: Telepistemology, Mediation, and the Design of Transparent Interfaces. In K. Goldberg (ed.). The Robot in the Garden. Telerobotics and Telepistemology in the Age of the Internet. MIT Press (2000) 312-329
14. Goldstein, I.: The genetic graph: a representation for the evolution of procedural knowledge. In D. Sleeman and J.S. Brown (eds, Intelligent Tutoring Systems. Academic Press, 1982.
15. Joyce, M.: Nonce Upon Some Times: Rereading Hypertext Fictions. Modern Fiction Studies 43(3) (1997) 579-597
16. Learner Model. IEEE Learning Technology Standards Committee (LTSC); http://ltsc.ieee.org/wg2/index.html
17. LOM (Learner Object Metadata). IEEE Learning Technology Standards Committee (LTSC); http://ltsc.ieee.org/wg12/index.html
18. Novak, J. D.: Clarify with concept maps. The Science Teacher, 58(7), (1991) 45-49
19. Perrin, M.: What Cognitive Science Tells us About the Use of New Technologies. Invited Talk given at the Conference on Languages for Specific Purposes and Academic Purposes: Integrating Theory into Practice. Dublin, 6-8 March (1998)
20. RDF (Resource description framework) standard: http://www.w3.org/RDF/
21. Semantic Web: http://www.w3.org/2001/sw/
22. SMIL, W3C standard, http://www.w3.org/AudioVideo/
23. W3C Recommendation: Authoring Tool Accessibility Guidelines 1.0 (3 February 2000); http://www.w3.org/TR/ATAG10/
24. Wu, H., De Bra, P.: Suficient Conditions for Well-behaved Adaptive Hypermedia Systems. Web Intelligence. Lecture Notes in AI. Vol. 2198. Springer. (2001) 148-152

A Methodology for Developing Adaptive Educational-Game Environments

Rosa M. Carro[1,2], Ana M. Breda[1], Gladys Castillo[1], and Antonio L. Bajuelos[1]

[1] Departamento de Matematica, Universidad de Aveiro,
3810, Aveiro, Portugal
{rosac,ambreda,leslie,gladys}@mat.ua.pt
[2] E. T. S. Informática, Universidad Autónoma de Madrid, Ctra. Colmenar Viejo km. 15,
28049, Madrid, España
rosa.carro@ii.uam.es

Abstract. In this paper we present a methodology for describing adaptive educational-game environments and a model that supports the environment design process. These environments combine the advantages of educational games with those derived from the adaptation. The proposed methodology allows the specification of educational methods that can be used for the game environment generation. The educational goals, the activities that the users can perform, their organization and sequencing, along with the games to be played and the game stories are selected or dynamically generated taking into account the user's features and behaviors.

1 Motivation

Educational computer-based games are those games that promote the growth of people's reasoning and the acquisition of skills and knowledge in a pleasant way [1].

Their background is related to pieces of knowledge that the users have to put in practice in order to reach the goals proposed in the games. From the first studies about the use of games in education [2] until now, they have proved that can constitute a very good resource of motivation [3] for the users to test the knowledge they own, improve it by practicing, and learn what they do not know while enjoying. Particularly, the use of multimedia resources, stories that present real or figured goals attractively, and agents that accompany the user during the game execution (motivating them to go on playing, providing feedback and so on) increases the learning achievements [4].

From a high-level point of view, there exist basically two different kinds of educational game environments: those composed by a fixed sequence of sceneries which the user has to interact with [5], and those who allow the user to select the game (s)he wants to play among a set of games [6]. In both cases, the whole game environment is developed ad-hoc. Adaptation exists in the sense that each concrete game's behavior depends on user actions, but the decisions about the next scenery or the available games at every moment are fixed during the game development phase, being the same for every user at runtime.

There exist some factors that affect the effectiveness of educational games. These are related to personal user's features, preferences and behaviors [7]. As it is well known, not all the users have the same preferences or styles while interacting with games and solving problems. From the game developer's point of view, there are several educational methods and strategies that can be applied during game-environment creation [8]. They are related to the kind of tasks proposed to the users, the sequencing among them and so on. Each developer may want to apply different methods depending on the features of the users the game is intended for. Moreover, (s)he can consider as necessary the use of different kind of multimedia games and storylines for each type of user.

In order to broaden the number of potential users and to improve the effectiveness of the games for each of them, we propose the development of *adaptive* educational game environments. In these environments the cognition activities that users have to perform, the difficulty of the problems behind the game, the sceneries presented and the organization of these elements, among others, can be dynamically selected or generated for each particular user depending on his/her personal features and behaviors. In such a way the advantages of using computer-based games in education [9] along with those that come from the adaptation [10, 11] can be exploited together.

In Sect. 2 of this paper we present a methodology that has been created for supporting the design of adaptive educational game environments along with the specification of the educational methods to be used in them. In Sect. 3 we propose a model that supports this methodology, and Sect. 4 shows the adaptation process carried out during the dynamic game environment generation. Finally, Section 5 contains the conclusions and future work.

2 The Proposed Methodology for the Environment Design Process

In order to assist the process of creating educational adaptive games we have developed a methodology that establishes a set of steps for the game environment design process. In the following subsections this methodology is presented, as well as an example about its application for developing an adaptive game environment.

2.1 Steps to Follow

The methodology establishes the following steps:
1. Identifying the *types of users* who the environment is directed to, by fixing the personal features that will be taken into account during the adaptation process and their possible values.
2. Specifying the game *goals* from an educational point of view, namely, the user's knowledge or skills needed to play the games or those that can be acquired/improved while playing them.

3. Creating or providing the *computer-based games*, indicating, for each of them, the learning goals involved and the type of users the game is intended for, in case they are specifically oriented to certain kinds of users. Games can be taken from existing game repositories, or generated and stored in one of them.
4. Establishing the educational method for each type of user, by:
   4.1. Determining the *activities* that will be proposed to the users. These activities can be of two different kinds: educational activities or relaxing activities. The former are those proposed with the purpose of motivating the acquisition of certain knowledge, that one described by the educational goals; the latter can be non-related to education, they all have the same goal ('relaxing') and can be included so that the users can relax after performing difficult tasks. For every activity the developer must specify its type, goals and the number of games that will be presented to the users to play with while performing the activity. Optionally, the name of the concrete game(s) can be specified. Otherwise, games will be selected from the ones in the game repository, selecting the games whose goals match with those indicated in the activity.
   4.2. Describing how the environment *structure* will be generated for each user at runtime. This requires the specification of i) the organization of activities for each type of user in *activity groups*, where several activities can be gathered ii) the sequencing mode for these activities execution and iii) the prerequisites that can be established among them.
5. Describing stories, where the game goals, activity feedbacks, agents and other multimedia elements can be included. These components are associated to the game structure components (activities and activity groups) and constitute altogether a story that can be independent from the concrete games presented to the users. In this case, the users can consider games as ways of achieving the story goals. Different stories can be created for distinct types of users, being included in a game environment by:
   5.1. Creating or providing *starting sceneries* that are presented to the users before they carry out an activity or access a group of activities. They present challenges and goals in an attractive way so as to catch the user's attention and make them get involved in the environment. The goals presented can be either related to the activity goals or fictitious, being part of a fantastic story.
   5.2. Developing or supplying *menu sceneries* that will be used for game menu generation. They can contain objects or agents that stimulates the users to select one activity among any set of available ones. Menu sceneries can be used for story construction by presenting fictitious goals that will be achieved if the user perform the activities, for example, or by motivating the users to go on playing for reaching the goal (whichever the goal is).
   5.3. Creating or supplying *feedback sceneries* for providing the users with comments about the activity execution, giving them a positive reinforce both when the results are good, to reward them, and also when they are bad, to motivate them to learn and go on playing. This comments should be inserted into the story explaining in an attractive way why the story goals have (not yet) been achieved.

5.4. *Classifying the games* according to their subject (i.e., animals, sports, etc.) so that games related to the same subject can be selected during the environment generation.

2.2 Ecotoons2: An Adaptive Educational Game Environment

The educational environment Ecotoons2 has been created starting from Ecotoons, an educational game (developed inside the frame of the Geometrix project) whose main goal is to promote the children mathematical reasoning development in an attractive and pleasant way. The game was conceived for children from 5 to 9 years old. Several experiences with Ecotoons, involving about 120 children from three different schools located in Aveiro, have proved that it is a well-designed game with respect to the interface usability [12], the motivational elements, and so on. In Ecotoons the stages are presented sequentially to all the users in the same way.

Ecotoons2 is an adaptive educational game environment that incorporates some of the games and resources of Ecotoons. This environment is intended for users from 5 to 18. By now, there have been established three different ranges: children from 5 to 9, those from 9 to 11, and users from 11 to 14.

Its main goal is to help and motivate users to construct knowledge about mathematical concepts and improve their mathematical reasoning. The educational goals involved in the game are related to mathematical concepts and operations such as counting, adding, subtracting, manipulating fractions, and so on. Ninety independent computer-based games that support the performance of these activities are being developed. Some of them are distinct games with the same goal, specifically developed for certain kind of users (i.e., younger users can add by counting and provide the solution by selecting among several numbers, while older ones should be able to solve problems by adding numbers and writing the result). All the games developed until now for the youngest are related to environment conservation while those provided for teenagers are related to sports and animals, among others. Each game has its own feedback messages that are shown to the users while they are playing it.

With respect to the educational method, in many cases educators have decided that mixing activities with different goals or letting the users to choose the order of activities is better than establishing a fixed sequence. Otherwise, users could get tired or bored while performing the same task for a long time, or feeling certain lack of freedom while interacting with the game. In other cases, the establishment of a fixed sequence of activities has been considered convenient.

There have been specified thirty activities, which have been organized in groups of five, resulting in six activity groups. These are grouped into three activity groups that compose the main one. The corresponding relations among them have been established in order to describe the game structure.

Stories are included by means of different starting and feedback sceneries that have been attached to each activity group. We have used the story of Ecotoons for sceneries generation. In the main activity group the starting scenery contains an agent that states the main goal of the whole game: "Saving the planet Platoon by avoiding that the Poluxes destroy it. If your help is positive, Poluxes will be transformed into Platoons. Otherwise, the planet will be lost forever". In every starting scenery, an agent presents the fictitious goal (what Poluxe can be converted, in the case of the three activity groups, or the planet area to be protected, for the six activity groups) and the way of achieving it. Feedback sceneries contain animations showing the Poluxe transformation or the area saved, along with the Platoon explanation of what is happening, depending on the score obtained while performing each activity. The menu sceneries are related to Platoon landscapes and agents.

3 The Adaptive Game Environment Specification Model

In order to support the previously described methodology we have developed a model for describing adaptive educational environments. These environments are generated on the fly. The main components of the model are related to the types of users, educational goals, computer-based games, educational methods and stories.

- The *types of users* the game is intended for are described by a series of *attributes*. The possible *values* for each attribute can be described by specifying the ranges of values or the set of possible discrete values (see Table 1).

Table 1. Establishing some user features and their possible values

Attribute	Values
Age	[5, 9) [9, 11) [11, 14]
Language	Portuguese/Spanish/English
Preferred-media	Sounds/Texts/Images/Animations

- An *educational goal* is specified by its *description* (a word or a sequence of words). Example: 'adding numbers'.
- A *computer-based game* is included by specifying its *identifier, description, goals, location, icon* (for menu generation), *difficulty* ('H' for high, 'M' for medium, 'L' for low and 'P' to indicate that the game can be generated from a template with parameters whose values can be set), *features* (list of descriptive game attributes such as the age of the users it is intended for, the predominant media, the language used in texts, sounds, etc.), and, optionally, *subject* (i.e., 'sports', 'animals', 'races', and so on). An example of a template-based game that is oriented to portuguese children from 5 to 9 can be seen in Table 2. When generating the game, the number of fishes that appear in each fishing rod is randomly selected from the range of possible values.

In order to describe the educational method of an adaptive game environment the following components are used:

- *Activity*: it is the basic unit of the game structure and represents a task to be performed. It is described by its *name, type* ('educational'/ 'relaxing'), *goals*, and, optionally, identifiers of *starting sceneries, menu sceneries,* and/or *feedback sceneries* (the way of describing sceneries is explained below). The *number of games* that should be played while performing the activity can also be specified (otherwise one game will be played). Table 3 shows an example of an activity with no sceneries associated. For the activity performance, one game whose goal is 'add' will be selected for each particular player.

Table 2. Game example: adding fishes

Attribute	Value
Identifier	Adding-fishes
Description	The user has to count the number of fishes that appear in three fishing rods, write the three numbers, and write the total number of fishes
Goals	Add
Location	/games
Icon	Fishing.gif
Difficulty	P
Features	[5-9), Portuguese
Subject	Ecology

Table 3. Activity example: adding numbers

Attribute	Value
Name	Adding-numbers
Type	Educational
Goals	Add

- *Activity Group (AG)*: it groups several activities or activity groups. It is described by its *name*. It may have associated *starting sceneries*, *menu sceneries,* and/or *feedback sceneries* that will be used for the story generation. This sceneries can be different depending on the type of user, so it is possible to associate several sceneries including the *condition* for each of them to be selected (which is related to the user's features). One of the AGs constitutes the *main* AG of the game environment. An example of an AG with associated sceneries (the same for every kind of user) is shown in Table 4.

Table 4. Activity Group example

Attribute	Value
Name	Oceanus-Place
Starting scenery	Saving-Oceanus
Menu scenery	Ocean
Feedback-OK scenery	Feed-OK-Oceanus
Feedback-Wrong scenery	Feed-Wr-Oceanus

- *Decomposition Rule (DR)*: it describes which activities or activity groups are part of a given activity group, and the order they should be performed at runtime, if any. It is possible to define several DRs for the same AG, showing different ways of decomposing it and/or different orders in which activities must be carried out. In this case, the DRs must include activation conditions that have to be satisfied for the DR activation. These conditions can be related to the user's features and/or behaviors while interacting with the environment. In such a way it is possible to specify different educational methods by providing each user with different activities for the same AG. It is also possible to combine the same activities in different ways for every type of user. Moreover, the use of conditions allows the decomposition of the same AG in different ways depending on the results obtained by the user while performing other activities. In order to describe a DR it is necessary to indicate the *AG identifier*, the *AGs and/or activities identifiers*, the *sequencing* mode among them (according to the sequencing modes proposed in [13], 'AND' means that the activities must be performed in the order they appear in the DR and 'ANY' means that they can be performed in any order) and, optionally, the *activation conditions,* related to user's features and/or behaviors (other activities execution). Optionally, it is possible to associate a weight to each subactivity, indicating the contribution of the score obtained by the user while performing the subactivity to the calculation of the score obtained in the activity group (by default the score will be calculated as the media of subactivity scores). Table 5 shows an example of two strategies for the same AG: while the order of activities for the youngest children will be fixed, children from 9 to 11 will be able to select, a priori, the activity they want to perform at every moment among those that appear in the DR. In addition, older children will have available the 'Subtracting-numbers' activity, which will not appear in the environment generated for younger ones.

Table 5. Decomposition Rule examples

Attribut	Value
Activity group	Oceanus-Place
Subactivities	Identifying-objects, Adding-numbers, Associating-objects, Ordering-numbers
Sequencing	AND
Activation condition	[5, 9)

Attribute	Value
Activity group	Oceanus-Place
Subactivities	Identifying-objects, Adding-numbers, Associating-objects, Ordering-numbers, Subtracting-numbers
Sequencing	ANY
Activation condition	[9, 11)

- *Prerequisite rule (PR)*: it describes the dependence relation that can exist among activities. By means of a PR it is possible to state that some activities should not be performed before doing other ones previously. A PR is composed by the *ac-*

tivity whose availability depends on the performance of other activities, the *prerequisite activities*, those that have to be performed before that one, and the *activation condition*, that indicates for which type of users the rule will be active, that is, in which cases the dependence relation will be taken into account. Optionally, it is possible to associate a weight to each prerequisite activity, indicating the minimum score that must be obtained during the activity execution for considering the prerequisite condition satisfied (by default it will be 5 in a scale from 0 to 10). Table 6 shows an example of a PR defined for children from 9 to 11 that establishes that they will not be able to perform the 'Subtracting-numbers' activity unless they have performed the 'Adding-numbers' one.

Table 6. Prerequisite Rule example

Attribute	Value
Activity	Subtracting-numbers
Prerequisites	Adding-numbers
Activation condition	[9, 11)

As for the story generation, sceneries are included in the model. These sceneries can be used for presenting the story, stating the fictitious or real goals at every moment, generating menus, providing feedback, etc.
- A *scenery* is described by its *name*, *type* ('starting'/'menu'/'feedbackOK'/ 'feedbackWrong'), *description*, *location* and the kind of users it is created for, that is directly related to the scenery *features*. If it is intended for every kind of users this attribute will be empty.

4 The Adaptive Environment Generation

Once the description of an adaptive educational game environment has been provided, it is possible to generate the components that will be presented to each particular user while interacting with it. The adaptation mechanism operates in two stages: at the beginning of the environment generation and at runtime.

4.1 First Stage: Structure Generation and Story Attachment

The environment structure is generated starting from the main activity group, considering the decomposition rules and user features in order to determine the activity groups or activities in which the main one is decomposed for this particular user. This process is repeated recursively until the game structure is generated. For every node of the structure (activities and groups of activities) it is checked whether it has any scenery associated. If it is the case, the scenery is attached to the activity. In case there are several sceneries available for the same node, the most suitable one for the user is selected.

In this stage the basic environment structure along with the story in front of it have been generated. This does not mean that all the activities are available. The activity availability will be decided for every user at runtime.

4.2 Second Stage: Selection of Available Activities and Games

While a user is interacting with the environment, the available activities at every moment are selected on the fly. This selection is done by taking into account the user's features and behaviors, along with the decomposition and prerequisite rules. For each set of available activities, a menu is generated so that the user can select the activity to be carried out. For each activity execution, the most suitable game supporting it is selected, considering the available games whose goals match the activity goals, their features and the user's characteristics. Once the user has selected an activity or the system has decided which one will be the next, the computer-based game will be presented/generated: if the game can be constructed starting from a template, it is dynamically generated; otherwise, the game is directly presented to the user.

The availability of activities and the difficulty of the games presented will depend on the user's actions and behaviors while interacting with the game environment.

5 Conclusions and Future Work

In this paper we have presented a methodology that establishes the suggested steps for describing adaptive educational game environments. These environments combine the advantages of educational games [9] with those derived from adaptation [10][11]. We have also presented a model that supports the adaptive environment design.

The environments described following this approach are dynamically generated taking into account the particular user's features and behaviors for the personalization of: i) the activities that are part of the environment, ii) their organization in the environment structure, ii) the order in which activities should be performed, if any, or the free activity selection, iii) the computer-based games that will be presented for activity performance, including their subject and difficulty, and iv) the displayed storyline.

The use of activities, activity groups and rules for the environment description allows the specification of educational methods. In such kind of environments, the users can acquire skills and improve their own knowledge in a personalized way. The educators can include the most appropriate educational methods, activities and games for each kind of user.

The separation among the activities to be performed and the games that support them makes it possible to select the most suitable games for every user while performing the activity. We have created a game repository with games labeled with their educational goals and difficulty. This makes possible the game reuse in different educational environments. Furthermore, existing games stored in game repositories can also be tagged and used in the environments generated.

By providing different sceneries for distinct types of users, it is possible to create several stories for the same activities, widening the possibility of attracting users' interest in playing the game. Sceneries can compose a fantastic story that can be used in different environments independently of the activities and the games behind them.

Currently we are experimenting with the use of the proposed methodology and model for different game environment generation. We are also considering the adaptation of the kind of game selected at every moment (educational vs. relaxing games), provided that some user features such as the age, the difficulty of the last activity performed and/or the score obtained by the user while performing it may affect the type of activity that should be proposed next. In the future we plan to create a model for the internal game components and behavior representation.

References

1. Klawe, M., Phillips, E.: A classroom study: Electronic Games Engage Children as Researchers. Proceedings of CSCL'95 Conference. Bloomington, Indiana (1995) 209-213
2. Gordon, A.: Games for Growth. Sc.Research Associates, Inc., Palo Alto, California (1970)
3. Malone, T. W.: What makes things fun to learn? A study of intrinsically motivating computer games. Cognitive and Instructional Sciences Series, CIS-7, SSL-80-11, Palo Alto Research Center, Palo Alto (1980)
4. Klawe, M.: Computer Games, Education And Interfaces: The E-GEMS Project. Invited Presentation at Graphics Interface 1999, Online Papers (1999). Available at http://www.graphicsinterface.org/proceedings/1999/20/
5. Breda, A.M., Bajuelos A.L., Castillo G, Lopes, M.: Computational Math Games Versus Learning. Proceedings of the International Conference on New Technologies in Science Education, Aveiro, Portugal (2001)
6. Hungry Frog Java Arcade Games. At http://www.hungryfrog.com/java/javamath.htm
7. McGrenere, J.: Design: Educational Electronic Multi-Player Games. A Literature Review. Thesis from the Department of Computer Science, Univ. British Columbia, USA (1996)
8. Gonzalez, C.S., Moreno, L., Aguilar, R.M., Estévez, J.I.: Towards the Efficient Communication of Knowledge in an Adaptive Multimedia Interface. Proceedings de Interactive Learning Environments for Children, Athens, Greece (2000). Available at http://ui4all.ics.forth.gr/i3SD2000/proceedings.html
9. Papert, S.: The Children's Machine, BasicBooks, New York, NY (1993).
10. Brusilovsky P., Kobsa A., Vassileva J. (eds.) Adaptive Hypertext and Hypermedia. Dordrecht: Kluwer Academic Publishers (1998) 1-43
11. Carro, R.M., Pulido, E., Rodríguez, P.: Dynamic Generation of Adaptive Internet-Based Courses. Journal of Network and Computer Applications. Academic Press. Available online at http://www.idealibrary.com. Vol. 22 (1999) 249-257
12. Reynolds, A., Martin, J.V.: Designing an educational computer game: Guidelines that work. Educational Technology, January (1988) 45-47
13. Carro, R.M., Pulido, E., Rodríguez, P.: TANGOW: a Model for Internet Based Learning. International Journal of Continuing Engineering Education and Life-Long Learning, UNESCO. Special Issue on "Internet based learning and the future of education" (2001). At http://www.inderscience.com/ejournal/c/ijceell/ijceell2001/ijceell2001v11n12.html

Multi-model, Metadata Driven Approach to Adaptive Hypermedia Services for Personalized eLearning

Owen Conlan[1], Vincent Wade[1,2], Catherine Bruen[2], and Mark Gargan[1]

[1] Knowledge and Data Engineering Group, Trinity College, Dublin
{oconlan, vwade, garganm}@cs.tcd.ie
http://www.cs.tcd.ie/research_groups/kdeg
[2] Centre for Learning Technology, Trinity College, Dublin
cbruen@tcd.ie
http://www.tcd.ie/CLT

Abstract. One of the major obstacles in developing quality eLearning content is the substantial development costs involved and development time required [12]. Educational providers, such as those in the university sector and corporate learning, are under increasing pressure to enhance the pedagogical quality and technical richness of their course offerings while at the same time achieving improved return on investment. One means of enhancing the educational impact of eLearning courses, while still optimizing the return on investment, is to facilitate the personalization and repurposing of learning objects across multiple related courses. However, eLearning courses typically differ strongly in ethos, learning goals and pedagogical approach whilst learners, even within the same course, may have different personal learning goals, motivations, prior knowledge and learning style preferences. This paper proposes an innovative multi-model approach to the dynamic composition and delivery of personalized learning utilizing reusable learning objects. The paper describes an adaptive metadata driven engine that composes, at runtime, tailored educational experiences across a single content base. This paper presents the theoretical models, design and implementation of the adaptive hypermedia educational service. This service is currently being successfully used for the delivery of undergraduate degree courses in Trinity College, Dublin as well as being used as part of a major EU research trial.

1 Introduction

In the past Intelligent Tutoring Systems (ITS) traditionally have embedded experts' knowledge in the structure of its content and applied appropriate design models. However, such systems have continually been criticized for believing that this is sufficient for effective learning to occur [13]. In reality, these early systems constrained the learner and limited the opportunities for the learner to investigate topics the ITS deemed to be of little relevance.

Later ITSs used knowledge about the domain, the learner, and about teaching strategies to support flexible individualized learning and tutoring [4]. One of the goals of these ITSs was to adaptively deliver content. The majority of such ITSs merge the content, narrative and learner modeling into a single engine, giving a system that adapts effectively yet is very difficult to repurpose.

Adaptive Hypermedia is a newer research domain [3]. Adaptive Hypermedia Systems (AHS) apply different forms of learner models to adapt the content and the links of hypermedia pages to the user [4]. While there tends to be a clearer separation of the learner model and content model in AHSs (as opposed to the integrated approach of ITSs) the narrative or pedagogical model in usually either embedded in the content or into the adaptive engine itself. This means that applying new or different pedagogical models, e.g. case based learning, simulations, etc., to the content model is more difficult and involves a re-authoring of the content model. This results in learning content that is difficult to reuse or an engine that is domain specific.

This paper proposes an approach that has a clear separation of content, learner and narrative models, and a generic adaptive engine that employs a multi-tiered AI model to achieve effective adaptation to the learner's requirements. The approach is to have very little semantics actually embedded in the adaptive engine itself. Therefore the pedagogic semantics that govern the narrative sequence of the learning experience are contained in a separate model. The adaptive engine reconciles the three models to compose, at runtime, the personalized course. Such dynamic construction of the learning experience is controlled by each learner via appropriate pedagogic instruments, e.g. indirect access to their learner model via an instrument. This approach enables multiple narrative models to be constructed to fulfill different learning goals, while these goals may be achieved from a common repository of content.

Section 2 presents the issues which impact on the development and representation of content within the Adaptive Hypermedia Service. Section 3 discusses the aspects of the learner which can be modeled to enable adaptation to the learner's preferences. Section 4 introduces the narrative model that facilitates the separation of content and structure and enables the course author to define how the service adapts to the learner's knowledge. Section 5 presents the Personalized Learning Service, an implementation of the multi-model, metadata driven approach to constructing Adaptive Hypermedia Services. Finally, Section 6 discusses the conclusions drawn from this research.

2 Content Issues

The main goal of the multi-model approach is to separate the learning content from the adaptive linking logic or narrative. This separation improves the possibilities of reusing a piece of learning content as the learning object (LO) is no longer specific to a given implementation or narrative model. A second goal (with respect to content) of this approach is to allow course designers to easily discover learning content in the content repository by providing appropriate descriptive metadata.

Metadata may describe both technical and pedagogical aspects of the LO. This information is not only useful to a course designer in selecting appropriate learning content, but can be used by an adaptive engine to select appropriate content where there may be many candidate LOs available to fulfill a learning or technical requirement.

2.1 Content Model for the Adaptive Service – The Content Model

The use of standards based metadata to represent the content model encourages the reuse of the learning objects outside of the adaptive hypermedia service. Content may also be imported into the services content repository from external repositories if that content has similar metadata associated with it. The content model utilized in the adaptive hypermedia service is based on IMS Learning Resource Metadata [9]. The IMS Metadata specification was chosen as the basis for the content model schema as it is based on the IEEE LOM specification and an XML binding is available.

Adaptivity is not, however, directly addressed by the IMS Metadata Specification and in order for the adaptive engine to choose between several candidate pieces of content (Sect. 2.3) it may be necessary for it to have further information about the learning objects. Within the EASEL [6] IST project (through which this research has been part funded) an extension to the IMS Metadata schema was developed. The extension consisted of the addition of a sub-section called Adaptivity to the Education section of the schema. This sub-section caters for user definable adaptivity types allowing the metadata creator to develop complex relationships and dependencies within the metadata description of the service [5].

From the perspective of a single reusable learning object, the adaptivity types might include competencies.taught, competencies.required and learningstyle. Included in each adaptivity type is the ability to reference, using a URI, an external resource that enables the metadata author to describe that type and any vocabularies or requirements associated with it.

2.2 Content Lifespan and Granularity

The separation of content from narrative eases the reuse of the learning objects and potentially increases their lifespan. For example, if many learning objects covering aspects of the Java programming language were developed three years ago then, if viewed as a complete course today, may be out of date with respect to the current version of the language. However, if viewed individually some of the learning objects (LO) may be reusable, e.g. those describing the control loops. If the narrative was embedded in the LOs then it may be more difficult to reuse them within another adaptive course.

The potential reuse of LOs is related to the granularity, or the scope, of the learning object. The smaller the granularity of the content the greater potential exists for the LOs reuse. One possible disadvantage of this approach is that if the fine grained LO, which the author terms pagelets, are poorly sequenced then they may appear to be inconsistent or incoherent. It is the function of the narrative author to ensure that the customized courses produced from the narrative contain pagelet sequences that maintain learning concept coherency and have a logical flow (Sect. 4).

2.3 Candidate Content Groups

The mechanism employed by the narrative to refer to content is to use an indirection, whereby the narrative doesn't refer to individual pieces of content (LOs) directly, but to candidate content groups. Each candidate content group contains learning objects that fulfill the same content requirement. The LOs in a candidate content group may differ technically (e.g. bandwidth requirements), in instructional approach or on any other axes on which the adaptive service may be adaptive. The decision as to which LO to deliver can be made at runtime based on some information about the learner (Sect. 3). The requirement for different candidates can be determined by an educational instructional designer, although the task of generating the content for the candidates is generally a collaborative process between the domain expert and the instructional designer.

3 Modeling the Learner

A learner/user model contains explicitly modelled assumptions that represent the characteristics of the student which are pertinent to the system. The system can consult the user model to adapt the performance of the system to each student's characteristics. User modelling allows the system to personalize the interaction between the student and the content. To achieve effective learning this personalization should put the content in a context that the student can understand and to which they can relate.

3.1 Prior Knowledge and Learning Objectives

The learner model should be capable of storing the prior knowledge and learning objectives of the learner to facilitate the personalized delivery of content based on the learner's experience and goals. This raises a number of questions –
- What vocabulary should be used to describe the prior knowledge and objectives?
- What level of detail does this vocabulary need to describe?

As the narrative model is constructed by an expert(s) in the knowledge domain it is up to them to use whatever vocabulary they feel best describes the knowledge domain for which they are building the narratives. As they are responsible for the mechanism(s) that are used to populate the learner model, e.g. a knowledge pre-test, all they need to ensure is that the vocabulary is consistent between the learner model and the narrative.

The granularity to which the vocabulary exists and the scope of the pagelets determine the level at which the engine can adapt to prior knowledge and learning objectives. For example, if a course author decides there are ten learning objectives in a course then the finest grain that the adaptive engine can personalize a course is at the scale of one of those objectives. This is true even if the pagelets are finer grained, as each learning objective may require several pagelets to fulfill it. On the other hand if there was a learning objective associated with each pagelet then the engine could personalize the course on a pagelet by pagelet basis. There is a balance between the vocabulary granularity and pagelet granularity that determines the level of content personalization that is achievable by the adaptive engine.

3.2 Pedagogical Considerations

Learning style is a term used to describe the attitudes and behaviors that determine an learner's preferred way of learning. Learning style preferences have implications for all types of learning, whether the learning is dedicated to the acquisition of knowledge through formal structured activities, e.g. lectures, case studies and books or through experiential learning, i.e. learning through experience [8]. For the online paradigm, as in traditional classroom situations, there is no consensus on how best to model the learner's preferred approaches to learning. Therefore, the approach taken in this design of the Adaptive Hypermedia Service (AHS) was to enable the instructional designers to impact the rendering of the personalized course at two levels –
- The structure/layout in which the content is placed.
- The type (or format) of content displayed.

To this end the AHS enables many candidate narratives, supporting different pedagogical approaches to structuring the content, to be associated with a single course. This association and an appropriate selection mechanism enables the AHS to deliver a personalized course that, while dealing with the same subject matter, can be structured in a way that best engages the learner's preferred learning styles. The subject matter, however, is not referred to directly in the narratives, but rather through the mechanism of candidate content groups (Sect. 2.3). At runtime the AHS can determine which candidate is most suitable (Sect. 5.4). The pedagogical approach used in the design and selection of the content can be defined by the instructional designer.

One such approach is the VARK (Visual, Auditory, Read/Write and Kinesthetic) [15] model that can influence the design of individual content candidates to emphasize one of these aspects – visual, auditory, read/write and kinesthetic. Using an appropriate instrument the learner model may be populated with these values. The AHS can reconcile the content model and the learner model to determine the appropriate candidate at runtime.

3.3 Describing the Learner – What to Model?

The learner model employs a similar mechanism to the content model enabling an extensible metadata framework where information pertaining to how the adaptive engine creates a personalized course may be placed. There is an Adaptivity subsection in the metadata model that enables the definition of new adaptivity types. For example, these types may include competencies.learned, competencies.required and learningstyle. As this is an extensible framework the domain expert, who describes the learning content requirements of a course, and the instructional designer, who describes the pedagogy requirements of the course, can define new adaptivity types to facilitate other forms of adaptivity they may wish to implement in the narrative.

The learner model also includes learner information such as forename, surname and a unique identifier (within the adaptive hypermedia service). When the Adaptive Hypermedia Service is integrating with a Learning Management System (LMS) it is usual that some of this information is retrieved from the LMS (Sect. 5.6).

4 The Narrative Model

The narrative model for a course describes the rules, developed by domain and pedagogical experts, which govern the range and scope of personalized courses that the adaptive engine can produce for learners. The narrative enables the course author(s) to separate the rules which govern how the personalized course will be generated from the content that will be included in that course.

4.1 Encapsulation of Domain Expertise

The narrative is a representation of the expert's knowledge of a domain. Narratives can be used to generate courses that differ in ethos, learning goals, pedagogical approach and learner prior experience from a common content repository. The vocabulary used to describe the learning concepts embodied in the course is that of the domain expert. As the narrative does not refer directly to individual pagelets, but rather to candidate content groups using this vocabulary, the domain expert can create the narrative without being constrained by pedagogical or technical delivery issues at the content level. The author can simply refer to the Candidate Content Group in the narrative and allow the adaptive engine determine which candidate from the group is most suitable for delivery.

Using a similar mechanism to the candidate content groups it is possible to have several candidate narratives for a single course. The candidates have the same ethos, learning goals and require the same learner prior knowledge, but differ in pedagogical approach. Where these kinds of pedagogical issues, i.e. those which impact the course structure, are implemented the process of developing the narratives is often a collaborative process between instructional designers and the domain expert. The Personalized Learning Service is capable of selecting a narrative based on learner model values (e.g. learning style) or on external factors (e.g. is a revision course required).

4.2 Coherent Personalized Course Structures

The primary goal of the narrative is to produce courses that are structured coherently and fulfill the learning goals for the course. It is, therefore, the domain expert's task to ensure that each learning goal has sufficient appropriate pagelets to fulfill that goal and that those pagelets are sequenced in such a manner that engages the learner.

From this perspective the domain expert must consider how the exclusion or inclusion of pieces or sequences of content will impact on the intelligibility of neighboring content and on the personalized course as a whole. To this end it is often useful to determine, before designing a narrative, what is the granularity of content personalization that is to be achieved, i.e. personalization on the section, page or paragraph level. It is also useful to determine what content, if any, is considered core material and should always be present in all personalized courses. With these two factors set, the expert has a framework in which to consider the impact of the inclusion or exclusion of content based on the learners' expertise and preferences.

4.3 Reconciling the Learner Model and the Content Model

As the vocabularies used to describe the knowledge domain and the learner's prior knowledge and learning objectives are determined by the expert (Sect. 3.1), that expert must ensure that those vocabularies are one common vocabulary or that there is a translation mapping available between the two vocabularies. The adaptive hypermedia service does not place any restrictions on what constitutes the vocabulary, only that the narrative model and any elements of the learner model that the expert wishes to reference share that vocabulary or that there exists an appropriate mapping between the narrative and learner model vocabularies. This enables the narrative to reconcile learner prior knowledge and/or learning objectives with candidate content groups.

This reconciliation enables the narrative to select appropriate candidate content groups based on the learner's prior knowledge and learning objectives. The narrative is not directly concerned with learning style issues; only with the learning concepts the final course should include to meet the learner's learning objectives. Learning style considerations are catered for by the appropriate selection of narrative (Sect. 5.3) and content (Sect. 5.4).

5 Personalized Learning Service

The Personalized Learning Service (PLS) has been developed as a service to deliver personalized educational courses based on the multi-model, metadata driven approach outlined in this paper. The PLS is currently being used to deliver personalized online courses in SQL (Structured Query Language) to final year undergraduate students in two degree programmes in Trinity College, Dublin and a trial of eighty students, over a period of two months, was been carried out to assess the students reaction to using an online adaptive hypermedia service. It is also being used within the EASEL [6] IST project to demonstrate the discovery and integration of Adaptive Hypermedia Services with traditional (static) online learning content.

5.1 Architecture

The architecture of the PLS has the three models – learner, narrative and content – as the basis of its design. The PLS utilizes three metadata repositories (Learner, Content and Narrative) and two information repositories (Content and Narrative). There are also two repositories that contain information about candidates – one dealing with Candidate Content Groups and one concerning Candidate Narrative Groups.

At the core of the PLS is the Adaptive Engine (AE). The AE uses the Java Expert System Shell (JESS) [10] with customized functions as the basis of its rules engine. The rules engines role is to produce a model for a personalized course based on a narrative and the learner model. The XML-based [16] personalized course model encapsulates the structure of the learner's course and contains the candidate content groups that fulfill the learner's learning requirements in accordance with the narrative.

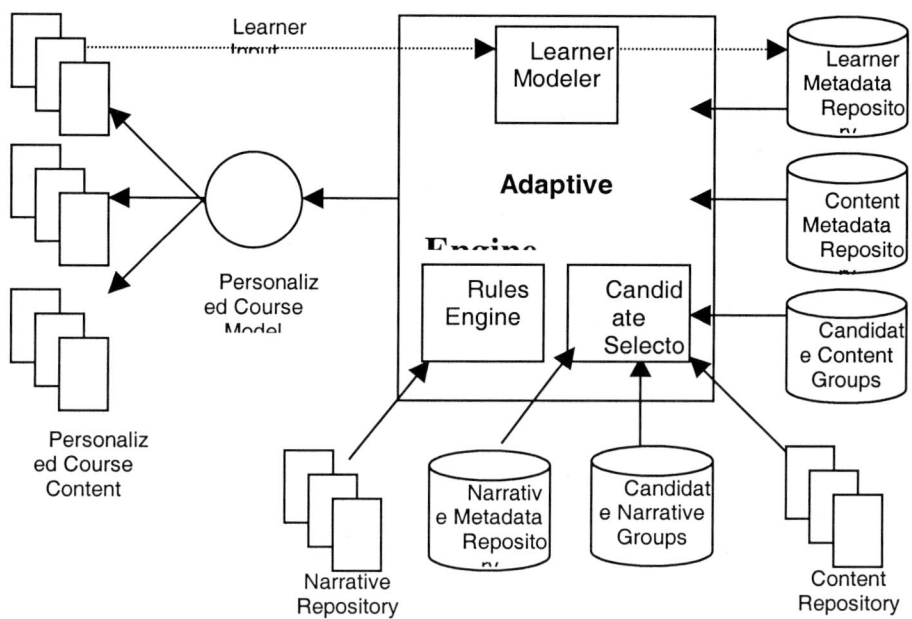

Fig. 1. Adaptive Hypermedia Service Architecture

The AE also utilizes a candidate selector for choosing the appropriate narrative by reconciling information in the learner model with the candidate narrative groups. The candidate selector is also used to choose the appropriate piece of content to deliver from a candidate content group when the personalized course content is being generated from the personalized course model (Sect. 5.4).

The AE has a learner modeler component that enables input from the course or pre-tests to be translated into changes in the learner's information. This component is used to populate the learner's model when the learner initially enters the Adaptive Hypermedia Service. It can also be used at runtime to modify the learner's model – these modifications may either be initiated by the learner or by the engine itself and can be initiated directly from the JSP.

5.2 Building the Learner Model

Before the PLS can create a personalized course for a learner it must have some appropriate information about that learner. This information is obtained by asking the student to complete an online instrument, typically a prior knowledge questionnaire, that determines both their prior knowledge of the domain and any pertinent learning style information. This instrument uses the learner modeler component of the AE to modify the learner model.

The design of any instruments that determine learner information is the responsibility of the domain expert and the instructional designer. The learner is asked to interact with the instrument on their first visit to the PLS. The learner can access the instrument at any stage during their learning and modify their answers. This process gives the learner an indirect mechanism to change their learner model and rebuild their personalized course accordingly.

5.3 Selecting the Narrative and Creating the Personalized Course

The first step in creating a personalized course model is to select an appropriate narrative. For each course there may be several narratives available to achieve the same learning objectives. These narratives differ in the pedagogical approaches used to structuring the content they implement. The adaptive engine calls the candidate selector to choose the best candidate narrative from the candidate narrative group for the course. The selection is based on the metadata in the Narrative Metadata Repository and on the learner's metadata. For example, if the learner's preferredcoursestructure is abstract the candidate selector will select the narrative that matches this preference most closely.

Once the narrative, which is represented by the JESS [10] language, is selected the rules engine is invoked to interpret the rule set. This rules engine has access to the learner model to determine which candidate content groups should be added. It can compare elements of the learner model with rules in the narrative. In the PLS the rules engine is primarily concerned with reconciling the learner's prior knowledge and learning objectives with appropriate candidate content groups.

The rules engine generates an XML representation of the personalized course model that is described in terms of organizational structures such as sections, modules or units (as determined by the narrative designer) and candidate content groups.

5.4 Selecting Content and Delivering the Course

Once the Personalized Course Model has been generated it needs to be translated into a structure and format that the learner can access easily. The appropriate candidates (chosen from the candidate content groups) need to be included in the delivered course as well. These steps are performed by passing the XML representation of the Personalized Course Model through as XSL [17] transformer. The transformer produces many Java Server Pages (JSP) from the XML representation. The JSPs give HTML form to the Personalized Course Model. During the transformation the candidate selector is called to choose the content that best fits the learner's VARK [15] preferences. The candidate selector chooses this content by comparing the prospective candidates metadata with the learner model and uses server-side includes to include the content in the JSP files. The course is delivered as HTML using the Jakarta Tomcat [14] JSP engine.

5.5 Initial Learner Trial Results

After completing the personalized SQL course, produced by the PLS, and a related database design project, the eighty final year undergraduate students who took part in the trial were asked to complete an evaluation questionnaire.

The evaluation of these results is currently being performed, but the initial findings have shown that –
- 30% of the students had no prior experience of online learning, while only 6% said they had much online learning experience.
- Over 80% said the personalized course generated represented the answers they gave in the online pre-test instrument.
- 60% of the students believed the online instrument gave them sufficient control over the content contained in the personalized course generated.
- 87% of the students were happy with how the content was structured in the personalized courses.

These results appear to show the students' satisfaction with the personalized courses generated by the PLS, although some of the comments on the evaluation questionnaires indicated that some students desired a finer level of content control than that offered via the online instrument.

Also observed was a behavior that was not originally anticipated – some students used the instrument to regenerate a personalized course for each study period. They interacted with the instrument is such a way that the personalized course produced contained only the content they wished to study for that period. This gave the students greater control over their learning, echoing some of the fundamental concepts of constructivism.

5.6 PLS as a Remote Third Party Service

In order to be called a service the Adaptive Hypermedia Service (AHS) must facilitate ease of integration with heterogeneous Learning Environments (LE) in such a way that learners are able to seamlessly launch and use the AHSs adaptive content from within their preferred LE, e.g. WebCT, Blackboard, etc. This process, as far as the learner's interaction with the LE is concerned, should appear no different from regular (LE native) content. It may be the case that the learner is studying content from both native and adaptive sources to achieve a learning objective. Within the EASEL [6] IST project the Personalized Learning Service has been successfully integrated with Fretwell-Downing Educations [7] Learning Environment using the Content Interworking API initially defined by the AICC [2]. The API version and data model utilized is a JavaScript implementation of the ADL SCORM [1].

The information exchanged between the LE and the PLS is learner identification, and performance and assessment information. The PLS requests the learner's identification from the LE when the service is initially launched and returns assessment information when the learner has completed their personalized course.

The PLS can be a Third Party Service residing on a separate server from the learning environment. The advantage of this approach it that there is a clear separation of responsibilities – the LE provides the learning support facilities and the PLS provides personalized content. If the learning support features of a Learning Environment are not required the PLS can be launched as a stand-alone service or integrated with other learning content.

6 Conclusions

This paper has presented an approach for developing Adaptive Hypermedia Services based on separation of the narrative, content and learner into individual models. This approach encourages the reuse of content, as the content does not embed the logic used to produce personalized courses. The pedagogical approach and course structure is instead embedded in the narrative model. This approach enables a single course to support many pedagogical approaches to structuring learning content. Also proposed is a mechanism to enable course authors to reference learning objectives, rather than individual pieces of content, from the narrative, thus facilitating the selection of learning content at runtime. This content is selected in accordance with the learner's content presentation preferences.

The paper also presents the Personalized Learning Service, an implementation of the multi-model, metadata approach. The PLS is currently being used to successfully generate and deliver personalized courses in SQL to eighty final year undergraduate degree students in Trinity College, Dublin. Presented are some initial evaluation findings from this trial.

Finally the paper discussed the PLS as a service, highlighting how the service approach enables personalized learning content to be integrated with existing learning content.

References

1. "ADL Sharable Content Object Reference Model", Version 1.2 , http://www.adlnet.org/.
2. "AICC CMI Guidelines for Interoperability", Revision 3.0.1, Release 24 November 1999.
3. Brusilovsky, P.: Methods and techniques of adaptive hypermedia. In P. Brusilovsky and J. Vassileva (eds.), Spec. Iss. on Adaptive Hypertext and Hypermedia, User Modeling and User-Adapted Interaction 6 (2-3), 87-129.
4. P. Brusilovsky. Adaptive educational systems on the world-wideweb: A review of available technologies. In Proceedings of Workshop "WWW-Based Tutoring" at 4th International Conference on Intelligent Tutoring Systems (ITS'98), San Antonio, TX, 1998.
5. Conlan, O., Hockemeyer, C., Lefrere, P., Wade, V., & Albert, D. (2001). Extending educational metadata schemas to describe adaptive learning resources. In Hugh In Proceedings of the twelfth ACM Conference on Hypertext and Hypermedia (Hypertext 2001), pp. 161-162, New York: Association of Computing Machinery (ACM), 2001.
6. Educators Access to Services in the Electronic Landscape (EASEL). EC IST project 10051, http://www.fdgroup.com/easel/.
7. Fretwell-Downing Education, http://www.fdlearning.com.
8. Honey, P. & Mumford, A.: The Manual of Learning Styles, 3rd Edition, 1992, ISBN 0 9508444 7 0.
9. IMS Learning Resource Metadata, Version 1.2, http://www.imsproject.com/metadata/.
10. Java Expert System Shell, Version 6.0, http://herzberg.ca.sandia.gov/jess/.
11. JavaServer Pages Technology, Sun Microsystems, http://java.sun.com/products/jsp/.
12. Marchionini, G.: The costs of educational technology: A framework for assessing change. In H. Maurer (Ed.), Proceedings of Ed-Media 95, World conference of educational multimedia and hypermedia, Graz, Austria.
13. Stauffer, K.: "Student Modelling & Web-Based Learning Systems", 1996.
14. Jakarta Tomcat, The Apache Software Foundation, http://jakarta.apache.org/tomcat/.

15. Fleming, N.D. (1995), I'm different; not dumb. Modes of presentation (VARK) in the tertiary classroom, in Zelmer, A., (Ed.) Research and Development in Higher Education, Proceedings of the 1995 Annual Conference of the Higher Education and Research Development Society of Australasia (HERDSA), HERDSA, Volume 18, pp. 308 – 313.
16. Extensible Markup Language, XML, http://www.w3.org/XML/.
17. Extensible Stylesheet Language, XSL, http://www.w3.org/Style/XSL/.

Adaptation and Personalization on Board Cars: A Framework and Its Application to Tourist Services[*]

L. Console, S. Gioria, I. Lombardi[+], V. Surano, and I. Torre

Department of Computer Sciences – University of Torino
Corso Svizzera 185 - 10149 Torino (Italy)
{luca.console, ila.torre}@di.unito.it

Abstract. In this paper we analyse the goals and problems that should be taken into account when designing adaptive/personalized services that must run on-board vehicles. This is, in fact, a very interesting and promising area of application where adaptation and personalization can provide unique advantages. We then introduce a framework and a multi-agent architecture for on-board services supporting different forms of user and context modelling and different forms of adaptation and personalization. Finally, to support our claims and framework, we discuss a specific prototype system for on-board tourist services.

1 Introduction

The convergence between the different information technologies has reached by now the automotive world. Manufacturers and suppliers of electronic systems have been reproducing, on cars, the whole of appliances and services of both home and office. The main problem they are facing now, is how such different devices - mobile phones, TV, computers, PDAs, new generation phones with internet access, CD and DVD players, GPS, information and entertainment systems -, can be integrated in dashboards and made compatible with the environment of a car and of a user who is driving. Indeed, the solutions implemented or proposed so far are only partially satisfactory and this integration is the subject of several research projects.

The project described in this paper aims at bringing a contribution to these research issues. The main claim of our work is that adaptation and personalization techniques can bring interesting contributions to research in this area. Roughly speaking, in fact, these methodologies and technologies can contribute to making information services on-board a car more useful and more compatible with the context of a vehicle and with the driving task since they can be successful in reaching the goal of providing "the right service, at the right time and in the right way, given the driver's ability/preferences and the current contextual conditions". The aim of our project is to support this claim. In more detail, we started analyzing the peculiar problems arising in this context; as a result we defined a framework for adaptive and

---

[*] The work described in this paper has been carried on in co-operation with Centro Ricerche Fiat and Magneti Marelli Electronic Systems.
[+] Current affiliation: Magneti Marelli Electronic Division

personalized services on-board cars; finally we experimented the framework implementing a prototype for providing personalized tourist information (information about hotels, restaurants, places of interests).

Although adaptation and personalization techniques have been applied to many contexts and domains, including mobile systems (see [3, 4, 9,] for reviews and [8, 6] for applications on mobile devices, dealing also with tourist information), the specific case of automotive systems has not received the attention it deserves. Some applications have been developed (e.g., [7, 10]), but there is no systematic study of the problems that have to be dealt with in this special case.

The paper is organized as follows: Sect. 2 analyses the problems and goals for on-board adaptation/personalization and introduces the framework we defined; Sect. 3 discusses how the framework has been used for implementing a tourist information service called MASTROCARONTE; Sect. 4 concludes the paper with a few words about implementation issues.

2 On-board Adaptation/Personalization: Goals and Framework

The starting point of our project was the analysis of the goals that must be taken into account when designing adaptive/personalized services (systems) on-board cars. This led us to the definition of a set of requirements for the design of our framework:

- Adaptation and personalization must focus on making a service effective and usable on a car where the driver has no time to navigate a space of alternatives, browsing or evaluating different options. This means that the system should be able to provide only the right service (information), at the right time and using the right communication system.
- The system should be very easy and intuitive to use (no effort should be required to comprehend at a glance what the system is communicating and the options that are open to the user) so that its use must not distract the user from her main task, driving. This means also that the system should not be intrusive, especially when it is not appropriate (e.g., driving conditions requiring maximum attention).
- The hardware and software limitations on-board must be taken into account. This is particularly critical as regards the interface since many I/O devices (such as keyboards or pointing devices) cannot be available.
- The services should be location based; this implies a connection with systems such as the GPS and the car navigation system.
- The system should be able to operate in different modes: on demand answering a user request or activating autonomously (if this is compatible with the situation).
- The system should adapt to at least two different aspects: (1) the user – adapting to her features (dimensions), some of which are general and domain independent (e.g., her capabilities or propensity to spend), while others depend on the specific service (e.g., her tourist interests) and (2) the context of interaction. The latter includes dimensions such as the car and driving conditions, the weather, the time of the day, the presence of other passengers (see next item) and is a peculiarity of the application on-board a car.
- The system should take into account that the same user may have different preferences in different situations or contexts (e.g., when travelling alone or with

the family, when travelling for business or for pleasure). This means that the system should be able to deal with multiple views of a user (on the user model).
- The system should support different forms of adaptation and personalization, each of them requires to take into account both the user's profile and the context:
    - *Content adaptation*: selection of the specific service to be suggested,
    - *Detail adaptation*: the amount of information to be presented (possibly on demand),
    - *Interface adaptation*: the interface and channels for presenting the information,
    - *Behavior adaptation*: the behavior of the system, especially as regards the autonomous activation and the autonomous suggestions.
- The user model should follow the user on multiple cars: an individual should receive personalized services on any car equipped with the system and the system should support multiple users of the same car. This means that the user model must be located on a portable support (e.g., a smart card) that can be inserted into any car on which the adaptive system is installed.
- The user cannot be involved too actively in the user modelling process; in particular, we cannot expect that this process can be performed in an interactive and co-operative way. The system must be able to get and exploit at best indirect (and weak) knowledge about the user's behavior.
- Multiple services should be supported on the same car and should be integrated into a unique interface (or unique device). This can be achieved if the services are based on a client/server model, where the client on the car connects to a server via the telephone line. This connection, however, can be critical since it may be unavailable (e.g., in a tunnel or in a remote area) and is quite expensive and slow. As a consequence, the number of connections and the amount of information to be transferred should be limited as much as possible. On the other hand we cannot expect to have powerful computing and storage resources on-board a car.

Architecture of the system. Starting from these goals, we designed a framework and architecture for on-board adaptive/personalised systems (Fig. 1). In the following we shall analyse the framework (using the tourist services application when needed to be more concrete). The architecture is designed to support multiple services; a specific server has to be set for each one of them. The architecture is constituted by a set of agents, distributed in part on the car and in part on the server.

The interaction between the user and the system is mediated by an interface agent running on the car.

The user model is stored on a smart-card that the user can insert into the system on any car. This supports mobility of the user. The model is initialised on the server using stereotypical information. The user model is then updated periodically by taking into account the user's behavior; this can be done either on the car or again on the server. This process is performed by an agent which takes into account statistics on the user behavior collected with the help of the interface agent. Performing the update on-board has the advantage that these data need not be transferred via the GSM line; however, in case the user has multiple cars, the statistics have to be stored on the smart card. On the other hand, performing the update on the server may allow the system to take into account data about the user collected on multiple cars and the behavior of other users (to implement co-operative approaches to user modelling).

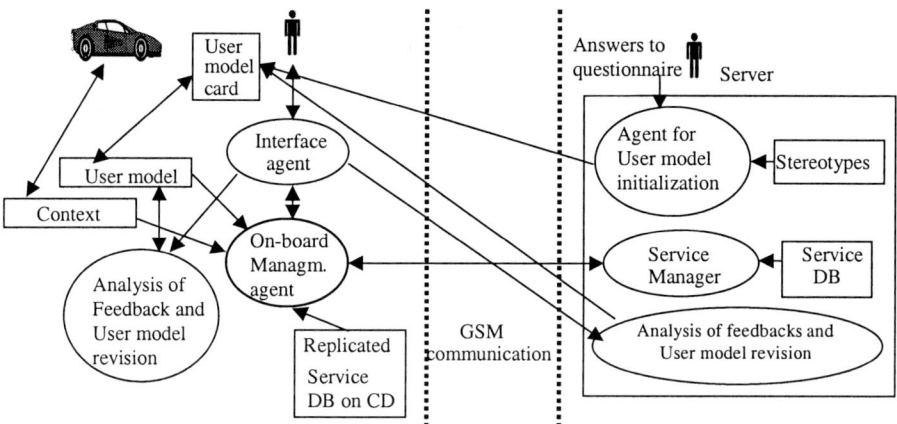

Fig. 1. An architecture for on-board adaptive/personalized services

The user model must contain at least two types of information
- Domain specific information, depending on the application. In the case of tourist services we maintain information about the user interests (e.g., for topics such as art, architecture, museums, natural parks, ...), preferences (e.g., about type of hotel or restaurant) and life-style (propensity to consume and spend).
- Domain independent information, concerning, e.g., the user capabilities, cognitive characteristics, preferences as regards the interface and the modes of interaction and the level of autonomy of the system.

The context model contains information about the context of interaction, that is:
- Information about the position of the car, obtained by the GPS installed on the car.
- Information about the driving conditions (e.g., speed, duration and direction of the travel, the fact that the car is inside a metropolitan area or not, estimated level of traffic, presence of passengers). These pieces of information can be obtained from trip computers and sensors on the car (possibly after some computation).
- Other useful information such as the date and time of the day or weather conditions (these can be obtained from sensors available on the car).

The service data base (DB) are located on the provider site. Whenever it is possible, a replication is distributed on a CD/DVD to be used on the car. In MASTROCARONTE the DB contains information about hotels, restaurants and places of interest (like in a tourist guide), augmented with information useful for personalization.

Three agents are in charge of adaptation/personalization: the interface agent and the on-board manager are on the car, and the service manager is on the provider's site. The on-board manager is responsible of deciding when a service has to be provided (after a user's request or activating autonomously). It also decides which portions of the user and context model are relevant for personalization. It then sends a request to the service manager agent on the server.

The service manager, given information about the user and context model, selects the appropriate personalized service (information) and sends it back to the car. In MASTROCARONTE it selects from the tourist database the hotels or restaurants or places of interest (depending on the type of request) that are most appropriate, given the user preferences and the context (position, time of the day).

The on-board manager receives these pieces of information and evaluates them according to the complete user model. In MASTROCARONTE it ranks the list of items received from the server given the complete user model.

If the service DB is replicated on the car, a protocol for reducing the amount of information to be transferred can be adopted: (i) the server only sends the keywords of the items to be presented (ii) the on-board manager can check if the information on the CD is up-to-date (the keyword is replaced at each update, so that if the keyword is available in the DB on the CD, then the information on the CD is up-to-date), (iii) it asks to transfer data from the server only if needed. This is the protocol adopted in MASTROCARONTE which uses a replicated tourist DB on a DVD on the car.

The interface agent is in charge of selecting the right medium and form of presentation, given the user and context model. For example, it may decide to use a voice synthesizer to provide information in safety critical situations (e.g., high traffic or speed) or to use the video display in other conditions (e.g., low speed, non metropolitan area, limited traffic). Moreover, it decides the amount of information and detail to be provided (detail adaptation).

This framework can be used to implement different types of services. In the following section we discuss in more detail MASTROCARONTE, which is the first prototype we implemented based on the framework.

3 MASTROCARONTE, an Application for Tourist Services

In this section we discuss MASTROCARONTE, a specific instantiation in the domain of tourist services of the framework discussed in the previous section. In the following we analyse in more detail the various agents and modules in Fig. 1.

User and Context Model
The analysis of the dimensions of the user to be modelled has been carried on using the methodology proposed in [11, 12]). The methodology suggests that an application is analysed by performing a decomposition of the adaptation goals and of the features of the application domain and context. The resulting matrix provides guidelines for choosing which aspects of the user are most useful (for achieving a given goal, in a given application domain and context). We performed this analysis on several potential applications on-board cars and this allowed us to single out the distinction between a portion of the user model which is common to (almost) all the applications (because it is mainly related to the goals of adapting the interaction with the user on a car) and a portion which is domain dependent.

The former includes dimensions such as the user cognitive characteristics (amount of information that she can read at a glance, level of attention that she can pay to the on-board information system, ...), her life style and propensity to spend and consume and preferences (e.g., on the interface, on the medium to be used in the interaction, on the level of initiative that the system may take..).

The latter includes, in the tourist service application, aspects such as the user's tourist interests (useful for selecting the most appropriate places of interests), her preferences concerning food or location or type and level of comforts of hotels/restaurants, and the propensity to spend under some specific conditions, such as kind of travel, (useful for selecting the most appropriate hotels or restaurants).

The approach we adopted for user modelling is a modular one, where different dimensions of the user are dealt with in a separate way (following a methodology already adopted in [1, 2]). This has several advantages since user modelling knowledge can be re-used in multiple applications for which the dimension is relevant. In MASTROCARONTE we considered three dimensions: *Cognitive characteristics, Interests, Life style*.

We defined stereotypes for these dimensions, starting from psychographic studies about the Italian population (and specifically about their cultural interests) published by Eurisko [5]. We thus have three groups of stereotypes:
- *Interests*. Starting from classificatory data such as the age, gender, type and field of work, hobbies and recent travels, these stereotypes make a first prediction on the user's interests in art (ancient or modern), technology, amusements, nature, ...
- *Cognitive characteristics*. This group of stereotypes uses classificatory data such as the user's age, education level, job and makes a prediction on the user's receptivity, a parameter used to determine the amount and detail of the information that can be presented to her.
- *Life style*. These stereotypes classify users according to their psychographic features, which include socio-demographic data and priorities. They make predictions about the user propensity to spend and consume and about the preferred types of tourist facilities (e.g., hotels and restaurants).

The user model is generated by matching the data provided by the user with the stereotypes and then generating and merging the corresponding predictions. In particular, each prediction regards a feature in the user model and corresponds to a probability distribution for the linguistic values of the feature.

For the sake of brevity we omit the details of this classification process (which is a fairly standard one based on probabilities and Bayesian classification, see [1]), and we only report an example of a fragment of a user model:

interest for art(modern) very-high: 0.4, high: 0.3, medium: 0.2, low: 0.1, null: 0
interest for architecture very-high: 0.2, high: 0.3, medium: 0.3, low: 0.1, null: 0.1
interest for shopping very-high: 0.1, high: 0.1, medium: 0.1, low: 0.4, null: 0.3
....
receptivity: very-high: 0.5, high: 0.4, medium: 0.1, low: 0, null: 0
propensity-to-spend: very-high: 0.1, high: 0.2, medium: 0.4, low: 0.3, null: 0

For example, the first line specifies that the probability that the user's interest for modern art is very high is 0.4, etc.

The user model is refined (or even revised) after tracking the user behavior. In particular, the system records the actions performed by the user whenever she receives a suggestion and in this way tries to infer the user's actual interests/preferences. We noticed that we cannot ask the user to provide direct feedback; nevertheless there are many events that can provide indirect (even if uncertain) feedback. For example, strong feedback can be obtained whenever the user makes a phone call or asks for further information about a place (this can be done using facilities integrated into our interface, see Fig. 2). Weaker feedback can be obtained from the GPS: from the position of the car (and in particular from that of the parking) the system can guess which are the places that the user actually visited.

Very roughly, the revision is performed in three steps:
- Feedback (direct and indirect ones) about the user's behavior are collected across time and stored on the memory card containing the user model, with different degrees of reliability associated with them.
- Statistics about the user's behavior are computed periodically. In particular, these statistics regard the type of places the user visited and their characteristics. For example, for places of interest we compute statistics about the type of places that have been visited (e.g., related to modern art or to architecture or to shopping; this information can be extracted from the tourist database, see next paragraph).
- A set of rules is activated periodically to compute, from the statistics above, new probability distributions for the features in the user model. For example, if the user visited all the time places which are highly relevant for modern art, we may get the following new probability distribution for the user interest in modern art:

   interest for art(modern) very-high: 1, high: 0, medium: 0, low: 0, null: 0

   This new distribution is then combined with the one in the current user model. The two contributions are weighed according to the following schema:
   - in the early phases of the use of the system (when the current user model mainly comes from stereotypes), the distribution computed using feedback about the user's behavior and the revision rules has a stronger impact;
   - this impact is progressively reduced and, after some time, the distribution in the current user model becomes the most relevant one, so that the rules can only perform a slight revision of the user model.

Database of Tourist Information

This database is a standard tourist database, augmented with additional information useful for performing a personalized selection of the items.

For hotels and restaurants, it maintains information about the category, style, level of price, type of amenities, look of the place, etc.

For places of interests it keeps track of how relevant the place is with respect to a set of categories (which are those in terms of which the interests of a user are classified in the user model, see above): art (ancient and modern), nature, architecture, technology, amusements, shopping, etc. The relevance is defined on a scale from 0 (not relevant) to 4 (highly relevant). For example, the "Museum of Cinema" of Torino (a museum concerning the history and techniques of Cinema), has the following attributes:

   relevance for: art (modern) = 4, technology = 3, amusements = 4

For each item we also keep track of its absolute location (in terms of GPS coordinates). Finally, each item is identified by a unique key, which is changed whenever a piece of information about the item is updated. The database is stored on the server and replicated on a DVD to be used on the car. Through the identifying key it is possible to discover, on the car, if the information on the DVD is up to date.

On-board Management Agent

This agent decides if and when the system must activate autonomously to provide recommendations to the user. This is decided given information in the user model (user preferences about the level of the system's autonomy and statistics about the situations in which the user likes to receive advice).

Whenever the system is activated, the agent is responsible of generating the query to be sent to the service manager. The query concerns one of the services (hotels, restaurants or places of interests) and includes information about the location (GPS coordinates) of the car and about the user model. The latter is the list of the interests/preferences for which the cumulative probabilities of the levels "medium", "high" and "very high" is over a threshold (0.66). Thus, the typical structure of a query is the following (using am abstract SQL):

Select identificationKey
From (restaurants OR hotels or placesOfInterest) {depending on the query}
Where   Location closeTo currentGPSposition AND
     Attrubutes includeAtLeastOneOf UserPreferences

The query is sent to the server to the information retrieval agent.

When it receives the answer from the server, the query management agent ranks the items in the reply. This is done by taking into account the preferences in the user model and the information about each item contained in the tourist database. Let us consider the case of places of interest. The ranking is obtained by computing a degree of match between each item (and in particular its degree of relevance with respect to the categories of interests, e.g., art(modern), architecture, ...) and the preferences in the user model (probability distributions regarding the same categories).

Service Manager Agent
The service manager agent is activated by a query sent from the car and is responsible of retrieving the items that are most appropriate, given the information about the car location and user's preferences carried by the query. It queries the database and returns the list of identifiers of the retrieved items. The selection takes into account:
- The location of the car: the items must be not farer than X km from the location of the car (the actual value of X depends on the location – metropolitan or not – and on the time of the day), possibly in the direction of the trip. In case the criterion is too restrictive (less than 10 items are retrieved), it is weakened and the distance doubled (this, however is applied only if the query was started by the user).
- Contextual information about the date and time so that all the items which are not open or accessible are discarded.
- The preferences of the user: only the items which have a relevance of at least 2 for at least one of the preference attributes associated with the query are retrieved.

Interface Agent
The interface agent is responsible of collecting requests from the user (who simply has three buttons for asking about hotels, restaurants or places of interests) and of presenting the list of suggested items as ranked by the on-board management agent.
 The adaptation of the presentation depends on three main aspects:
- The context in which the interaction is taking place, that is the driving conditions (e.g., speed, traffic, metropolitan area vs. motorway, weather, time of the day).
- The user's cognitive characteristics. These include long term information stored in the user model (i.e., the user receptivity which estimates the amount of information that the user can read at a glance) and short term information concerning the user tiredness (estimated given the time of the day and the number of hours driven).
- The user preferences concerning the style and layout.

The user interface agent evaluates these conditions every time it receives from the query management agent a list of ranked items to be presented to the user. The decision to be made is the choice of the presentation format, which corresponds to choosing how many items to list in a page and how many pieces of information and services to associate with the selection of each item. In order to simplify the process, we decided to define a fixed set of presentation formats so that the interface agent must select the most appropriate one among these formats. We use XML for the exchanges of information and each format is defined by a style-sheet; thus, the generation of the presentation simply amounts to the application of the selected style to the ranked list of items. In the current prototype we defined five style-sheets.

Examples of presentation are showed in Fig. 2. All the screenshots refer to the same driver but those in the first row refer to driving conditions that are less critical than those in the second row. The screenshots on the left correspond to the list of items presented to the driver (ten per page in the first case, four per page with larger fonts in the second). The screenshots on the right refers to the details about one item (a restaurant in this case) with a personalized ranking ("Voto" on a scale from 1 to 5) and the possibility of activating other services (e.g., "Chiama" for making a phone call or "Strada" for getting the route from the navigation system). Notice that in the second row the number of available services is reduced.

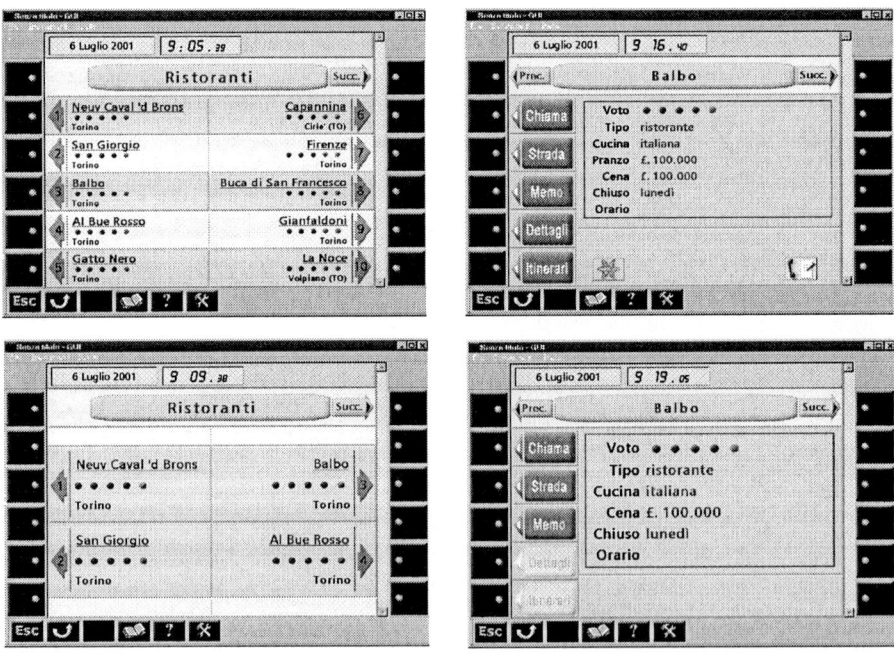

Fig. 2. Examples of interaction

4 Summary and Implementation Issues

In the paper we introduced a framework that addresses the goals and problems to be taken into account when designing adaptive/personalized services on board vehicles and we discussed an instance of the framework in the area of tourist services.

The framework has been implemented as a multi-agent system, where the agents running on the car are embedded in the VxWorks real time operating system used by Magneti Marelli on its car navigation systems. In particular, we implemented the agents using CLIPS (a rule-based system developed by NASA), embedding CLIPS-based agent in VxWorks. All exchanges of information are based on XML schemas. The prototype of MASTROCARONTE runs on a PC emulation of the CONNECT car navigation system by Magneti Marelli, installed on cars of the Fiat group (the black buttons in Fig. 2 correspond to the physical buttons in the dashboard of the car).

References

1. L. Ardissono, L. Console, I. Torre: An Adaptive System for the Personalized Access to news, in *AI Communications*, Vol 14, no. 3, 2001, pp. 129-147.
2. L. Ardissono, A. Goy, G. Petrone, M. Segnan, P. Torasso: Tailoring the recommendation of tourist information to heterogeneous user groups, in *Springer LNCS 2266*, pp. 280-295.
3. P. Brusilowsky: Methods and Techniques of adaptive hypermedia. In *User Modelling and User Adapted Interaction* 6 (2-3): 1996, pp 87-129.
4. P. Brusilowsky: Adaptive Hypermedia. In *User Modelling and User Adapted Interaction* 11 (1-2): 2001, pp 87-110.
5. G. Calvi: *Indagine Sociale Italiana, rapporto Eurisko*, Franco Angeli, 1986
6. B.N. De Carolis, F. de Rosis: in Proc. *Worksop on AI in Mobile Systems*, Seattle 2001.
7. C-N Fiechter, S. Rogers: Learning subjective functions with large margins. In *AAAI Spring Symposium on Adaptive User Interfaces*, Stanford March 2000, AAAI, pp. 40-47.
8. J. Fink, A. Kobsa, A. Nill : Adaptable and adaptive information for all users, including disabled and elderly people, in *New review of Hypermedia and Multimedia*, Vol. 4, 1998, pp. 163-188.
9. A. Kobsa, J. Koenemann, W. Pohl: Personalized hypermedia presentation techniques for improving online customer relationships, in *The Knowledge Engineering Review*, 2001.
10. C.A Thompson, M. Göker: Learning to Suggest: The adaptive place advisor. In *AAAI Spring Symposium on Adaptive User Interfaces*, Stanford March 2000, AAAI, pp. 130-135.
11. I. Torre: A modular approach for user modelling. In *Adaptive Hypermedia and Adaptive Web-Based Systems* 2000 (AH 2000), *Springer LNCS 1892*, pp. 414-420.
12. I Torre: Goals, tasks and Application domains as the guidelines for defining a framework for User modelling", in *Springer LNAI 2109*, pp. 260-264.

Adaptive Authoring
of Adaptive Educational Hypermedia

Alexandra Cristea and Lora Aroyo

Department of Computer Science
Eindhoven University of Technology
Eindhoven, The Netherlands
{a.i.cristea, l.m.aroyo}@tue.nl
http://wwwis.win.tue.nl/~{alex, laroyo}

Abstract. In this paper we propose a set of development guidelines for an *adaptive authoring environment of adaptive educational hypermedia*. This set consists of relevant and necessary functionalities and architectural features of authoring systems (AS) for adaptive teaching and/or learning environments (LE). We extracted the core functionalities by analysing MyEnglishTeacher (MyET) and AIMS - two independently designed and built AS for adaptable/ adaptive LE. The extended core led us to a *concept-based layered approach* with respect to *concept-* and *attribute-level adaptation*, as well as *lesson* and *presentation adaptation*. We believe that providing adaptive authoring support for adaptive hypermedia will have a strong impact on the authors' motivation and efficiency in performing their tasks and consequently will increase the popularity of adaptive hypermedia.

1 Introduction

To keep up with the high demands in educational software and LE, it is already widely accepted by the educational community that the future of such environments lies in *adaptability* and *adaptivity* [11,13,18,19]. These high demands reflect also on the authoring environments, general purpose or application oriented. At present, AS for adaptive LE are almost non-existent, mainly because of the field novelty and the growing demands– making any authoring system for LE outdated before it is used. However, with the ripening of the field, *standardization of adaptive and adaptable techniques and methods* [10,15,16,22] is starting to preoccupy the research community, and AS become a serious need. Still, it is not reasonable to expect teachers to skilfully apply adaptation to their new on-line courses. Transition from linear, book-like courseware is not easy. Teachers are confronted with the heavy task of designing contents alternatives, adaptation techniques and ultimately, the whole user-interaction mechanism. It is clear that for adaptive courseware the authoring tool has to offer tuneable complexity and automatically perform many of the authoring tasks.

In this paper, we build upon our previous research by shortly reviewing two AS for adaptable/ adaptive LE, MyET and AIMS, which we designed and built independently. From our experience with these two systems we are extracting a set of functionalities that are relevant and necessary for AS for adaptive teaching and/or LE. Given the complexity of the authoring task such environments [14], we independently came to the conclusion that the authoring tool has to be also adaptive to the teacher. Therefore, we extend our previous research to an *adaptive authoring framework* based on the above-mentioned necessary functionalities.

2 Two Methods for Authoring Support of Adaptive Courseware

In this section we are presenting the two independently designed, developed and tested systems for courseware authoring, with special focus on adaptive courseware: (a) MyET [9], developed at the University of Electro-Communications in Japan, and (b) AIMS [2], developed at Twente University in The Netherlands. In both MyET and AIMS concept mapping paradigm [4,7] is used as a main structure to organise the subject domain terminology and to link to course items (lessons, exercises, documents). We outline the common features shared by these systems with respect to course content organization, maintenance and presentation, with the purpose of *reusability* and *student adaptation*. Our evaluation framework is based on the: (a) *general course structure*; (b) *text presentation and structure*; (c) *lesson composition*; (d) *authoring views and (e) student adaptation facilitation*. Due to lack of space, we have skipped the analysis of tests and exercises creation, structuring and linking.

2.1 General Course Structure

The information exchange from tutor to system means input of lessons, texts, links, but also asking for help in editing, etc. The data from the tutor is stored in a structured way, as shown in Figure 1. Input can be *audio, video, graphic* or *text*.

Teacher-name
AUDIO FILMS PICTURES LESSON
113-1 115-1 119-1 123-1 190-1 196-1 65-1
114-1 118-1 119-2 123-2 190-2 197-1 67-1
EXERCISES conclusion keywords
title TEXTS explanation pattern
TEXT1 TEXT2
exercise1 keywords pattern

COURSE: <name> <description>
INSTRUCTOR: <name>
DOMAIN: <name>
TOPIC-1: <name> <description>
MAIN-TEXT: <link>
TASK-1-1: <name> <keywords> → TEXT(s)
...
TASK-1-N: <name> <keywords> → TEXT(s)

(a)   (b)

Fig. 1. Data structure in MyET (a) ; Course structure in AIMS Course Editor (b)

a. In MyET, the first three inputs have also a text version in the lesson and with automatically generated index. Each lesson object is subdivided into *exercises, conclusion, keywords, title, explanation, pattern to learn* and *text objects*. These are further subdivided into *exercise, keywords, pattern, title* and actual *main text*.
b. A related structure appears in Fig. 1b. The teacher in AIMS creates the course structure as part of an information model, defining the *subject domain* (course

terminology/concepts), *library* (collection of texts), *course* (lessons and exercises) and *user profile* objects and expressing all the links between them and their components [3]. Each course *lesson* is divided into *exercises*, which are directly related to subject domain concepts and this way also to related documents (texts). This domain-specific structuring and concept-based linking are provided [17].

2.2 Text Presentation and Structure

The smallest block / object in the course structure is a TEXT.

In MyET, each text also has (next to text body), some obligatory attributes: a *short title, keywords, explanation, patterns to learn, conclusion* and *exercises*. This way, not only titles and keywords but also explanation and conclusion files are used for search and retrieval. Moreover, the corresponding text to any video/audio recording allows any non-text resource to be retrieved via a text-based search.

The authors in AIMS are offered the choice to select *keywords from the domain terminology* they have created as a concept map. These keywords also make the link directly to the lessons (course structure of course topics and exercises). The AIMS library editor provides the authors with presentation and instructional formats to map each course related material in such a way that it is both *task-* and *use-oriented* [2].

2.3 Lesson Composition

One or more texts (with multimedia or not) build a LESSON object. In MyET, each lesson also has (beside of texts, etc.) the following attributes: *title, keywords, explanation, conclusion, combined exercises* (generated automatically or not). This structure is very similar to the text object structure.

A text or lesson is generically called 'SUBJECT' in MyET or 'TOPIC' consisting of course 'TASKS' in AIMS.

2.4 Student Adaptation Issues

In the MyET environment, adaptation to the students' needs meant interpreting the concept maps and the links created by the teacher. A *global agent* would copy the map to create a global student model that would serve as a guide for all students. Moreover, a *private agent* would make its own copy and alter it with respect to the student's needs and based on the interaction with the student. The system agents work based on the embedded rule/knowledge systems. They act as learning objects, which can adaptively change their representation of the subject space [10].

The adaptation to the students' needs in AIMS is performed with a team of collaborating agents with respect to (a) *user-oriented presentation of the information*, based on the general work progress of the student on the course, and (b) *students' search activities*. This is realised by refining the student search query according to the current course task context, by adjusting the search result presentation with relevance to the course task and by providing students with alternative view of the results and thus alternative ways to build a conceptual structure of the course knowledge [2].

2.5 Courseware Views for Authors

Once a map has about 50 subjects representing a number of concepts with their links, it is impossible to get a sensible display in one map [1]. To manage the complexity we designed extra courseware views showing different sub-sections: "views" of whole graph, with reduced information (*"bird's eye views"*); one concept and its "star"-links (all concepts currently linked to it) (*"fisheye views"* [9,11]); non-linked concepts: *"floating"*-concepts [10]; one concept and its *"star"-linked documents* (texts) [3]; all *link types* currently in use [2]; all *concepts ordered alphabetically* by name, by description and category; the *place in the concept map* of every newly defined concept.

3 Our Concept Mapping Layered Approach to Adaptive Authoring

From the analysis and extraction of common proprieties of the two AS, a more intuitive division seems therefore to be to separate the course material into concepts [2,10], as derived from the *concept-mapping* paradigm [7]. A low level concept should represent an *atomic piece of content/ information* that has an independent semantics. This atomic unit can be labelled with one concept. Collections of concepts can, of course, build *composite concepts*, generating a *concept hierarchy*. Concepts can be related to each other at any level of the hierarchy. The creation of these building bricks is the role of the course designer [3,9]. The division of the content into concepts only gives us the primitive building blocks of the courseware. Putting these building blocks together with different sequences generates different presentations or *lessons*. This can be done by a course designer or by a teacher. In a more advanced environment it can be automatically generated by a system [10].

At this level, we would only speak of *adaptive navigation support*. That is because *adaptive presentation* is (normally) at a lower level than the concept level and binds actually parts (fractions) of concepts with each other. Clearly, it makes no sense to just transform parts of concepts into sub-concepts, as it is possible that they make no sense but in the context of the atomic concept (so have no independent semantics attached).
- *Example:* Consider, for instance, the case of the introduction to some text. This is a construct that appears very often and that can be dropped in later versions of the browsing (or used together with other introductory fragments in an introductory chapter). However, this construct usually has no independent meaning.

The solution is quite obvious [9]: the concept can be sub-divided into its *attributes*. These can be anything from a concept name to alternative contents or fragments.

By dividing/mapping the course content into a concept hierarchy, and the concepts into a set of attributes, the adaptation has only to deal with *concept-level adaptation* and *attribute adaptation*. The advantage is that it can all be performed (and viewed) from a high level and does not need separate consideration of different conditions written within the text, which are more difficult to re-use by other authors. Basically, the adaptation becomes only a matter of combining concept attributes into *pages* (pieces of information that can be show at a time), *chapters* and *subchapters*. This way, the adaptation is only at a content level (equivalent to adaptive presentation), while the navigation is only dependent on the presentation format. We will return to these issues in Section 3.1 (e.g., short pages will mean that the "next" button within the same lesson appears more often, but the content of the page is shorter [20]).

3.1 Lesson Map

A lesson map is, in the simplest case, the lesson sequence that tells the student how the lesson should proceed (according to the teaching style, learning style or learning goals). In a more general case (Figure 2), the lesson map is a directed (not necessarily a-cyclic) graph with at least one beginning (START) and at least one ending state (GOAL). Circles here represent either whole concepts, or concept attributes.

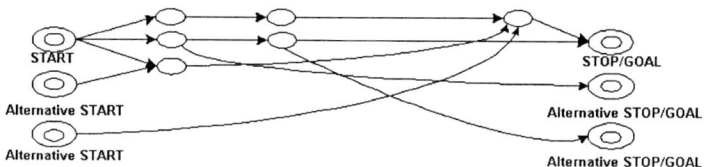

Fig. 2. Alternatives 'start' and 'stop' positions for the lesson map

The START and STOP positions do not have to be unique. The user model (UM) based adaptation engine determines the selection between alternatives.

In Figure 3 we present a sketch of the concept mapping layered approach to lesson adaptation. A lesson X is composed of some concept fragments (attributes) that are grouped into chapters (here, 2). At presentation, there is another separation into pages (here, 6 pages). The latter is presentation means dependent (e.g., laptop screen browser, hand-held device, etc.).

It is interesting to note that, although the fragments themselves have no semantics (and therefore could not have been subdivided into concepts), they can be addressed via the concepts they belong to.

3.2 Authoring Adaptive Courseware with Concepts

Next we present two types of concept editing processes. This way we show that the transition from classical course editing - to pure concept editing style is an easy one.

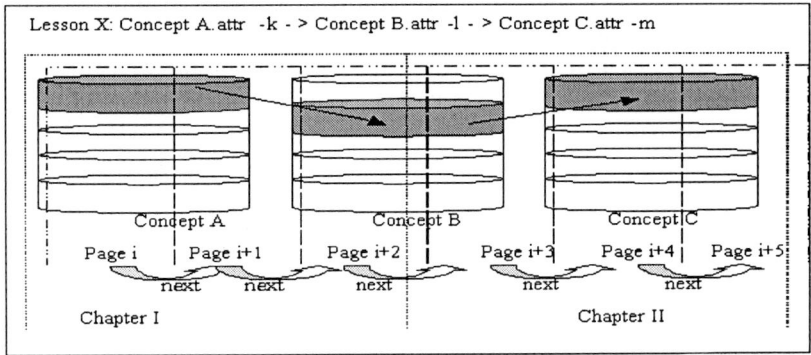

Fig. 3. Lesson adaptation: *lesson* X (straight line square), composed of, e.g., 3 *concepts* A, B and C (cylinders), with *attributes* (darkened cylinder); presentation order shown by directed connections between attributes; lesson has 2 *chapters*, that contain (parts of) concepts (dotted line squares). In chapters information is presented (in browser window, e.g.) in *pages* (point-dotted line squares). "Next" buttons at page level are navigation support for presentation only.

3.2.1 Concept–Based Authoring in Traditional Order

In order to make the transition from traditional editing to concept editing easier a concept-based authoring tool should be able to allow, in extreme cases, pure traditional editing. In this section we present a five-step procedure for concept editing in traditional order, illustrated in Figure 4.

1. First, the author writes sequentially the text of the course/lesson together with the respective multimedia. The instructor can stop the process here or at any of the next steps and let the system automatically perform the rest of the steps and show the results again to the teacher for approval, or to another author for reusing.
2. The content is divided and organised into a *concept structure*. First, the concept hierarchy of concepts, sub-concepts and atomic concepts is created, where the atomic concepts are the smallest semantically indecomposable building blocks within this structure. Further, the main attributes of the concepts are filled in, such as concept name and content and possibly any other related attributes [9].
3. Adaptive features are added by writing a separate rule-base [22] or setting importance coefficients and weights [10] and generating at least one *lesson map* (sequence). In some cases it may be necessary here to return to STEP 2 in order to refine the division granulation or to STEP 1 to add more concepts/ material.
4. The author can define the different items to display depending on certain conditions (only mentioned in the separate rule-base, started at STEP 3: lesson maps).
   ➢ At first glance, we have here *alternatives* (such as alternative texts in different languages for the same concept/ lesson/ etc.) or *conditionals* (such as additional information that is only presented if "conditions are right" – classical adaptive presentation). However, from the adaptive engine point of view, this distinction cannot be meaningful, as conditionals can be seen as alternatives, where, if the condition is not satisfied, nothing is displayed (instead of an alternative). Here we don't discuss the cases where empty information pages re-

sult due to, e.g., bad authoring. This is a matter of presentation means adaptation and not user-modelling adaptation.

After new attributes have been generated the author can return to STEP 3 to refine the rules. If necessary, s/he can jump to STEP 2 to refine granulation of division or to STEP 1 to add more concepts/ material.

5. The author creates the lesson maps following the procedure from Section 3.1.

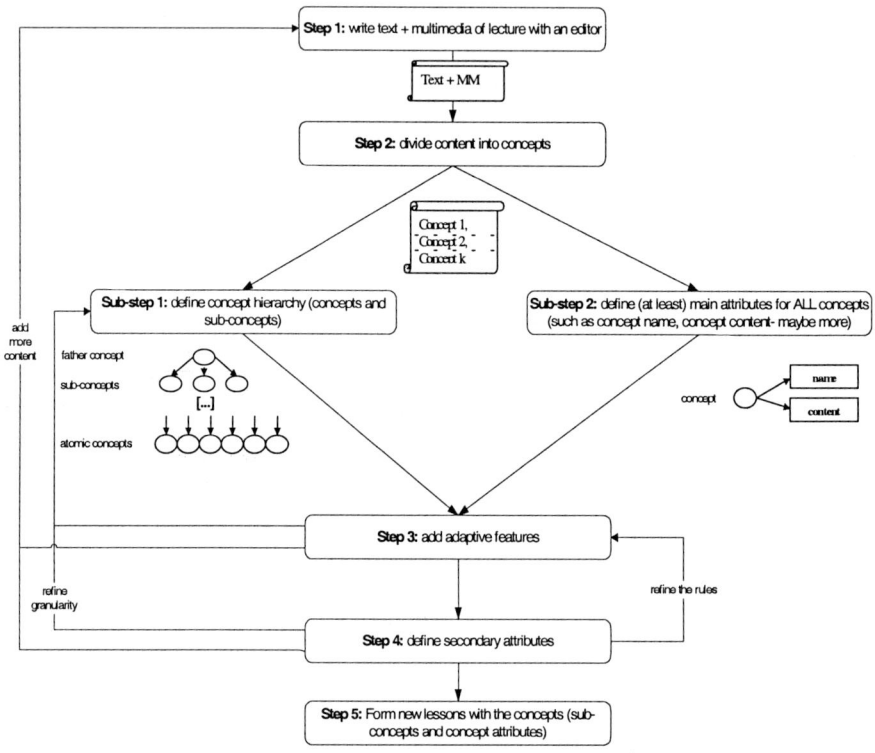

Fig. 4. Concept-based editing: traditional order

The procedure above allows the author to be as precise and detailed as s/he wants but at the same time, it allows him/her to do as little authoring as possible. This is realized by the clear division between the authoring stages. An author/ teacher can be just content creator – or the creator of non-adaptive hypermedia (STEP 1). Other authors nevertheless can reuse and refine the created content, by performing the steps starting from STEP 2. In this way, we have accomplished several goals:
  ➢ Simple authoring, yet
  ➢ Complex results; moreover
  ➢ Collaborative authoring.

The latter is made possible by the semantic structure, based on a flexible, growing common ontology based on well-annotated concepts (as concept attributes can also take over the role of concept annotations).

Moreover, the transition from STEP 1 to STEP 2 is not unique and loops to refine the granulation of the concepts are possible – so, subdivisions of higher level into lower level concepts – as long as the units obtained still have an independent semantics. This structuring is in the sense of the Semantic Web, while the division of contents into concepts, with their attributes and links is similar to the RDF W3C standard recommendations (of separating resources, literals and properties).

3.2.2 Non-traditional Authoring: Direct Concept Editing

The previously presented method is only to make the bridge between traditional (classical) editing and concept-based editing. In a purely concept oriented editor, an author would follow the following steps:
STEP 1: write concepts + concept hierarchy
STEP 2: define concept attributes (define main and extra attributes)
STEP 3: fill concept attributes (write contents)
STEP 4: add content related adaptive features regarding UM (des. alternatives, conditions)
STEP 5: define format (presentation means-related; define chapters)
STEP 6: add adaptive features regarding presentation means (define pages).

3.3 Resulting Layers, Author Adaptation and Automatic Processing per Layer

Concluding from this procedural explanation, it is clear that the courseware resulting will have a *layered structure* as illustrated in Figure 5.

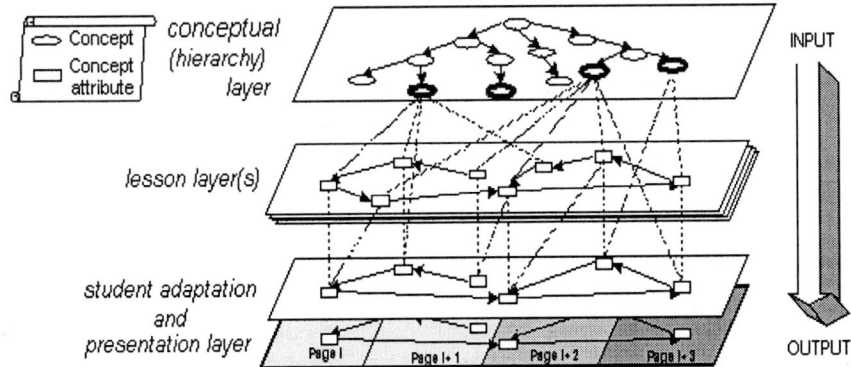

Fig.5. Authoring adaptation layers

1) The first layer is the conceptual layer, with
   a) a first sub-layer of *atomic concepts*, which cannot be changed anymore. *Adaptation and automatization at this level can mean search of related (possibly identical) concepts, in order to warn the author that the new concept s/he wants to define possibly already exists. Also, this is the moment to automatically establish connections between concepts (computed by system via heuristics [9] and approved by the author).*

b) a second sub-layer of composite concepts, which are sets of concepts of atomic granulation or larger, and which have a *hierarchical structure*. Course designers and/or system can change this hierarchy automatically. In this layer, connections as *relatedness connections* [10] also appear.

The system can perform concept – sub-concept adaptation by helping in suggesting relevant higher concept classes, etc.

2) The second layer contains *lessons* (the hierarchy of chapters, sub-chapters and the directed graph called lesson – Section 3.1). This represents the way and the order in which the concepts should be taught. Note, that the lesson layer deals with concept attributes and not necessarily directly with concepts. This allows having both adaptive navigation support and adaptive presentation within the same layer and guarded by the same mechanism. The system can search for alternative existing orders and make the author attentive to other possibilities or inquire in a dialog with the author for the possibility that the order is not compulsory.

3) The third layer contains

a) a UM-based sub-layer, an *adaptation engine* that specifies what material should be presented and when (under which conditions or equivalent sets of conditions – Section 3.4).

From this point, user adaptation means student adaptation.

b) a sub-layer, formed by the *presentation means based adaptation*. This adaptation part is concerned with the formatting so that the information appears nicely in the page, with questions such as the ideal page length – so where chapters should be cut to form pages, how and where multimedia presentations should appear, colours, fonts, etc. These matters should, in the simplest authoring version, be generated fully automatically in order to simplify the task of authors. Of course, such issues should also be designable by authors, if necessary [20] Here, rhetorical structure adaptation should be overlayed.

4 Conclusions

Providing adaptive authoring for adaptive hypermedia is quite a crucial task as the authoring process involves, beside of what was mentioned in this paper, also a number of other complicated tasks, such link-checking (e.g., issues of *termination* and *confluence* [22]) which become almost impossible for a human to keep track of. Therefore, next to the adaptation support with respect to the content organization and presentation, an important issue is also the provision of support *tools to analyse and monitor the information input by the author*. The editing environment must provide support for a number of editorial tasks, such as information search and retrieval, information visualisation, selecting, restructuring, annotating information with metadata, generation of adaptive user feedback and user preferences information. In order to make the course related content and knowledge to be most efficiently maintainable it is of a vital need for the authors to be provided with facilities to view the content from different perspectives and to perform various analyses and statistics on it.

Note that the few authoring systems which allow auhoring of adaptive hypermedia are quite restrictive. The well-known InterBook shares the concept-based approach, but relies only on the simple overlay model, and is based on a strict prerequisite structure [6]. A more advanced system, Tangow [8], has a top-down approach (whereas here we describe a bottom-up one), and requires a predefined set of concept (here, task) attributes – whereas here we allow more flexibility.

We obtained from the analyses and tests of two separate, independent systems (MyET and AIMS) a framework of a concept-based, layered architecture and guidelines for adaptive hypermedia, in concordance with the stratified hypermedia structure for information disclosure [5]. This way we set the basis towards standardization-based authoring [15, 16, 21].

References

1. Ackerman, F., Eden, C., Cropper, S.: Cognitive Mapping – a user guide, http://www.banxia.com/depapsum.html (1993)
2. Aroyo, L., Dicheva, D.A.: Concept-based approach to support learning in a Web-based support environment, In: Moore, J. (eds.) Proc. of AIED'01, Leipzig: IOS Press (2001) 1-12
3. Aroyo, L., Dicheva, D., Velev, I.: Conceptual visualisation in a task-based information support system, In: Bourdeau, J., Heller, R. (eds.): Proc. of EdMedia'00 Conf. (2000) 125-130
4. Beyerbach, B.: Developing a technical vocabulary on teacher planning: preserves teachers' concept maps, Teaching and Teacher Education, Vol. 4 (4) (1988) 339-347
5. Bruza, P. D., Van der Weide, T. P.: Stratified Hypermedia Structures for Information Disclosure. The Computer Journal, Vol. 35 (3) (1992) 208-220
6. Brusilovsky, P., Schwarz, E., Weber, G.: A Tool for Developing Adaptive Electronic Textbooks on WWW, WebNet'96
7. Buzan, T., Buzan B.: The Mind Map Book: How to Use Radiant Thinking to Maximize Your Brain's Untapped Potential. New York: Plume (1996)
8. Carro, R. M., Pulido, E., Rodriguez, P.: Designing Adaptive Web-based Courses with TANGOW, ICCE'99, v. 2, 697-704
9. Cristea, A., Okamoto, T.: MyEnglishTeacher–A WWW System for Academic English Teaching. ICCE'00, Taiwan (2000)
10. Cristea, A. I., Okamoto, T.: Object-oriented Collaborative Course Authoring Environment supported by Concept Mapping in MyEnglishTeacher, Edu. Tech. & Society 4(2) (2001)
11. De Bra, P., Brusilovsky, P., Houben, G.-J.: Adaptive Hypermedia: From Systems to Framework. ACM Computing Surveys, http://wwwis.win.tue.nl/~debra/public.html (1999)
12. Dicheva, D., Aroyo, L.: An approach to intelligent information handling in Web-based learning environments. In: Arabnia, H. R. (ed.), Proc. of ICAI'00 Conf. (2000) 327-333
13. Fink, J., Kobsa, A., Schreck, J.: Personalized Hypermedia Information Provision through Adaptive and Adaptable System Features. Mullery, A. et al (eds.)Springer (1997) 456-467
14. Höök, K., Karlgren, J., Waern, A., Dahlbäck, N., Jansson, C-G., Karlgren, K., Lemaire, B.: A Glass Box Approach to Adaptive Hypermedia, Journal of UMUAI, 6 (1996) 157-184
15. IEEE P1484.6 Course Sequencing Working Group: http://ltsc.ieee.org/wg6/index.html
16. IEEE P1484.2 Learner Model Working Group: http://ltsc.ieee.org/wg2/index.html)

17. Murray, T. et al.: MetaLinks - A Framework and Authoring Tool for Adaptive Hypermedia. S. Lajoie and M. Vivet (eds.): AIED'99, (1999) 744-746
18. Okamoto, T., Cristea, A., Kayama, M.: Future integrated LE with Multimedia. JCAI, Advanced information technologies for learning in the APR. Vol. 17 (1) (2001) 4-12
19. Opperman, R., Rashev, R., Kinshuk: Adaptability and Adaptivity in Learning Systems, Knowledge Transfer (Volume II) (Ed. A. Behrooz), 1997, pAce, London, UK, pp173-179
20. SMIL, W3C standard, http://www.w3.org/AudioVideo/
21. W3C Recommendation: Authoring Tool Accessibility Guidelines 1.0 (3 February 2000): http://www.w3.org/TR/ATAG10/
22. Wu, H., De Bra, P.: Sufficient Conditions for Well-behaved Adaptive Hypermedia Systems. Proc. of WI Conf. Lecture Notes in AI. Vol. 2198. Springer-Verlag. (2001) 148-152

Hypermedia Presentation Adaptation on the Semantic Web

Flavius Frasincar and Geert-Jan Houben

Eindhoven University of Technology
PO Box 513, NL-5600 MB Eindhoven, The Netherlands
{flaviusf, houben}@win.tue.nl

Abstract. Web Information Systems (WIS) present up-to-date information on the Web based on data coming from heterogeneous sources. In previous work the Hera methodology was developed to support the design of a WIS. In this paper we target the design of an intelligent WIS. For this reason the Hera methodology is extended with two kinds of hypermedia presentation adaptation: adaptability based on a profile storing device capabilities and user preferences, and adaptivity based on a user model storing the user browsing history. While adaptability is considered to be static, i.e. the presentation is fixed before the browsing starts, adaptivity is dynamic, i.e. the presentation changes while the user is browsing it. The models used in Hera and their adaptation aspects are specified in RDF(S), a flexible Web metadata language designed to support the Semantic Web.

1 Introduction

The Web is the most rapidly growing information source. As huge amounts of data are today stored in the "deep web" (searchable databases), there is an increasing need to automate the presentation of this data. Designed originally for human consumption, the Web is nowadays augmented to target machines. In the Semantic Web [1] era, Web data will evolve from *machine readable* to *machine understandable*, i.e. it will have associated semantics described by its metadata.

The Web can be accessed through a number of different devices (PC, Laptop, WebTV, PDA, WAP phone, WAP watch etc.) each having its own capabilities (display size, memory size, network speed etc.). At the same time, the user preferences (desired layout, navigation patterns etc.) and browsing history can be taken into account during the presentation generation.

Web Information Systems (WIS) [2] offer Web presentations of data typically coming from heterogeneous sources (relational databases, object-oriented databases, XML repositories, WWW etc.). In order to generate an appropriate hypermedia presentation (hyperdocument), the presentation needs to be tailored to specific device capabilities and user preferences.

The Hera methodology [10, 11] supports the design of a WIS. It distinguishes three important design steps: conceptual design that produces the conceptual model of the integrated data, application design that focuses on the navigational or logical aspects of the hypermedia application, and presentation design that gives an abstraction of the physical level of the application. The heart of Hera is the Application Model, a model inspired by Relationship Management Methodology (RMM) [12, 13]. In previous work [9] we built a prototype using the Hera methodology based on XML.

This paper extends Hera by considering the adaptation of the presentation with respect to devices capabilities and user preferences stored in a profile (adaptability). Moreover, we target also the automatic generation of adaptive presentations based on user browsing history stored in a user model (adaptivity). In our methodology the different models lead to a lot of metadata that describe different aspects of the application. Semantic Web technology appears to be a natural solution to represent this metadata. As there is not yet a W3C recommendation for a semantic markup language (only a note on DAML+OIL [5]) we base our future prototype on RDF(S) [3, 15].

The rest of the paper is structured as follows. In Sect. 2 we introduce the Hera methodology and discuss its individual design activities. The artifacts produced by Hera activities are: Conceptual Model, Application Model, and Application Model with Adaptation, presented in Sects. 3, 4, and 5, respectively. Section 5 distinguishes two kinds of adaptations: adaptability described in Subsect. 5.1 and adaptivity described in Subsect. 5.2. Section 6 concludes the paper.

2 Hera Methodology

The Hera methodology is a model-based Web Engineering [16] method for designing WIS. Figure 1 depicts the four different activities of the proposed method: Conceptual Design, Application Design, Adaptation Design, and Presentation Design. The newly introduced activity Adaptation Design is further decomposed in two sub-activities: Adaptability Design and Adaptivity Design.

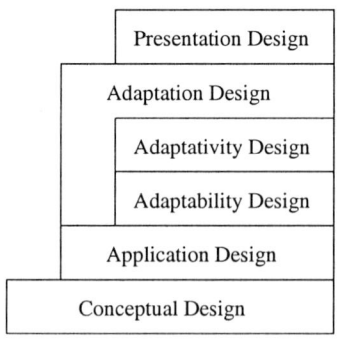

Fig. 1: Hera Methodology

Each activity has specific design concerns and produces a model which is an enrichment of the model built by the previous activity. Hera models are represented in RDFS [3], the schema language for RDF [15]. There are several reasons that motivated us to choose RDF(S). RDFS offers the subclass/subproperty mechanisms useful for building taxonomies for classes/properties. As RDFS is expressed in RDF, it has all the benefits of property-centric models like extensibility and sharability. Extensibility enables the building of each model on top of the previous one and sharability fosters re-use of the developed models. There exist already Composite Capability/Preference Profiles (CC/PP) [14] vocabularies (in RDF(S)) for modeling device capabilities and user preferences which ease the burden of defining new ones.

Conceptual Design provides a common representation for the schema of the retrieved data. A WIS gathers data from multiple sources each having its own dialect. In order to be able to further process this data one needs to define a uniform semantics for it. This semantics is captured in the Conceptual Model (CM) as an application specific ontology. The basic elements in the CM are concepts and concept relationships. Concepts have properties to describe their features.

Application Design is concerned with the navigational aspects involved in the hypermedia presentation of the retrieved data: the structure of the hyperdocument. It extends the CM with navigational views that build the Application Model (AM). The basic elements in AM are slices and slice relationships. Slices are units of presentation for data contained in one or more concepts from CM.

Adaptation Design adds adaptation features to the previously defined AM. We distinguish two kinds of adaptation: adaptability and adaptivity. Both condition the appearance of slices and the visibility of slice relationships. Adaptability does it based on information about device capabilities and user preferences prior to browsing. Adaptivity uses information about the user browsing history stored in a User Model (UM) during the browsing of the presentation. Adaptability is considered to be static, i.e. the presentation is fixed before browsing starts, while adaptivity is dynamic, i.e. the presentation changes while the user is browsing it.

Presentation Design takes into consideration the physical aspects of the presentation. In the Presentation Model (PM) we define slice appearance in terms of regions [10]. The basic elements in PM are regions and region relationships. Regions are rectangular shaped areas that present some data from one or more slices. Slice relationships are materialized by navigational, spatial, or temporal region relationships which can be synchronized. PM is outside the scope of this paper, nevertheless we acknowledge the need of extending the adaptation aspects also to the PM (e.g. font colour, page layout etc.).

3 Conceptual Model

The Conceptual Model (CM) presents a uniform view of the domain semantics for the input data sources. It is an application specific ontology that will constitute the basis for the subsequent data transformations. The retrieved data is so-called "instance data", as it represents specific instances of the concepts defined in the ontology. CM specifies in a hierarchical manner the concepts (classes) in the domain and the relationships among them. These relationships are expressed as class properties (slots). One can associate logic to this ontology that will enable reasoning about CM, e.g. the transitivity of some properties enables the derivation of new properties which can be used at a later stage in our design process.

For CM serialization we were inspired by the RDF(S) representation of ontologies built with Protege-2000 [17]. Protege-2000 is a graphical tool intended for defining ontologies without having to know any ontology language. This graphical representation can be saved in a Protege-extended RDF(S). Figure 2 presents an example of CM that corresponds to a subset of the Rijksmuseum catalogue in Amsterdam.

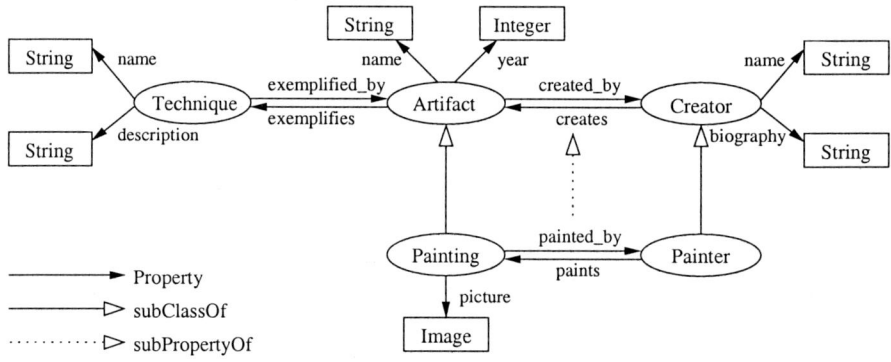

Fig. 2: Conceptual Model

As RDF(S) has its own modeling limitations, we added two new properties to characterize RDF(S) properties that represent relationships: the cardinality (single or multiple) of a relationship and the inverse of a relationship. We also defined a hierarchy of Media classes that have specific properties to be used in the Adaptation Design phase. Example 1 shows an instance of the Image class: the image dimensions (pix_x and pix_y) can be considered in adapting the presentation to the display size.

Example 1. Media Type

```
<Image about="http://www.example.com/sunset.jpg"
       pix_x=326
       pix_y=230
       ...
</Image>
```

4 Application Model

The Application Model (AM) describes the navigational view over CM. The AM is the most abstract form of the presentation. We define meaningful presentation units called slices and relationships among them. The simple slices contain only a concept attribute (concept property that points to a media item). Complex slices are defined in a tree-structure manner having simple slices as leaves [12, 13]. We distinguish two kinds of slice relationships: aggregation and reference [9]. Reference relationships are also called links as usually they are materialized to hyperlinks (navigational relationships in the Presentation Model). Each slice belongs to a certain concept from CM. While the reference relationships do not leave the context of a certain concept, aggregation relationships can link slices belonging to different concepts. The designer needs to carefully specify the relationships from the CM, which make such a slice embedding possible. For relationships having cardinality single-many the access structure Set (of slices) is used.

Figure 3 describes a part of the AM for the Rijksmuseum example, i.e. two complex slices Slice.technique.main and Slice.painting.main.

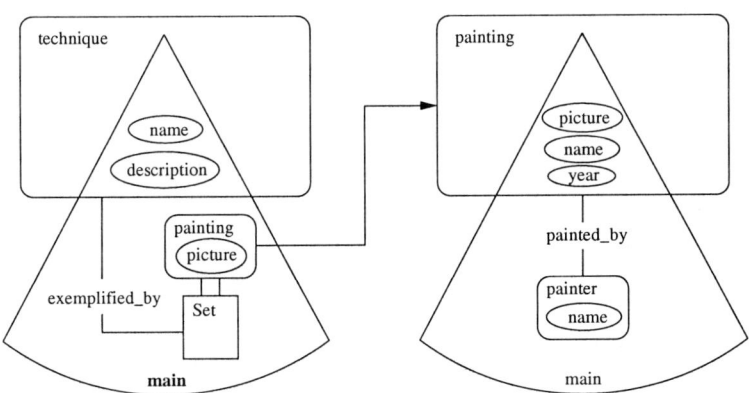

Fig. 3: Application Model

Slice.technique.main has two attributes from the concept technique, i.e. name and description and an attribute from painting, i.e. picture. Since the relationship exemplified_by (inherited from CM) has cardinality "single-many" one needs to add an access structure, e.g. Set. Note that the previous attributes are slices on their own, i.e. simple slices. Each picture has a reference (link) to the Slice.painting.main that describes the current painting. This description includes the picture, name, year, and the name of the painter the painting was painted_by. We chose a very simple AM example but rich enough to show, in the next section, different kinds of presentation adaptation.

5 Adaptation in the Application Model

A WIS can be accessed through a multitude of devices and by different users. Each device has its own capabilities (display size, memory size, network speed etc.). Every user has specific preferences (desired layout, navigation patterns etc.) and browsing history with respect to a particular presentation. An intelligent WIS needs to take into account these constraints (abilities) coming from both devices and users, and adapt the presentation accordingly.

The adaptation we consider in this paper is based on conditioning the appearance of slices in the AM (and derived, the visibility of slice relationships or links). Figure 4 shows two examples of slice conditioning, one for adaptability and one for adaptivity. Both examples will be discussed at the level of RDF(S) in the following two subsections.

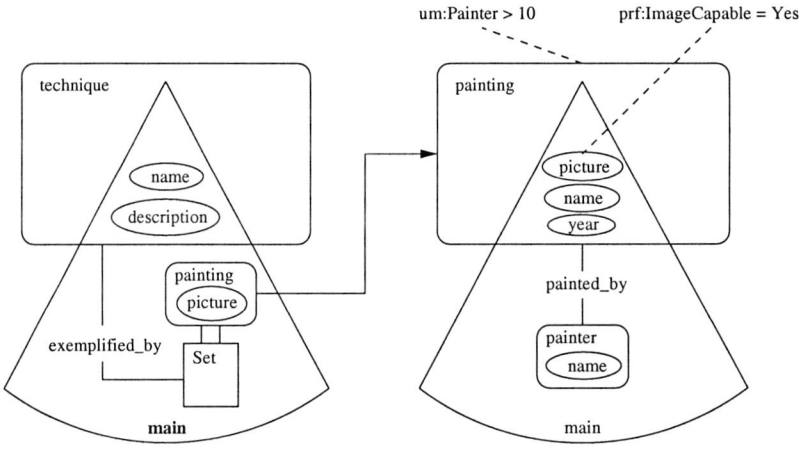

Fig. 4: Adaptation in the Application Model

Example 2 illustrates the definition of the condition for slice appearance in RDFS. A link pointing to a slice that has the appearance condition unfulfilled will be hidden [7].

Example 2. Slice Condition

```
<rdf:Property rdf:ID="condition">
    <rdfs:domain rdf:resource="#Slice"/>
    <rdfs:range rdf:resource="#Literal"/>
</rdf:Property>
```

We consider two kinds of presentation adaptation: *adaptability* and *adaptivity*. Adaptability means conditioning the appearance of slices and the visibility of slice relationships based on device capabilities and user preferences stored in a Profile. Adaptivity takes into account the user browsing history stored in a User Model (UM) to condition the appearance of slices and links during the browsing of the presentation. While we consider adaptability to be static, i.e. the presentation is fixed prior to browsing, we consider adaptivity to be dynamic, i.e. the presentation changes while the user is browsing it.

Two existing techniques fit well in the Hera methodology to model the two kinds of adaptation mentioned above. For adaptability the Composite Capability/Preference Profile (CC/PP) [14] offers a framework to model profiles that characterize device capabilities and user preferences. The AHA (Adaptive Hypermedia Architecture) system [6] adds adaptivity functionality to a hypermedia presentation based on UM.

5.1 Adaptability

Adaptability is the adaptation that considers the device capabilities and user preferences stored in a Profile. A Profile contains attribute-value pairs used by the Hera system to determine the most appropriate presentation for the retrieved data items. Example 3 shows how to build a Profile using two vocabularies, the CC/PP [14] UAProf (User Agent Profile) vocabulary [18] developed by WAP Forum to model device capabilities, and our own vocabulary for describing user preferences.

Example 3. Device/User Profile

```
<Description rdf:about="Profile">
    <ccpp:component>
        <prf:HardwarePlatform>
            <prf:ImageCapable>No</prf:ImageCapable>
            <prf:ScreenSize>600x400</prf:ScreenSize>
            ...
        </prf:HardwarePlatform>
    </ccpp:component>
    <ccpp:component>
        <up:UserPreferences>
            <up:Language>English</up:Language>
            ...
        </up:UserPreferences>
    </ccpp:component>
</Description>
```

A Profile has a number of components, each component grouping a number of attributes. In the previous example we defined two CC/PP components. The `HardwarePlatform` component has two attributes, `ImageCapable` that specifies if the device is able to display images and `ScreenSize` that defines the dimensions of the device display. The `UserPreferences` component has one attribute `Language`, the language the user prefers. Example 4 illustrates an adaptability condition that models the presence of `Slice.painting.picture` in AM based on the ability of the device to display images.

Example 4. Adaptability Condition

```
<rdfs:Class rdf:ID="Slice.painting.picture"
            slice.condition="prf:ImageCapable=Yes">
   <rdfs:subClassOf rdf:resource="#Slice"/>
</rdfs:Class>
```

In an adaptability condition, one can use the media properties defined in Example 1, e.g. one can test if the dimensions of a particular image fit the size of the screen. Note that the adaptation based on user preferences can be treated in the same way as the adaptation based on device capabilities.

5.2 Adaptivity

Adaptivity [4] is the dynamic adaptation that considers the user browsing history stored in a User Model (UM). AHAM (Adaptive Hypermedia Application Model) [8], a Dexter-based reference model for adaptive hypermedia, defines in the Storage Layer three models: the Domain Model, the Teaching Model later on renamed Adaptation Model [19], and the User Model (UM). We use the AHA system to add adaptivity functionality to our methodology. In Hera, the Domain Model will have as atomic concepts slice instances, which stand for both AHAM pages and fragments, and as composite concepts class instances from CM and additional concepts introduced by the application author. The UM contains attribute-value pairs: for each concept from DM a value (from 0 to 100) is associated. The Adaptation Model contains adaptation rules based on the Event-Condition-Action paradigm (like in active databases) that can be executed by the software from the AHA engine.

In Hera when the user visits a certain (page) slice, update rules get triggered that in the end determine the appearance. A slice is desirable if its appearance condition evaluates to true. The desirability of a slice included in another slice implies its appearance in the presentation. Standard AHA functionality implies that a link pointing to a desirable page is displayed in "good" colour ("blue" for active) if it was not visited before, or "neutral" colour ("purple" for visited link) if it was visited before, while "bad" colour ("black" for hidden link) is used if the link points to an undesirable page.

The appearance condition in adaptivity for the slice Slice.painting.main, illustrated in Example 5, models the desirability of the slice based on the interest of the user for the painting's painter.

Example 5. Adaptivity Condition

```
<rdfs:Class rdf:ID="Slice.painting.main"
            slice.condition="um:Painter > 10">
   <rdfs:subClassOf rdf:resource="#Slice"/>
</rdfs:Class>
```

Initially, all concepts from UM have their values set to 0. Example 6 shows an update rule expressed in RDF.

Example 6. Update Rule

```
<um:Slice.painting.main>
    <aha:updatelist>
        <aha:SetOfConcepts>
            <aha:item><um:Painting aha:update="+80"/></aha:item>
            <aha:item><um:Painter aha:update="+40"/></aha:item>
        </aha:SetOfConcepts>
    </aha:updatelist>
</um:Slice.painting.main>
```

Suppose that when seeing the slice `Slice.technique.main`, the user is interested in a particular painting description and clicks its link, which for the moment is a link to an undesirable slice (condition not fulfilled), as are all the `Slice.painting.main` instances. Before this slice `Slice.painting.main` is actually visited, the corresponding update rule is triggered. First, the value of the particular instance of `Slice.painting.main` (i.e. associated to the chosen painting) is updated to 35 (default update for a undesirable slice). Then, the values of the Painting and Painter instances from DM (note that these concepts were present also in the CM) corresponding to this particular slice instance have their values updated by 80% and respectively 40% of the slice update increment.

As opposed to AHA which specifies update rules for instances, in Hera we specify update rules based on classes (rules are defined at schema level, because the particular instances are not known beforehand). Nevertheless, the Hera update rules will become instance update rules (as in AHA) at runtime.

When after visiting the slice describing a particular painting, the user would go back to `Slice.technique.main`, the user would observe that all the paintings related to the painter of the previously chosen painting are now active links pointing to desirable slices (the condition is fulfilled since the Painter value was updated; $40\% \times 35 = 14 > 10$).

6 Conclusion and Further Work

The Hera methodology has been extended with adaptation models (Profile and User Model) that condition the slice appearance in the Application Model. During the different activities that compose our methodology there are a lot of ontologies involved: Conceptual Model, Domain Model, Profile etc. RDF(S) proves to be a flexible language for modeling, but as we saw, it has also its own shortcomings (we added RDF(S) extensions to cope with them). The Semantic Web promises a richer Web where data will have semantics associated to it. This semantics can be fully exploited in an adapted automatic generation of hypermedia presentations. In the future we plan to include these new emerging Semantic Web standards like DAML+OIL in the modeling of the different ontologies involved in our processes. A prototype based on RDF(S) that experiments with the proposed Hera methodology is under development.

References

1. Berners-Lee, T.: Weaving the Web. Orion Business, London (1999)
2. Bieber, M., Isakowitz, T., Vitali, F.: Web Information Systems. Communications of the ACM, **41(7)** (1998), 78–80
3. Brickley, D., Guha, R.V.: Resource Description Framework (RDF) Schema Specification 1.0. W3C (2000), http://www.w3.org/TR/rdf-schema
4. Brusilovsky, P.: Adaptive Hypermedia. User Modeling and User-Adapted Interaction **11(1/2)**, Kluwer Academic Publishers (2001), 87–110
5. Connolly, D., van Harmelen, F., Horrocks, J., McGuinness, D.L., Patel-Schneider, P.F., Stein, L.A.: DAML+OIL (March 2001) Reference Description. W3C (2001), http://www.w3.org/TR/daml+oil-reference
6. De Bra, P., Aerts, A., Houben, G.J., Wu, H.: Making General-Purpose Adaptive Hypermedia Work. In Proc. WebNet 2000 World Conference on the WWW and Internet, AACE (2000), 117–123
7. De Bra, P., Brusilovsky, P., Houben, G.J.: Adaptive Hypermedia: From Systems to Frameworks. ACM Computing Surveys, **31(4es)** (1999)
8. De Bra, P., Houben, G.J., Wu, H.: AHAM: A Dexter-based Reference Model for Adaptive Hypermedia. In Proc. The 10th ACM Conference on Hypertext and Hypermedia, ACM Press (1999), 147–156
9. Frasincar, F., Houben, G.J.: XML-Based Automatic Web Presentation Generation. In Proc. WebNet 2001 World Conference on the WWW and Internet, AACE (2001), 372–377
10. Frasincar, F., Houben G.J., Vdovjak, R.: An RMM-Based Methodology for Hypermedia Presentation Design. In Proc. Advances in Databases and Information Systems, LNCS 2151, Springer (2001), 323–337
11. Houben, G.J.: Hera: Automatically Generating Hypermedia Front Ends for Ad Hoc Data from Heterogeneous and Legacy Information Systems. In Proc. Third International Workshop on Engineering Federated Information Systems, Aka and IOS Press (2000), 81–88
12. Isakowitz, T., Kamis, A., Koufaris, M.: Extending RMM: Russian Dolls and Hypertext. In Proc. 30th Hawaii International Conference on System Sciences, Computer Society Press (1997)
13. Isakowitz, T., Stohr, E., Balasubramanian, P.: RMM: A Methodology for Structured Hypermedia Design. Communications of the ACM, **38(8)** (1995), 34–44
14. Klyne, G., Reynolds, F., Woodrow, C., Ohto, H.: Composite Capability/Preference Profiles (CC/PP): Structure and Vocabularies. W3C (2001), http://www.w3.org/TR/CCPP-struct-vocab
15. Lassila, O., Swick, R.R.: Resource Description Framework (RDF) Model and Syntax Specification. W3C (1999), http://www.w3.org/TR/REC-rdf-syntax
16. Murugesan, S., Deshpande, Y., Hansen, S., Ginige, A.: Web Engineering: A New Discipline for Web-Based System Development. In Proc. First ICSE Workshop on Web Engineering, ACM Press (1999), 1–9
17. Noy, N.F., Sintek, M., Decker, S., Crubezy, M., Fergerson, R.W., Musen, M.A.: Creating Semantic Web Contents with Protege-2000. IEEE Intelligent Systems, **16(2)** (2001), 60–71
18. Wireless Application Group: User Agent Profile Specification. WAP Forum (1999), http://www.wapforum.org/what/technical/SPEC-UAProf-19991110.pdf
19. Wu, H., De Bra, P., Aerts, A., Houben, G.J.: Adaptation Control in Adaptive Hypermedia Systems. In Proc. International Conference on Adaptive Hypermedia and Adaptive Web-based Systems, LNCS 1892, Springer (2000), 250–259

User Data Management and Usage Model Acquisition in an Adaptive Educational Collaborative Environment

Elena Gaudioso and Jesus G. Boticario

Dpto. de Inteligencia Artificial
Universidad Nacional de Educacion a Distancia
Senda del Rey, 9; Madrid, Spain
{elena,jgb}@dia.uned.es

Abstract. In this paper we describe the basis of aLF (*active learning framework*) an environment for web-based distance learning on the web and how it can be extended with a user modelling subsystem aimed at providing an adaptive response which can meet users' knowledge state, preferences and goals. We concentrate on user data collection and its further processing to create a user model. Furthermore, as regards the user modelling task, we claim that a combination of different machine learning algorithms should perform better than individual methods. To support our approach we will provide some preliminary experimental results.

1 Introduction

Distance education takes place when a lecturer and student(s) are separated by physical distance. The proliferation of accesses to the Internet has made the World Wide Web (WWW) an ideal environment for lecturer-student communication with no restrictions of time and space. When a web site is designed to support certain courses it is called an *educational web site*. Educational web sites reduce student isolation by offering a number of communication channels, usually newsgroups, e-mail, mailing lists and chats. They may also provide the necessary course material that can be downloaded by the students, offer HTML pages that guide students through the course contents or provide references to other information sources, as well as many other educational possibilities.

Often the content provided by an educational web site is fully static. The HTML page navigation sequence, the set of references, and the newsgroup messages are the same for every student on the course. This homogeneous response is provided to students with changing needs and whose level of experience on the subject being taught and on the use of resources available on the website are different. Furthermore, adaptation is essential in distance education because students are isolated and have a wide variety of backgrounds and interests. Therefore an environment that adapts to each individual student appears to be desirable. In order to solve this problem, the web-based adaptive educational systems [3] carry out an adaptation based on a user model, representing the user's knowledge state, preferences and goals. These are not entirely new kinds of systems, they borrow heavily from adaptive hypermedia systems.

Adaptive hypermedia systems [4] apply different forms of user models to adapt the contents and the hypermedia page links to the user. The main goal of this adaptation is to provide the user with efficient access to the site by first presenting the links that should be of interest. Adaptive hypermedia application in educational systems is a very hot research area. According with [4], many interesting adaptive educational hypermedia systems have been developed and reported during the last eight years. An interest to provide distance education over the Web has been a strong driving force behind these research efforts. The introduction of the Web has impacted both the number and the type of systems being developed. All the early system were essentially lab systems, built to explore some new methods that used adaptivity in an education context. In contrast, several more recent systems provide complete frameworks and even authoring tools for developing web-based courses.

Traditionally adaptation decision in adaptive systems was based on taking into accounts various characteristics of their users represented in the user model. Currently the situation is different. A number of adaptive web based systems are able to adapt to something else than user characteristics. Kobsa et al. [7] suggest to distinguish adaption to user data, usage data, and environment data. User data comprise the traditional adaptation target, various characteristics of the users. Usage data comprise data about user interaction with the systems that can not be resolved to user characteritics (but still can be used to make adaptation decisions). Environment data comprise all aspects of the user environment that are not related to the users themselves. To achieve a good adaptation it is neccesary to collect correctly the data that will be used to construct the user models.

To summarise, although distance learning benefits from the use of the educational web sites, it poses several challenges regarding the management of student collaboration and the adaptation of the contents to student needs. Within this context, an interesting and relatively new area is the adaptation to students with regard to their activities. In this paper we will describe aLF (active learning framework), a system for web-based distance learning developed to support the requirements for collaborative work between all the different students in a course delivered in aLF.

We aim to describe how to provide advice to students in their collaborative work with fellow students. For this we construct a usage model. We will describe the user data collection and its further procesing to form a user model and we also suggest that, as regards the user modelling task, a combination of different algorithms should perform better than individual methods, providing some experimental support.

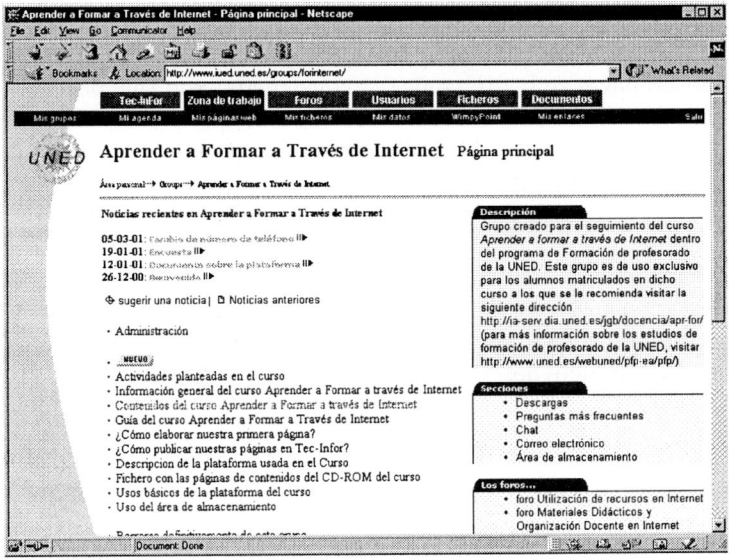

Fig. 1. aLF course workgroup

2 An Environment for Web-Based Distance Learning

2.1 Overview

Our research is developed in a distance-learning university (UNED[1]) with over 180,000 students and a traditional distance-education model. In this context there is a set of educational requirements and needs to be fulfilled that are different for each student. Distance-education tools have been shown to be useful in such situations and, particularly, web-based adaptive educational systems seem to be one of the best solutions.

A platform called aLF (*active learning framework*) has been developed in order to support the requirements for collaborative work between all the different communities involved. The platform builds upon the ArsDigita Community System [2], a multiplatform and open source set of tools for constructing web-based applications. aLF is composed of a Web server connected to a relational database and a set of TCL (*Tool Command Language*) scripts allowing management of the interaction with the data model. The database does not only store the user personal information and the contents they send, but also serves to structure potentially everything that is happening in the site.

Another key feature of aLF is that it offers different views based on user navigation and actions through the site. All kinds of information on users can thus be gathered with TCL scripting language. The scripts can interface with the

---

[1] http://www.uned.es
[2] http://www.arsdigita.com/. Related web sites built with ArsDigita http://www.arsdigita.com/pages/customers

database so that this information can be easily stored and retrieved on demand. TCL scripts can also contribute to maintaining a dynamic environment, since they enable web pages to be dynamically constructed and this process can make use of the database information if required. Users registered on aLF are grouped into workgroups (see Fig. 1). The administration of each workgroup is done by the person in charge who may not be the web site manager. The setting up of these kind of workgroups is particularly useful for distance learning since it allows different university departments, courses, study groups and research groups to be managed.

aLF workgroups offer several services thus allowing a learning and collaborative environment to be easily set up, such us forums, chat rooms or shared file storage area. A complete description of the services that offers aLF can be found at [1].

3 An aLF Course Experience

We will now describe an experience of a distance course being taught through aLF. The goal of this course was precisely to teach the use of the Internet in education. We set up a group in aLF for the students on the course; this group had a bulletin board, news service, chat, file-storage area and a personal webpages storage area where the students could publish their own web pages.

Regarding the conceptual organization of the contents, it was based on the proposal made by Roger Schank in the ASK system [10]. The course concepts were organized as a conceptual network where each node was a course concept for the student to learn and the arcs represented certain links between concepts such as, prerequisite, consequence, example or exercise. These links were presented by several questions or options that the student could choose . The course contents were represented by a set of HTML pages, each one corresponding to one concept in the course conceptual network. This conceptual network, the goals of the course, and other elements were represented by an XML page that the system may interpret to construct the student knowledge model. For each student on the course, the system stored a model of the contents that the student had already learned. For this course the system assumed that a student had learned a concept if he/she had successfully done a test or had simply visited the pages related to the concept. The system guided the student through the contents of the course according his/her conceptual model; in this paper we are not going to describe it further since it is described elsewhere [2].

First we presented the students with a survey in order to evaluate how familiar they were with educational software or the Internet. In most cases the students were in turn lecturers interested in the use of the Internet in education, and on the whole, they had little experience in the use of computers and Internet services. However, as the course proceeded we realised that we had a very hetereogenous group of students.

Consequently, the course lecturers had to closely monitor the students on the course. The lecturers solved (on demand) the difficulties that arose. They proposed several activities (such as sending a message to the bulletin board) in order to guide the students more closely.

Although there was also the possibility of contacting the lecturers by phone or face-to-face, the main channels of communication were the course bulletin boards and electronic mail. The lecturer also visited the chat room established for the course to detect if the students had difficulties in the course.

We have also discovered that students do not collaborate among themselves except when they use the chats and send personal e-mails. If this lack of collaboration could have been foreseen, lecturers could have suggested scenarios or tasks where students were encouraged to interact.

These problems could have been avoided if the system had detected student difficulties, such as problems in the use of the course services and student similarities. Then lecturers could have been informed of these problems right from the very beginning and they could have set up subgroups of students with similar characteristics, needs and interests. The system could also automatically do this.

Thus our proposal for a personalized environment is based on a cooperative tutorization scheme. In this scheme the lecturer, besides solving the doubts of the students in a personalized way, is responsible for improving collaboration between the group components.

As we have seen before the lecturers proposed several activities through the forums of the course. So it is very important to monitor the student correctly to control the user performance in the course, thus we have to acquire some kind of usage model of the user to describe his/her user interaction with the forums and with any other service in the web site. All this proccess will be describe in the next section.

4 Adaptation and User Modelling in aLF

4.1 Usage Model in aLF

At first, the main problem within the web-based adaptive systems were the user data collection. However, nowadays, more and more systems are capable to monitor the user actions to record the complete user interactions [8, 11].

It is important to point out that aLF manages all the services through the database. Information about the messages sent to a forum or a bulletin board, the tickets sent to the project management tool, the appointments in the calendar, the annotations to a particular news in the board or the conversation in a chat, are stored in the database, so a great amount of information on the interaction of a user with the platform is available. Another key feature of aLF, is that all this data is stored separately in tables of the database, and that differs from traditional web logs in which we only usually store the urls accessed by the user.

We are now to describe the user features that we consider to construct the user model in aLF. They can be divided in two fundamental groups, personal data and usage data. In the first group we include typical user attributes such us, `user-id`, `first-names`, `last-name`, `screen-name`, `e-mail`, `url?`, `portait?`,

Table 1. Usage features related to the user interaction with the system

Feature	Description
n-sessions	Number of sessions of the user
msg-to-other-forums	Number of messages that the user may have sent to other forums
msg-to-group-forum	Number of messages that the user may have sent to the forums of the group
email-alerts-out?	Determines if the user has activated some alerts in forums out of the course
email-alerts-aprfor?	Determines if the user has activated some alerts in the forum of the course
wp-presentation?	Determines if the user has constructed a presentation
bm?	Determines if the user has bookmarks in aLF
num-msgs-chats-aprfor	Number of messages that the user have sent to the chat of the course
num-msgs-chats-out	Number of messages that the user have sent to chats out of the course
num-entrances-chat-aprfor	Number of entrances to the chat of the course
num-entrances-chat-out	Number of entrances to chats out of the course
files-personal-storage-area	Number of files in the user personal file storage area
files-group-storage-area	Number of files in the file storage area of the group
groups-other?	Number of groups that the user is registered
num-news-sent	Number of news that the user has sent
num-static-pages-visited	Number of pages that the user has visited
average-session-duration	Duration of the user's sessions duration
spam?	Determines if the user has sent a email to the whole group or to the teachers

bio?, and several attributes describing certain users preferences (obtained from an initial survey) such us do-you-have-interest-in-teleeducation, do-you-have-interest-in-collaborative-environments,... and users background (obtained also from an initial survey) such us computer-use-skill-level, internet-use-skill-level, knowledge-about-computers, use-of-internet-resources.

In the second group we include all those attributes that allows us to determine certain characteristics in the user interaction with the system and they are described in Table 1.

However, as we have seen before, the course activities are controlled through the forums of the course, so it is neccessary a closer control in the user messages to the forum (all these last features allow us to determine the usefullness of the contributions of the user to the forum.). So we consider the following features:

- num-threads-user-started: Number of threads that the user has began.
- num-threads-started-and-not-replied: Number of threads that the user has began and his partners have not replied.
- num-threads-user-in-and-tutor: Number of threads in which the user and the tutor have participated.

- `num-threads-user-finished`: Number of threads that the user has finished
- `num-replies-to-user-messages`: Number of replies to user messages
- `fellows-replayed-user-messages`: List of users that have replayed a particular user messages

With all this information we can determine some user characteristics that are not directly observable from the data gathered by aLF. This features will be the result of some machine learning tasks and we will be described in next section.

4.2 Learning Some Features in the User Model

As we have seen before, there are some features of the user model that are not directly observable from the data in the database. These features are very useful in order to give the user some recommendations about his collaboration within the course.

Currently the recommendations of the system are very simple. We focus in determining the level of activity of the user in the course and the possibility that a particular user may fail the course. With these features, the system may recommend a user to participate more in the course, or may alert the teacher that a user is going to fail.

Each of these attributes constitutes a separate machine learning task. The particular data used in learning the value of these two attributes is taken from user interaction with the web site.

First the goal is to learn a set of user profiles in order to infer the level of activity that the user is going to exhibit. We measure this activity taking into account a certain period of time and from the data described in Table 1. A set of three categories is defined corresponding to the low, medium and high activity profiles.

Extracting and preparing data from the aLF database, we composed a training set of instances as input data to the learning algorithm. Each instance corresponds to a user and includes information about his behavior in his first one or two interactions (some of the attributes have been described earlier). As result of this process, we obtained a dataset of 125 instances described each by 21 attributes and labeled with a class value indicating the level of activity in the forum of the course (this training data were constructed taking account the labeled data constructed by external tutors of the course).

However, in a web environment there are a great variety of interaction data. Single classifiers would fail in some regions of the training data or would be accurate in others (competence region). If we have certain classifiers with distint competence regions, we can combine them in order to achieve a better performance, such a combination is usually called *ensemble of classifiers*.

So for our experiments we consider three classifiers; a decision tree learner (C4.5), a rule set learner (C4.5Rules) and a Bayesian learner (Naive Bayes). To asses the individual performance of each of the algorithms, we performed a 10-fold cross validation test. This procedure divides the available data into 10

Table 2. Error rate from 10-fold cross validation for each learning algorithm with the standard deviations

Algorithm	Accuracy
C4.5	13.46 (6.02)
C4.5Rules	24 (5.58)
Naive Bayes	42.37 (8.24)
Best Classifier	7.34 (5.08)

subsets of instances and successively takes one different subset as the test set, using the remaining instances in the training set. In this manner, the algorithm is ran 10 times learning with a subset of the 90% of instances and tested with the remaining -unseen- 10%. The average of accuracies can be taken as an estimate of the accuracy of the system for the dataset.

Table 2 shows the final results for each of the algorithms together with an estimate of the upper bound that we could obtain if we pick up the best algorithm for each testing instance. To compute this accuracy, we simply recorded a correct prediction for all the instances for which at least one of the algorithms made a correct guess.

As we can observe in the Table 2, the individual performance of any of the algorithms is not outstanding. However, the room for improvement by using a combination of these algorithms is huge.

Taking into account that an ensemble of classifiers will perform better than a single classifier, there are a lot of work done directed to improve the accuracy of certain learning tasks [5]. In our case, the user model construction implies several learning tasks with very heterogenous data, we need some kind of mechanism to improve the learning accuracy of the user modelling subsystem and the flexibility to achieve a good performance in possible new learning taks.

So, following [9] we are modifying the user model construction and we are constructing an ensemble formed by several classifiers constructed by running cross-validation with a particular training set and c4.5. For each classifier and each testing set, we store the prediction made by the classifier for a particular instance in the testing set, and the correct prediction for that instance. For each classifiers we have a referee that predicts with the set described before (using c4.5 also) if its corresponding classifier will make a correct prediction. We combine the solution given by the different classifiers that is supposed to be correct (acording to their referes' prediction), by simply mayority voting. The results of our preliminary experiments are shown in Table 3.

Table 3. Error rate of the c4.5 classifier and the corresponding ensembles

Algorithm	Error rate
Ensemble with 5 classifiers	12.11 (8.34)
Ensemble with 10 classifiers	12.82 (6.57)
Ensemble with 30 classifiers	12.20 (6.79)

At the moment we have only focused in choosing the best response for a particular learning task. To learn the best algorithm for each of the learning task involved in the user model construction is in turn another learning task. One related work is [6], who present an approach to combine multiple learning agents that constructs a preference table which is updated according the performance of each individual agent. Although the results are not very relevant at the moment because we have not yet enough interaction data, we are currently working in this direction, together with using simpler approaches in order to get further insight on this problem.

5 Conclusion and Future Work

aLF, the platform described in this paper, is especially intended to facilitate the development of workgroups on the Web. What differentiates aLF from all other initiatives is that it provides an integrated framework for all the Internet services through HTML pages, storing all the information about the interactions of the user in a database which allows a processing of that data to be done.

Although aLF is not only intended to serve for educational purposes, it is specially useful in the establishment of on-line courses since it provides many integrated services such us forums or file storage areas. However, supporting distance education with educational web sites, does not guarantee that the students will find the required information or will engage in effective collaborative learning behavior. So, it is needed some kind of adaptation to help the users in the variety of tasks he/she is expected to solve such as self-assessment exercises, collaborative tasks, or practical exercises.

In order to access all the relevant data arising from each user's interaction, aLF draws up a complete register among the members of a group of users. Although we have only discussed data preparation at a cursory level, this is not a trivial problem as pointed out in related areas such as web mining [8]. Storing information about the user behavior on a database should serve better to model his preferences than, for example, simply using the navigation traces in web logs. However, this information may be also more difficult to manage and prepare for the user modeling stage.

Currently, the recommendations of the system are simple (tell the student to visit a forum, or alert the teacher that a user seems to fail the course) but it can be expanded given the information the system is gathering about the student's collaborative activities, such as, level of expertise in the use of the services, preferences and interests. A possible scenario could be, if the student is having trouble with topic X (perhaps as indicated by failing the online competency test on topic X), the system might suggest contacting a student, by email, who has shown competency and interest in topic X (as evidenced by this latter student's contributions to forums about topic X)). Also, the system could encourage students to participate in chats/etc. about topic X. Or simply encourage the student to participate in activities other than forums - e.g., chats - when there is evidence that the student has not done so. This advice can be useful in having the student be part of the learning community and all its attendant benefits.

We have shown that all these features are better infered from the past user interaction applying machine learning techniques. In addition the complexity of the learning tasks in these contexts lead us to explore more ellaborated solutions based upon combining different learning techniques.

References

1. Jesus G. Boticario, Elena Gaudioso, and Carlos Catalina. Towards personalised learning communities on the web. In Kai Hakkarainen Pierre Dillenbourg, Anneke Eurolings, editor, *European Perspectives on Computer-Supported Collaborative Learning. Proceedings of the First European Conference on Computer-Supported Collaborative Learning*, pages 115–122. Maastricht McLuhan Institute, 2001.
2. Jesus G. Boticario, Elena Gaudioso, and Felix Hernandez. Adaptive navigation support and adaptive collaboration support in webdl. In *Proceedings of the International Conference on Adaptive Hypermedia and Adaptive Web-based Systems*, number 1892 in Lecture Notes in Computer Science (LNCS), pages 51–61, Trento, Italy, August 2000. Springer Verlag.
3. Peter Brusilovsky. Adaptive educational systems on the world-wide-web: A review of available technologies. In *Proceedings of Workshop WWW-Based Tutoring at Fourth International Conference on ITS (ITS'98)*, San Antonio, TX, August 1998. MIT Press.
4. Peter Brusilovsky. Adaptive hypermedia. *User Modelling and User Adapted Interaction*, 11(1):87–110, 2001.
5. Joao Gama. *Combining classification algorithms*. PhD thesis, Facultad de Ciencias, Universidad de Porto, Portugal, 1999.
6. J. Ignacio Giraldez, Charles Elkan, and Daniel Borrajo. A distributed solution to the pte problem. In Giuseppina C. Gini and Alan R. Katritzky, editors, *Predictive Toxicology of Chemicals: Experiences and Impact of AI tools, Papers from the 1999 AAAI Spring Symposium, TR SS-99-01*, pages 82–85. AAAI Press, March 1999.
7. A. Kobsa, J. Kownemann, and W. Pohl. Personalized hypermedia presentation techniques for improving online customer relationships. Technical Report 66, German National Research Cetner for iNformation Technology, St. Augustin, Germany, 1999.
8. B. Mobasher, R. Cooley, and J. Srivastava. Web mining: Information and pattern discobery on the world wide web. In *Proceedings of the Ninth International Conference on Tools with Artificial Intelligence (ICTAI97)*, 1997.
9. J. Ortega. Exploiting multiple existing models and learning algorithms, 1995.
10. Roger C. Schank and Chip Cleary. *Engines for education*. Lawrence Erlbaum Associates, Hillsdale, New Jersey, 1995.
11. Gerhard Weber and Marcus Specht. User modeling and adaptive navigation support in www-based tutoring systems. In *Proceedings of the Sixth International Conference on User Modeling*, pages 289–300, Chia Laguna, Sardinia, Italy, June 1997.

Personalizing Assessment
in Adaptive Educational Hypermedia Systems

Evangelia Gouli, Kyparisia Papanikolaou, and Maria Grigoriadou

Department of Informatics and Telecommunications, University of Athens,
Panepistimiopolis, GR-15784 Athens, Greece
{lilag, spap, gregor}@di.uoa.gr

Abstract. In this paper, we present a comprehensive framework for assessment, developed through the web-based module named PASS-Personalized ASSessment, which can be integrated in an Adaptive Educational Hypermedia System to provide personalized assessment. PASS estimates learner's performance through multiple assessment options - pre-test, self-assessment and summative assessment - tailored to learner's responses. The adaptive functionality of PASS, which is mainly based on the adaptive testing and the adaptive questions techniques, is described. The first results from the formative evaluation of PASS are encouraging, concerning the total number of questions posed to estimate learner's knowledge level, which is usually less than the maximum needed and the accuracy of the outcome results compared to the estimations of the expert-tutor.

1 Introduction

Educational assessment is a process of drawing reasonable inferences about what learners know on the basis of evidence derived from observation of what they say, do or make in selected situations [8]. An important consideration affecting the design of the assessment is the purpose on which it will be used. Two broad purposes served by assessment are *the assessment to assist learning* usually referred as *formative assessment* and *the assessment of individual achievement* usually referred as *summative assessment*. Formative assessment is part of the developmental process of learning and assesses the quality of learning while summative assessment assesses the quantity and retention of learning following the completion of a unit of instruction [5, 8].

In a web-based distance learning setting, information derived from both assessment approaches as well as the learner's interaction with the system can be stored by the learning environment for further exploitation: (*i*) by *learners* to observe their personal learning progress and to decide how to further direct their learning process, and (*ii*) by *tutors* to individually support learners and formulate judgments about the quality and the effectiveness of the provided content.

Moreover, when the learning environment is an Adaptive Educational Hypermedia System (AEHS) [1], assessment provides a way to estimate learners' knowledge level and skills through learners' responses in tests, characteristics that are usually used as sources of adaptation. Thus, the generation of assessment tests tailored to learners' responses could mainly enhance the adaptation of a system in this educational context and extend its adaptive capabilities. Several techniques have been recently used in learning environments introducing adaptation to the assessment process such as adaptive testing [11] and adaptive questions [2].

In this paper, we propose a comprehensive framework for assessment, developed through the web-based module named PASS-Personalized ASSessment. Multiple assessment options tailored to the learner's responses are provided: *(i)* pre-testing and self-assessment that correspond to the formative assessment, and *(ii)* summative assessment. The assessment process is based on the central idea of the adaptive testing and the adaptive questions techniques. The PASS module can be integrated in any AEHS with certain characteristics.

The paper is organized as follows. In Sect. 2, a description of the adaptive testing and the adaptive questions techniques is provided. Then, in Sect. 3, the PASS module is presented and in Sect. 4, the functionality of PASS module is described according to the proposed framework of the assessment. In Sect. 5, experimental results from the formative evaluation of PASS module are discussed and in Sect. 6, the paper ends with concluded remarks and plans for further research.

2 Adaptation in Assessment

The enhancement of the assessment process with adaptive capabilities is meaningful for at least two reasons: *(i)* the assessment process becomes dynamic and individualized, as it is adapted to the learner's performance, and *(ii)* the number of questions required to estimate learner's knowledge level is usually reduced, resulting in a less tedious assessment process. The *adaptive testing* and the *adaptive questions* techniques, which can be used to introduce adaptation in the assessment process, are presented below.

Adaptive Testing involves a computer-administered test in which, the selection/presentation of each question and the decision to stop the process are dynamically adapted to the learner's performance in the test [11], [4].

Computerized adaptive testing relies on Item Response Theory [11]. In the adaptive testing procedure, a learner answering questions correctly (or incorrectly) will be gradually administered more difficult (or easier) questions. Questions are selected so that their difficulty matches the learner's estimated knowledge level. The questions that provide most amount of "information" about the actual knowledge level of the learner are usually those with difficulty similar to the learner's knowledge level, as it is estimated by the system, and low guessing factor. The learner's knowledge level estimation depends on the number of questions answered correctly and on the difficulty level of the answered questions. The assessment process will hopefully reach an accurate estimation of the learner's knowledge level after a number of questions posed.

Several approaches exploit the idea of adaptive testing. Huang in [4] describes an adaptive testing algorithm, CBAT-2, that generates content-balanced questions and the SIETTE system [10] is a Web-based testing system with adaptive capabilities.

Adaptive questions technique defines a dynamic sequence of questions depending on learner's responses. Specific responses or learner's performance to certain questions trigger the next series of questions according to several predefined rules, in contrast to the adaptive testing technique, where the triggered question is the one that provides the most amount of "information" about the learner's actual knowledge level.

The adaptive questions technique uses a pool of questions, which are highly structured. Questions are grouped in different classes according to criteria specified by the tutor, such as specific learning outcomes. Furthermore, each class may contain a number of subclasses with different characteristics, such as the difficulty level of their questions. Classes/subclasses are triggered following a certain sequencing mainly determined by the learner's responses. Each time a class/subclass is triggered, all its questions are posed.

Adaptive questions have been used mainly in computer-assisted surveys. Pitkow and Recker in [9] showed that Web-based adaptive questionnaires can reduce the number and complexity of questions posed to users. Furthermore, in CATES [2], "adaptive questionnaires" are used to assess Web users' attitudes.

3 PASS - A Personalized ASSessment Module

PASS is a web-based assessment module, aiming to estimate learner's performance and to assess specific learning outcomes, which are congruent with the learner's learning goal. To this end, it provides multiple assessment options. Tutors can use it in order to define the assessment specifications and to have a detailed overview of the learners' performance and progress. Learners can use PASS for taking a pre-test, self-assessment and summative assessment tests (multiple assessment options) tailored to their responses. PASS can be integrated to any AEHS with a structured domain knowledge and a learner model that keeps information about the navigational behaviour of the learner.

PASS module has been integrated and evaluated in a simulated environment of INSPIRE [7]. INSPIRE is a web-based Adaptive Educational Hypermedia System, which aims to facilitate distance learners during their study, providing them with personalized support. Based on the learning goals that the learner selects, INSPIRE generates lessons that correspond to specific learning outcomes, accommodating the knowledge level of the learner and his/her learning style.

In order to follow the functionality of the different components comprising the PASS module, we provide a brief description of the domain knowledge of INSPIRE. This is represented in three hierarchical levels of knowledge abstraction [7]: learning goals, concepts and educational material. The outcome concepts, which are the most important concepts of a learning goal, are associated with a number of prerequisite concepts. The educational material of an outcome concept is organized in three different levels of performance [6]: *Remember level* (associated with learner's ability to recall the provided content), *Use level* (associated with learner's ability to apply the provided content in specific problems) and *Find level* (associated with learner's ability to propose and solve original problems). On each particular level of performance, one or more educational material pages, comprising of multiple types of knowledge modules, such as examples, theory presentations, exercises, activities, are provided.

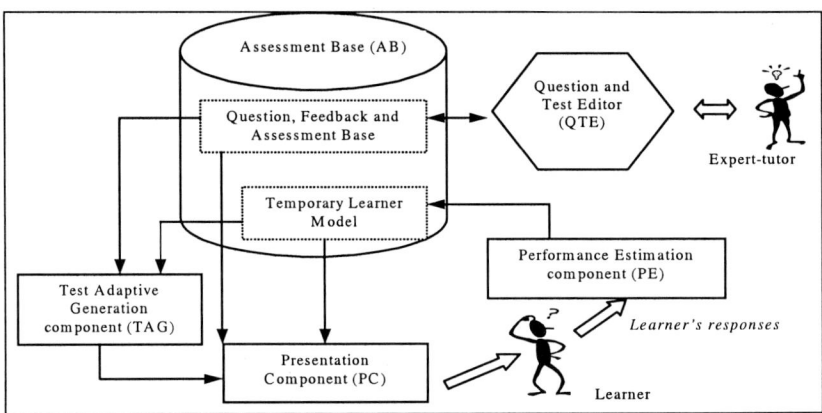

Fig. 1. Schematic of the PASS module

The schematic of the PASS module is illustrated in Fig 1. It is comprised of the following components:
- *Assessment Base* (AB): a data storage, which contains a pool of questions with a variety of parameters, assessment parameters and a Temporary Learner Model (TLM). The TLM stores all the information regarding the learner's interaction with the PASS module and the temporary estimations concerning the knowledge level of the learner.
- *Question and Test Editor* (QTE): a tool that allows tutors to define: (*i*) the questions, (*ii*) the feedback provided to the learner for each of the alternative answers of the question, (*iii*) the question's parameters such as the initial difficulty level, the number of alternative answers, the level of performance (in this case: Remember, Use, Find) that the question assesses, (*iv*) the assessment parameters such as the maximum number of questions in each particular test, the minimum number of questions for each level of performance, the degree of confidence in the estimated knowledge level, the termination criteria, and (*v*) the weight of each educational material page and of each prerequisite concept denoting their importance for the outcome concept. The QTE allows the tutor to concentrate on authoring questions and relieves him/her of the strain of technological details.
- *Test Adaptive Generation* (TAG): selects the appropriate question to be posed to the learner according to: (*i*) the questions' parameters, (*ii*) the assessment parameters, and (*iii*) the current estimation of the learner's knowledge level recorded on the TLM. It takes all the required information from the AB and following the algo-

rithm of the selected assessment option, it selects the "best" next question/class of questions. Furthermore, the TAG uses multiple termination criteria in order to terminate the assessment procedure (see Sect. 4 for more details).
- *Performance Estimation* (PE): estimates the learner's performance level and updates the TLM (see Sect.4 for more details).
- *Presentation Component* (PC): presents the question selected by TAG and the appropriate feedback according to the learner's response. Also, it provides a graphical and a text-based representation of the learner's learning progress.

4 PASS Module's Functionality

PASS, as an assessment module, provides a variety of evidence to support educational decision making, offering three assessment options: (*i*) pre-testing, (*ii*) self-assessment on the content that the learner has already studied, and (*iii*) summative assessment on the overall content. These options, in the context of AEHSs, can provide essential information about the learner's performance in different stages of the learning process. The adequate exploitation of this information can mainly enhance the dynamic adaptation of an AEHS towards: (*i*) personalizing the content that will be delivered to the learner, and (*ii*) providing adaptive navigational support through the content.

Pre-testing functionality. Pre-testing has been designed: (*i*) to provide a preview of the subject matter, (*ii*) to investigate the learner's prior knowledge in the provided content, (*iii*) to diagnose learning difficulties in the prerequisite material, and (*iv*) to initialise the learner's temporary model.

To fulfil the above aims, the three following categories of questions have been specified: (*i*) questions assessing learners' prior knowledge on the subject matter by providing a preview of it, (*ii*) open questions providing information about learners' experience and prior knowledge on related subjects, and (*iii*) questions assessing learners' knowledge on the prerequisite material.

Specifically, the technique of adaptive questions is adopted for the selection/presentation of questions assessing learners' knowledge on the prerequisite material (3rd category of questions). This technique is adopted in order to enable the learners to refrain from frustration, which is usually caused when they are asked to answer questions the level of which is above their knowledge. In the proposed approach, a class of questions is specified for each prerequisite concept of an outcome concept. For each particular class, a number of subclasses is defined, aiming to: (*i*) assess the level of learners' performance, and/or (*ii*) draw meaningful inferences through learners' responses. The rules that trigger the next class/subclass of questions are based on: (*i*) the percentage of learners' correct responses, and/or (*ii*) qualitative criteria defined to draw specific inferences about the gaps in the learners' knowledge.

An overview of the way the pre-testing is provided through the PASS module is described below (not yet fully implemented). Once the learner has decided to take a pre-test, the TAG selects the first two categories of questions and the PC presents them to the learner. Next, the TAG applies the adaptive questions procedure, for questions assessing learners' knowledge on the prerequisite concepts, taking into account the learner's responses. The TAG triggers the appropriate classes/subclasses of questions following certain rules. All the questions of each triggered subclass are posed. When the assessment procedure is completed for a class, the PE estimates the learner's knowledge level for the particular prerequisite concept with which the class is associated. Then, a new class of questions is triggered. A qualitative model, which classifies learner's knowledge level to one of the four levels of proficiency {Insufficient (In), Rather Insufficient (RI), Rather Sufficient (RS), Sufficient (S)} is used.

Following the termination of the pre-testing, the PE estimates the prior knowledge level of the learner on each outcome concept by taking into account: (*i*) the percentage of correct responses on questions presenting a preview of the subject matter, (*ii*) the learner's knowledge level estimation for the prerequisite concepts of the outcome, and (*iii*) the weights of the prerequisite concepts denoting their importance for the outcome with which they are associated. This estimation is used as an initial estimation of the learner's knowledge level in the adaptive testing procedure, which is performed during the self-assessment and the summative assessment.

Self-assessment and summative assessment functionality. Self-assessment aims to stimulate the learner to contemplate and reflect on the content that s/he has studied, to assess the learner's performance and to provide immediate and informative feedback. Summative assessment intends to evaluate the learning outcomes of the instruction by indicating an end mastery of the learning outcomes for each outcome concept. The learner has always the option to select self-assessment or summative assessment. Moreover, the system has the ability to propose the most appropriate one, according to the navigational behaviour of the learner through the content i.e. in case the learner has not visited all the provided material of an outcome concept, self-assessment is proposed for the outcome.

The construction of the self-assessment and the summative assessment tests is dynamic, depending on the current knowledge level of the learner. Moreover, in self-assessment, the navigational behaviour of the learner through the content is also considered. The assessment procedure takes into account the content that the learner has visited as well as the time that s/he has spent studying the material. Thus, the AEHS needs to keep such kind of information in the learner model. In summative assessment, questions associated with the prerequisite concepts and questions relevant to each outcome concept, are posed.

The technique of adaptive testing is adopted for self-assessment and summative assessment. The assessment procedure in both these approaches works as follows:
- 1st step: The TAG looks for an initial estimation of the learner's knowledge level in the TLM. If no estimation exists, an average is assumed.
- 2nd step: Depending on the assessment option selected, i.e. self-assessment or summative assessment, the maximum number of questions to be posed for each performance level (Remember, Use, Find) is estimated. In the case of self-assessment, the weight of each educational material page (see in Sect. 3, QTE) and the navigational behaviour of the learner, are taken into account. In the case of

summative assessment, just the weight of each educational material page is considered.
- 3rd step: The TAG selects the candidate questions according to the assessment option, the navigational behaviour of the learner and the minimum and maximum number of questions for each performance level. Questions that are associated with important educational material pages (pages with higher weight) have a greater chance of being chosen.
- 4th step: For each candidate question, the TAG calculates the Item Characteristic Curve (ICC) and the Item Information Function (IIF) based on the current estimation of the learner's knowledge level, the difficulty level of the question and the guessing factor [11] (the discriminatory power is omitted). The ICC represents the probability that the learner with a certain knowledge level will be able to provide a correct answer and the IFF is a representation of the amount of "information" provided by each question about the learner's knowledge level. According to the weight of each educational material page and the amount of "information" provided by each question, the TAG selects the "best" question. Usually, questions with difficulty similar to the learner's knowledge level and low guessing factor provide the most amount of "information". In the proposed approach, the difficulty level of each question is initially assigned by the tutor and as the question is used in the assessment procedure, it is re-estimated according to the number of times that it has been answered correctly or incorrectly [4]. The calibration of the difficulty level of questions is necessary.
- 5th step: The PE, according to the learner's response, estimates his/her knowledge level. The knowledge level is adjusted by a quantity, which depends on the previous estimation of learner's knowledge level and on all his/her previous responses. The PE classifies learner's knowledge level for each outcome concept of the selected learning goal, to one of the four levels of proficiency: {In, RI, RS, S}.
- 6th step: The TAG terminates the assessment procedure when any of the following predefined criteria is met: (*i*) when the number of questions posed exceeds the maximum number of questions defined for the test (see Sect. 3, QTE), (*ii*) when all the questions in the AB have already been posed, (*iii*) when the degree of confidence in the estimated learner's knowledge level is high, (*iv*) when the number of questions posed exceeds the maximum number of questions estimated for each particular level of performance (see 2nd step).

Steps 4 and 5 are repeated until the termination criteria are met. For a detailed description of the algorithm, which is followed by the above assessment procedure, see [3]. At the end of the assessment procedure, information on the learner's achievement and charts showing the learner's progress over the learning process are provided and stored in the system for further exploitation by the tutor.

5 Experimental Results

The first stage of the formative evaluation of the PASS module aims to check the validity of its estimations concerning the knowledge level of the learner and the efficiency of the proposed procedures. The study, performed in this context, focused on the module's estimations provided on the self-assessment and summative assessment options, which were compared to: (*i*) the diagnostic process of an expert-tutor, and (*ii*) the simplified process of accounting the percentage of right answers, a method adopted in many AEHSs. In order to check the validity of the estimations, we examined the accuracy of the outcome results, i.e. the percentage of learners who were classified by PASS into the same level of proficiency as classified by the expert-tutor. The efficiency of the assessment procedure used in the summative assessment option (the same procedure is used in self-assessment) was examined through the total number of questions posed to the different learners.

The students' data used in this study have been obtained from an experiment, which was performed as a part of the evaluation of INSPIRE at the Dept. of Informatics and Telecommunications, University of Athens. In this experiment, twenty undergraduate students used INSPIRE for two hours in order to study the learning goal "Describe the Role of Cache Memory and its basic operations". Once the students had studied the educational material of the outcome concept "Mapping Techniques", they were asked to submit an assessment test on the particular outcome (summative assessment). The professor of the "Computer Architecture" course who had the role of the expert-tutor assessed these tests. The estimations of the expert-tutor were based on the general impression given by the tests, the difficulty of the questions, the number of correct answers on each performance level and the comparison between students' answers.

Students' answers on the test were also provided to PASS and the expert-tutor assigned the required parameters. The maximum number of questions posed in the test was assigned to 15. The initial difficulty of the questions was assigned according to the level of performance that the question assessed, e.g. for questions assessing the Remember level of performance, the initial difficulty was 0.3. For question's difficulty calibration, data from the final exams of the course "Computer Architecture" were used. The initial knowledge level of the students was assumed as {RI}. The scale of the four levels of proficiency, i.e. {In, RI, RS, S} was experimentally set. This scale provides results, which are closer to the estimations of the expert-tutor. The study was also performed by classifying learner's knowledge level to five and to six levels of proficiency. We found that if four levels of proficiency are considered then the accuracy of the estimations is higher compared to the other two approaches.

Additionally, we estimated the students' knowledge level based on the percentage of correct answers, according to heuristic rules i.e. if the percentage of correct answers is between 0-25% or between 26-50% or between 51-75% or over 75% then the proficiency level is estimated as {In} or {RI} or {RS} or {S} correspondingly.

Figure 2 shows the summative assessment results obtained from the classification of 20 students into the four levels of proficiency using the three estimation approaches. Unfortunately, none of the students' proficiency level has been characterized as {S}. The reader may notice that for 17 out of 20 students, the proficiency level estimations, resulted from the PASS module, coincide with the expert-tutor's estimations. On the other hand, for only 4 students, the expert-tutor's estimations coincide with estimations resulted from the percentage of correct answers approach.

Although the sample is rather small to reach a safe conclusion, the experimental results imply that the student's proficiency level estimations provided by PASS follow the expert-tutor's estimations with high accuracy.

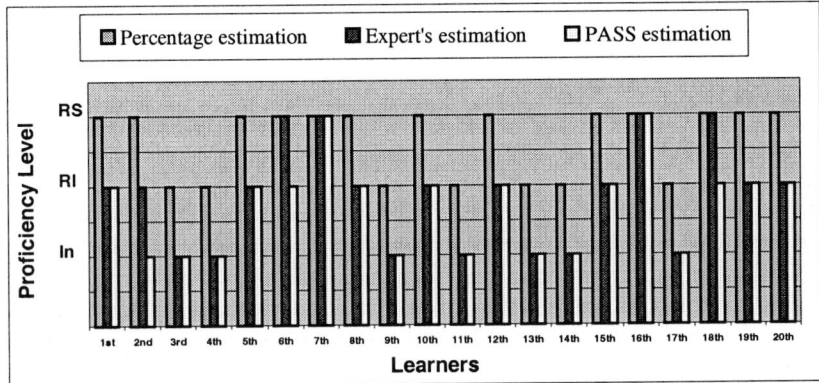

Fig. 2. The proficiency level of 20 students on the concept "Mapping Techniques" as it is estimated by: *(i)* calculating the percentage of students' correct responses, *(ii)* the expert-tutor, and *(iii)* the PASS module.

Furthermore, another interesting point, which we considered, was the total number of questions that were posed to each student, a parameter that mainly affects the testing time. Figure 3 shows the total number of questions posed to students in order to estimate their proficiency level. The reader may notice that 11/20 students answered less than 15 questions. These results imply that less time is needed to take the assessment test since fewer questions are required to achieve an acceptable accuracy. Furthermore, Fig. 4 shows the relationship between the average number of questions posed and the estimation of student's level of proficiency. The initial students' proficiency level was assumed as {RI} and as we have mentioned above, questions were selected in a way that their difficulty was similar to the student's knowledge level. The reader may notice, in Fig.4, that for students with a proficiency level estimated as {RS}, the average number of questions posed was less, compared to those with a

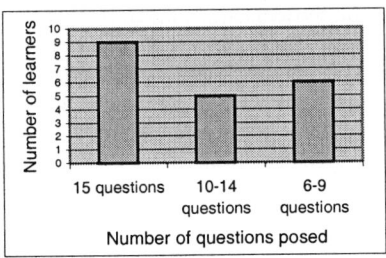

Fig. 3. Number of questions posed by the PASS module

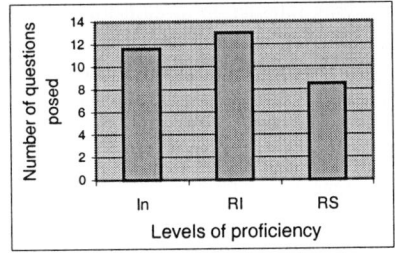

Fig. 4. Average number of questions posed for each level of proficiency

lower level of proficiency, i.e. {In} or {RI}. One possible explanation is that students with lower levels of proficiency usually guess the answers, so the assessment procedure needs to pose more questions for estimating accurately their knowledge level.

6 Conclusions and Further Research

In this paper, we presented PASS, a web-based and easy to integrate in an AEHS, assessment module. PASS offers three assessment options tailored to learner's responses: pre-testing, self-assessment and summative assessment. The technique of adaptive questions has been adopted for pre-testing. The discriminative characteristics of the self-assessment and summative assessment procedures adopted in PASS are: the adoption of the adaptive testing technique, the consideration of the learner's navigational behaviour, the re-estimation of the difficulty level of each question each time it is posed (initially assigned by the expert-tutor), and the consideration of the importance of each educational material page.

The experimental results from the formative evaluation of PASS, even performed on a limited test group, have been encouraging and indicate that the estimations on learners' proficiency are close to the expert-tutor estimations. We have also shown that a reduction in the number of questions posed can be achieved, especially for learners with higher levels of proficiency, resulting in a reduction of the testing time.

Our future plans, apart from the evaluation of the PASS module with a wider group of learners, include the completion of the pre-testing implementation and the adaptation of the feedback provided to the learners' according to their performance.

References

1. Brusilovsky, P.: Adaptive and Intelligent Technologies for Web-based Education. In: Rollinger, C., Peylo, C. (eds.): Special Issue on Intelligent Systems and Teleteaching. Kunstliche Intelligenz, Vol. 4 (1999) 19-25
2. Chou, C.: Constructing a computer-assisted testing and evaluation system on the World Wide Web–the CATES experience. IEEE Transactions on Education 43(3)(2000) 266-272
3. Gouli, E., Kornilakis, H., Papanikolaou, K., Grigoriadou, M.: Adaptive Assessment improving interaction in an Educational Hypermedia System. In: Avouris, N., Fakotakis, N. (eds.): Advances in Human-Computer Interaction I. Proceedings of the PanHellenic Conference with International Participation in Human-Computer Interaction (2001) 217-222
4. Huang, S.: A Content-Balanced Adaptive Testing Algorithm for Computer-Based Training Systems. In: Frasson, C., Gauthier, G., Lesgold, A. (eds.): Intelligent Tutoring Systems, Third International Conference, Springer (1996) 306-314
5. Kommers, P., Grabinger, S., Dunlap, J.: Hypermedia Learning Environments. Instructional Design and Integration. Lawrence Erlbaum Associates (1996)
6. Merril, D.: Component Display Theory. In: Reigeluth, C.M. (eds.): Instructional design theories and models: An overview of their current status. Lawrence Erlbaum Associates, Hillsdale NJ (1983) 279-333

7. Papanikolaou, K., Grigoriadou, M., Kornilakis, H., Magoulas, G.: INSPIRE: An INtelligent System for Personalized Instruction in a Remote Environment. In: Reich, S., Tzagarakis, M.M., De Bra, P. M.E. (eds.): Hypermedia: Openness, Structural Awareness and Adaptivity. Lecture Notes in Computer Science Vol. 2266, pp. 215-225. Springer-Verlag, Berlin (2002)
8. Pellegrino, J., Chudowsky, N., Glaser, R. (eds): Knowing what students know: The Science and Design of Educational Assessment. National Academy of Sciences, National Academy Press, Washington (2001)
9. Pitkow, J., Recker, M.: Using the Web as a Survey Tool: Results from the Second WWW User Survey. Computer Networks ISDN Systems 27(6) (1995) 809-822
10. Rios, A., Millan, E., Trella, M., Perez-de-la-Cruz, J., Conejo, R. : Internet Based Evaluation System. In: Lajoie S., and Vivet M. (eds.): Artificial Intelligence in Education, Open Learning Environments, New Computational Technologies to Support learning Exploration and Collaboration. Frontiers in AI and Applications, Vol 50. IOS Press (1999) 387-394
11. Wainer, H., Dorans, N., Eignor, D., Flaugher, R., Green, B., Mislevy, R., Steinberg, L., Thissen, D. (eds): Computerized adaptive testing: A primer. 2nd edition. Lawrence Erlbaum Associates, Hillsdate NJ (2000)

Visual Based Content Understanding towards Web Adaptation

Xiao-Dong Gu[1,*], Jinlin Chen[2], Wei-Ying Ma[3], and Guo-Liang Chen[1]

[1] Dept. of Computer Science, Univ. of Sci. & Tech. of China,
230027, Hefei, China
gxd@mail.ustc.edu.cn
[2] School of Information Science, Univ. of Pittsburgh,
Pittsburgh, PA 15260 USA
jlchen@pitt.edu
[3] Microsoft Research Asia
Beijing 100080, China
wyma@microsoft.com

Abstract. Web content structure is proposed to facilitate automatic web page adaptation in this paper. By identifying the logic relationship of web content based on layout information, web content structure effectively represents authors' presentation intention. An automatic top-down, tag-tree independent approach to detect web content structure is presented. It simulates how a user understands web layout structure based on his vision. Comparing to other content analysis techniques, our approach is independent to physical realization and works well even when the physical structure is far different from layout structure. Besides, our approach is an $O(n)$-time process which is much more efficient comparing to other approaches with $O(n^2)$-time complexity. Furthermore, our approach is tag tree independent, which means it can be applied to web contents of arbitrary physical realization formats. Experiments show satisfactory results.

1 Introduction

Web publishing is playing a more and more important role for information distribution today. When creating a new web page, the author first decides what to present, i.e., the semantic content. He then further decides how to present the information. Finally, a markup language is used to realize the presentation, which gives a physical structure to the content. Considering the whole process, we have XML to represent semantic structure and many markup languages such as HTML to represent physical structure. However, we still lack an effective way to represent presentation structure, which indicates authors' intention towards the presentation logic of web content.

Furthermore, with the exponential growth of information and increasing diversity in terms of devices and networks in today's web, it becomes increasingly pressing to access desired contents accurately and conveniently. Various content adaptation technologies [1-4,13,14] have been developed for this purpose. One crucial issue for content adaptation is the need to effectively represent and understand presentation structure of web pages. Many web content analyzers have been proposed to extract structural information from web pages either manually [5-8] or automatically [9-11]. However, a big problem with these approaches is that they try to extract structural information from HTML tag tree directly, which often leads to unstable results because HTML tags were designed for both presentational and structural representation. Besides, most of them are bottom-up approaches which are time consuming. In addition, these approaches are only suitable for HTML documents.

To solve these problems, we first propose the web content structure, which attempts to represent author's presentation intention by identifying the logic relationship of web content based on visual layout information. An automatic top-down, tag-tree independent approach to detecting web content structure is then presented. It simulates how a user understands the web layout structure when he browses a page such as objects' size, position, color, background, etc. A projection-based algorithm is applied to segment a web page into blocks. Blocks are further divided into sub-blocks or merged if they are visually similar. In this way we avoid the breaking of logical chunks. Comparing to other existing approaches, our approach is independent of physical realization and performs even when the physical structure is different from visual layout structure. Besides, our approach is an $O(n)$-time process which is much more efficient comparing to the $O(n^2)$-time process in [11] (n is the number of basic objects). In addition, our approach is tag tree independent, which can be applied to contents with various physical realization formats.

This paper is organized as follows. In Sect. 2 we will first introduce the web content structure. It is followed by the automatic detection of web content structure in Sect. 3. Experimental results and conclusions are given in Sects 4 and 5, respectively.

2 Web Content Structure

When designing a web page, the author first collects all the basic objects for the page. A basic object is the smallest unit of a web page, which cannot be further divided to perform some certain functions. He then groups related basic objects together to achieve a major function. This group of objects is called a composite object. Composite objects can be further grouped into a more complex one. This is a recursive process until all the objects in a web page are grouped together. During this process the author also needs to consider how to visually separate the composite objects.

Based on the analysis above, to fully express the presentation design of a web page, web content structure should represent the layout structure of a web page, which is the result of dividing and subdividing the content of a web page into increasingly smaller part, on the basis of presentation. Layout structure includes the structure of composite objects and how they are separated from each other. Similar to the description of document representation in [12], the basic model of web content structure is described as below:

A web page • can be represented by a triple

$$\bullet = (\bullet, \bullet, \bullet). \tag{1}$$

where $\bullet = \{\bullet_1, \bullet_2, \ldots, \bullet_n\}$ is a finite set of objects, including basic objects and composite objects. Each composite object can be viewed as a sub-content structure. $\bullet = \{\bullet_1, \bullet_2, \ldots, \bullet_j\}$ is a finite set of separators in visual representation, including horizontal and vertical separators. • is the relationship of every two objects in O and can be expressed as:

$$\bullet = \bullet \times \bullet \cup \{NULL\}. \tag{2}$$

Suppose $\bullet_i, \bullet_j \in O$, $\bullet(\bullet_i, \bullet_j) \bullet NULL$ indicates that $\bullet_i$ and $\bullet_j$ are exactly separated by the separator $\bullet(\bullet_i, \bullet_j)$, or we can say that the two objects are adjacent to some extent. Otherwise there exists other object between $\bullet_i$ and $\bullet_j$.

Based on the definition above, authors can easily represent their presentation design in a formulas manner.

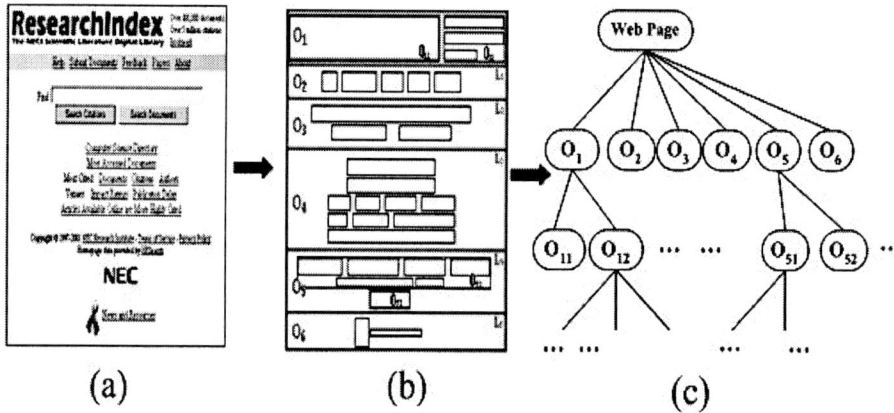

Fig. 1. An example of web content structure

Figure 1 gives an example of web content structure, in which

$$O = \{O_1, O_2, O_3, O_4, O_5, O_6\}$$
$$\Phi = \{L_1, L_2, L_3, L_4, L_5\}$$

$$\delta = O \times O \to \Phi : \delta \begin{pmatrix} (O_1, O_2) \\ (O_2, O_3) \\ (O_3, O_4) \\ (O_4, O_5) \\ (O_5, O_6) \\ else \end{pmatrix} = \begin{pmatrix} L_1 \\ L_2 \\ L_3 \\ L_4 \\ L_5 \\ NULL \end{pmatrix}$$

In the page L_1-L_5 are all horizontal separators, O_1-O_6 are all Composite Objects, which can be further subdivided. For example, O_1 can be divided into two sub-blocks O_{11} and O_{12} by a vertical separator.

3 Automatic Web Content Structure Detection

Since web content structure reflects authors' intention directly, it plays a crucial role for content understanding. Therefore, detecting web content structure from existing web pages is very important for content adaptation. Although it is desirable that additional information be added for the generation of web content structure during the authoring stage, authors often decide not to do so. Thus, it is important that web content structure can be automatically detected.

In this section, we describe a top-down tag-tree independent approach to detecting web content structure based on page visual presentation. Our proposed approach simulates how a user understands the web layout structure when he browses a page. Below is the detailed description to the algorithm.

3.1 System Structure

Web content structure detection is a reverse process to web authoring. We start from physical structure of web content to find out the presentation scheme. The detection of web content structure is to analyze and establish the quintuple of (1), i.e. •, • and • defined in Sect. 2.

Figure 2 illustrates the framework of our approach. The detection process is the division and repeated subdivision of a web page into increasingly smaller parts (objects). The detected structure can be visually represented by a geometric tree as in

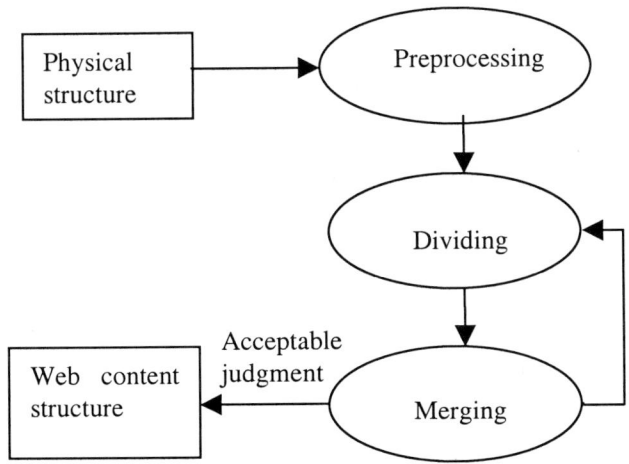

Fig. 2. Web content structure detection

Fig. 1 (c). To construct web content structure, first basic objects are extracted from the physical structure (tag tree). We then preprocess the basic objects to find out decoration objects and group similar ones to reduce complexity. Then based on web visual representation, the whole page is divided into blocks through projection. Adjacent blocks are merged if they are visually similar. This dividing and merging process continues recursively until the layout structure of the whole page is constructed. Below we will first introduce the two major components in our system: dividing and merging. We then give a brief introduction to preprocessing module.

3.2 Dividing Blocks via Projection

Projection is applied to divide a block into smaller sub-blocks. Projection refers to the mapping of a web page into a waveform whose value is the sums of the values of the object weights along projection axis. All objects in a web page are contained in rectangular blocks. Blanks are placed between these rectangles. Thus, the projection profile is a waveform whose deep valleys correspond to the blank areas of the web page. A deep valley with a width greater than an established threshold can be considered as separator between objects. The process of projection is performed recursively until all objects are located. Figure 3 (a) gives an example of projection. Every object is projected along a projection axis. The sub-lines in the projection axis without any objects projecting into indicate the separators (see L_1 and L_2 in Fig. 3 (a)).

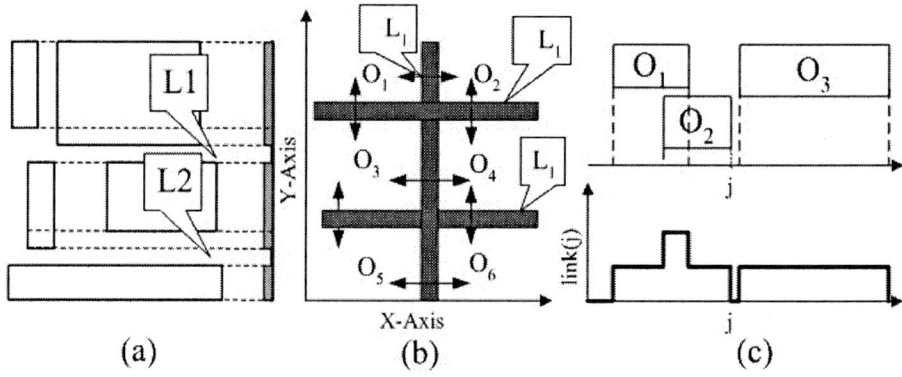

Fig. 3. Using projection to divide block

Figure 3(c) explains the details of the projection process. Let $\{O_1, O_2, \ldots, O_n\}$ be the n objects in a block, and s_i, e_i be the starting and ending point of O_i along a projection axis. Our goal is to find out all separators $\bullet = \{L_1, L_2, \ldots, L_t\}$ along the projection axis. Let link[j] be the judge value of point j at the projection axis. Then the weight value of O_i (1 by default) is added to link[s_i]. Similarly, the weight value of O_i is deducted from link[e_i]. Point j is considered a separator point if link[j] is zero. Below is the detailed algorithm.

Step 1: Let C be the set of the starting and ending points of all the objects. C = $(\cup_i \{s_i\}) \cup (\cup_i \{e_i\})$, and |C| = K;
Step 2: Sort C into ascending order;
Step 3: Let link[0] = 0, we then project all the objects onto the projection axis:
for (j = 1; j <= K; j++)
    link[j] = link[j-1]+c-d;

where c is the number of objects with starting point at C[j], and d is the number of objects with ending point at C[j]. This repetitive expression realizes the projection process in current block. If there are totally c objects starting at point j, the sum of the weights of these c objects should be added to link[j-1] to get link[j]. Correspondingly, if there are totally d objects ending at point j, the sum of the weights of these d objects should be deducted from link[j-1] to get link[j].

Since default weight is equal to 1 for each object, the resulting values of the sum of weights are c and d, respectively. More fine-grained weight can be assigned to compute link[j] for more accurate result.

Sub-line C[j]+1...C[j +1]-1 is a separator if link[j] is 0. This means that there is no object in the area between Sub-line C[j]+1...C[j +1]-1.

Our algorithm requires O(n) time because each step above costs O(n) time. Comparing to the $O(n^2)$-time required in [11], our approach significantly reduces the computational complexity.

Using the algorithm above, we detect separators $L_1[0...t_1-1]$ in X-axis and $L_2[0...t_2-1]$ in Y-axis. Then the division in current level is:

$$O = \{O_1, O_2, ..., O_{(t_1+1)(t_2+1)-1}\}$$

Sub-blocks are indexed from left to right as shown in Fig. 3 (b);

$$\Phi = L_1[0...t_1-1] \cup L_2[0...t_2-1]$$

$$\delta(O_{i(t_1+1)+j}, O_{i(t_1+1)+j+1}) = L_2[j] \quad (0 \leq i \leq t_2, 0 \leq j < t_1)$$

$$\delta(O_{i(t_1+1)+j}, O_{(i+1)(t_1+1)+j}) = L_1[i] \quad (0 \leq i < t_2, 0 \leq j \leq t_1)$$

As can been seen in Fig.3(b), projection in Y-axis reveals two horizontal separators L_1 and L_2 while in X-axis reveals one vertical separator L_3. These three separators divide current block into six sub-blocks: $O_1 \sim O_6$. The seven bidirectional arrows represent the relationship between sub-blocks and separators. Thus •,•,• are all detected.

3.3 Merging Sub-blocks via Layout Similarity

Since the division method above is only related to the position of objects, the separators detected may break a holistic object. Therefore the merging of some adjacent sub-blocks is necessary.

Simulating human's decision on whether two objects are similar, we use visual similarity to decide whether two objects are holistic and should be merged. For basic objects, if two objects are of different media type, their similarity x=0. Otherwise, x is related to the media type. Below is an example of basic text objects. In a similar way we can compute the similarity for basic objects of other media types.

- Starting from $x=1.0$, we first compare key HTML attributes (like <H1> ...<H6>, <A>). If not equal, $x = x*Modifier\_key$.
- Compare alignment and other common attributes. If not equal, $x = x*Modifier\_Common$
- Compare font size attribute. If not equal, $x = x*Modifier\_Size$.
- Compare styles (bold, italic, underline...). If not equal, $x = x*Modifier\_Style$.
- Compare font face. If not equal, $x = x*Modifier\_Face$.
- Compare text length, we have the following modification method:

$$x = x * \left(\frac{\min(length1, length2)}{\max(length1, length2)} \right)^{factor\ Adjust}$$

To calculate the similarity of two composite objects, we use an approximate similarity measurement to compare two element strings that enables weighted mismatches and omissions (skips). Weight of skipping may differ from element to element, because some of the objects (such as those with attributes like <H1>...<H6>) could be more important than others, and thus skipping of them would be costly (a small weight) or not allowed (zero weight).

Some additional rules are used to modify visual similarity between objects for our application based on the definition of visual similarity above:

1) Distance is an important factor for human to decide visual similarity. Let d be the distance between two objects. The larger d is, the less their visual similarity is. Let x be the visual similarity obtained above, a monotonic degressive function Dist_Modifer(d) is applied to embody the impact of distance to similarity:

$$x = x \cdot Dist\_Modifer(d)$$

2) Color has great influence for human to decide visual similarity. Two objects with the same distinguished color and background color (different from those of surrounding objects) are considered as a whole. Thus, $x=1$ if adjacent objects have the same color and background color. Otherwise x remains its original value.

Based on the visual similarity between two adjacent objects, we can then decide whether to merge them or not.

3.4 Preprocessing

Preprocessing is necessary to prevent decoration objects from enveloping separators and prevent unexpected separators (e.g., shadowed separator in Fig. 4 is unexpected if the dotted rectangle is a tightly-united object) from breaking object integrity.

By preprocessing we can not only decrease the opportunity of detecting unexpected separators, but also reduce the problem scale thus speedup the whole process.

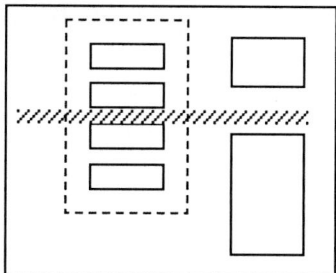

Fig. 4. Unexpected separator

4 Experimental Results

To evaluate our proposed approach, we randomly selected 50 web pages from popular sites listed in http://www.yahoo.com. We run our web content structure detection over these pages and the results are listed in Table 1.

Table 1. Experiment results with a test set of 50 pages

DETECTING RESULTS	NUMBER OF DOCUMENT
Correct	45
Acceptable	4
Failed	1

Totally the layout structures of 45 (90%) pages are correctly detected. Some apparent chunks are missed for 4(8%) pages. In most of these cases, one logical chunk is broken into two or more segments. These segments are usually well separated by a big white space from surrounding segments. Human consider these segments as a whole chunk mostly according to their semantic meaning. Therefore, this is not strictly the fault of our algorithm. Our detector fails to provide proper analysis to the page because the page is confused in visual representation that even human eyes cannot partition it correctly.

One benefit with our approach is that it is independent of how the web page is realized in HTML tag-tree. Figure 5 gives an example. The left side bar (indicated in dotted rectangle and was actually detected as a navigation list), which should be one logical chunk, is actually realized with two HTML tables, which leads to misdetection in tag-tree based approach [11]. But with our approach the side bar is detected as a whole.

Fig. 5. Our approach successfully detects the side bar as a whole while tag-tree based approaches fail in this case because the tags are spread across different part of HTML file.

5 Conclusions

In this paper the web content structure was proposed for web authoring, adaptation and information retrieval. By identifying the logic relationship of web content based on visual layout information, web content structure can effectively represent authors' presentation intention. An automatic top-down, tag-tree independent algorithm to detect web content structure was presented. It simulates how a user understands the web layout structure based on its visual representation. Comparing to other approaches, our method is independent of physical realization and works well even when the physical structure is far different from visual structure. Besides, our approach is an $O(n)$-time process which is much more efficient than other approaches with $O(n^2)$-time complexity. Experiments show satisfactory results.

References

1. Ma, W.Y., Bedner, I., Chang, G., Kuchinsky, A., and H.J.Zhang. A Framework for Adaptive Content Delivery in Heterogeneous Network Environments. in Proc. MMCN2000 (SPIE Vol.3969), San Jose, USA (2000) 86-100.
2. Chen, J.L., Yang, Y.D., and Zhang, H.J.: An Adaptive Web Content Delivery System, in Proc. AH2000, Springer (2000) 284-288.
3. Smith, J.R., Mohan, R., and Li, C.S.: Scalable Multimedia Delivery for Pervasive Computing, in Proc. of the 7th ACM International Conference on Multimedia (1999) 131-140.
4. Bickmore, T.W., and Schilit, B.N.: Digestor: Device-independent access to the World Wide Web, in Proc. WWW6 (1997) 655-663.
5. Hammer, J., Garcia-Monlina, H., Cho, J., Aranha, R., and A. Crespo: Extracting semistructured information from the web, in Proc. PODS/SIGMOD'97 (1997) 18-25.
6. Ashish, N., and Knoblock, C.: Wrapper generation for semi-structured Internet sources, in Proc. PODS/SIGMOD'97 (1997) 8-15.
7. Simth, D., and Lopez, M.: Information extraction for semi-structured documents, in Proc. PODS/SIGMOD'97 (1997) 117-121.
8. Nestorov, S., Abiteboul, S., and Motwani, R.: Inferring Structure in Semistructured Data, in Proc. PODS/SIGMOD'97 (1997) 39-43.
9. Embley, D.W., Jiang, Y., and Ng, Y.K.: Record-Boundary Discovery in Web Documents, in Proc. SIGMOD'99, Philadelphia PA (1999) 467-478.
10. Lim, S.J., and Ng, Y.K.: An Automated Approach for Retrieving Hierarchical Data from HTML Table, in Proc. CIKM'99, Kansas City, MO (1999) 466-474.
11. Yang, Y.D., and Zhang, H.J.: HTML Page Analysis Based on Visual Cues, in Proc. of the 6th International Conference on Document Analysis and Recognition, Seattle, USA (2001)
12. Tang, Y.Y., Cheriet, M., Liu, J., Said, J.N., and Suen, C.Y.: Document Analysis and Recognition by Computers, Handbook of Pattern Recognition and Computer Vision, World Scientific Publishing Company (1999)
13. Chen, J.L., Zhou, B.Y., Shi, J. Zhang, H.J., and Wu, Q.F.: Function-based Object Model Towards Website Adaptation, Proc. of the 10th International World Wide Web Conference, Hong Kong, China (2001) 587-596.
14. Yang, Y.D., Chen, J.L., and Zhang., H.J.: Adaptive Delivery of HTML Contents, in WWW9 Poster Proceedings (2000) 24-25.

Knowledge Modeling for Open Adaptive Hypermedia

Nicola Henze and Wolfgang Nejdl

University of Hannover
ITI- Rechnergestützte Wissensverarbeitung
Appelstr. 4
D-30167 Hannover
{henze,nejdl}@kbs.uni-hannover.de
http://www.kbs.uni-hannover.de/~{henze,nejdl}

Abstract. This paper proposes a knowledge modeling approach for adaptive, open corpus hypermedia systems. Our approach towards adaptive, open corpus hypermedia is based on interpreting standard metadata of learning objects. For each corpus of documents integrated into the open adaptive hypermedia system (OAHS) we are calculating subgraphs of the ontology for estimating the user's knowledge with respect to this corpus. This enables the OAHS to understand the knowledge contained in learning materials, to make estimations about an individual user's knowledge state and to learn the prerequisite knowledge required for learning objects from given structures in the materials.

1 Introduction

Hypermedia systems have become more and more popular as tools for user driven access to information. Adaptive hypermedia systems bring together ideas from hypermedia systems and intelligent tutoring systems, and enable personalized access to information.

Recently, many approaches like SCORM [15], LOM [7] or IMS [1] begin to standardize information for learning. They introduce metadata descriptions for so called learning objects which are entities containing some learning material. This metadata is e.g. an identifier, the creator of this material, the language, keywords describing its content, the interactivity level of this material, etc. In LOM there are currently about 80 metadata attributes defined. With these standardized descriptions of learning materials it is possible to build large learning repositories in which teachers and students will be able to store or retrieve valuable materials for learning, for preparing courses etc. Current approaches are e.g. ARIADNE [3] or EDUTELLA [8].

The individualization of the access to large learning repositories is a great challenge for adaptive hypermedia. Normally, adaptive hypermedia systems work on a closed set of materials which are often described by proprietary metadata and whose adaptational functionalities are tailored to the current application.

The shift towards adaptation for open learning repositories will require to interpret the standardized metadata of the learning objects accordingly and to find generalizations of adaptational functionalities which can handle the demands of open learning repositories.

In this paper we present an approach towards open adaptive hypermedia systems (OAHS). Our approach is driven by the claim to learn as much as possible from standard learning descriptions (such as keywords) and from structures in the learning materials (like reading sequences). This is motivated by the nature of open learning repositories where authors of learning objects should have a minimum overhead as possible for adding their learning objects into the repository. For a definition of adaptive hypermedia systems we follow [4]:

Definition 1 (Adaptive Hypermedia System [4]). *"By adaptive hypermedia systems we mean all hypertext and hypermedia systems which reflect some features of the user in the user model and apply this model to adapt various visible aspects of the system to the user."*

Definition 2 (Open Adaptive Hypermedia System). *An open adaptive hypermedia system (OAHS) is an adaptive hypermedia system which operates on an open corpus of documents.*

The definition of OAHS includes that the system must be able to adapt hypermedia documents to individual needs of a user regardless of the origin of the materials: The materials may belong to some set of course materials, may be a sequence of pages from a tutorial, may refer to content on personal home pages, or, generally spoken, may be learning objects from an an arbitrary corpus of documents.

The approach choosen here stems from research in adaptive hypermedia. We see a strong relation to the area of Open Hypermedia Systems (OHS) [9], too. Research in OHS focusses on cross-application access, on distributed hypermedia and group work by developing e.g. advanced hypermedia data models and hypermedia protocols [2]. So far as the authors know there has not been any attempt to systematically apply adaptation strategies from adaptive hypermedia research on top of open hypermedia - however this might be a very fruitful combination (see for example [6]).

2 Adaptation in Open Corpus Hypermedia

Hypermedia systems can be described as a set of nodes (containing multiple forms of media such as text, video, audio, graphics, etc.) which are connected by links [14]). Consequently there are generally two aspects of hypermedia systems which can be adapted to a user: the content (content level adaptation), and the links (link level adaptation). By adapting the content for a user, the document's content is tailored to the needs of the user, for example by hiding too specialized information or by inserting some additional explanations. By using link level adaptation, the user's possibilities to navigate the hypermedia documents are personalized. Techniques for content level and link level adaptation are for example described in [4].

In case of open corpus hypermedia we face a large collection of learning objects. As many authors can add arbitrary learning objects to an open learning repository it is highly probable that we have an oversupply of information. Thus for link level adaptation in OAHS it will be a central issue to decide which is the best learning object for a user. For content level adaptation in OAHS the metadata of a specific learning object must deliver information to redesign the presentation of the learning object itself. A user of an OAHS might be a teacher or a student as well. To consider students as users is very common in adaptive educational hypermedia. However it is an important issue to support teachers as users of an OAHS in the process of both storing and retrieving *qualified* learning objects. In this paper we will focus on personalized access to learning objects for students. Characteristics for a "best learning object" are e.g.

- current situation
  E.g. a student might want to prepare an exam, to learn or to refresh her knowledge.
- current interest
  E.g. a learning goal, a teaching goal.
- current knowledge state
  This is the most used characteristic in adaptive educational hypermedia and very important for student modeling.
- current learning experience
  E.g. based on previous studies. curriculum, general education.
- learning style
  E.g. problem-based, constructivist.
- presentation style
  E.g. graphics, textual descriptions, audios, animations.
- preferred author / corpus
  Individual preferences for a specific way of presentation or a teaching style.

Most of the above stated characteristics have successfully been used in adaptive hypermedia systems so far. The main new characteristic for OAHS is "preferred author / corpus" which we think will play an important role during the access to open learning repositories. For example, a student favors a specific teacher and her way to explain things. Or a student wants to make sure that he masters all topics of the class he is currently enrolled in.

3 Knowledge Modeling for OAHS

The knowledge of a user is the main source of information for adaptation in educational hypermedia. Based on the user's actual knowledge state, selection of information takes place, examples are proposed, reading sequences are generated and next learning steps are calculated for and presented to the user.

A knowledge model for OAHS has to fulfill the following requirements: It must be

1. universally valid
   Throughout the different corpora of the learning repository
2. expandable
   E.g. learning objects on new topics may be added to one of the corpora
3. expressive
   The knowledge contained in one single corpus must be describable as a valid model on its own.

Ontologies have been developed in Artificial Intelligence to facilitate knowledge sharing and reuse and therefor meet the first requirement. There are many definitions of ontologies in literature. We follow Gruber [10]

Definition 3 (Ontology [10]). *"An ontology is a formal, explicit specification of a shared conceptualization."*

By generating the ontology as a shared conceptualization we had to find a way to support different views on the categorization of concepts which we want to illustrate by an example from the domain of Java Programming: "implements" is used within a class declaration for implementing an interface. Therefor "implements" can be expected to occur in the ontology nearby "interfaces" or "class declaration". But one can take the point of view that "implements" is a Java keyword thus a person looking up Java keywords in the ontology can expect to find "implements" there, too. All these different viewpoints on the classification of "implements" are valid. In addition, as we will see in Sect. 4.1, the neighborhood of an entity in the knowledge model is a rich resource for improving the rating of relevance of learning objects during the retrieval process. Thus we allow multiple occurrences of concepts in the ontology-based knowledge model.

Ontologies are able to meet the second requirement for the knowledge model as well. As the example of the Java domain shows, new concepts are likely to appear (there have been many new developments in the past, for naming one: the migration from "AWT" to "Swing" in the Java Programming Language). However, applying an ontology for knowledge modeling in OAHS includes that the adaptation strategies and algorithms that we define must be capable to understand and to deal with new concepts which have been added to the ontology.

In order to model the knowledge of each individual corpus there are two different strategies possible: We can apply a separate ontology for each corpus and construct the overall ontology by ontology mapping [13]. The other strategy is to use one common ontology and express the knowledge described in each of the corpora as subgraphs of the ontology by labeling the nodes accordingly. We decided for the latter approach as it allows us to easily compare the knowledge of a user in relation to each of the corpora.

3.1 Assessment of Knowledge

If we employ an ontology-based knowledge model we have to rethink the way a user can acquire knowledge in an OAHS. In OAHS $\mathcal{U}$ can learn by using learning materials from different courses.

Example 1. User $\mathcal{U}$ can read about object-oriented programming in the course materials of her class and then starts writing her first Java program with aid of the Sun Java Tutorial [5].

Thus the knowledge of $\mathcal{U}$ must be estimated by rating her/his knowledge in a broader context, not solely in terms of the curriculum of one course or one set of learning materials.

To assess $\mathcal{U}$'s knowledge about a concept a with respect to some corpus $\mathcal{C}$ we determine a minimal topic-subgraph of the ontology. This topic-subgraph contains at least the topic a and all its child nodes. If neither one of the child nodes nor a itself are contained in the corpus we add recursively parent nodes of a to the subgraph until one parent node is contained in the corpus. Now we can assess the knowledge of $\mathcal{U}$ with respect to some corpus $\mathcal{C}$ in the following way: A concept which is contained in $\mathcal{C}$ can either be learned (value 1) or not learned (value 0). The knowledge of a concept not contained in $\mathcal{C}$ is estimated by the ratio of the number of learned concepts in the topic-subgraph which belong to $\mathcal{C}$ by the number of all concepts in the topic-subgraph which belong to $\mathcal{C}$.

Example 2. In Fig. 1 we interpret the knowledge of $\mathcal{U}$ in relation to corpus $\mathcal{C}$ as follows

- Fig. 1A: $\mathcal{U}$'s knowledge of topic "a" in respect to corpus $\mathcal{C}$: $a|_\mathcal{C} = 1$
  $\mathcal{U}$'s knowledge of topic "b" in respect to corpus $\mathcal{C}$: $b|_\mathcal{C} = 1$
  $\mathcal{U}$'s knowledge of topic "c" in respect to corpus $\mathcal{C}$: $c|_\mathcal{C} = 1$
- Fig. 2A: $a|_\mathcal{C} = 1$, $b|_\mathcal{C} = 0.5$, $c|_\mathcal{C} = 0$
- Fig. 3A: $a|_\mathcal{C} = 1$, $b|_\mathcal{C} = 0.5$, $c|_\mathcal{C} = 0$, $d|_\mathcal{C} = 0.5$
- Fig. 4A: $a|_\mathcal{C} = 1$, $b|_\mathcal{C} = 0.33$, $c|_\mathcal{C} = 0$, $d|_\mathcal{C} = 0$
- Fig. 5A: $a|_\mathcal{C} = 1$, $b|_\mathcal{C} = 1$, $c|_\mathcal{C} = 1$
- Fig. 6A: $a|_\mathcal{C} = 0$, $b|_\mathcal{C} = 1$, $c|_\mathcal{C} = 0.5$

Representation in one ontology

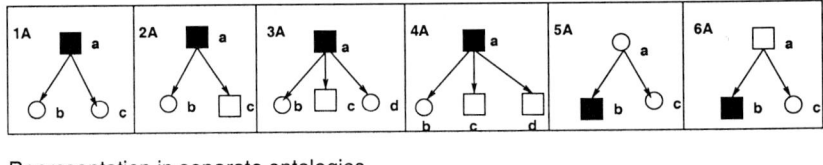

Representation in separate ontologies

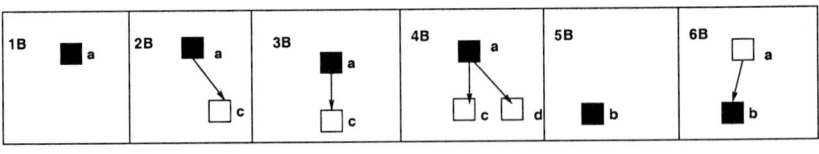

○ not read & not contained in corpus C   □ not read & contained in corpus C
● read & not contained in corpus C   ■ read & contained in corpus C

Fig. 1. Assessment of knowledge in an ontology-based knowledge model

3.2 Used Metadata of Learning Objects

The concepts in the knowledge model define a *controlled vocabulary* for describing the knowledge of the application domain and can be used for metadata annotation of the learning objects (LOM, category General, data element 1.6 Keywords) (see Fig. 2). The learning objects themselves are solely described and identified by a set of keywords describing their content.

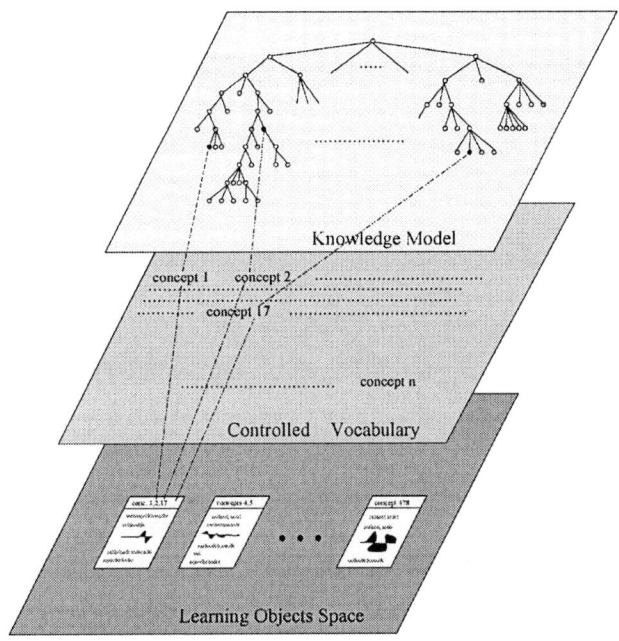

Fig. 2. The role of the Controlled Vocabulary

We have implemented an early prototype of an OAHS which proves the applicability of our approach. This prototype is an adaptive hypermedia system on Java Programming, the *Java Hyperbook* [1]. The Java Hyperbook is an adaptive system which uses course materials from an undergraduate course on Java Programming held at University of Hannover and guides the student through the course by showing next reasonable learning steps, by selecting projects, generating and proposing reading sequences, annotating the educational state of information, and by selecting useful information, based on a user's actual goal and knowledge [11].

The adaptation component of this prototype was based on a separate knowledge model which described the learning dependencies in our Java course. The documents of the hypermedia system were annotated by a short metadata de-

---

[1] http://www.kbs.uni-hannover.de/hyperbook

scription which contained a set of keywords describing the content of each document. To prove the openness of the Java Hyperbook, we added the content of the Sun Java Tutorial [5], a freely available online tutorial, to the Java Hyperbook. The Java Hyperbook was capable to adapt to both corpora [12]. However the coding of learning dependencies in the knowledge model has shown to be a drawback by the simultaneous integration of different corpora: Each collection of learning materials might follow their own learning / teaching strategy and therefor might define different learning dependencies. Our approach was functioning very well for our Java course and the Sun Tutorial but is not generalizable. Thus we claim that for OAHS we need an independent knowledge model like the ontology-based knowledge model proposed above.

4 Prerequisite Estimations and Enhanced Retrieval

In this section we will discuss two applications of the above presented ontology-based knowledge modeling approach for improving the retrieval of learning objects and for making estimations on prerequisites required for learning objects. We therefor need the following definition:

Definition 4 (Content Map). *Let $\mathcal{CV}$ be the set of topics contained in our ontology-based knowledge model (the controlled vocabulary). Let O be some set of learning objects. Then*

$$I : \mathcal{O} \to \mathcal{P}(\mathcal{CV}) \setminus \{\emptyset\}$$

is the content map, which gives for each learning object $\in \mathcal{O}$ the set of keywords of this resource, e.g. the values of the metadata attribute 1.6 General, keywords from LOM ($\mathcal{P}$ is the power set).

4.1 Enhanced Information Retrieval

An ontology defines a context for each of its topics x: topics "nearby" x describe details or more general aspects of x. This observation can be used for enhancing the retrieval of learning objects. Each query for learning objects can be checked in the following way: if all topics of the query are handled in the learning object (which means that they are contained in the learning objects metadata) we are done. Otherwise we rate how "near" the topics covered by this object are to he query by determining the minimal distance from each keyword from the learning object to the set of query terms in the graph of the ontology.

More formally: Let O be some learning object, and $\{q_1, \ldots, q_n\}$ the query set. An x, y *up-down path* in a directed graph G is the edge disjoint union of a continuously directed x, z path and a continuously directed z, y path for some z. The *up-down distance* $d_G(x, y)$ is the minimum number of edges an x, y up-down path may have, and $+\infty$ if there is no such path. d_G is reflexive and symmetric, but, in general, does not satisfy the triangle inequality. For each keyword $k \in I(O)$ we define the following weighting function $w(k)$:

$$w(k) := min\{d_G(k, q_1), \ldots, d_G(k, q_n)\}$$

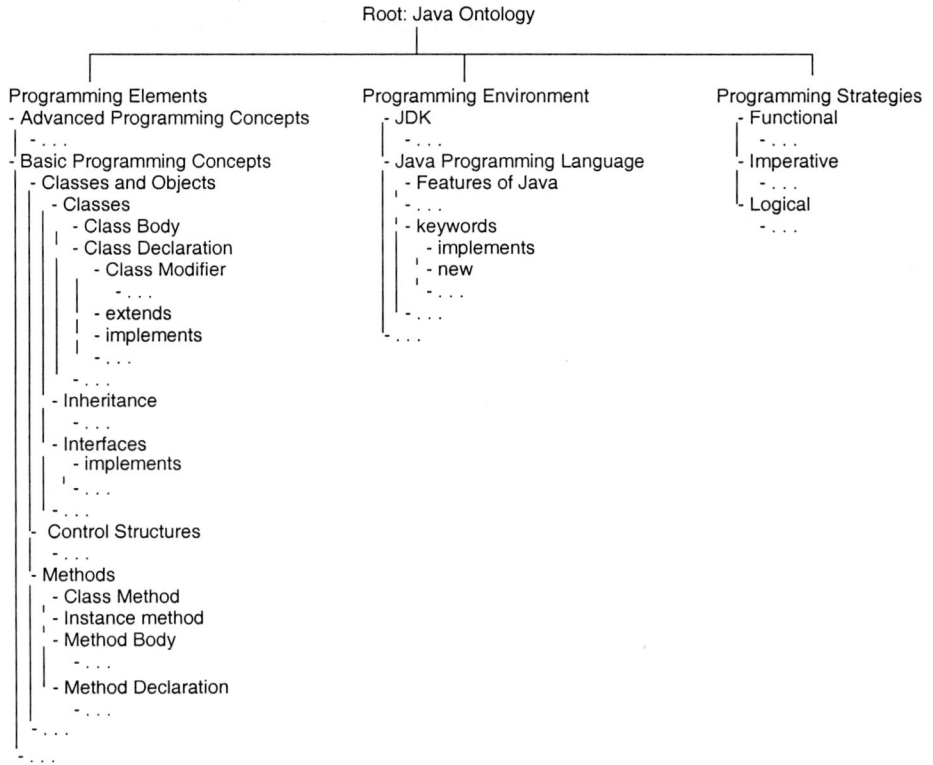

Fig. 3. Part of the ontology for the Java domain knowledge

Example 3. Let q_s be a search query, $q_s = \{\text{"implements"}\}$, and let O_1, O_2 be two learning objects, $I(O_1) = \{\text{"keywords","interfaces","implements"}\}$, and $I(O_2) = \{\text{"class declaration", "class body", "implements"}\}$. Then

$$w(O_1) := \frac{\sum_{k \in I(O_1)} w(k)}{|I(O_1)|}$$
$$= w(\text{"keywords"}) + w(\text{"interfaces"}) + w(\text{"implements"})$$
$$= \frac{1+1+0}{3} = 0,\bar{6}$$

$$w(O_2) := \frac{\sum_{k \in I(O_2)} w(k)}{|I(O_2)|}$$
$$= w(\text{"class declaration"}) + w(\text{"method declaration"}) +$$
$$w(\text{"implements"})$$
$$= \frac{1+5+0}{3} = 2$$

As $w(O_1) < w(O_2)$ we expect that object O_1 will fit better to the users information need than O_2. In a normal keyword-based query we can not further distinguish between O_1 and O_2.

4.2 Knowledge Estimation Based on Reading Sequences

We claim that structured materials deliver useful information with great potential for adaptation. Here we will consider the structure "reading sequences" which is a predefined sequence of learning objects defined by some author.

A reading sequence links together some closed set of learning objects. For each element in the sequence we calculate the knowledge that a (hypothetic) user has gained before starting with this element:

Let $O_1, \ldots, O_n$ be a sequence of learning objects in some corpus C and $\mathcal{CV}$ be the set of topics contained in our ontology-based knowledge model. $\forall i \in \{1, \ldots, n\}$: Mark all topics $k \in \mathcal{CV}$ with: $\exists j, j < i$, and $k \in I(O_j)$ as "read" (marking all topics contained on the previous steps of the sequence). Whenever we want to retrieve a learning object out of some sequence we compare the required knowledge (as calculated above) with the user's actual knowledge state (as proposed in Sect. 3.1). This allows the estimation whether the user lacks some knowledge to successfully work with this learning object, whether the user has the required prerequisite knowledge to work with this object or whether the user has already learned the content of the learning object. This enables the adaptive presentation of learning objects covering prerequisite knowledge, or the presentation of hints indicating that the content of some learning object is assumed to be known to the user.

In case that we have one or more reading sequences which cover *all* documents of a corpus, we can make the following knowledge estimation: Let again $O_1, \ldots, O_n$ be a sequence of learning objects in some corpus C and $\mathcal{CV}$ be the set of topics contained in our ontology-based knowledge model. Then $\forall i \in \{1, \ldots, n\}$:

1. Mark all topics $q \in \mathcal{CV}$ with: $\exists j, j < i$, and $q \in I(O_j)$ as "read" (marking all topics contained on the previous steps of the sequence)
2. Mark all topics $q \in \mathcal{CV}$ with $\exists j, j \leq n$, and $q \in I(O_j)$ as "contained" (marking all topics contained in the overall sequence).
3. $\forall k \in \mathcal{CV}$: Estimate the knowledge of a (hypothetic) user who has followed the sequence by

$$\text{knowledge}(k) = \frac{\#\text{ "read" topics in the subgraph of k}}{\#\text{ "contained" topics in the k-subgraph}}$$

Here the k-subgraph is the subgraph of the ontology containing the node "k" and all its children.

The above stated calculations are statical and user independent and allow us to estimate the knowledge which is required to successfully learn each learning object of the sequence. This necessary prerequisite knowledge can then be compared to a user's actual knowledge state.

5 Conclusion and Current Work

In this paper we discussed the use of ontologies for user and knowledge modeling in open adaptive hypermedia systems (OAHS). Our approach settles on extracting as much information as possible from standard metadata descriptions like SCORM as resources for adaptation in OAHS. This avoids to burden the authors of learning objects with too extensive descriptions of the objects. In addition we expect these standard metadata to be widely used for describing learning objects. Exemplary we described improved retrieval of learning objects in open learning repositories and the derivation of learning dependencies by investigating reading sequences. Current work concentrates on setting up an interface to the EDUTELLA framework to provide personalized access to learning objects.

References

1. Lom: Draft Standard for Learning Object Metadata. http://www.imsglobal.org/.
2. K. M. Anderson and S. A. Sherba. Using open hypermedia to support information integration. In *Proceedings of OHS7 - the 7th International Workshop on Open Hypermedia Systems, held in conjunction with Hypertext 2001, Danmark*, 2001.
3. Ariadne: Alliance of remote instructional authoring and distributions networks for europe, 2001. http://ariadne.unil.ch/.
4. P. Brusilovsky. Methods and techniques of adaptive hypermedia. *User Modeling and User Adapted Interaction*, 6(2-3):87–129, 1996.
5. M. Campione and K. Walrath. *The Java Tutorial*. Addision-Wesley. http://java.sun.com/docs/books/tutorial/.
6. L. Carr, S. Bechhofer, C. Goble, and W. Hall. Conceptual linking: Ontology-based open hypermedia. In *Proceedings of the Tenth International World Wide Web Conference*, Hongkong, May 2001.
7. Draft Standard for Learning Object Metadata. http://ltsc.ieee.org/wg12/doc.html.
8. Edutella, 2001. http://edutella.jxta.org/.
9. K. Grønbæk and R. H. Trigg. *From Web to Workplace: Designing Open Hypermedia Systems*. The MIT Press, 1999.
10. T. R. Gruber. A translation approach to portable ontology specifications. *Knowledge Acquisition*, 5:199–220, 1993.
11. N. Henze and W. Nejdl. Extendible adaptive hypermedia courseware: Integrating different courses and web material. In *Proccedings of the International Conference on Adaptive Hypermedia and Adaptive Web-Based Systems (AH 2000)*, Trento, Italy, 2000.
12. N. Henze and W. Nejdl. Adaptation in open corpus hypermedia. *IJAIED Special Issue on Adaptive and Intelligent Web-Based Systems*, 12, 2001.
13. J. Park, J. Gennari, and M. Musen. Mapping for reuse in knowledge-based systems. In *Eleventh Workshop on Knowledge Acquisition, Modeling and Management*, 1998. http://ksi.cpsc.ucalgary.ca/KAW/KAW98/KAW98Proc.html.
14. R. Rada. *Interactive Media*. Springer, 1995.
15. Scorm: The sharable content object reference model, 2001. http://www.adlnet.org/Scorm/scorm.cfm.

Adaptive Navigation for Learners in Hypermedia Is Scaffolded Navigation

Roland Hübscher[1] and Sadhana Puntambekar[2]

[1] Department of Computer Science and Software Engineering, Auburn University,
107 Dunstan Hall, Auburn, AL 36849-5347, U.S.A.,
roland@eng.auburn.edu,
http://iis.cse.eng.auburn.edu/~roland/
[2] School of Education, Program in Instructional Media and Technology, University of Connecticut, U-64, 249 Glenbrook Ave., Storrs, CT 06269-2004, U.S.A.,
sadhana@uconnvm.uconn.edu,
http://www.sp.uconn.edu/~sadhana/

Abstract. Adaptive navigation support can be of great help in large hypermedia systems supporting learners as well as users searching for specific information. A wide variety of adaptive mechanisms have been implemented in existing adaptive hypermedia systems that provide better and better suggestions to the user what hyperlinks to follow. We suggest that adaptive navigation support should *scaffold* a learner in an educational hypermedia system to select the appropriate links. We show that this implies that selecting a link is an educationally relevant activity that should not always be reduced to a trivial task by powerful adaptive mechanisms. It follows that learners require sometimes different kinds of adaptive navigation support than users looking for information. Finally, we will suggest how to extend current mechanisms to provide scaffolded navigation support to learners.

1 Introduction

With the advent of the World-Wide Web, hypermedia systems have become a widely used and dominating way of providing information and educational content to users. Hypermedia has been recognized as having great potential in providing content to learners because relationships between concepts can be made explicit with hyperlinks, and the same material can be organized along different dimensions presenting the material to be learned from different views [1]. The non-linear nature of hypertext environments offers opportunities as well as certain difficulties for learning, thus making the design of such systems both complex and challenging. The flexible nature of hypertext makes it necessary for designers to provide learners with some kind of navigational support. Researchers believe that learning from hypertext puts a greater cognitive load on learners [2]. Readers have to acquire specific strategies such as knowing where they are, deciding where to go next and building a cognitive representation of the network structure, in order to cope with the specific constraints of a non-linear presentation. Hyperlinks allow each individual learner to traverse and explore the content in a way that fits his or her interests and learning goals at any particular time. In a hypertext system, the reader is actively engaged in creating both meaning and structure.

The reader constantly makes decisions about where to go next. However, this added flexibility, compared to books which are often read in a more or less linear fashion, can also cause problems seriously impacting the pedagogical benefits of a hypermedia system. It is quite easy for the learner to lose orientation and therefore not knowing how the current page fits into the big picture and what hyperlinked path to follow.

Adaptive hypermedia attempts to solve these problems by individualizing the presentation of the content for each user and by providing personalized navigation support. The goal of both approaches, personalized presentation and navigation, is to reduce the cognitive load for the user. Learners with different goals and knowledge may be interested in different information or prefer examples from different domains. They also may want navigate along different paths depending on their goals and prior knowledge. This is especially important in educational systems to make sure the learner sees those content relevant to his or her learning goals. Furthermore, adaptive navigation can help prevent users from getting lost in large systems.

Adaptive hypermedia systems (AHS) approach these problems with adaptive presentation of the information and adaptive navigation. Adaptive presentation mechanisms decide how the information is delivered most appropriately to the user considering factors like user expertise, media preferences, learning goals, interests, and so forth stored in a user model [3]. The user model is learned by the AHS over time using various information sources like questionnaires, quizzes, navigation behavior of the user, and others. The basic idea of adaptive navigation is to constrain the options of where to go next to a smaller set of relevant choices making sure the user will end up at a hypermedia page that is appropriate to his or her task.

Examples of navigation support are the "next" or "continue" links which are, according to the AHS, the best and possibly only choice [4], sorted lists of links where earlier links are better choices [5], annotated links reflecting some important status like 'the user is ready to follow it or not' or 'it leads to redundant or irrelevant material' [6], or link hiding where only those links are made accessible that the system considers relevant to the user [7].

Each of these mechanisms is based on a user model which is a description of the user's preferences, knowledge, skills, characteristics, learning goals, etc. and a pedagogical model that suggests what the user should visit under what circumstances [8]. Too often, the pedagogical model is rather implicit and built into the adaptive algorithm [9]. Much of the current research focusses on providing better user models and better algorithms for providing appropriate navigation support by ordering the content according to some scheme.

In this paper, we would like to revisit the assumption that the better suggestions we can give to the user, the better the system serves its purpose. Of course, on the one hand, it is obvious that the better the adaptive mechanisms are, the better the system is. On the other hand, it is not obvious that more accurate advice is indeed better for a user—or, more specifically, a learner—under all circumstances.

This paper is not about what can and cannot be done. It is about how adaptive navigation should be designed for specific users, especially for learners. We do not need to propose new mechanisms—many good ones already exist. However, we want to make explicit that efficiently getting to the right page should often not be the overriding goal of adaptive navigation support for learners.

Consider the following hypothetical AHS. Let's assume that the user model and adaptive mechanisms are so good that the system can almost always provide exactly one link to the page that is best for the user to visit next. In an information-seeking task, this is of course great because the user will find immediately what he was looking for, possibly without ever thinking about what he was looking for at all. But is this also a good system for a learner? We will come back to this question at the end of this paper.

2 Adaptive Navigation

Throughout this paper, we will consider two types of tasks—learning and information seeking–that cover a large class of activities AHS are used for. A learner who uses an AHS to learn about a certain concept executes a learning task. It is the system's goal to make sure that the learner will understand well enough the concept and all the necessary prerequisite concepts. On the other hand, if the user is only interested in finding the relevant information, then we consider the task to be supported by the AHS an information-seeking task. Many systems support both types of tasks, however, it is not necessarily the case that both types of tasks should get the same adaptive navigation support.

Next, we will review existing adaptive hypermedia mechanisms. Then we will discuss what navigation support information-seeking and learning tasks require. We will argue that the objectively best suggestions the adaptive mechanism can provide are not necessarily the ones from which learners benefit the most.

2.1 Adaptive Mechanisms

Adaptive navigation deals with the problem of the user having to select a link among the many possibilities. Often, there are too many possibilities and it is very difficult for the user to choose an appropriate link. Adaptive navigation reduces the number of choices using various mechanims. Some of the most frequently used ones are link ordering, link hiding, link annotation and the use of the "next" link [10]. All these mechanisms constrain how and from how many links the user can choose to go to the next page in the hypermedia system.

The most restrictive mechanism is the "next" or "continue" link that the AHS recommends as leading to the most relevant next page. This allows the user to turn to the next page as easily as in a book, i.e., there is no need to think about where to go next. If this were the only link provided, the hypermedia system would be reduced to an individual, though completely linear structure, indeed even more linear than a textbook. However, in combination with other mechanisms, as for instance in InterBook [11], the "next" link can be useful.

The previous idea can be somewhat relaxed and instead of suggesting just one link, an ordered list of links can be provided where the first link is the most relevant for the user, according to the system, and the last one the least relevant. This approach provides some choice to the user, but in return, requires him or her to make a conscious decision which link to choose. However, Guzdial found evidence in WebCAMILE, a web-based collaboration system, that users tend to choose the first item in a list simply because it is the first item in the list [12]. In this case, and no real decision has to be made. Thus, the sorted list may not be that qualitatively different to "next" link approach.

Another widely used approach is link hiding where links that should not be followed are simply hidden, e.g., on a WWW page by presenting the link text as simple text [13]. This approach has the advantage that it does not impose an external ordering on the links, yet the binary approach—a link is either hidden or visible—does not allow for great expressiveness. Therefore, this approach was extended resulting in annotated links, another way to support learners.

Annotated links are hyperlinks that are further tagged with some information that can be taken advantage of by the user to decide whether to follow it or not. For instance, the tag can provide further information about the difficulty of or relevance of the information on the page the link leads to [6]. This allows the user to make a more informed decision about which link to follow and it does require less trial-and-error behavior.

All these adaptive mechanisms constrain the number of choices for the learner. The less choice, the easier the decision will be for the user. The annotated-link approach, however, does not just reduce the set of choices but provides further information to the user supporting the decision making process to choose a good next hypermedia page, i.e., a page relevant to the current goals.

2.2 Navigation Support for Information Seekers and Learners

Now, which one of those mechanisms is the best? This question needs to be answered from two directions. First, empirical evidence needs to be collected and second, the tasks the adaptive navigation is supposed to support need to be analyzed to understand what kind of support they require. This paper focuses on the latter of the two issues where we look at the tasks of learning and of finding information.

An information seeker is a person who is interested in quickly and easily finding relevant information. Adaptive hypermedia can be extremely helpful if the user model is accurate. In this case it can make sure that the user is never confronted with irrelevant information and thus, the search space that the user has to explore to find the information can be made quite small. The more accurate the user model, the more powerful the adaptive algorithms and the more constraining the mechanisms, the better the system will support the user. This is consistent with many AHS's approaches.

The case where the user is a learner is more complicated, but extremely important because many AHS target learners. Of course, many educational systems must also support information-seeking tasks. A learner not only needs to understand concepts and principles but also has to place the new knowledge in context, often requiring prerequisites that will enable her to understand the current concepts. This definition can be extended such that it is not necessarily the user's goal to learn but whoever made the learner use the hypermedia system.

Supporting a learning task requires the learner to focus much more on the process of acquiring the necessary knowledge and skills than just on finding a certain location in the hypermedia system. The learning task, especially the examples and practice exercises, should be as authentic as possible, i.e., relevant to the learner's interests. In addition to the concept to be learned, the learner also needs to be provided with all the prerequisite knowledge that she has not learned yet. Furthermore, the order in which these different concepts, examples and exercises are visited is dependent on the employed teaching methodology, which in turn may be dependent on the learner's history and the material to be learned. Although the learning process should not be dragged out forever, minimization of time is not as important as when looking for information. Furthermore, the learner needs to be challenged, yet nor frustrated by the difficulty of the material. Of course, this will cause some decent cognitive load for the learner without which learning could not occur. This does not imply that AHS need to be designed to make them difficult to use. However, the learner must be encouraged to make non-trivial decisions and reflect, for instance on what he or she is learning, how this ties into previous knowledge, and why it is useful for accomplishing the actual learning goal. In other words, adaptive navigation for learners should be viewed as scaffolded navigation.

2.3 Scaffolded Navigation

Scaffolding in the context of learning has originally been defined by as an "adult controlling those elements of the task that are essentially beyond the learner's capacity, thus permitting him to concentrate upon and complete only those elements that are within his range of competence" [14]. Scaffolding has been linked to the work of soviet psychologist Lev Vygotsky, although he never used the term scaffolding. According to Vygotsky, a novice learns with an expert, and learning occurs within the novice's Zone of Proximal Development (ZPD). ZPD is defined as the "distance between the child's actual developmental level as determined by independent problem solving and the higher level of potential development as determined through problem solving under adult guidance and in collaboration with more capable peers" [15]. Enabling the learner to bridge this gap between the actual and the potential depends on the resources or the kind of support that is provided. Instruction in the ZPD can therefore be viewed as taking the form of providing assistance or scaffolding, enabling a child or a novice to solve a problem, carry out a task or achieve a goal "which would be beyond his unassisted efforts" [14].

Adaptive navigation can be viewed as a method to provide scaffolding to a learner navigating through a large hypermedia system. Scaffolding in this context then implies the following among other things [16, 17].

- The learner must be aware of and interested in the goal of the learning activity.
- Continuous assessment of the learner needs to be used to calibrate the support.
- Scaffolding fades away over time and the learner must take control of the task.
- The learner needs to be actively involved in the learning process.

We will now discuss each of these characteristics with respect to adaptive navigation support in adaptive hypermedia systems.

The learner must be aware of and interested in the goal of the learning activity. The learner needs to have a choice of selecting links that deal with more authentic problems. For instance, it is important that the user selects the example that he or she is more familiar with, if there is more than one example illustrating the same point. An AHS can accomplish this by providing all the examples illustrating the same point and the user can choose, or, if the user model contains information about the preferences, it can simply provide the one example it knows the learner is interested in. The latter solution is more efficient whereas the former requires and allows the learner to make a decision. It is important that the learner has to make a decision if there is a potential educational benefit in doing so.

Continuous assessment of the learner needs to be used to calibrate the support. The difficulty of the decision which link to select needs to be adapted to the learner so that it is in the ZPD. In other words, providing a set of possibly annotated links needs to be viewed as posing a problem to the learner that the learner should be able to solve, yet it must not be too simple to be pointless activity. This implies that making it as simple to the learner as possible to select a correct next page should not be the goal. It is important for a learner to figure out what knowledge, information sources, case studies, etc. are relevant. For instance, in Problem-Based Learning, finding out what the relevant knowledge to learn is, is at the heart of this learning methodology [18, 19].

Scaffolding fades away over time and the learner must take control of the task. A very important part of scaffolding is that it fades away as the learner learns to select the proper next page. A user model that takes the learner's behavior into account can take care of this part automatically. Since the basic idea of adaptive navigation is to constrain the learner's options, it implies that the constraints need to be relaxed as the learner gains more expertise. Of course, these constraints must not be relaxed to violate usability guidelines.

The learner needs to be actively involved in the learning process. This implies that the learner should not be spoon-fed with the correct choices, but should be actively involved in the decision process of where to go next. This adds yet another strong argument against over-constraining the choices for the user. The learner should not just passively follow the lead of the system but should make the decisions, or should at least, over time assume control.

Several important observations can be made. First, fading scaffolding maps quite well to the adaptive nature of AHS. Second, selecting a link should be regarded as a problem to be solved if the decision is educationally relevant. And third, reducing the difficulty of selecting the right link as much as possible is not always the right thing to do. Actually, it is important that the learner is allowed to make mistakes for two reasons: it provides him- or herself some valuable feedback and the AHS can use it to improve the user model based on the learner's apparent misconception.

The central observation is that selecting a link is sometimes an educationally relevant task that needs to be scaffolded. Therefore, making it as easy as possible is not adequate in such a situation. Selecting the link needs to require the learner to reflect upon what is important to learn or read about next. How will this information at the other end of the hyperlink help with respect to the learning goals? We therefore suggest that the link-selection task needs to be put into a context that supports the learner to make the right decision.

We suggest that the context consists of prompts and questions that are adaptively selected together with the set of links. Assume, the learner is working on a problem where she has to figure out when an object hits the ground when dropped from a certain height. Now, should we provide just links related to velocity and acceleration or also links to mass? An AHS will recommend against going to the pages about mass as they are irrelevant for this problem. However, we provide both sets of links plus the contextual prompt "Does a heavy item fall faster than a light one?". Of course, the question needs to be phrased so that the learner can answer it, i.e., it must be at the right level with respect to the ZPD.

3 Conclusions

We have made the argument that adaptive navigation for learners in hypermedia is scaffolded navigation. We have provided a largely theoretical argument whose implications are backed up by the empirically well-established educational value of scaffolding [20, 21].

Adaptive hypermedia systems use adaptive navigation mechanisms to support the users to find their way around in large hypermedia systems. They make sure that the users find the relevant information and that learners are exposed to all the relevant concepts to understand a certain goal concept. However, it is important to keep in mind that a learner is not just interested in efficiently getting to the page describing the goal concept. The learner needs work hard to understand all the prerequisite knowledge and learn these concepts in some pedagogically appropriate order. Reducing the information seeker's cognitive load is great, however, doing the same for the learner is not always beneficial to him or her. This implies that the use of too much navigation support can be detrimental to the learner because it frees him or her up from thinking [22].

We therefore recommend that adaptive navigation support be separated into two categories. The first category deals with navigation simply to get to a certain location in the system as quickly and easily as possible, i.e., this is navigation for navigation's sake. The second category deals with educationally related decision problems where the learner needs to decide what information source, what concept, what method, and so on, would be more relevant for the current task at hand. In this case, the learner needs to be scaffolded so that he or she learns to make the right decisions, i.e., chooses the relevant information sources, tools, etc. We accomplish this annotating the adaptively selected links with appropriate prompts and questions scaffolding the learner to make a good choice.

Let's revisit the hypothetical system suggested earlier. We assumed that the user model and adaptive mechanisms are so good that the system can almost always provide exactly one link to the page that is best for the user to visit next. This is potentially a great system for an information seeker. However, if the system is supposed to support learners, then this hypothetical system boils down to an individualized book that requires to be read in exactly one order. This way we lose most of the educational advantages of hypermedia. Furthermore, the learner is not required at all to reflect on why she is reading what she is reading, she has no opportunity to make mistakes and recognize them as useful feedback. In other words, a system that is optimal in some "adaptive sense" is surely not that useful for a learner anymore.

References

[1] Rand J. Spiro, Paul J. Feltovich, Michael J. Jacobson, and Richard L. Coulson. Cognitive flexibility, constructivism, and hypertext: Random access instruction for advanced knowledge acquisition in ill-structured domains. *Educational Technology*, May:24–33, 1991.

[2] P. Wright. Cognitive overheads and prostheses: Some issues in evaluating hypertexts. In R. Furuta and D. Slotts, editors, *ACM Conference on Hypertext*, pages 1–12. ACM Press, 1991.

[3] Peter Brusilovsky. Adaptive educational systems on the World-Wide-Web: A review of available technologies. In *4th International Conference in Intelligent Tutoring Systems*, San Antonio, TX, 1998.

[4] Elmar Schwartz, Peter Brusilovsky, and Gerhard Weber. World-wide intelligent textbooks. In *ED-TELECOM'96 - World Conference on Educational Telecommunications*, pages 302–307, 1996.

[5] Peter Brusilovsky, Elmar Schwarz, and Gerhard Weber. Elm-art: An intelligent tutoring system on World Wide Web. In C. Frasson, G. Gauthier, and A. Lesgold, editors, *Intelligent Tutoring Systems (Lecture Notes in Computer Science)*, volume 1086, pages 261–269. Springer Verlag, Berlin, 1996.

[6] Gerhard Weber and Markus Specht. User modeling and adaptive navigation support in WWW-based totoring systems. In A. Jameson, C. Paris, and C. Tasso, editors, *User Modeling: Proceedings of the Sixth International Conference (UM97)*, pages 289–300, Cagliari, Italy, 1997. Springer Verlag.

[7] Paul De Bra. Design issues in adaptive web-site development. In *2nd Workshop on Adaptive Systems and User Modeling on the WWW*, pages 29–39, Banff, 1999.
[8] Paul De Bra, Geert-Jan Houben, and Hongjing Wu. AHAM: a dexter-based reference model for adaptive hypermedia. In *Proceedings of the 10th ACM Conference on Hypertext and Hypermedia*, pages 147–156, 1999.
[9] Roland Hübscher. What's in a prerequisite. In *International Conference on Advanced Learning Technology (ICALT 2001)*, Madison, 2001.
[10] Peter Brusilovsky. Efficient techniques for adaptive hypermedia. In C. Nicholas and J Mayfield, editors, *Intelligent hypertext: Advanced techniques for the World Wide Web*, volume 1326 of *Lecture Notes in Computer Science*, pages 12–30. Springer Verlag, Berlin, 1997.
[11] Peter Brusilovsky, Elmar Schwartz, and Gerhard Weber. A tool for developing adaptive electronic textbooks on www. In *WebNet-96*, San Francisco, 1996.
[12] Mark Guzdial, Cindy E. Hmelo, Roland Hübscher, Kris Nagel, Wendy C. Newstetter, Sadhana Puntambekar, Amnon Shabo, Jennifer Turns, and Janet L. Kolodner. Integrating and guiding collaborations: Lessons learned in computer-supported collaborative learning research at Georgia Tech. In *Computer Support for Collaborative Learning*, Toronto, 1997.
[13] Paul De Bra and L. Calvi. AHA! An open adaptive hypermedia architecture. *The New Review of Hypermedia and Multimedia*, 4:115–139, 1998.
[14] D. Wood, J. Bruner, and G. Ross. The role of tutoring in problem solving. *Journal of child psychology and psychiatry*, 17:89–100, 1976.
[15] L. S. Vygotsky. *Mind in Society*. Harvard University Press, Cambridge, 1978.
[16] A. S. Palincsar. Keeping the metaphor of scaffolding fresh - a response to C. Addison Stone's "the metaphor of scaffolding: Its utility for the field of learning disabilities". *Journal of Learning Disabilities*, 31(4):370–373, 1998.
[17] C. A. Stone. The metaphor of scaffolding: Its utility for the field of learning disabilities. *Journal of Learning Disabilities*, 31(4):344–364, 1998.
[18] Howard S. Barrows. *How to Design a Problem Based Curriculum for the Preclinical Years*. Springer Verlag, New York, NY, 1985.
[19] Roland Hübscher, Cindy E. Hmelo, N. Hari Narayanan, Mark Guzdial, and Janet L. Kolodner. Mcbagel: A shared and structured electronic workspace for problem-based learning. In *Second International Conference on the Learning Sciences*, Evanston, IL, 1996.
[20] A. L. Brown and A. S. Palincsar. Reciprocal teaching of comprehension strategies: A natural history of one program for enhancing learning. In J. D. Day and J. G. Borkowski, editors, *Intelligence and Exceptionality: New directions for theory, assessment, and instructional practice*. Ablex, Norwood, NJ, 1987.
[21] A. S. Palincsar and A. L. Brown. Reciprocal teaching of comprehension-fostering and monitoring activities. *Cognitition and Instruction*, 1(2):117–175, 1984.
[22] Roland Hübscher and Sadhana Puntambekar. Navigation support for learners in hypertext systems: Is more indeed better? In Johanna D. Moore, Carol Luckhardt Redfield, and W. Lewis Johnson, editors, *Artificial Intelligence in Education: AI-ED in the Wired and Wireless Future*, pages 13–20. IOS Press, 2001.

Pros and Cons of Controllability: An Empirical Study

Anthony Jameson[1] and Eric Schwarzkopf[2,*]

[1] DFKI / International University in Germany
[2] DFKI, the German Research Center for Artificial Intelligence

Abstract. A key usability issue with systems that adapt to their users is *controllability*: the ability of the user to determine the nature and timing of the adaptation. This paper presents an empirical study of the trade-offs involved in an attempt to ensure a suitable degree of controllability. Within an adaptive hotlist for a conference web site, two mechanisms for providing users with recommendations of conference events were compared: *automatic* vs. *controlled updating* of recommendations. In an experimental setting, each of 18 users worked with both variants of the adaptive hotlist, as well as with a nonadaptive variant. The users differed markedly in their responses to automatic vs. controlled updating. A number of reasons for these differences could be found in the objective and subjective data yielded by the study. The study illustrates how preferences for different forms of user control can be influenced by factors ranging from stable individual differences to unpredictable features of a situation. General implications for the design of controllable adaptive systems are discussed.

1 Is Maximal Controllability Always Best?

One of the main usability issues in connection with systems that adapt to their users concerns *controllability*. For example, Norman [5] wrote in an influential article: "An important psychological aspect of people's comfort with their activities—all of their activities, from social relations, to jobs, to their interaction with technology—is the feeling of control they have over these activities and their personal lives" (p. 69). The relationships between controllability and other usability issues with user-adaptive systems have been discussed by Wexelblat and Maes [8] and by Jameson [3, section 4].

One plausible policy for designers of user-adaptive systems is to give users maximal control over all aspects of system adaptation. For example, Kay [4] discusses many ways in which learners can be given control over learner-adapted teaching systems. But as Kay also points out (p. 121), simply maximizing control in all respects may not always be the best policy: Some users may have generally less desire for control than others; and making the user exercise too much control may lead to distraction and time-wasting.

Similarly, Trewin [7] discusses the controllability trade-offs involved with agents that help users to configure aspects of an operating system or an input device such as a keyboard. For example, a physically impaired user may not be able to operate a keyboard even well enough to initiate and control the configuration process; so fully

---

[*] The research described here is being supported by the German Ministry of Education and Research (BMB+F) under grant 01 IW 001 (project MIAU). Björn Mittelsdorf and Marie Norlien made essential contributions to the empirical study.

				Recommendations for Hotlist: *Update*		
Sun 14:10–14:30	DC	Patrick Gebhard	Enhancing Embodied Intelligent Agents With Affective User Modelling	*View Session*	*Remove*
Mon 11:00–11:30	Paper	Neal Lesh, Charles Rich, Candace L. Sidner	Collaborating with Focused and Unfocused Users Under Imperfect Communication	*View Session*	*Accept* or *Reject*
Mon 13:30–15:30	Poster	Piotr J. Gmytrasiewicz, Christine L. Lisetti	Emotions and Personality in Agent Design and Modelling	*View Session*	*Remove*
Mon 13:30–15:30	Poster	Detlef Küpper, Alfred Kobsa	User-Tailored Plan Presentation	*View Session*	*Accept* or *Reject*

Fig. 1. Example hotlist from the UM 2001 web site.
(The first and third entries were added by the user; the second and fourth, shown in the system in a red font, are recommendations made by the system. Italicized words represent hyperlinks, referred to in this article as "buttons".)

autonomous system adaptation may actually give the user more control overall than if she were required to control the configuration process.

Although there has been much discussion among researchers about controllability, some of it quite heated, there is a dearth of systematically gathered evidence about what users themselves think about these issues. The present study aims to provide such evidence within the context of one particular adaptive hypermedia system. Section 2 introduces the system, Sect. 3 describes our empirical study, and Sect. 4 presents and discusses the results.

2 The Hotlist and Its Recommendation Component

The Eighth International Conference on User Modeling, UM 2001, held in July of 2001, was the latest in a biennial series of conferences concerning user-adaptive systems (see [1]). It offered the following *conference events*: 3 invited talks, 3 tutorials, 19 full paper presentations, 21 poster presentations, and 12 doctoral consortium presentations. The conference web site (http://dfki.de/um2001) introduced a variety of adaptive features, of which only the *hotlist* will be examined in the present study. The hotlist (see Fig. 1) is basically a specialized bookmarking tool that helps a potential attendee put together a list of personally relevant conference events. Once the user has explicitly added some events to the hotlist, the system can insert a set of *recommendations*—essentially, a set of similar events that this user might be interested in.

The recommendations are computed with a naive Bayes classifier (see, e.g., [6]), using as features a set of 22 domain-specific key concepts such as *Machine Learning*. If the user clicks on the *View Session* button for a recommended event to see its full description, she will also see a simple "explanation" of the recommendation in terms of the system's estimates of the user's interest in the individual key concepts associated with the event. Further details concerning the recommendation mechanism must be omitted here for reasons of space; they are not required for an understanding of the results that will be presented below.

After evaluating a recommendation, the user can choose to *Accept* the recommendation, making it into a normal hotlist entry; or to *Reject* it, causing it to disappear from the hotlist.

At various times, the system *updates* the set of recommendations: It removes any recommendations currently in the hotlist and replaces them with a (perhaps overlapping) set that is based on all of the user's relevant actions so far. Different ways of controlling this updating process were compared in our empirical study.

3 Empirical Study: Issues and Method

It would be possible to design a study to determine what type of control was really best for users in the long run. But it is equally interesting to find out how users deal with and respond to each system variant during an initial encounter of just a few minutes. After all, users often briefly try out a system—or an option within a system—and decide on the basis of a small sample of experience whether to continue using it.

Moreover, the goal of the empirical study is not to determine the accuracy or overall utility of the hotlist recommendations. Instead, it is assumed (as will be confirmed) that the recommendations have only modest accuracy, as is the case with many recommender systems, because of the severely limited evidence on which they are based. The question is: How much control do users want to have when dealing with these imperfect recommendations?

Subjects

Subjects were 17 students and 1 recent graduate from Saarland University and the International University in Germany. Only subjects were recruited whose major or minor course of study had some affinity with the topic of user modeling (e.g., computer science, information science, or psychology), so that the experimental task (to be described below) would be motivating and manageable to them; but the large majority had little or no specific knowledge of the field. The number hours per week that subjects reported spending in the world-wide web averaged 12.9, with a standard deviation of 10.8. All subjects were male. They received 15 German marks for their participation.

System Variants Studied

Three variants of the hotlist were used:
- *Controlled updating of recommendations.* This is the variant shown in Fig. 1: The user explicitly requests each update of the recommendations by clicking on the *Update* button at the upper right.
- *Automatic updating of recommendations.* In this variant there is no *Update* button; the system updates the recommendations automatically whenever the user adds or removes a hotlist event or accepts or rejects a recommendation.
- *No recommendations*: In this variant, the user can use only the basic hotlist, adding or removing events but receiving no recommendations.

In a within-subject design, each subject used all three variants of the hotlist, the order of use being counterbalanced as is described below. This type of design was chosen over a between-subject design because of (a) our expectation (confirmed during the study) that individual differences would be very large; and (b) our desire to hear the comparative

Instructions (paraphrase):

You are working as a research assistant at the nearby research institute [name given]. A number of more senior researchers at this institute are considering attending the UM 2001 conference, which will take place 3 months from now.

To spare these researchers the time of familiarizing themselves with the conference site and program, the director has asked each of them to send you an email message in which they characterize the topics that they are interested in.

For each such message, your job is to build up a list of relevant conference events, which you will email back to the researcher in question. On the basis of this list, the researcher will decide whether he or she considers it worthwhile to attend the conference.

Example email message:

From: Anna Reiter <[local email address]>

Subject: What I'd like to see at UM 2001

For me, the most important methodological approach in the area of user modeling is machine learning. Often, methods from this category are applied in web-based systems, or in systems that select specific news stories for individual users. I'm *not* interested in these last two types of application of machine learning.

Anything that deals specifically with the improvement of automobile safety would be especially interesting to me.

Another thing I'm interested in is systems that model some type of psychological state of the user, such as emotions or stress.

Best regards, Anna Reiter

Fig. 2. Paraphrase of the key instructions (left) and one of the three fictitious email messages used as a sketch of an interest profile (right).

comments of subjects who had experienced all three variants. Learning effects could not be avoided with this design. But the counterbalancing measures described below ensured that such learning effects could not lead to overall differences in the results for the three variants; and we will also see that the observed differences among subjects are not explainable in terms of learning effects.

Each subject spent only a limited amount of time with each variant: about 4 minutes of introduction plus 7 minutes of measured use. A serious conference visitor might spend considerably more time constructing a personal conference schedule. On the other hand, the shorter amount of time seems typical of the time that a user might spend trying out the hotlist recommendations before deciding whether to continue using them to create a complete schedule.

Material

The experimental task assigned to the subjects was designed to overcome two obstacles:
  1. Subjects have considerably less familiarity with the topic of the conference than a potential conference visitor would typically have.
  2. Because of the within-subject design, each subject has to search the conference site with respect to three different configurations of interest.

The left-hand side of Fig. 2 summarizes the way in which the experimental task was introduced to each subject; the right-hand side of the figure shows one of the three fictitious email messages employed. Each of the three messages had a similar style and structure, and it described interests for which it was approximately equally easy to find relevant conference events. The interests expressed were in part strongly related to the hotlist recommender concepts, but for the most part subjects had to look at the detailed information about an event in order to decide whether it was really relevant. This situation appears to be typical of the way in which real potential conference visitors use the hotlist.

Orders of Presentation

Each of the 6 possible orders of the 3 system variants was employed equally often (i.e., for 3 of the 18 subjects). Each of the 3 fictitious interest profiles was used equally often in the 1st, 2nd, and 3rd temporal position and equally often together with each system variant.

Procedure

Each subject participated individually with the guidance of an experimenter. In an introductory phase that lasted between 20 and 25 minutes, the experimenter explained that the investigators had developed various methods for searching for information in a conference web site and that they were interested in evaluating and improving them with a view to possible use in other sites. The experimenter then summarized some basic ideas of the field of user modeling and explained the fictitious situation. Using an example email, the experimenter gave an explanation of the web site and the hotlist, frequently stopping to allow the subject to try out the system's functions.

In each of the three main trials, the subject first read one of the emails from a hypothetical colleague and then was allowed 7 minutes to build up a hotlist for that colleague, starting with the system initialized for a new user (with an empty hotlist). In the system's log files, a record was kept of all pages visited and all actions taken in relation to the hotlist. The experimenter took notes on other observable aspects of the subject's behavior. At the end of the 7 minutes, the experimenter saved the hotlist to disk in its printable form.

After the three main trials, the subject typed in answers to a number of questions about his use of the system, some of which are discussed below. Finally, subjects were asked for further comments during a debriefing.

Despite their lack of knowledge about user modeling, subjects reported no major difficulties in understanding the fictitious interest profiles or in evaluating individual events with regard to these profiles.

4 Results

4.1 Quantitative Objective Results

Although the key variable of interest is subjects' subjective evaluation of the two types of updating, some objective results will give us a general picture of the way in which they used the hotlist.

Figure 3 shows that subjects were just about equally (un)successful with all three variants in finding relevant events to add to the hotlist. The rather small overall number of events found is consistent with the limited amount of time that subjects had available to process each interest profile.

Figure 4 shows the differences between the two system variants that included recommendations, in terms of how the system presented recommendations and how users responded to them. It is not surprising that automatic updating led to about 4 times as

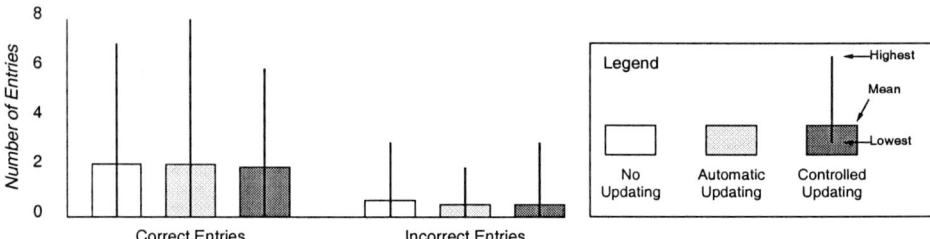

Fig. 3. Mean numbers of correct and incorrect entries in the final hotlists produced by subjects with the three system variants.

(The maximum numbers of correct entries for the three interest profiles were 12, 14, and 18 respectively, but some correct entries were difficult to identify as such. The upper and lower ends of the vertical line segment in the middle of each bar indicate the highest and lowest values, respectively, that were found among the 18 values obtained for the 18 subjects.)

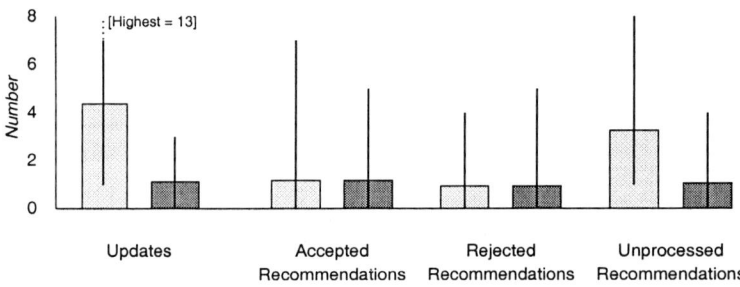

Fig. 4. Objective results concerning the appearance and processing of recommendations with automatic and controlled updating.

(Legend as for Fig. 4.)

many updates of the hotlist, since it involves utilizing just about every opportunity for an update.

Although subjects using controlled updating experienced only 30% as many hotlist updates as those using automatic updating, they received 59% as many recommendations: By the time they had gotten around to requesting an update, it was likely to contain more new recommendations than a typical automatic update.

On the average, subjects accepted and rejected exactly the same number of recommendations using the two variants. The big difference is that with automatic updating, many more recommendations were never responded to explicitly at all (this difference, shown in the right-hand pair of bars in Fig. 4, is highly significant by a Wilcoxon rank-sum test: $Z = -3.03, p < 0.01$). As the logs confirm, in many cases these recommendations were swept away by an automatic update after the subject had made some change to another aspect of the hotlist.

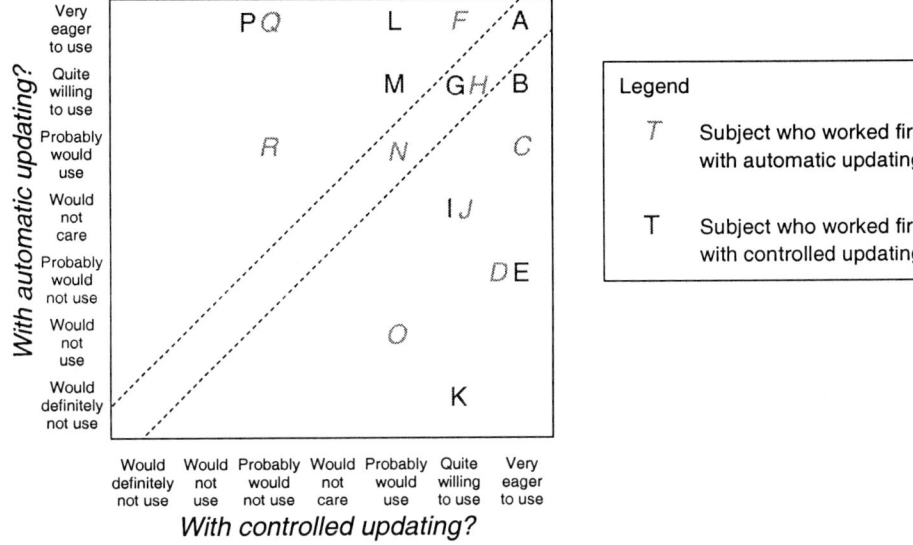

Fig. 5. Scattergram of subjects' expressed preferences for two updating methods.
(Each letter represents the responses of one subject. With respect to each method, the question was: "If you had to perform more searches, what would you prefer to do: use the recommendations (that is, have them displayed, and follow up on at least some of them); or not use the recommendations (that is, turn them off or not request them in the first place)?".)

4.2 Attitudes Toward the System Variants

Figure 5 gives an overview of the subjects' responses to two questions that were designed to reveal (indirectly) their preferences for controlled vs. automatic updating. Given the emphasis in previous literature on the importance of controllability, we might expect to see a statistically significant tendency for subjects to prefer controlled updating. (With a within-subject design involving 18 subjects, a moderately strong tendency could have been detected.) Instead, the most important conclusion to be drawn from Fig. 5 is that users responded in very different ways to the questions. Given a sufficiently large sample of subjects, we could no doubt find a statistically significant preference for one type of adaptation or the other. But it is more important to understand the reasons for the differences in users' responses, using all of the available types of data: their responses to the rating scales in the questionnaire; the verbal comments that they typed into the questionnaire and made during their work or during the debriefing; and the detailed records of the interaction that can be found in the system logs. This type of analysis inevitably involves qualitative interpretation.

Subjects Who Preferred Controlled Updating

Subject K (cf. Fig. 5) is typical of users who have a strong general desire to remain in control of the interaction with a system. He wrote "I am used to updating information manually" and "I hate having the information appear automatically". K's behavior, as it is revealed by the log files, is consistent with his attitude: With controlled updating, he requested 1 update of the recommendations and proceeded to accept or reject each of the 3 recommendations that appeared. With automatic updating, he received 8 recommendations in 4 updates, and he was able to follow up on only 4 of them (1 per update).

Subject A—the most successful subject of all in terms of the number of relevant events found—showed an attitude and a strategy similar to that of K with controlled updating. But unlike K, he was able to follow up on the recommendations equally thoroughly in the automatic updating condition, accepting or rejecting 11 out of the 12 presented—simply because the system happened to present only about 1 new recommendation after each update. Consistent with this result, A expressed an equally strong willingness to work with both system variants. He mentioned two advantages of automatic updating that will be discussed below, and he stated that his true preference would be to switch back and forth at will between the two variants.

Subject O had quite a different reason for preferring controlled updating: On the whole he found the recommendations to be of little value, accepting only 1 of the total of 5 that he received. Accordingly, his attitude toward both of the variants with recommendations was relatively negative (cf. Fig. 5). But he was especially critical of the variant with automatic updating, saying that the burden of having to read the recommendations may be even greater than that of reading through the detailed event descriptions. Note that a reasonable strategy is for the user to start paying attention to the recommendations only when the user has reason to believe that the system's model has achieved a reasonable level of accuracy. In both system variants, the user can indeed always decide whether to follow up on the recommendations; but with automatic updating, the user pays a price for the recommendations even when he or she is ignoring them, in terms of screen clutter and longer system response times.

Subjects Who Preferred Automatic Updating

The clearest preference for automatic updating was shown by subject P (see Fig. 5). He volunteered the comment that "If you are not accustomed to press the update button periodically or after a decision you just made, you'll miss topics."

Similarly, Subject L commented spontaneously on two advantages of automatic updating: First, he found it "too time-consuming to press the button each time". Second, L appreciated the fact that the automatically generated recommendations always represented the system's most up-to-date model of his interests.

Subject Q illustrated a somewhat different drawback of controlled updating: The danger that the user may forget about updating entirely. Indeed, while using the variant with controlled updating he had completely forgotten about recommendations, using instead just the basic hotlist, as he himself noticed later.

Table 1. Summary of the potential advantages of each variant of the hotlist recommender that came to light in the empirical study.

Potential advantage	Precondition(s) for advantage to apply
Controlled updating:	
1. The user's feeling of control over the interaction with the system is enhanced.	The user has a general desire to control interactions.
2. The user can follow up on more than one recommendation in a given set.	The user receives relatively large, nonoverlapping sets of recommendations. The user pursues the strategy of looking at all of the recommendations in each set.
3. System response times can be faster because of less frequent updating.	Technical conditions make system response time an important factor. The user would not choose to request an update at every opportunity.
4. The user can restrict updates to situations in which the system's model of her interests is assumed to have useful accuracy.	The user can assess the likely accuracy of the system's user model.
5. A smaller amount of irrelevant text appears in the hotlist.	The user finds recommendations distracting although they are clearly distinguishable from normal hotlist entries – perhaps because of limited available screen space.
Automatic updating:	
1. The user is regularly reminded that new recommendations are available.	The user's strategy does not provide for regular consideration of the recommendations. The user has not yet learned that hotlist actions typically result in new recommendations.
2. The user is spared the effort of clicking on a button to obtain new recommendations.	The user's hotlist–related actions are sufficiently numerous that new recommendations are frequently available.
3. The recommendations displayed always reflect the system's most complete model of the user's interests.	The accuracy of the system's user model tends to improve significantly with each modification to the hotlist.
4. The user cannot overlook the availability of the recommendation feature.	The user is not yet accustomed to using recommendations.

5 Discussion

Whenever a choice between controlled and automatic adaptation arises, each solution is likely to have its own potential advantages over the other one. The specific potential advantages of automatic and controlled updating that emerged from our study are summarized in Table 1.

As this table illustrates, the relative importance of each of these advantages may depend on various types of conditions:
1. The nature of the application and of the adaptation involved.
2. Individual differences among users in terms of preferences, experience, and ways of approaching the tasks in question.
3. Relatively stable contextual factors such as the speed of an internet connection.
4. Essentially random situational factors such as the nature of the information retrieved during a small number of search attempts.

One general design implication is that an attempt to deal with the controllability problem should begin with an analysis of the reasonably stable, predictable conditions that are likely to be relevant. For example, Trewin [7] discusses different controllability mechanisms that are appropriate for different types of configuration task.

A second approach to providing suitable controllability is to allow users to choose the type of control that they desire (see, e.g., [8, "Issue 4"]). For example, if our hotlist included a button for toggling between automatic and controlled updating, those users who had a clear, strong preference for one type of updating might be quickly satisfied. But a user cannot in general be expected to be able or willing to take into account all of the relevant considerations (e.g., the entire set listed in Table 1).

To a certain extent, the factors identified as relevant can be taken into account by the system itself. For example, our hotlist recommender could compute at any moment the expected utility of an automatic update, taking into account factors such as the length of the delay that would be caused by the update and the number of recommendations in the hotlist that the user has not yet processed. The user could then be allowed to set an expected utility threshold that must be exceeded before an automatic update is performed. (A similar approach was realized in the LUMIÈRE prototype; cf. [2].)

Given the nature of the factors that tend to be involved, neither the designer nor the user nor the system—nor all of them working together—will in general be able to ensure that the right degree of controllability is available all of the time. It should be anticipated that frustrations like those experienced by our subjects with respect to both of the adaptive variants will in some cases occur; and the possibility should be taken into account that they may cause a user to abandon a system entirely.

Although this last point sounds discouraging, taking into account the limited predictability of users' behavior and responses may be an important step toward an adequate solution of the problem of giving users appropriate control over adaptation.

References

1. Mathias Bauer, Piotr Gmytrasiewicz, and Julita Vassileva, editors. *UM2001, User Modeling: Proceedings of the Eighth International Conference.* Springer, Berlin, 2001.
2. Eric Horvitz, Jack Breese, David Heckerman, David Hovel, and Koos Rommelse. The Lumière project: Bayesian user modeling for inferring the goals and needs of software users. In Gregory F. Cooper and Serafin Moral, editors, *Uncertainty in Artificial Intelligence: Proceedings of the Fourteenth Conference*, pages 256–265. Morgan Kaufmann, San Francisco, 1998.
3. Anthony Jameson. Adaptive interfaces and agents. In Julie A. Jacko and Andrew Sears, editors, *Handbook of Human-Computer Interaction in Interactive Systems.* Erlbaum, Mahwah, NJ, 2002. In press.
4. Judy Kay. Learner control. *User Modeling and User-Adapted Interaction*, 11:111–127, 2001.
5. Donald A. Norman. How might people interact with agents? *Communications of the ACM*, 37(7):68–71, 1994.
6. Michael Pazzani and Daniel Billsus. Learning and revising user profiles: The identification of interesting web sites. *Machine Learning*, 27:313–331, 1997.
7. Shari Trewin. Configuration agents, control and privacy. In *Proceedings of the ACM Conference on Universal Usability*, pages 9–16, Arlington, Virginia, U.S., 2000.
8. Alan Wexelblat and Pattie Maes. Issues for software agent UI. Unpublished manuscript, available from http://wex.www.media.mit.edu/people/wex/, 1997.

Personis: A Server for User Models

Judy Kay, Bob Kummerfeld, and Piers Lauder

Department of Computer Science
University of Sydney, Australia, 2006
{judy, bob, piers}@cs.usyd.edu.au

Abstract. A core element of an adaptive hypertext systems is the user model. This paper describes Personis, a user model server. We describe the architecture, design and implementation. We also describe the way that it is intended to operate in conjunction with the rest of an adaptive hypertext system.

A distinctive aspect of the Personis user model server follows from our concern for making adaptive systems scrutable: these enable users to see the details of the information held about them, the processes used to gather it and the way that it is used to personalise an adaptive hypertext. We describe how the architecture supports this.

The paper describes our evaluations of the current server. These indicate that the approach and implementation provide a workable server for small to medium sized user collections of information needed to adapt the hypertext.

Keywords: Server for user profile/model, Security and Privacy of User Models, User Modelling, Personalisation, User Control

1 Introduction

Adaptive hypertext relies on the availability of information about the user as a foundation for its adaptivity. This paper describes our approach to building a server for such user models. The motivation for such a server follows from the nature of the information in a user model, the difficulties associated with building good user models and the way that such models might be used in a range of applications.

First consider the nature of user modelling information. Because it constitutes personal data, it needs to be treated rather differently from other parts of an adaptive hypertext system: it is subject to far tighter requirements for security of the information. For systems to move out of the laboratory, it will have to meet legal requirements such as the European Community Directive on Data Protection[2] It is in the spirit of such legislation that users be able to access and control their own data. A server makes sense for the provision of the required security at the same time as ensuring user access and control.

---
[2] $http://www.doc.gov/ecommerce/eudir.htm$ (visited Jan 2002)

Another important problem for user modelling is that it takes considerable time and effort to build up a detailed user model. When users first comes to an adaptive hypertext system, they either have to accept a generic interface initially or they have to provide information about themselves. A server should enable the reuse of the user model across applications. In particular, suppose the user explores one adaptive hypertext to do some substantial activity such as learning how to program in C [1]. When they move to another adaptive hypertext system that teaches Java, it would be useful for that system to be primed with the user model that has already been built up.

For the most part, work on personalisation has placed the user model within an application. For example, there have been several user modelling shells: GUMS [2,3] and its successor, GUMAC [3]; BGP-MS [4] UMT [5] and in the area of student modelling, TAGUS [6] These systems explored many issues in building generic tools for managing user models. They did not provide a server for reuse of user model information across applications. A recent review of generalised support for user modelling [7,8] concluded that we have yet to see a user model server that addresses the needs for ensuring the user's privacy, control and ability to scrutinise their user model and the processes for personalisation.

There has been some work on user model servers. Orwant built a system [9] with user models in a Lisp-like language. Orwant took care to encrypt the user model during transmission. Paiva also built a server [10] which could support multiple teaching agents. A rudimentary form of user model server is provided by Hailstorm[3]. This initiative is an indication of the recognition of the value of a user model.

Interestingly, Hailstorm is described with a focus on user control: 'It puts users in control of their own data and information, protecting personal information and providing a new level of ease of use and personalisation.' It allows a registered user to store personal data in a standard form with standard access methods on a central server provided by Microsoft. Access to the information is provided through a standard set of services using the Simple Object Access Protocol (SOAP) and is based on the earlier 'Passport' system for storing user names and passwords. It seems to be intended for broad tasks: address book, email, diary, documents, device settings. It is claimed to give users control over the data while retaining privacy. However, the architecture presents both a single point of failure and a single point of security vulnerability. It is described as a simple data store, without inferencing ability.

Several of these systems, including BGP-MS, UMT and TAGUS, had interfaces for the use of the developer to scrutinise the models as they built and debugged them. However, the representation and reasoning mechanisms were not designed for the user to scrutinise them.

The goal of the Personis project is to explore ways to support powerful and flexible user modelling and at the same time to design it, from its foundations, to be able to support user scrutiny and control. Our underlying representation of the user model [11,12] collects *evidence* for each component of the user model.

---

[3] $http://www.microsoft.com/net/hailstorm.asp$ (visited Jan 2002)

In large scale field testing [12] we have demonstrated that many users can and do scrutinise their user models. In a relatively short eight-week study, some users scrutinised the full range of details of the user model, including the meanings of the components of the model, the details of evidence about each one, the details of the evidence sources and the reasoning used to infer component values. In this paper, we describe the way that the Personis server builds upon this foundation to provide a user model server that can support scrutability for adaptive hypertext systems.

In Sect. 2, we describe the architecture of the Personis server and the way that the server fits into the architecture of an adaptive hypertext system. Section 3 gives an overview of its application in a simple recommender application. We report results of some evaluations of the current Personis server in Sect. 4 and Sect. 5 has discussion and conclusions.

2 Architecture of a Personis-Based Adaptive Hypertext System

2.1 High Level Architecture of Several Adaptive Hypertext Systems

Figure 1 shows the way that a Personis server can support reuse of the user models over a series of adaptive hypertext systems. This illustrates four main ideas that we now describe: the server itself; generic scrutiny tools that enable the user to see and control their own user model; a collection of adaptive hypertext applications; and the *views* which are the conceptual, high level elements shared between the server and each application.

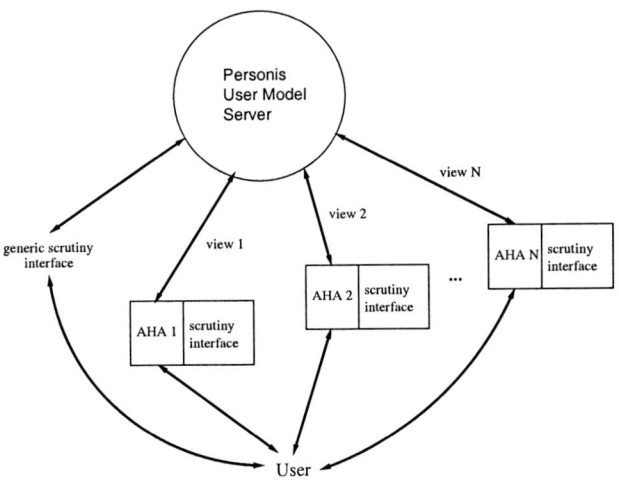

Fig. 1. Personis Server Architecture

In keeping with our previous work, our architecture includes provision for tools for the user to scrutinise their user model. This might include an interface to explore the details of each component of the model, as in the um toolkit [12] and we envisage additional tools for exploring large user models [13] We do not focus on the range of these tools in this paper. We do, however, note that such tools are important to our approach. The figure shows the user interacting with the *generic scrutiny interface* and this, in turn, interacting with the server. In fact, as the figure suggests, interfaces that support user scrutiny of the user model operate as a special type of adaptive interface. (These tools may well be adaptive hypertext applications in their own right.)

Figure 1 shows each adaptive hypertext application with two parts: the core of the adaptive hypertext which enables the user to do some task such as learn to program; and, in addition, we show a scrutiny interface associated with that adaptive hypertext application. This structure is important. If a user model server were to be in practical use, we would expect that the user model for each individual would steadily grow to be quite substantial. Although we are committed to supporting the user's scrutiny of that model, we expect that users will generally want to explore their model in the context of their interaction with a particular application. So, for example, the user might be using an adaptive hypertext that teaches the programming language, C. As they do so, they might wonder why it presented information in a particular way. They might also see a friend using the same system and if its adaptation for that friend is different, our user might want to explore why. In this type of user-scrutiny, the answers to their questions will typically involve the interaction of the adaptive hypertext application and the user model. So, it makes sense to provide support for the user to scrutinise the adaptivity within the context of the adaptive hypertext application.

Issues of scale and comprehensibility give another reason for supporting scrutiny of the user model within the adaptive hypertext application. For the case of the C hypertext, the user would probably be primarily interested in those parts of the user model that are used by that application. Since this will be a small part of a full user model, it is a more manageable and relevant aspect to explore. Our architecture requires that scrutability be supported in the application.

The last element of Fig. 1 is the *views* of the user model available to each adaptive hypertext application. For example, the leftmost application in the figure might need just a few components of the user model. Our architecture allows the definition of a view that defines just these components. Another application will typically use a different view. The application writer would define those parts of the user model needed by their application and these would be defined in views established for that application.

Importantly, these views have an interaction with the design of the access control for the server. Personis allows the user to define just which applications are allowed to see each part of the user model. The user can also control the information sources that should be made available to each applications. So, for example, the user model may contain evidence from several sources about the user's knowledge of programming. That user could decide to make only the information from certain sources available to an application. Another user might make a different decision. Access control information is stored with the user model in the object database.

In particular, suppose an application like AHA1 in the figure teaches about C and it collects data from the user's answers to quiz questions. It provides this to the user model as evidence about the user's knowledge. Further, suppose that AHA2 teaches about a somewhat related subject, Java programming. The user can control whether AHA2 is allowed to access user model evidence that was provided to AHA1. The user can also control just which components of the model are available to AHA2. This means that if AHA2 requests information about the user's knowledge of Java, this will only be provided if the user has made it available to AHA2.

2.2 Internal Architecture of Server

The internal architecture of a Personis server is depicted in Fig. 2. The user model information is held as an object database. This stores the user model in a representation that has the same conceptual foundation as the um toolkit [12] The basic element is the *component* and each has an associated list of *evidence*. Each piece of evidence is tagged with information about its source. The object database also manages the structuring of user models into *contexts* which give a hierarchical structuring of the component namespace. It also holds objects which define the views of Fig. 1. Any context can define a view which includes components from any part of the user model context hierarchy.

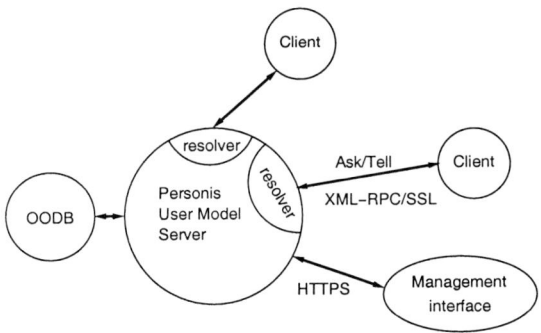

Fig. 2. Personis Server Architecture

The object database also holds the access control information. The establishes access rights to for applications and users. Each aspect can be controlled at the common levels of readable and/or writable.

The server needs to handle large numbers of clients simultaneously. To achieve this, the current implementation is an object layer over a relational database. Internally, objects in the database are referenced using an Object Identifier that is resolved to a server address. This allows parts of user models to reside on different servers. It is envisaged that users would want to keep most of their personal model on a local system under their control. They can then choose to allow selected information to be stored on servers outside their direct control.

As shown in Fig. 1, a view defines a collection of components and an application can ask for the values of these components or send evidence about these to the user model. As shown in Fig. 2, this communication between server and client operates with remote method calls using the XML-RPC[4] protocol over SSL (secure socket layer).

In addition, the server provides a management interface implemented with HTML, HTTP and SSL protocols and accessible from any web browser. The management interface for the user model server has several functions. It provides a status display for the running server and allows reconfiguration. It also allows a suitably privileged user to create and manipulate user model definitions as well as create new user models for individuals according to a previously created definition. It also provides interfaces for setting and altering access control.

The user model server is designed to be scalable to a large number of users, each with large models. Access to model objects by an application is extremely simple with only one line of program code typically required to acquire a complete set of component values corresponding to a view.

The remaining element of Fig. 2 is the *resolvers*. These follow the approach of the um toolkit where the generic user model simply holds the uninterpreted collection of evidence for each component. It is only at runtime that the application uses a resolver to interpret the evidence available to it and conclude the value of a component. A default resolver is available but specialised resolvers can be associated with an application. So, as shown in Fig. 2, one client adaptive hypertext system might use one resolver. Another client might use another and so interpret the same component differently. To take a simple example, Resolver A might treat the user's self-assessment of their knowledge as highly reliable. Resolver B might give higher reliability to the user's performance on quizzes. Then, suppose Rebecca is a the user who is quite knowledgeable about C control structures as evidenced by quiz performance. Suppose that she lacks confidence and rates her knowledge as low in this area. An application which uses Resolver A will treat her as not knowing C control structures. One that uses Resolver B will treat her as knowing them. Note that, Rebecca could decide that evidence derived from her quiz results was not to be made available to either of these applications: in that case, the server would not present evidence to the resolvers and associated applications would operate as if Rebecca's user model had no quiz results.

---

[4] *www.xmlrpc.org*

2.3 Application View of Personis

The basic API for the user model server is simple and elegant. Remote method calls using the XML-RPC protocol (and possible future use of SOAP) provides user model access to any application with a client side XML-RPC implementation. The basic client API consists of three calls:

`um = access(odbname, user, password)`

The `user`, `password` and `odbname` are strings. The system maps the odbname to a server address.

`components = um.ask(context, view, resolverident)`

The `context` is a list of context names giving a path to the required context. The `view` is either a simple string indicating a view name, or a list of names of components. The resolver ident is the name of a resolver located at the server to resolve the values. If the resolver ident is omitted a default is used.

`um.tell(context, component, evidence)`

The `evidence` is a list containing the type of the evidence, an optional expiry time, and the value of the component.

An application can collect resolved values for a complete set of components, as defined by a view, using an `ask` statement. Combined with a statement to connect to the server and one to close the connection the entire interaction with the server is three lines of code.

3 Overview of User Model Server

We now illustrate the architecture in an example application: a "Personal Jazz Channel" that provides users with personalised jazz programmes.

Like many such systems, it asks the user to prime its user model by answering a small set of carefully chosen question. This screen is shown in Fig. 3.

From this, the system sends a collection of evidence to Personis. That evidence is tagged as being given by the user, via the Personal Jazz Channel query interface.

Then, the PJC application makes inferences about other CDs, styles and artists. Each of these generates a piece of evidence which is tagged as inferred and added to the user model by the Personal Jazz Channel application. This very simple process enables the system to have a rich set of preference data from a small set of questions.

At this point, a personal streaming audio channel is created with a mix of tracks conforming to the user's modelled preferences. During normal interactions, the Personal Jazz Channel adds new pieces of evidence about tracks the user allows to play, those that are skipped and so on. Each time the user comes to the Personal Jazz Channel, they log in and the system sets up a connection with

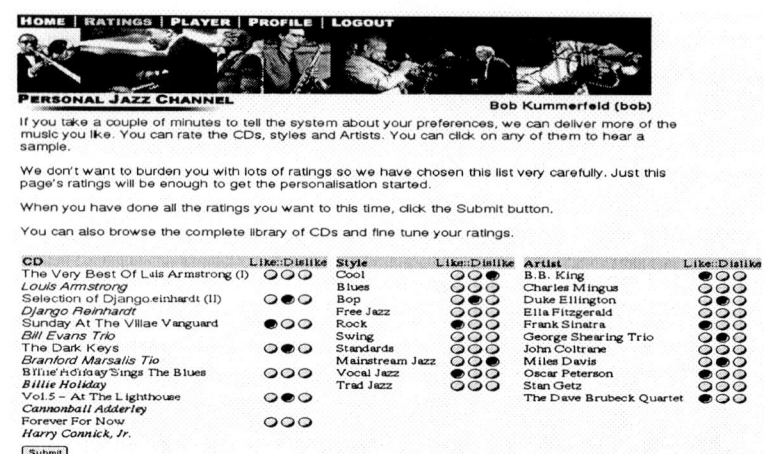

Fig. 3. Example rating screen for a personalised jazz channel

the Personis server and *asks* for the user model view it needs to perform its personalisation.

The Personal Jazz Channel application interacts with the Personis server to gather relevant model information. For example, to gather all the resolved values for jazz styles the following lines of code connect to the server, retrieve the values and close the connection:

```
um = access(odbname, user, password)
styles = um.ask(context=["music","jazz","styles"])
um.close()
```

In this case the context is 'music->jazz->styles' and the default *view* for the context is all the components in that context. The um.ask call will return a dictionary of resolved values. Each element of the dictionary is a tuple containing the resolved value, the name of the resolver used and the time it was resolved.

The Personal Jazz Channel operates in the way illustrated in Fig. 1. In addition to its job as a typical customised application, it also has an interface to support scrutability. At any time, the user is able to examine and change the personal information held by the system by selecting the *Profile* button at the top of the screen. This brings up a screen like that shown in Fig. 4.

From the point of view of our architecture, there are some important aspects to point out. Firstly, we note that it is an essential aspect of the architecture that the Personis server and each of its associated adaptive applications is loosely related. The authors of the application are responsible for it. Different applications will be created by different people and will work differently. The user needs to explicitly allow an application to access relevant views in the user model. The user may decide that the security of some systems is effective enough that it is acceptable to allow them access to substantial amounts of the user model. On the other hand, a user may be less happy with the security protection in another

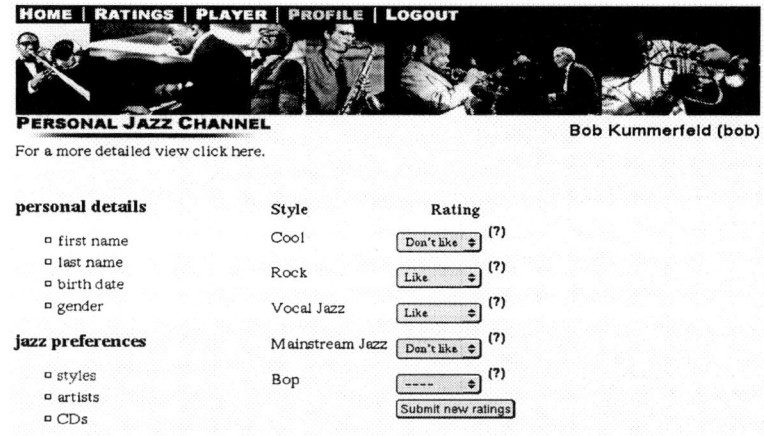

Fig. 4. Profile information: the user has selected *styles* from the list at the left and see sees the user model components for styles of music.

system: that application might be authorised to access only a limited part of the user model and only information derived from a few of the evidence sources.

4 Evaluation

The current server has had very little work to optimise performance but still performs at an acceptable level. A test application performing 10000 accesses achieved the following number of transactions per second:

tell (new value each time)	26/sec
ask (single component)	17/sec
ask (view with 2 components)	13/sec

Each of the ask operations used a default resolver (most recent given evidence value).

The server was running on an 850Mhz Duron processor with 512MBytes memory. The user model being accessed had approximately 50 components arranged in 15 (sub)contexts. The database would have cached the complete model after the first access and so the figures quoted show performance for the client/server protocol and the internal data structure search and overhead.

Investigation has shown that the XML-RPC protocol is a major overhead. This is mainly due to the poor performance of the general purpose XML parser used in the implementation. We feel that significant performance gains can be made with a hand crafted parser. We feel strongly that the use of a standard protocol such as XML-RPC is warranted since it provides access to the Personis server from a wide range of programming languages.

From the application programmers point of view the Personis server is very easy to use. Only a handful of lines of code are required to retrieve the resolved values of a sets of components. In a similar way, it is very straightforward to add evidence to existing components.

5 Conclusion

The underlying design of the Personis user model server is based upon the primary requirement that users have access to their user model and control over it. In addition, it has been designed to provide support for user modelling with an elegant but powerful programmer interface. It is novel in its design being explicitly focussed on user control and scrutability.

References

1. Kay, J., and Kummerfeld, R.J.: An individualised course for the C programming language. Online Proceedings: *http://www.ncsa.uiuc.edu/SDG/IT94/Proceedings/Educ/kummerfeld/kummerfeld.html*, Elsevier (1994)
2. Finin, T. W.: GUMS - a general user modeling shell. In: Kobsa, A., Wahlster. W. (eds.): User models in dialog systems. Springer-Verlag, Berlin (1989) 411–431
3. Kass, R.: Building a user model implicitly from a cooperative advisory dialog. User Modeling and User-Adapted Interaction. **1** (1991) 203–258
4. Kobsa, A., and Pohl, W.: The user modeling shell system BGP-MS. User Modeling and User-Adapted Interaction **4** (1995) 59–106
5. Brajnik, G., and C Tasso, C.: A shell for developing mon-monotonic user modeling systems. International Journal of Human-Computer Studies **40** (1994) 36–62
6. Paiva, A., and Self, J.: TAGUS - a user and learner modeling workbench. User Modeling and User-Adapted Interaction **4** (1995) 197–228.
7. Kobsa, A.: Generic User Modeling Systems. User Modeling and User-Adapted Interaction - Ten Year Anniversary Issue **11** (2001) 49–63
8. Fink J., Kobsa, A.: A Review and Analysis of Commercial User Modeling Servers for Personalization on the World Wide Web. User Modeling and User-Adapted Interaction - Special Issue on Deployed User Modeling **10** (2000) 209–249
9. Orwant, J.: Heterogenous learning in the Doppelganger user modeling system. User Modeling and User-Adapted Interaction **4** (1995) 59–106
10. Machado, I., Martins, A., Paiva, A.: One for all and all for one: a learner modelling server in a multi-agent platform In: Kay, J (ed): User Modeling: Proceedings of the Seventh International Conference, UM99. Springer Wien, New York (1999)
11. Kay, J.: Accretion representation for scrutable student modelling. In: Gauthier, G., Frasson, C., VanLehn, K. (eds.) Intelligent Tutoring Systems (2000) 514–523
12. Kay, J., The um toolkit for cooperative user modelling. User Modeling and User-Adapted Interaction **4** (1995) 149–196
13. Uther, J., On the visualisation of large user models in web based systems. Phd Thesis, Department of Computer Science, University of Sydney (2001)

The Munich Reference Model for Adaptive Hypermedia Applications

Nora Koch and Martin Wirsing

Ludwig-Maximilians University of Munich
www.pst.informatik.uni-muenchen, Germany
{kochn,wirsing}@informatik.uni-muenchen.de

Abstract. Although adaptive applications are increasing in popularity, there are only a few approaches that focus on their generalization or the specification of a reference model. Trying to fill this gap, this paper presents a reference model for adaptive hypermedia applications, similar to AHAM. The main novelty of our approach is an object-oriented specification written in UML (Unified Modeling Language) which integrates both an intuitive visual representation and a formal unambiguous specification in OCL (Object Constraint Language). Our reference model is defined as an extension of the Dexter Hypertext Reference Model including user modeling aspects and rule-based adaptation mechanisms.

Keywords. Adaptive Hypermedia, Reference Model, Visual Modeling, UML, Formal Specification, Constraint Language, OCL.

1 Introduction

An adaptive hypermedia system is a set of nodes and links that allows one to navigate through the hypermedia structure and that dynamically "adapts" (personalizes) various visible aspects of the system to individual user's needs, preferences or knowledge [2]. These applications include an explicit representation of properties of the user. This paper presents a reference model for these adaptive hypermedia applications. The contribution of the paper is twofold. Firstly, we provide an object-oriented formalization for such a reference model. Secondly, we include a graphical representation of this model.

The objective of a reference model is to find common abstractions to the current systems and to provide a basis for the development of these applications. It is named Munich Reference Model, continuing with the tradition of choosing names of places for the reference models related to the hypermedia field, such as the Dexter Model [4], the Amsterdam Model [5] or the Dortmund Family of Hypermedia Models [9].

Adaptive hypermedia systems are first of all hypermedia systems, therefore our reference model is based on the widely used Dexter Model for hypertext systems. It includes the same three layers, but enhanced with adaptation functionality. The key aspects of the Munich Reference Model are inclusion of a user model and an adaptation model as part of the Storage Layer, the dynamic acquisition of user behavior, a dynamic rule-based adaptation and a user behavior triggered Run-Time session. To our knowledge there is only one other reference model for adaptive applications: AHAM [3,12], which is semi-formally defined with tuples. The Munich

Model takes an object-oriented software engineering point of view whereas AHAM takes more a database point of view. Our architecture is similar to the architecture of the AHAM reference model, where user models are always structured as tables. The AHAM adaptive engine is included in the adaptation model of our reference model as data and functionality are integrated in the object-oriented approach. An important contribution of AHAM is the adaptation rule language.

Our focus is, as already mentioned, the formal and visual description of the reference model. The Dexter Model was formalized by Halasz and Schwartz [4] in the specification language Z, early in the nineties. Since then, the use of object-oriented methodologies gained in dissemination and importance. In addition, more emphasis is now put on visual modeling languages making models more intuitive. These were our motivations to select the Unified Modeling Language (UML) – standard for object-oriented modeling – for the formalization of the Munich Reference Model. On the one side, the UML [10] provides the notation and techniques (diagrams) for the visual representation. It has the advantage of showing the relevant concepts at a glance, how they are organized and how they are related to each other. This augments the intuitive comprehension. On the other side, the Object Constraint Language (OCL) which is part of the UML, is used to supplement the semi-formal graphical representation with formally written semantics information.

The Munich Reference Model constitutes the basis for the UML-based Web Engineering (UWE) approach that focus on development of adaptive hypermedia applications [6,7]. UWE includes a design method and the description of a development process that covers the whole life-cycle of these applications. This reference model was used in the development of SmexWeb, a framework for implementing adaptive learning systems on the Web [1]. SmexWeb supports all type of dynamic adaptations, i.e. content, link and presentation adaptation.

This paper is an outline of the specification of the Munich Reference Model; the complete version is included in [6]. It is organized as follows: Section 2 gives an overview of the Munich Reference Model. Section 3 presents the specification of the domain. Section 4 introduces the extensions to include user modeling and adaptivity. Section 5 briefly presents the specification of a hypermedia session management. Finally, in the last section some conclusions are outlined.

2 An Overview of the Reference Model

The Munich Reference Model preserves the three-layer structure of the Dexter Model describing the network of nodes and links and the navigation mechanism. It extends the functionality of each layer to include the user modeling and adaptation aspects. The Run-Time Layer, the Storage Layer and the Within-Component Layer are represented as UML subsystems as it is illustrated in Fig. 1.

- The *Run-Time Layer* contains the description of the presentation of the nodes and links. It is responsible for user interaction, acquisition of user behavior and management of the sessions.
- The *Storage Layer* has more functionality than just storing information about the hypermedia structure. To support adaptation the Storage Layer is divided into three sub-models:

- The *Domain Meta-Model* that manages the basic network structure of the hypermedia system in terms of mechanisms by which the links and nodes are related and navigated. The nodes are treated as general data containers.
- The *User Meta-Model* manages a set of users represented by their user attributes with the objective to personalize the application.
- The *Adaptation Meta-Model* consists of a set of rules that implement the adaptive functionality, i.e. personalization of the application.

- The content and structure within the hypermedia nodes are part of the *Within-Component Layer*, which is not further detailed as its structure and content depend on the application.

The functionality of adaptive hypermedia systems is specified by three types of operations included in the classes of the reference model:

- *Authoring operations* are needed by adaptive hypermedia systems to update components, rules and user attributes, e.g. to create a link or a composite component, to create a rule, to add an user attribute to the model, to delete components or rules.
- *Retrieval operations* are required to access the hypermedia domain structure and the User Model, e.g. to get a component, to get all rules triggered by a user's behavior or another rule.
- *Adaptation operations* are used to dynamically adapt the User Model content to the user behavior and to adapt the presentation to the current state of the User Model, e.g. the adaptive resolver, the constructor or the rule executor.

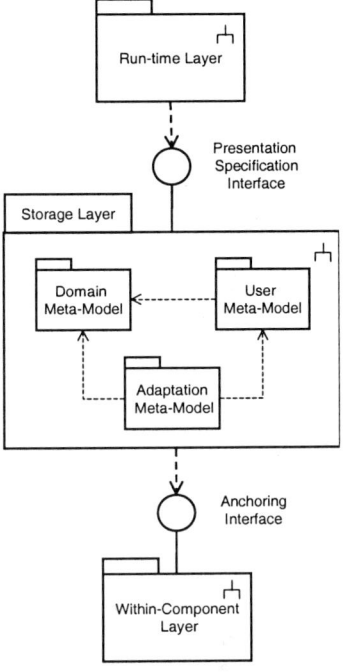

Fig. 1. Architecture of Adaptive Hypermedia Applications

The remainder of this paper presents the visual specification (slightly simplified) of the layers of the reference model and includes a few constraints of the formal specification out of a total of seventy constraints that comprise the complete specification of the Munich Reference Model [6].

3 Specification of the Domain Model

The Domain Meta-Model describes the structure of a hypermedia as a finite set of components together with three main operations, a *resolver*, an *accessor* and a *constructor*. These concepts are modeled by a *class Domain* and a *class Component*. Every component has a globally unique identity *(class UID)*. With the operations *resolver*, *accessor* and *constructor* it is possible to "retrieve" and "construct" adaptive components. The accessor operation allows one to "access" a component given its

UID. UIDs "resolve" to a component. This way UIDs provide a guaranteed mechanism for addressing any component in the hypermedia domain. As in the Dexter Model, this addressing is accomplished in a indirect way based on the entities called anchor *(class Anchor)* consisting of two parts: an anchor ID *(class AnchorID)* and an anchor value *(class AnchorValue)*. The anchor value is an arbitrary value that specifies some location within a component. The anchor ID is an identifier that uniquely identifies the anchor within the scope of the component.

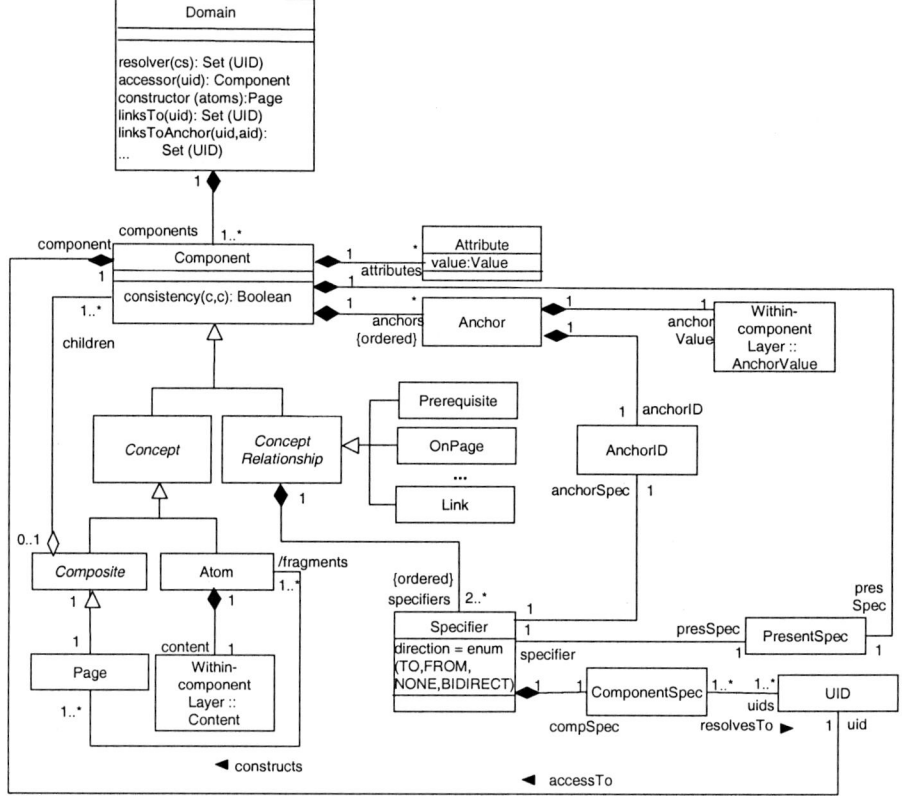

Fig. 2. View of the Domain Meta-Model of the Munich Reference Model

The visual specification of the Domain Meta-Model of the Munich Reference Model is represented by an UML class diagram. Part of it is shown in Fig. 2. Note that for classes belonging to another package, the name of the package is included before the class name, e.g. Within-Component-Layer::AnchorValue. As examples, the classes Component and Domain are described with some more detail below.

Component. A component is an abstract representation of an information item from the application domain. It is represented by an abstract *class Component*. A component can either be a concept *(class Concept)* or a concept relationship *(class ConceptRelationship)*. A concept, in turn, can either be an atom *(class Atom)* or a composite *(class Composite)*. A concept relationship can be a link *(class Link)* or a prerequisite *(class Prerequisite)*, or a is-part-of relation *(class On page)*, etc. This inheritance hierarchy is shown in the UML class diagram (Fig. 2). The component information consists of attributes *(class Attribute)*, a presentation specification *(class Present Spec)* and a sequence of anchors *(class Anchor)*. The UML visual specification is insufficient to model the "type consistency" between components. Therefore, the following OCL constraint is added to the specification to express that two components are "type consistent" if both are of the same type.

    context Component :: consistency (c1:Component, c2:Component):Boolean
    post: result = c1.oclIsTypeOf(Composite) and c2.oclIsTypeOf(Composite)
            or c1.oclIsTypeOf(Link) and c2.oclIsTypeOf(Link)
            or c1.oclIsTypeOf(Atom) and c2.oclIsTypeOf(Atom)
            or .....

Domain. The domain is represented by a *class Domain*, which is a composition of objects of type *Component*. The class *Domain* includes two operations for links and anchors ensuring the navigation functionality of the hypermedia system. These are the *linksTo* and the *linksToAnchor* operations. The *linksTo* operation returns the set of links that resolve to a specific component. The *linksToAnchor* obtains the set of links that resolve to a specific anchor. The following is the OCL specification of the pre-condition and post-condition of *linksTo*. The post-condition expresses that *result* consists of the set of all *Link* identifiers such that one of the component specifications of the corresponding Link resolves to the given UID.

    context Domain :: linksTo (uid : UID) : Set (UID)
    pre: components → exists (c : Component | accessor (uid) = c)
    post: result = UID.allInstances → select (lid : UID |
            Component.allInstances → exists (link :Component |
              link.oclIsTypeOf (Link) and link = accessor (lid)
            and ComponentSpec.allInstances → exists (cs :
            ComponentSpecs | link.specifiers.compSpecs → includes (cs)
              and uid = resolver (cs))))

4 Modeling Adaptive Hypermedia Applications

The Munich Reference Model includes adaptation and user modeling functionality. The User Meta-Model defines the user attributes and attribute-values that are relevant to the adaptive application. The adaptive mechanisms are specified in the Adaptation Meta-Model and they are responsible for adaptive content, adaptive links and adaptive presentation. The presentation specification builds pages out of page fragments, taking into account the adaptive mechanisms.

4.1 The User Meta-Model

The User Meta-Model describes the structure of the individual models of each user and how these models are administrated. User modeling comprises initialization, updating and retrieval of the current state of a User Model. The User Meta-Model is modeled as a subsystem that consists of a class *UserManager* and a set of *Users* and operations *initializer, updater* and an *evaluator*. Fig. 3 depicts the classes of the User Meta-Model subsystem and its relationship to the Domain Model.

A user of an adaptive hypermedia application is modeled by a class *User*, which is related through an aggregation association to a *UserIdentification* and to a set of *User Attributes*. The user ID identifies the user uniquely in the universe of the application. With the user attributes the system provides a representation of the user's characteristics that are relevant for the application. One can distinguish different types of information contained in user models: user's knowledge, user's preferences, user's background experience, user's tasks, etc., summarized in two categories: "user knowledge related to the domain components" and "user general characteristics".

The first group includes domain dependent attributes while those of the second group are domain independent. The second group includes knowledge not related to the components, such as background knowledge and preferences. Classification like this can be found in Hynecos [11] and SmexWeb [1]. We model these two groups of user's characteristics with *Class DependentAttr* and *Class IndependentAttr*. The separation has the advantage that the domain independent attributes can be shared with other applications. The following constraint defines the invariant for a domain independent User Model, i.e. all user attributes are independent of the domain.

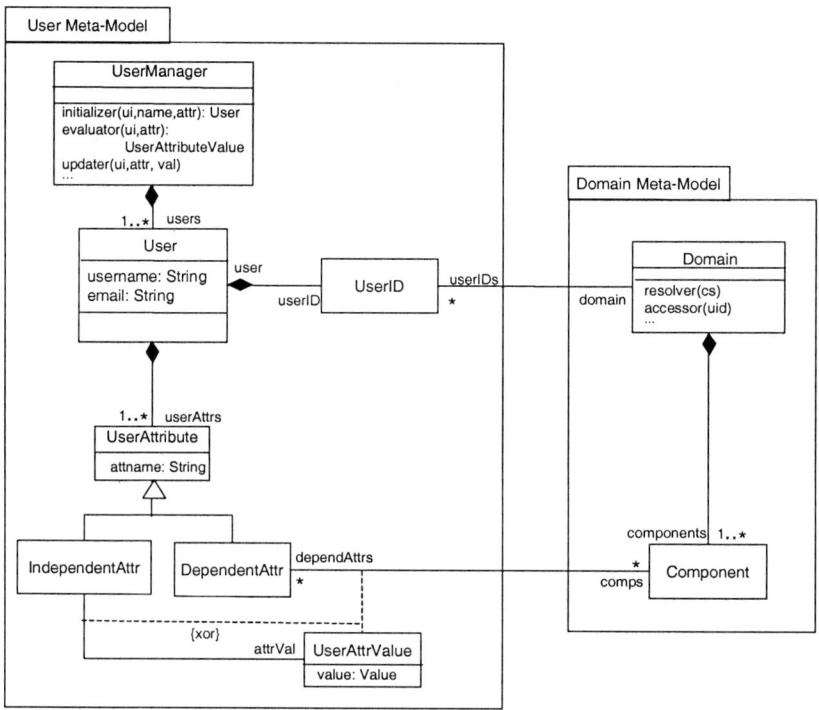

Fig. 3. View of the User Meta-Model of the Munich Reference Model

context User
inv domain independent user model:
   userAttrs → forAll (uat:: UserAttribute |
      uat.oclIsTypeOf (IndependentAttr))

Let us mention here only the formalization of one functionality related to the User Meta-Model subsystem: the registration of a new user. We define an *initializer* operation that creates a new instance of class *User* for each new user that registers to the adaptive hypermedia application and assigns a given set of attributes to this user.

context UserManager :: initializer (userIdentification:UserID, n:String,
              defaultAttrs: Set(UserAttribute)) : User
post: result.oclIsNew and users = users@pre → including (result)
      and result.userID = userIdentification and result.username = n
      and result.userAttrs = defaultAttrs

4.2 The Adaptation Meta-model

The adaptation is performed using a set of rules, such as in most adaptive hypermedia applications; typical examples of rule-based adaptation is supported by the frameworks AHA [3] and SmexWeb [1]. These rules determine how pages are built and how they are presented to the user. The Adaptation Meta-Model is specified by a UML class diagram, which is depicted in Fig. 4.

The core elements used to model the adaptation are the class *Adaptation* and the class *Rule*. The class *Adaptation* includes three main operations: an *adaptation resolver*, a *finder* and a *trigger*. The first one "resolves" a component specification into a UID of an appropriate component that builds an adapted page. The second one implements a trigger mechanism that returns all the rules triggered by one given rule, i.e. the rules to be used at a given time. The first rule to be used is triggered by the user behavior. The *executor* operation of the class *Rule* allows the system to select the appropriate components, and to perform content-adaptation, presentation-adaptation and link-adaptation as well as to update the User Model. These operations play the role of the adaptive engine in AHAM.

The specification of the Adaptation Meta-Model is supplemented with a set of OCL constraints. For example, the following OCL invariant assures the dynamic update of the User Model: For at least one user attribute there exists a rule that modifies an attribute value of the User Model.

context Adaptation
inv dynamic update of the user model:
   Rules.allInstances → exists (r:Rule | r.oclIsTypeOf (AcquisitionRule)
      and r.action.elements → exists (m: ModelElement |
         m.values.oclIsTypeOf (UserAttributeValue)
         and m.modified))

An object of class *Rule* consists of one condition (class *Condition*), one action (class *Action*) and attributes, such as phase and propagate proposed by De Bra et. al [3]. *phase* determines whether rules are applied before or after the User Model is updated while *propagate* with a value true allows the system to trigger other rules. Conditions and actions are expressions containing model elements and operators.

ModelElements are defined by two attributes: an element identifier (*elementID*) and a Boolean value (*modified*) which indicates whether the model element is being modified in the actual action. Only certain types of model elements, i.e. User Model attribute values and presentation specifications can have a *modified* value true.

Our formalization of rules is very general, thus our reference model does not prevent problems with confluence and termination of rule-based systems. Depending on the chosen rule language, rule applications may be non-terminating and non-confluent. These problems can be analyzed in each case using different approaches, such as those used in rewriting systems or in the active database field.

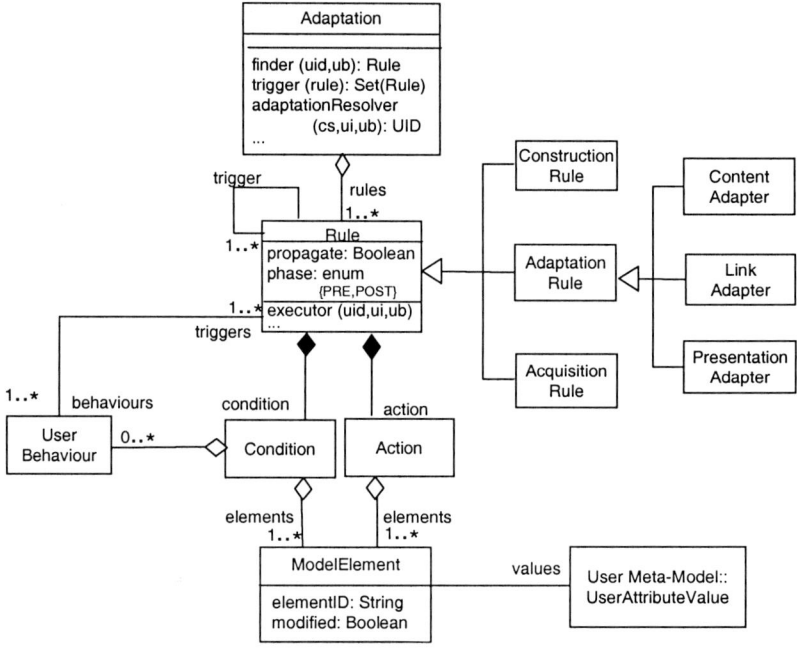

Fig. 4. View of the Adaptation Model of the Munich Reference Model

Rules are classified according to their objectives into: construction rules, acquisition rules and adaptation rules [6]. Adaptation rules adapt content, links or the presentation of the application. They differ in the executor method. The different types of rules are represented as a hierarchy of rules as it is shown in the class diagram of the Adaptation Model (see Fig. 4).

5 Session Management

The Run-Time Layer manages different sessions for the users generating and presenting the instances of pages. The Run-Time Layer describes how the components are presented to the user. This presentation is based on the concept of instantiation of a component, i.e. a copy of the component is cached to the user. The

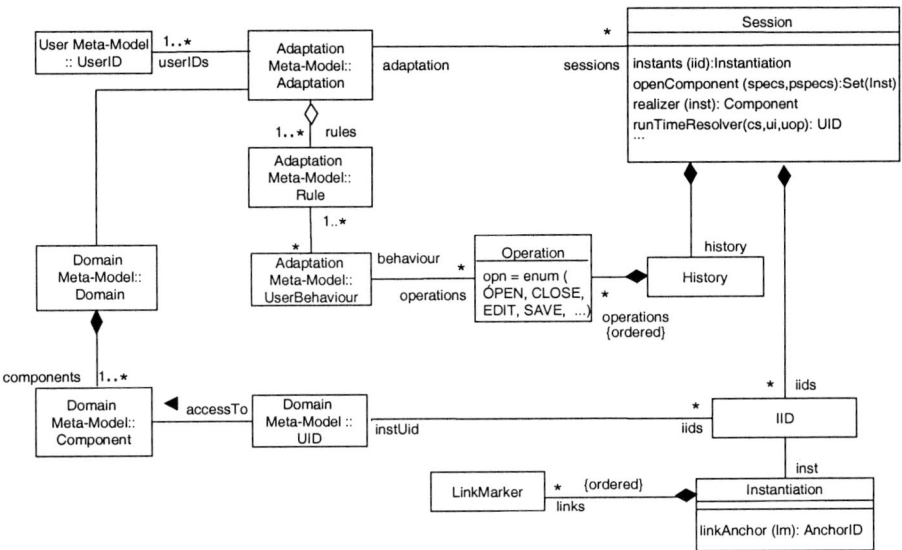

Fig. 5. View of the Run-Time Layer of the Munich Reference Model

copy receives an instantiation identifier (class *IID*). It should be noted that more than one instantiation for a component may exist simultaneously and that a user may be viewing more than one component.

Instantiation of a component also results in instantiation of its anchors. An instantiated anchor is known as a link marker. These concepts are modeled with the *classes Instantiation, IID,* and *LinkMarker.* In order to keep track of all these instantiations the Run-Time Layer uses an entity session (*class Session*) as shown in Fig. 5. A session can be open or closed and in a session the user can perform operations, such as open a component that results in the creation of an instantiation, edit an instantiation and follow a link. All these operations that result from the user interactions are recorded in a history which constitutes the basis of the observation of the user behavior and the adaptation mechanism. As example a constraint for the *instantiator* operation is shown. Given an UID of a component, the function returns an instantiation of the component that is part of the session. The presentation specification is a primitive in the model, which contains information about how the component is to be presented by the system during instantiation (see Figures 5 and 2).

      context Session :: instantiator (uid: UID, ps: PresentSpec): Instantiation
      pre: adaptation.domain.components → includes (accessor(uid))
      post: result = iids.inst → select (ins:Instantiation |
            ins.presSpec = ps and ins.iid.instUID = uid) → asSequence → first

Figure 5 depicts part of the Run-Time Layer for adaptive hypermedia systems. The UML class diagram shows how core classes of the Domain Meta-Model, the User Meta-Model and the Adaptation Meta-Model collaborate with classes of the Run-Time Layer.

6 Conclusions and Future Work

In this paper we introduced an object-oriented reference model for adaptive hypermedia applications – called Munich Reference Model. It constitutes the basis of our UWE engineering approach for adaptive Web applications [6,8]. This model was defined in parallel to the development of SmexWeb. SmexWeb is a framework for adaptive Web learning applications [1]. The architecture of this model is similar to the AHAM architecture, i.e. it extends the Dexter model by including an user model and an adaptation model in the Storage Layer as well as adapting the domain model and the Run-Time Layer.

We presented an integrated visual and formal specification of the reference model. The model is visually represented using UML notation and is formally specified in OCL. UML was chosen as it is the de facto standard modeling language. A visual representation is missing when other kind of specification, e.g. Z or VDM are selected [4]. OCL is part of the UML and is used for the specification of invariants for the model elements and for the specification of pre-conditions and post-conditions on operations describing the adaptive functionality.

Acknowledgment. We thank the reviewers for their valuable feedback and their requests for additional explanations.

References

1. Albrecht F., Koch N. and Tiller T. (2000). SmexWeb: An Adaptive Web-based Hypermedia Teaching System. *Journal of Interactive Learning Research*. Kommers P. & Mizoguchi R. (Eds.).
2. Brusilovsky P. (1996). Adaptive Hypermedia: An attempt to analyze and generalize. *Proceedings of First International Conference on Multimedia, Hypermedia and Virtual Reality 1994*. Brusilovsky P. & Streitz N. (Eds.) LNCS 1077, Springer, pp. 288-304.
3. De Bra P., Houben G.-J., and Wu H. (1999). AHAM: A Dexter-based Reference Model of Adaptive Hypermedia. *Proceeding of the ACM Hypertext Conference*, pp. 147-156.
4. Halasz F. and Schwartz M. (1990). The Dexter Hypertext Reference Model. NIST Hypertext Standardization Workshop.
5. Hardman L., Bulterman C. and Rossum G. (1994). The Amsterdam Reference Model. *Communications of the ACM 37(2)*.
6. Koch N. (2000). Software Engineering for Adaptive Hypermedia Systems: Reference Model, Modeling Techniques and Development Process. *PhD. Thesis*, Uni-Druck.
7. Koch N. (2002). An Object-Oriented Hypermedia Reference Model. *In Information Modeling for Internet Applications,* van Bommel P. (Ed.), to appear.
8. Koch N. and Wirsing M. (2001). Software Engineering for Adaptive Hypermedia Applications? *Third Workshop on Adaptive Hypertext and Hypermedia at the UM'2001*.
9. Tochtermann K. and Dittrich G. (1996). The Dortmund Family of Hypermedia Systems. *Journal of Universal Computer Science*.
10. UML: The Unified Modeling Language. Version 1.3. (1999). http://www.omg.org/uml
11. Vassileva J. (1994). A Practical Architecture for User Modeling in a Hypermedia-based Information System. *Proceeding of the 4th International Conference on User Modeling*.
12. Wu H., De Bra P., Aerts A. and Houben G.-J. (2000): Adaptation Control in Adaptive Hypermedia Systems. *Proceedings of the Adaptive Hypermedia and Adaptive Web-based Systems*. Brusilovsky P, Stock O., Strapparava C. (Eds.). LNCS 1892, Springer, pp. 250-259.

Tracking Changing User Interests through Prior-Learning of Context

Ivan Koychev

FhG - FIT.ICON
D-53754 Sankt Augustin, Germany
phone: +49 2241 14 2194, fax: +49 2241 14 2146
ivan.koychev@fit.fraunhofer.de

Abstract. The paper presents an algorithm for learning drifting and recurring user interests. The algorithm uses a prior-learning level to find out the current context. After that, searches into past observations for episodes that are relevant to the current context, 'remembers' them and 'forgets' the irrelevant ones. Finally, the algorithm learns only from the selected relevant examples. The experiments conducted with a data set about calendar scheduling recommendations show that the presented algorithm improves significantly the predictive accuracy.

1 Introduction

Recently, many systems have been developed that recommend information, products and other items. These systems try to help users in finding pieces of information or other objects in which the users could be interested [8]. In a similar way, adaptive hypermedia systems build a model of the goals and preferences of each user and use this model to adapt the interaction to the needs of the user [3]. Many of those systems use machine learning methods for learning from observations about the user [15]. However, user interests and preferences can change over time. Some of the systems are provided with mechanisms that are able to track drifting user interests [1, 5, 9, 11, among others]. The problem of learning drifting user interests is relevant to the problem known as concept drift in the area of machine learning. The next section discusses different approaches about learning drifting concept and their applications for learning about users.

In this paper it is assumed that the user interests do not only change, but also possibly recur. The user interests can be quite wide and the user can currently focus her attention on a small subset of her broad interests. For example, the whole set of user interests in the case of Internet browsing can include interests that are relevant to her job, as well as her hobbies, etc. Even the user's job related interests could be quite extensive and interdisciplinary. A system that assists the user in web browsing should be flexible enough to recognize what her current interests are and provide her with relevant recommendations. A possible approach is to learn about current user interests from a time window that includes recent relevant observations only. However, if the current user interests often change, a precise user profile cannot be learned from a small set of relevant recent observations only. Hence, the system can search for past episodes where the user has demonstrated a similar set of interests and try to learn a more precise description of the current user interests, 'remembering' relevant and 'forgetting' irrelevant observations.

This paper presents such an algorithm for tracking changing user interests and preferences in the presence of changing and recurring context. First, the algorithm learns about current context. Subsequently, it selects past episodes that are relevant to this context and eventually it learns concept descriptions from the selected examples.

The next section discuses different approaches for tracking changes developed in areas of machine learning and user modeling. Section 3 presents a two-level learning algorithm that is applicable to learning changing and recurring user interests and preferences. Section 4 presents experiments of the designed algorithm with real data about calendar scheduling preferences as well as with an artificial data set.

2 Related Works

This section briefly introduces different approaches developed for tracking changing (also known as shifting, drifting or evolving) concepts. Such systems use different forgetting mechanisms to cope with this problem. Usually it is assumed that if the concept changes, then the old examples become irrelevant to the current period. The concept descriptions are learned from a set of recent examples called time window. For example, a software assistant for scheduling meetings is described in Mitchell et al. [11]. It employs induction on a decision tree to acquire assumptions about individual habits of arranging meetings. The learning method uses a time window to adapt faster to the changing preferences of the user. A system that learns user's interest profiles by monitoring web and e-mail habits is described in Grabtree and Soltysiak [15]. This research shows that user's interests can be tracked over time by measuring the similarity of interests within a time period.

An improvement of the time window approach is the use of heuristics to adjust the size of the window. Widmer and Kubat [17] use a time window with a flexible size, which is adapted dynamically. The window size and thus the rate of forgetting is supervised and dynamically adjusted by heuristics that monitor the learning process. Klingenberg and Renz [17] investigate the application of such an approach in the area of information retrieval.

Maloof and Michalski [10] have developed a method for selecting training examples for a partial memory learning system. The forgetting mechanism of the method selects extreme examples that lie at the boundaries of concept descriptions and removes from the partial memory examples that are irrelevant or outdated for the learning task. The method uses a time-based function to provide each instance with an age. Examples that are older than a certain age are removed from the partial memory.

Nevertheless, pure time window approaches totally forget the observations that are outside the given window, or older than a certain age. The examples which remain in the partial memory are equally important for the learning algorithms. This is abrupt and total forgetting of old information which in some cases can be valuable.

System use different approaches to avoid loss of useful knowledge learned from old examples. The CAP system [11] keeps old rules till they are competitive with the new ones. The architecture of FLORA systems [17] assumes that the learner maintains a store of concept descriptions relevant to previous contexts. When the learner suspects a context change, it will examine the potential of previous stored descriptions to provide better classification.

An intelligent agent called NewsDude that is able to adapt to changing user interests is presented in Billsus, and Pazzani [1]. It learns two separate user models: one represents the user's short-term interests and the other represents the user's long-term interests. The short-term model is learned from the most recent observations only. It represents user models that can adjust more rapidly to the user's changing interests. If the short-term model cannot classify the story at all, it is passed on to the long-term model. The purpose of the long-term user model is to model the user's general preferences for news stories and compute predictions for stories that could not be classified by the short-term model. This hybrid user model is flexible enough to consider changes in user interests and keeps track of long-term user interests as well. Chiu and Webb [4] have used a similar approach - a dual student model for handling concept drift.

Webb and Kuzmycz [14] suggest a data aging mechanism that places an initial weight of 1 on each observation. In a similar way Koychev and Schwab [9] have used a gradual forgetting function that provides each observation with a weight according to its appearance over time.

An approach for tracking changing concepts that employs two-level learning algorithms is presented in [16]. The assumption is that the domain provides explicit clues as to the current context (e.g. attributes with characteristic values). A two-level learning algorithm is presented that effectively adjusts to changing contexts by trying to detect (via meta-learning) contextual clues and using this information to focus the learning process. Another two-level learning algorithm assumes that concepts are likely to be stable for some period of time [6]. This approach uses batch learning and contextual clustering to detect stable concepts and to extract hidden context.

The approach presented in this paper also employs a two-learning level. However, it does not assume that the attributes represent current context explicitly. It starts from the assumption that the recent observations are able to provide information about current context. The recent relevant observations cannot be sufficient to learn an accurate description of the concept, but the learned description is accurate enough to be able to distinguish the past episodes that are relevant to the current context. Then the algorithm constructs a new training set, 'remembers' relevant and 'forgets' irrelevant examples. Finally, the concept description is learned from this set of examples.

3 Tracking Changes through Prior-Learning of Context

When the concept drifts and possibly recurs, we can use time window based forgetting mechanisms. However, the recent examples that represent the current context can be insufficient for learning accurate descriptions. Therefore, if the context recurs, then remembering the 'old' examples that are relevant to the current context should enlarge the size of the training set and thus improve the predictive accuracy. However, the context is frequently hidden and explicit indicators about its changes and recurrences cannot be discovered easily. Hence, in such cases the aim should be to learn more about the current context and then to search for old observations that were made in a similar context. An algorithm that makes use of this idea consists of the following three steps:

1. *Learning about current context.* A relatively small time window is used to learn a description of the current context (e.g. learning a description of the user interests based on the recent observations about the user).

2. *Remembering relevant past episodes.* The learned description in step 1. is tested against the rest of the training set. The episodes that show a predictive accuracy that is greater than a predefined threshold are selected (i.e. selecting the episodes that are relevant to the current context).

3. *Learning from context-related examples.* The new data set selected in step 2. is used for learning a new description of the current user interests, which is expected to be more accurate.

Let's call this algorithm COPL (COntext Prior Learning algorithm). The COPL algorithm requires a predefinition of the following settings:

- *The size of the time window* used in step 1. This time window should be long enough to allow a sufficiently accurate description of the current context to be learned, as well as short enough to be able to track fast changing user interests. Some enhancements like adaptive time window [17] can be employed aiming at improving predictive accuracy.

- *The episode selection criterion* for step 2. This criterion should be able to distinguish the episodes that are relevant to the learned context in step 1. The criterion should be resistant to noise in the sequence of examples.

- *The threshold for the episode-selecting criterion* in step 2. After the episode selection criterion has been established, a suitable threshold should be defined, which should assure as much as possible that only the relevant old examples be selected.

- *The learning algorithms* used in steps 1. and 3. The same or different learning algorithms can be used in those steps.

Those settings should be defined empirically and based on preliminary investigation of the application domain. The implementation of the algorithm described in the next section gives an example of such definitions.

The next section presents the results from experiments that compare the designed algorithm where the main idea is to extend the set of examples by recovering relevant past examples as opposite to the CAP and FLORA approaches where the model was extended by past rules.

4 Experiments

This section present results from experiments with the COPL algorithm. Two data sets are used in the experiments. The first one contains data from a real use of a calendar manager tool aiming at helping the user to scheduling meetings [Mitchell et al. [11]. The second one is an artificial data set [13] that is used in many papers in the area of Machine Learning dedicated to concept drift (e.g. [10, 17], etc.)

Mitchell et al. [11] have developed a software assistant that helps schedule a particular user's calendar: a calendar manager called CAP (Calendar APprentice). CAP learns the users' scheduling preferences through routine use, enabling it to give customized scheduling advice to each user. It can be considered as an analogy to a human secretary who might assist someone in managing a calendar. CAP employs induction on decision tree to acquire assumptions about individual habits of arranging meetings. The learning method uses a time window to adapt faster to the changing preferences of the user. The newly generated rules are merged with old ones. The rules that perform poorly on the test set drop out of the list.

The user's scheduling preferences depend very much on a hidden context. Some of this context can be assumed and explicitly presented and used for improving predictive accuracy (e.g. academic semesters, etc.). However, there are many other events and conditions that can influence the meeting schedule and which cannot be explicitly represented by an attribute space (e.g. room availability, the schedule preferences of other participants of a meeting and many others). Under this condition, the predictive accuracy of the system can oscillate with very high amplitude. A more comprehensive investigation and analysis of the specifics of the domain can be found in Mitchell et al. [11].

The section below presents the results from experiments conducted with the CAP data set[1]. The attributes used for describing the calendar events in the current experiments are listed in Table 1. The task is to predict the following meeting characteristics:

- *Duration* - the duration of the meeting in minutes e.g. 30, 60, 90, etc. (number of values legal - 13);

- *Day-of-week* - the day of the week of this meeting; e.g. Monday, Thursday, etc. (number of legal values - 6);

- *Location* – the place where the meeting is held; e.g. weh5409 (number of legal values - 142);

---

[1] http://www.cs.cmu.edu/afs/cs.cmu.edu/project/theo-5/www/cap-data.html

- *Start-time* - the time at which the meeting begins, in military time; e.g. 930 (9:30am), 1400 (2pm), etc. (number of legal values - 21);

Table 1. The list of features that are used for describing calendar events.

Third-most-common-time-last-60-days-this-meeting-type
Third-most-common-time-last-60-days
Second-most-common-time-last-60-days-this-meeting-type
Second-most-common-time-last-60-days
Most-common-time-these-attendees-last-60-days
Most-common-time-these-attendees
Most-common-time-last-60-days-this-meeting-type
Most-common-time-last-60-days
Most-common-day-these-attendees-last-60-days
Most-common-day-these-attendees
Duration-of-next-meeting-with-these-attendees
Duration-of-last-meeting-with-these-attendees
Day-of-week-of-next-meeting-with-these-attendees
Day-of-week-of-last-meeting-with-these-attendees
Required-seminar-type
Required-course-name
Required-speakers
Single-person?
Action
CMU-attendees?
Group-attendees?
Position-attendees
Department-attendees
Sponsor-attendees
Known-attendees?
Duration
Day-of-week
Location
Start-time

The settings of the algorithm listed in the previous section are defined for the conducted experiments as follows:

- The size of the time window: Preliminary experiments show that for different prediction tasks the size of the window that produces best predictive accuracy can be quite different. For the given data set the best accuracy is reached for the window of the following size: Location - 200; Duration - 350; Start-time - 350; Day-of-week - 400.

- The episode selection criterion for step 2. The criterion used in this implementation selects the examples e_j for the new data set taking into account the average predictive accuracy in its neighborhood. In particular, a small episode around the example which includes the previous two and next two examples, is used. An event will be selected for the new training set $e_j \in S_{new}$ if the average predictive accuracy for this episode is greater than or equal to a predefined threshold τ.

- The threshold for the episode-selecting criterion in step 2. is set up to $\tau = 0.6$ in all experiments.

- The learning algorithm used in steps 1. and 3. is Induction on Decision Tree (aka ID3) [12]. This algorithm was used in CAP, which makes the comparison between different approaches clearer. This algorithm produces an explicit user profile (e.g. set of rules) that is understandable for the user. This is an important advantage from the viewpoint of user modeling.

Table 2. Comparison of predictive accuracy for the User.

Prediction task	CAP	ID3-FM	COPL (ID3)
Location	64%	58%	67%
Duration	63%	71%	79%
Start-time	34%	39%	48%
Day-of-week	50%	52%	66%
Average	53%	55%	65%

Table 2 presents the results from experiments with data for User 1. In this experiment a new description of user preferences is learned after each 10 meetings. The learned description at each step is tested on the next 10 meetings. The line in the table presents the accuracy of prediction for different learning tasks. The results are compared with the CAP. The average predictive accuracy of the ID3 with full memory (ID3-FM) to some extent outperforms the CAP. This is slightly surprising, because CAP is designed to track changing user preferences better than a simple learning algorithm. An explanation of this phenomenon is that some implementation details like attribute selection criteria and used pruning method can change the outcome of the algorithm. The use of one level time window, even with an adaptive size, does not improve the predictive accuracy because the user preferences alternate very often and with high amplitude. The comparison between full-memory learning algorithm (ID3-FM) and the presented two-level learning algorithm is fully compatible because the same implementation of the basic learning algorithm is used. The results from the experiments show that the context-learning algorithm is able to improve the average predictive accuracy for each feature. All those improvements are significant (using t-test with $\alpha = 0.01$).

Figure 1 shows the results from experiments for the predicted features. It can be seen that the user's preferences can change abruptly, which leads to a dramatic decrease of the predictive accuracy. The presented two-level algorithm tracks changes better than the basic algorithm and produces a significantly improved average accuracy.

Experiments with this data set, which use the Winnow and Weighted-Majority algorithms, were reported in Blum [2]. The Winnow with a large feature set reaches the best average accuracy, which is equal to that reached by the algorithm in the presented experiments. However, these algorithms are not suitable for producing explicit user profiles, which is considered to be important in the area of user modeling.

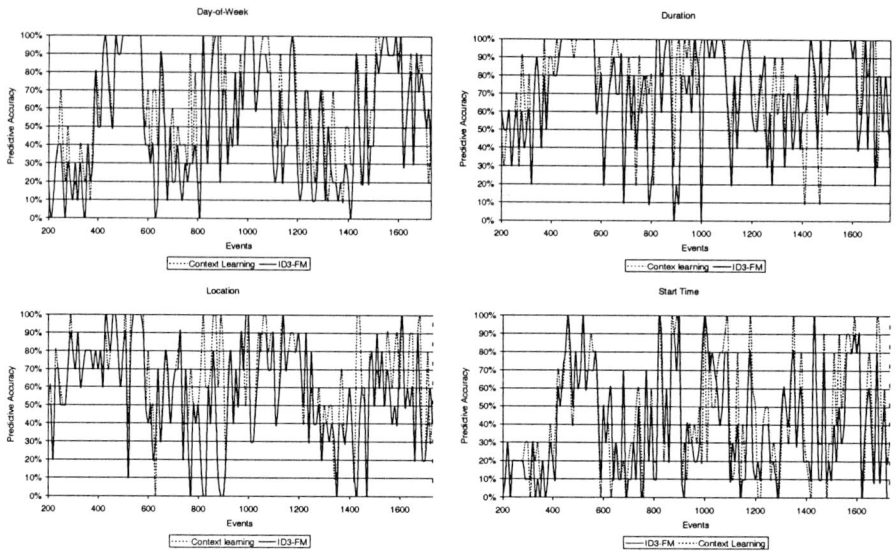

Fig. 1. The improvement in predictive accuracy for the predicted features.

To compare the presented approach with FLORA3, which is able to recover 'old' rules learned in a similar context [17], experiments were conducted also with STAGGER data set [13]. The instance space of a simple blocks world is described by three attributes *size* = *{small, medium, large}*, *color* = *{red, green, blue}*, and *shape* = *{square, circular, triangular}*. There is a sequence of three target concepts (1) *size* = *small* and *color* = *red*, (2) *color* = *green* or *shape* = *circular* and (3) *size* = *(medium or large)*. 120 training instances are generated randomly and classified according to the current concept. The underlying concept is forced to change after every 40 training examples: (1)-(2)-(3). A concept description is learned from initial n examples. After each learning phase the predictive accuracy is tested on an independent test set of 100 instances. The result are averaged over 10 runs. The concept recurrence is simulated by generating this sequence three times: (1)-(2)-(3)-(1)-(2)-(3)-(1)-(2)-(3) [17].

The parameters for the COPL algorithm in this experiment are set up as follows: the size of the time window used at step 1 is 18; the episode selection criteria and the related threshold remain the same as above; and the used learning algorithms at step 1 and 3 is Naïve Bayes Classifier (NBC) to demonstrate the ability of the presented two-level algorithm to work with other learning algorithms.

Table 3 compares the presented algorithm with FLORA3 [17]. On the basic data set (1-120) the FLORA3 produces a slightly better accuracy (i.e. non significant difference). On recurring concepts (i.e. examples 121-360) both algorithms perform better than the ones that do not recover the context (e.g. FLORA2 [17]- 81.5%). The COPL (NBC) algorithm benefits from the recurrence of context better than FLORA3 (see columns *121-240* and *241-360* of Table 3). Moreover, the predictive accuracy of the presented algorithm increases when context recurs, which shows that it really takes advantage of context recurrence. For example, on second recurrence of the concept (see column *241-360* of Table 3) the COPL algorithm produces a significantly better (using t-test with $\alpha = 0.01$) average accuracy than FLORA3.

Table 3. Comparison between FLORA3 and COPL (NBC) on recurring context.

Algorithm\Examples:	2-120	121-240	241-360
FLORA 3 context	85.9%	85.4%	83.5%
COPL (NBC)	85.3%	85.6%	87.1%

5 Conclusion

The paper describes a two-level learning algorithm that is able to track changing user interests and preferences through prior-learning of context. The algorithm benefits from the recurrence of the context by remembering the relevant observations and forgetting the irrelevant ones. The presented approach provides a general framework for dealing with changing and recurring user interests that can be used with different machine learning algorithms. Conducted experiments with recommendations about calendar scheduling demonstrate that the approach is able to improve the predictive accuracy significantly. Additional experiments conducted with an artificial data set demonstrate that the presented algorithm really makes use of context recurrence and increases the predictive accuracy when the context recurs. Further investigations of the episode selection criterion and designing a mechanism for its threshold detection are expected to improve the predictive accuracy of the algorithm additionally.

The presented two-level learning algorithm can be embedded in any type of adaptive hypermedia system where some observations during the interaction with the user have been collected and then used to learn about the user. The knowledge learned about the user can then be used to adapt the interaction to the needs of that user. Providing the user with adequate recommendations in the presence of fast changing user's interests and preferences is, for example, vital for many contemporary recommendation systems. Future applications of the algorithm are expected to provide fruitful ideas for the development of mechanism for dynamical adaptation of the algorithm parameters.

References

1. Billsus, D., and Pazzani, M. J.: A Hybrid User Model for News Classification. In Kay J. (ed.), UM99: Proceedings of the Seventh International Conference on User Modeling, Lecture Notes in Computer Science, Springer-Verlag (1999) pp. 99-108.
2. Blum, A.: Empirical Support of Winnow and Weighted-Majority Algorithms: Results on a Calendar Scheduling Domain. Machine Learning 26 (1997): 5-23.
3. Brusikovsky, P. Adaptive Hypermedia. User Modeling and User-Adapted Interaction 11 (2001) 87-110.

4. Chiu, B. and Webb, G.: Using Decision Trees for Agent Modeling: Improving Prediction Performance. User Modeling and User-Adapted Interaction 8 (1/2) (1998) 131-152.
5. Grabtree, I. and Soltysiak, S.: Identifying and Tracking Changing Interests. International Journal of Digital Libraries vol. 2 (1998) 38-53.
6. Harries, M. and Sammut, C. Extracting Hidden Context. Machine Learning 32 (1998) 101-126.
7. Klingenberg, R. and Renz, I.: Adaptive information filtering: learning in the presence of concept drift. AAAI/ICML-98 Workshop on Learning for Text Categorization, TR WS-98-05, Madison, WI, (1998).
8. Kobsa, A., Koenemann, J. and Pohl, W.: Personalized Hypermedia Presentation Techniques for Improving Online Customer Relationships. The Knowledge Engineering Review, 16(2) (2001) 111-155.
9. Koychev, I. and Schwab, I.: Adaptation to Drifting User's Intersects - Proceedings ECML2000/MLnet workshop: ML in the New Information Age, Barcelona, Spain, (2000) pp. 39-45.
10. Maloof, M. and Michalski, R.: Selecting examples for partial memory learning. Machine Learning 41 (2000) 27-52.
11. Mitchell, T., Caruana, R., Freitag, D., McDermott, J. and Zabowski, D.: Experience with a Learning Personal Assistant. Communications of the ACM 37(7) (1994) 81-91.
12. Quinlan, R.: Induction of Decision Trees. Machine Learning 1 (1986) 81-106.
13. Schlimmer, J. and Granger, R.: Incremental Learning from Noisy Data. Machine Learning 3, Kluwer Academic Publishers (1986), 317-357.
14. Webb, G. and Kuzmycz, M.: Feature-based modelling: a methodology for producing coherent, consistent, dynamically changing models of agents' competencies. User Modeling and User-Adapted Interaction 5(2) (1996) 117-150.
15. Webb, G. Pazzani, M. and Billsus, D. Machine Learning for user modeling. User Modeling and User-Adaptive Interaction 11 (2001) 19-29.
16. Widmer, G.: Tracking Changes through Meta-Learning. Machine Learning 27 (1997) 256-286.
17. Widmer, G. and Kubat, M.: Learning in the presence of concept drift and hidden contexts: Machine Learning 23 (1996) 69-101.

Prediction of Navigation Profiles in a Distributed Internet Environment through Learning of Graph Distributions

Dirk Kukulenz

Kiel University, Institute of Computer Science,
Preusserstr. 1-9, 24105 Kiel, Germany
dku@ks.informatik.uni-kiel.de

Abstract. Collaborative filtering techniques in the Internet are a means to make predictions about the behaviour of a certain user based on the observation of former users. Frequently in literature the information that is made use of is contained in the access-log files of Internet servers storing requested data objects. However with additional effort on the server side it is possible to register, from which to which data object a client actually navigates. In this article the profile of a user in a distributed Internet environment will be modeled by the set of his navigation decisions between data objects. Such a set can be regarded as a graph with the nodes beeing the requested data objects and the edges being the decisions. A method is presented to learn the distribution of such graphs based on distance functions between graphs and the application of clustering techniques. The estimated distribution will make it possible to predict future navigation decisions of new users. Results with randomly generated graphs show properties of the new algorithm.

1 Introduction

In many applications in the field of Internet research it is important to estimate the relevance of data objects available in the Internet for a specific user or a group of users. In the field of *content-based learning* the estimation is based on the behaviour of a specific user. *Collaborative filtering* techniques make it possible to learn from former usages of other users in order to make predictions for a new user. These estimations can e.g. be used to make navigation on an Internet site easier, to improve the quality of web sites or to find groups of consumers or interest groups.

In [10] a procedure is presented to apply a collaborative filtering technique for the creation of index lists, i.e. new web pages containing lists of hyperlinks relevant for a certain topic, that are based on sets of requested data objects. In [2] a navigation support system is presented that learns from search words and browsing decisions of users, applying a reinforcement learning technique. In [14] and [12] techniques for presending documents on the WWW are described that apply different kinds of Markov-learning techniques.

The information that is known about a specific user in the case of [10] and [14] is the log data of Internet servers. Each request is stored in the so-called access-log file containing information about the time of a request, the IP-address of a client and the (IP-address of the) requested data object. However, different caching strategies are used in the Internet, with the intention to reduce net traffic and to increase the speed of requests. As a consequence, not all requests of clients actually reach the original server. Thus only a subset of requested data objects of a specific client is known on the server's side.

In [14] the actual navigation path is estimated using the access-log information. Here we will however use an idea presented in [2] to register the actual set of navigation decisions of a client on the server's side. A specially developed proxy server in the connection between server and client modifies each requested web page in a way that all hyperlinks point to that proxy server. The new links contain additional information like the originally requested page, the page where the link is located and and an id-number assigned to the client. By this means navigation decisions of Internet users on the considered website can be registered on the server's side. This method makes it also possible to register the number of navigation decisions in a distributed Internet environment, i.e. the navigation decisions between data objects on a number of Internet servers.

Our collaborative filtering procedure is based on these sets of navigation decisions of users. In the field of data mining algorithms are presented to find sets with high frequencies [1]. Related to that, in [6] an algorithm is presented to find frequent navigation sequences in the Internet. The approach described here is based on the distances between patterns. A set of navigation decisions can be regarded as a set of directed edges between data objects. These edges constitute a graph structure with vertices being the requested data objects and the edges being the decisions. In the field of pattern recognition different distance functions between graph structures are presented e.g. in [9], [4], [13]. We will use one of these functions together with an application of nearest neighbourhood clustering [7] to estimate the shape of the distribution of the graph profiles. Knowing this distribution simple classification procedures can be applied to classify a new profile and thereby to predict future decisions. The advantage of this technique compared to Markov models, as presented e.g. in [14], is that we don't have to consider the order of a Markov process. Such a predefinition may cause classification errors or otherwise cause an unnecessary increase of complexity.

In the next section the technique for the estimation of graph distibutions and the prediction technique of future navigation decisions will be described. In Sect. 3 some estimation examples with randomly generated graphs are presented showing properties of the distribution estimation and the prediction technique. Section 4 gives a summary and mentions further research issues.

2 Estimation of Graph Distributions

2.1 Definitions and Model

As described in the introduction, the information that can be acquired about a specific Internet user on the server's side with the described method is the set (or at least a subset) of his navigation decisions. These navigation decisions take place between certain data objects being available on the considered Internet site, like web pages, images, scripts, etc . Let 'D' denote the set of data objects in the Internet site, having an (own) URL address.

A user profile, measured by the agent, is then a graph structure:

Definition 1. *A (profile-) graph or navigation profile is a 4-Tupel $G=(V,E,\mu,\nu)$. V is a set of nodes and $E \subseteq V \times V$ is a set of edges. Function $\mu : V \to L_V \subset D$ assigns labels to the nodes. Function $\nu : E \to L_E$ assigns labels to the edges. Let $<G>$ be the set of all graphs following the preceding definition. This set will be denoted as 'graph space' based on D. Let $\{G\} \subseteq <G>$ denote a set of graphs.*

L_V is a subset of D or a set of pointers to D. The edges considered here are in the most common case hyperlinks that are present on certain web pages, Java applets or scripts. However, with the help of a search engine, the user can get from one data object to possibly any other object.

In the following sections the definitions of a subgraph, a graph and subgraph isomorphism, graph-edit operations and an error correcting subgraph isomorphism are used that are common in the field of graph theory or artificial intelligence and that are presented e.g. in [3] and [9].

2.2 Characterizations of Graph Distributions

It is our aim to classify a new profile graph according to a set of former profiles supplied by users. For this purpose it is helpful to know the distribution of graph profiles or at least to get an idea of the shape of this distribution. It is possible to regard $<G>$ as a discrete set and to assign a probability value to each element depending on the relative frequency. However, graphs may be similar according to certain aspects which may not be taken into account by the discrete formulation.

It is very likely that people having the same question in mind produce similar navigation profiles that are however slightly distorted because of Internet caching, different starting points or different searching strategies. Vice versa, similar profiles are likely to result from similar questions or intentions of users which is the main assumption we make [5], [8]. We therefore assume that the profiles are distributed in a way that one or a number of profiles in some 'places' in the graph space have a high likelihood and the other profiles being more and more distant from one of these 'central' profiles have a decreasing likelihood with respect to a distance function that will be defined in Sect. 2.3. This distribution can then be characterized by a function:

$$Charac1 : \{G\} \longrightarrow \{1,..n\}$$

Here, every profile is associated with one of the clusters. Another method is to consider the centers of the clusters and to take into account some characteristics of the inner cluster structure. A characterization of the graph distribution is then the set of these cluster properties:

$$Charac2: \bigcup_{i=1,..n} \{(\mu_i, \sigma_i, A_i)\},$$

where μ_i is the center graph of cluster i, σ_i is a measure for the distribution within the cluster, e.g. the mean value of the distances of the elements in the cluster i from the center element μ_i and A_i is the number of elements in the cluster. The center values μ_i can easily be found from $Charac.1$ by determining the element in the cluster with the smallest sum of the distances to all the other elements in the same cluster.

In the following we will use a simplification of the graph distribution characterization $Charac2$ by taking only the center elements into account. We define: $Charac2' : \bigcup_{i=1,..n} \{\mu_i\}$.

2.3 Graph Metrices

The 'shape' of the graph distribution as being characterized by $Charac1$ or $Charac2$ depends strongly not only on the data elements but also on the distance measure between graphs. Several definitions of graph distances are known from the field of pattern recognition.

A simple idea to define such a distance function is to count the number of identical nodes. To achieve a better segmentation of the set of graph profiles however, the structure of the connections, i.e. edges in the graphs, should be taken into account, too. A measure for such a structural similarity is the size of the largest common subgraph. In [4] it was shown that for two non-empty graphs G_1 und G_2 and the largest common subgraph $lcS(G_1, G_2)$ the function

Definition 2. $d(G_1, G_2) := 1 - \frac{|lcS(G_1,G_2)|}{max(|G_1|,|G_2|)}$

has the mathematical properties of a metrics ($|.|$ denotes the number of nodes in a graph). A similar graph distance was defined in [13]. The disadvantage of this metrics is that possible similarities between different nodes can't be taken into account. Such similarities between the type of nodes that are considered here, i.e. data objects, have been examined for textual data in the field of information retrieval [11]. They are important for the automatic indexing of web pages for the realization of search engines. One well-known distance measure is the *tfidf-*Norm, in which text pages are converted into vectors of weights of words that can be compared with the help of the cosine between the vectors.

A distance measure for two graphs G_1 and G_2 making it possible to take such similarities into account is the following function, where Δ is a set of graph-edit operations and C is a cost function for the edit oprations as described in [9]:

Definition 3. $d(G_1, G_2) := min_\Delta\{ C(\Delta) \mid$ there exists an error-correcting-subgraph-isomorphism f_Δ from G_1 to $G_2\}$

The distance function in definition 3 is not symmetric. In order to create a symmetric distance function it is possible to take the minimum of $d(G_1, G_2)$ and $d(G_2, G_1)$.

In the following we will however work with the distance in definition 2 which is easier to implement and faster to compute.

2.4 Estimation of a Graph Distribution

The previously defined metrices or distance functions can now be applied to estimate the shape of a graph distribution considering the distribution characterization $Charac2'$ in Sect. 2.2. The navigation graphs can be clustered using a common clustering technique like nearest neigbourhood clustering as described in [7] and by using one of the distance functions given in Sect. 2.3. Further investigations concerning the shape of the inner cluster distributions according to $Charac2$ in Sect. 2.2 can then be made.

In order to measure the quality of such a distribution estimation it may be helpful to determine the distance between a real distribution that is known in advance and an estimation of this distribution. Let $G_1,..G_n$ be the elements in $\{G\}$, $H_1,..H_m$ ($m \leq n$) be the real cluster centers characterizing the graph distribution and $d(G_1, G_2)$ be the distance between two graphs according to one of the definitions in Sect. 2.3. Let $\delta(G) := min\{d(G, H_j) | j = 1,..m\}$ with $G \in \{G\}$.

Definition 4. *Given an estimation of the cluster centers $\hat{H}_1,..\hat{H}_m$, let err* $:= \sum_{i=1,..m} \delta(\hat{H}_i)$.

Obviously, err decreases, if the estimation result gets better i.e. the estimated cluster centers move towards the real ones.

Knowing the estimated distribution of navigation graphs we can describe a prediction technique to find future navigation steps of a specific user if we assume that the new profile follows the same distribution as the former ones. One way is to compare the new navigation profile to the estimated cluster centers and to find the closest center. Given the estimated cluster centers $\hat{H}_1,..\hat{H}_m$ and the new profile G, in this method $d1_j := d(G, \hat{H}_j)$ has to be minimized in j where $d(G, \hat{H}_j)$ is a distance of G to the cluster center $\hat{H}_j$ as defined in Sect. 2.3. This center element $\hat{H}_j$ can then be expected to have a high relevance for the user.

A further possibility is to take into account the absolute probability that a user profile belongs to a cluster. This probability can be estimated by the relative number of elements in the cluster. The minimization of $d2_j := d(G, \hat{H}_j) \frac{1}{1+A_j/A}$ in j takes this absolute probability into account, where A is the number of observed profiles, A_j is the number of patterns in cluster j. These functions will be tested in the following section. The basic steps of the estimation and prediction algorithm are:

- Data acquisition

Distribution estimation (offline)

- Computation of the distance matrix
- Clustering procedure
- Distribution estimation

Prediction (online)

- Registration of a new (partial) user profile
- Computation of distances to the estimated cluster centers
- Classification of the new profile according to the estimated distribution and a classification function
- Prediction of future navigation decisions according to the classification results

The distribution estimation as described above can be done offline. For most of the applications like navigation support, the prediction step has to be done in real-time.

3 Simulation Results with Randomly Generated Graphs

It is our aim to show some of the properties of the described distribution estimation and classification with randomly generated navigation profiles where the distribution (i.e. $Charac2'$ in Sect. 2.2) of the original data is known in advance and can be compared to the estimation results. The simulation process starts by defining a graph space $< G >$ as defined in Sect. 2.1. A number of graphs will then be computed randomly with equal distribution, the number of nodes being identical and a fix number of edges. These graphs represent the real center graphs. Then a sequence of graphs will be computed presenting the simulated graph data. Each graph is obtained by randomly choosing one of the real center graphs and a number for the label errors. The error value is chosen according to a discrete Gaussian $N(0, \sigma)$ distribution. The simulated graph is computed by changing a number of node labels of the center graph, equal to the number of label errors.

In Fig. 1 the dependence of the estimation quality according to definition 4 on the number of graphs in the sequence of navigation profiles is shown. The number of elements in D is 30, the number of nodes in each graph is 25, with 30 edges. The graphs were computed from 2 original graphs (m=2), constituting the real distribution characterization. The number of identical simulations was 10. In Fig. 1 each value is the mean value of the estimation errors in the identical simulations. The graph metrics applied here for the clustering and the estimation quality measurement is the subgraph metrics in definition 2. As can be expected, the estimation error decreases, when the number of graphs increases since more information about the distribution is available for the estimation process.

In a second experiment we examined the prediction quality supposing that the distribution characterization is already known. A number of profiles were

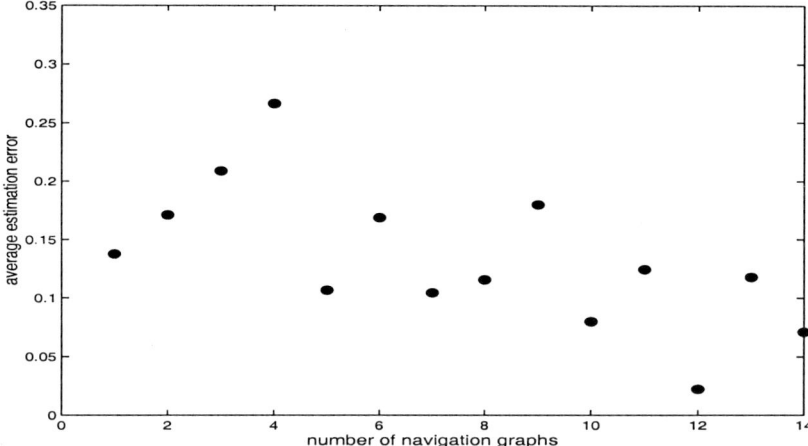

Fig. 1. Dependence of the estimation error on number of graphs

generated, following this distribution as described above. The percentage ($\times \frac{1}{100}$) of missclassifications was determined, denoted as 'classification error'.

Figure 2 shows the classification error based upon the minimization of $d1$ (•) and $d2$ (+) in Sect. 2.4. In the experiment the deviation of label errors is changed. As can be seen, the prediction based upon minimization of $d2$ shows better results for higher values of the label error. This result was expected since more information about the shape of the distribution is used in the case of $d2$.

4 Conclusion and Further Aspects

In this article an estimation technique was presented that applies clustering of a set of graphs based on a definition of a distance between graphs. This process provides a characterization of the distribution of graphs which is difficult to describe directly. This characterization can then be applied for a relevance estimation presuming that the new navigation graph follows the same distribution.

Some characteristics of the algorithm like the convergence for an increasing number of patterns were shown by means of randomly generated graphs. The advantage of the use of simulated data is the knowlege about the distribution that can't be known for real data.

Compared to Markov modelling this estimation method has the advantage that a multi-step-prediction can easily be done and that not only sequences of navigation steps but also navigation graphs i.e. sets of navigation steps can be taken into account. A graph modelling of user decisions can be of advantage if e.g. caching strategies in the Internet cause distorted navigation profiles or if the actual set of navigation decisions has to be considered.

One problem to discuss when recommending navigation decisions is the so-called 'snowball effect'. If the system learns a wrong path and presents it to other

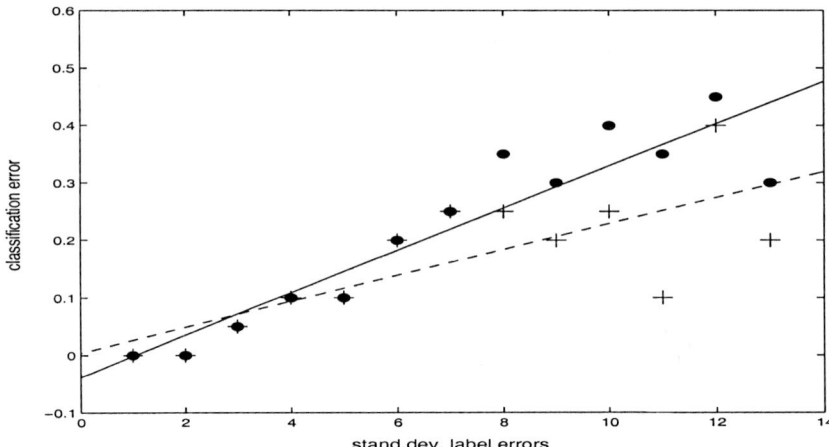

Fig. 2. Classification experiment of user profiles by minimizing d1 (•) and d2 (+) in Sect. 2.4.

users, they may also follow this wrong path and the system will learn again the wrong path. This problem however becomes only important if a high percentage of users actually use the support system. The registration of navigation decisions described in Sect. 1 is also possible for users who don't apply the support system.

There are more refined methods conceivable to describe a distribution of graphs. A first improved method is given in definition 2.2, however further improvements should be developed. Different and more refined graph distances can be defined e.g. taking into account node distances as described in definition 3. Additionally the prediction quality has to be examined closely for real data. The time requirements of the prediction algorithm are very important because this step has to be done in real-time if the prediction result is used e.g. for a navigation support tool. Further improvements of the system with respect to learning from additional information about a user or the Internet site are of interest.

References

1. R. Agrawal, T. Imielinski, and A. Swami. Mining association rules between sets of items in large databases. In *Proc. of the ACM SIGMOD Conference on Management of Data*, 1993.
2. R. Armstrong, D. Freitag, T. Joachims, and T. Mitchell. Web watcher: A learning apprentice for the www. In *AAAI Spring Symposium on Information Gathering from Heterogeneous, Distributed Environments*, pages 6–12, 1995.
3. Bollobas. *Graph theory*. Springer, 3 edition, 1999.
4. H. Bunke and K. Shearer. A graph distance metric based on the maximal common subgraph. In *Pattern Recognition Letters*, volume 19, pages 255–259, 1998.
5. E. Carmel, S. Crawford, and H. Chen. Browsing in hypertext: A cognitive study. In *Transactions on System, Man and Cybernetics*, volume 22, pages 865–883, 1992.

6. M. Chen, J.S. Park, and P.S. Yu. Data mining for path traversal patterns in a web environment. In *Proc. of the 16th ICDCS*, volume 16, pages 385–392, 1996.
7. B.S. Everitt. *Cluster Analysis*. Edward Arnold, 3 edition, 1993.
8. C. Hoelscher and G. Strube. Web search behavior of internet experts and newbies. In *World Wide Web Conf*, volume 9, 2000.
9. B. Messmer and H. Bunke. *Efficient graph matching algorithms for preprocessed model graphs*. PhD thesis, Bern University, 1996.
10. Mike Perkowitz and Oren Etzioni. Towards adaptive web sites: Conceptual framework and case study. *Artificial Intelligence*, 118(1–2):245–275, 2000.
11. G. Salton. Developments in automatic text retrieval. *Science*, 253:974–979, 1991.
12. R. Sarukkai. Link prediction and path analysis using markov chains. In *Intern. World Wide Web Conf.*, 2000.
13. W.D. Wallis, P. Shoubridge, M. Kraetz, and D. Ray. Graph distances using graph union. In *Pattern Recognition*, volume 22, pages 701–704, 2001.
14. I. Zukerman, D.Albrecht, and A.Nicholson. Predicting users' requests on the www. In *UM99 – Proceedings of the Seventh International Conference on User Modeling*, 1999.

EDUCO - A Collaborative Learning Environment Based on Social Navigation

Jaakko Kurhila[1], Miikka Miettinen[2], Petri Nokelainen[2], and Henry Tirri[2]

[1] Department of Computer Science
University of Helsinki, Finland
Jaakko.Kurhila@cs.helsinki.fi

[2] Complex Systems Computation Group
Helsinki Institute for Information Technology, Finland
{Miikka.Miettinen, Petri.Nokelainen, Henry.Tirri}@hiit.fi

Abstract. Web-based learning is primarily a lonesome activity, even when it involves working in groups. This is due to the fact that the majority of web-based learning relies on asynchronous forms of interacting with other people. In most of the cases, the chat discussion is the only form of synchronous interaction that adds to the *feeling* that there are other people present in the environment. EDUCO is a system that tries to bring in the sense of other users in a collaborative learning environment by making the other users and their the navigation visible to everyone else in the environment in real-time. The paper describes EDUCO and presents the first empirical evaluation as EDUCO was used in a university course.

1 Introduction

When Dourish and Chalmers introduced the concept of *social navigation*, they stated it to be "navigation because other people have looked at something" [4]. The concept has evolved since then (see e.g. [8] for an overview of the topic), and various categories of social navigation have emerged (direct – indirect [3], intended – unintended [6]). Today, many of the systems incorporating social navigation use *collaborative filtering*. It means that these "systems provide the user with recommendations of their likely interest in data items on the basis of 'interest matches' derived from ratings from the set of users" [5]. Examples of such recommender systems include various web-stores, where the customer is recommended a product based on the actions of previous customers.

In the area of web-based learning, recommender systems based on collaborative filtering can have a positive impact on the overall learning process. However, these systems do not address the problem of the feeling of being alone in a web-course. Commercial or even research-level course delivery systems [1] have rarely taken this into consideration. There are various collaborative virtual environments [2] that include the "feeling" of other users, but the solutions are not necessarily directly applicable to web-based learning.

EDUCO is a system that visualizes other live users currently present in the learning environment. Navigation and initiating synchronous or asynchrornous discussions have been made as simple as possible. The movement from one document to another in the environment is updated for every participant in real-time, thus adding to the feeling of truly live action. Research on workspace awareness has notified this as an important issue in groupware [12].

The EDUCO system has been tested in one advanced university course. A detailed description of the system, the study setting and the results are discussed in the subsequent sections.

2 EDUCO

Before going into the system description of EDUCO, a few concepts should be clarified. A *user* is a learner participating in a course in a web-based learning environment using EDUCO. A *document* is an HTML-file within EDUCO that is visible to the users. Documents have visual representations on the screen, and they can be grouped into *document clusters*. An *instance of* EDUCO means a fixed set of document clusters, i.e. a unique course within the EDUCO learning environment. An *administrator* of EDUCO is a person responsible for an instance of EDUCO. It is typical that the administrator of EDUCO is the teacher of the course. Only an administrator can add users or documents to an instance of EDUCO. The document clustering is also conducted by the administrator. The administrator can also assign group information to the users, thus forming various *user groups*. The group information and the document clustering are static unless the administrator makes the required changes to the system.

The user interface of EDUCO consists of six views of which only one is visible at a time. The views are map, chat, search, alarm, preferences and help. The screen layout when using EDUCO is presented in Fig. 1. The six views of EDUCO are presented in a tool resembling a handheld computer (upper-left corner in Fig. 1, now in "map" view). The largest area is reserved for documents gathered into an instance of EDUCO (right-hand side of the web-browser in Fig. 1). The space below the EDUCO tool is for the comments provided by the users.

"Map view" presents the document clusters of an instance of EDUCO. Every document is visible, and the clusters are distinct. Documents are presented as paper-icons. The users in an instance of EDUCO are presented as coloured dots. The dot is located next to the document the user is currently viewing. When a user places the mouse pointer on top of a document or a dot representing a user, a tool tip text appears showing the name of the person or the document. In Fig. 2 the pointer is on a document called "Where did all the people go?". Double clicking a document opens the document into the right-hand side of the browser window and moves the dot representing the user to a corresponding location on the map view of every user in the EDUCO instance.

The rectangle at the bottom of the map view in Fig. 2 is a magnifying glass included in the map view. The purpose of the magnifying glass is to make it easier for the users to click on the dots or documents while navigating.

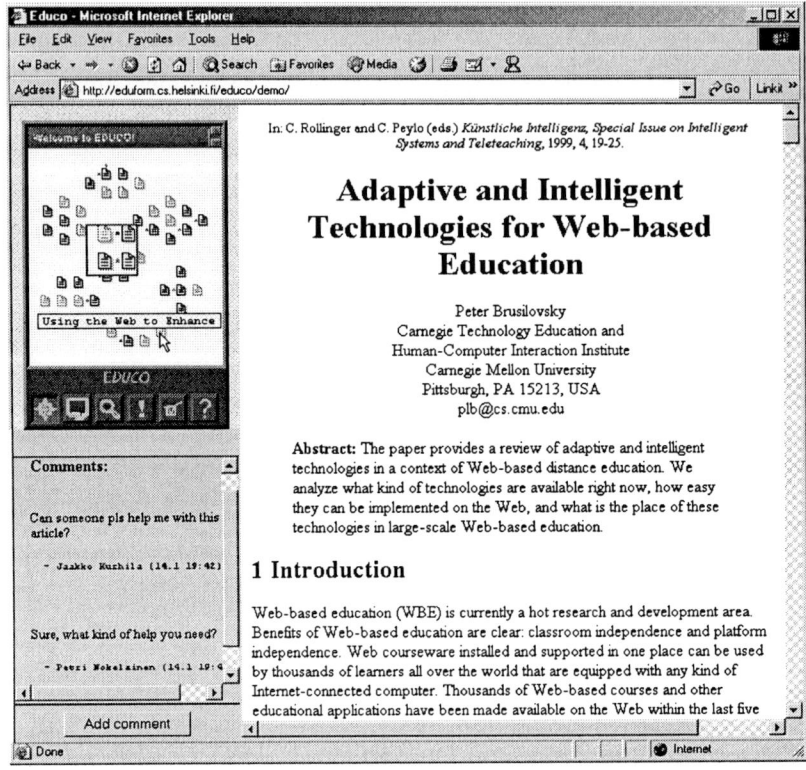

Fig. 1. The user interface of EDUCO.

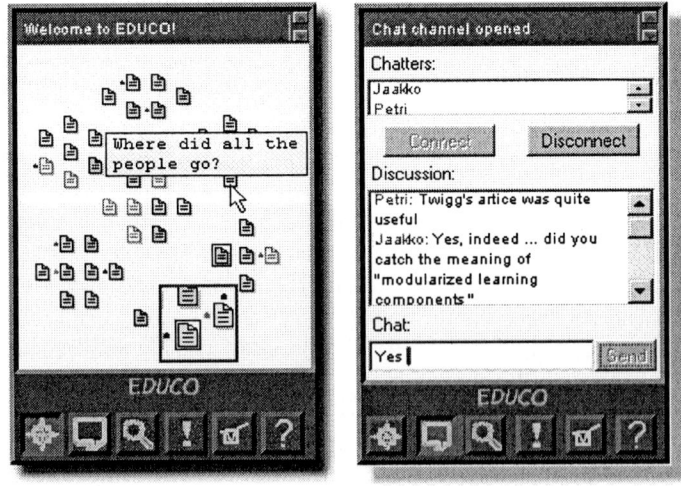

Fig. 2. The "map" and "chat" views of EDUCO.

The colours of the dots indicate different group memberships or types of user profile. The groups are assigned according to some metric the administrator of the EDUCO instance wishes to choose. For example, the groups can be assigned based on the students' interest in various topics within the course topics.

The documents change their colour on the map depending on how much they have been read in relation to the other documents. The colours range from bright (heavily read) to dimmed (not heavily read), as presented in Fig. 2. This way the user can get the "footprint" information at a glance and does not have to stay online and constantly watch where the other users navigate.

When in map view, clicking a user or a document symbol once selects it for further use. The further use can, for example, be a "Chat", which is the second view (Fig. 2). Any user can easily initiate a chat discussion with other users simply by clicking the corresponding user symbol and then clicking the "Connect" button in the chat view. The chat can be initiated with one to n other users. The restriction is that one person can be involved in only one chat channel at a time.

Chat is a form of synchronous communication in EDUCO. Depending on the situation, asynchronous discussions might sometimes be more useful. Therefore, every user in EDUCO has the possibility to write a comment when viewing a document. The comment is visible to users navigating to that document, i.e. the comments are document-specific. Other users can comment on the comment, thus continuing the chain of comments as illustarted in Fig. 1.

The third view is "Search". Users can search for other users and documents in an instance of EDUCO. When a user searches another user or a document, the results are shown textually in search view (Fig. 3) and graphically in map view by highlighting the corresponding user or document (the same effect as clicking a user or a document *once* in map view). The highlighting is illustrated in Fig. 2 where the magnifying glass is on a highlighted document. In addition to finding documents on the map, the operation of the search makes it easy to initiate a chat with a specific user.

"Alarm view" gives users the possibility to set up an alarm that is triggered if the requested condition occurs. For example, if a user seeks another user who is also interested in a certain document or topic, he or she can tell the system to give a notifying message when someone else arrives at the document. Alarm is a versatile tool, since the user can make different combinations of the three possible triggering events: users, group members and documents. Figure 3 shows the alarm view where the user is about to set the alarm to trigger if a user named "Demo user" or someone from group 2 arrives at the document named "Adaptive and Intelligent Technologies". Other highly used combinations include notifying if a certain user enters the system or if someone arrives to a specific document.

The last two views are "Preferences" and "Help". While viewing "Preferences", the user is allowed to change personal settings in the system. The settings include preferred nickname within the chat (in case the user wants to stay anonymous in the chat), and whether the user is visible to other users. If the user chooses to make her own navigation invisible in EDUCO, it automatically

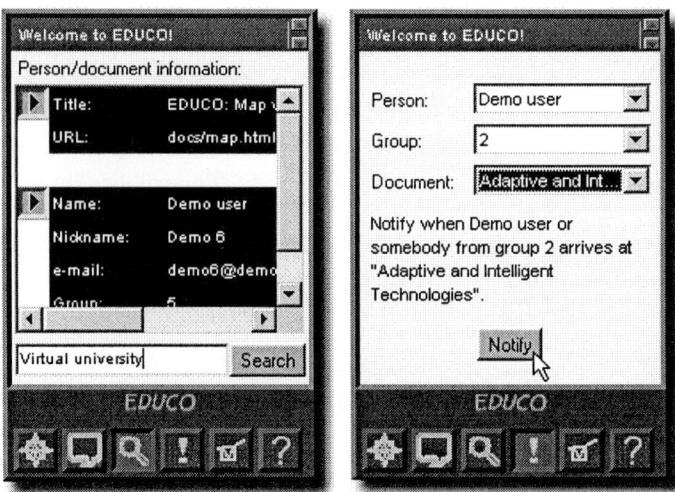

Fig. 3. The "search" and "alarm" views of EDUCO.

means that she cannot see the other users. Help view provides information about the system in general (Fig. 4)

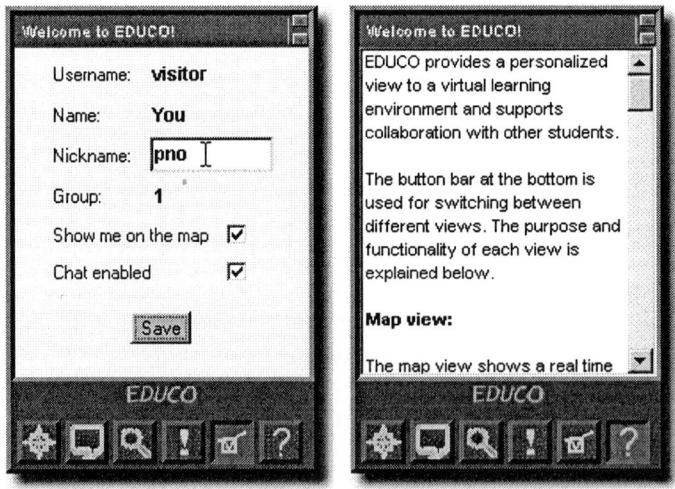

Fig. 4. The "preferences" and "help" views of EDUCO.

3 Educo Architecture

From a technological point of view, EDUCO consists of a socket server, a Java applet for every user and several CGI-scripts. The most important task of the server is to keep track of the state of the distributed system and inform the clients as changes occur. The changes include navigation from one document to another. If one of the users moves to another page, the new location has to be sent to everyone currently present in EDUCO. The implementation of this kind of communication scheme without delays requires that the clients maintain an open socket connection to the server throughout the session.

Besides managing connections as well as user and document information, the server forwards chat messages to their recipients and takes care of various bookkeeping activities related both to its own functioning and logging the users' actions for research purposes.

To avoid copyright issues and to make the use of EDUCO simpler for the administrator (course teacher), we have taken the approach that the documents (HTML-files) for a particular instance of EDUCO do not need to be copied to the EDUCO server. Instead, they can be located anywhere on the Web. To operate properly, the server still needs to know which document the user is reading to be able to send that information to all the other users in that instance. The operation has to work even when the users navigate along the hyperlinks in the documents and are not using the map view by double-clicking the document symbols. We have solved this problem by using the EDUCO server as a proxy. It means that the documents are routed through the server instead of being sent to the client directly from their actual location. This requires two additional operations: clients are informed about the new location of the user and all of the links in the document are changed so that they point to their destination indirectly through the proxy. If the user then clicks one of these links, the same procedure is repeated in a recursive fashion.

Commenting the documents in an instance of EDUCO is technically based on the use of ordinary HTML-forms. Each document has an associated comment file, which is opened to its designated frame every time a user navigates to that document. The server keeps track of modifications and the visits of individual users. This way the documents that have been commented after the last visit can be distinguished visually from those that contain only comments the user has already seen.

As mentioned above, the documents change their colour on the map view depending on how much they have been read in relation to the other documents. The total time all users have spent reading each document is recorded by the server on an hourly basis. The change in the colour of an individual document is determined by the distance of its moving average for the last 24 hours from the same average for all the documents. Heuristic methods have been devised to make the colouring of the documents operate sensibly at the very beginning of the course and during the silent periods (weekends, holidays etc.). It is also appropriate to eliminate the disturbing effect of very long reading times by setting an upper bound after which the additional time is ignored. The value for the upper bound can be the same for all documents or adjusted according to the differences in the lengths of the documents.

4 Study Setting

The course structure. The first empirical evaluation of EDUCO was conducted during a course entitled "Web-based learning" given at the University of Helsinki, Finland. The course is an advanced course in Computer Science studies. Twenty-four students participated in the course, some of them adult learners with varying backgrounds and degrees but most of them were CS majors. The type of the course was a "seminar" which means that the students have to pick a topic, prepare a 10-page paper on the topic and present it to the teacher and other students in the course. In addition, there were some short weekly assignments to complete.

There were only two face-to-face meetings during the course. The first was an initial meeting where the structure and requirements for the course were explained and the EDUCO system was introduced. The second face-to-face meeting was the final meeting where the students presented their papers. Everything else between the initial and final meeting was conducted on-line using EDUCO.

Only the real-time social navigation of the system was studied and not the use of the "footprint" information. Because of the small student population participating in the course, we fixed a primary time slot to make sure that there would be people in EDUCO at the same time. However, the time slot was not restrictive in any way.

Forty-three documents were first gathered into the instance of EDUCO to serve as a starting point for the topics in the course. The documents were clustered according to the six general areas to be covered: history of web-based learning, society and web-based learning, research findings, teaching and studying in a web-based course, course delivery systems, and providing adaptation in educational systems.

The data set for the study was gathered in three stages: (1) a pre test after the start of the course measured motivational level and learning strategies, (2) users' actions were logged during the course, and (3) a post test after the course measured how students' expectations met the reality.

Pre test. Motivational profiling in this study is based on the Motivated Strategies for Learning questionnaire (MSLQ), which is developed on the basis of a motivational expectancy model [7]. MSLQ measures both motivational factors and learning strategies. The motivation section (A) of MSLQ consists of 17 items that were used to assess students' value for a course, their beliefs about their skill to succeed in the course, and their anxiety about tests in the course. A 5-point Likert-scale ranging from 1 ("Not at all true of me") to 5 ("Very true of me") was used for all items.

The theoretical model of motivation [10] is constructed out of six factor solution: (1) Intrinsic goal orientation, (2) Extrinsic goal orientation, (3) Meaningfullness of studies, (4) Control beliefs, (5) Efficacy beliefs, and (6) Test anxiety

occupied	occ_no	url	id	time_min	id_group
0	0	http://ijhcs.open.	mj	8,00	Group 2
1	4	http://ausweb.scu.	m	2,00	Group 3
0	0	http://194.100.30.	va	1,00	Group1
1	2	http://www.educaus	k	3,00	Group 2

Fig. 5. A sample of the filtered EDUCO log file.

[11]. We expected to find a similar structure in the sample data and thus to be able to construct sensible motivational groups.

Users' actions during the course. The user log from EDUCO (time stamp, user id, action) was recorded during the course from September 24 to November 20, 2001. The filtered log file of 1832 recorded actions (Fig. 5) was analysed in order to find what effect EDUCO's visual social navigation information had on the users' navigation behaviour.

The main level problem was operationalised into the following two sub-level propositions: firstly, did the users in general prefer occupied (someone else at the document, "occupied" = 1 in Fig. 5) documents over unoccupied (the document is "free" from other users, "occupied" = 0) ones? Secondly, did the users based on their pre test motivational group membership ("id_group") prefer occupied documents over unoccupied ones?

Post test. An email survey consisting of 17 open propositions was conducted two weeks after the course in December 2001. Propositions measured users' experiences and expectations towards web-based education together with attributes related to EDUCO (usability issues, user interface, functionality etc.).

5 Results

Pre test. The analysis of the "A" section of the motivational pre test questionnaire was carried out with a Bayesian dependence modeling tool named B-Course[1] [9]. The results indicated that the theoretical model of six factors [11] was a viable solution for this small number data set. Based on the motivational level scores on six dimensions, respondents were divided into three groups:

- Group 1 ("Blue", N=10) characteristics: (2) Extrinsic goal orientation, (6) test anxiety and (3) meaningfullness of studies.
- Group 2 ("Green", N=8) characteristics: (5) Efficacy beliefs, (1) intrinsic goal orientation and (3) meaningfullness of studies.
- Group 3 ("Red", N=6) characteristics: (4) Control beliefs and (1) intrinsic goal orientation.

---
[1] B-Course URL http://b-course.cs.helsinki.fi

The classification accuracy of the theoretical model [10] was confirmed with both a linear and nonlinear discriminant analysis (87.5% of original and 75.0% of cross-validated grouped cases were correctly classified). There was no statistical signifigance between the group memberships of male and female respondents.

The group descriptions with clear explanations were published on the course web-site for all the participants, so that the students were able to use the information when completing weekly assignments or choosing a study partner.

Users' actions during the course. After filtering out the entry document from the log file, the analysis of the data (total number of logged events = 1832) indicated that the users preferred unoccupied documents (943 requests, 51.5%) over occupied ones (889 requests, 48.5%). The number of simultaneous readers in occupied documents varied from one to six with the following request frequencies: one reader (501 requests, 56.5%), two readers (268 requests, 30.2%), three readers (75 requests, 8.5%), four readers (35 requests, 3.9%), five readers (7 requests, 0.8%), and six readers (1 request, 0.1%). The results revealed no gender-related differences.

The results proved ($\chi^2 = 13.29$, p=0.01) that the respondents selected documents based on their pre test motivational group membership (Fig. 6). Members of the "Blue" group preferred unoccupied documents (N=496, 55.5%) over occupied ones (N=398, 44.5%). Students belonging to the "Green" group made no distinction between documents. This result is in balance with the group characteristics that emphasize intrinsic goal orientation and efficacy beliefs. Members of the "Red" group preferred occupied documents (N=234, 55.1%) over unoccupied ones (N=191, 44.9%) indicating a tendency towards social navigation.

The third part of the log file data analysis focused on the reading times per document. The values of "Time" variable were categorised into six classes: 0–2, 2–5, 5–10, 10–30, 30–60 and 60–90 minutes. Reading sessions that lasted over 90 minutes were excluded from the analysis. This part revealed interesting group specific results. Members of the "Green" group spent the least time (x=2.7 min) per document compared to other groups ($\chi^2 = 19.38$, p=0.04). This result sup-

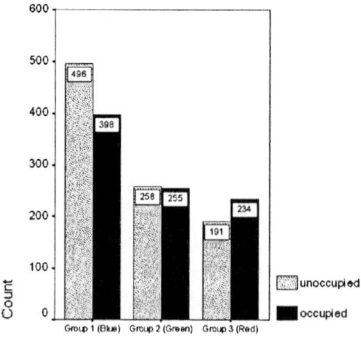

Fig. 6. Social navigation preferences based on pre test motivational group membership.

ports the "result-oriented" label of the group members. There was no difference in reading times between the "Blue" (x=3.2 min) and the "Red" (x=3.6 min) group.

Post test. The third phase of this study was to analyse the propositions of the post test (the total number of propositions was 17). The total number of answers to the post test questionnaire was 17 (71%) out of 24. The sample data consisted of five female and twelve male students.

Results of the post test show that EDUCO was seen as a useful tool in the matters like adaptation to respondents learning, cognitive and motivational strategies, and means to implement collaborative actions.

> "It was very useful to see what documents other users were reading, it gave me many hints and saved time."
> "It was truly nice to be able to see what the most interesting document at the moment is and who is reading it."
> "Actually, in several cases I wanted to start a chat conversation with someone reading the same hyperdocument with me ...I guess this is social navigation?"

The presence of EDUCO increased task-related participation and was a valued tool for those who had difficulties to participate in face-to-face meetings:

> "The learning material was easy to access."
> "EDUCO gives more flexibility to the studying process."
> "It was possible for me to participate in this course and carry out all those tasks regardless of my domicile."

The real time interaction of EDUCO also elicited negative comments:

> "EDUCO hindered the formation of REAL social contacts!"
> "Chat never beats traditional face to face meetings."

EDUCO's tools for seeking work mates (group membership, search function) were truly useful for most of the respondents:

> "I was in a blue group, and when another blue was looking for a mate, I replied instantly. He had already chosen an article, I glanced at it and found that it was suitable for me too."
> "I had a group proposal via email message. As my forthcoming work mate had the same colour as I did, it was easy to make the decision to start collaboration. Afterwards I thought that I agreed so quickly because of the same motivational group, normally it takes more consideration. But to be honest, the topic was the most important factor."

6 Conclusions

EDUCO, a system based on social navigation for web-based learning, has been beneficial for some users. Moreover, using a system like EDUCO opens up other important issues as well. The teacher of a web-course has an opportunity to re-think the learning process as a whole. Recent pedagogical approaches such as just-in-time learning can benefit, for example, from the possibility in EDUCO to form *ad hoc* study groups based on the motivational group information and the interest expressed for a certain topic. The students themselves are in control of forming the groups, thus shifting the emphasis towards peer-assisted and learner-centered education.

References

1. Brusilovsky, P. and Miller, P.: Course Delivery Systems for the Virtual University. In T. Tschang and T. Della Senta (Eds.): Access to Knowledge: New Information Technologies and the Emergence of the Virtual University, pages 167-206. Amsterdam: Elsevier Science (2000).
2. Churchill, E., Snowdon, D. and Munro, A.(Eds): Collaborative Virtual Environments. Springer (2001).
3. Dieberger, A.: Social Navigation in Populated Information Spaces. In A. Munro, K. Höök and D. Benyon (Eds.), Social Navigation of Information Space, pages 35-54. London: Springer (1999).
4. Dourish, P. and Chalmers, M.: Running Out of Space: Models of Information Navigation. In Proceedings of HCI'94 (1994).
5. Dourish, P.: Where the Footprints Lead: Tracking Down Other Roles for Social Navigation. In A. Munro, K. Höök and D. Benyon (Eds.), Social Navigation of Information Space, pages 15-34. London: Springer (1999).
6. Forsberg, M., Höök, K. and Svensson, M.: Footprints in the Snow. Position paper for 4th ERCIM Workshop User Interfaces for All. http://ui4all.ics.forth.gr/UI4ALL-98/forsberg.pdf (1998).
7. Garcia, T. and Pintrich, P.: Regulating Motivation and Cognition in the Classroom: The Role of Self-Schemas and Self-Regulatory Strategies. In D.H. Schunk and B.J. Zimmerman (Eds.), Self- Regulation of Learning and Performance: Issues and Educational Applications. Hillsdale, N.J.: Erlbaum (1994).
8. Munro, A., Höök, K. and Benyon, D.: Footprints in the Snow. In A. Munro, K. Höök and D. Benyon (Eds.), Social Navigation of Information Space, pages 1–14. London: Springer (1999).
9. Nokelainen, P., Silander, T., Tirri, H., Tirri, K and Nevgi, A.: Modeling Students' Views on the Advantages of Web-Based Learning with Bayesian Networks. Proceedings of the 10th International PEG2001 Conference, pages 202–211 (2001).
10. Ruohotie, P.: Conative Constructs in Learning. In P. Pintrich and P. Ruohotie (Eds.) Conative Constructs and Self-Regulated Learning, pages 1-30. Saarijärvi: Learning and Change Series of Publications (2000).
11. Ruohotie, P., Nokelainen, P., Tirri, H. and Silander, T.: Modeling Student Motivation and Self-regulated Learning with Bayesian Networks. In P. Ruohotie, P. Nokelainen, H. Tirri and T. Silander (Eds.) Modeling Individual and Organizational Prerequisites of Professional Growth, pages 174–195. Saarijärvi: University of Tampere (2001).
12. Wang, H. and Chee, Y.S.: Supporting Workspace Awareness in Distance Learning Environments: Issues and Experiences in the Development of a Collaborative Learning System. Proceedings of the International Conference on Computers in Education (ICCE2001), pages 1109–1116. Seoul, Korea: Incheon National University of Education (2001).

GOOSE: A Goal-Oriented Search Engine with Commonsense

Hugo Liu, Henry Lieberman, and Ted Selker

MIT Media Laboratory
20 Ames St., E15-320G
Cambridge, MA 02139, USA
{hugo, lieber, selker}@media.mit.edu

Abstract. A novice search engine user may find searching the web for information difficult and frustrating because she may naturally express search goals rather than the topic keywords search engines need. In this paper, we present GOOSE (goal-oriented search engine), an adaptive search engine interface that uses natural language processing to parse a user's search goal, and uses "common sense" reasoning to translate this goal into an effective query. For a source of common sense knowledge, we use Open Mind, a knowledge base of approximately 400,000 simple facts such as "If a pet is sick, take it to the veterinarian" garnered from a Web-wide network of contributors. While we cannot be assured of the robustness of the common sense inference, in a substantial number of cases, GOOSE is more likely to satisfy the user's original search goals than simple keywords or conventional query expansion.

1 Introduction

The growth of available content on the World Wide Web makes it necessary for everyone to use tools, not experience, to find things. Major search engines like Google and Yahoo have made great progress in indexing a large percentage of the content on the web so that it is searchable. However, the user interface to the search process is usually just a text input box waiting for input. The user interfaces in most of today's search engines still rely on a grammar of set operators and keywords, and for good results, the user is expected to be able to fill the box with the right keywords and in the right combination. This situation prompts the question: instead of having the user conform to the search engine's specifications, why not make the search engine adapt to how the user most naturally expresses his/her information needs, so that even inexperienced users can perform an effective search?

1.1 An Experiment

To learn some qualities an intuitive search engine interface should have, we asked four search engine novices and four experienced search engine users to perform several tasks using the Yahoo search engine. Whereas experienced users chose precise keywords likely to isolate the types of web pages they were looking for, novice users reverted to typing their search goal into the keyword field in natural language. For example, one search task that users were asked to perform was to find people on the web who shared the user's own interests. One novice user submitted the query: "I want to find other people who like movies," and obtained many irrelevant and unwanted search results on the topic of movies. In contrast, a more experienced user formed the query: " +'my homepage' +'my interests' +'movies' " and was able to get many relevant results. The experienced user chose not only a keyword ("movies") on the topic of the search, but also two keywords ("my homepage", "my interests") differentiating the context in which the topic keyword should appear. In choosing these keywords, the experienced user used her expertise to guide a series of inferences from the search goal. In interviewing the user, we learned that the inference chain, or thought process, that she went through looked something like this:

I want to find people online who like movies.
Movies are a type of interest that a person might have.
People might talk about their interests on their homepage
People's homepages might start with "my homepage".

This prompted us to further reasoning. As with all of the inference chains used by the four experienced users, this inference chain has the following property: Most of the steps in the inference chain are statements that arguably fall under the "common sense" knowledge domain, things that most people know to be true (in this case, only the last step is somewhat domain-specific knowledge); however, the knowledge of how to connect these commonsense facts to infer a good search query is where search engine expertise is required.

Even the experience of these few subjects point to out that novice searchers are confusing the search engine with the approach that they naturally communicate with. Simple improvements might be to: 1) allow the user to formulate the search query as a statement of the user's search goal, and from that, the search engine must make the necessary inference to arrive at the appropriate keywords, and 2) allow the user to express the search query in natural language.

To meet the second criterion, the search engine needs to have natural language parsing capabilities. The first criterion is trickier. If we are to expect the search engine to assume the burden of performing the inference, we might give it knowledge about the world that most people know (commonsense), and also some knowledge about what a good search query is, something that experienced search engine users know (expertise).

GOOSE is a goal-oriented search engine organized around the concept of a search goal. Enriched with commonsense knowledge, search engine expertise, and natural language parsing capabilities, it assumes the burden of translating a user's search goal into a good query.

In this paper, we will first present some background on this project, followed by descriptions of the GOOSE user interface and internal mechanism, a sample user scenario, and preliminary user test results. We will then proceed to discuss some future work of personalizing the commonsense and conclude.

2 Background

Previous approaches to query improvement have for the most part employed three techniques: 1) expanding the topic keyword using thesauri and co-occurrence lists [7, 10] 2) relevance feedback [11], and 3) using hand-crafted question templates [1]. Though the first approach shows promise for queries that return limited results, expanding keywords does not necessarily improve the relevance of the search results. The second approach does a better job of improving relevance, but complicates the task model by adding additional search steps. In addition, neither the first nor the second approaches address the weaknesses of keywords as the basis of the user interface. The third approach, as used by Ask Jeeves [1], offers the user a more intuitive natural language interface, but answerable questions must be anticipated in advance and a template for each question must be handcrafted. For this reason, we don't believe that this approach is easy to scale.

Our approach is significantly different from all the aforementioned approaches. In our system, the original query is a natural language statement of the user's search goal, and the reformulation step involves natural language parsing of this statement, followed by inference to generate the query that will best satisfy this goal. Unlike thesauri-driven keyword expansion, our system is not merely adding new keywords, but is actually performing inference and composing an entirely new search query that would best fulfill the user's goal. Compared with relevance feedback, the user interface we propose is automatic, and does not require additional steps in the task model. Finally, unlike handcrafted question templates, we believe that our approach of using a freely available, ever-growing, and vast source of commonsense knowledge to perform *reasoning* over the original query is a more scalable approach, and allows for many levels of inference, compared to the fixed, one-level of inference associated with question templates.

2.1 Source of Commonsense

The idea of using commonsense reasoning to improve user interfaces has been extensively explored by Minsky [5]. The commonsense knowledge used by our system comes from the Open Mind Commonsense Project [8] – an endeavor at the MIT Media Laboratory that aims to allow a web-community of teachers to collaboratively build a database of knowledge using diverse representations, and to explore ways to use this knowledge to make computer applications more intelligent and context-aware. Using the Open Mind Commonsense website, web collaborators input simple facts about the world, expressed as simple English sentences, which are organized into an ontology of commonsense relations.

2.2 Ordinary Commonsense vs. Application-Level Commonsense

When we refer to the commonsense knowledge used in GOOSE, we mean two things. The first is ordinary commonsense, which encompasses the things that people normally consider to be known by everyone, such as "sugar tastes sweet," or "if someone hits you, you may feel pain." The second is application-level commonsense, that is, knowledge specific to a domain, and considered to be commonsense in that domain. An example of application-level commonsense in our web search engine domain is: "espn.com is a website which provides news about sports." Both types of commonsense can be easily solicited through the Open Mind website interface because each piece of knowledge is expressed in simple English. In addition, some application-level commonsense can be mined from the World Wide Web.

3 User Interface

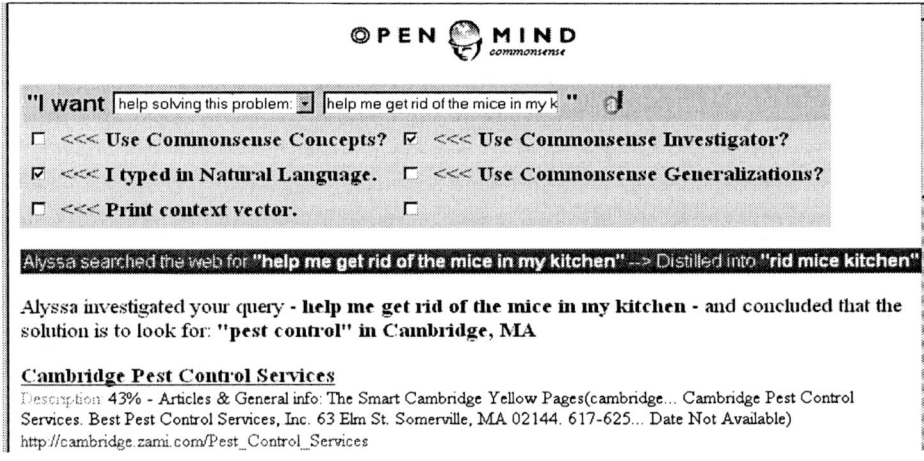

Fig. 1. A screenshot of the current User Interface for GOOSE, where search goals must be manually disambiguated.

Arguably the most intuitive interface would simply allow the user to type the entire search goal as a sentence in natural language. Our system must then understand that goal and have the expertise to know how to reformulate the goal into a good query. Unfortunately, the expertise in our system is currently not complete enough to be able to interpret arbitrary goals, so instead we have created some templates that encapsulate search engine expertise for the common categories of goals.

GOOSE's user interface (Fig. 1) asks the user to select the goal of his/her search from a pull-down menu, and enter a query that completes the sentence begun by the search goal. Currently five search goals exist, and they are:

1. "I want help solving this problem:"
2. "I want to research…"

3. "I want to find websites about…"
4. "I want to find other people who…"
5. "I want specific information about the product/service…"

Because the knowledge associated with each goal category is modular, it would be relatively easy to add new search goals. Without an extensive usability study, it is unclear exactly how much coverage these categories of goals provide, and how many may eventually be needed; however, we believe that some of the categories listed above are generic enough to support any goal. Therefore, the issue of scaling up is not likely to be limited so much by the number and types of available search goals as by the diversity and coverage of the commonsense knowledge available for inference. One limitation of this type of interface is the lack of ability to state multiple goals and overlapping goals, but this is addressable if we allow more than one goal to be active at a time, and devise a method for combining search results obtained through multiple goals.

4 Mechanism

Given a search goal and search query, GOOSE performs four major internal steps before results are returned to the user: 1) Parsing the query into a semantic frame [6]; 2) classifying the query into a commonsense sub-domain; 3) reformulating the query through commonsense inference guided by expertise templates; 4) and re-ranking results using commonsense concepts.

4.1 Parsing to Frames

After the user executes the search query, GOOSE parses the query to fill the slots of a semantic frame, which provides a concise, stereotyped representation of the original query. Representing the original query as a frame makes commonsense reasoning easier because the most important features of the query are extracted. An example is given in Table 1.

Table 1. An example of a filled semantic frame for the goal, "I want help solving this problem:" and the query, "My cat is sick and wheezing"

Slot Name	Slot Value
Problem Attribute	[Sick, Wheezing]
Problem Object	[Cat]

As suggested by this example, each search goal needs its own unique set of semantic frames. This is true because different aspects of each query are useful to accomplishing different search goals. In the above example, identifying the problem attribute and problem object is most useful to identifying a solution through commonsense reasoning. The set of all semantic frame templates represents a part of the expertise that experienced users possess. Currently, each of the five search goal categories has one semantic frame, but as the system scales, more frames are likely to be added.

It is worth pointing out that our system's parsing of the natural language query differs from the ways in which other search engines handle unstructured text input. A typical search engine throws out a list of stop words and treats the remaining words as keywords [9], but our approach tokenizes, part-of-speech tags, parses the entire query, and translates the parse tree into a filled semantic frame.

4.2 Classification

In addition to parsing the original query to frames, a classifier examines the original search goal and determines the commonsense sub-domain that can provide the most applicable knowledge when performing commonsense reasoning. Examples of sub-domains for the "I want help solving this problem" search goal include "personal health problems," and "household problems." Each sub-domain contains both ordinary and application-level commonsense knowledge.

Classification is performed in a relatively straightforward way. Each sub-domain is described by the commonsense concepts it covers. A search goal is classified into all sub-domains, which match the concepts contained in it. Multiple sub-domain matches can be safely merged.

We have chosen to group the commonsense used for GOOSE into sub-domains to help disambiguate certain words and concepts. Another advantage of sub-domains of commonsense is the savings in the run-time of the inference, a benefit of a smaller search space.

4.3 Reformulation

In this step, we take the filled semantic frame and apply reasoning over the chosen commonsense sub-domain. In our current implementation, reasoning takes place as an inference chain, implemented as a depth-first search, guided by heuristically motivated rules that help direct the inference so as to avoid unnecessary searching. Inference terminates when an application-level rule has fired. Again, application-level rules are a component of search engine expertise. When the inference terminates, we will have the reformulated search terms that we need.

Once the query has been successfully reformulated, it is submitted to a commercial search engine and the result is captured for further refinement.

4.4 Re-ranking

Using GOOSE's concept vectors, a list of weighted words and phrases representative of the concepts contained within the search query, GOOSE re-ranks the search results so that the hits most relevant to the search query are given higher priority.

This concept-based re-ranking step is similar to the query expansion approach proposed by Klink [3], except that in our case, it is only used as a refinement of existing search results.

Where commonsense inference fails to infer any query from the search goal, keywords from the search goal are extracted and passed to the commercial search engine. In such cases, query refinement with commonsense concept vectors can serve as a back-up mechanism, because such refinement may still lead to improved results over the baseline where GOOSE is not used at all.

5 A Scenario

Having explained the GOOSE user interface and mechanism, let us imagine a typical user scenario. Suppose that a novice user has a sick pet and wants to find ways to remedy the problem. She does not know how to form a good search query, so she decides to try her search on GOOSE. She chooses the goal, "I want help solving this problem:" and types in the query, "my golden retriever has a cough." Using the semantic frame defined for this particular goal, GOOSE fills the frame as follows:

Problem Attribute: [cough]
Problem Object: [golden retriever]

The classifier examines the query and determines that the commonsense subdomain to be used is "animals." Performing inference over the "animals" subdomain, the following inference chain is invoked:

1. A golden retriever is a kind of dog.
2. A dog may be a kind of pet.
3. Something that coughs indicates it is sick.
4. Veterinarians can solve problems with pets that are sick.
5. Veterinarians are locally located.

The first three steps in the inference chain are ordinary commonsense, while the last two steps are application-level commonsense. GOOSE takes the result of the inference and submits the reformulated query, "Veterinarians, Cambridge, MA" to a commercial search engine. The locale that was added is a personalization, and must be obtained through a user profile. After search results are returned, commonsense concept vectors are used to refine the results so that search hits containing the concepts closest to "veterinarian" appear higher in the search results.

The user finds what she was looking for in the first page of results and never had to explicitly choose the keywords that brought her to what she was looking for.

6 Preliminary User Tests

We conducted preliminary user tests asking four search engine novice users to form queries for a few simple search tasks. Due to the limited search goal categories available in the current implementation, we focused on the categories and commonsense sub-domains that the system knew how to handle. The query being inputted into the GOOSE UI was sent to both GOOSE as well as directly to the Google commercial search engine. Users were then asked to rate the relevance of the first page results on a scale of 1 (most irrelevant) to 10 (most relevant). In cases where commonsense inference failed to infer a search query from the search goal, commonsense concept vectors were still used to reorder the search results. Table 2 presents some of the results.

Table 2. Preliminary user test results. Participants formed 2 queries each for each search task.

Search Task	# successful inferences	Avg. score GOOSE	Avg. score Google
Solve household problem	7 / 8	6.1	3.5
Find someone online	4 / 8	4.0	3.6
Research a product	1 / 8	5.9	6.1
Learn more about	5 / 8	5.3	5.0

Our test results suggest that for novice search engine users, GOOSE on average produced more effective first-page results than Google, a leading commercial search engine. The problem solving goal category is where inference showed the most promising results, as demonstrated by the search task "solve household problem." However, the high rate of failure of the inference in producing a query suggests that GOOSE is still very brittle in the current implementation and only works well under very constrained domains for which organized commonsense knowledge exists, such as personal health and household problems. Many more domains and goals must be supported before any extensive user tests can performed, but these initial results are encouraging.

One fundamental limitation of using the commonsense knowledge for inference is illustrated by the result for the "research a product" search task. In this task, some users chose to search for trademark names of products, such as "the Total Gym", and "TurboTax". In such cases, commonsense inference will not be of help because trademark product names are not part of the knowledge base. This task, however, seems to be particularly suitable to a keywords approach, as Google received relatively high marks on this task. GOOSE received similar marks because although it could not be helpful in this case, it did not hurt the results either.

The results of this preliminary user test are promising. In future user tests, we hope to measure the intuitiveness of the proposed user interface, the usefulness of GOOSE to already experienced users, and have a head-to-head comparison against other query enrichment techniques such as keyword expansion and relevance feedback.

7 Conclusion

In this paper, we presented an adaptive search engine interface that can use commonsense to perform inference over user's search goal, in order to generate an effective query. While the commonsense inference is not complete, it can still be useful. GOOSE is a fail-soft application, in that, in the case it fails to produce a better query for the user, it will just produce the same results the user would have obtained anyway. So the argument can be made that GOOSE can be useful, even if the commonsense reasoning is brittle, because GOOSE can help some of the time, and it won't hurt the rest of the time.

As we continue to scale the commonsense coverage of GOOSE, we face several pointed issues. First, classification into commonsense sub-domains becomes less accurate as the number of sub-domains increases. Second, it will become increasingly difficult to define commonsense sub-domains that are of the right size and that do not overlap with existing sub-domains. One radical solution to the two above-mentioned problems would be to not only allow overlapping sub-domains, but to go so far as *fostering* many diverse and competing representations of commonsense, each with strengths and weaknesses, which will compete with each other in their reasoning of a particular query. In this model as suggested by Minsky [5], commonsense coverage will be increased, and reasoning will be more robust because it will exploit the complementary strengths of different representations.

Third, as the number of commonsense statements increase, inference will take combinatorially longer and be more prone to noise because the search space will have increased. To overcome these problems, we need to give the inference process more guidance via pruning techniques, and give it the ability to recognize when it is on the wrong path to the goal, or when it does not know enough to reach the goal. One possibility for guided inference is to valuate candidate inference chains that will result from different inference paths, much like a chess-playing program valuates board positions that result from different moves. However, this approach assumes that it is feasible to devise good ways to valuate an inference chain, which is a non-trivial problem.

From the preliminary user tests, we have learned more about the fundamental limitations of using commonsense to help the user compose search queries. First, the commonsense knowledge in Open Mind contains only about 400,000 facts, which do not assume equal distribution of the knowledge over diverse topics. Minsky estimates that somewhere on the order of 15 million pieces of knowledge may be needed in order to be comparable to what humans possess. Obtaining and organizing knowledge on that scale will be a huge challenge, not to mention efficiency issues that that scale creates. The second major limitation of commonsense is that it will probably not tell GOOSE about all the specific topics needed to perform inference, such as trademarked products, what specific companies do, etc. It can only help to reason about concepts and problems that we encounter in everyday life. Without speculation of the difficulty of doing so, if we can mine specific knowledge from other resources or the web, it may be possible to connect this knowledge to the inference mechanism.

8 Future Work

As of now, GOOSE is not yet robust or helpful enough although it has the potential to be. In addition to the scaling issues discussed above, we are working toward two goals: personalizing the commonsense, and automatic detection of goal categories.

One way to consider the role "common sense" plays in the system is to think of it as a generic user model, because it represents knowledge in everyone's head (everyone within a particular culture). We can customize the user model by adding personal commonsense to the system such as "Mary is my sister." Personalizing commonsense is logical, because the notion of what "common sense" is varies from one person to another. GOOSE may be able to utilize personal commonsense to better interpret the user's search goals and produce more relevant results. An example of personalization currently used by the system is the placement of the locale keyword in the query to accompany a local business. "Veterinarian Cambridge, MA" is one example. However, we can also imagine subtler examples of how personal commonsense can influence inference. For instance, if a user has a broken VCR, she might want search results for either do-it-yourself resources or electronics repair shops. Depending on the type of person she is, she might want one type of result or the other or both.

Personal commonsense can be stated as simple English sentences, so it is easy to add to the system. The real challenge is in devising a way to collect the information. For instance, we can imagine with the broken VCR example, that the user may be shown two sets of search results, and her preferring one set or the other set may then enter the appropriate piece of personal commonsense into the system. Other ways to enter personal commonsense can include an interview wizard, mining information about the user from a homepage, or getting shared information from some other context-aware application that is also learning personalizations about the user. ARIA [4], a photo agent also being developed at the MIT Media Lab, is an example of such application.

The second goal is to eliminate the explicit goal selection task by automatically classifying queries into goal categories. This may first require the coverage of the goal categories to be validated, and may necessitate more robust natural language processing in order to parse the unconstrained input. Alternatively, we may be able to apply shallow IR techniques such as support vector machines to perform the classification.

In the end, we hope to create a much more intuitive and personalized search experience for all web users, and to utilize the lessons learned here about commonsense reasoning so as to be able to apply its benefits to other domains and applications.

References

1. Ask Jeeves, Inc..: Ask Jeeves home page. (2002). http://askjeeves.com/.
2. Belkin, N.J.: Intelligent information retrieval: Whose intelligence? In: ISI '96: Proceedings of the Fifth International Symposium for Information Science. Konstanz: Universtaetsverlag Konstanz. (1996). 25-31.

3. Klink, S.: Query reformulation with collaborative concept-based expansion. Proceedings of the First International Workshop on Web Document Analysis, Seattle, WA (2001).
4. Lieberman, H., Liu, H.: Adaptive Linking between Text and Photos Using Common Sense Reasoning. In Proceedings of the 2nd International Conference on Adaptive Hypermedia and Adaptive Web Based Systems, Malaga, Spain (2002).
5. Minsky, M.: Commonsense-Based Interfaces. Communications of the ACM. Vol. 43, No. 8 (August, 2000), Pages 66-73
6. Minsky. M.: A Framework for Representing Knowledge. MIT, (1974). Also, In: P.H. Winston (Ed.): The Psychology of Computer Vision., McGraw-Hill, New York, (1975).
7. Peat, H. J. and Willett, P.: The limitations of term co-occurrence data for query expansion in document retrieval systems. Journal of the ASIS, 42(5), (1991), 378--383.
8. Singh, P.: The Public Acquisition of Commonsense Knowledge. AAAI Spring Symposium, Stanford University, Palo Alto, CA, (2002).
9. Shneiderman, B., Byrd, D., and Croft, B.: Sorting out searching: A user-interface framework for text searches, Communications of the ACM 41, 4 (April 1998), 95-98.
10. Voorhees, E.: Query expansion usin lexical-semantic relations. In Proceedings of ACM SIGIR Intl. Conf. on Research and Development in Information Retrieval. (1994) 61-69.
11. Xu, J. and Croft, W.B.: Query Expansion Using Local and Global Document Analysis. In Proceedings of the Nineteenth Annual International ACM SIGIR Conference on Research and Development in Information Retrieval, (1996). pp. 4-11.

On Adaptability of Web Sites for Visually Handicapped People

Mercedes Macías, Julia González, and Fernando Sánchez

Escuela Politécnica. Universidad de Extremadura.
Avda. Universidad s/n, 10071, Cáceres, Spain
{mmaciasg, juliagon, fernando}@unex.es

Abstract. Currently, the great majority of content published on the Internet is inaccessible to visually impaired users. Although designers have guidelines that guarantee the accessibility of pages constructed as well as software tools to facilitate this task, it is necessary to consider the user's perspective too, allowing him/her to participate in the restructuring or presentation process of contents. There are few software tools which are able to do this. In this paper we present KAI (Accessibility Kit for the Internet) that considers both the user and the designer. It classifies the different components of a published Web page and presents them to the user according to his/her needs. KAI is based on a new language, BML (Blind Markup Language) that helps authors to develop better structured pages. It provides two levels of independence: original Web code and user browser or navigation platform. KAI includes a mixed audio/touch browser (WebTouch) that enables selective reading of contents. The proposed accessibility kit uses several accessibility metrics to ensure that those pages transformed by KAI are more accessible than the original ones. In this paper we give an overview of the overall system.

1 Introduction

When the World Wide Web service was created and HTML became its main support, only some people could guess what today constitutes one of the most valuable researching or working instruments of present society. Some of the best qualities that this service offers are availability and immediate diffusion of information published on the Internet. These characteristics are supposed to be especially useful for users with some types of disability.

However, the terms availability and accessibility are not synonyms. Anybody can obtain the information published on the net but not everyone has the ability to obtain it in the same way or in the same quantity or quality. Most of the time, users with disabilities must overcome an endless number of accessibility obstacles in order to reach the same level as users without disabilities. In the case of visually handicapped people, a conventional computer cannot be used in a conventional way. First of all, these users need technical assistance to use hardware (Braille lines, Braille printers) or software (screen magnifiers, screen readers). Second, the majority of browsers used to surf the net use a graphical approach that hinders the work of the screen readers mentioned above. The few specific text-only or voice browsers which exist do not contain the information provided by the structure of the original page. Finally, the Web page itself may be badly organised or incompletely or incorrectly coded in HTML, making it impossible for the user to access to its content.

Conscious of these problems, several companies and associations are working on guidelines and recommendations for software and hardware engineers, Web browser and authoring tool developers and Web page designers. Fortunately, governments are also trying to minimise these difficulties in public websites.

The accessibility research group of the University of Extremadura is developing a project for people with visual handicaps. It improves the accessibility of information published on the net. The aim of this paper is to present an overview of this project.

The rest of the article is as follows: in Sect. 2 related works are considered. In Sect. 3, the main ideas of our proposal are outlined. Finally, in Sect. 4 we summarize and present ideas for future works.

2 Motivation

When one surfs the Internet with certain regularity and visits different Web pages, one realises that there are almost as many ways to present the information, as there are Web page designers. With such variety, authors have something in common: they try to structure the Web page content in such a way that it invites Web surfers to read it.

Structuring different contents of a Web page goes far beyond the mere aesthetic function. Structures help users to perceive the information better, understand more quickly the ideas behind them, and make conclusions. Many times, the designer unconsciously chooses a determinate structure for a certain type of content. For instance, a group of statistical data is usually assigned to a table, since this structure better enables its comprehension. Despite the importance of the Web page content's structure, very few books about Web design and publication on the net refer to this aspect. However, all of them explain how to construct different structures from a technical point of view, generally in HTML.

As a reference of the variety of Web pages and designs, the Web Accessibility Initiative (WAI) of the World Wide Web Consortium (W3C) has compiled some Guidelines of Accessibility for Web page authors [1], authoring tools creators [2] and Web browser designers [3]. Their final objective is to make Web pages more accessible. These guides constitute excellent resources that every author should be familiar with, although it is impossible to force anybody to follow a guideline when designing a Web page. This is the reason why WAI has also created an evaluation and repairing working group, which is in charge of compiling information about software tools that evaluate, repair or transform Web pages [4]. This helps not only Web designers, but also users, to build a more accessible Web page.

These tools can be classified into two main groups. The first one contains tools *oriented to Web designers*. Among this group of tools, there are:

- *Evaluation* tools: They usually perform a static analysis of a Web page by evaluating its accessibility and returning a report. One example is Bobby [5], which guarantees that a page complies with all the standards of accessibility recommended by the section WAI of W3C.
- *Repairing* tools: Once the errors of accessibility on a Web page have been identified, repairing tools help the designer to correct them. One example is Tidy [6]. It detects and cleans the syntactic errors found in HTML and XML files, warns of accessibility problems and replaces all the presentation tags with style rules in CSS.

The second group contains tools *oriented to the users*, allowing their participation in the final presentation style of a Web page. Users are able to enhance their browsers by personalising certain characteristics of presentations. Some of these tools are integrated in the user's browser even though the majority work on the server. Among this group of tools there are:
- *Filtering* tools: their task consists in eliminating certain elements that could be inaccessible while giving the user the possibility of deciding what these elements are. One example is Muffin [7], which offers the user various configurable filters to eliminate *cookies*, GIF animations, advertisements, Java applications, JavaScript, and add/eliminate/modify some HTML tags.
- *Transformation* tools: it is not enough to eliminate the elements that seem to be inaccessible at first glance. Occasionally, some of them can be recovered if they are transformed correctly [8,9,10].

The tool proposed in this article classifies, evaluates, filters, repairs, restructures, transforms and presents the content of a Web page to the user. Moreover, it does all this in a personalised way. It is a software tool oriented to both, the user and the designer. In next section an overview of KAI is given.

3 KAI

3.1 A General Overview

KAI is a personalised environment for surfing the net. Users with a visual handicap decide how to access the content of a Web page. They can choose both the contents they are interested in, and the way they are presented. KAI classifies, filters and restructures the contents of any existing Web page in order to eventually present them to the user as he/she desires.

Beforehand, it is necessary to identify all the components of a given page. Nowadays, HTML hinders this identification since it is a permissive language. In other words, it allows one to obtain the same visual presentation of one component of a page though several language elements. For example, the component *table* should be constructed with the HTML element <TABLE>, but the designer could also scan the table and place it in the Web page with the HTML element <IMG>, so the table would be treated as an image. Designers could also use certain combinations of ASCII characters to obtain a similar effect, but only visually. And in many authoring tools, the element <TABLE> is used to distribute the different contents in a certain visual way, but not to build a real table. A screen reader is able to read the content of an element <TABLE> but it can not read the content of an image. And the way in which it reads a sequence of ASCII characters is no longer valid.

Faced with these difficulties, we have developed a new language to construct accessible Web pages, called BML, Blind Markup Language, upon which KAI relies. KAI also offers an accessible authoring tool to simplify the process of making accessible Web pages. The language BML has been developed following the specifications of the meta-language XML. It is very simple. Its fundamental function is to code the real components of a Web page, like the table mentioned above, but not those HTML elements used to achieve them.

The creation of an audio/touch platform (WebTouch), which can represent the structure of a Web page, has also been proposed. This platform permits users with visual handicaps to access the contents selectively, rather than sequentially.

Figure 1 shows the outline of the architecture supporting KAI.

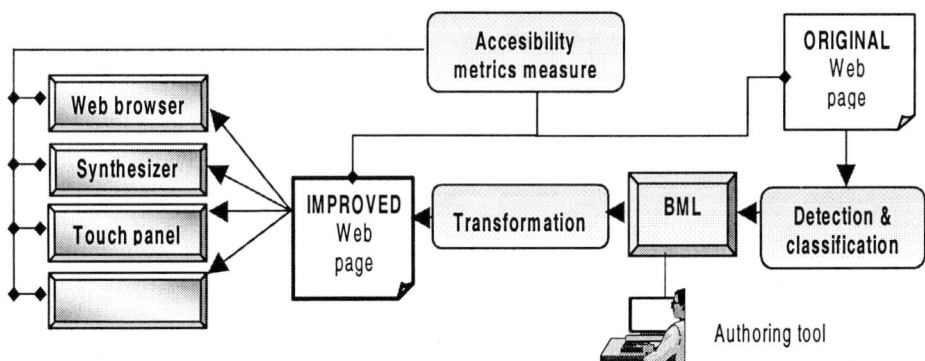

Fig. 1. A general overview of KAI

Traditionally, a client accesses a Web page through a connection with a server. The server sends to the user the code of the page he/she wishes to visit but the user's browser is responsible for the interpretation of this code and its final presentation. We suggest that the browser could transform the original code, improving it as an added service to their users.

Our transforming tool performs several tasks:
- It transforms the source code of the web page from HTML or XML to the intermediate language BML. This transformation is achieved by classifying the content and the structures of the page. In order to do this, techniques of pattern recognition and source code analysis are used. These techniques are necessary to correctly identify the real components of a web page, such as the table mentioned above, which can not be coded as a table but as an image.

- Once the contents and structures are classified and coded in BML, they can be filtered, repaired, restructured and presented according to the user's preferences or needs which have been previously identified.
- If the user's browser does not support XML, KAI transforms the BML code to HTML again. Then the Web page is ready to be sent. We would like to emphasise that the final visual aspect of the Web page could be identical to the original. The difference is that the components are now conveniently tagged. For example, a structure table would be marked correctly, with an element <TABLE>, so that the screen reader could read it in the appropriate way. Of course, the final browser may not be a traditional one, for example WebTouch. Then, BML is translated to the appropriate structures supported by this platform.

During this transformation process, different accessibility metrics based on the standard ISO9126-1 [11] and the model discussed in [12,13] are applied. These metrics allow us to establish a ranking of web pages according to their accessibility. This feature is very useful for search engines. After transforming the original page into an improved one, the user can compare the accessibility level between the original page and the new one. Finally, when the page is presented in one specific browser, the *quality in use* can be measured to know if the result is satisfactory for the end-user.

Next we give several details of BML, WebTouch and the metrics used.

3.2 The BML Language

BML has been developed following the XML specifications. It has been designed to build Web pages independently from the presentation device and the technology used. Besides, isolating the contents of a page from the aspects of presentation permits the extraction of the structures that support them. This separation of aspects: contents, presentation and structures, is fundamental in order to achieve easily transformable pages. Thus, all the users obtain the same information, independently from the senses they use: sight, hearing and/or touch.

This language is very simple and its simplicity plays an important role in the correct coding of the different components of an existing Web page. Besides, BML gives KAI total independence from the original language of the Web page (HTML or other), and from the language used when sending a page to the user (HTML, XHTML, XML,..., with CSS or XSL).

In addition, this language offers:
- An *authoring tool that guarantees that the Web page constructed is accessible*. Simply, it only constructs accessible Web pages. At first, Web designers constructed their pages in HTML language directly, and for this reason, there were very few designers. Now, there are many authoring tools to help designers construct sophisticated Web pages. Although the majority of tools build pages based on HTML language, the designer can use them without knowing this language. Anybody can be a designer, if he/she is able to see. Generally, once the page is finished and the author wants to verify whether it is accessible or not, he/she must use another specific tool. Many elements might result inaccessible and the majority of

authoring tools can not prevent this situation. In general, the designer has to repair the inaccessible elements in HTML by hand, thus making it difficult for many designers.
- *An authoring tool which is accessible itself.* This means that anybody can be a Web designer. Even a visually handicapped person will be able to design a Web page in a very attractive way.
- BML serves as a reference to restructure any Web page on the net, increasing its degree of accessibility.
- The possibility of configuring specific style sheets for different output devices, technologies or versions. Therefore, users are able to obtain the contents of any Web page based on their previous preferences, which can be changed dynamically.

3.2.1 The Elements of BML.

The definition of BML includes the existence of a group of components that constitute the basis of any Web page. Two criteria have been followed to consider a possible element of BML:
- *Identifiable*: a component is identifiable when any user, regardless of the presentation device used, is able to recognise it. The visual (images, bright signs) and auditory perspectives have both been kept in mind. Sight and hearing are senses that are regularly used in the perception of Web pages. Nevertheless, BML language considers an element identifiable from haptic or tactile points of view too (Braille, raised symbols, movements, or vibrations).
- *Functionality*: a well-defined function must also be considered. This means that each component can provide additional information enhancing its own content. A component has a well-defined functionality when all users are able to perceive the same function.

For example, a *link* would be a component of a Web page. It is identifiable by any user both in a visual and auditory way. Its function is to connect the current page with another point on the network. Therefore, the component *link* constitutes a clear element of the language.

Each component plays a role within a Web page. The elements of the language can be classified according to this role:
- *Constructive* elements: when combined correctly, they can compose any Web page. There are two different types of constructive elements:
  - *Elemental* constructors: these elements represent the simple components within a Web page. They are not the result of any combination. They include: *Text, Image, Sound, Email Address, Link, Button, Control or Touch*. For example, the last one collects components from the Web page that provides information of interest to the user from the tactile point of view. Although this tactile aspect is not yet commonly used in Web pages, some examples can be seen in [14].
  - *Structural* constructors: they combine elemental constructors and add some complementary information regarding such association. The following elements are included in this group: List, Table, Form, Sub-window or Group.
- *Organizational* elements: this type of element helps the user to surf a Web page by orienting him/her. For example, the element Abstract of a Web page provides in-

formation such as the summary, the authors, the languages available, the data of creation or publication, etc. Another organizational element is Directory, which guides the user through the different contents of the Web page in order to facilitate surfing.
- *Semantic* elements: in this case, they are embedded in constructive elements, giving them added meaning and functionality, such as *Language, Date or Telephone*. This last element allows the user to navigate among the different telephone numbers in a Web page, for example.

Besides its role, each component has a different relationship with the user. With respect to this connection, different structures or elements of the BML language could be classified in the following way:
- *Interactive* structures: These structures permit the user to actively participate in the information process. For example, *Email* would be a clear interactive element, since it allows the user to activate it and contact its owner.
- *Navigational* structures: They allow the user to surf through the interior or exterior of a page that is being visited. For example, the element *Directory* offers a table of contents to guide the user.
- *Information* structures. In this case, structures give the users the content they are seeking. For example, *Text* uses to be the main container of information.
- *Meta-information* structures. They offer additional information about the content that is being visited. For example, *Abstract* gives the user additional information about the languages available or the date of creation of the Web page.

Table 1 classifies some of the elements of the BML language according to the two criteria explained above: the role carried out in the interior of a Web page and its relation with the user.

Table 1. Classification of some elements of the BML language

	ELEMENTS			
	CONSTRUCTIVES			
	Elemental	Structural	ORGANIZAT.	SEMANTIC
INFORMATION	Text Image Sound Touch	Form Sub-window		
META-INFORMATION		Group List Table	Section Extract	Language Date
INTERACTION	Button Control E-mail address			Phone
SURFIN	Link		Directory	

3.3 The Audio/Touch Browser

KAI provides an audio/touch browser (WebTouch) in which the structure of a Web page is represented. This browser includes several buttons so users can interact with the different elements of a web page. Thus, a blind user can obtain information and surf the net just like other users who are not visually impaired. Visually-handicapped users can access the contents of a Web page more selectively, thus complementing their usual tools that already offer certain ability to select information like the voice browser HomePage Reader [15] or the popular screen reader Jaws [16].

Nowadays, we rely on both graphic and auditory platform simulators. A touch simulator is being developed with the help of a touch mouse, which produces different textures when it passes over distinct representations of Web page's components. Consequently, the user is provided with general information about the content's structure. The first version of WebTouch is being finishing at the time of writing this paper.

3.4 Accessibility Metrics Measure

One of the main goals of KAI is to ensure that the final page is better than the original one in terms of accessibility. In ISO 9126, the quality of a product is high-levelled defined into six main characteristics: functionality, reliability, usability, efficiency, maintainability, and portability. In our case, we are interested in *functionality* and *usability*. Moreover, we introduce the concept of *quality in use* that can be defined as the capability of the software to enable specified users to achieve specified goals with effectiveness, productivity, safety and satisfaction in specified context of use. We focus on the issue of choosing metrics to measure these characteristics, especially in the case of visually impaired users.

For example, and regarding to images, several measures to take into account when fixing the accessibility level of a given page are:
- Image count: it helps to measure the amount of provided visual information.
- Different image count: counts the non-repeated images.
- Percentage of image redundancy: the relation between the amount of different images and the image count. An image repetition may be interpreted as the level of redundancy of visual information.

$$PercentageImageRedundancy = 100 * \left(1 - \frac{DifferentImageCount}{ImageCount}\right) \quad (1)$$

But each image can have associated an alternative text, which is used to give extra information or simply when it is not possible to display or see the image. We can also define several measures regarding the alternative text:
- Number of images with alternative text.
- Percentage of presence of alternative text. This metric is calculated as follows:

$$PercentagePresenceAlternativeText = 100 * \frac{\#ImageswithAlternativeText}{ImageCount} \quad (2)$$

- Number of images with descriptive alternative text.
- Percentage of presence of descriptive alternative text.
- Percentage of descriptive alternative text.

Of course, there are other measures that are taken into account but it is impossible to mention all of them here.

4 Conclusions and Future Work

Throughout this paper, we have presented several tools that help to solve problems that visually handicapped users experience when accessing information published on the Internet. Some of these problems can be analysed from the Web designer's position and others from the user's perspective. Then, KAI has been presented, a proposal that face the problem from both sides.

Designers can use the language BML and its accessible authoring tool to create accessible Web pages. At the same time, users can personalise the environment for surfing by deciding what information they want and how they want to receive it. Thus, KAI classifies the contents of a Web page in relation to the elements of the language BML and the user's preferences, enabling him/her to increase the degree of accessibility of any Web page. The audio/touch browser (WebTouch) facilitates Web surfing and the user's ability to perceive the content's global aspect and its distribution within a Web page.

We are currently developing personalised metrics that permit us to determine the degree of accessibility and the degree of transformability that a Web page has, in relation to the needs of a user.

The metrics could be integrated in a search engine, so that besides the data that these tools already offer, searching could be filtered in relation to a user's predefined threshold of accessibility or transformability.

References

1. Chisholm, W., Vanderheiden, G. and Jacobs, I: Web Content Accessibility Guidelines 1.0., W3C Recommendation,
http://www.w3.org/TR/WAI_WEBCONTENT/, 5/5/1999.
2. Treviranus, J., McCathieNevile, C., Jacobs, I., Richards, J.: Authoring Tool Accessibility Guidelines 1.0., W3C Recommendation,
http://www.w3.org/TR/ATAG10/, 3/2/2000.
3. Jacobs, I., Gunderson, J., Hansen,E.: User Agent Accessibility Guidelines 1.0., W3C Working Draft, http://www.w3.org/TR/UAAG10/, 22/6/2001.
4. Web Accessibility Initiative. Evaluation, Repair, and Transformation Tools for Web Content Accessibility. W3C. http://www.w3.org/WAI/ER/existingtools.html
5. CAST, Welcome to Bobby 3.2., CAST, http://www.cast.org/bobby

6. Raggett, D.: Clean up your Web pages with HTML TIDY, W3C, http://www.w3.org/People/Raggett/tidy, 4/8/2000.
7. Muffin, World Wide Web Filtering System 0.9., http://muffin.doit.org/
8. Vorburger, M.: ALTifier Web Accessibility Enhancement Tool, http://www.vorburger.ch/projects/alt, 1998-1999.
9. Gunderson, J.: Web Accessible. http://slappy.cs.uiuc.edu/fall99/team5, 1999-00.
10. Cascado et al: Web adaptor for the visually handicapped, Grupo de robótica y Tecnología de computadores aplicado a la Rehabilitación. Facultad de Informática. Universidad de Sevilla. Proceedings of Iberdiscap2000.
11. ISO/IEC 9126-1: 2001 (E), International Standard Software Engineering - Product Quality- Part 1: Quality model.
12. Olsina, L.: Web Engineering: A Quantitative Methodology for Quality Evaluation and Comparison of Web Applications, Doctoral Thesis (in Spanish), Ciencias Exactas School, UNLP, La Plata, Argentina. 2000, April.
13. Olsina L., Gonzalez-Rodriguez, J., Lafuente G., Pastor, O.: Toward Automated Web Metrics. Proceedings of WQS2001, Anais do VIII Workshop de Qualidade de Software, October, RJ, BR, pp.74-86.
14. Logitech, IFeel Mouseman, http://www.logitech.com.
15. IBM, IBM Home Page Reader. http://www-3.ibm.com/able/hpr.html.
16. Henter Joyce, Jaws for Windows, http://www.hj.com/JAWS/JAWS.html.

A Framework
for Filtering and Packaging Hypermedia Documents

Lucimar C. Martins, Tatiana A.S. Coelho, Simone D.J. Barbosa,
Marco A. Casanova, and Carlos J.P. de Lucena

Informatics Department, Pontifical Catholic University of Rio de Janeiro
Marquês de São Vicente, 225 – 22453-900 – Rio de Janeiro – Brazil
{lucimar, tati, sim, casanova, lucena}@inf.puc-rio.br

Abstract. Despite great effort in attempting to develop systems that personalize both content and presentation, there are still some important challenges related to information filtering, packaging and formatting that adapt to user's goals, interests and presentation preferences. This paper addresses these issues by proposing a three-level framework that achieves a high degree of separation of concerns. The framework dissociates the packaging process from the filtering and formatting processes, and thus facilitates the implementation, user testing and fine-tuning of the system representations and algorithms.

1 Introduction

The feeling of being "lost in hyperspace" is familiar to most Web users. The excessive amount of information confuses us to the extent of not knowing where we are and forgetting what we were looking for when we started browsing.

Many applications related to e-learning, e-commerce and information retrieval have been designed so as to adapt both content and navigation access to the users' supposed knowledge [7,8], to their preferences and goals [1,2,3,9,11,13], to their tasks and receptivity [4,5,15]. Many of these references illustrate the increase in efficiency that certain adaptation techniques bring about [12,17].

Despite great effort in attempting to develop systems that personalize both content and presentation, there are still some important challenges, some of which are related to:

- acquisition and representation of relevant document and user information;
- information filtering that takes into consideration such information;
- information packaging and formatting that adapt to user's presentation preferences, his current browsing device and network conditions.

In this context, the primary contribution of this paper is to propose a three-level framework that achieves a high degree of separation of concerns, by dissociating the *packaging* process from the *filtering* and *formatting* processes. We also illustrate a possible use of our framework through an instantiation called *MyNews*, which is a personalized electronic newspaper.

A high degree of flexibility, provided by the framework, is necessary because the success of adaptive systems relies heavily on the choice of representations and algorithms adequate to the underlying domain and application. The evaluation of this success must be done empirically, by means of user testing, which may require further fine-tuning. The final goal is to achieve a high level of user acceptance and satisfaction, with minimal redesigning and code rewriting.

This paper is organized as follows. Section 2 presents an overview of the proposed framework. Section 3 describes the user, document and packaging models. Section 4 discusses the process of information filtering. Section 5 describes information packaging. Finally, Section 6 presents the conclusions and suggests directions for future research.

2 Framework

The idea of separation of concerns [18] provides a major motivation for the definition of a framework for personalized filtering and packaging of hypermedia documents. Our goal is be able to analyze issues related to document and user modeling, information filtering and information packaging, as independently as possible.

This approach makes it easier to build a variety of applications in diverse domains, by deriving multiple instantiations of the framework using different algorithms and configurations. This characteristic is essential to adaptive applications, since user satisfaction can only be empirically verified, and a great amount of tweaking and fine-tuning may thus be necessary, according to the successes or limitations of each configuration.

In order to illustrate the proposed framework and personalization processes, we will use an instantiation of the framework, called *MyNews*, for the domain of electronic newspapers. *MyNews* creates a personalized newspaper that selects adequate content and presentation structures to be delivered to its users.

In the following subsections, we will present the architecture of the proposed framework and a brief description of its hotspots.

2.1 Architecture

The overall goal of the architecture presented in this section is to outline the adaptation process the available content goes through, from being requested by the user to finally being presented to him. This process takes into account document, user, packaging and formatting models.

Figure 1 presents a functional architecture of a document personalization system. A user starts by requesting a personalized view of the set of documents contained in the repository. This request is processed by the *Interface Subsystem* and dispatched to the *Filtering Subsystem*, which is responsible for creating an ordered set of documents, based upon the user and document models. These models will be discussed in Sect. 3.1 and 3.2, respectively.

The *Packaging Subsystem* is responsible for regrouping, reordering and restructuring the filtered set of documents, based on the packaging model described in Sect. 3.3.

The *Formatting Subsystem* creates the final layout and visual design of each document, according to the formatting model. This task relies heavily on the expertise of graphics designers and will not be further discussed in this paper.

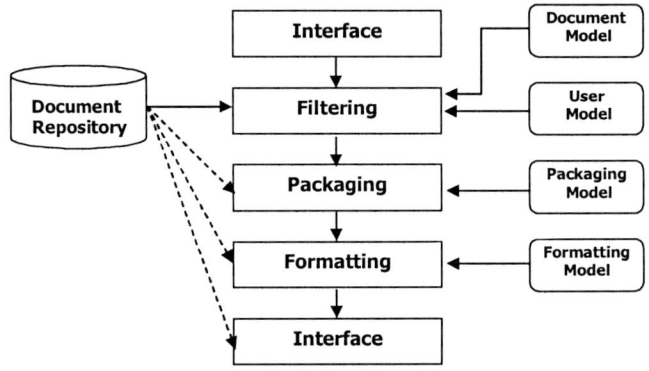

Fig. 1. Functional architecture.

2.2 Hotspots

Our framework contains several hotspots to achieve a high degree of separation of concerns. Whereas the basic architecture is invariant, the models and algorithms may differ from one domain or application to another.

The framework hotspots are as follows:

- **document model**: defines the documents' structure, including metadata that help classify the documents in various ways.
- **user model**: allows the definition of constraints related to each metadata, i.e., acts as a definition of views upon the document model.
- **filtering algorithm**: constructs a query by combining the document and user models, and returns the ordered set of documents computed as most relevant to the user.
- **packaging model**: defines which portions of the document's structure should be presented, and in which arrangements or presentation structures.
- **packaging algorithm**: uses the packaging model to regroup and rearrange the filtered set of documents, as well as to restructure the documents.
- **formatting model**: defines how each document should actually look like when presented to the user, including platform dependencies.
- **formatting algorithm**: uses the formatting model to create the final presentation layout of the documents.

3 Models

3.1 Document Model

The document model is any hypermedia model that defines the documents' structure, including metadata attributes that reflect characteristics of the documents. The definition of each metadata domain must include comparison and metrics operators that permit defining precise filtering algorithms.

In the context of *MyNews*, documents are structured into: title, subtitle, authors, summary, image and whole text. The metadata domains are:

- the *semantic metadata domain* is represented by a labeled directed graph, in which a node label represents a theme in the domain, and an arc label represents the strength of the connection between two nodes. The distance between two nodes A and B is the weighed sum of the arcs in the shortest path between A and B. Figure 2 presents a sample semantic graph;
- the *importance metadata domain* is the integer interval [1,10] and indicates the importance of a document, where 1 means the highest importance. This metadata determines the relation between a document and its corresponding theme;
- the *temporal metadata domain* is a set of timestamps and allows the computation of a document's obsolescence.

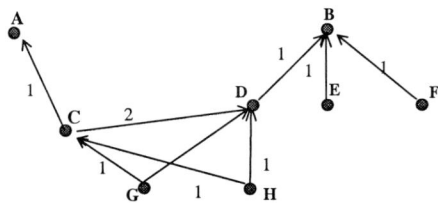

Fig. 2. Part of the semantic metadata domain with the themes of an electronic newspaper.

3.2 User Model

The user model must contain information about the preferences and goals of a user when using the system. It depends on the document model. The user model may be provided directly by the user through a questionnaire, or implicitly inferred by the system, which then needs to monitor his interaction behavior.

In the *MyNews* example, the user model consists of a triple (S,I,T), where:

- S is a list of themes that interest the user, taken from the themes listed in the semantic metadata domain;
- I indicates the minimum importance of the documents to be retrieved.
- T is a set of constraints on the obsolescence of the documents.

Suppose that the user is interested in theme A and that he wishes to view all news pieces (any importance value between 1 and 10) that were inserted in the last 3 days. The user model could then be represented by the triple *({A},10,{t <3})*.

3.3 Packaging Model

The packaging model specifies:

- the groups into which the filtered set of documents will be partitioned;
- the order of the groups and the order of the documents within each group;
- the document views, which define the components that will be retained and passed to the formatting process, in addition to references or links to other document views.

A *document view* specifies a different structure for a document, that may reorder or even omit its components.

In *MyNews*, the document views are represented as in Fig. 3.

```
dv1 = {title, subtitle, link}
dv2 = {title, subtitle, summary, link}
dv3 = {title, subtitle, summary, image, link}
dv4 = {title, subtitle, image, whole text}
```

Fig. 3. Document views used in *MyNews*.

In the example, we define a very simplistic packaging model as follows. The model contains the following groups:

- the *front page* contains news pieces with rank less than 6 (see Sect. 4 for the definition of rank);
- for each theme T in the user model, there is group, called *thematic group T*, containing all filtered news pieces whose theme is T.

The front page is always the first group and the thematic groups are listed by alphabetical order of their theme. The news pieces within each group are listed by rank order, as computed by the filtering algorithm.

For the first three documents in the front page, the packaging model retains the components defined in view dv3 of Fig. 3; for all other documents in the front page, it uses view dv1. The thematic groups use view dv4 for their documents. In addition, for the documents in the front page, the hyperlinks in views dv1 and dv3 point to the corresponding news pieces in the thematic groups.

An alternative packaging model for *MyNews* would, for example, use only view dv1 for all documents and hyperlink each view to the document's full version in the document repository. A second and more sophisticated model would take into account limitations of the platform and indicate to use views dv1 and dv2, instead of views dv3 and dv4, respectively, if the platform has a small presentation area.

4 Filtering

The filtering algorithm creates an ordered subset of the set of available documents, based on a *ranking function* that maps each document into its *rank*. according to their metadata values and the goals and interests represented in the user model. Intuitively, the filtering algorithm correlates the documents' metadata with the user model, creating an ordered subset of documents that supposedly interest the user the most.

The definition of the ranking function is an interesting issue. In order to verify that a certain document is indeed relevant to the user, a great deal of user testing must be done, and the ranking function will probably need to be fine-tuned for best results.

Returning to our running example, recall from Sect. 3 that the user model is the triple *({A},10,{t <3})*. Consider a ranking function that combines the semantic and importance metadata and is defined as $P[U](x) = \sqrt{(D_s[U](x))^2 + (D_I[U](x))^2}$, where $D_s[U](x)$ corresponds to the shortest distance between the theme labeling document $\underline{x}$ and the themes of interest to the user, and the value $D_I[U](x)$ represents the importance of document $\underline{x}$.

Table 1 shows a possible result of the filtering process, where the rank column contains the document rank, computed by the above function, and all other columns correspond to the document metadata and document components.

Table 1. A sample set of documents resulting from the filtering process.

Document	rank	theme	importance	obsolescence	title
Doc2	2.24	C	1	3-Dec-2001	Wall Street...
Doc1	3.16	A	3	5-Dec-2001	Dolly...
Doc4	3.16	A	3	3-Dec-2001	Crisis in...
Doc53	5.10	A	5	3-Dec-2001	Research...
Doc18	7.21	D	6	4-Dec-2001	Christmas sales...
Doc7	10.05	A	10	1-Dec-2001	New clones...

5 Packaging

Packaging comprises three major processes, grouping, ordering and document restructuring, and is driven by the packaging model.

The first step partitions the set of documents returned by the filtering process into several groups, according to the criteria defined by the packaging model. The second step reorders the groups, and the documents within each group. It may directly follow the documents' rank order or it may be recomputed as a function of both the rank and some of the documents' attributes. For instance, the documents may be presented in reverse chronological order, indicating the recency of events, independently of their relative importance. The final step selects which components of each document will be passed to the formatting process.

Thus, the packaging process results in a sequence of tuples containing: a group descriptor, a sequence of documents, the corresponding document view and the "target" document views, in case the selected view contains links.

In the *MyNews* example, using the packaging model of Sect. 3.3, the documents shown in Table 1 will be rearranged as follows:

- *front page:* contains documents doc2, doc1, doc4 and doc53, in this order;
- *Thematic Group A:* contains document doc1, doc4, doc53 and doc7, in this order;
- *Thematic Group C:* contains document doc2;
- *Thematic Group D:* contains document doc18.

The documents in the front page retain the following components:

- the first three documents - docs2, doc1 and doc4 – follow view dv3 in Fig. 3, that is, they retain the title, subtitle, summary and image, if any;
- the last document, d53, follows view dv1, that is, it retains the title and subtitle.

The documents in Thematic Groups A, C and D follow view dv4, that is, they retain the title, subtitle and the whole text.

This result may be represented as the following sequence:

[
    (front page$_a$, [doc2, doc1, doc4], dv3, dv4),
    (front page$_b$, [doc53], dv1, dv4),
    (thematic group A, [doc7], dv4),
    (thematic group D, [doc18], dv4)
]

Figure 4 schematically shows the final result of the packaging process, including the hyperlinks between the filtered documents. Note, however, that the document views used in Fig. 4 do not imply any formatting scheme. They are used just for illustrative purposes.

6 Conclusions

In this paper we have defined a framework that helps design personalization systems. Our major contribution was to organize the framework into three levels that achieve a high degree of separation of concerns, by dissociating the packaging process from the filtering and formatting processes.

The framework facilitates the implementation, user testing and fine-tuning of the system representations and algorithms. The filtering process, for example, has three hotspots - the filtering algorithm, the document model and the user model – that can be instantiated in different ways. Likewise, the packaging process has two hotspots – the packaging model and the packaging algorithm.

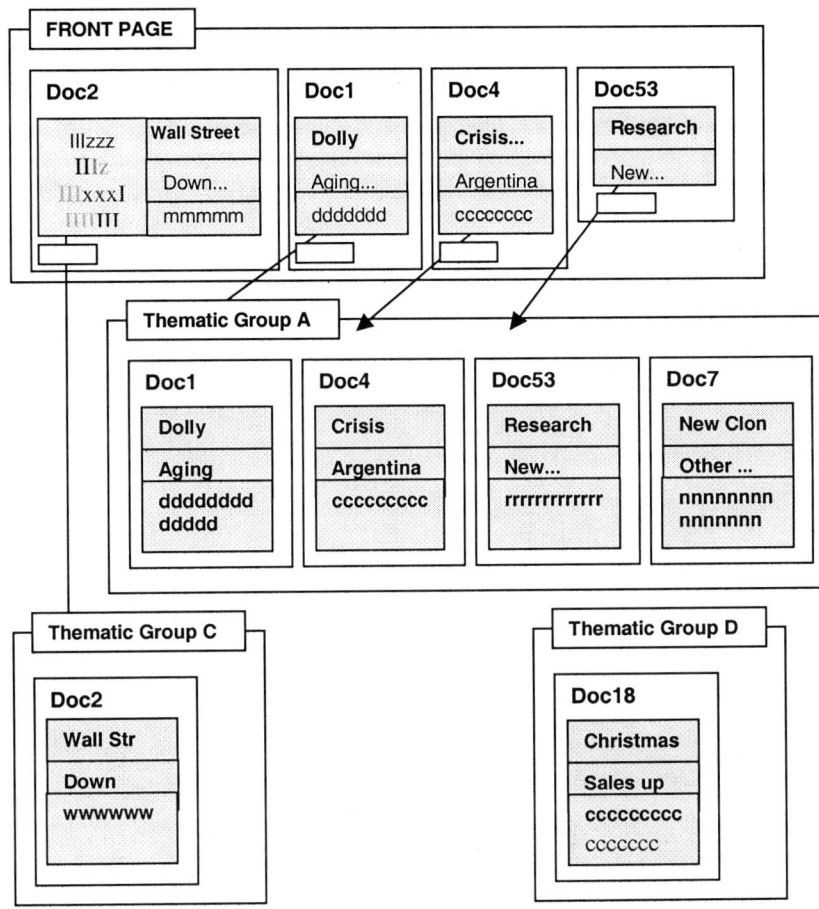

Fig. 4. Packaging of the documents in Table 1.

If we consider the filtering process, our approach is similar to other approaches in the literature. It aims to select the documents (topics and news) that are most relevant to each user.

In our framework, we introduce the packaging level, which allows us to define the abstract organization of the selected information, by selecting and organizing relevant elements of the filtered documents.

Our framework may be used as a resource for analyzing existing approaches to personalized systems. Ossenbruggen's work on *Cuypers* [16] decomposes what we call formatting level according to their algorithms for automatic generation of the final multimedia presentation. If we can design algorithms to generate an adequate semantic structure based on communicative intentions, our packaging process would be able to provide the input for their prototype. Our packaging process would be thus positioned before the *Cuypers Engine*.

Our work is somewhat similar to the IMMPS proposal [6], which defines a Standard Reference Model for Intelligent Multimedia Presentation Systems. Their *design layer*, however, encapsulates our packaging level and, to some extent, our formatting level as well.

The approach described in [3] proposes an electronic newspaper that allows the personalization of the content and presentation detail of the news item based on receptivity (a dimension used for estimating the amount of information that a user might read). In place of our packaging process, their approach provides only two different types of pages for organizing information: index pages and news pages. Our instantiation, *MyNews*, maintains the distinction between the packaging and formatting processes, allowing editors and designers to experiment more easily with alternative solutions.

We are currently implementing the framework described in Sect. 2, with the *MyNews* instantiation [15]. We plan to investigate an alternative framework where the packaging process drives filtering. Also, we plan to extend the framework to address the problem of processing specific user requests, such as keyword searches.

Acknowledgments

Lucimar Martins would like to thank CAPES for supporting her work. Tatiana Coelho and Simone Barbosa thank CNPq for supporting their research.

References

1. Ardissono, L., and A. Goy. *Tailoring the Interaction with Users in Electronic Shops*. In J. Kay, ed.: UM99 User Modeling: Proceedings of the Seventh International Conference. Wien New York: Springer-Verlag, 35-44, 1999.
2. Ardissono, L., Console, L., and I. Torre. *On the application of personalization techniques to news servers on the WWW*. In: Lecture Notes in Artificial Intelligence N. 1792. Berlin: Springer Verlag, pp. 261—272, 1999.
3. Ardissono, L., Console, L., and I. Torre. *Strategies for personalizing the access to news servers*. Working Notes of the Adaptive User Interfaces. Spring Symposium of AAAI (Technical Report SS-00-01), pp. 7-12, Stanford, CA, 2000, AAAI Press.
4. Billsus, D. and M. Pazzani. *User Modeling for Adaptive News Access*. User Modeling and User-Adapted Interaction 10(2-3), 147-180, 2000.
5. Billsus, D., Pazzani, J., and J. Chen. *A Learning Agent for Wireless News Access*. Proceedings of the 2000 International Conference on Intelligent User Interfaces, 2000, Pages 33 - 36.
6. Bordegoni, M., Faconti, G., Maybury, M.T., Rist, T., Ruggieri, S., Trahanias, P., and M. Wilson. *A Standard Reference Model for Intelligent Multimedia Presentation Systems*. Computer Standards & Interfaces, 18(6-7):477-496, December, 1997.
7. Bradley, K., Rafter, R. and **B.** Smyth. *Case-Based User Profiling for Content Personalization*. Book: AH. 2000.

8. Brusilovsky, P. and D. W. Cooper. *ADAPTS: Adaptive hypermedia for Web-based performance support system*. Proceedings of the 2nd Workshop on Adaptive Systems and User Modeling on the WWW. 1999.
9. Cingil, I., Dogac, A., and A. Azgin. *A broader approach to personalization*. Communications of the ACM 43(8):136--141, August 2000.
10. Fayad, M., Schmidt, D., and Johnson, R. *Building Application Frameworks*, Wiley Computer Publishing, 1999.
11. Fink, J., Kobsa, A., and J. Schreck. Personalized Hypermedia Information Provision through Adaptive and Adaptable System Features: User Modeling, Privacy and Security Issues. Proc. of the Workshop Adaptive Systems and User Modeling on the World Wide Web of the 6th Int. Conf. on User Modeling, Chia Laguna, Sardinia, June 1997.
12. Hof, R. D., Green, H., and Himmelstein, L. *Now it's YOU WEB*. Business Week, pages 68-74, October 5, 1998.
13. Kamba, T., Bharat, K., and M. C. Albers. *The Krakatoa Chronicle – An Interactive, Personalized, Newspaper on the Web*. In Proc. of the Fourth International World Wide Web Conference, pp. 159-170, Nov 1995.
14. Khan, L., and D. McLeod. *Audio Structuring and Personalized Retrieval Using Ontologies*. In Proceedings of IEEE Advances in Digital Libraries, Library of Congress, Washington, DC,May 2000.
15. Martins, L.C. *Personalização de Visões sobre Documentos Hipermídia*. Technical report in preparation. Informatics Department, Pontifical Catholic University of Rio de Janeiro, 2002.
16. Ossenbruggen, J.V., Geurts, J., Cornelissen, F., Rutledge, L., and Lynda Hardman. *Towards Second and Third Generation Web-Based Multimedia*. In The Tenth International World Wide Web Conference, pages 479-488, Hong Kong, May 1-5, 2001
17. Parsaye, K. *PQ: The Personalization Quotient of a Website*. Published by personalization.com. NovuWeb, Inc. 2000.
18. Tarr, P., Ossher, H., Harrison, W., and S. Sutton. *N Degrees of Separation: Multi-Dimensional Separation of Concerns*. Proceedings 21st International Conference on Software Engineering (ICSE'99), May 1999.

Adaptation in an Evolutionary Hypermedia System: Using Semantic and Petri Nets[1]

Nuria Medina-Medina[1], Lina García-Cabrera[2], Mª José Rodríguez-Fortiz[1], and José Parets-Llorca[1]

[1]Depto. L.S.I. E.T.S.I. Informática. Universidad de Granada. SPAIN
{nmedina, mjfortiz, jparets}@ugr.es
[2]Depto. Informática. Universidad de Jaén. SPAIN
lina@ujaen.es

Abstract. In this paper a classification of adaptive hypermedia systems is presented. Advantages and disadvantages of these systems are also discussed. As a consequence, the need of evolution is argued. An adaptive and evolving hypermedia system is presented and outlined, where the user model is formalized by means of Petri Nets. Finally, an example shows how in our proposal the user model is initialized and updated during the browsing and how adaptation is carried out over the conceptual structure of navigation.

Keywords. Hypermedia System, Adaptation, Petri Net, Evolution, SEM-HP model

1 Introduction: A Taxonomy of Adaptive Hypermedia Systems

Adaptive hypermedia systems (AHS) appeared with the purpose of improving the usability of traditional hypermedia systems. Most of them facilitate the activity of the user, because they adapt the system to some user features. The design of an adaptive hypermedia system suggests four interrogations concerning adaptation: What? Whom? How? When?. Following De Bra [8,25] three elements are implicit or explicitly presented in most adaptive hypermedia systems: domain model, user model and adaptation model. Depending on the answer to the previous questions, the author will design these elements. Table 1 summarizes the approaches followed in literature from different points of view and relates each criterion to the most important solved interrogation.

On the basis of the revision and analysis realized over the current situation of adaptive hypermedia systems, we observe a lot of benefits due to adaptation features, which convert these systems in very powerful tools. Also, we notice some problems; for instance the entire life cycle (design, construction and maintenance) of adaptive hypermedia systems are not enough considered and the authoring-tools do not incorporate mechanisms that facilitate changes in the system during and after its construction. Considering these two problems of AHS and the fact that hypermedia systems should change continuously, we propose an evolving approach to the

---

[1] This research is supported by MEIGAS, a project financed by the Spanish MCT (TIC2000-1673-C06-04) which is a subproject of the DOLMEN project (TIC2000-1673-C06).

Table 1. A taxonomy of adaptive hypermedia systems

Criterion	Types			
Application domain What?	*General adaptive hypermedia systems:* The documents include very different subjects			
	Specific adaptive hypermedia systems: All the documents explain concepts of an uniform information domain. ADAPTS [5] is an adaptive diagnostics and personalized technical support project, ELM-ART [7] is a Lisp course, PUSH project [9] reorganize a manual on an object-oriented software development method			
Adaptation to Whom?	User	**Representation of the user model**	*Pairs (attribute/value).* AHA [24,25]	
			Bayesian model. KBS Hyperbook [14]	
			Probabilistic and episodic approach. ATS [21]	
			Petri Net [Our proposal]	
	User group	*Personalized recommendations.* Approach of Johan Bollen[4]		
		Recommendations to user groups. INTRIGUE [2]		
	Others. For instance, adaptation to different kinds of devices in mobile technology [1]			
Adaptive methods [6] What? How?	*Adaptive navigation*	*Guidance*	*Local or Global*	
		Orientation support	*Local or Global*	
		Personalized views		
	Adaptive presentation	*Additional explanations*		
		Prerequisite explanations		
		Comparative explanations		
		Explanation variants		
		Sorting		
Kind of prerequisites [16] How?	*Pedagogical prerequisites:* State relationships between concepts related to learning			
	Prerequisites as ordering mechanism: Try to establish a partial order between pages			
Integrating of information from different origin What?	*Open adaptive hypermedia systems:* These systems can integrate information resources located anywhere in the WWW. KBS Hyperbook [14]			
	Closed adaptive hypermedia systems			
Interactivity with the adaptivity When? How?	*Adaptable hypermedia systems:* User model is only updated after an explicit solicitation of the user			
	Adaptive hypermedia systems: The user model is automatically updated as the user browses and the content and the link structure are adapted to it		*The user can have some control over the adaptive behavior of the system.* PUSH [9]	
			The user can't have any control over adaptation	
	Adaptable/Adaptive hypermedia systems. Approach Intensional Hypertext [23]			
Creating hypermedia documents When? How?	*Dynamic AHS:* Documents are dynamically created under user demand			
	No dynamic AHS: Documents exist before of their use, though their presentation is adapted to each user			
	Mediating between adaptive and dynamic hypermedia. Macronodo Approach [18]			
Navigation history How?	*Explicit history representation.* A kind of navigation rule uses path history [15]			
	The representation of user browsing path is not explicit			
Contextual information Whom?	*User context:* Role of the user in a group, physical localization, etc.			
	Textual context: Surrounding phrase, paragraph or document			
	Spatial context: User browsing path through the hyperspace before arriving at present page. Context-based approach [3]			

construction and maintenance of adaptive hypermedia systems. We have two main reasons in doing this. The first reason is that AHS are software systems and the quality of the obtained product depends on the quality of the development process. Consequently, we propose a software engineering approach in the development of adaptive hypermedia systems. This process is divided in four phases that we consider inherent to the design of a conceptual and navigational system. We will further explain this process.

The second reason in taking one such approach stems from the fact that the preparation of hyperdocuments includes a lot of changes, additions and updates carried out by the authors; this implies that the author needs change mechanisms. Therefore, we consider that user adaptation in current AHS should be completed with mechanisms of evolution [22]. Adaptation carried out by AHS is adaptation to different users, however evolution implies the possibility of changes in the system, which are produced by the developer in order to improve the system. Transformations happened in the system context would determine which are the changes that the author (developer) must carry out in the system.

In this paper we present the main features of our approach, called SEM-HP and the integration of adaptation features using Petri Nets. In Sect. 2 the main characteristics of the model are briefly outlined including adaptive features. Section 3 presents an example of adaptation, and finally the related works, conclusions and further work are considered.

2 SEM-HP: Evolutionary and Adaptive Hypermedia System

SEM-HP [13] is a systemic, evolutionary and semantic model for the development of adaptive hypermedia systems. It is systemic because it conceives a hypermedia system as a set of interacting subsystems. It is semantic because it offers a flexible semantic approach which allows to author characterizes his information domains. An explicit semantic representation increases the possibilities of adaptation and evolution.

Joining the two reasons discussed in the previous section, we propose a evolutionary and iterative development process for adaptive hypermedia systems, where each phase integrates changes of the system structure produced by the developer in a flexible and consistent way:

- *Conceptual phase.* The author constructs conceptual and information worlds.
- *Presentation phase.* The author selects different presentations of a concrete conceptual and information world.
- *Navigation phase.* The author states how the reader can browse the offered information.
- *Learning phase.* The author resolves the aspects of adaptation. Here, the author answers the four essential questions: What? Whom? How? When?, i.e., he must decide representation, initialization and updating of the user model and adaptive techniques.

2.1 Architecture of SEM-HP

In SEM-HP an adaptive hypermedia system is conceived as composed of four interrelated and interacting systems, each one corresponding to a development phase [12]:

Memorization System. It is in charge of the storage, structuring and maintenance of the knowledge that the AHS offers. The main element of this system is the Conceptual Structure (CS). The CS is a semantic net, in which, nodes and links are labeled with semantic meanings. The CS has two types of nodes: concepts and items. Concepts are labeled ideas and items contain pieces of information, which are related to the concepts. Links in the CS are relationships among concepts or among concepts and items. The author can change the CS after or during its construction, in order to do it, evolutionary actions are provided which allows the creation, deletion or modification of concepts, items or relationships.

Presentation System. This system allows a selection of subsets of concepts, items and relationships included in the conceptual structure.

Navigation System. It uses as basis the CS of the presentation system and allows the addition of special order restrictions in the graph. These restrictions are expressed in temporal logic and they state a partial order between the pieces of information offered by the system, i.e., they provide a partial order of the items. Considering the CS and these order restrictions a Petri Net [19] is automatically constructed, which allows an operational navigation. Evolution is carried out deleting or modifying restrictions.

Learning System. Adaptation of the hypermedia system according to an user model is carried out by this system. Also in this system, evolution is needed because the author can modify, add or delete adaptation rules or user model updating rules. Furthermore, when the author modifies the CS in the knowledge system or he changes order relationships in the navigation system, these changes can imply changes in some elements of the learning system. In SEM-HP these last changes are carried out automatically by the system, facilitating the work of the author and guarantying the system coherence. For example, if the author adds new concepts in the CS, these concepts will be included into the user model, with the objective of keeping track of the knowledge level of the user about these concepts.

The three first systems are fully described and formalized in [13]. The user adaptation performed by the learning system is described in paragraph 2.3 and exemplified in Sect. 3.

2.2 Evolution in SEM-HP

Because adaptive hypermedia systems offer knowledge captured by their authors, they change frequently. In order to carry out these changes, a set of evolutionary actions is provided by SEM-HP model [13]. The author uses the different evolutionary action depending on the modifications that he needs. In the SEM-HP model, a set of restriction that the system must satisfy at any moment exists. In order to keep the consistency, an evolutionary action only will be executed if it fulfils the set of restrictions. In addition, new restrictions can be added by the author to this set, it will be performed through a special kind of evolutionary actions which restrictions are named *meta-restrictions*. The model also takes into account that the modifications of an element into a system (memorization, presentation, navigation or learning) can imply some modifications in other elements of the system itself or of others systems. These two situations are named respectively *internal propagation of changes* and *external propagation of changes*.

2.3 User Adaptation in SEM-HP

Obviously, the learning system supports the greatest charge of adaptation. It initializes and maintains the user model, and performs adaptation. Both navigation adaptation and presentation adaptation is supported by SEM-HP. In this paper, we focus on the navigation adaptation. In SEM-HP, the main browsing mechanism is the conceptual structure. Therefore, it will be the recipient of the navigation adaptation.

Table 2 shows the information stored in the user model. The third column of the table indicates what user features are taken into account in SEM-HP. We think that the user models considered in literature include two types of features: 1) Variable features which change frequently during navigation -rows 1 to 5- and 2) Stable features whose changes are long term -rows 6 to 9-. Variable features are represented by a Petri Net, except the goal which is not considered at present. Stable features are stored apart from the Petri Net.

Table 2. User model in SEM-HP

Information	Description	SEM-HP?
Goal	Information that the user wants to know	NO
Knowledge	User knowledge value about each item. 0 <= N:Integer <= 100	OK
Read	Items read by the user	OK
Read number	Readings number of each item	OK
Ready to read	Items that can be read by the user	OK
Subject experience	User knowledge about the conceptual domain of the system	OK
Navigation experience	Practice of the user in the use of hypermedia systems	OK
Preferences	Predilections and tastes of the user	OK
Personal data	Data as name, age, sex, profession, etc.	OK

Navigation adaptation techniques are applied over the conceptual structure of navigation, in order to tailor it to user features:
- *Links annotation*. In the current conceptual structure (CS), each item previously visited is annotated with both the number of visits and a violet color. In addition, concepts and items are annotated indicating the user knowledge level about them.
- *Links hiding and disabling*. An item only can be reached if the user knows its prerequisite items. When it does not occur the item is hidden and disabled.
- *Personalized CS*. In the presentation phase, the author creates different views of the same CS. For each user the view that better tailors his knowledge and preferences is selected.

3 Adaptation in SEM-HP: An Example of Use

The following example describes how both adaptation of conceptual structure and updating of the user model is performed in SEM-HP, using a Petri Net.

Step one. A conceptual structure (CS) is created by the author. Concepts are represented as circles. Items -documents offered to the reader- are represented as squares. Arrows are relationships among concepts and lines are relationships among concepts and items. Conceptual relationships means prerequisites between concepts. In Fig. 1, the arrow from *C3* to *C4* declares that if the user knows the concept *C3* can read the concept *C4*.

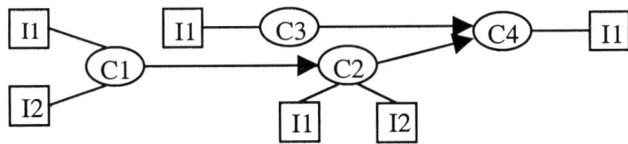

Fig. 1. Example of conceptual structure. Circles and squares are labeled

Step two. The system generates automatically order restrictions among items, these order restrictions are written in propositional temporal logic. We will call them *order rules*. Because relation concept-item has cardinality N-N, an item is identified using the name of the concept and its name. Table 3 shows the four rules automatically generated from CS of Fig. 1. The first rule states that the order prerequisite for the item *C2.I1* is the previous lecture of item *C1.I1* or item *C1.I2*.

Table 3. Order rules: Order restrictions among items of the CS

1) C1.I1 or C1.I2 → C2.I1	3) C2.I1 or C2.I2 → C4.I1
2) C1.I1 or C1.I2 → C2.I2	4) C3.I1 → C4.I1

Step three. Order rules can be modified by the author, if desired. An order rule can be deleted, its logical operators can be altered or it can be extended by the author. For instance, the author modifies the second rule (substitutes or for and), he extends the third rule and he deletes the fourth rule of the table 3.

Table 4. Modifications performed by the author, using a graphic interface

Modifications	Final set of order rules
2) **C1.I1 and C1.I2** → C2.I2 3) **C1.I1 and C3.I1 and** (C2.I1 or C2.I2) → C4.I1 4) ~~C3.I1 → C4.I1~~	1.a C1.I1 or C1.I2 → C2.I1 2.a C1.I1 and C1.I2 → C2.I2 3.a C1.I1 and C3.I1 and (C2.I1 or C2.I2)→C4.I1

Step four. The influence of an item over knowledge of its associated concept is defined by the author for each item in the CS. In the example, the author has decided that both item *C1.I1* and item *C1.I2* have the same weight upon the knowledge of the concept *C1*, however *C2.I1* has more weight than *C2.I2* upon concept *C2*.

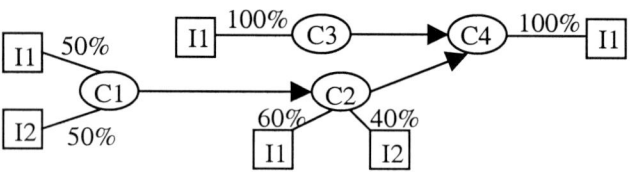

Fig. 2. Weights defined by the author

Based on these weights, the system generates automatically a set of *weight rules* in order to calculate user knowledge about each concept at every moment. Knowledge about a concept is based on knowledge about its associated items. Table 5 displays the generated weight rules. The function K returns the knowledge value of the argument (item or concept).

Table 5. Weight rules generated from Fig. 2

K(C1) = 50%K(C1.I1) + 50%K(C1.I2)	K(C3) = K(C3.I1)
K(C2) = 60%K(C2.I1) + 40%K(C2.I2)	K(C4) = K(C4.I1)

<u>Step five</u>. Knowledge prerequisites are defined by the author for each order rule generating the *knowledge rules*. In order to do it, the author establishes knowledge thresholds for each prerequisite item into an order rule. The knowledge threshold of an item says what is the lowest knowledge value required for it in the current rule. Figure 3 shows the definition of knowledge thresholds for the rule 3.a of table 4. The required items (left part of the rule) are identified by means of prohibition signs. The head of the rule is identified by means of a smiling face. The author writes knowledge threshold next to each prohibition sign. In the example, the author has decided that the user will be ready to read *C4.I1* if the user knowledge about *C1.I1* is equal to 100 and *C3.I1* is higher than 40 and *C2.I1* higher than 50 or *C2.I2* higher than 30.

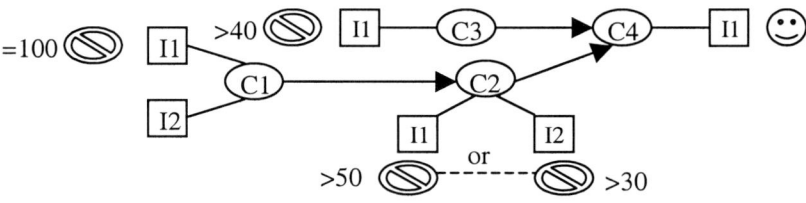

Fig. 3. Knowledge rule *3.b* generated from the order rule *3.a*

The following table shows the set of knowledge rules defined from rules of table 4.

Table 6. Knowledge rules

1.b. K(C1.I1)>40 or K(C1.I2)> 60 → C2.I1	2.b. K(C1.I1)>75 and K(C1.I2)>50 → C2.I2
3.b. K(C1.I1)=100 and K(C3.I1)>40 and (K(C2.I1)>50 or K(C2.I2)>30) → C4.I1	

Step six. The author states how the user knowledge about items increases during navigation. In each rule a smiling face marks the current item and a ring marks those items whose knowledge value will be updated due to a visit to the current item. Symbol + represents a relative update (an increase). Symbol = represents an absolute update (fixed value). Symbol % represents a percentage on the knowledge value of the smiling item. Figure 4 implies: each time that item *C1.I1* is visited its knowledge value is increased on 50 and knowledge value of item *C3.I1* is increased on 50% of the current knowledge value of *C1.I1*. In this example, the full knowledge of *C1.I1* requires two visits.

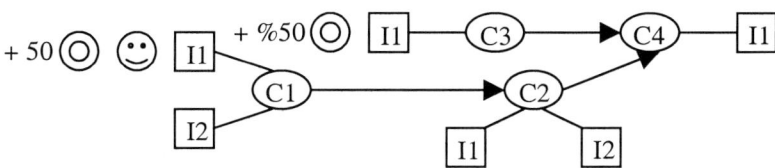

Fig. 4. Graphic interface for the update rule: *Visit(C1.I1)→ InK(C1.I1, 50), InK(C3.I1, 50%K(C1.I1))*

The rules generated are called *update rules* and are represented internally using logic. The predicate Visit(Cc, Ii) will be true when the item Ii associated to the concept Cc will be visited by the reader. The function FixK(Cc.Ii, N) establishes the knowledge value of item Cc.Ii to value N (0<=N<=100). The function InK(Cc.Ii, N) increases the knowledge value of the item Cc.Ii on value N (the result is normalized between 0 and 100). The visited item is always updated at first place.

Table 7. Internal representation of update rules defined by the author

Up11 Visit(C1.I1)→InK(C1.I1, 50), InK(C3.I1, 50%K(C1.I1))	*Up22* Visit(C2.I2)→InK(C2.I2, 25)
Up12 Visit(C1.I2)→FixK(C1.I2, 100), InK(C3.I1, 10%K(C1.I2))	*Up31* Visit(C3.I1)→FixK(C3.I1, 100)
Up21 Visit(C2.I1)→FixK(C2.I1, 100), InK(C3.I1, 10%K(C2.I1))	*Up41* Visit(C4.I1)→FixK(C4.I1, 100)

Step seven. Based on previous information (from step 1 to step 6) a Petri Net (PN) is generated automatically by the system. This PN represents and updates the user model described in section 2.3. The PN is obtained applying an adaptation of the algorithm, which transforms temporal logic formulas in a Petri Net, explained and demonstrated in [20]. The PN integrates the user model, knowledge rules and update rules (Fig. 5).

In SEM-HP, the user navigates by selecting items in the CS. The selection of an item is represented by means of a **transition** in the PN. Therefore, *knowledge rules* are split as conditions of the transitions, depending on logical operators and following [20]. Consequently, an item can't be selected if its prerequisites are not satisfied. An *update rule* is associated to the output arc of the transition that leads up to the selected item. So when the reader visits an item this update rule is executed. There are four types of **places** in the PN:

- *User-selection place.* There is a sole place of this type in the PN. This place determines what the user selection is, that is to say, what is the fired transition in the PN. It has always one token. There is an input arc to each transition. In order to conserve the token there is an output arc from each transition.
- *Item places.* Each item Cc.Ii in the conceptual structure has associated an item place in the PN. It represents the item and stores the user knowledge value of this item. In Fig. 5: C1.I1, C1.I2, C2.I1, C2.I2, C3.I1 and C4.I1 are item places. Initially each one of them has one token, but each visit to the item increases its number of tokens in one. Therefore, the number of visits is equal to the number of tokens minus one. There is an output arc to each transition whose condition evaluates the knowledge of this item. There is an input arc, which has associated the update rule, that must be executed in each visit to this item.
- *Starting places.* A starting place for each item Cc.Ii without knowledge prerequisites exists. C1.I1 Start, C1.I2 Start, C3.I1 Start in Fig. 5. It has always one token. There is an input arc to the transition, which leads up to the item place Cc.Ii.
- *Assistant places.* This type of place represents a condition, which is part of a complex knowledge rule. In Fig. 5: X. Initially these places have no tokens, it means that the represented condition is not satisfied.

Figure 5 shows the PN generated by the system. For clarity reasons only the interaction of the user-selection place with one transition is shown. An arc with a double arrow represents one input and one output arcs. *Upci* is the *update rule* of the table 7, which is executed when item Cc.Ii is visited.

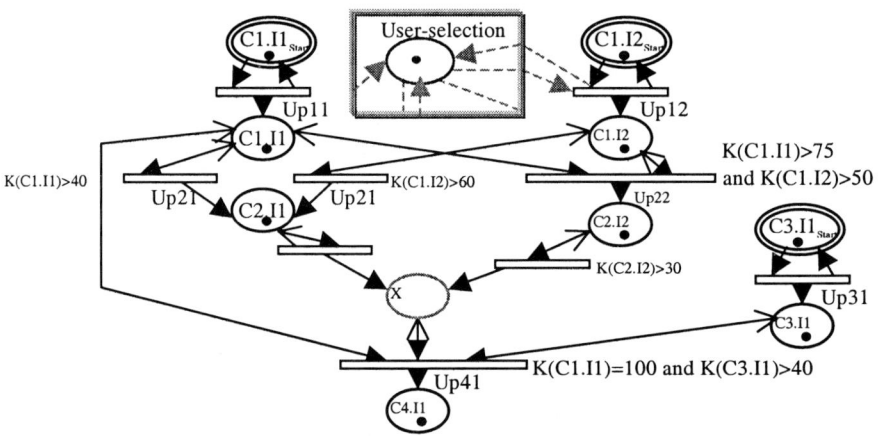

Fig. 5. Petri Net automatically generated

<u>Step eight</u>. Firing the Petri Net both adaptation and user model updating is carried out while the user navigates. Figure 6.a displays the initial CS. In the PN, only the item places C1.I1, C1.I2 and C3.I1 can be visited firing the transitions from the user selection place. Therefore, items *C2.I1*, *C2.I2* and *C4.I1* are hidden and disabled in the CS of navigation to avoid that the reader selects them. Initially, items and concepts are annotated with knowledge value 0.

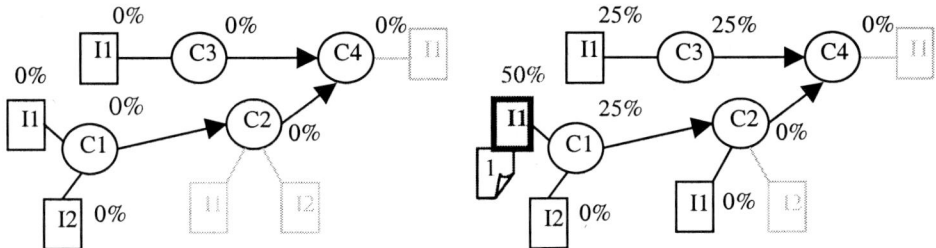

Fig. 6.a Initial CS disabling the forbidden items   **Fig. 6.b** CS after item *C1.I1* is visited

The rule *Up11* is executed when the user selects the item *C1.I1*. This rule increases the knowledge of both *C1.I1*(in 50) and *C3.I1*(in 50%50). Consequently, the knowledge on concepts C1 and C3 has been increased. In the PN, the condition which enables the transition to *C2.I1* will be true. Then in the CS, the item *C2.I1* will be visible and the item *C1.I1* is annotated indicating one visit (Fig. 6.b).

4 Related Work, Conclusions and Further Work

Hypermedia models that use finite state machines different from Petri Nets have been proposed in the scientific literature. For instance, HMBS [10] is a hypermedia model based on statecharts. We use Petri Nets because have an inherent mechanism of execution, whereas the classical formalism of statecharts is not executable. Statecharts are more focused on specification of the structure and static browsing semantic of hypermedia systems, for this purpose we use the conceptual structure and the logic rules.

The caT model [17] is a context-aware hypertext model, which also uses Petri Nets. CaT extends Trellis hypertext model [11], using a high-level PN in order to authoring, browsing and analysing dynamic documents. It supports user adaptation to changes in environmental information (localization, time, etc.). However, the caT model follows an approach very different from our proposal, because it builds directly the PN-based document structure, without constructing a conceptual structure, neither performing conceptual and presentation phases. Moreover, caT does not support adaptation to user knowledge, due to that it does not establish knowledge rules and does not update the user knowledge during navigation. Another difference is that in our case the PN represents the variable features of the user model while in caT the user model is a globally visible file used in the PN, which contains the less dynamic data of the user such as work organization. In addition, caT and the works referenced in table 1 [1-9, 14-16, 18, 21, 23-25] do not offer mechanisms of evolution.

Following the taxonomy of table 1, the SEM-HP model can be characterized as a model that allows the creation of open systems with a generic application domain, in these systems both evolution and user adaptation is performed. Evolutionary modifications can be carried out on the created system by the author in a flexible way, due to the evolution mechanisms supported in the model. In addition the user model is represented by means of a Petri Net, both adaptive navigation and adaptive presentation is supported, the prerequisites between items are used as order mechanism and navigation history is implicitly represented by means of the Petri Net. However, the hypermedia systems designed using the model are not dynamic because the information items are *a priori* established.

Our future work will be centered around three main problems related to the dynamic construction of presented information: a) How can the system find out the user goals? b) How can we represent and update the user subjective experience and item difficulty over the Petri Net? c) How can the system generate items in a dynamic way depending on the user goals and user experience? At present the last two problems are partially considered in the model by means of certain item properties which characterize the information items and dynamic composition of items, but this approach requires further refinements.

References

1. Alatalo T. Peräaho J. A Modelling Method for Designing Adaptive Hypermedia. 3rd Workshop on Adaptive Hypertext and Hypermedia. UM2001. Sonthofen, Germany. July 13-17, 2001.
2. Ardissono L. Goy A. Petrone G. Segnan M. Torasso P. Tailoring the Recommendation of Tourist Information to Heterogeneous User Groups. 3rd Workshop on Adaptive Hypertext and Hypermedia. Hypertext'01. Aarhus, Denmark. August 14-18, 2001, LNCS 2266, pp. 280-295.
3. Bailey C. El-Beltagy S. Hall W. Link Augmentation: A Context-Based Approach to Support Adaptive Hypermedia. 3rd Workshop on Adaptive Hypertext and Hypermedia. Hypertext'01. Aarhus, Denmark, August 14-18, 2001.
4. Bollen J. Group User Models for Personalized Hyperlink Recommendations. LNCS 1892– Int'l Conference on Adaptive Hypermedia and Adaptive Web-based Systems.,pp. 39-50. Trento. 2000.
5. Brusilovsky P. Cooper D. ADAPTS: Adaptive Hypermedia for a Web-based Performance Support System. 2nd Workshop on Adaptive Systems and User Modeling on the WWW. Canada, 1999.
6. Brusilovsky P. Methods and Techniques of Adaptive Hypermedia. User Modeling and User-Adapted Interaction, 6: 87-129. Kluwer Academic Publishers. 1996.
7. Brusilovsky P. Weber G. http://www.psychologie.uni-trier.de:8000/projects/ELM/elm.html
8. De Bra P. Houben G. Wu H. AHAM, A Dexter-based Reference Model for Adaptive Hypermedia. ACM Conference on Hypertext and Hypermedia, pp. 147-156. 1999.
9. Espinoza F. Höök K. A WWW Interface to an Adaptive Hypermedia System. Conference on Practical Application of Agent Methodology (PAAM'96). London. April, 1996.
10. Ferreira-De Oliveira C. Santos-Turine M. Masiero P. A Statechart-Based Model for Modeling Hypermedia Applications. ACM Transactions on Information Systems. April, 2001.
11. Furuta R. Stotts D. Trellis: A Formally-defined Hypertextual Basis for Integrating Task and Information. Olson G.M. et al. editors. Coordination Theory and Collaboration Technology, 2001.
12. García-Cabrera L. Parets-Llorca J. A Cognitive Model for Adaptive Hypermedia Systems. 1st Int'l Conf. on WISE. Workshop on WWW Semantics, pp. 29-33. Hong-Kong, China. June, 2000.
13. García-Cabrera L. SEM-HP: A Systemic, Evolutionary, Semantic Model for Hypermedia System Development (in Spanish). Ph Thesis. November, 2001.

14. Henze N. Nejdl W. Bayesian Modeling for Adaptive Hypermedia Systems. ABIS99, 7.GI - Workshop Adaptivität und Benutzermodellierung in Interaktiven Softwaresystemen 29./30.9. 1999. Otto-von-Guericke-Universität Magdeburg.
15. Hijikata Y. Yoshida T. Nishida S. Adaptive Hypermedia System for Supporting Information Providers in Directing Users through Hyperspace. 3rd Workshop on Adaptive Hypertext and Hypermedia. Hypertext'01. Aarhus, Denmark. August 14-18, 2001, LNCS 2266, pp. 322-326.
16. Hübscher R. What's in a Prerequisite. Int'l Conference on Advanced Learning Technology (ICALT 2001). Madison, WI, USA. 2001.
17. Na J. Furuta R. Dynamic Documents: Authoring, Browsing, and Analysis Using a High-Level Petri Net-Based Hypermedia System. ACM Symposium on Document Engineering'2001, pp.38-47. Atlanta, Georgia. November, 2001.
18. Not E. Zancanaro M. The MacroNode Approach: Mediating Between Adaptive and Dynamic Hypermedia. Int'l Conference on Adaptive Hypermedia and Adaptive Web-based Systems (AH'2000). Trento. August, 2000, LNCS 1892, pp. 167-178.
19. Peterson J. Petri Net Theory and the Modeling of Systems. Prentice-Hall. Englewood Cliffs, 1981.
20. Rodríguez-Fortiz M. Software Evolution: A Formalisation Based in Predicate Temporal Logic and Coloured Petri Nets (in Spanish). Ph Thesis. October, 2000.
21. Specht M. Oppermann R. ATS – Adaptive Teaching System a WWW-based ITS. U.Timm (Eds.). Workshop Adaptivität und Benutzermodellierung in Interaktiven Softwaresystemen: ABIS 98.
22. Torres-Carbonell J. Partets-Llorca J. A Formalization of the Evolution of Software Systems. Computed Aided Systems Theory, EUROCAST'99. Pp. 269-272. Vienna. September, 1999.
23. Wadge B. Schraefel M. A Complementary Approach for Adaptive and Adaptable Hypermedia: Intensional Hypertext. 3rd Workshop on Adaptive Hypertext and Hypermedia. Hypertext'01. Aarhus, Denmark. August 14-18, 2001, LNCS 2266, pp. 327-333.
24. Wu H. De Bra P. Aerts A. Houben G. Adaptation Control in Adaptive Hypermedia Systems. Adaptive Hypermedia Conference (AH2000), LNCS 1892, pp. 250-259. 2000..
25. Wu H. Houben G. De Bra P. Supporting User Adaptation in Adaptive Hypermedia Applications. On-line Conference and Informatiewetenschap 2000 (InfWet2000). De Doelen, Rotterdam. 2000.

Evaluating the Effects of Open Student Models on Learning

Antonija Mitrovic and Brent Martin

Intelligent Computer Tutoring Group
Computer Science Department, University of Canterbury
Private Bag 4800, Christchurch, New Zealand
{tanja,bim20}@cosc.canterbury.ac.nz

Abstract. In previous work [10], we reported on an experiment performed in the context of SQL-Tutor, in which we analysed students' self-assessment skills. This preliminary study revealed that more able students were better in assessing their knowledge. Here we report on a new study performed on the same system. This time, we analysed the effect of an open student model on students' learning and self-assessment skills. Although we have not seen any significant difference in the post-test scores of the control and the experimental group, the less able students from the experimental group have scored significantly higher than the less able students from the control group. The more able students who had access to their models abandoned significantly less problems the control group. These are encouraging results for a very simple open model used in the study, and we believe that a more elaborate model would be more effective.

1 Introduction

Self-assessment is one of the meta-cognitive skills necessary for effective learning. Students need to be able to critically assess their knowledge in order to decide what they need to study. The same skill is also important for students to assess the difficulty of the problem they are working on, and to decide whether to abandon to problem or keep working on it. Intelligent educational systems must support the acquisition of meta-cognitive skills in order to support deep learning, and therefore must also support the acquisition of self-assessment skills.

In previous work [10], we hypothesized that more able students were better when assessing their own knowledge than their less able peers. This hypothesis is in accordance with findings from other studies [1]. In order to evaluate the hypothesis, we analysed students' self-assessment skills in the context of the SQL-Tutor system. The system was modified slightly to allow for data collection. We focused on situations when students abandoned the problem they were working on, and asked for a new problem. In such situations, students were asked two questions. Firstly, we asked the student to specify the reason for abandoning the current problem. Three possible replies were offered: the student may think that the current problem was too easy or too difficult, or may simply want to work on a problem of a different nature. The student was then asked to specify what kind of problem they would like to work on next. For this purpose, problems were characterized by the clause, so seven options were available, one for each clause of the SELECT statement, plus the *any clause* option. The results of the data analyses performed supported our hypothesis.

In this paper, we report on a new experiment conducted in the context of the same system. We were interested in using open student models as a way to support self-assessment skills. We begin by overviewing related work in Sect. 2, and then introduce SQL-Tutor briefly in Sect. 3. SQL-Tutor provides a facility for students to select problems on their own, which requires students to be able to assess their own knowledge. Section 4 describes the experiment performed, and is followed by a description of the findings in Sect. 5. The conclusions are presented in the final section.

2 Related Work

Metacognition includes the processes and activities involved with awareness of, reasoning and reflecting about, and controlling one's cognitive skills and processes. A number of studies showed that better metacognitive skills result in improved problem solving and better learning [2, 6, 7, 15, 16], and that such skills can be taught [3, 6].

White et al. [16] define metacognition as consisting of three fundamental components: *knowledge about knowledge* (including cognitive and social expertise), *regulatory skills*, needed to monitor and control knowledge and *development expertise,* which allows students to reflect and improve knowledge. Their hypothesis is that students need to be conscious of theories for socio-cognitive processes for learning. In [16] they present SCI-WISE, a system that supports inquiry learning. In this type of learning, students cycle through several stages, starting by formulating a question, followed by the generation of hypotheses, and experimentation. After that, collected data is analysed, and students develop a model on the basis of results of analysis, and finally evaluate the model by applying it in a novel situation. The system supports inquiry learning by asking the student to explicitly state the purpose of each action and provide a justification for it. The system provides a simulation environment in which to perform experiments, and incorporates several agents, each of which specializes in a particular metacognitive process, such as inventing, collaborating and analysing, and advises the student in relevant situations. The student develops his/her own theory of scientific inquiry by modifying the agents so that they reflect student's beliefs. In order to test his/her theory, the student then engages in a physics project, during which agents provide advice. The student evaluates the agents' behaviour, which may result in the modification of the theory.

Most of the metacognitive research focuses on self-explanation, which is a skill of "generating explanations and justifications to oneself to clarify an example solution" [2, 7]. Self-explanation enables students to focus on general principles by examining specific examples [6]. Aleven and Koedinger [1] evaluate students' abilities to identify situations when help is needed and to ask for appropriate help. They show that not all students possess this skill, and recommend several ways in which the system may support students in acquiring it.

Reflection is a metacognitive skill in which students examine their own knowledge. This metacognitive skill is encouraged by allowing the student to inspect and, in some cases, to modify the student model. Several projects focused on the effects of opening the student model on students' learning [4, 5, 8, 9]. The efforts range from simply visualizing the model, to actively involving the student in the modeling process through negotiation or collaborative construction of the model. In these systems, the student model is not just a source of knowledge about the student of value to the system, but becomes an important learning resource in its own right.

The representations used to visualize the student model range from simple skillometers to very complex ones. Skillometers allow for an easy to understand, high-level overview of the student model, and have been used in ELM-ART [4] and cognitive tutors [1]. In addition to just showing the student model at a high level, some systems allow the student to challenge and negotiate the content of the model. This process is referred to as open interactive [8], collaborative [5], cooperative [9] or participative [12] student modelling. Such approaches use more complex representations of the student model based on conceptual graphs [8], Bayesian networks [17], tree structures [9], tables [5] and Prolog clauses [14]. These projects differ in the content of the student model, representation chosen for visualizing the model, the type of interactions (inspection or negotiation) and the mechanism for dealing with conflicts. The area is still just emerging, and proper ways of evaluating developed systems is yet to be identified. In all projects only very limited evaluation has been done, the results of which are not irrefutable.

3 SQL-Tutor

SQL-Tutor is an intelligent educational system aimed at university-level students learning SQL. For a detailed discussion of the system, see [11]; here we present only some of its features. SQL-Tutor consists of an interface, a pedagogical module, which determines the timing and content of pedagogical actions, and a student modeller, which analyses student answers. The system contains definitions of several databases, and a set of problems and the ideal solutions to them. SQL-Tutor contains no problem solver. To check the correctness of the student's solution, SQL-Tutor compares it to the correct solution, using domain knowledge represented in the form of more than 500 constraints. It uses Constraint-Based Modeling [13] to model knowledge of its students. Students may work their way through a series of problems for each database, or ask the system to select a problem on the basis of his/her student model.

4 The Study

The purpose of this study was to determine the effect of a simple open student model on students' learning and self-assessment skills. Let us first describe the way we visualize the student model. The student model in SQL-Tutor is implemented as an overlay on top of the constraint base. There are currently more than 500 constraints in the system, and therefore it is not possible to visualize information about each constraint. Instead, we have decided to compress the student model into a simple structure that resembles the structure of the SELECT statement. The student is shown six skillometers, which show the student model in terms of the six clauses of the SELECT statement. For each clause, we find all the relevant constraints, and compute the *coverage* (the percentage of constraints that the student has used) and *correctness* (i.e. the percentage of all relevant constraints that the student has used correctly). These two percentages are visualized as shown in Fig. 1.

We focus on situations when students abandon the current problem and ask for a new one. In such cases, the students were asked the same two question as in the preliminary study: to specify the reason for abandoning the current problem, and to specify the type of the problem they would like to work on next. The available options were the six clauses of the SELECT statement (*SELECT, FROM, WHERE, GROUP BY, HAVING,* and *ORDER BY*), plus the *any clause* option. For the experimental group, if the student's selection of the problem type was different from the one suggested by the system, the student was shown the open model, and asked whether they wanted to continue with the type of problem they specified, or whether they would prefer to switch to the system's suggestion.

The participants were enrolled in an introductory database course at the University of Canterbury, New Zealand, in the second half of 2001. Prior to the experiment, all students listened to four lectures on SQL and had two labs on the Oracle RDBMS. During the experiment, there were 4 additional lectures on SQL, and a series of four

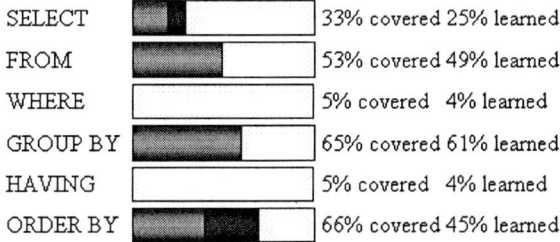

Fig. 1. The visualization of the student model

more labs. The experiment required the students to sit a pre-test, which was administered in a lecture on 10 September 2001. The pre-test consisted of three multichoice questions. All three questions contained the text of the query, and some solutions. The students were asked to classify the solutions as correct or incorrect. The maximum mark for the pre-tests was 9.

The students who sat the pre-test were given user accounts to use in SQL-Tutor from September 12, and were randomly allocated to one of the three possible versions of the system. The experiment was designed to combine two evaluations into one: the evaluation of an enhanced constraint and problem set, and the evaluation of the open student model. The control group served as the control group for both studies. The problem selection group is not of importance for this paper, and the experimental group is the group that had access to the open student model.

The interaction with the system was voluntary. The course involved a test on SQL a month after the system was introduced to the class. The post-test consisted of three questions of similar nature and complexity as the questions in the pre-test, and was administered in a lecture, on 9 October 2001.

5 Results

This section presents the results of the analyses performed on the data collected in the experiment. Section 5.1 presents the general findings about how students learnt with SQL-Tutor. Data analyses relevant to our hypotheses are discussed in Sect. 5.2.

5.1 Learning with SQL-Tutor

Out of 159 students enrolled in the course, 100 sat the pre-test. Table 1 gives the number of students in each group, their pre-test scores, and some additional information about their logs. The mean score for the pre-test for the whole class was 5 (out of 9, SD=1.36). The t-test reveals there are no significant differences between the pre-test scores, which means that the three groups are comparable. The problem selection group is of no importance for this paper, so we report on the control and experimental groups only.

As the usage of the system was voluntary, 80 students actually logged on to SQL-Tutor. Table 1 gives the number of students in each of the groups who sat the pre-test, and also the number of students who actually used the system. However, some of these students have only briefly looked at the system. We excluded the logs of 9 students who attempted no problems, and the number of valid logs is given in the table.

Table 1. The three groups

Group	Students	Pre-test mean (SD)	Accounts used	Valid logs	Post-test
Control	34	4.82 (1.44)	29	24	12
Experimental	33	5.12 (1.41)	23	21	12
Problem selection	33	5.06 (1.25)	28	26	14

There were 101 students who sat the post-test (mean=5.99, SD=1.60). In the post-test, the students were asked whether they have used SQL-Tutor and, if they have, to specify their account. The mean score on the post-test for students who have used SQL-Tutor was 6.42 (SD=1.50), which is higher than the overall mean. The mean score of the students who have not used SQL-Tutor was 5.67 (SD=1.61). However, we cannot claim that SQL-Tutor was responsible for this higher mean, as the participation in the study was voluntary, and the students who participate are usually more motivated.

Although we asked students to specify the account if they used the system, some students have not done that. The last column in Table 1 contains the number of students in each group who specified their account names. These are the only students whose pre- and post-test results we were able to match. Table 2 contains the statistics for the pre- and post-test results for those students only. It can be seen that the scores for the experimental group are slightly higher, but not significantly.

Table 2. Pre- and post-test results for the students who can be matched

Group	Matched tests	Pre-test mean (SD)	Post-test mean (SD)
Control	12	4.42 (1.24)	6.42 (1.38)
Experimental	12	4.50 (1.17)	6.67 (1.56)

Table 3[1] gives some simple statistics gathered from the valid logs. The number of sessions ranged from 1 to 13, and the lengths of individual sessions ranged from 1 minute to almost four hours. The total interaction time ranged from 5 minutes to more than ten hours. The *Total solved* column gives the mean number of problems the students have solved during all sessions, which ranges from 1 to 70. *Problem/session* gives the average number of problems students have seen in a session (ranges from 1 to 40). *Solved/session* gives the averages for the number of solved problems (the minimum for solved problems per session is 0, the maximum is 35), while the percentage of problem completion is given in the next column. On the average, the control group needed slightly more time per solved problem than the experimental group. None of the reported numbers are significantly different.

Table 3. Statistics about the sessions

Group	Sessions	Session length (min)	Total time (min)	Total solved	Problem /session	Solved /session	% prob. solved /session	Mins per solved
Contr (24)	4.7 (3.28)	39 (41)	183 (189)	20.5 (15.2)	5.3 (3.1)	4.4 (3.3)	77.6 (21.7)	8.6 (5.2)
Exper. (21)	4 (2.66)	36 (32)	144 (125)	22.8 (18.8)	6.7 (3.8)	5.6 (3.7)	77.1 (18.2)	7.2 (3.7)

5.2 Analyzing the Self-assessment Skills

We also analysed the effects of the open student models with respect to students' abilities. Each group was split into two subgroups, with less and more able students, depending on their scores on the pre-test. Students who scored above the average (5 or more marks) on the pre-test were put into the *more able* group, while the students who scored 0 to 4 marks were put into the *less able* group. Table 4 contains statistics about the subgroups, which are of similar sizes. There is no significant difference on

---

[1] Standard deviations are given in parentheses.

the pre-test scores between the less able and more able students in the control and the experimental groups. The results on the post-test for the more able students are not significantly different. However, the scores on the post-test for the less able students in the experimental group are significantly better than the results of the less able part of the control group (t=1.43, p<0.1). This result suggests that the less able students benefit more from open student models.

The logs also contain the data relevant to our hypothesis. Out of 45 logs we analysed, 12 students did not abandon any problems. These students interacted with the system for a shorter time (105 minutes on average) and solved 16 problems. However, they solved all the problems they attempted. The remaining 33 students abandoned some problems. Whenever a student asked for a new problem before completing the current one, the system asked the two questions. Each student was asked these questions at least once, and at most 40 times, and the means for the four subgroups are given in Table 4 in the *Questions* row. Out of the total of 242[2] abandoned problems, 93 (38.4%) were from the more able students, and 149 were from the less able students. Therefore, less able students are much more likely to abandon a problem. The more able students from the experimental group have abandoned significantly less problems than the more able students from the control group. However, there is no significant difference between the two groups of less able students. This might suggest that the more able students were encouraged to complete the problems by being exposed to their student models.

Table 4. Statistics for the groups of students with different prior knowledge

	Control		Experimental	
	Less able	More able	Less able	More able
Pre-test	3.6 (0.5)	5.6 (0.9)	3.7 (0.5)	5.6 (0.9)
Post-test	5.9 (1.5)	7.2 (0.8)	7 (1.5)	6.2 (1.6)
Time	164 (135)	321 (229)	169 (142)	115 (107)
Problems solved	19.8 (10.4)	28.8 (17.2)	27.4 (26.2)	19.4 (14.4)
Questions	7.1 (4.1)	10.87 (13.2)	8.5 (5)	3.9 (3)
0 attempts	5.1 (2.9)	7.6 (11.2)	4.7 (2.8)	2.1 (1.6)
0/new problem	1.6 (1.1)	2.2 (3.6)	1.1 (0.7)	1.5 (1.5)

The number of attempts before abandoning the problem ranged from 0 (the total of 165 cases) to 13 (an average of 1.43). The *0 attempts* row in Table 4 gives the mean number of cases when students abandon the current problem without attempting it. The numbers reported here are a bit misleading, as they include all problems, not just the new problems. In other words, the student might attempt a problem, and then abandon it, only to receive the same problem again, and then abandon it for the second time. Such a problems is counted twice. The following row (*0/new problem*) counts each problem only once in such situations. It can be seen that the more able students in the experimental group attempt to solve problems more often than the

---

[2] Although we use the word "problem" here, we refer to situations when the student abandons the current problem, and get the two questions. It may be the case that the student abandons the same problem several times, so the total number reported here does not equal to the number of distinct problems abandoned.

more able students from the control group; however, the differences are not significant.

The distribution of answers to the first question is given in Fig. 2. The control group students thought that the problem is too easy more often than experimental group students, especially the more able ones, although the inspection of the logs very often contradicts the reason they specified.

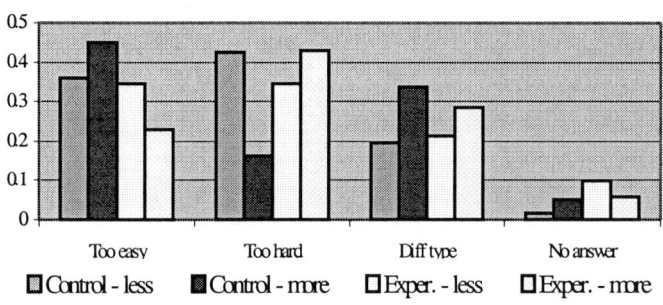

Fig. 2. The distribution of answers for question 1

Figure 3 shows the distribution of answers to the second question. As we hypothesized, less able students are not good at identifying the kind of problem to work next, and therefore they specify *any clause* most often (in 54.69% of the cases in the control group, and 40.98% in the experimental group).

After answering the second question, the students in the experimental group were shown the summary of their student models if their selection of a clause to work on next differed from the system's selection. The number of such cases for the two subgroups are given in the *No of cases* column in Table 5. In those situations, the students were asked to specify whether they wanted to go on with their selection, or adopt the system's suggestion. The following column gives the percentages of the total number of questions when the student's selection differed from the system's one. Although the more able students have opinions about what they should be doing that more often varies from the system's suggestion, compared to the less able students, the difference is insignificant. The percentages of cases when the student accepts the system's suggestion (last column in Table 5) is almost identical for the more and less able students. When comparing the experimental group with the control group, there is no significant difference in the percentages of cases when more able student's selections differ from system's selections.

Table 5. The statistics for the two subgroups of the experimental group

Group	No of cases	% of questions	Student agrees	% agree
Exper. - more able	2 (2.69)	57.25 (42.57)	0.75 (0.70)	51.56 (51.94)
Exper. - less able	3.70 (3.40)	35.78 (31.70)	1.80 (1.64)	57.5 (42.94)
Control – more able	8.25 (11.37)	42.20 (28.20)	N/A	N/A
Control – less able	5.44 (4.44)	41.20 (20.62)	N/A	N/A

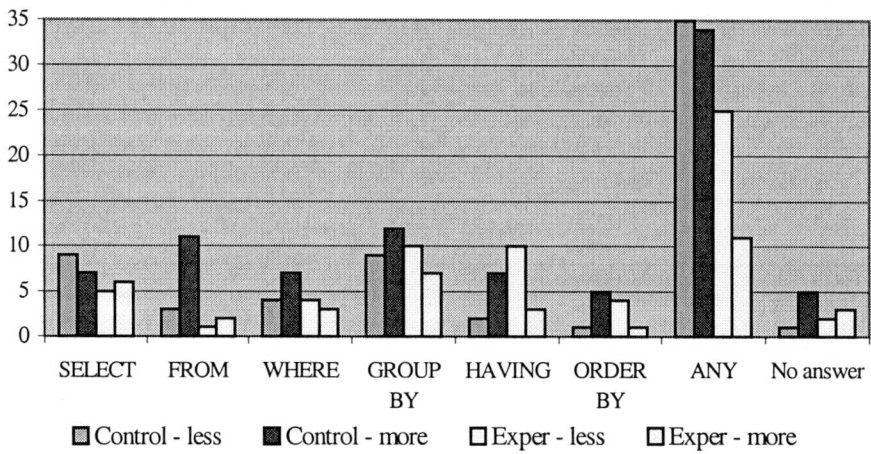

Fig. 3. The distribution of answers for Question 2

6 Conclusions

We presented a study of the effects of open student models on student self-assessment skills. Although we have not seen any significant difference in the post-test scores of the control and the experimental group, the less able students from the experimental group have scored significantly higher than the less able students from the control group. The more able students who had access to their models abandoned significantly less problems than the more able students from the control group, and had stronger opinions on what they should work on next, which often varied from the system's suggestions.

Overall, these results suggest that the open model may have improved the performance of the less able students, and that it may have boosted the self-confidence of the more able students, such that they abandoned fewer problems and judged their own abilities more readily. Alternatively, more able students in the experimental group may have specified a clause more often *in order to view the model*, which would suggest that they judged it to be beneficial. Such results are encouraging given the simplicity of the open student model developed for this study. Our students only received a high-level overview of their knowledge, and they could not challenge it or make any modifications. We believe that a more sophisticated open student model would be more effective, and plan to conduct a new study along these lines in the future.

Acknowledgements

The work presented here was supported by the University of Canterbury grant U6430.

References

1. Aleven, V., Koedinger, K. (2000) Limitations of Student Control: Do Students Know When They Need Help? Proc. ITS'2000, Springer-Verlag, pp. 292-303.
2. Aleven, V., Koedinger, K., Cross, K. (1999) Tutoring Answer Explanation Fosters Learning with Understanding. In: Lajoie, S.P., Vivet, M. (eds): Proc. AIED'99, pp. 199-206.
3. Bielaczyc, K., Pirolli, P., Brown, A.L.: Training in Self-Explanation and Self-Regulation Strategies: Investigating the Effects of Knowledge Acquisition Activities on Problem-solving. *Cognition and Instruction*, 13(2) (1993) 221-252.
4. Brusilovsky, P., Schwarz, E., Weber, G. (1996) ELM-ART: an Intelligent Tutoring System on World Wide Web. Proc. ITS'96, pp. 261-269.
5. Bull, S., Brna, P. (1997) What does Susan Know that Paul Doesn't? (and vice versa): Contributing to each other's student model. Proc. AIED 97, pp. 568-570.
6. Chi, M. T. H., Bassok, M., Lewis, M.W., Reinmann, P., Glaser, R. (1989) Self-Explanations: How Students Study and Use Examples in Learning to Solve Problems. *Cognitive Science*, 13, 145-182.
7. Conati, C., VanLehn, K.: Further Results from the Evaluation of an Intelligent Computer Tutor to Coach Self-Explanation. Proc. ITS'2000, Springer-Verlag, (2000) 304-313.
8. Dimitrova, V., Self, J., Brna, P. (2001) Applying Interactive Open Learner Models to Learning Technical Terminology. Proc. UM 2001, Springer, pp. 148-157.
9. Kay, J. (1995) The UM toolkit for cooperative user modelling. *User Modelling and User-Adapted Interaction*, 4, 149-196.
10. Mitrovic, A. Investigating students' self-assessment skills. Proc. UM-2001, Sonthofen, July 2001, Springer-Verlag LNAI 2109, pp. 247-250.
11. Mitrovic, A., Ohlsson, S.: Evaluation of a Constraint-based Tutor for a Database Language. *Int. J. on Artificial Intelligence in Education*, 10(3-4), (1999) 238-256.
12. Morales, R., Pain, H., Conlon, T. (2001) Effects of Inspecting Learner Models on Learners' Abilities. Proc. AIED 2001, pp. 434-445.
13. Ohlsson, S.: Constraint-based student modeling. In: Greer, J.E., McCalla, G (eds): *Student modeling: the key to individualized knowledge-based instruction*, (1994) 167-189.
14. Paiva, A., Self, J. (1995) TAGUS – a user and learner modelling workbench. *User Modeling and User-Adapted Interaction*, 4, 197-226.
15. Swanson, H.L.: Influence of Metacognitive Knowledge and Aptitude on Problem Solving. *J. Educational Psychology*, 82 (1990) 306-314.
16. White, B.Y., Shimoda, T. A, Frederiksen, J.R. (1999) Enabling Students to Construct Theories of Collaborative Inquiry and Reflective Learning: Computer Support for Metacognitive Development. Int. Journal on AI in Education, vol 10, 151-182.
17. Zapata-Rivera, J.D., Greer, J.E. (2000) Inspecting and Visualizing Distributed Bayesian Student Models. Proc. ITS'2000, Springer, pp. 544-553.

Ephemeral and Persistent Personalization in Adaptive Information Access to Scholarly Publications on the Web

Stefano Mizzaro and Carlo Tasso

Artificial Intelligence Laboratory
Department of Mathematics and Computer Science
University of Udine
{mizzaro, tasso}@dimi.uniud.it

Abstract. We show how personalization techniques can be exploited to implement more adaptive and effective information access systems in electronic publishing. We distinguish persistent (or long term) and ephemeral (or short term) personalization, and we describe how both of them can be profitably applied in information filtering and retrieval systems used, via a specialized Web portal, by physicists in their daily job. By means of several experimental results, we demonstrate that persistent personalization is needed and useful for information filtering systems, and ephemeral personalization leads to more effective and usable information retrieval systems.

1 Introduction

Oversupply of information constitutes a well known phenomenon that is progressively becoming worse and that threatens Web usefulness. Other related issues are information waste (documents published on the Web do not always reach the appropriate readers, or reach them too late), and low information quality (the amount of available information is increasing, but its quality is decreasing). These problems are very general, and affect all kinds of Web contents, i.e., information to be accessed, products to be purchased, and services to be exploited. Personalization allows a more effective information access: end users can be delivered personalized information, tailored to their individual needs, and, more generally, it enables a more effective and efficient transfer of the published information from the authors to the most appropriate readers.

At the University of Udine, we have been investigating the issue of personalization in information access for several years [1, 8, 9, 10, 20, 22]. In this paper, we present the most recent results concerned with the application of adaptive and personalized information access to the electronic publishing field, and more specifically in scholarly publishing. We claim that personalization is needed and useful in information access, and especially in scholarly publishing, where users (i.e., researchers) are interested in it for two important reasons: (i) detecting newly published information which is relevant to their interests and preferences, and (ii) accessing stored information for satisfying specific information needs. However, this twofold situation requires a novel approach, in which two distinct and complementary personalization techniques (i.e., ephemeral and persistent personalization) are applied together to meet user's requirements.

This paper is structured as follows. Section 2 briefly describes the world of scholarly publishing, and the heavy changes introduced in it by the Web. In Sect. 3 we present a short overview of information access approaches, and discuss how personalization techniques can be useful in this field. In Sects 4 and 5 we show the application of personalization techniques to information access to scholarly publications. Section 6 closes the paper and sketches some future developments.

2 Scholarly Publishing and the Web

The communication mechanism adopted by science today arose in the 17th Century, with the publication of the first scientific journals. Since about 1930, the dissemination of scholarly information is based on peer review, that usually assures a high quality of the published papers. Internet has changed, and is changing, this situation [3]. Now a peer reviewed journal can be distributed by electronic means, and the peer reviewing can take place completely electronically, drastically reducing time and money for publishing (see, e.g., JHEP at jhep.sissa.it or Earth Interactions at EarthInteractions.org). Many publishers now allow their subscribers to electronically access the full text of the papers published on standard journals. Beyond modifying the standard scholarly journals and proceedings, the Web has also introduced a new way of disseminating scholarly knowledge: *e-prints*, i.e., open online repositories of scholarly papers (see, e.g., arXiv.org, mainly about physics, or cogprints.soton.ac.uk, about disciplines concerning cognition). The repositories usually contain *preprints*, i.e., electronic versions of submitted papers made publicly available before review, acceptance, and, possibly, publication.

The exploitation of the Web has also highlighted another essential characteristic of scholarly publications, i.e., their hypermedia nature. A rich hypertext structure is provided by both the citations across publications and the references (to chapters, sections, figures, and so on) within each publication. Multimediality is also important since it leads to a more effective communication, and even though still limited today, it will increase in the next years. Another aspect that further extends the richness of the hypermedia structure is the storage (easy obtainable on electronic media) of a publication as a multilayered document (dlp.cs.berkeley.edu), that includes the various versions of a document, the slides and presentations resulting from it, the referees' and readers' comments, and any other remark about the document. This provides a richer information on the topic at hand, and adds more hypermedia information as links among the various layers.

All these new means available to authors allow an ever growing rate of production of scholarly articles (see, e.g., the arXiv usage statistics: arXiv.org/show_stats). The new Web-based approach guarantees easier access, more powerful and richer means of information seeking, and better timeliness, but it features also some drawbacks (e.g., the quality of preprints is not assessed by a peer review process) and poses some new problems (copyright problems, social and legal acceptance, and so on). However, after a slow start [15], the impact of scholarly publishing is steadily increasing [11].

As a result, the scholar is nowadays overloaded by a large amount of highly structured hypermedia information, in the form of scholarly publications, online repositories, commentaries, and so on. In this scenario, it is important to allow the scholar: (i) to stay up-to-date, being notified when new information on some topics of interest is published, and (ii) to quickly and easily find, on demand, information on specific topics. Both goals can be approached by advanced personalization techniques, as shown in the next section. Personalization plays indeed a fundamental role not only for the highly subjective nature of the information seeking process, but also because the job of a researcher is highly innovative, it does not conform to any standard behavior, and it is therefore quite different for each researcher.

3 Personalized Information Access

Information access is the process exploited by a seeker who wishes to find and retrieve some data/information which satisfies an *information need*. It is common to distinguish between two kinds of information access:

- *Information retrieval* (*IR*) [2] is characterized by a static database of documents, a short term information need, and a query made up by a few (usually less than two) terms. Web search engines are the most known instance of IR systems. It is well known that IR is a difficult task [4], since users have to specify in a query something that they do not know (if they knew it, they wouldn't be searching for it).
- *Information filtering* (*IF*) [14], on the other side, is characterized by a dynamic database (actually an incoming flow of documents) and a long term and rather static information need. Users of IF systems are more motivated to express their information needs as more accurate and complete descriptions that will last for longer time. These descriptions are usually called *user profiles* (or *models*), and are made up by a lot of data: concepts, relationships among them, weights, etc.

Web personalization is the process of selecting, preparing and delivering Web contents for a given user, by taking into account his specific needs and preferences [23]. Personalization means delivering to the user the most relevant contents, in the most adequate way, and at the most appropriate time. A personalization system is based on three main functions, which all can be performed in a personalized way: selection, visualization, and delivery. In order to be personalized, all the three functions have to be supported by specific information about the user, which is included in a user profile and has to be available when the personalization process takes place. In this paper we deal only with the first of the three functions, i.e., selection of the most appropriate content.

Personalization techniques are very numerous and are ranging from simple user-controlled customization of Web content, to autonomous system-controlled adaptation [17, Reader's Guide, p.6]. We distinguish two types of personalization [23]: *persistent* (or *long term*), i.e., based on a user profile which lasts over time and is stored in a persistent information structure; and *ephemeral* (or *short term*), which is not based on a persistent user profile. The main differences are the temporal features of the process aimed at building and managing the user profile. In persistent personalization, the user profile is incrementally developed over time and at the end of each session it is stored in order to be used later on in subsequent sessions. Usually, but not necessarily, the information exploited for building the profile comes from various sources, it concerns different aspects of the user, and it is often extended by means of (possibly sophisticated) reasoning or learning processes. In ephemeral personalization, the information used to build the user profile is gathered during the current session only, and is immediately exploited for executing some adaptive process aimed at personalizing the current interaction. At the end of each session, the user profile is lost, and no information about the user is stored in a persistent way for later use.

Information access systems should and can exploit both kinds of personalization [4, 12]. We propose here a twofold approach. On the one side, personalization in IF means capturing the long term information interests and preferences of the user, in order to tailor the selection process to the specific personal characteristics. On the other side, in IR persistent personalization is not feasible, since in that context information needs have a short term nature and are different, for the same user, in the different sessions. However, ephemeral personalization can be used in an effective way, with the goal of modeling the search session, rather than the information need, for immediately providing personalized support during the searching session. The idea of long and short term modeling in information access is not new (see, e.g., [7]), however it has been considered from the IF perspective only, i.e., it consists in building user profiles across a shorter or longer period of time (a limited number of sessions or very many sessions), and the profiles, in both cases, model only the topics interesting for the user. Our approach is innovative for two reasons: (i) short term modeling is performed through ephemeral personalization, restricting the scope of observation to the current session only, and (ii) we do not build a model of the information need (difficult, if not impossible, during just one session), but rather a session model. This novelty allows to provide adaptive support to the user, as it will be shown in Sect. 5.2.

We have experimented this twofold approach in scholarly publishing portals for physics. We chose that community since the physics (especially high energy physics) field seems well ahead in exploiting the full potential of web publishing (no surprise, since the Web was born at CERN, one of the major physics institutions worldwide): the above cited arXiv repository (formerly known as xxx) is already a used, valid, and widely accepted media for physics and astronomy fields [11], and the SPIRES (www.slac.stanford.edu/spires/hep) citation index is almost three times more complete than the ISI well known database. In the next sections we present an application of persistent and ephemeral personalization within the Torii vertical portal (torii.sissa.it) on physics, which has been developed in the 5th FP IST project TIPS (Tools for Innovative Publishing in Science), see tips.sissa.it.

4 Persistent Personalization in Information Filtering

In previous work, we have developed and evaluated several content-based filters [18] for persistent personalization. Among them [1, 20, 22], the most effective has been the information agent *ifT* (*information filtering Tool*) [20], which is based on the user modeling shell *UMT* (*User Modeling Tool*) [10]. The work presented here concerns the exploitation of ifT in the Torii portal.

4.1 Content-Based Filtering through ifT

ifT exploits lightweight natural language processing and co-occurence-based semantic networks for building long term user profiles and for evaluating the relevance of text documents with respect to a profile. The main mechanism for building user profiles exploits explicit relevance feedback provided by the user on both positive and negative examples. The learning capabilities of this mechanism have been evaluated by means of several laboratory experiments [1]. In one of them, four subjects received

2000 documents (20 each day, for 100 days) on various computer science topics. Each subject was interested in some specific area(s) of computer science, and ifT was filtering and ranking the incoming documents according to their relevance. Initially the user profile was empty, and the user was allowed to 'explain' his interests through relevance feedback only. Throughout the experiment, standard precision and recall were measured. Fig. 1 shows the evolution of precision over time (100 sessions): dots represent the observed data, the irregular line represents the moving-average of order 5, and the regular line is an interpolation curve. The results show good learning capabilities (a precision of 80% is reached after 8 sessions), as well as a very high final precision value which saturates at about 92% in the interpolation model.

Another significant application of ifT has been developed within the *ifWeb* system for filtering Web documents [22]. The system includes the information agent *ifSpider*, aimed at the autonomous navigation of the Web for searching documents relevant to a specific user profile. The navigation performed through hyperlinks is opportunistic: only the paths including documents which feature relevance scores above a given threshold are considered.

ifWeb has been evaluated in several laboratory experiments. In one of them, devoted to assess its ranking capabilities, each subject was initially defining a profile through relevance feedback given on 4-6 documents, and then he was performing a series of nine sessions with ifWeb. After each session, the subject was requested to provide the correct ranking of the documents given by ifWeb, and human and system rankings were compared. Fig. 2 shows precision (continuous line) and the ndpm measure [24], which evaluates the difference between the two rankings (good performance is indicated by decreasing values). After the first sessions, as precision reaches good values, the ndpm starts to decrease, indicating the capability to produce a better ranking.

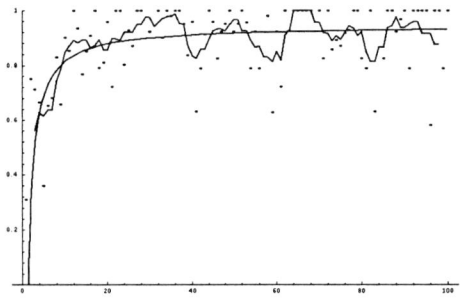
Fig. 1. Precision of ifT over 100 sessions.

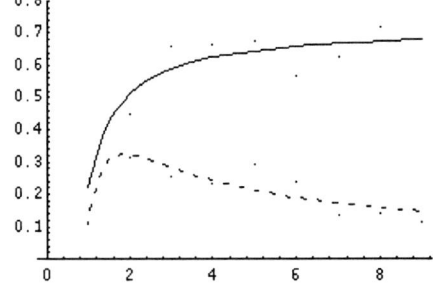
Fig. 2. Precision and ndpm measures of ifWeb over 9 sessions.

4.2 Exploiting Content-Based Filtering in Electronic Publishing

Given the performance reached by ifT, we decided to adopt ifT as the filtering engine of the Torii portal. More specifically, the problem approached with persistent personalization has been the high (and currently increasing) rate of incoming documents: about 100-200 new e-prints are submitted every day and included in arXiv, which is available in Torii. Normal users (researchers in high energy physics) are used to start the working day by browsing the long list of new e-prints. By adding a personalized filtering engine to Torii, each user can define one or more profiles related to his interests, and all the new incoming information is automatically filtered. In this way, Torii displays (in the first positions) only the documents which best match user's interests. Information overload is then reduced, as well as the cognitive load of analyzing many documents every day. Fig. 3 shows a snapshot of the Torii portal.

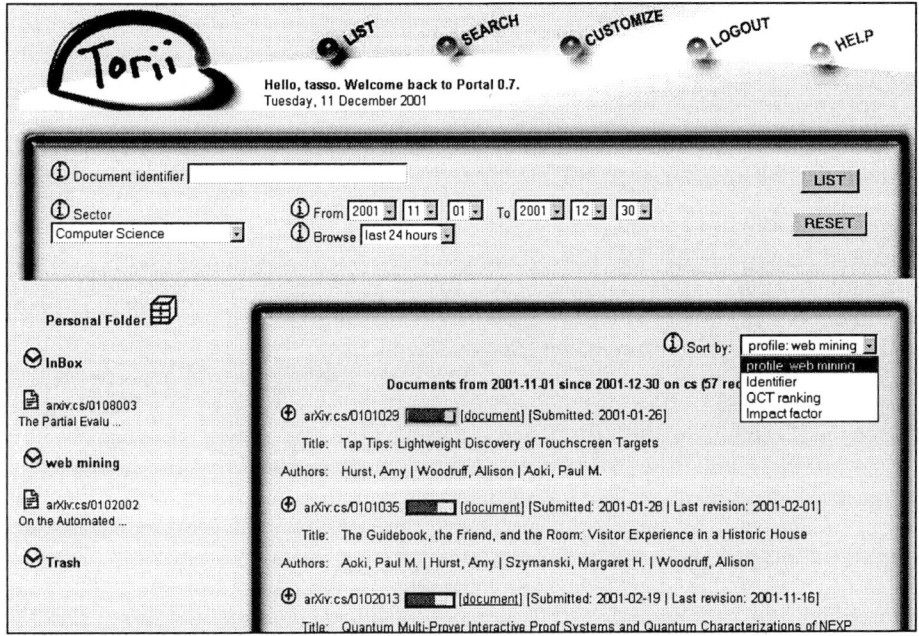

Fig. 3. Torii portal: documents ranked by the ifT filtering engine.

The relevance measure produced by ifT and exploited in Torii is a unique figure (see the bars shown in Fig. 3) which combines the document *topicality* value, i.e., a measure of how much concepts relevant for the user are present in the considered document, and the *conceptual coverage* value, i.e., a measure of how many of the concepts relevant for the user are present in the considered document.

Torii has undergone a first validation phase through field testing in July 2001. Twenty users were using the system for 29 days. All their sessions have been monitored and tracking logs of all actions acquired. Final interviews were also delivered. Cognitive filtering was working well and judged well by the users, who proposed to extend the system with the possibility to rank any set of documents (possibly coming as the result of a search in one of the available collections) by means of ifT. SISSA (the managing institution of Torii), has decided to use the filtering engine ifT as a standard tool available to all users of their portal.

5 Ephemeral Personalization in Information Retrieval

5.1 Supporting Users of IR Systems

The interactive nature of IR is advocated since years [16] and is now widely accepted: between the user and the IR system a dialogue takes place [6], during which the user should receive adequate support [4]. The help should be provided proactively by the system and suggestions should be given "on the background", with the user retaining the control of the interaction [5]. A basic kind of support is *terminological* help, which identifies and suggests to the user terms that improve the query [13, 19]. Another kind of support is *strategic* help, which provides to the user useful hints on how to improve the strategy adopted for organizing the searching process (see a survey of this issue in [9]).

We propose to use ephemeral personalization techniques to provide both strategic and terminological support to IR users. We have been doing research on this issue for several years. We implemented the FIRE prototype [8] that, by means of thesauri, is capable of suggesting to the users of a boolean IR system alternative terms to better (re)formulate their information needs. After a carefully designed laboratory experiment involving 45 participants, we had evidence that terminological help alone is useful, but needs to be complemented by strategic help.

On the basis of these results, we added to FIRE a Strategic Aid Module (SAM) capable of providing to the users suggestions on which strategies are more likely to be effective in a certain situation [9]. SAM is based on a collaborative (between the user and the system) view of the session: users know their needs, judge the relevance of the retrieved documents, select the terms to be added to the query, and retain the control of the session; the system monitors users' actions and provides contextual suggestions, proposing alternative routes, emphasizing mistakes (e.g., term spelling), and so on. SAM is based on a detailed conceptual model of the session, made up by representing user actions, the current situation of the session, and the set of feasible and more appropriate suggestions. By exploiting a knowledge base, the current situation of the session is inferred from the actions made by the user, and personalized suggestions are selected on the basis of the current situation. We performed two laboratory experiments (one in which we simulated the activity of the users of the previous FIRE experiment, and one that involved six new participants), both of which showed that strategic support is useful, well accepted, and it allows users to learn the best strategies.

5.2 Supporting Users of IR Systems on the Web

Following the positive evaluations of the two prototypes mentioned above, we decided to apply ephemeral personalization to an IR system deployed in a real setting: we implemented the Information Retrieval Assistant (IRA), a system providing various kinds of suggestions to users that are searching the paper and e-print database available in the Torii portal. IRA exhibits some innovative features with respect to the previous two prototypes. It fully integrates terminological and strategic suggestions. The underlying IR system is a probabilistic one (Okapi, see web.soi.city.ac.uk/research/cisr/okapi/okapi.html) in place of a boolean one, and it works on an underlying full text database, containing almost 200,000 scholarly documents about physics (as opposed to the bibliographic, and smaller, database used in the previous experiments). IRA is designed to be deployed in a real life environment, and used by physicists in their daily job. IRA can also be easily tailored to be used with other IR systems.

However, the most important innovative features in IRA are on the conceptual side, and concern the new models on which ephemeral personalization, i.e., both terminological and strategic suggestions, is based. The sorted term lists suggested in terminological help are obtained by a new spreading activation algorithm capable of browsing heterogeneous, dynamically generated, and integrated thesauri, starting either from the last inserted search term, or from the set of all the search terms used by the user so far. This new version of terminological help has shown, by means of an experimental evaluation involving six participants, significant improvements with respect to the terminological help previously used in FIRE: more terms are suggested (since more term sources are used), they are more adequate to the current context and ranked in a better way (mainly for two reasons: the synergy among the different term sources and the new spreading activation algorithm).

The enhanced reasoning process for suggestion generation is represented in Fig. 4. Each user *action* (i.e., any operation performed by the user, such as term insertion/removal/modification, search in the database, document reading, relevance judgment, etc.) on the Okapi user interface is notified to IRA by Okapi. IRA monitors these time-stamped actions and builds a model of the session history, that is made up by a sequence of interleaved actions and states. A *state* is a set of parameters describing the current state of the system, like number of terms in the query, number of retrieved, read, and judged (as relevant or not relevant) documents, etc. At each state, i.e., after each action, a new set of situations is inferred. A *situation* is a history pattern, or an abstract description of the session history. Situations can be very simple, like 'insertion of a zero posting count term in the query' (a term that is not contained in any document), or they can concern a longer time interval, like 'two consecutive searches with no changes to the query'. Moreover, they can be more

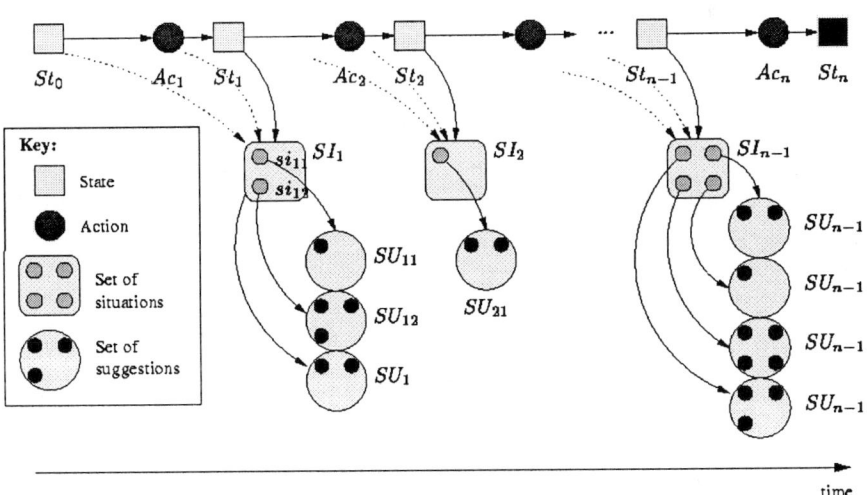

Fig. 4. IRA reasoning process.

abstract and difficult to infer certainly, like 'user not reading the content of the retrieved documents'. Situation derivation is triggered by the last user action, but takes into account the whole session history.

From each situation, a set of *suggestions* is derived. One of the most important suggestions is terminological help, but IRA suggestions also include simple *hints*, that merely make aware the user of alternative actions (like reminding the user to have a look at the full text of the documents, or to judge, by clicking on the appropriate button, the relevance of the read documents), and more complex *advices*, that are carried out collaboratively by the user and IRA (like author search, that suggests to look for documents written by the same author as the documents already judged relevant by the user). IRA suggestions are always contextual and are provided in two kinds of situations: *critical* (i.e., the user is experiencing some problem, as repeatedly retrieving no documents, or not making progress) and *enhanceable* (i.e., when the user could follow other – possibly more – appropriate alternative routes). Finally, IRA suggestions are ranked and proposed to the user as two types of textual descriptions, a short one and a longer one displayed on demand. They are shown in IRA own window on the background, thus allowing the user to maintain the control of the interaction with the IR system. The user can either accept the suggestions received (e.g., he can insert into the query some new relevant term provided by terminological help), or can ignore them. IRA knowledge bases by now contain 33 actions, 28 situations, and 20 suggestions, and are still being extended.

We performed a first laboratory evaluation that highlighted some positive qualitative results: the sample users that used IRA are satisfied with the adequacy, timeliness, comprehensibility, and usefulness of the suggestions. Moreover, as foreseen, terminological help is especially appreciated. IRA is now being deployed and used by real end-users, and another more extensive evaluation of it will take place in the next months.

6 Conclusions and Future Work

In this paper we have shown how persistent and ephemeral personalization techniques can be exploited to implement more adaptive and effective information access systems. More specifically, the research presented here approaches two problems of the user of a scholarly publishing system: the need to be timely and accurately updated about new relevant information and the request for adequate, effective and easy-to-use support during search of archive information. Several experimental results show that persistent personalization is useful for information filtering systems, and ephemeral personalization leads to more effective and usable information retrieval systems.

So far, we have kept separated the two approaches, but they naturally complement each other. Therefore, we plan to integrate them in various ways: the long term user profile can be used in IR, e.g., to rank the retrieved documents in a more personalized way; vice versa, the suggestions can be useful during the initial construction of the profile, or during feedback iterations. We also believe that these personalization techniques can be fruitfully applied also outside the scholar community, for instance in the more general context of electronic publishing, where various media such as newspapers, magazines, news agencies, and so on are continuously fed with new information. Finally, the quality of information is another important issue, that we have not considered in this paper, and that we are approaching with a collaborative work approach [21].

References

1. F.A. Asnicar, M. Di Fant, C. Tasso, User Model-Based Information Filtering, in M. Lenzerini ed. *AI*IA 97: Advances in Artificial Intelligence – Proc. of the 5th Congress of AI*IA*, LNAI 1321, Springer, Berlin, D, 1997, 242-253.
2. R. Baeza-Yates, B. Ribeiro-Neto, *Modern Information Retrieval*, Addison-Wesley, New York, NY, USA, 1999.
3. C.W. Bailey, Jr., Scholarly electronic publishing bibliography - Version 40: 12/12/01, http://info.lib.uh.edu/sepb/sepb.html, visited 5/1/02.
4. N.J. Belkin, Helping People Find What They Don't Know, *Comm. of the ACM* 43(8), 2000, 59-61.
5. N. Belkin, C. Cool, D. Kelly, S.-J. Lin, S.Y. Park, J. Perez-Carballo, C. Sikora, Iterative exploration, design and evaluation of support for query reformulation in interactive information retrieval, *Information Processing and Management* 37(3), 2001, 403-434.
6. N. Belkin, C. Cool, A. Stein, U. Thiel, Cases, scripts, and information-seeking strategies: On the design of interactive information retrieval systems, *Expert Systems with Applications* 9(3), 1995, 379-395.
7. D. Billsus, M.J. Pazzani, User Modeling for Adaptive News Access, *User Modeling and User-Adapted Interaction Journal* 10(2-3), 2000, 147-180.
8. G. Brajnik, S. Mizzaro, C. Tasso, Evaluating User Interfaces to Information Retrieval Systems: a Case Study on User Support, *Proc. of the 19th Annual International ACM SIGIR Conference*, Zurich, CH, 1996, 128-136.
9. G. Brajnik, S. Mizzaro, C. Tasso, F. Venuti. Strategic help in user interfaces for information retrieval, *J. of the Am. Soc. for Information Science and Technology*, 2002, in press.
10. G. Brajnik, C. Tasso, A shell for developing non-monotonic user modeling systems, *International Journal Human-Computer Studies* 40, 1994, 31-62.
11. C. Brown, The E-volution of Preprints in the Scholarly Communication of Physicists and Astronomers, *J. of the Am. Soc. for Information Science and Technology* 52(3), 2001, 187-200.
12. W.B. Croft, S. Cronen-Townsend, V. Lavrenko, Relevance Feedback and Personalization: A Language Modeling Perspective, *DELOS Workshop: Personalisation and Recommender Systems in Digital Libraries*, 2001, www.ercim.org/publication/ws-proceedings/DelNoe02/.
13. E.N. Efthimiadis, Query expansion, *Annual Review of Information Science and Technology (ARIST)*, M. E. Williams ed., vol. 31, 1996, 121-187.
14. U. Hanani, B. Shapira, P. Shoval, Information Filtering: Overview of Issues, Research and Systems, *User Modeling and User-Adapted Interaction* 11(3), 2001, 203-259.
15. S.P. Harter, Scholarly communication and electronic journals: An impact study. *J. of the Am. Soc. for Information Science* 1998, 49(6), 507-516.
16. P. Ingwersen, *Information Retrieval Interaction*, Taylor Graham, London, UK, 1992.
17. A. Jameson, C. Paris, C. Tasso eds., *User Modeling – Proc. of the 6th Intl. Conference UM97*, Springer-Verlag, Wien New York, 1997.
18. T. Malone, K. Grant, F. Turbak, S. Brobst, M. Cohen, Intelligent information sharing systems, *Comm. of the ACM* 43(8), 1987, 390-402.
19. R. Mandala, T. Tokunaga, H. Tanaka, Query expansion using heterogeneous thesauri, *Information Processing & Management* 36, 2000, 361-378.
20. M. Minio, C. Tasso, User Modeling for Information Filtering on Internet Services:

Exploiting an Extended Version of the UMT Shell, *UM96 Workshop on User Modeling for Information Filtering on the World Wide WEB*, Kailua-Kona, Hawaii, USA, January 1996.
21. S. Mizzaro & P. Zandegiacomo Riziò. An automatically refereed scholarly electronic journal: Formal specifications. *Informatica - An International Journal of Computing and Informatics* 24(4), 2000, 431-438.
22. C. Tasso, M. Armellini, Exploiting User Modeling Techniques in Integrated Information Services: The TECHFINDER System, in E. Lamma and P. Mello eds., *Proc. of the 6th Congress of the Italian Association for Artificial Intelligence*, Pitagora Editrice, Bologna, I, 1999, 519-522.
23. C. Tasso, P. Omero, *La personalizzazione dei contenuti Web: e-commerce, i-access, e-government*, Franco Angeli, Milano, I, 2002.
24. Y.Y. Yao, Measuring retrieval effectiveness based on user preference of documents, *J. of the Am. Soc. for Information Science* 46(2), 1995, 133-145.

Fuzzy Linguistic Summaries in Rule-Based Adaptive Hypermedia Systems

Miguel-Ángel Sicilia[1], Paloma Díaz[1], Ignacio Aedo[1], and Elena García[2]

[1] Laboratorio DEI, Computer Science Department, Universidad Carlos III de Madrid
Av. Universidad 30, 28911 Leganés (Madrid), Spain
{msicilia, pdp}@inf.uc3m.es, aedo@ia.uc3m.es
http://www.dei.inf.uc3m.es
[2] Computer Science Department, Universidad de Alcalá de Henares
Ctra. Barcelona km. 33.600, 28871 Alcalá de Henares (Madrid), Spain
elena.garciab@uah.es

Abstract. Rule-based adaptive hypermedia systems personalize the structure of the hypermedia space using an inference mechanism that operates on a specific knowledge representation about its users. Approximate quantifiers are very frequently used in human language expressions that entail the summarization of a large number of facts. We describe how quantified expressions can be used in adaptation rules to specify common adaptation behaviors, enhancing rule's expressive power for the human expert. Those quantified expressions can be implemented through fuzzy quantification mechanisms operating on fuzzy linguistic labels and relations, and can be integrated as extensions in general-purpose rule-based adaptive hypermedia systems.

1 Introduction

Adaptive hypermedia systems (AHS) personalize the information, links and navigation features of the hypermedia space by using knowledge about its users, represented in a user model. Several *adaptation techniques* can be used for this goal, which are in turn abstracted in *adaptation methods* at a conceptual level (as defined in [2] and extended in [3]). In addition, a particular technique can adapt different aspects of the hypermedia structure (aspects that are called *adaptation technologies*). More specifically, rule-based AHS use an inference mechanism to implement adaptation and/or user modeling behaviors, resting on some kind of knowledge representation model. These systems can be considered as general-purpose ones when they are defined on a conceptual AH architecture as in [22]. In many cases, adaptation rules are defined by domain experts (e.g. marketing directors in Web recommendation systems or teachers in educational AHS), in a process of knowledge acquisition that results in a reusable and easily modifiable knowledge base about the intended adaptation behavior of the system. Indeed this approach is taken in several Web personalization engines [6]).

In this paper, we describe a general-purpose syntax and execution semantics for using fuzzy quantifiers in rule-based AHS. Although different theories of uncertainty representation have been applied in user modeling [11, 17], quantified expressions have not been applied as a general-purpose rule-modeling construct, even though their closeness to human language expression suggests that they could significantly enhance the rule definition process. The use of quantifiers in adaptation rules can be helpful for different adaptation technologies, and can be used also for the task of user modeling. In [19], an application of fuzzy linguistic quantified expressions is described for the specific user-modeling task of classifying users of a Web application in vague categories (fuzzy *stereotypes*), based on their navigation history. In this work, we focus on the description of adaptation behaviors using quantified expressions.

The rest of this paper is structured as follows. Section 2 describes fuzzy quantified expressions in rules and how they can be applied to extended-for-fuzziness AH models. Examples of adaptation methods that can be implemented using them are described in Sect. 3, along with the most relevant implementation details. Finally, conclusions and future research directions are provided in Sect. 4.

2 Fuzzy Quantified Rules in Adaptive Hypermedia

2.1 Quantified Expressions and Rule Formulation

Approximate quantifiers like '*almost all*' or '*many*' are very frequently used in human language, and serve the important purpose of abstracting from details, and summarizing a large number of evidences into a global view [12]. A quantified linguistic expression can be specified as an expression in the form "$Q\ X$" in the case of *absolute* quantification (for example, 'quite a few visits') or in the form "$Q\ X\ are\ Y$" in the case of *relative* – or *proportional* – quantification (for example, 'most visits are short'). Both X and Y are natural language nouns or phrases, which, for our purposes, must refer to user or domain model information that can be crisp or vague, and that must be interpreted in the context of a specific AH schema. Those expressions can be integrated in the antecedent of a rule, in the general form "if $Q\ X$ then <<*action*>>", where *action* stands for the activation of a specific adaptation technology, or the addition of an inferred fact to the user model.

Fuzzy quantified expressions can be added to existing adaptation rule syntax to enrich the expressiveness of the rule language. An experiment was carried out to gather some evidence about the appropriateness of including quantifiers in the syntax of the adaptation rules. We focused on a specific and basic *adaptation technology*, namely a *direct guidance*, a kind of *adaptive navigation support* [2]. Both computer specialists and non-technical experts were included in the population (although experience in using the hypermedia technology we're analyzing – the Web – was considered mandatory). In consequence, we partitioned the sample according to two different user profiles: technicians and non-technicians. The objective of the study was to find how frequently natural language quantifiers were used in the formulation of simple adaptation rules. A scenario was developed in which the main page of a research group's Web site was described. The site had a navigation bar in a left frame that guided the user to different sections of the site. Participants were asked to write down 'if/then' rules in natural language to perform direct guidance to sections to which the user might be interested in, based exclusively in previous navigation history. Results showed that eighty three percent of the thirty participants used a quantifier (as 'most', 'many' and 'often') to describe the rule (either referring to frequency of visits, sessions or interactions in general), with no significant difference between the two user profiles. Although this is only a small experiment, it reveals the importance of quantifiers in human expression – a review of available evidence is in [16].

2.2 Fuzzy Linguistic Quantifiers

Zadeh's sigma-count operator [24] is the earliest operational definition of the concept of linguistic quantifier in terms of the theory of fuzzy sets and possibility theory. Although this and other fuzzy linguistic definitions of quantifiers do not achieve perfect linguistic adequacy (see, for example, [7]), a number of application exists that prove their usefulness in modeling natural language constructs. The approach presented here uses sigma-count and OWA operators, but other quantification mechanisms can be used either, with no impact in the conceptual semantics of the adaptation methods.

Most existing approaches define fuzzy linguistic quantifiers as fuzzy subsets of the non-negative real numbers (absolute quantifiers) or of the unit interval (proportional or relative quantifiers), and therefore can be considered as fuzzy numbers. In consequence, a quantifier Q is represented either as a mapping $\mu_Q : R^+ \to I$ or $\mu_Q : I \to I$ respectively, where I is the unit interval. From an information modeling viewpoint, an essential difference exists between absolute and relative quantifiers, since the former are entity-dependent, that is, their definition is tied to the subject on which they're applied (we can consider that four are definitely *many* cars for a buyer but four is not many if we're expressing a football team's supporters number). In addition, it can be instance-dependant in the following sense: if we're measuring the user's visits in a *Web site*, *many* visits depend on the particular site we're considering. As a consequence, we can use the notation μ_Q^x to denote quantifier Q applied to subject x.

Example definitions as *S-functions* of the absolute quantifier *'many'* (applied to visits) and the relative one *'most'* are provided in Fig. 1, defined as Zadeh's *S-functions* $S(x;10;55;100)$ and $S(x;0.6;0.75;0.9)$ respectively.

Given a domain D of elements (in our case, elements in the user or domain model, for example, the set of users or nodes in our AH system), a unary quantification mechanism in the form:

$$M : X \in \wp(D) \to R^+$$

where $\wp(D)$ is the fuzzy power set of D, provides a way of representing a summary of the cardinality of a fuzzy subset of elements in that domain through a real number.

This numeric summary can then be matched to a quantifier Q to obtain the degree of conformance of the quantified expression, thus achieving the transformation:

$$Q: X \in \wp(D) \to I$$

The definition can be extended to *n-ary* quantifiers, but we're only concerned with unary (absolute) and binary (relative) quantifiers. Zadeh's sigma-count is one of those quantification mechanisms, with the following absolute and relative formulations:

$$sigma - count\,(X) = \sum_{e \in D} \mu_X(e)$$

$$sigma - count\,(X_2 / X_1) = sigma - count\,(X_2 \cap X_1) / sigma - count\,(X_1)$$

In the relative formulation, X_I is the subset on which the proportion is computed. Additional details about the computation of linguistic summaries can be found, for example, in [18].

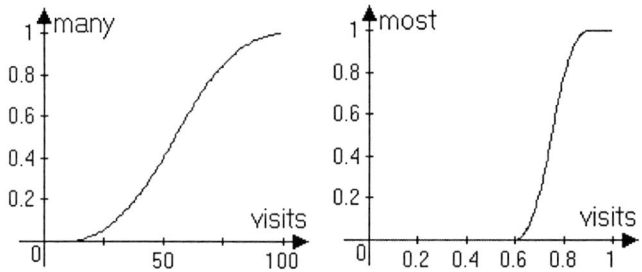

Fig. 1. Example quantifiers: *many* and *most*

The other quantification mechanism we have used is based in Yager's proposal based on the Ordered Weighted Averaging (OWA) operator [23], only for proportional ones (we do not describe it here in detail, since it does not introduce changes in rule formulation).

2.3 Fuzzy Quantified Rules in an AHS

Adaptation techniques are characterized by a specific kind of knowledge representation and a specific adaptation algorithm. In this subsection, we describe a minimal abstract model that supports fuzzy linguistic labels and common fuzzy inference techniques, which can be implemented with a generalized fuzzy relation model framework (see, for example, [15]). This partial model could be combined with those from generic user models [13], or general purpose AHS like [22].

We'll assume a common division of our AH model in three components: the User Model (UM), the Domain Model (DM) and the Adaptation Model (AM). We also assume that an object model exists defining the entities in the three components in terms of classes, associations and other common object-oriented modeling constructs.

The three model's components can be described with attributes in a relation as described in [22], but we describe here a more abstract rule syntax, that could easily be mapped onto these more specific schemas. In addition, some specific fuzzy types are introduced as extensions in the model, namely:
- Independent terms, for example, *frequent*, that is defined by an associated membership function $\mu_{frequent}$. Each term is defined on a domain that, in our case, could be groups of users or some entity belonging to the domain model.
- Linguistic labels picked from predefined label sets. For example (*bargain, cheap, somewhat cheap, medium-priced, somewhat expensive, expensive, unaffordable*) as price description. This second model construct allow us to store only references to the specific label in a label set.

Label sets fulfil some properties: (1) they must form totally ordered sets with odd cardinality $T_g + 1$, in the form $LS_g = \{s_i\}, i \in \{0, ..., T_g\}$ such that the set is ordered: $s_i \geq s_j$ if $i \geq j$; (2) it exists a negation operator: $Neg(s_i) = s_j$, such that $j = T_g - i$, and (3) it exists maximization and minimization operators: $Max(s_i, s_j) = s_i$ if $s_i \geq s_j$, and $Min(s_i, s_j) = s_i$ if $s_i \leq s_j$. Label sets are specially well suited to model and aggregate user's preferences, since they've been extensively used in processes of group decision making (see for example [9]), and can be also used in content rating [5].

The set of users of our UM is denoted by $U=\{u_i\}$. Each user has a set of attributes each of them with an associated domain (including label sets), and can be included in one or more sets that represent associated information about the user. In the formulation of adaptive rules, with the general syntax $C \rightarrow A$, the set of antecedents (C) express conditions on the user model and the context in which the adaptation is performed, and actions (A) are updates on the UM (*user modeling* rules) or dynamic adaptation behaviors (*adaptation* rules). We describe here only the syntax of antecedents, in which the quantifiers are inserted. An antecedent can have the following formulations:

```
instance.attribute op expression
instance op expression
```

Where valid instances are the user currently connected (u_i), the current navigation context (c_i), an entity in the DM, or one of the groups defined by linguistic independent terms g_{term}. The context is a placeholder for navigation specific information, including session information and characteristics of the DM. Attributes are defined on entities on a domain, and operators (*op*) and expressions are defined on that domains (e.g. character string, number comparison and the like). Association relationships between entities in the model are considered as a special kind of attribute, that denotes the collection of instances associated to the instance. An example of 'crisp' antecedent is u_i.age>20, and an example of a simple fuzzy expression is u_i is loyal. We'll focus here only on fuzzy attributes and its applications and on fuzzy antecedents that are used in standard fuzzy rules like Mamdani *min* implication [21] (antecedents in the same rule are implicitly connected by *and* operators). Expressions regarding fuzziness include the following:
- Membership of the user in a group: u_i includedIn g_{term}, e.g. 'includedIn *frequent*' or 'includedIn *advanced*'.

- Fuzzy label sets domains, with two forms: `u`$_i$`.att op label`, e.g. '`likesLongNews` is *high*', and `u`$_i$`.rel a`$_j$` op label`, where `rel` is a (fuzzy) relationship between the user and some other entity, from which `a`$_j$` is an instance v.g. '`interestIn` music is *low*'.

Quantification can operate on that expressions; Table 1 describes the main alternative syntaxes and examples (fuzzy subsets are in italics), which can be considered as extensions of existing *data design* notations in hypermedia development methods [4] with imprecise (or vague) information (according to Smets [20]).

Table 1. Example of quantified expressions that can be used in rules

Syntax	Example	Scenario
`Q g`$_i$	Many *positive_answers*	Suppose the system is asking its users for opinion about a new feature, and positive answer is defined as a fuzzy set on a ten-point scale valuation obtained through a form.
`Q g`$_i$` are g`$_j$	Most *frequent_users* are *beginners*.	Proportional quantification.
`Q instance.att` `Q instance.rel [instance]`	Few [user's] visits Few [user's] visits to channel A.	Queries about the absolute amount of current user's visits, and the relative amount of visits to an specific section.
`Q instance.att are g`$_k$ `Q g`$_h$` instance.att are g`$_k$	About half the [user's] sessions are *short*. Most *excellent* [user's] assignment are *short*.	Query about the typical session of the current user, and query about the correlation of assignment scoring and length for a user.

The first and second syntaxes are related to subpopulations or groups of entities (characterize user's groups or global domain entities descriptions). The rest are about countable evidence related to a particular entity (i.e. a specific user or hypermedia node).

3 Adaptation Methods and Techniques Using Fuzzy Quantifiers

A quantifier is specified as a predefined function and its parameters (if other functions need to be specified, MATHML[1] content markup could be used instead). For example:

```
<fuzzy:quantifier>
    <fuzzy:quantName>most</fuzzy:quantName>
    <fuzzy:quantKind>relative</fuzzy:quantKind>
    <fuzzy:sFunction initRange=0 endRange=1 >
        <fuzzy:par1>0.6</fuzzy:par1>
        <fuzzy:par2>0.75</fuzzy:par2>
```

---

[1] <http://www.w3.org/TR/MathML2/>

```
            <fuzzy:par3>0.9</fuzzy:par3>
        </fuzzy:sFunction>
</fuzzy:quantifier>
```

Linguistic labels can be defined in a similar way, but they need to be defined on attributes of 'the user' or an entity in the DM. For example, 'loyal' users can be defined by a left linear function on attribute `numberOfPurchasesYear` as follows:

```
<fuzzy:label>
    <fuzzy:labelName>loyal</fuzzy: labelName>
    <fuzzy:entity> user </fuzzy:entity>
    <fuzzy:attribute>numberOfPurchasesYear</fuzzy:attribute>
    <fuzzy:definition>
        <fuzzy:lFunction range=numberOfPurchasesYear >
        <fuzzy:par1>2</fuzzy:par1>
        <fuzzy:par2>10</fuzzy:par2>
        </fuzzy:lFunction>
    </fuzzy:definition>
</fuzzy:label>
```

Note that the domain of the fuzzy set is the user entity. Information about the schema (attributes and associations) of UM and DM models are defined in the persistence mechanism, so we only need to specify the entity.

Label sets can be defined in a similar way with a `<fuzzy :labelSet>` tag that includes several label definition, all of them on the same attribute or association.

We have used the *Fuzzy Java Toolkit*[2] for the implementation of rules (inference is performed in two phases, one for user modeling and the second for adaptation), mixed with our SHADOWS framework for handling fuzzy types in relational databases. Independent terms are stored as fuzzy relations, which are implemented in a straightforward manner in a relational database by adding attributes to the users table or by including an additional table for each term (both representations are allowed in our implementation). Linguistic label sets are implemented as metadata and values are stored as pairs of keys (*label_set, label*). In what follows some examples of rules are given; we have specified adaptation rules in a XML syntax that we have tried to keep close to the ongoing research effort of RuleML[3] [8] (although that effort considers fuzzy logic as one of its future target semantics, it does not support currently fuzziness).

Preferences in Information Browsing Contexts
Ad-hoc fuzzy quantified expressions have been used to personalize presentation preferences (number, text size and reading complexity of recommendations) in browsing environments with potentially large information spaces [14]. In this case, the user provides indirect feedback about his/her preferences by rating the items he visited so that evidence can be found over time with common-sense rules in the form "if *most*

---

[2] <http://www.iit.nrc.ca/IR_public/fuzzy/fuzzyJToolkit.html>
[3] <http://www.dfki.uni-kl.de/ruleml>

long news are rated poorly [by the user] then tend to select shorter ones". Adaptive technologies implemented this way can act as a second filter for a basic information retrieval function. The rule antecedent can be codified as follows:

```
<rule>
    <_head>...</head>
    <_body>
        <and><atom>
                <_opr> <rel>most</rel> </_opr>
                <var>large(user.newsVisited)</var>
                <var>poor(user.newsVisited@)</var>
        </atom></and>
    </_body>
</rule>
```

Where 'most' refers to the previously defined quantifier, 'long' is a single label defined on each news' text length and 'poor' is one of the labels in a fuzzy label set 'ratings' (note that they're extensions to RuleML syntax). As news ratings are link attributes of the association between User and News classes, the *'at sign'* is used according to the ONN notation described in [1].

Examples on Adaptive Navigation Support
Adaptive hypermedia technologies can be performed with quantified rules as a technique when exploiting quantitative information about user's browsing history or habits. For example, a simple *direct guidance* [2] behavior can be implemented for the homepage of a university research group that has several sections (e.g. teaching, research, people and resources) with a rule in the form 'if most user sessions browse teaching nodes then <<directly guide the user to that section>>':

```
<_body><and><atom>
            <_opr>   <rel>most</rel>   </_opr>
            <var>user.sessions</var>
            <var>teaching-related(user.sessions)</var>
    </atom></and></_body>
```

As a second example, *adaptive annotation* techniques can augment a link with some kind of information about the node behind the link. A rule like the following can activate a longer description or visual differentiation for links that are not frequently visited or are shortly visited by the user:

```
<_body><and><atom>
            <_opr>   <rel>few</rel>   </_opr>
            <var>user.visits</var>
        </atom>
        <atom>
            <_opr>   <rel>few</rel>   </_opr>
            <var>long(user.Visits)</var>
        </atom>
</and></_body>
```

Note that in this latter case, the first quantification is operating on a crisp set, but both *atoms* yield a fuzzy membership grade due to the application of the quantifier.

Adaptation based on User's Knowledge
Quantifiers can help in specifying vague or compensatory criteria in adaptive text presentation, for example, in the case of adaptive educational systems, a specific hypermedia node n explaining knowledge item k is showed to user u only if a set of knowledge prerequisites are fulfilled. Then, we have a (fuzzy) relationship between users and knowledge items (i.e. a user 'knows' an item with a specified grade), and another (possibly fuzzy) relation between knowledge items. If we define *prerequisites* as a term defining the fuzzy subset of the knowledge items that are k's prerequisites and *currentKnowledge* as the fuzzy subset of items user u knows, we can relax the presentation criteria with expressions in the form 'if *most prerequisites* are *currentKnowledge* then <<show the item>>'. The rule antecedent can be expressed as follows:

```
<_body><and>
        <atom>
        <_opr>   <rel>most</rel>   </_opr>
            <var>prerequisite(context.item)</var>
            <var>user.currentKnowledge</var>
        </atom>
</and></_body>
```

Note that the context is used to refer to the item that is connected to the node that the system is deciding to show or not. The fuzziness of the association `currentKnowledge` implicitly defines a fuzzy subset, and therefore this rule has the semantics of the last example in Table 1.

4 Conclusions and Future Work

Quantified expressions enhance the expressive power of rule languages due to its closeness to human language expressions. In the formulation of adaptation rules in AHS, quantified expressions can be used as adaptation methods to specify a number of adaptation technologies. Finally, fuzzy quantification mechanisms can be used to implement adaptation techniques based on quantification, operating on a fuzzy knowledge representation that includes linguistic label sets and fuzzy relations.
Current markup interchange languages for rules need to be complemented to be able to express adaptation rules that operate on complex user and/or domain models. We have defined our own semiformal language combining `RuleML`, `ONN` and extensions to the first, and currently a formal definition is in progress.

Future research will address the formulation of complex quantified expressions, applied to general nominal phrases that can involve implicit queries in the user model. In addition, the linguistic adequacy of quantifier implementations should be experimentally validated to ensure they have an appropriate behavior in diverse mentally validated to ensure they have an appropriate behavior in diverse adaptation contexts, using usability testing techniques (as is common in the field [10]).

Acknowledgements

This work is supported by "Dirección General de Investigación del Ministerio de Ciencia y Tecnología", project number TIC2000-0402.

References

1. Blaha, M. and Premerlani, W.: Object-Oriented Modeling and Design for Database Applications. Prentice Hall, Upper Saddle River, New Jersey (1998)
2. Brusilovsky, P.: Methods and techniques of adaptive hypermedia. User Modeling and User- Adapted Interaction, **6**(2/3), Kluwer Academic Publ., The Netherlands (1996) 87–129
3. Brusilovsky, P.: Adaptive Hypermedia. User Modeling and User-Adapted Interaction **11**(1/2), Kluwer Academic Publ., The Netherlands (2001) 87–110
4. Díaz, P., Aedo, I., Montero, S.: Ariadne, a Development Method for Hypermedia. In: Proceedings of the 12th International Conference on Database and Expert Systems Applications (DEXA'01) (2001) 764–774
5. Dodero, J. M., Sicilia, M.A., García, E.: A Fuzzy Aggregation-Based Reputation Model for e-Learning Exploitation of Public Domain Resources. In: Proceedings of the 4th International ICSC Symposium on Soft Computing and Intelligent Systems for Industry (SOCO/ISFI'2001), Paisley, Scotland, UK (2001)
6. Fink, J. and Kobsa, A.: A Review and Analysis of Commercial User Modeling Servers for Personalization on the World Wide Web. User Modeling and User-Adapted Interaction **10**(3/4), Kluwer Academic Publ., The Netherlands (2000) 209–249
7. Glöckner, I. and Knoll, A.: A Framework for Evaluating Fusion Operators Based on the Theory of Generalized Quantifiers. In: Proceedings of the 1999 IEEE International Conference on Multisensor Fusion and Integration for Intelligent Systems (MFI '99), Taipei, Taiwan (1999)
8. Grosof, B.N.: Standarizing XML Rules. In: Proceedings of the Workshop on E-Business & the Intelligent Web (IJCAI 2001), Seattle, USA (2001)
9. Herrera, F., Herrera-Viedma, E., Verdegay, J. L.: Aggregating Linguistic Preferences: Properties of LOWA Operator. In: Procceedings of the 5th IFSA World Congress 1995, Sao Paulo, Brasil (1995) 153–156
10. Höök, K.: Evaluating the Utility and Usability of an Adaptive Hypermedia System. Journal of Knowledge-Based Systems **10**(5) (1998)
11. Jameson, A.: Numerical Uncertainty Management in User and Student Modeling: An Overview of Systems and Issues. User Modeling and User-Adapted Interaction, **5**, Kluwer Academic Publ., The Netherlands (1996) 193–251
12. Kacprzyk, J., Zadrozny S., Yager R.: A fuzzy logic based approach to linguistic summaries of databases. Intl. Journal of Applied mathematics and Computer Science **10**(4) (2000)
13. Kobsa, A.: Generic User Modeling Systems. User Modeling and User-Adapted Interaction **11**(1/2), Kluwer Academic Publ., The Netherlands (2001) 49–63

14. López, L., Sicilia, M.A., Martínez, J.J., y García, E.: Personalization of Web Interface Structural Elements: A Learning-Scenario Case Study. In: Proceedings of the 3rd Mexican International Conference on Computer Science (ENC'01), Aguascalientes, Mexico (2001)
15. Medina, J. M., Pons, O. and Vila, M.A.: GEFRED: A Generalized Model of Fuzzy Relational Databases, Information Sciences, **76**(1/2) (1994) 87–109
16. Moxey, L.M. and Sanford, A.J.: Communicating Quantities: A review of psycholinguistic evidence of the control of perspective by quantifying expressions. Applied Cognitive Psychology, **14** (2000) 237–255
17. Presser, G. Personalization of Newsletters Using Multistage Fuzzy Inference. In: Proceedings of the Fuzzy Days Conference, Lecture Notes in Computer Science **2206**, Springer-Verlag (2001) 629–636
18. Rasmussen, D., Yager, R.R.: SummarySQL: A Fuzzy Tool For Data Mining. Intelligent Data Analysis, Elsevier (1997)
19. Sicilia, M.A., Dodero, J.M.: User Stereotype Modeling for Approximate Reasoning-Based Adaptive Enterprise Portals. In: Proceedings of the 10th European-Japanese Conference on Information Modeling and Knowledge Bases, Sääriselka, Finland (2000) 177–184
20. Smets, P.: Imperfect information: Imprecision-Uncertainty. In: Motro, A., Smets, P. (eds.) Uncertainty Management in Information Systems: From Needs to Solutions, Kluwer Academic Publishers (1997) 225–254
21. Tsoukalas, L.H., Uhrig, R.E.: Fuzzy and Neural Approaches in Engineering. John Wiley & Sons, New York (1996)
22. Wu, H., De Kort, E., De Bra, P.: Design Issues for General-Purpose Adaptive Hypermedia Systems. In: Proceedings of the ACM Conference on Hypertext and Hypermedia, Aarhus, Denmark (2001) 141–150
23. Yager, R.R.: Connectives and quantifiers in fuzzy sets. Fuzzy Sets and Systems, **40** (1991) 39–75
24. Zadeh, L.A.: A Computational Approach to Fuzzy Quantifiers in Natural Language. Computing and Mathematics with Applications, 9(1) (1983) 149–184

The Plight of the Navigator:
Solving the Navigation Problem for Wireless Portals

Barry Smyth[1] and Paul Cotter[2]

[1] ChangingWorlds Ltd.
Trintech Building
South County Business Park
Leopardstown, Dublin 18, Ireland
barry.smyth@ChangingWorlds.com

[2] Smart Media Institute
Department of Computer Science
University College Dublin
Belfield, Dublin 4, Ireland
paul.cotter@ChangingWorlds.com

Abstract. The wireless Internet, as epitomized by the first generation of WAP-enabled phones and portals, has failed to meet user expectations, resulting in limited take-up, and poor revenue growth for mobile operators. A combination of factors has been responsible: unreliable early handsets; poor content; slow connections; and portals that were difficult to use and navigate. Today, the first 3 of these issues have been solved (or are about to be) by improved handsets, high-quality content and high-speed infrastructure such as GPRS. However, portal usability remains a key problem limiting the ease with which users can locate and benefit from wireless content services. In this paper we describe how personalized navigation techniques can greatly enhance the usability of information services in general, and WAP portals in particular, by personalizing the navigation structure of a portal to the learned preferences of individual users, and how this has resulted in increased WAP usage in live user trials.

1 Introduction

The wireless Internet, as represented by the current generation of WAP portals (see www.wapforum.org) and WAP-enabled mobile phones, has failed to live up to the marketing hype. Poor usability is a key problem, due mainly to poor portal design, and exacerbated by limited device functionality, bandwidth, and content. However, the bandwidth and content issues have largely been, or are being, resolved, and the current generation of phones offer users improvements over the original models. However, poor portal design remains an issue. The core problem is that the menu-driven nature of WAP portals, whereby users access content services by navigating through a series of hierarchical menus, means that users are spending a significant amount of their time on-line navigating to content. That this frustrates users and limits the efficiency of mobile information access should be clear. But the fact that most mobile operators charge users for their navigation time (as well as their content time) simply adds insult to injury. The result: WAP offers poor value-for-money.

Recent studies highlight the scale of this usability problem and the gross mismatch between user expectations and WAP realities. For example, the Neilson-Norman WAP Usability Report [6] indicates that while the average user expects to be able to access relevant content within 30 seconds, the reality is often closer to 150 seconds.

In this paper we present an automated solution to this navigation problem (used in the ClixSmart Navigator™ system developed by ChangingWorlds Ltd.[1]) that allows navigation effort to be reduced by more than 50% by personalizing a WAP portal to the needs and preferences of users, based on their historical usage. We show that for every 1 second of navigation time saved, users invest an additional 3 seconds accessing content, which provides strong practical evidence for improved user experiences, in addition to the obvious incremental revenue benefits for operators.

2 Click-Distance as a Model of Navigation Effort

The length of time that it takes a user to access a content item can be viewed as a good independent measure of navigation effort. Moreover, we suggest that the navigation effort associated with an item of content depends critically on the location of that item within the portal structure, and specifically on the number of navigation steps that are required in order to locate and access this item from a given starting position within the portal (typically the portal home page).

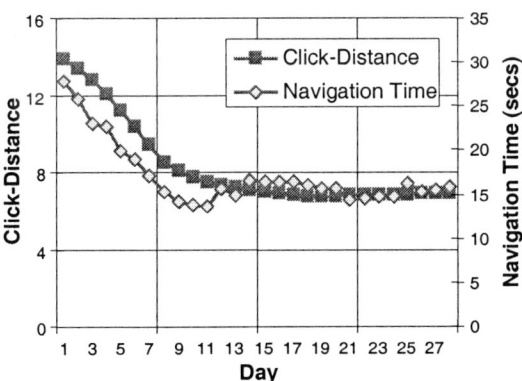

Fig. 1. A plot of click-distance versus navigation time shows a clear correlation between both measures of navigation effort.

With the current generation of WAP phones, there are two basic types of navigation steps. The first is the *menu select*: the user clicks to select a specific menu

---

[1] The authors of this paper would like to thank the Navigator team in ChangingWorlds, Elizabeth McKenna, Nigel Hanby, James Reilly, Paul McClave, Michael Kerrigan, and Creina Mahon, for their hard work and dedication to this product.

option. The second is a *menu scroll*: the user clicks to scroll up or down through a series of options. Accordingly, an item of content within a WAP portal can be uniquely positioned by the sequence of selects and scrolls needed to access it, and the navigation effort, associated with this item can be simply modeled as *click-distance*, the number of these selects and scrolls (see Eq. 1).

$$\text{For content item, } I, \quad Click - Dis\tan ce(i) = Selects(i) + Scrolls(i) \quad (1)$$

Although this simple model of navigation effort assumes equal weights for scrolls and selects, when we evaluate click-distance in comparison to navigation time by analyzing the behaviour of live-users on commercial WAP portals, we find a near-perfect correlation. Fig. 1 presents the results of a recent evaluation (6 weeks of WAP usage for 100 users - see Sect. 4) that results in a correlation coefficient of 0.92 between click-distance and navigation time. Thus, the click-distance of a content item is a strong predictor of the navigation time associated with its access.

Our strategy for decreasing navigation effort is to reduce the click-distance of the content items that a given user is likely to be interested in by promoting these items (or the links that lead to them) to higher positions within the portal menu structure.

3 Personalized Navigation

The basic idea behind our personalized navigation technique is to use a probabilistic (Markov) model of user navigation to predict the probability that a given menu option o will be selected by a given user u given that they are currently in menu m, and based on their past navigation history; that is, we wish to compute $P(o|m)$ (the *access probability of o given m*) for all options o accessible from m (either directly or indirectly, through descendant menus). Put simply, when a user arrives at menu page m, we do not necessarily return the default options, $o_1, ..., o_n$, instead we compute the options, $o'_1,...,o'_k$, that are most likely to be accessed by the user given that they have navigated to m; that is the k menu options accessible from m that have the highest access probabilities. This can mean promoting certain menu options, which by default belong to descendant menus of m, up to m. The size of the final personalized menu is constrained by some maximum number of options, k, and the constituent options of m are ordered according to their access probabilities.

3.1 Profiling Navigation Histories

To construct an accurate picture of a user's navigation history it is necessary to track and store the user's accesses to individual menu options. This is efficiently achieved through the use of a so-called *hit table*; see Fig. 2(a) for an example of a partial menu tree and corresponding hit table entries. This hash table is keyed according to menu id and stores a list of accesses made by that user to options within that particular menu. For example, Fig. 2(a) indicates that the particular user in question has accessed option B of menu A 10 times and option C 90 times.

In fact, we need two tables: a global static hit table that is initialized with respect to the default portal structure (Fig. 2(b)); and a user hit table that records each user's particular history on the portal. The static table makes it possible to deliver the standard menu structure early on but this will eventually be over-ridden by the personalized menu once the access probabilities build. Moreover, the default hit values that are set in the static hit table make it possible to control the *personalization latency* – low values mean that personalization takes effect very quickly, while large values make the system less sensitive to user activity.

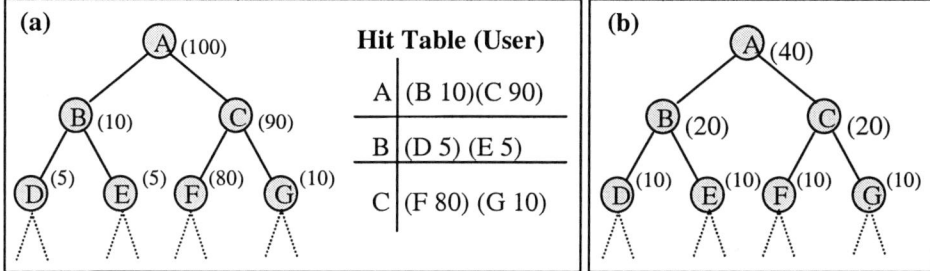

Fig. 2. (a) A partial menu tree and corresponding user hit table; (b) Represents a static menu tree feeding a static hit table.

3.2 Constructing a Personalized Menu

To construct menu m we use a Markov model to identify the k most probable options from m; that is the k options with the highest $P(o|m)$. We take account of the hit values listed for each option in both the static and user hit tables. For the data shown in Fig. 2 the following access probabilities are determined:

$P(B|A)$ = (20+10)/(40+100) = 0.214
$P(C|A)$ = (20+90)/(40+100) = 0.786
$P(D|A) = P(B|A)P(D|B)$ = (30/140)(10+5)/(20+10) = 0.107
$P(E|A) = P(B|A)P(E|B)$ = (30/140)(10+5)/(20+10) = 0.107
$P(F|A) = P(C|A)P(F|C)$ = (110/140)(10+80/20+90) = 0.642
$P(G|A) = P(C|A)P(G|C)$ = (110/140)(10+10)/(20+90) = 0.142

So in descending order of access probability we have C, F, B, G, D, and E. And for $k=3$, C, F, and B are selected, in order, for menu A.

3.3 Promotion and Demotion

This personalized navigation method supports two basic types of menu adaptation, which we call *promotion*. A menu option may be promoted *within* the context of its default menu; that is, its relative position may be changed. A promotion *between* menus occurs when a menu option is promoted into an ancestral menu. Promotions (and conversely *demotions*) are side effects of the probability calculations. For instance, in the above example link *F* is promoted to *A*'s menu – and in theory links can be promoted from deeper levels once their probabilities build sufficiently.

Of course if *F* is subsequently selected from *A*, it is added to *A*'s entry in the user's hit table. So the next time that menu *A* is created, and *P(F|A)* needs to be computed we must account for the new data on *F* (see Fig. 3(a) for example). Specifically, assuming a single access to *F* as an option in *A*, we get:

$$P(F|A) = 1/101 + (110/141)(10+80/20+90) = 0.009 + 0.638 = 0.647$$

3.4 An Efficient Algorithm for Computing Promotable Options

The complexity of the proposed method depends on the complexity of the process that identifies the *k* most probable options for the menu, *m*. This can mean examining not just the options of *m*, but also all the options contained in menus that are descendents of *m*. Fortunately, a more efficient algorithm is possible once we recognize that,, by definition *P(o|m)* is always greater than or equal to *P(o'|m)* where *o'* is an option of a menu, *m'*, which is itself a descendent of *m* through *o*. This means that we can find the *k* most probable nodes for menu *m* by performing a depth-limited breadth-first search over the menu tree rooted at *m*. Moreover, we only need to expand the search through an option *o'* if *P(o'|m)* is greater than the kth best probability so far found.

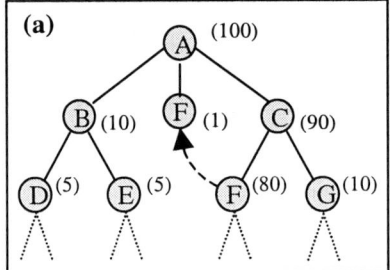 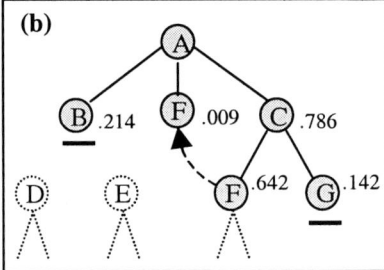

Fig. 3. (a) Option *F* has been promoted to menu *A* from menu *C* and accessed once; (b) Cutting-off search at *B* and *G* during the personalization of *A*..

For example, as Fig. 3(b) indicates, during the calculation of the access probabilities for *A*'s descendants with k=2, search can be initially cut-off at option *B*, since B's children cannot have access probabilities greater than 0.214, which is the probability of the kth best option found so far (*B* itself). Similarly, after computing the access probabilities for *C's* options (*F* and *G*), search can be cut-off at *G* since its probability is less than the 0.642, the *new* k^{th} best option. In practice this technique can result in significant reductions in search effort allowing probabilities to be computed on-the-fly without a noticeable impact on the personalization time.

4 Experimental Evaluation

The following evaluation is based on live-user field trials on European WAP portals. The standard trial consisted of a 2-week *profiling period* in which no personalization took place but the behaviour of the users was monitored in order to profile their navigation patterns. The remaining 4 weeks are divided into two 2-week *personalization periods*. During this time profiling continued but in addition, personalization was switched on so that users experienced a new portal structure that was adapted to their navigation preferences. The trial consists of approximately 100 trialists from a variety of backgrounds and with a range of mobile usage habits and handsets.

4.1 Click-Distance

Figure 4 shows how click-distance changed during the trial. It presents the average user click-distance from the portal home page to each of the user's top 3 content sites, during each trial period. The results show that the default click-distance of 13.88 for the static portal (experienced during the profiling period) dropped significantly by over 50% to 6.84 during the first personalization period and by a further 2% for the final two weeks of personalization. These results show two things: first that significant click-distance reductions are possible; and secondly, that these reductions are realized very rapidly, in this case within the first two weeks of personalization.

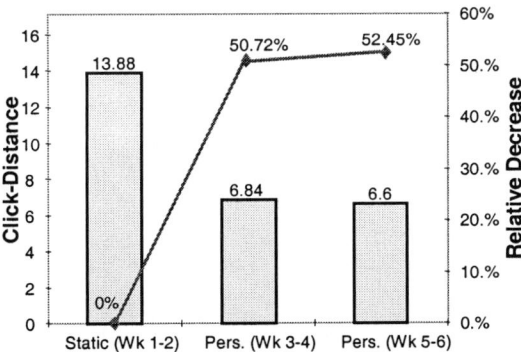

Fig. 4. Comparative click-distance results for the profiling and personalization periods.

4.2 Navigation vs Content Airtime

Figure 5 shows the reduction in average daily navigation time for the trialists. We find that over the 4-week personalization period (weeks 3-6) average daily navigation time has reduced by 36%. During the initial static (profiling) period users were spending an average of 56.42 seconds navigating to content each day, and this fell to only 35.99 seconds for the 4 weeks of personalization. Indeed if we look at the results for the final two weeks of personalization (weeks 5-6) in comparison to the first two weeks of personalization (weeks 3-4) we see that the benefits of personalization are incremental, with navigation time reducing from an average of 36.55 seconds (weeks 3-4) to 35.43 seconds (weeks 5-6).

When we look at the airtime spent by users accessing content pages (see Fig. 6) we find that there is a significant increase as a result of personalization. Over the 4-week personalization period (weeks 3–6) average daily user content time increases by nearly 17%. During the static period the average daily content time per trialist was 312.46 seconds compared to 364.55 for the 4-week personalization period. Moreover, if we again look at the content time for the final two trial weeks (as opposed to the final 4 weeks) we find a relative increase of more than 22% (content time of 382.62 seconds). In other words, the relative change in content time for the final two weeks of the trial (22.45%) has more than doubled in comparison to the first two weeks of personalization (10.89%); as personalization proceeds so too do the benefits increase.

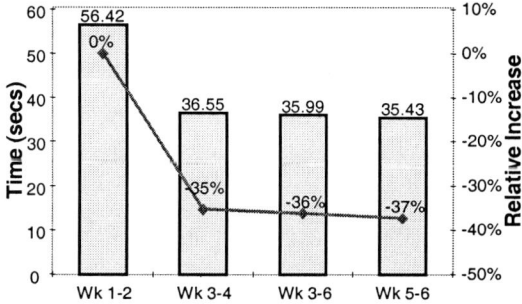

Fig. 5. Comparative navigation airtime results for the profiling and personalization periods.

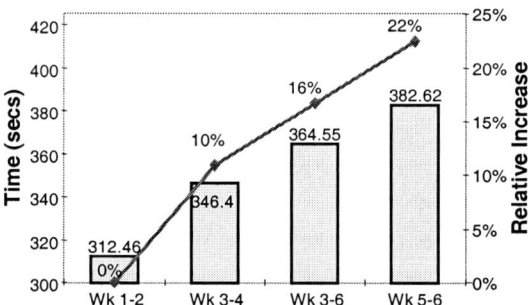

Fig. 6. Comparative content airtime results for the profiling and personalization periods.

These results show that users are willing to trade savings in navigation time for increases in content time. For every second of navigation time saved the average user increases their content time by 3 seconds – by the final two weeks of personalization the average user has saved 22.99 seconds of navigation time but increased their content time by 70.16 seconds. There are obvious benefits here for the mobile operator from a revenue point of view, not only in terms of existing airtime-based charging models but also as operators move to content-based charging models.

4.3 Page Impressions

Figure 7 illustrates that, as a result of personalization, the average number of daily page impressions per user increases by 35% by the end of the trial (the 29.4 average daily page impressions per user in the static period grows to 39.65 during the final 2 weeks of personalization).

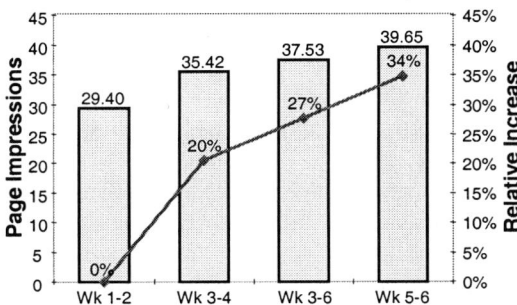

Fig. 7. Comparative page impression results for the profiling and personalization periods.

Once again, as with the airtime results, we have separately reported the average results for the final 2 weeks of personalization in addition to the normal 4-week period in order to emphasise that the page impression count is continuing to increase as personalization proceeds. For instance during the first 2 weeks of personalization the page impression count increases by 20% compared to the static period. Thus, there is an additional 15% rise associated with the final 2 weeks of personalization.

4.4 Discussion

The results presented in this paper represent only a small subset of the personalization benefits learned from the trial, and for reasons of space it has been necessary to omit many other important results. In addition similar usage increases have been found for other important statistics including the average number and length of user sessions and the number of unique accesses to content sites. Very briefly: the average number of daily sessions per user increased by 31%; average session length increased by 25%; and the average number of user accesses to content sites increased by 30%.

Finally, it is worth pointing out that while the above results are based on a 100-user trial, qualitatively and quantitatively similar results are being found from a much broader 100,000-user trial that is underway at the time of writing.

5 Related Work

In general, with the advent of the Internet and the reality of the information overload problem, there has been significant attention given to how personalization techniques can be used to filter information more precisely according to the learned preferences of individual users. Many different application domains have been investigated from news articles [2] to TV programs [9], and a range of techniques has been developed including content-filtering, collaborative filtering, and probabilistic methods [7]. For the most part, research has focused on content personalization, that is, the prioritization of content items within particular content domains. This is in contrast to work described in this paper where the focus is on navigation (see also [8]).

In the navigation area the work of Perkowitz [4] has addressed the related so-called *shortcut link problem* in traditional web sites, and attempts to make shortcut recommendations from a page P to another page Q based on how often Q is viewed by users after P in some navigation trail. An alternative approach to shortcut recommendation is taken in the SurfLen [3] and PageGatherer [5] systems. This time page links are suggested based on page request co-occurrences with past sessions. Briefly, the basic idea is to suggest the top k pages that are most likely to co-occur with pages that the user has visited in their current session. These techniques have been used to good effect in adaptive Web sites as a means of generating automatic index pages or for inserting shortcut links into existing pages and we believe they could be equally well-applied to personalizing navigation on wireless devices. More recently, the wireless navigation problem has also been considered by Anderson et al. [1] who have investigated Naïve Bayesian and Markov modeling techniques to make navigation link recommendations as a way of automatically repurposing Web pages for wireless devices. The particularly interesting feature of this work is the explicit use of a recommendation metric that not only accounts for the relevance of the navigation link in question but also the level of navigation effort that can be saved by recommending this link, a feature that could also be incorporated into the technique presented in this paper.

The above represents an abbreviated list of related research in the area of personalization and for reasons of space it has not been possible to provide a more complete analysis. The above techniques share some motivations, objectives and technical features with our approach. However it is also worth pointing out that the research in this paper is currently deployed as part of an enterprise-level solution for mobile operators capable of handling millions of users and real-time personalization. The ClixSmart Navigator™ product by ChangingWorlds Ltd. also includes a wide range of sophisticated administration and reporting tools for the mobile operator in order to control the level and type of personalization offered. It is also worth pointing out that the probabilistic personalization technique describe here is just one of a number of personalization methods currently supported by the Navigator system. Additional approaches include, for example, collaborative recommendation techniques that allow navigation links to be recommended based on the navigation patterns of related users (see www.changingworlds.com for further information).

6 Conclusions

The current incarnation of the mobile Internet, which is largely based on WAP (wireless application protocol) phones and portals, has met with only limited success. One of the most significant problems facing mobile users is the time it normally takes to locate relevant content. Many mobile portals have average click-distances in excess of 15 and recent studies have shown that many users are taking an average of 120 seconds to perform many common content access tasks, while the users themselves are expecting access times of about 30 seconds. This has resulted in frustrated users and limited WAP up-take and usage.

In this paper we have described a personalized navigation technique, developed by ChangingWorlds Ltd. as part of its ClixSmart Navigator™ solution for mobile operators, that can actively adapt the structure of a portal to match the preferences and needs of individual users in order to radically reduce portal click-distance on a user-by-user basis. Specifically we have shown how click-distance can be reduced by over 50% and how the corresponding navigation time can be reduced by nearly 40%.

From an end-user point of view, the result is a WAP portal that is easier to use and that delivers superior value-for-money. In turn, this leads to increased usage by users and the results reported here highlight content time increases of over 20% and page impression increases of 35%. Furthermore, for each second of navigation time that is saved, the average user is willing to invest an additional 3 seconds in content time to deliver significant increases in overall airtime. Crucially, this means improved incremental revenue opportunities for mobile operators alongside improved user loyalty and reduced churn.

As mobile operators attempt to shift from pure airtime-based charging models (where navigation time is charged at standard rates) to content-based charging models (where navigation time not charged for, or charged at a reduced rate), ClixSmart Navigator ensures that revenue levels are maximized by increasing content time in favour of reduced navigation times. At the same time, network resources that would have been utilized in the service of navigation are being more profitably re-deployed in the service of content.

References

1. Anderson, C., Domingos, P., and Weld, D. Adaptive Web Navigation for Wireless Devices. In: Proceedings of the 17th International Joint Conference on Artificial Intelligence. Seattle, WA (2001).
2. Billsus, D. ,Pazzani, M.J. and Chen, J. A learning agent for wireless news access. Intelligent User Interfaces (2000) 33-36
3. Fu, X., Budzik, J., and Hammond, K. Mining Navigation History for Recommendation. In: Proceedings of the Conference on Intelligent User Interfaces (2000).
4. Perkowitz, M. Adaptive Web Sites: Cluster Mining and Conceptual Clustering for Index Page Synthesis. PhD Thesis, Department of Computer Science and Engineering. University of Washington. (2001).
5. Perkowitz, M. and Etzioni. Towards Adaptive Web Sites: Conceptual Framework and Case Study. Journal of Artificial Intelligence. **118**(1-2) (2000).
6. Ramsey, M. and Nielsen, J. The WAP Usability Report. Neilsen Norman Group (2000).
7. Reiken, D. Special Issue on Personalization, Communications of the ACM. **43**(8) (2000)
8. Rucker, J. and Polanco, M.J. Personalized Navigation for the Web. Communications of the ACM. **40**(3) (1997) 73-75.
9. Smyth & Cotter. Wapping the Web: A Case-Study in Content Personalization for WAP-enabled Devices. In: Proceedings of the 1st International Conference on Adaptive Hypermedia (AH2000). Trento, Italy. (2000)

Towards an Adaptive Web Training Environment Based on Cognitive Style of Learning: An Empirical Approach

Maria A. M. Souto[1], Regina Verdin[2], Ricardo Wainer[2], Milton Madeira[2],
Mariusa Warpechowski[1], Karine Beschoren[3], Renata Zanella[3],
Juarez Sagebin Correa[3], Rosa M. Vicari[1], and José Palazzo M. de Oliveira[1]

[1] PPGC/UFRGS, Instituto de Informática, Caixa Postal 15.064, CEP 91501-970 Porto Alegre, RS, Brasil, Fax: +55(51)3316.7308
 {Souto, Mariusa, Rosa, Palazzo}@inf.ufrgs.br
[2] UNISINOS, Faculdade de Psicologia, Caixa Postal 275, CEP 93022-000, São Leopoldo, RS, Brasil, Fax: +55(51)590-8268
 {Regina, Wainer, Madeira}@cirrus.unisinos.br
[3] CRT Brasil Telecom, CEP 91430-001, Porto Alegre, RS, Brasil, Fax: +55(51)3378-4828
 {Renata, Karine, Jsagebin}@crt.net.br

Abstract. The paper presents an investigation about the learner's cognitive profiles in the context of Tapejara Project[1]. In this investigation, we have assumed that the learner's Cognitive Style of Learning (CSL) actually influences his/her cognitive behavior while performing a long distance Web course. The paper describes the empirical procedures used to generate the learners' cognitive profiles and his/her associated learning behavior that must be considered in the adaptive Web training environment. The training target population refers to the Telecommunications Company's employees. The learner's CSL assessment was obtained from the statistical analysis of the Ross Test data [14]. The CSL learning behavior was obtained from the statistical analysis of the navigational log data in an experimental training module designed for this purpose. The statistical results have shown five CSL groups, their style dimensions and the correlation between each CSL group and their navigational behavior in the Web training module.

1 Introduction

Nowadays, long distance corporate training via the Web is an increasingly necessary issue to be considered. From a corporation's viewpoint this means to minimize training expenses and not taking much time of its employees; from an employee's viewpoint this means flexibility to choose time and place to accomplish the training.

Usually, commercial training Web systems mainly address hypermedia appeals to keep online learners interested and self-motivated to proceed, but they leave a gap between a learner's cognitive profile and the assistance provided by the system to the

---

[1] The Tapejara Project - Intelligent Training System in the Internet – is a consortium of two Universities and a Telecom company supported by Brazilian Research Council, CNPq, under the ProTeM-CC framework.

remote user. To overcome this, many researchers have attempted to define which individual differences actually influence learning in that system [4,6,7,10,11]. For example, [10] investigates *how individuals manage learning in interactive Web learning environments designed to support learning orientations*; [11] has attempted to *determine what combination of non-linearity and advance organizers work best for learners with given levels of self-regulation.*

The Cognitive Style of Learning (CSL) is *an individual aspect that describes the way in which a person habitually approaches or responds to the learning task* [13]. According to [4, 5, 13], a person's cognitive style is considered one of the most stable user's characteristics overtime, influencing a person's general attainment or achievement in learning situations. This stability is manifested in the use of hierarchies' processes in information treatment and strategies the learner uses when acquiring new information through a hypermedia system.

Besides, matching the cognitive style to the domain content in hypermedia systems is a pedagogical form to make the comprehension easier and lead the learner to choose his/her preferred mode to process information [12, 13]. This occurs because the cognitive style interacts with the content structure and processes the information in some differentiated way, which means the use of a specific learning strategy for each cognitive style [8]. Knowing the cognitive styles and their associated learning strategy enable the instructional designer to develop learning resources close to the learner's profiles.

A wide number of cognitive style dimensions has been generated by psychologists researchers such as the *field-dependency-independency* - Witkin and Asch, 1948 - *Wholist-analytic, verbal-imagery* - Riding and Cheema, 1991 - etc. A review of these styles can be found in [13]. We have found out in literature, at least two authors [3, 6] that have been investigating the cognitive style construct as an important aspect to be considered in the adaptation of the system characteristics to the user's cognitive style in an assisted hypermedia environment.

In the I-Help project, [3] has used cognitive style classification to integrate the learner's characteristics to be considered in the Intelligent-Help environment to *match learners who have help requests with potential peer helpers*. Bull [3] has used both of Riding and Cheema's cognitive style dimensions: verbal-imagery and wholist-analytic. These cognitive style dimensions were assessed using a five-item questionnaire. The author doesn't have any conclusive results about the use of the learner's cognitive style in the system yet.

Ford and Chen, [6], have investigated the correlation between field-dependency/independency cognitive style and learning behavior, and learning outcomes, while a group of learners were performing a learning task. This task includes using a hypermedia system to learn how to design a web home page. The Cognitive Style Assessment - CSA – (the instrument used in this experiment and designed by Riding's) was accomplished to determine levels of field-dependency/independency. The authors also used Study Preferences Questionnaire (SPQ) to assess levels of *holist* or *serialist* style dimension. The main conclusion of the study is that field-dependency/independency cognitive style dimensions were linked to strategic differences in navigation.

Like the works mentioned above, the Tapejara Project uses the learner's CSL as source of a user's information to enable adaptation of a hypermedia system's characteristics to his/her cognitive style. Our approach is based on two psycho pedagogical constructs: *cognitive style of learning* - Atkinson 1998; Riding 1991,

Riding 1997 - and *learning trajectory* [9]. The CSL characterizes a pattern of cognitive actions represented by the *learning trajectory* that can be concretely observed through the index variables of performance behavior during the learning practice. The study of these *trajectories* is accomplished through the analysis of the learners' interactions with the training environment during a free process of learning, i.e. a learning phase without the interference of any artificial or human tutor [9].

In order to assess the target learner's CSL, we have used the Ross test as described in Sect. 3. The main objective of this test is approaching the cognitive superior abilities, based on Bloom's taxonomy of the educational processes in the cognitive domain. According to this, we have aimed to take advantage of Bloom's taxonomy, which can make the tasks of planning learning experiences easier. Up to now, the statistical results have showed five CSL groups, their style dimensions and the correlation between each CSL group and their navigational behavior in the Web training module. Based on these research outcomes, we have been developing the training environment aiming to adapt the didactic resources to the learner's profile. In the next stage, we are planning to integrate in the environment an artificial agent collection, whose roles will correspond to (i) monitoring a learner's trajectories; (ii) perform the learner's cognitive diagnostic; and (iii) provide learning strategies to adjust to the learner's CSL.

This paper is organized as follows. In Sect. 2 we present the adaptive model, in Sect. 3 we detail the empirical procedures of CSL class generation, in Sects 4 and 5 we detail, respectively, the domain content and the empirical results about CSL classes behavior. Finally, in Sect. 6, conclusions and the next research activities are described.

2 The Adaptive Model

According to [2], we presume that important issues should be considered in developing an Adaptive Hypermedia System, such as: adapting where and why (application area and adaptations goals); adapting what (user features); how (methods and techniques), etc. Up to now, we have worked on the processes of design and development of a Web training environment to support learners' cognitive aspects modeling the CSL and to adjust domain content to this important learner feature.

The purpose of the Tapejara Project Web training environment is to provide the necessary support to the learner's style of interaction with a specific knowledge space represented by HTML pages with wide and rich didactic material. Based on this interaction, the system identifies a learner's cognitive style and starts adapting the instruction to the needs of the style, presenting suitable paths to the learner's individual features of learning, looking for optimal learning results.

In order to support training adapted to learners' cognitive style, the learner model integrates information from the learners. For example: the Web log of the learner's interactions; a set of index variables obtained from the Web log; and the learner's most likely cognitive style pattern. These index variables highlight cognitive actions and a learner's behavior while browsing the training environment pages. Indexes are organized in three categories: (i) navigational indexes (i.e. didactic resources and preferable forms of presentation); (ii) temporal indexes (i.e. time spent in the whole training module and in the module activities); and (iii) performance indexes (i.e. total learner attempts to perform an exercise and the final evaluation grade). We assume that each cognitive style presents a similar behavior related to the index values. This means that we have a learning path pattern for each cognitive style.

The main requirements of a Web training adaptive environment is a computational architecture that: supports the identification of a learner's cognitive pattern based on his/her interactions with the training environment; knows the domain organization in the Web; knows the psycho pedagogical rules to support the learner's cognitive diagnostic; and knows the appropriate pedagogical strategies assigned to each learner's cognitive pattern. In this article we focus on important empirical results of the Project towards the Web training adaptive environment architecture. These results consist of: (i) the CSL classes; (ii) the domain content; and (iii) the CSL classes' preferences.

3 The Cognitive Styles of Learning Classes

3.1 Applying the Psychological Ross Test

For learners' styles classification we chose a psychological test – The Ross test [14]. The test was conceived to measure the psycho pedagogical abilities relevant to the Upper Cognitive activities referred by [1]. The main focus of [1] was the Educational Processes Taxonomy in the cognitive domain. The Ross Test assesses three psycho pedagogical abilities (*Synthesis*, *Analysis* and *Evaluation*), underlying eight cognitive processes: *analogy*, *deductive reasoning*, *absent premises*, *abstract relations*, *sequential synthesis*, *questioning strategies*, *relevant and irrelevant analysis of information* and *attributes analysis*. The main emphasis of the test is on the individuals' abilities to deal with abstractions from a verbal base. The ability to elaborate concepts from abstractions with verbal elements is a major component of the upper cognitive processes. The test requires the subject to perform a variety of tasks that reflect these abilities.

The Ross test consists of a set of questions subdivided in two parts with four sections each. The subjects had to answer on a separate answer sheet. The maximum time for completion varied from 7 to 12 minutes, depending on the section. The test was applied in a sample composed of 231 employees randomly chosen from different departments of the Telecommunications Company.

Data collection through the Ross test lasted six months and collective sessions were composed of at least 2 and at most 10 subjects in each meeting. Each meeting lasted for one hour and a half, being divided in two successive sessions (of 45 minutes and 32 minutes, respectively), with a break of 15 minutes between sessions. The application setting was accomplished in a room at the company, especially prepared for the application, with artificial illumination, good ventilation and excellent control of external stimuli. The applicators were psychologists, trained in the application procedure and responsible for all the initial report, as well as the reading of the test instruction's manual that was standardized for this procedure.

3.2 Analyzing Data from Ross Test

Data analysis was performed at three moments. At the first one, the Ross test was assessed at three validity levels: (i) from the whole 105 test items (Alpha of Crombach=0.923); (ii) from the eight Cognitive Processes (Alpha of Crombach=0.8429); and (iii) from the three cognitive abilities (Alpha of Crombach=0.8364). This means that the Ross test was consistent and trustworthy. In order to validate the Ross test to the target population, the main adaptation consisted of classifying the individuals according to their performance ranges on different test sections, instead of considering the item numbers at each section.

At the second moment we have proceeded with *factorial analysis*. The factors analyzed were related with the eight cognitive *processes* and the three *abilities* assessed by the Ross test. The cognitive process *Analogy*, which underlies the *Analysis* ability, explained 72.61% of the total variance. The processes *abstract relations* and *sequential synthesis*, which underlie the *Synthesis* ability, explained 39.41% and 33.87%, respectively. The process *deductive reasoning*, which underlies the *Evaluation*, explained 62.97% of the total variance. The processes mentioned were the most predominant factors in each *ability* assessed.

In the *cluster* analysis the subjects were grouped by similarities in performance levels in each of the cognitive *processes* and *abilities* assessed. This statistical analysis has generated five clusters in a range of [0, 5] in the dendrogram.

The cognitive styles were generated based on empirical procedures, using the *factorial* analysis results and the *cluster* analysis. The representative CSL classes established are: (i) *Analogue-Analytical*; (ii) *Concrete-Generic*; (iii) *Deductive-Evaluative*; (iv) *Relational-Synthetic* and (v) *Indefinite style*. The nomenclature used to refer the five CSL classes highlights the most characteristically cognitive *process* and psycho pedagogical *ability*.

Table 1 shows the performance levels in the three pedagogical *abilities* in each CSL. The subjects that were assessed as 'superior' performance level (4 or 5) in *Analysis* ability were classified as *Analogue-Analytical* style. The subjects that were assessed as 'inferior' performance level (1 or 2) in *Analysis* ability were classified as *Concrete-Generic* style. This could mean that the group tends to work with the whole information and uses less abstraction than the *Analogue-Analytical* group. The subjects that were assessed as 'superior' in *Evaluation* ability, 'medium-inferior' in *Synthesis* ability and 'medium' *Analysis* ability were classified as *Deductive-Evaluative* style and so on.

The fifth group was very heterogeneous, without a performance similarity in the abilities and cognitive processes assessed by the Ross Test. To our surprise the Ross test was not sufficiently refined to group subjects according to their performance in the cognitive abilities. We are aware that the solution for this problem would be to use another test that could assess the same cognitive aspects as the Ross test does, but that would enable to utilize another grouping criteria. However, due to Project schedule time limitations, we decided to investigate only the navigational pattern of this group and labeled it as *Indefinite* CSL class.

Table 1. Cognitive Style Groups by Performance (4-5 superior, 3 medium, 1-2 inferior)

CSL Class	Subject	Sample %	Psycho Pedagogical Abilities		
			Ability 1 (Analysis 73%)	Ability 2 Synthesis 10,6%	Ability 3 (Evaluation 14,02%)
Analogue-Analytic	109	47,19	4 or 5	-	-
Concrete-Generic	60	25,97	1 or 2	-	-
Deductive-Evaluative	24	10,39	3	1, 2 or 3	4 or 5
Relational-Synthetic	07	3,03	3	4 or 5	1, 2 or 3
Indefinite Style	31	13,42	3	1,2,3 e 4	1,2,3,4 e 5

4 The Domain Content

Up to now, the main objective related to domain content has been to develop a Web experimental training module in order to analyze and generate the CSL classes preferences. The design and development of this training Web module integrates a multidisciplinary Project teamwork: psychologists, pedagogues, Web designers and a domain content specialist.

According to training demands of the Telecommunications Company, the Telecommunications course was chosen to be the first one. An initial module of TDMA (Time Division Multiple Access) was chosen as experimental module. TDMA has a medium difficulty level. This module was developed assuming that the learners have as pre-requisite a working knowledge on multiplex technology.

The non-tutorial interface's module of TDMA (Time Division Multiple Access) was developed to prevent the learner inducement to a particular navigation style. This approach enables the investigation about learners' CSL classes preferences, behavior and learners' performance.

Figure 1 shows the module's initial page, composed of two layers. In the top-left position there are three buttons corresponding to the didactic resources, presentation forms and final evaluation options. On the other part of the page there is a layer with didactic resources offered to the learner such as *concepts*, *examples*, *exercises* and *evaluation review*. The learner has to choose the didactic resources better suited to his/her CSL. After a learner's selection the presentation forms are presented using the same graphical interface as the initial page.

The domain content was designed using traditional didactic practices like: concepts presentation instruments, examples, exercises, evaluation review and final evaluation. For each didactic resource, there is a presentation form set. These presentations include textual, graphical and schematic forms or a mixture of all these. In a set, each presentation form refers to the same content being explained. The presentation forms varieties make possible to each learner to construct a customized trajectory which best fits the specific CSL.

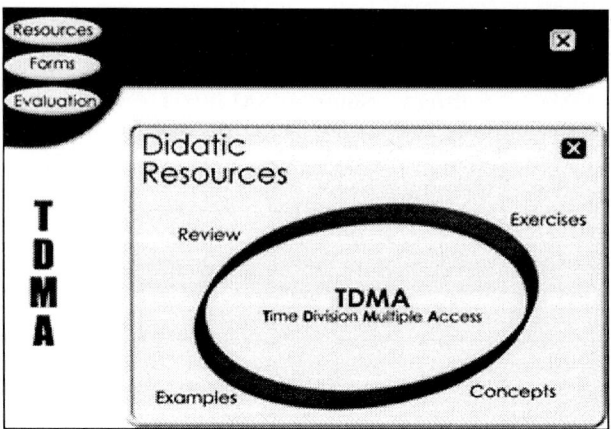

Fig. 1. The TDMA Initial Page

5 The Empirical Results about CSL Classes Behavior

In order to identify the generated CSL classes' behavior or preferences, we have carried out the investigation of learners while browsing the TDMA Web training pages. The sample learners were selected from the most typical ones of each CSL class. We obtained respectively from the representative groups: *Analogue-Analytical* class - 10 subjects; *Concrete-Generic* class - 7 subjects; *Deductive-Evaluative* class - 8 subjects; *Relational-Synthetic* class - 3 subjects and *Indefinite Style* class–7 subjects.

Before TDMA training module submission, the learners were advised about (i) the purpose of the investigation; (ii) the TDMA module characteristics; and (iii) their flexibility to make choices while browsing the training module.

All training environment information was recorded in the application database. The learner Web log was application-dedicated and the learners' interactions were sequentially recorded in a global log file. The log file recorded data/hour of the interaction, learner's and Web page visited identifications. Specifically, exercises a learner attempted and final evaluation information were recorded in another database file. The training environment used a client/server model. The client was developed using Web pages and Javascript/PHP tools and the Web server was implemented using servlets Java. The database access used JDBC connection.

There had been had a number of issues in preprocessing logged data before the learner navigation patterns and preferences were analyzed. These include: (i) cleaning/filtering the raw data to eliminate irrelevant items (i.e. learner menus accesses, connection faults records and application information pages); (ii) grouping individual page accesses into semantic units (i.e. learner session accesses); (iii) integration of various data sources such as user CSL, age, instructional level and gender; (iv) transforming alphanumeric codes into numeric; and (v) calculating time spent in each Web page he/she visited.

In order to accomplish the statistical analysis, the learners' Web log data were grouped by CSL classes. In this investigation, the independent variable was the learner's CSL, and the dependent variables were learner's preferences related to *didactic resources* (i.e. concepts pages, exercises, examples and evaluation review) and *presentation forms* (i.e. textual, graphical, schematic). The statistical analysis included descriptive analysis (i.e. mean/standard deviation/range), ANOVA analysis and Correspondence analysis. The ANOVA results have showed non-significant differences between CSL classes concerned with didactic resources preferences ($\alpha > 0.05$), except that the *Indefinite* CSL class have shown a significant preference for *exercises of filling the blanks* presentation form compared with *Concrete-Generic* CSL class ($\alpha = 0.016$).

Comparing the total navigation time in the experimental module, the *Relational-Synthetic* CSL class took more time than *Concrete-Generic* CSL class ($\alpha = 0.097 < 0.10$) and comparing the mean navigation time in the *exercises* Web pages, the *Relational-Synthetic* CSL class took more time than *Concrete-Generic/Analogue-Analytical* CSL classes ($\alpha = 0.089 < 0.10$). We have observed that the *Deductive-Evaluative* CSL class took more time than *Analogue-Analytical* CSL class at performing *final evaluation* ($\alpha = 0.051 < 0.10$). Comparing the total pages accessed, the *Relational-Synthetic* CSL class has accessed more pages than the *Deductive-Evaluative/Indefinite* CSL classes ($\alpha = 0.058 < 0.10$).

Nevertheless, the main differences between CSL classes were better observed from the Correspondence analysis at the first twenty learner's actions as Fig. 2 shows. Figure 2 shows also the local associations among the cognitive styles (AA, CG, DA, RS, EI) and Didactic Resources (1, 2, 3, 4, 5). These associations are outlined in the graphical representation. The *Analogue-Analytical* and *Indefinite* CSL classes, (AA) and (EI), have predominantly used the *Concepts* didactic resources (1). This preference differentiates these CSL classes from the others. The *Concrete-Generic* CSL class (CG) has predominantly used the *exercise* didactic resource (2), making this preference a significant characteristic of the class. The *Relational-Synthetic* CSL class (RS) has predominantly used the *evaluation review* didactic resource (4). Finally, the *Concrete-Generic* and *Relational-Synthetic* CSL classes, (CG) and (RS) respectively, have predominantly used the *example* didactic resource (3).

Before concluding the Correspondence Analysis, we have verified the learner *presentation forms* preferences at the first twenty actions as Fig. 3 shows. The *Analogue-Analytical* CSL class (1) has predominantly used concept pages that use outlined texts and graphics (111) and evaluation review (402). The *Concrete-Generic* CSL class (2) has predominantly used example pages that use comparative blocks of texts and graphics (305), concept pages that use texts and graphics (107) and concept pages that present schema with questions (109).

The *Deductive-Evaluative* CSL class (3) has predominantly used evaluation review (401) and example pages with schema and graphics (303). The *Indefinite* CSL class (5) has predominantly used filling the blanks exercises (204) and textual questioning example (302). Finally, the *Relational-Synthetic* CSL class (4) has predominantly used simple choice exercises (203), relating columns exercises (202) and example pages with texts and graphics (301).

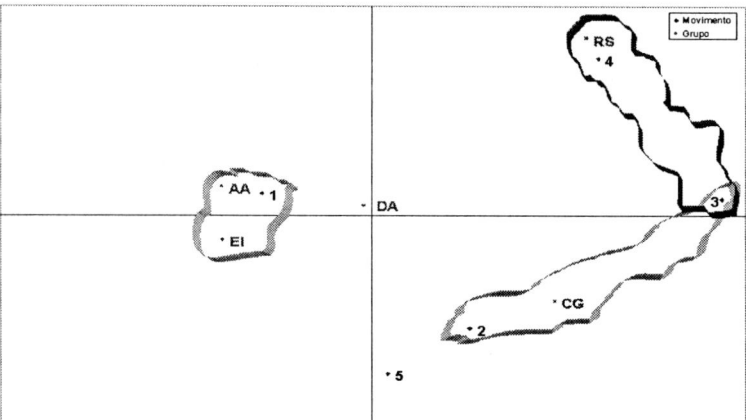

Fig. 2. The Correspondence Analysis Related to Didactic Resources Preferences

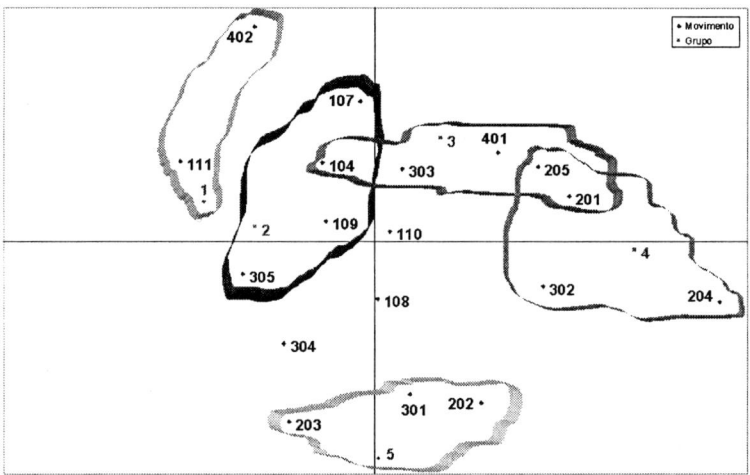

Fig. 3. The Correspondence Analysis Related to Presentation Forms Preferences

6 Conclusions

The adaptive Web training environment demands investigation of a multidisciplinary team such as psycho-pedagogical researchers, Web designers, content domain specialists, and technology information intelligent systems designers. This is a great challenge not only concerning experts' knowledge, but also concerning cooperation requirements between them. In our investigation, we have attempted to contribute in this area proposing a new methodology to generate the learner's cognitive profiles to be considered in the adaptation of systems characteristics to the learner's cognitive features. This work was totally based on empirical procedures that have worked with a specific target population, the Telecommunications Company's employees, and partner of the Tapejara Project.

The study of CSL classes' behavior consists of another contribution of our work. This process has included a statistical analysis in order to identify the main features associated to each CSL classes, concerning its pedagogical actions while browsing a training Web module. All knowledge obtained from this investigation will give us the background to develop Web training environment contents. Afterwards, we aim to propose an artificial agent collection to assist the log distance training, suggesting to the learner the strategy that best fits his/her cognitive style. We do hope that this adaptation model will benefit the learner's training over the Web, making his/her learning process easier.

References

1. Bloom, B.: Taxonomia de Objetivos Educacionais – Domínio Cognitivo. Porto Alegre: Ed. Globo, 1972.
2. Brusilovski, P.: Methods and techniques of adaptative hypermedia. In: Brusilovsky, Peter et al. (Ed.). Adaptative Hypertext and Hypermedia, Netherlands, p. 1-43, 1995.
3. Bull, S., Greer, J.: Peer Help for Problem-Based Learning. In: International Conference on Computers in Education, Vol. 2. Taipei, Taiwan (2000) 1007-1015.
4. Dufresne, A., Turcotte, S.: Cognitive Style and its Implications for Navigation Strategies. In: World Conference on Artificial Intelligence and Education, AI-ED'97, 8, Proceedings ... Amsterdam: IOS, 1997.
5. Fierro, A.: Personalidad y Aprendizaje en el Contexto Escolar. In C. Copll; J. Palacios; A.Marchesi (ed). Desarrollo psicológico y educación, II. Psicologia de la educación. Madrid: Alianza, 1990.
6. Ford, N. & Chen, S.Y.: Individual Differences, Hypermedia Navigation, and Learning: an Empirical Study. Journal of Educational Multimedia and Hypermedia 9(4). 281-311, 2000.
7. MacGregor, S. K.: Hypermedia navigation profiles: cognitive characteristics and information processing strategies. Journal of Educational Computing Research, 20(2). 189-206, 1999.
8. MacLoughlin, C.: The Implications of the Research Literature on Learning Styles of the Design of Instructional Material. Australian Journal of Educational Technology, 15(3), 222-241, 1999.
9. Madeira, M.; Diehl, E.; Verdin, R.; Wainer, R.; Fraga, T.: Learner Cognitive Modeling in Intelligent Tutoring Systems for Distant Learning in the Internet. In: XXVIII Interamerican Congress in Psychology. Chile, Santiago Del Chile, 2001.
10. Martinez, M.; Bunderson, V.: Building Interactive World Wide Web (Web) Learning Environments to Match and Support Individual Learning Differences. Journal of Interactive Learning Research, 11(3), 163-195, 2000.
11. Mcmanuns, T.F.: Individualizing Instruction in a Web-Based Hypermedia Learning Environment: Nonlinearity, Advance Organizers, and Self-Regulated Learners. Journal of Interactive Learning Research 11(3), 219-251, 2000.
12. Riding, R. & Grimley, M.: Cognitive Style and Learning from Multimedia Materials in 11- year Children. British Journal of Educational Technology, 30(1), 43-59,1999.
13. Riding, R. & Rayner, S.: Cognitive Styles and Learning Strategies. London: David Fulton Publishers, 2000.
14. Ross, J. D.; Ross, C. M.: Test Ross of Cognitive Processes. São Paulo: Institute Pieron de Psicologia Aplicada, 1997.

Automated Personalization of Internet News

Aditya V. Sunderam

2412 Harvard Yard Mail Center
Cambridge, MA 02138, USA
sunderam@fas.harvard.edu

Abstract. A systems approach to the automatic and adaptive personalization of Internet news is described. Implemented on the client side as a lightweight, transparent software system, this approach is based on *implicit* user feedback, thereby preserving privacy while avoiding the constant recustomization needed in explicit schemes. The system consists of two modules: (1) a profiling agent, which unobtrusively monitors news reading patterns to track interest in different topics while acting as a proxy server on the user's computer; (2) and an action agent, which uses the profile information to retrieve, filter, and present news articles. A prototype of the system was implemented and evaluated over a two week period. Precisions (the percentages of relevant articles returned by the system) ranging from 60-95% were observed for profiles representing various combinations of interests. The system also responded very well to simulated changes in user interests, returning rapidly increasing numbers of articles relevant to newly developed interests.

1 Introduction

The Internet has the potential to be a highly effective and timely medium for news, especially news that is personalized for individual users. Given its highly interactive and customizable nature, in theory, users could construct their own "newspapers" by assembling an ideal mix of articles from multiple websites. However, creating such a personalized newspaper is currently impractical, due to the sheer volume of news and the required expertise, tools, and computational resources. Therefore, users must settle for generic front-pages that are created by human editors at Internet news sites; readers scan these index pages and click on articles of interest for in-depth reports. There are several major drawbacks to this mode of newsreading. Manual selection of interesting articles is tedious and time-consuming. Multiple sites must be scanned to ensure comprehensiveness. Moreover, because news sites constantly update their index pages, scanning must be frequent to avoid missing important articles. These drawbacks suggest that new, automated approaches be pursued to make Internet news more effective. A pragmatic scheme for the automated and adaptive personalization of Internet news that addresses these issues is presented in this paper.

1.1 The Basis for Automatic, Adaptive, Personalization

Generally, an individual's interests determine the types of news articles that he or she is likely to read. Automated approaches to news personalization may be based on this premise; articles that a user recently found interesting could be used to automatically gauge the relevance of new articles. Further, changes in reading patterns could be used to detect and adapt to changing interests. For Internet news read via a web browser, several parameters can be measured to quantify the user's degree of interest in an article. Combining these measures with the characteristics of the articles themselves, a "profile" of the user could be created, representing his or her interests. Such a profile could then be used as a basis of comparison for future articles; articles that closely match the profile are likely to appeal to the user.

1.2 Background

The system described herein draws upon the fields of software agents and information filtering and retrieval (IF and IR). Agents are used within this project in a heuristic and pragmatic manner; informal notions of inference, preference, and persistence are utilized as in Letizia [12] and Apt [4]. Concepts from IF and IR are used more explicitly, especially those employed in retrieval systems to select relevant documents from a given set in real-time [1]. Specifically, news articles are considered documents, characterized as in IF and IR systems by a set of keywords $K = \{k_1, k_2, k_3, ..., k_n\}$, and described by a corresponding frequency vector: $D = \{d_1, d_2, d_3, ..., d_n\}$, where d_i denotes the number of occurrences of keyword k_i. This project also uses a standard IR metric to express similarity between two documents, viz. the angle, or cosine, metric,

$$Similarity(X, Y) \equiv \cos\theta = \frac{\sum_{i=0}^{n} x_i y_i}{\mid X \mid\mid Y \mid},$$

where x and y are the two document vectors, (the frequencies in each document of all words in either document [6]). If each vector is visualized in n-dimensional space, the angle between the vectors is small for similar documents and large for dissimilar ones. Thus, higher values for $\cos\theta$ imply greater similarity between the documents.

1.3 Project Concepts

A key idea in this project is that the structure of "profiles" representing user preferences can be designed in a manner that facilitates the selection of relevant incoming news articles. The user profile is represented as a keyword-weight vector, a set of numerical values indicating the user's relative interest in topics associated with corresponding words. For example, the profile of a user interested *only* in politics would have high scores for words such as "Clinton", "Congress", and "Republicans", while words common to other topics would have lower scores.

The profile can thus be thought of as a composite representation of the user's ideal document (a canonical personalized newspaper), reflecting all the user's interests. Over time, the user's interests and priorities may change. As this occurs, the user's profile should also change. A second key idea in this project is that the profile is automatically maintained to be accurate and current by continually monitoring reading patterns and adapting the profile as appropriate. Adaptation is accomplished by comparing the user's expected and actual level of interest in an article and adjusting the profile accordingly.

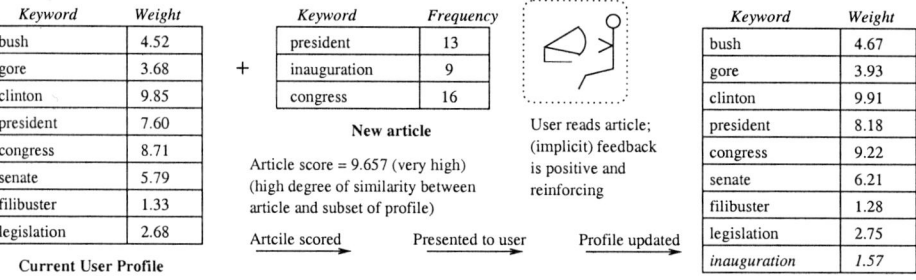

Fig. 1. News personalization schema

The concepts underlying the news personalization approach proposed in this project are illustrated by the schematic example in Fig. 1. It shows the steady-state profile of a user interested only in politics, the scoring and presentation of the article to the user, and the eventual update of the profile with adjusted scores and newly encountered keywords. In a different scenario, low-scoring articles or those ignored by the user would result in attenuation of appropriate keyword weights in the profile. The details of this process, including transparent measurement of user interest, the scoring algorithm, profile maintenance, and inclusion of new topics are discussed in the following sections.

1.4 Related Work

Among the many approaches to personalization, expert-system strategies are the most automated. The Fishwrap and ZWrap systems developed at MIT were successful implementations of such strategies and served as valuable foundations for subsequent projects [2, 3]. However, those systems were not adaptive; changes in user interests were not automatically detected and reconciled. At the opposite extreme are commercial systems, such as MyYahoo! [7] and MyExcite, which are highly dependent on user input. These schemes tend to rely heavily on user selection (from short, fixed menus) of news topics; at the portals, human editors simply sort news articles into appropriate topic categories. In addition to being too rigid, these approaches require the storage of personal preference data on content-provider servers and lack the ability to adapt to changing interests. Most other systems, including the popular PTV [9] and News Dude [5] services, also require explicit user input.

2 Design and Implementation

This project proposes a new approach to adaptive, automated personalization of Internet-based news that is implemented as an associated software system. Several sources continually provide news on their web pages[1]. Articles from these sources typically include a headline, a byline, narrative text, pictures, and embedded links. A user usually selects articles to read based on the headline and the byline. Articles are read for varying lengths of time depending on interest in the topic, length of the article, number of pictures, and other factors. The user may also follow embedded links related to the article, indicating deeper interest in the topic. The model proposed in this project is based on the premise that observation of such behavior can be used to quantify the user's interest in a given article. This characterization is the foundation for selecting future articles.

2.1 System Design

The system was designed to consist of two software agents, small programs that run transparently and unobtrusively on the user's computer. The first is the "profiling" agent, which monitors the user's degree of interest in various topics. The profiling agent characterizes articles based on keywords, as described earlier. To estimate the user's degree of interest in a given article, it uses measures of (1) *immediacy* (time between seeing a headline and clicking on it), (2) *detail* (time spent reading an article), (3) *comprehensiveness* (number of embedded links followed), and (4) *focus* (percentage of topical articles read). These measures are used to continually update the user's profile, so that it always reflects the user's most current interests. As a result, when the user's interests evolve or change, the system adapts quickly and automatically to the new interests.

The second program is an "action" agent. The action agent uses the profile to filter incoming news streams. Each new article is scored against the user's profile. News items likely to be of compelling interest to the user are presented in a prioritized list. The profiling agent also monitors the user's reaction to the news presented by the action agent, in addition to monitoring news that is read directly from the web. Both agents run on the user's computer (i.e. on the client side), where the profile is also stored. Therefore, content providers do not have access to the user's preferences, ensuring privacy. Further, analysis and scoring of news articles against individual profiles is performed locally, thereby distributing the computational load. Finally, client-side implementation allows the user to obtain personalized news from multiple news sites and sources, in contrast to server-side implementations which force loyalty to a single source.

---

[1] At present, HTML-based webpages are assumed; it is expected that future XML versions will assist the system and improve its efficacy.

2.2 Prototype Implementation

The action agent is implemented as a continuously running background process on the client computer. One module within this program periodically (every 15 minutes) retrieves the front page of targeted news sites, by issuing HTTP GET requests. The HTTP response is parsed to extract all the embedded URLs. Any new URLs are piped to an analysis module that characterizes articles and scores them against the user's profile. This module first fetches the content of each new article and parses the page by removing certain standard HTML tags (links, javascripts, tables, images). From the remaining text, two vectors of length n, $K = \{k_1, k_2, k_3, ..., k_n\}$ of keywords and $A = \{a_1, a_2, a_3, ..., a_n\}$ of corresponding frequencies, are created. Keywords appearing in the article but not in the profile are set aside for later addition to the profile. Next, subvector P' of the user profile P is constructed, such that $P' = \{p_1, p_2, p_3, ..., p_n\}$, where p_i is the profile weight of keyword k_i. The article score is computed as the cosine of the angle θ between A and P'. Pointers to high-scoring articles are then inserted into a custom-made web page for later presentation to the user. New keywords encountered within the article that are not in the profile are added to the profile (with a weight of zero) after the article is scored. As the user reads more articles containing these words, the profiling agent will appropriately update their weights. Note that articles presented by the system, as well as those read directly from the Internet, are included in this process. In this way, the system adapts automatically to (1) newly developed interests in pre-existing topics and (2) user interest in newly emerging news topics.

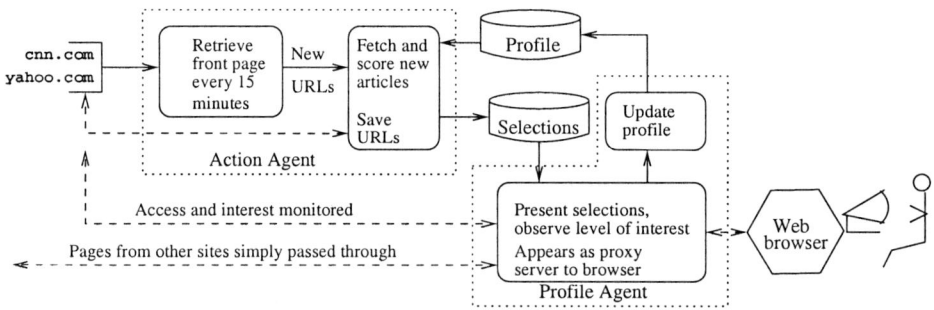

Fig. 2. Prototype Implementation

A schematic of the prototype implementation is shown in Fig. 2. In the prototype, the profiling agent is positioned as an intermediary (on the client computer) between the user's browser and the Internet. The profiling agent acts as a minimalistic web-proxy server and appears as such to the browser. This scheme exploits the built-in proxy options of web browsers, thereby obviating the need for software modifications and causing no disruptions to the user's browsing experience. The profiling agent reads in the current user profile and executes an infinite loop, relaying HTTP requests and responses between the browser and the Internet. For retrievals of interest (news from selected sites in this case), it logs the reaction time rt (time between seeing a headline and clicking on it), dwell ratio dr (time spent reading divided by article length), number of embedded links followed lf, and rank rk (the order of selection of a given article from a set of headlines). Note that the nature of the HTTP protocol facilitates collection of this data through observation of the browser's network connections. Proxy servers, positioned between the browser and the web, can monitor both the content and timings of all interactions and can thus transparently collect the required measurements.

The data collected by the profiling agent is used to track the user's interests and changes therein. Low values of rt and rk, coupled with high values of dr and lf indicate continued high interest or increased interest in the topic exemplified by the article. Conversely, articles that are not viewed at all or are viewed for a short duration indicate decreasing interest. To quantify the degree of interest, an article score metric that indicates increasing, decreasing, or constant interest is developed. It is computed as $Score = \frac{c_1 \times dr \times n}{rt \times rk} + c_2 \times lf$, where n is the length of the article vector and c_1 and c_2 are adjustable constants. This implicit user evaluation of the article is used to update the profile $P = \{p_1, p_2, p_3, ..., p_m\}$ as follows. First A is scaled to A' such that $|A'| = Score$. For each $a'_j \in A'$, such that keyword k_j is in the article and in the profile, p_j is updated according to the equation $p_j = \frac{c_3 \times p_j + a'_j}{c_3 + 1}$, where c_3 is a constant. Informally, the relevant parts of the profile are updated using a weighted average of the old profile and the current article, which has been scaled to reflect the user's degree of interest (as measured by the implicit score for this article). Since the old profile represents a historical measure of the user's interest in the topic of the current article, this weighted averaging process tracks the user's degree of focus in this topic. Since this scheme updates the user's profile based on every article read, the profile is always kept up to date.

3 Evaluation

Traditional measures [6] of IR and IF system performance were used to evaluate the prototype, since the selectivity of the system in personalizing news is analogous to the retrieval of appropriate documents from a large set. The most important performance metric is *precision*, defined as $precision = \frac{\|\{retr\} \cap \{rel\}\|}{\|\{retr\}\|}$ where $\{retr\}$ is the set of returned articles, $\{rel\}$ is the set of all relevant articles in the document set, and $\| x \|$ represents the size of set x. Precision indicates the probability that a retrieved document is relevant and is the most important measure because the primary goal of IF and IR systems is to return as many relevant articles as possible. Another metric, which characterizes the proportion of relevant articles that have been retrieved, is *recall*, defined as: $recall = \frac{\|\{retr\} \cap \{rel\}\|}{\|\{rel\}\|}$. In other words, recall is the ratio of the number of relevant articles returned to the total number of relevant articles. Two other measures are sometimes used to complement precision and recall. The first is $fallout = \frac{\|\{retr\} \cap \{rel\}\|}{\|\{rel\}\|}$, which is the fraction of non-relevant articles returned. The second is the density of relevant articles in the entire document set: $generality = \frac{\|\{rel\}\|}{\|\{all\}\|}$, an inherent characteristic of the document set rather than a true performance measure. Generality provides an estimate of topic distribution in a given document set.

3.1 Methodology

During live operation, the system retrieves and filters articles for a user who then provides implicit feedback through his or her reading patterns. In order to simulate this process for several hypothetical users and evaluate the system, the following methodology was adopted. First, a document set consisting of 3695 articles was assembled by continuously harvesting newly generated articles from two popular news sources, cnn.com and dailynews.yahoo.com. As an initialization process, the document set was analyzed to determine the list of common words. A base profile was then created, consisting of all "content" words, i.e. words in the document set that were not in the list of common words. An initial weight of zero was assigned to all words in the profile. For the experimental document set, the profile consisted of 25,000 words.

Table 1. Article counts and distribution by topic

Topic	Russia	Stocks	Tennis	Politics	MidEast	Total(5 topics)	Entire set
No. of Articles	135	239	73	166	85	698	3695
Generality	3.65%	6.46%	1.98%	4.49%	2.30%	18.9%	100%

Five news topics were chosen for the evaluation process: *Russian affairs, financial news, tennis, domestic politics*, and *the Middle East*. Table 1 shows the number of articles corresponding to each topic in the document set of 3695 articles, along with generality measures for each. Profiles were then created for multiple users with one, two, and three interests and with a change from one interest to another, by using "training articles", simulating a new user's selection of articles in a topic of interest; in live operation, the profiling agent would accomplish this through observation of browsing patterns.. Training articles relevant to a given user's interest(s) were selected from the document set and assigned values for each of the feedback metrics. Realistic ranges for these metrics (reaction time, rank, dwell ratio, and links followed) were obtained through empirical observation and by querying real users. Simulated values for experimental profiles were then chosen randomly from within those ranges. For each of the hypothetical users, profiles were created (using the scoring formula developed in Sect. 2.2) with 1, 5, 10, 15, 20, 25, 30 and 35 training articles. These profiles were then used to filter the entire document set for articles relevant to each interest, combination of interests, or change in interests. *Precision* and *recall* were computed for each set of returned articles. The number of articles returned for a given test profile ($\| \{retr\} \|$) ranged from 15 to 32 and was determined by the generality of the topic(s) in the document set.

3.2 Results

The results of these experiments are very encouraging. Experiments using 35 training articles exhibited precisions in the range of 79-100%, and those using as few as 5 training articles exhibited precisions of 60-95% in most cases. Values of recall were mostly in the 60-70% range, and fallout was extremely low (less than 1%) in all cases; these positive results were obtained despite relatively low levels of generality (ranging from 2% for tennis articles to 6% for articles concerning the stock market). For space reasons, the remainder of the discussion concerns only precision, the most important retrieval metric.

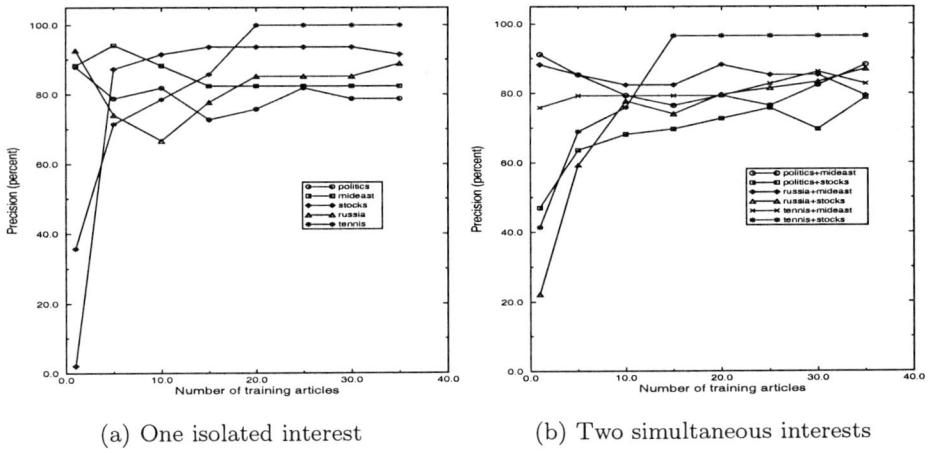

(a) One isolated interest   (b) Two simultaneous interests

Fig. 3. Precision vs. Training Articles

Observed values of precision for varying numbers of training articles are shown in Fig. 3a and 3b for each of the five news topics treated individually, and for topics taken two at a time – representing users with one and two simultaneous interests respectively. Precisions are uniformly high in all cases, except in a few isolated instances when only one training article was used. This indicates that the filtering algorithm, though simple, is very effective. Results for profiles simulating three or more simultaneous interests are also very good, as may be seen in Fig. 4a. These results are particularly significant since they are representative of the multiple, varied interests of the average news reader.

Fig. 4b plots precision versus the number of training articles when a hypothetical user switches from one interest to another, measuring the system ability to automatically adapt. The graph shows the selection of residual, undesired articles about the original topic (dashed lines, unfilled symbols), as well as the selection of desirable articles about the new topic (solid lines, filled symbols). The general trends are clear; as the number of training articles (for the new topic) increases, greater precision is observed in the number of "new-topic" articles selected. Simultaneously, the numbers of "old-topic" articles retrieved decrease. The rate at which new topic precision increases (and old topic precision de-

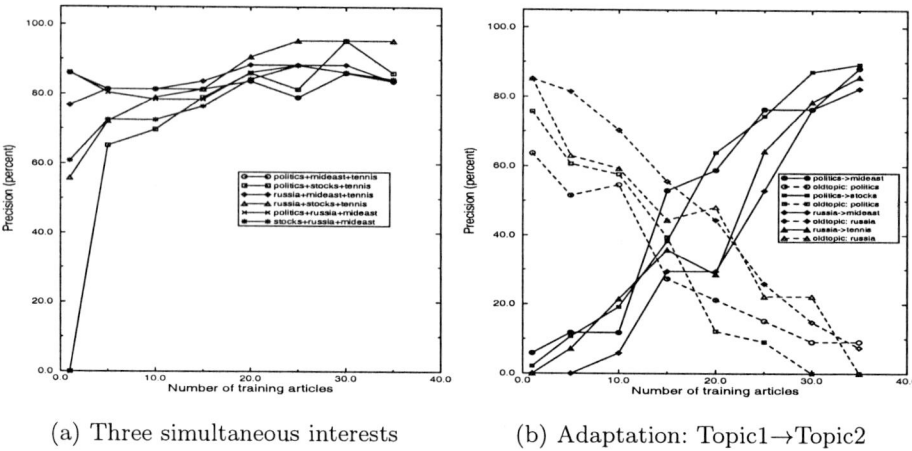

Fig. 4. Precision vs. Training Articles

creases) is high, indicating that the system adapts quickly and effectively. For example, three of the five new topics achieve precisions of 60% or more with 20 training articles, while all achieve precisions of 80% or more with 35 training articles. Overall, these graphs are consistent with the expected behavior of the average user, who develops new interests not instantaneously but over a period of several days.

4 Conclusions

An agent-based software framework for automatic, adaptive personalization of Internet-based news was designed and implemented. By standard performance measures, the system achieves a high level of efficiency and is effective in adaptive filtering. The major strength of the system is its use of *implicit* relevance feedback to determine user interests and changes therein. This project also emphasizes other important issues. Privacy is achieved by a client-side implementation, and a proxy-based profiling agent can be deployed with minimal effort and disruption. During operation, the system is unobtrusive and transparent, and consumes negligible resources.

The system has some limitations. The current version requires the analysis of a few articles before it can handle entirely new topics. Thus, when presented with news concerning an unusual, unexpected event (i.e. articles containing previously unencountered words), the first few articles may not be forwarded to the user. However, if the user profile implies interest in this new topic or if the user reads a few articles on this topic through direct browsing, the system will adapt and subsequent articles will be presented. Techniques to detect and include new topics, alternative similarity detection algorithms, and proactive notification mechanisms are among the ongoing and future enhancements being considered.

According to recent statistics, the Internet encompassed about 147 million hosts in January 2002 [11] and is doubling in size every year [8]. With this growth, the information overload problem is only worsening. Addressing this situation in the context of text-based news is an important step forward. News represents a large volume of constantly changing information, and individuals have selected subsets of interests, which themselves change over time. This project has shown that a reasonable solution can be developed in such an arena.

Acknowledgements

I would like to thank Dr. Walter Bender for giving me a summer internship opportunity in the MIT Media Lab and for introducing me to news editing systems. I am also indebted to the RSI AlumReader program for feedback and comments on earlier versions of this paper.

References

1. Baeza-Yates, R., and Berthier Ribeiro-Neto. "Modern Information Retrieval." Addison-Wesley, 1999.
2. Bender, Walter. "Read All About It in the Daily You." *Communicating Business*, Forward Publishing, London, United Kingdom, 1995. Also available at: http://nif.media.mit.edu/papers/forward.html.
3. Gruhl, D. and W. Bender. "A New Structure for News Editing." *IBM Systems Journal* **39**, nos. 3&4, pp. 569–588 (2000).
4. Shearin, Sybil, and Henry Lieberman, "Intelligent Profiling by Example", *Proceedings of the International Conference on Intelligent User Interfaces (IUI 2001)*, Sante Fe, NM, January 2001.
5. Hirsh, Haym, et al. "Learning to Personalize." *Communications of the ACM*, **43**(8), pp. 102-106, August 2000.
6. Losee, Robert M. "Text Retrieval and Filtering: Analytic Models of Performance." Kluwer Academic Publishers, Boston, MA, 1998.
7. Manber, Udi, et al. "Experience with Personalization on Yahoo!" *Communications of the ACM*, **43**(8), pp. 35-40, August 2000.
8. Salus, Peter. "Internet Growth Rate." *Matrix News*, **10**(3), March 2000. Also available at: http://www.mids.org/mn/1003/growth.html.
9. Smyth, Barry and Paul Cotter. "A Personalized Television Listings System." *Communications of the ACM*, **43**(8), pp. 107-111, August 2000.
10. Tryon, R. and D. E. Bailey. "Cluster Analysis." McGraw-Hill, 1970.
11. Internet Software Consortium, "Internet Domain Survey, January 2002: Number of Hosts Advertised in the DNS", http://www.isc.org/ds/WWW-200201/index.html, January 2002.
12. Lieberman, Henry. "Letizia: An Agent That Assists Web Browsing", *Proceedings of the 1995 International Joint Conference on Artificial Intelligence*, Montreal, Canada, August 1995.

Conceptual Modeling of Personalized Web Applications[*]

Silvia Abrahão[1], Joan Fons[1], Magalí González[2], and Oscar Pastor[1]

[1] Department of Information Systems and Computation
Valencia University of Technology
Camino de Vera s/n, P.O. Box: 22012, E-46020 - Valencia, Spain
{sabrahao, jjfons, opastor}@dsic.upv.es
[2] Department of Informatics and Electronics
Catholic University of Asuncion
Tte. Cantaluppi y Tte. Villalón. C.C. 1683- Asuncion, Paraguay
magali@dsic.upv.es

Abstract. The demand for web applications that take into account the different needs and interests of the users has been increasing. Personalization can involve a wide-range of approaches and techniques to design the end-user experience. This paper discusses the use of conceptual modeling techniques in a software production process for the design of personalized web applications. This process is driven by an Object-Oriented Web-Solutions Modeling approach (OOWS) that properly captures the specific characteristics of web applications. We place special emphasis on the primitives of a navigational model that provides personalization patterns to capture and represent the semantics of this kind of application.

1 Introduction

The World Wide Web (WWW) has introduced a new software environment characterized by rapid changes in technology and the need for defining personalized applications for specific user requirements. Adaptation is the way to define rules that allow web applications to give an appropriate response in accordance with user profiles, navigation history, target devices, network connections, etc. E-commerce applications are representative examples of systems where the adaptation to new environments and requirements is a critical factor. In this context, automatic software production environments have become a significant way to accelerate the development process and reusability capacities. Thus, today ther is a need for dynamic adaptation of the applications with regard to the preferences of the user.

Nowadays, the approaches that address some kind of personalization vary widely [1]: from simple page generation strategies to complex content-based prediction systems, pattern recognition of user behavior, machine-learning algorithms, and data mining. Most of these approaches consider personalization

---

[*] Research supported by the CICYT Project, with ref. TIC2001-3530-C02-01 and the WEST Project (CYTED Program), subprogram VII.18)

issues from an implementation point of view. According to [12] the current techniques for collecting user information are explicit profiling, implicit profiling and legacy data. The most used widely techniques for analyzing information are rule based and filtering techniques.

However, we consider the use of conceptual modeling techniques to be important in the appropriate treatment of the inherent complexity of web applications. In [3] and [7], customization issues in web application development are discussed pointing out the need for modeling methods to develop customizable web applications. The WSDM method [8] is an audience-driven approach that defines information objects based on the information requirements of the users to develop a web application. In [4] the authors shows how to specify personalized web applications by defining different scenarios according to user profiles or preferences. In [2], a modeling language for designing web applications is proposed. It provides a personalization model where users and groups can be explicitly specified in the structure schema of the information.

In the same way, our proposal provides a contribution in this context claiming that conceptual modeling should include personalization features for the development of sound and robust web applications. In the context of the OO-Method project [9, 10], efforts have been oriented towards the development of a new model to enrich this object-oriented software production method with the required expressiveness to specify web applications. This model proposes a set of high level abstraction primitives to define the navigation semantics of applications. We focus on the integration of navigational design and conceptual modeling, which together could be used as input for an automatic software production environment. All this information is used to provide precise methodological guidance for going from the Conceptual Space to the Solution Space (represented by the final software product). The objective of this paper is to show how the OOWS-Modeling approach supports the specification of personalized web applications.

This paper is organized in four sections. Section 2 gives a general overview of the OOWS approach. Section 3 presents the primitives used to express specific features in conceptual modeling for customized web applications. Finally, Sect. 4 provides the conclusions and work in progress.

2 The OOWS-Modeling Approach

OOWS [11] is an extension of the OO-Method [9, 10] approach to develop web applications. The OO-Method is enriched with a navigational model to capture navigational semantics for different audiences. The OOWS approach comprises two major steps: *Specifying the System* and *Developing the Solution*. In the first step, a conceptual model of an application is built in terms of the problem space. At first, this step includes requirement collection using a Use Case [6] approach. Then, the conceptual model is built using an Object Model (object structure), a Dynamic Model (valid object lives and object interaction), a Functional Model (behavior description) and a Navigational Model (navigation structure). These models describe the object society from four complementary points of view within a well defined OO framework. In the Developing the Solution step, a strategy for component generation to integrate the solution (the final software product) is defined. In this step, a functional equivalent to the specification web-based application can be obtained in an automated way.

2.1 The Navigational Model

The Navigational Model allows for the definition of a *navigational view* over the Object Model. It captures the navigation semantics of a web application using a UML-like [5] notation.

The navigational model is essentially composed of a **Navigational Map** that represents the global view of the system for an agent (potential end-user). It is represented by a directed graph in which the nodes are the **Navigational Contexts** and the arcs are the **Navigational Links** defining valid navigation paths.

A Navigational Context allows to define the content and presentation of a user interaction. It represents the point of view that this user has over a subset of the object model. It is composed by **Navigational Classes** and **Navigational Relationships**. A navigational class defines which attributes and operations of an object model class will be shown for the given agent. Navigational relationships connect navigational classes and they describe valid navigation paths over object relationships.

There are two kinds of navigational contexts: exploration contexts and sequence contexts. The first one are contexts that can be reached at any moment, independently of the current context. Sequence contexts can only be reached by following a predefined sequence of navigational links. Finally, presentation patterns can also be specified to "format" the output presentation.

In OOWS it is possible to access the "connected user" with the application in the navigational model by using the **Active Agent** primitive. With this primitive, it is possible to define expressions that depend on part of the information from this user. For example, in a population filter one can use the expression `#RegisteredUser#.ShoppingBasket` to access only the `ShoppingBasket` for the connected user (assuming there is a `RegisteredUser` class, a `ShoppingBasket` class and an aggregation relationship between them which is defined in the Object Model).

In addition, the **Active Agent** has a predefined **Session** property that automatically collects information about user interactions with the application (such as the navigation paths followed, the objects selected, the operations performed, etc.) that can also be used to construct dynamic expressions.

3 Designing Personalized Web Applications

In the conceptual modeling phase of a web application [3, 4], personalization can be performed at three levels: the information *content* level (which information is available for a given user interaction), the *presentation* level (how this information is shown) and the *navigation* structure level (navigation structure).

Personalization for each of these levels can be seen from two different aspects: *static* and *dynamic*. Static personalization is fully defined at design time. Dynamic personalization depends on a runtime condition. Additionally, two levels of granularity can be defined in accordance with the applicability to a *group* of users (user profile) or to an *individual* user. Another characteristic of the personalization is the *environment adaptation*, changing or adapting the application interface depending on the target resources (device, location, network connection, etc.).

Through its abstraction primitives the OOWS approach allows static personalization with respect to the content, presentation and navigation levels. For dynamic personalization it only allows personalization with respect to the content and navigation level. It is possible to consider individual or group granularity.

3.1 Static Personalization

Navigation static personalization is obtained by linking a navigational map with an agent, predefining its navigation structure at design time. Navigational contexts allow the content personalization for this agent by specifying its navigational classes (attributes and operations), navigational relationships and population filters. Presentation patterns specified for a navigational context define the static personalization for the presentation level.

Group personalization is achieved by providing a navigational map for each user type (agent) detected in the navigational model. Therefore, agents of this type share all the characteristics of this map. However, defining individual personalization is not allowed.

3.2 Dynamic Personalization

Dynamic personalization allows for the definition of rules and characteristics at the conceptual level that must be evaluated at runtime depending on the current interactive user. OOWS proposes the **Active Agent** primitive for this purpose, enabling access to the "active user" and the user's **Session** (collection of interactions performed by the user with the application).

Content dynamic personalization is represented by defining population filters over the navigational classes involving some properties of the current interactive user (for example, accessing the user's `ShoppingBasket` or showing the user's navigation path to the current context using the user's **Session** property).

We consider that there is no need to specify navigation dynamic personalization. However, the navigational model can implicity capture this semantic enabling each user to define a subset of their navigational map. The application could even automatically show the user's most frequent navigational paths (without disabling all other navigation possibilities).

4 Conclusions

In this paper, we have presented how the OOWS approach deals with the design of personalized web applications. We argue that conceptual modeling of this kind of applications is a practice from a software engineering point of view that allow us to design applications which are more maintainable and extensible. Currently, we are extending our modeling language with new customization patterns that permit the construction of flexible web applications. We are also defining translation patterns for different target architectures, taking into account the personalization aspects captured at the conceptual level. Future work involves the extension of the modeling language to specify security features and integrity validation of the navigational model with respect to the other elements of the conceptual model.

References

1. Special Issue on Personalization. *Communications of the ACM*, 43(8), 2000.
2. Bonifati A., Ceri S., Fraternali P., and et al. Building Multi-device, Content-Centric Applications Using WebML and the W3I3 Tool Suite. In *19th International Conference on Conceptual Modeling (ER'00)*, Salt Lake City, USA, 2000. Springer-Verlag.
3. Kappel G., Retschitzegger W., and Schwinger W. Modeling Customizable Web Applications - A Requirement's Perspective. In *Proc. of Kyoto International Conference on Digital Libraries: Research and Practice*, November 2000.
4. Rossi G., Schwabe D., and Guimaraes R. Designing personalized web applications. In *Proc. of the WWW10*, Hong Kong, May 2001.
5. Object Management Group. Unified Modeling Language Specification Version 1.4 draft. Technical report, www.omg.org, February 2001.
6. Jacobson I., Christerson M., Jonsson P., and Overgaard G. *Object Oriented Software Engineering, a Use Case Driven Approach*. Addison -Wesley. Reading, Massachusetts, 1992.
7. Koch N. and Wirsing M. Software engineering for adaptive hypermedia applications. In *3rd Workshop on Adaptive Hypertext and Hypermedia*, 2001.
8. De Troyer O. and Leune C. WSDM: A user-centered design method for Web sites. In *Proc. of the 7th International World Wide Web Conference*, 1997.
9. Pastor O., Insfrán E., Pelechano V., Romero J., and Merseguer J. OO-Method: An OO Software Production Environment Combining Conventional and Formal Methods. In *9th Conference on Advanced Information Systems Engineering (CAiSE'97)*, pages 145–159, Spain, June 1997. Springer-Verlag.
10. Pastor O., Gómez J., Insfrán E., and Pelechano V. The OO-Method Approach for Information Systems Modelling: From Object-Oriented Conceptual Modeling to Automated Programming. In *Information Systems*, volume 26(7), pages 507–534, 2001.
11. Pastor O., Abrahao S., and Fons J. J. Object-oriented approach to automate web applications development. In *2nd International Conference on Electronic Commerce and Web Technologies (EC-Web'01)*, Munich, Germany, Septiembre 2001. Springer-Verlag.
12. IBM High-Volume Web site team. Web Site Personalization. January 2000.

On Evaluating Adaptive Systems for Education

Rosa Arruabarrena, Tomás A. Pérez, J. López-Cuadrado, J. Gutiérrez,
and J.A. Vadillo

Dpto. de Lenguajes y Sistemas Informáticos, Universidad del País Vasco (UPV-EHU)
Apdo. 649. 20080 San Sebastián, Spain
{jiparsar,jippefet,jiplocuj,jipgusej,jipvazoj}@si.ehu.es
http://www.ji.si.ehu.es/groups/hyper/

Abstract. In this paper we have gathered some interesting techniques to evaluate educative systems. Our main purpose is to evaluate HEZINET, an adaptive hypermedia system for education available commercially. Therefore, we also include a system evaluation plan to identify which types and techniques of evaluation will be needed in order to accomplish it.

1 Introduction

HEZINET is an Adaptive Hypermedia System [1] to learn Basque language. It automatically compiles exercises adapted to the concepts covered by the nodes that the student has already visited using the Item Response Theory and AI techniques [2]. The system has been validated and more than 2000 copies have been sold by now. However, we think that we can improve HEZINET. In order to do that, we have planned to perform different evaluations. At the moment we consider two uses of the system that we want to differentiate. On the one hand, the system is used as a distance learning system available on Internet to the subscribed students (we will call it HEZINET-D for short). On the other hand, it is also being used in intranets by students in Basque academia as an extra support to the traditional Basque classes (we will call HEZINET-C for short).

Until now, we have already made a usability test using surveys. The conclusions lead to some changes of location of functionality in the interface and to include some other contents to adapt to very beginners in Basque [3]. Now, together with the company that sells HEZINET we are interested in evaluating the effectiveness of the system and the advantages of the adaptation it provides [4].

This paper presents a wide study of strategies for software validation, types of evaluation to be considered when assessing computer assisted learning and concrete techniques to perform them. More detailed techniques are presented in [5]. A detailed overview on techniques that focus mainly on adaptation can be found in [6]. Finally, we present a plan to evaluate both versions of HEZINET.

2 Validation Strategies

Software validation focuses on demonstrating that programs meet their requirements. We call the processes that check this *validation strategies*. In [7], several validation strategies are presented, such as (a) *Proofs of Correctness,* that consist of validating and verifying programs using formal proofs of correctness; and (b) *Criterion Based Validation,* that is commonly used in software engineering (here the system is considered successful if it displays no major inadequacies within its intended application environment); (c) *Expert Review,* in which a person (the expert) observes the whole system, parts of it and/or its behaviour and identifies its deficiencies; (d) *Certification,* that is based on techniques for software quality and deterministic rules; (e) *Empirical Proofs,* that use experience of user with the system as a measure.

3 Evaluation

The evaluation of an educational system is a process of data gathering to determine the quality or the value of the instruction, its weaknesses and its strengths [8]. In [7,9,10] different dimensions of evaluation of such systems are presented. Two of them are the *Evaluation Paradigms,* that monitor what the evaluation goals are and the *Evaluated Elements* that classify those parts of the educational system to be assessed. Both are presented in detail in the following paragraphs.

There are mainly three evaluation paradigms: (1) *Formative Evaluation,* which is oriented to detect weak points at early stages of the development of the product in order to modify and improve it; (2) *Summative Evaluation,* that addresses punctual assessments of effectiveness of the finished application. The evaluation parameters are goals, benefits and costs; (3) *Integrative Evaluation,* which measures the level of integration between the educational software and other learning materials and methods into the context overall.

If one looks at the elements being observed, three kinds of evaluation could be distinguished: (1) *Internal Evaluation* that implies that the system itself is assessed (for instance, different components of the system can be evaluated, such as the architecture, the intermediate processes, as well as the behaviours of and the relations among the previous); (2) *External Evaluation,* that means that only elements out of the learning system are assessed, such as, student achievements or the affective impact of the system; (3) *Global Evaluation,* that evaluates components and impact on users.

4 Evaluation Techniques

Evaluation techniques are concrete methods to carry out the validation of the system. Four most common ones are [10,11]: (1) <u>*Comparison*</u>: is based on comparing the characteristics of the system versus some standard or other system (for example, there are methods, such as *golden standard, theoretical corroboration, empirical corrobo-*

ration, duplication, Turing test, sensitivity analysis and *benchmarking*). (2) <u>Contact with users</u> whose objective is to collect data about how the user interacts with the system, his/her behaviour and attitude (for instance, one can use *interviews*, *surveys*, *questionnaires*, *focus groups*, *nominal groups*, and *tests*). (3) <u>Data analysis,</u> that consists on reviewing, studying and assessing groups of data about certain characteristics. The information collected, processed and reported should be systematically reviewed and handled, and if any errors found, those should be corrected [12]. (4) <u>Pilot testing</u> which involves studying the performance of the system with potential end users. Depending on the number of users that are evaluated, we distinguish *one-to-one testing*, *small-group testing*, *field testing* and *beta testing*.

5 Evaluation of HEZINET

To evaluate the effectiveness of both versions of HEZINET and taking into account [6,13,14], we have established a plan to: (1) improve the tools associated to the system; (2) assure that the adaptation results in better performance; (3) check the impact of the system as a motivating element of learning; (4) attract users affectivity and retain the interaction with them as long as possible; (5) achieve excellent performance of students from the knowledge acquisition point of view, either using the system alone or transferring this acquisition to other contexts different from the computer; (6) guarantee that the system does not mislead students, independently from their computational skills, and that students can locate the desired contents either in HEZINET or in other related pedagogical material available.

We planned to perform several interface evaluation loops (internal summative evaluation) to measure different features. Although it could be considered formative, because the results will improve the product, we consider that the product has been already developed, and that we are working on a new version of the system.

The plan is to create two groups of students (those involved with HEZINET-D and the ones with HEZINET-C). First, we check how students use the elements of the interface by means of (1) questionnaires detect weak points of the interface; (2) contacts with experts in Human Computer Interaction for alternative solutions to the identified problems and (3) empirical corroboration to choose the best prototype by means of (4) pilot testing on both populations. Therefore, our aim is to check if the new design solves the problems detected without interfering the rest of users. Once the new interface is validated, and if it were required, it will be integrated into a new version.

To assess the affective impact of HEZINET, we will use open-ended questionnaires, in which users should indicate which elements are more helpful and pleasant. This evaluation (external and summative) could result in a reorganisation of the contents or in an inclusion of more multimedia courseware.

To evaluate the system's effectiveness, we are interested in finding the differences among the learning results obtained from three populations: students from HEZINET-D, from HEZINET-C and from those that learn attending regular classes at school but without any tool of this sort. In order to conduct this (external summative) evaluation, we should analyse the user model. We will compare the data obtained from each population to check if any type of correlation among them exists. Concretely, whenever it would be possible, we will handle data from the system logs, from lists of results in tests completed at schools, in an anonymous way, and from the list of marks obtained in official tests of linguistic capability. As a result of the analysis, the hypotheses that correspond will be established.

To verify the suitability of HEZINET-C within an institution like an academy of languages, it is important to assess whether the educational methods include the application as one more tool inside the classes or as an additional supporting service. We will conduct an (external integrative) evaluation using (1) interviews to students and teachers and (2) data gathering by direct observation.

We consider that it is very complicated to evaluate the integration of HEZINET-D students and the learning material they may handle. Nevertheless, we could give some advice about the work environment for a good learning.

6 Conclusions

Although it is not usual to evaluate systems after they are already in use, the goals of the education can vary and, perhaps, it is necessary to make certain adjustments to the initial proposed topics.

It is important not only to evaluate the system but also to value the integration within the context where the learning will take place. Some synergies can be obtained thanks to the integration, which can do the system's potential be even higher than the expected one if the application were considered only separately.

In this paper we have presented a wide study of types of evaluations that appear in educational systems. In the same way, it focuses on, possibly, the most interesting elements to conduct an evaluation of an educational adaptive hypermedia system. We have also discussed different goals we can consider and the system elements on which centre the study. Moreover, we also report about the techniques to be used to obtain a successful evaluation. Among these techniques, types of evaluations and strategies we have picked out the most interesting ones to evaluate HEZINET.

Future work, as well as conducting the proposed evaluation plan, includes projects to adapt HEZINET to other languages such as Spanish and French, since the system is successful.

References

1. Brusilovsky, P. (2001). "Adaptive Hypermedia". User Modeling and User-Adapted Interaction.Special Issue on: Ten Year Anniversary Issue 11(1/2): 87-110
2. Pérez, T.A., López, R., Gutiérrez, J., González, A.: Learning Basque in a Distance-adaptive way. Computers and Education in the 21st Century. Kluwer Academic Publishers, Dordrecht, The Nederlands (2000) 251-262

3. Villamañe, M., Gutiérrez, J., Arruabarrena, R., Pérez, T.A., Sanz-Lumbier, S., Sanz-Santamaría, S., López-Cuadrado, J., Vadillo, J.A.: Use and Evaluation of HEZINET; A System for Basque Language Learning . In: Lee, C.-H., Lajoie, S., Mizoguchi, R., Yoo, Y.D., du-Boulay, B. (eds). Proceedings of the 9th International Conference on Computers In Education (ICCE/SchoolNet2001), Seoul (South Korea) (2001)
4. Karagiannidis, C. and D. G. Sampson (2000). Layered Evaluation of Adaptive Applications and Services. International Conference on Adaptive Hypermedia and Adaptive Web-Based Systems: AH2000, Trento (Italy), Springer-Verlag Berlin Heidelberg.
5. Arruabarrena, R., T. A. Pérez, et al. (2001). Compendio de técnicas para evaluación de sistemas hipermedia adaptativos. Simposium Internacional de Informática Educativa, SIIE, Viseu, Portugal.
6. Weibelzahl, S.: Evaluation of Adaptive Systems. UM2001: Proceedings of the eighth International conference on User Modeling, Springer: Berlin (2001)
7. Mark, M.A., Greer, J.E.: Evaluation Methodologies for Intelligent Tutoring Systems. International Journal of Artificial Intelligence in Education, 4(2/3) (1993) 129-153
8. Tessmer, M.: Planning and Conducting: Formative Evaluations. Kogan Page Limited. London (1993)
9. Draper, S.W., Brown, M.I., Henderson, F.P., McAteer, E.: Integrative evaluation: an emerging role for classroom studies of CAL. Computers and Education, 26, (1-3) (1996) 17-32
10 Murray, T.: Formative Qualitative Evaluation for "Exploratory" ITS Research. International Journal of Artificial Intelligence in Education, 4(2/3) (1993) 179-207
11 Harvey, J.: LTDI Evaluation Cookbook. Learning Technology Dissemination Initiative. Edinburgh (1999)
12 Frechtling, J., Sharp, L.: User-Friendly Handbook for Mixed Method Evaluations. NSF, Arlington, VA (1997)
13 Chin, D. N.: Empirical Evaluation of User Models and User-Adapted Systems. User Modeling and User-Adapted Interaction 11(1-2) (2001) 181-194
14 Shute, V.J., Regian, W.: Principles for Evaluating Intelligent Tutoring Systems. International Journal of Artificial Intelligence in Education, 4(2/3) (1993) 245-271

Recommending Internet-Domains Using Trails and Neural Networks

Tobias Berka, Wernher Behrendt, Erich Gams, and Siegfried Reich

Salzburg Research - SunTREC
Jakob-Haringer-Strasse 5/III
5020 Salzburg
AUSTRIA
{tberka, wbehrendt, egams, sreich}@salzburgresearch.at

Abstract. This paper discusses the use of artificial neural networks, trained with patterns extracted from trail data, as recommender systems. Feed-forward Multilayer-Perceptrons trained with the Backpropagation Algorithm were used to assign a rating to pairs of domains, based on the number of people that had traversed between them. The artificial neural network constructed in this project was capable of learning the training set to a great extent, and showed good generalizational capacities.

1 Introduction

In today's information society, people are faced with the problem of navigating information spaces every day. This creates a need for effective navigational aids.

Recommender systems provide means for assisting users in the decision making process (for a discussion of recommender systems see [5]). These systems are the technical response to the fact that we frequently rely on other peoples' experience when confronted with a field where we have little or no knowledge. It is a recent development to view the process of navigation in the Internet not as an isolated activity of a single user, but to make the combined knowledge of individual users available to others.

The notion of a *trail* is an established concept in the field of hypertext navigation. A trail is a sequence of *trailmarks*, each consisting of a *node* (representing a document), the *activity* performed by the *user* and other properties such as *time* and *duration*.

$$Trailmark = (node, activity, time, duration, user)$$

For a concise definition of trails and trail-based systems see [3].

The recommender system described in this article has been developed for the *Trailist* research project, as proposed in [4], which aims at assisting the user in navigation with a variety of trail based systems. These system are unified in the *TrailBlazer* framework, an agent based platform for integrating various components addressing trail assessment, recommending and linking the platform into the users' applications. We used an early stage of this framework for prototyping.

If we focus on the documents in a set of trails, they form a "universe of navigational behaviour" for the respective community, consisting of n documents. These documents reside in k Internet-domains. For our purpose of developing a recommender system which is handling the "What's Related" problem from a trail based approach, we have a significant reduction of complexity if we reduce the trail induced dependencies between documents to dependencies between domains (since $k \ll n$). Once these domain dependencies have been established we can reduce the relationship between two documents, which are to be compared, to the domains, in which they are residing, thus increasing the probability of hitting a part within the knowledge base.

We take a somewhat different approach of constructing a recommender system than the classical collaborative filtering algorithms (see e.g. [1]) by using Artificial Neural Networks, or ANNs, to extract information about rules in trails. This approach utilizes a characteristic property of ANNs, which is the distributed encoding of information in the weights of the connections. The hypothesis is that the ANN will be able to generalize over the set of domain pairs, thus being capable of rating and recommending appropriate target domains.

2 Using ANNs for Comparative Internet-Domain Name Rating

The ANNs used for our experiments were all feed-forward Multilayer-Perceptrons trained with the Backpropagation Algorithm (as proposed in [6]). They were designed and trained using the Stuttgart Neural Net Simulator (SNNS v 4.2, see http://www-ra.informatik.uni-tuebingen.de/SNNS/).

We used proxy access logs as an initial source of trail data. We extracted all successful GET accesses of the research and development team of an IT enterprise and split them into (anonymous) user trails. These user trails were then analyzed in order to generate training data as described below:

If $N(d_1, d_2)$ is the number of times the domain names d_1 and d_2 appear as neighbors in a trail, then the relation rating r computes as follows:

$$r(d_1, d_2) = \left(1 - \frac{1}{1 + N(d_1, d_2)}\right)^n,$$

where n has to be adjusted to sufficiently stretch the output interval for a better differentiation between the results. If the function s assigns the binary encoding to every pair of domain names, a learning task L is defined as follows:

$$L = (\ (s(d_1), s(d_2))\ ,\ r(d_1, d_2)\ )$$

The learning behaviour of the ANN suggests monthly re-training update steps. Since the training sets represent a statistic evaluation of the trail data of an observation period, too short update steps will not allow the generation of representative training sets. Too long update steps would result in too large training sets, which implies unacceptable learning times. The ANN was always initialized randomly before re-training to avoid that the algorithm gets trapped in local minima. We extracted some 30,000 training tasks per monthly log file. After training with the training set generated from one month, the ANN correctly classified some 86.5% of this training set. The same net correctly classified as much as 84.5% of the training set generated from the following month, even though these training sets only contain 15.1% of equivalent domain name pairs. This suggests a reasonable generalizational capacity, though further analysis will be necessary to study the interpolation and extrapolation behaviour.

3 Experiments

In order to test the ANN, we integrated a sidebar into Netscape 6.2 to display the recommender's results in a user-friendly manner, and used a breadth-first traversal in the hypergraph-neighborhood of the current HTML document to obtain a search space, an algorithm which is time consuming. It is obvious that the response times may vary greatly based on the speed of the Internet connection and the performance of the user's computer.

First test runs performed by ten users with varying IT skills and educational backgrounds with the prototype of the *TrailBlazer* framework indicated that the algorithm's time consumption is acceptable, if it can be used in a "single shot" manner, being launched by the user to find related domains to the current HTML document. Another important issue is the presentation of the algorithm's results. Since the algorithm parses a great number of documents, simply displaying the domain name or title of the HTML document residing at that address may lack transparency, a problem which can be avoided by presenting the results in a manner similar to search engines (by displaying link target title, meta-data or excerpts).

The advantage of the algorithm is that it can exploit the generalizational capability of the ANN, and thus operate on unknown and yet uncharted regions of the net that are not part of the knowledge base, which clearly distinguishes it from other approaches to the "What's Related" - problem (see e.g. [2]).

4 Perspectives

Further features of the system will incorporate other methods of search-space generation. These algorithms will be based on user trails, bookmarks, browsing history, link databases, web connectivity charts, search engine results and other sources of URLs, and thus Internet-domains, and will provide a significant increase in system performance. Due to the fact, that we were "short of trail data" at this early stage of the Trailist project, and had not yet connected the system to existing online databases, we had to generate the hyper-graph neighborhood of an HTML-document seed by hypertext parsing, even though it is an extremely time consuming way of search-space generation, and loses the content independence of the trail-based approach.

Another possible use of the ANN, besides recommending related domains, could be part of a "distance measurement system" for trailmarks, which could be useful for trail selection in a certain radius of the current document, thus increasing the probability of encountering other trails in the process of hypermedia navigation. The ANN would be performing the distance measurement on the domain name level of the trailmarks' nodes.

Summarizing, we have shown how ANNs trained with patterns extracted from user trails can be used to recommend Internet-domains, described the first experiments and outlined future extensions of the system. Even though the behaviour of the ANN has to be studied more thoroughly, with a special focus on the interpolation and extrapolation behaviour on partly or totally unknown Internet-domain pairs, first results indicate that the system is able to operate on yet unknown domains.

Acknowledgements

This work has been supported in part by the Austrian *Fonds zur Förderung der wissenschaftlichen Forschung* (FWF) under grant No. P14006-INF.

References

1. John S. Breese, David Heckerman, and Carl Kadie. Empirical analysis of predictive algorithms for collaborative filtering. In *Proceedings of the Fourteenth Conference on Uncertainty in Artificial Intelligence*, pages 43–52, July 1998.
2. Jeffrey Dean and Monika R. Heinzinger. Finding related pages in the world wide web. In *Proceedings of the Eigth World-Wide Web Conference*, pages 1467–1479, 1999.
3. Siegfried Reich, Leslie A. Carr, David C. DeRoure, and Wendy Hall. Where have you been from here? Trails in hypertext systems. *ACM Computing Surveys — Symposium on Hypertext (published as electronic supplement)*, 31(4), December 1999.
4. Siegfried Reich and Erich Gams. Trailist - focusing on document activity for assisting navigation. In *Proceedings of the Twelfth ACM Conference of Hypertext and Hypermedia*, pages 29–30, August 2001.
5. Paul Resnick and Hal R. Varian. Recommender systems. *Communications of the ACM*, 40(3):56–58, March 1997.
6. D. Rumelhart, G. Hinton, and J. McClelland. Learning internal representations, 1986.

Learning Grammar with Adaptive Hypertexts: Reading or Searching?

Angela Brunstein, Jacqueline Waniek, Anja Naumann, and Josef F. Krems[1]

Technische Universität Chemnitz, Institut für Psychologie
Allgemeine und Arbeitspsychologie, D-09107 Chemnitz, Germany
{Angela.Brunstein,Jacqueline.Waniek,Anja.Naumann,Josef.Krems}@phil.tu-chemnitz.de

Abstract. Using adaptive hypertext as a learning tool, the present study addresses the question of the effects of different processing goals, especially the goal of general *reading* a hypertext as opposed to the goal of *searching* for specific information, on learning content and skills at English grammar. Twenty students with German as mother tongue processed the present continuous chapter of the Chemnitz InternetGrammar. It has been shown that *readers* answer a higher amount of questions about details and, more importantly, they answer them in more detail than *searchers*. Nevertheless, *searchers* tend to produce more elaborated answers to complex questions than *readers*. Both groups performed better on skill tests after the session, showing no effect of the performed task. Based on this experimental evidence, the requirements on adaptive learning tools are discussed.

1 Introduction

Adaptive hypertext has some interesting properties that make it suitable as a learning tool [1], e.g. it's possibility to adapt the lecture online to the learner. In the domain of foreign language education web based systems exist, that provide features beyond conventional learning material, striving to impart declarative and procedural aspects. For example, the Chemnitz InternetGrammar (http://www.tu-chemnitz.de/phil/InternetGrammar) combines grammatical rules, actual examples from politics and grammar exercises adapted to the proficiency of the learner.

It is often reported that the processing goal is an essential factor for navigating and learning with hypertext, e.g. in [2]. Also, the influence of the learner's goal sometimes dominates the influence of hypertext design [3,4, but 5]. Or it is at least postulated that different forms of design may be appropriate for different goals [6]. So the study of Dee-Lucas and Larkin [7] has shown that a high degree of segmentation of the hypertext led to a deeper understanding of the content while a low degree of segmentation led to a broader knowledge with subjects searching for details and solving problems.

---

[1] This study was supported by German Research Foundation Grant KR 1057.

It is assumed here that the guidance of different instructions associated with more or less specific goals is responsible for reported effects of both goals and interaction between goal and design by constraining the mental representation of the content.

Two plausible goals for using hypertext systems are *reading* chapters of a learning system and *searching* for details within them. *Reading* a hypertext without specific instruction requires to decide which information is essential. However, there are only few navigation decisions. S*earching* for details within the hypertext requires to decide where to go next to find the desired information. However, *searchers* do not have to separate central and secondary information already given by the task [7].

Therefore *readers* should develop a broader mental representation of the content and searchers should demonstrate a deeper understanding of the content [4]. Therefore *readers* should answer more factual questions in more detail. In contrast, *searchers* should answer questions in less detail altogether. However, they should answer complex questions more completely. This pattern should be shown only for declarative knowledge since the specific *searching* instruction focuses on rules and not on skill acquisition. So the benefit of the hypertext should be the same for *searchers* and *readers* in respect to application of the learned facts.

2 Methods

20 students of the Chemnitz University of Technology took part in the study. All students were native speakers of German. On average they solved 10 out of 21 items of a performance test on English grammar before processing the text.

One chapter dealing with the present continuous of the Chemnitz InternetGrammar was adapted to the experimental setting. Learning the present continuous is a challenging task for German students, since the German language lacks a verbal representation of the feature (+continuous).

The hypertext was created using Hypercard 2.4.1. The stack contained 75 cards for rules, examples and exercises. The headings of the topics were presented as a navigation tool on the left side of each card. Tabs above link the card to the corresponding rules', examples' or exercises' card. Buttons below lead respectively to the previous and next card.

The study was conducted on iMacs with 64 MB RAM. Factual knowledge was measured by a questionnaire consisting of 24 detailed questions, skill level was measured by performance tests each consisting of 14 items. The questionnaires were presented as paper and pencil tests.

All subjects processed the chapter for 30 minutes and navigated freely within the hypertext. The time seems to be enough to read all cards once, but it doesn't prove to be sufficient to get all details.

The study was conducted in group-sessions of up to six subjects at a time. The *searching* group of 10 subjects was instructed to answer the questions corresponding to the text online. The *reading* group was instructed to process the chapter to learn about the present continuous and afterwards to answer the questions by recall. Both groups performed a skill test before and after processing the chapter. Altogether a session lasted about one hour.

3 Results

Factual Knowledge. As expected, *readers* answered a higher amount of detailed questions than *searchers*. The former on average answered 21 out of 24 questions, while the latter had an average of 14 answers. This difference is statistically significant: $F(1,32) = 14.65$, $p < 0.001$. Interestingly, missing data occurred more often within the second half of the questionnaire for the *searchers* (10 at the beginning, 4 at the end) but not for the *readers* (each 11) ($F(1,32) = 9.95$, $p < 0.001$).

Also as predicted the *readers* answered detailed questions more accurately than the *searchers* according to the number of answers ($F(1,16) = 10.59$, $p < 0.005$). The *readers* attained an average of 19 marks out of 48, whereas the *searcher* reached only 13 marks. Looking only at the answers where the subjects report all necessary details, the effect disappears: In this case the *readers* gave a complete answer in 7 out of 24 cases while the *searchers* did so in 9 cases.

Skills. Both groups performed better after processing the chapter (66% of the items answered correctly) than before (56% of the items answered correctly) ($F(1,16) = 4.16$, $p < 0.05$). The processing goal had no influence whatever on this gain ($F(1,16) = 0.44$). However, subjects performed better only in respect to hits (correctly inserted verb forms), but not in respect to correct rejected verb forms. *Readers* and *searchers* on average gained 29% and 13% respectively ($F(1,16) = 7.62$, $p < 0.01$) in respect to hits. The difference between readers and searchers was not remarkable ($F(1,16) = 1.13$, $p = 0.31$). In respect to correct rejections subjects performed at a level of 77% correct answers before and 76% after processing the continuous chapter.

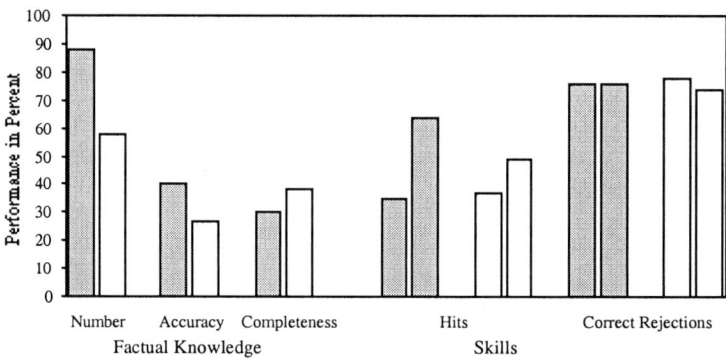

Fig. 1. Performance of *readers* (dark columns) and *searchers* (light columns) on *factual knowledge* and *skills test* in percent. Factual knowledge is illustrated by the number of answers, accuracy and completeness of answers. Skill level is illustrated by hits before and after processing and correct rejections before and after processing of the chapter.

4 Discussion

Discussing intelligent and adaptive educational systems is usually aimed at adapting the system to the learner. Therefore it is essential to characterize constraints on the learner's behavior as precisely as possible, e.g. the processing goal.

This study has shown that knowledge acquisition is affected by goals even with exactly the same hypertext design: *Readers* answered more factual questions in more detail while *searchers* tended to give more complete answers. There was no difference between both groups with respect to acquired skills. The subjects improved their hit rate but not their rejection rate.

For adaptivity in eLearning the results show the following: First, it can be useful not only to manipulate the appearance of the system but also to guide learners through the material by instruction relevant to their goals.

Second, the learning system should adapt itself to the type of relevant knowledge and to the complexity of desired information. That concerns adaptive sequencing, presentation and navigation.

Third, the acquired knowledge doesn't need to develop consistently as seen with performance tests. This means that there is a need for segmenting and differentiation of the given feedback for problem solving and solution support.

And last, adaptive systems should manage omissions differently depending on if they indicate lack of knowledge or insufficient time management. So they should offer more information for hard tasks and less information for time problems.

Altogether, this study shows differentiated effects of the learner's goal on knowledge acquisition and the need for intelligent guidance by an adaptive learning system.

References

1. Brusilovsky, P.: Adaptive and Intelligent Technologies for Web-based Education. Künstliche Intelligenz, Vol. 4/99. arenDTap Verlag, Bremen (1999) 19-25
2. Chen, C., Rada, R.: Interacting with Hypertext: A Meta-Analysis of Experimental Studies. Human-Computer-Interaction **11** (1996) 125-156
3. Foltz, P.W.: Comprehension, Coherence, and Strategies in Hypertext and Linear Text. In: Rouet, J.F., Levonen, J.J., Dillon, A.P., Spiro, R.J. (eds.): Hypertext and Cognition. Erlbaum, Hillsdale, NJ (1996) 109-136
4. Wiley, J.: Supporting Understanding through Task and Browser Design. Proceedings of the Twenty-third annual Conference of the Cognitive Science Society. Erlbaum, Hillsdale, NJ (2001) 1136-1141
5. Shapiro, A.M.: The Effect of Interactive Overviews on the Development of Conceptual Structure in Novices Learning from Hypermedia. Journal of Educational Multimedia and Hypermedia **9** (2000) 57-78
6. Dee-Lucas, D.: Instructional Hypertext: Study strategies for different types of learning tasks. Proceedings of the ED-MEDIA 96. AACE, Charlottesville, VA (1996)
7. Dee-Lucas, D., Larkin, J.H.: Hypertext Segmentation and Goal Compatibility: Effects on Study Strategies and Learning. Journal of Educational Multimedia and Hypermedia **9** (1999) 279-313

SIGUE: Making Web Courses Adaptive

Cristina Carmona, David Bueno, Eduardo Guzman, and Ricardo Conejo

Departamento de Lenguajes y Ciencias de la Computación
Universidad de Málaga
{cristina,bueno,guzman,conejo}@lcc.uma.es

Abstract. Most of the information of the WWW is not adaptive, rather it is dispersed and disorganized. On the other hand, the creation of an adaptive course is a complex task. SIGUE is an author tool that makes possible to build adaptive courses using existing web pages. This means that if there is a lot of information on the web about the same topic the author doesn't have to design the content of a specific course, he can reuse these pages to build his own course, taking the best pages for the concepts he wants to explain. The author can also construct adaptive courses reusing previously non-adaptive ones. SIGUE provides an enhanced interface for the student, controls his interaction, and annotates the visited links in a student model.

1 Introduction

Nowadays, there are many tutorials on the WWW that let students acquire knowledge on a specific subject. Most of them are not adaptive. Because of the freedom and the disorganization of the Web, a user can navigate freely in the pages of a course, and even in pages not related with the course. These problems have been stated several times and have been clearly summarized in [1], which points out four main problems: Disorientation, Cognitive overload, Narrative flow, and Content readiness. One of the characteristics that make a tutorial system adaptive is the possibility of modifying the sequencing or presentation of the course for each user according to their knowledge or preferences. Also the ability to recommend which unit they should do next. In this article we present SIGUE. This system is an author tool on the Web that can convert courses that weren't adaptive into adaptive ones. The original course could be a set of static pages build in as a course or existing pages from different sources. This lets authors make courses with the best information on the Web about a subject. SIGUE provides a student's interface that assists the students with adaptive tools when they navigate through the web pages. Another aspect of adaptivity is the multilingual interface of SIGUE, currently available in Spanish and English. SIGUE can also be integrated as a component of MEDEA [2]. MEDEA is an open system to develop Intelligent Tutorial Systems. It is composed of independent educative modules coordinated by a core that controls the instruction of the student. MEDEA can decide with is the best module to explain a concept in each moment. There are other modules, like SIETTE [3] which create tests to assess the estimated knowledge of the student. There are several tutorial systems on the Web that are adaptive and can guide the student through the learning process (i.e. ELM_ART [4], or Metalinks [5], just to mention a few). The main difference between these systems and SIGUE is that SIGUE has not been developed as a content authoring tool with adaptive features, but as an authoring tool to reuse previously developed non-adaptive material, turning it into adaptive material.

2 The SIGUE System

SIGUE has two main modules, the author tool (SIGUEAUTOR) and the student tool (SIGUE), which is used by the student to study the course. Both of them are accessible through a WWW interface

2.1 The Author Module (SIGUEAUTOR)

The author module lets human tutors to create their Web courses through SIGUE. The domain model of the system and the way that users can create adaptive courses are explained in the following subsections.

Domain Model. The author tool can create a course defining the domain model associated to it. For a specific course the domain model is a hierarchy of concepts. Various URLs can be associated with each concept and the relationship to other concepts can also be defined. For SIGUE two relationships have been defined: "belongs to" and "prerequisite of". This gives an idea of the order in which concepts should be visited, which is the sequence of the curriculum. The number of pages (URL) to describe a concept is unlimited. It is necessary to indicate the kind of information that each page contains (theory, examples or exercises) and the difficulty (easy, normal or hard).

Creation of Courses. Once the domain model is created and all the concepts and relations have been defined, the author has to associate pages to each concept. The authoring tool lets the user navigate freely, but supervised. The pages visited by the user are processed by a parser that modifies the links in accordance with SIGUE. The parser modifies regular links and forms. When the author finally finds an appropriate page for a concept he only has to click a button to add it to the course. The author can also define a glossary of terms for the course with synonymous. When a term defined in the glossary appears in any page of the course, a link is automatically included to show the definition of this term. Courses in SIGUE can have different modes of operation. The author decides how adaptive the course will be and must set the mode of operation accordingly. There are four predefined modes: (a) Disable all the links in the pages shown to the student. He will be able to do the course by accessing documents only through the concept tree; (b) Leave all the links of the pages, this lets users navigate freely even in pages not related to the course; (c) Enable only the links that give references to pages that belongs to the course. (d) Full adaptive. The links will be enabled according to the user model. Only those links corresponding to concepts that the user is ready to learn will be activated. To construct an adaptive course, it is necessary to define the prerequisite relationship of the concepts. It is important to remark that the author of a course in SIGUEAUTOR doesn't necessarily need to be the author of the HTML pages that he associates to his courses. One of the main ideas of this system is to reuse and compile pages that are related to a topic, but are located in different sites on the WWW, and add adaptive features to create a course with them.

2.2 The Student Module (SIGUE)

Once the course has been developed with SIGUEAUTOR, it will be available to students in SIGUE. While connected to the web through SIGUE, the student will see the hierarchical structure of concepts created by the author. Each time he selects a node he will see the main page associated with this concept. Before showing any page of the course, the HTML document is parsed and the links and submission forms are redirected to the SIGUE engine that acts as a supervisor between the user and the WWW. All links and forms are modified according to the strategy selected by the author for the course. The system will also include new references for the terms of a glossary defined by the author. If the course is fully adaptive, a student model is created for each user. In this model SIGUE stores the student's navigation path for each concept of the course. For each concept it shows two indicators. (a) The estimated background of the student visiting this concept, that is, if he's prepared or not to read it, according to previous pages that have been visited. (b) The percentage of pages related to that concept that he has already visited. SIGUE makes estimations of the knowledge based on the percentage of visited pages for each concept. So, if the percentage of URLs visited for a concept is less than the minimum the status of the concept is "empty"; if this percentage of visited pages is bigger than the maximum, the status is "full". The intermediary case is shown as "half-full". The status of a concept is associated to the percentage of pages the user has studied within a concept. This information is shown to the user by a progress bar that appears next to each concept. The level of preparation necessary for a user to visit a concept is reflected by using colors in the nodes of the concept tree. They can be green, red or orange. The color of the node is decided using the status of the prerequisites in this way: *Green*: A concept has this status when all the prerequisites are shown to have their status as "full". The user is ready to learn it. *Red*: This will be the color if at least one of the prerequisites of a concept is "empty". It indicates that the user is not ready to study the concept. *Orange*: This indication will appear when no empty prerequisites exist. Nodes with this color could be studied but finishing all the prerequisites first is recommended. The student model is updated after each interaction, every time the user visits a page. This update is reflected in the concept tree, modifying the status and color of nodes accordingly. The aim of SIGUE is to guide the student's navigation, and support it with adaptive annotation, but at the same time let him move freely through the pages of the course. This is why access to any page is permitted for the user even if this is not recommended (red). When a concept is red, it won't change its color until its prerequisites have been visited, even if the user has already visited the documents associated to this concept. The student also has the freedom to visit pages through the concept tree or through the activated links of each page. The activated links correspond to the glossary and to the recommended concepts (green). This means that if there is a link in one page to a page of a concept that is not recommended (red, orange) the authors can decide whether this link should be activated or disabled. Another important characteristic used to guide students is the inclusion of a simple planner that the student can use to get the best recommendation for the next document to view from the concept he is studying. This mechanism is designed for "two buttons users". These are the NEXT and BACK buttons. An evaluation module can replace the simple mechanism used by SIGUE, when SIGUE is used as a component of the MEDEA architecture.In this case the navigation frame provided by SIGUE is replaced by MEDEA's navigation frame. The SIGUE component receives a temporary student model each time it is activated by a call from MEDEA, and this information is used to control the links on the main page.

3 Conclusions and Future Works

The web is a great source of information, but it is dispersed and hard to find. The advantage of SIGUE is the possibility of taking the best parts of each tutorial; compiling them in the order the author thinks is best; organizing them; adding relationships and glossary terms; and providing a learning environment in which the student is always oriented because someone (the course author) has followed the path before him and has provided some marks. The author can also decide the degree of freedom that the user should have while navigating, according to the characteristics of his expected audience. The adaptive features of SIGUE can also be used to convert static tutorials into adaptive tutorials. SIGUE is an independent and adaptive component, with author and student modules that can be integrated into MEDEA. If a better measure of the knowledge is needed it can be taken from MEDEA. At present the prototype of SIGUE is fully functional and can be used freely. Future work on SIGUE will be directed towards improving the estimation of user understanding by analyzing their navigation behavior. SIGUE could also a workbench to compare the results and the satisfaction of users studying a course in an adaptive way or not. It is available for trial at http://www.lcc.uma.es/SIGUE

References

1. Murray, T. Shen, T. Piemonte, J. Condit, C. Tibedau, J.: Adaptivity for conceptual and narrative flow in hyperbooks: The Metalink system. *Adaptive Hypermedia and Adaptive Web-based system.* Lecture Notes on Computer Science 1892, Berlin (2000) 155-166
2. Trella, M., Conejo, R., Bueno, D.: MEDEA: Una arquitectura basada en componentes para el desarrollo de Sistemas Tutores Inteligentes en Internet. *CAEPIA 2001.* (2001) 469-478
3. A.Rios, E.Millán, M.Trella, J.Perez-de-la-Cruz, R.Conejo, Internet Based Evaluation System, en: *Artificial Intelligence in Education,* IOS Press, Amsterdam (1999) 387-394
4. Weber, G., Specht, M.: User Modeling and Adaptive Navigation Support in WWW-Based Tutoring Systems. *Proceedings of the Sixth International Conference on User Modeling, UM97.* Springer Wien New York (1997) 289-300
5. Henze, N. Nejdl, W.: Adaptivity in the KSB Hyperbook System. *Proceedings of the 2nd Workshop on Adaptive Systems and User Modeling on the WWW.* (1999)

An Ontology-Guided Approach to Content Adaptation in LEO: A Learning Environment Organizer

John W. Coffey

The Institute for Human and Machine Cognition
The University of West Florida
Pensacola FL 32514
jcoffey@uwf.edu

Abstract. This paper describes new capabilities of a nonlinear course presentation program entitled LEO: a Learning Environment Organizer. A Knowledge-based Instructional Assistant combines knowledge of the learner's attainment with knowledge of various attributes of the instructional media in order to make recommendations of media that might benefit the learner. This work describes an ontology to represent the basic conceptualization of the learning system, and how that representation is used to match potentially useful instructional content to student profiles. Recommendations of media are based upon multi-parameter similarity measures between media content and capability attainment.

1 Introduction

This work describes new enhancements to a program entitled LEO, a non-linear Learning Environment Organizer [6]. LEO is an advance organizer [1] that presents links to instructional media that contain content pertinent to the topic. This basic system is augmented by a Knowledge-based Instructional Assistant that exploits annotations of the content in a course and a student's emerging attainment profile in order to suggest instructional materials that might be beneficial to the student.

The approach in this work is based upon the idea of an ontology [9] for a learning environment that tracks student progress. The ontology creates a common parlance that is utilized by the various parts of the system including the testing component and the Instructional Assistant. The remainder of this paper presents a brief description of the Knowledge-based Instructional Assistant, an ontology for an instructional system that tracks student progress, and the means through which the ontology is used to map attainment deficiencies to instructional resources.

2 Recent Related Work on Adaptive Learning Systems

A substantial amount of literature exists on adaptive learning systems. Brusilovsky [3] presents a survey of adaptive educational hypermedia. He enumerates several current systems and describes adaptation in terms of adaptive navigational support and adaptive presentation. He further describes adaptation relative to a learner's knowledge, interests and individual traits. De Bra & Ruiter [7] describe a well-realized, general adaptive hypermedia engine that can be used to adapt instructional content for students. Their system, AHA!, determines user interest levels in topics and also tracks what users have read to determine preparedness for subsequent items. Castells & Macias [5] describe PEGASUS, an adaptive hypermedia modeling system that is based upon a domain-specific ontology that is enumerated by the author. Their system has a domain model that is rendered in XML that describes a semantic network of domain objects. An explicit presentation model is updated from presentation templates and the user model as the user traverses through system.

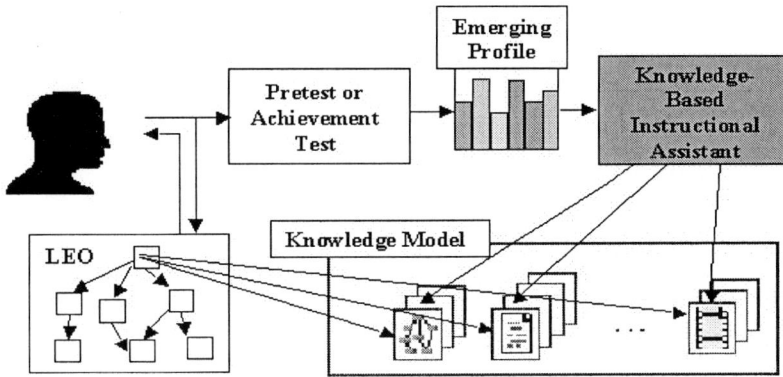

Fig. 1. The Knowledge-based Instructional Assistant.

3 A Knowledge-Based Instructional Assistant

The ideas in this work leverage the integration of LEO with the multimedia knowledge modeling software suite "CMapTools" [4]. Knowledge models created with CMapTools are comprised of many learning resources such as texts, graphics, video and web links, etc. Figure 1 presents a graphic depiction of LEO with links to a CMapTools knowledge model and with the Knowledge-based Instructional Assistant indicating recommended media. The user starts with a pretest to establish baseline knowledge for the course. The baseline is updated as the student works through the course within LEO, submitting deliverables and taking tests that are evaluated.

On the basis of the attainment profile and catalogued attributes of the instructional content, the Knowledge-based Instructional Assistant determines instructional content to recommend. The student can access recommended content through the links between topics and content in LEO itself, or from a comprehensive list of recommended resources that displays by individual topic, or by all the topics in the course.

4 An Ontology-Guided Approach to Content Adaptation

Cognitive and computer scientists borrow the notion of ontology, study of the nature of being or existence, from the philosophy field. In computer/cognitive science context, an ontology is generally held to be a formal representation of a conceptualization of a domain [8], a common parlance or vernacular for a knowledge domain.

In the modeling of an instructional system, generic attributes such as students, testing resources and learning resources form templates for domain-specific topic areas and descriptors of competencies in these topic areas. The ontology is comprised of five basic entities: *Student, Competency, Attainment, LearningResource*, and *TestResource*.

This basic representation provides a framework for domain-specific *areas of competency* and specific *dimensions of competency* within an area. Ratings for these measures can be any range that the user of the system chooses. For example, Likkert scale values on the range from 0 to 5 might be used.

5 Identifying Relevant Instructional Content

The process of matching possibly useful instructional materials to a user profile that is employed here was suggested by weighted nearest-neighbor [11] similarity measures utilized in case-based reasoning approaches. The fundamental idea is to employ a matching procedure [2] to identify a set of potentially useful instructional materials, and then to rank-order the set [10].

In an instructional system, the goal is to create matches on the basis of student strengths and weaknesses in topic areas and to suggest resources that vary along the various dimensions of competency in the area. As an example, a competency area in a Data Structures class would be an understanding of linked lists. Various competency dimensions within the area might include a theoretical understanding of the ideas surrounding the data structure, the ability to program various operations on the data structure, the ability to analyze various algorithms from code, etc.

The method described here creates matches between test questions and instructional resources. This approach is utilized to make recommendations from a simple, minimal student profile that records student performance on the questions. For questions on which the student has performed poorly, the similarity measure can be applied to find the learning resources that are most appropriate. Initially, the search space of relevant learning resources is reduced by a string match on the descriptors of the test question of interest (TR_j) and the set of resources (LR) to identify $LR' \subset LR$. A similarity measure of the following sort is then applied to assess the similarity of a given resource from LR' to the test question under consideration:

$$\text{Difference}(TR_j, LR'_k) = \sum_{i=1}^{n} WCD_i * (TR_jD_i - LR'_kD_i)^2 \quad (1)$$

In formula 1, TR_j is the *jth* TestResource, LR'_k is the *kth* Learning Resource from the string-matched subset of LR, WCD_i is the weight assigned to the *ith* competency dimension, TR_jD_i is the value of the *jth* test question with regard to competency dimension i and LR'_kD_i is the value of the *kth* learning resource with respect to competency dimension i. This analysis is a summation of squared, weighted distances between the various dimensions of competence supported by a learning resource and the same dimensions in a test question.

6 Summary and Future Work

This work describes a new approach to online course structuring and instructional content adaptation that is embodied in LEO, a Learning Environment Organizer. LEO is enhanced with an instructional assistant that suggests content that might be appropriate to a particular student. The student may access recommended materials by noting recommendations in navigational links to content materials from individual topics in the organizer or by viewing a list of suggestions pertaining to a given topic.

The adaptation approach starts with a basic ontology for common elements in an adaptive instructional domain. The approach identifies orthogonal ontological elements of content areas and dimensions of attainment within an area. The common ontology provides a generic framework within which context-specific vernacular can be mapped.

The approach described here employs a multi-parameter similarity measure to match test questions to content. This is a minimal approach that is the most subject to automation, but the least flexible. Future work will address ways to allow for a more comprehensive student profile that will allow the assessment of student attainment both across the various dimensions of an individual content area as well as across content areas on an individual attainment dimension. Also, the approach will be applied to additional knowledge domains in order to draw conclusions regarding the sorts of competency areas and dimensions that are identified.

References

1. Ausubel, D.P.: Educational Psychology: A Cognitive View. Rinehart and Winston, NY (1968)
2. Borg, I., Lingoes, J.: Construction of SSA Representations. In Multidimensional Similarity Structure Analysis. Springer-Verlag, New York: (1987)
3. Brusilovsky, P.: Adaptive Hypermedia. User Modeling and User-Adapted Interaction. Vol 11. 87-110, Kluwer Academic Publishers, The Netherlands (2001)
4. Cañas, A. J., Coffey, J. W., Reichherzer, T., Hill, G., Suri, N., Carff, R., Mitrovich, T., & Eberle, D.: El-Tech: A performance support system with embedded training for electronics technicians. *Proceedings of FLAIRS'98*, Sanibel Island, FL, (1998)
5. Castells, P., Marcias, J. J.: An Adaptive Hypermedia Presentation Modeling System for Custom knowledge Representastions. Proceedings of WebNet 2001, (2001)
6. Coffey, J.W.: LEO: A Learning Environment Organizer to accompany Constructivist Knowledge Models. Unpublished doctoral dissertation, The University of West Florida, Pensacola, FL. (2000)
7. De Bra, P., Ruiter, J.: AHA! Adaptive Hypermedia for All. Proceedings of WebNet 2001, World Conference on the WWW and Internet. Orlando, FL, October 23-27, (2001)
8. Genesereth, M.R., & Nilsson, N.J.: Logical Foundations of Artificial Intelligence. Morgan Kaufmann, San Mateo, CA (1987)
9. Gruber, T.A.: A Translation approach to Portable Ontology Specifications. Knowledge Acquisition, Vol 5 (1993) 199-220
10. Kolodner, J., Leake, D. A.: Tutorial Introduction to Case-based Reasoning . in Case-based Reasoning, Experiences, Lessons and Future Directions. D. Leake (ed.). AAAI Press, (1996)
11. Spalazzi, L.: A survey on case-based planning, AI Review, (16) 1 (2001) 3-36

A Scrutable Adaptive Hypertext

Marek Czarkowski and Judy Kay

Basser Department of Computer Science,
University of Sydney, Australia
{marek,judy}@cs.usyd.edu.au

Abstract. This paper describes Tutor/ADAPT, a working model and framework for scrutable adaptive hypertext. This enables the user to scrutinise the system to determine how the document was adapted. They are also able to control the adaptation by altering the user model at any time in the interaction. The user can see which parts of the user model have been used to control aspects, which appear in the document. The system has three major parts: an authoring tool; the web based interface; and ATML is the language used for adaptive hypertext source documents. This paper describes the user view, especially the scrutability support.

1 Introduction

This paper describes the Tutor/ADAPT framework for constructing and displaying *scrutable* hypertext. By scrutable we mean that the reader can explore the interface to determine what has been adapted. There has been considerable work in making user models accessible [1,2,3,4,5,6]. This work takes a step beyond that, making the *processes* also scrutable.

The hypertext author creates adaptive teaching material using an editor, which creates pages in the language ATML, a mark-up to HTML 4.0, which conforms to XML 1.0 [7]. Later the student can use the web-based interface to make use of the teaching materials. This is like a conventional adaptive hypertext system. The novel aspect of Tutor is that the user can scrutinise each part to see what has been customised to them.

2 System Overview

On starting a new course, users are asked questions. This very simple mechanism establishes their initial user-model. Next, students see an interface with teaching material like that shown in Figure 1. The icons across the top offer various facilities, including a course map, teacher's news page, a notes editor, glossary, the personal profile discussion room, log out and, at the far right, help. Figure 1 shows the hypertext as it would appear if a student had answered *none* to the question *How many examples would you like to see for each new concept*.

The system requires material marked up in ATML (Adaptive Teaching Mark-up Language). ATML provides a standard framework for authoring adaptive teaching hypertext material, allowing the author to include adaptive content and adaptive navigation features in the material. The author creates a course in an editor, which aids, and in some cases automates, the creation of ATML documents.

The author uses simple ATML syntax to create highly dynamic HTML content. When the user requests an ATML page, the system processes the user's profile and translates the ATML content into HTML 4.0, including the required JavaScript1.2 and CSS1.0 code which implement the dynamic HTML features. The resulting HTML is displayed in the browser.

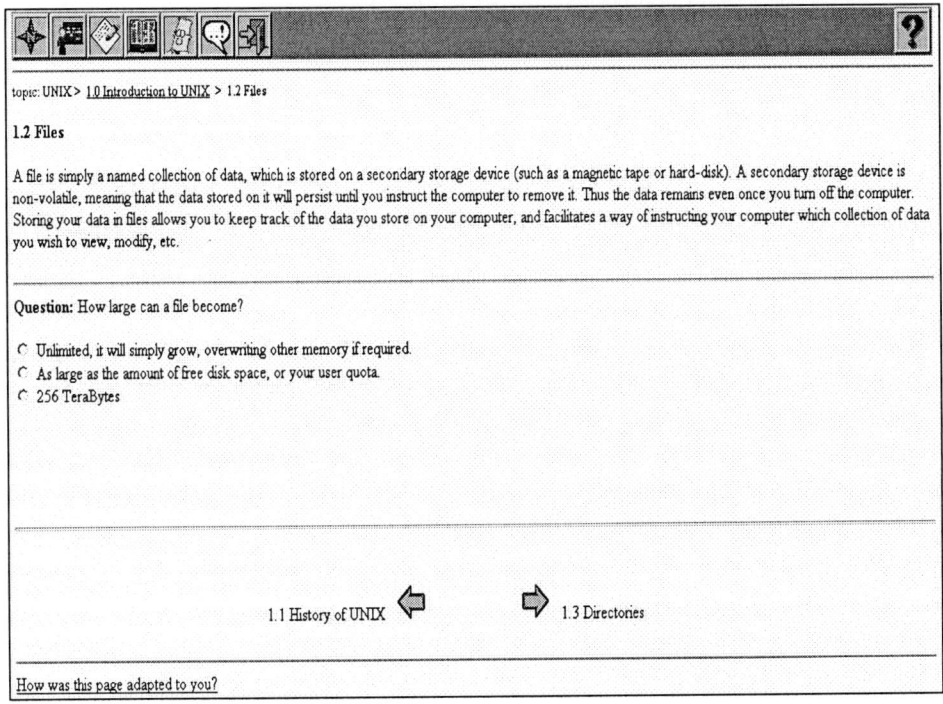

Fig. 1. Sample lesson as seen by user who does not wish to be shown examples.

3 Scrutability

At the very bottom of each page of adapted material is a link, *How was this page adapted to you?*. As in Fig. 1 this is below the navigation arrows and a horizontal line. If there has been no adaptation, this is indicated with the message *There was no adaptation of this page*. Where there has been adaptation, the bottom of the screen expands to list the set of page adaptations with a separate entry in the adaptation explanation. Each entry indicates if *content* (lesson text) or *navigation* (navigation arrows) has been *included* or *excluded*. The text is also colour coded with descriptions for content displayed in green and those for excluded content in red.

The user is able to query the system to scrutinise exactly what was included or excluded. If the user clicks on the text *[highlight]* the interface indicates the part of the page content adaptively included by highlighting the background of the relevant material in green. If the user wanted to see what they missed out on in their adapted hypertext, they select the *Show all text* hyperlink. The system reloads the page ignoring the adaptation criteria and the user profile to display all the content available on that page (see Fig. 2). The user can select *[hide explanation]* at the bottom of the screen. It then reverts to revert to the usual form as in Figure 1.

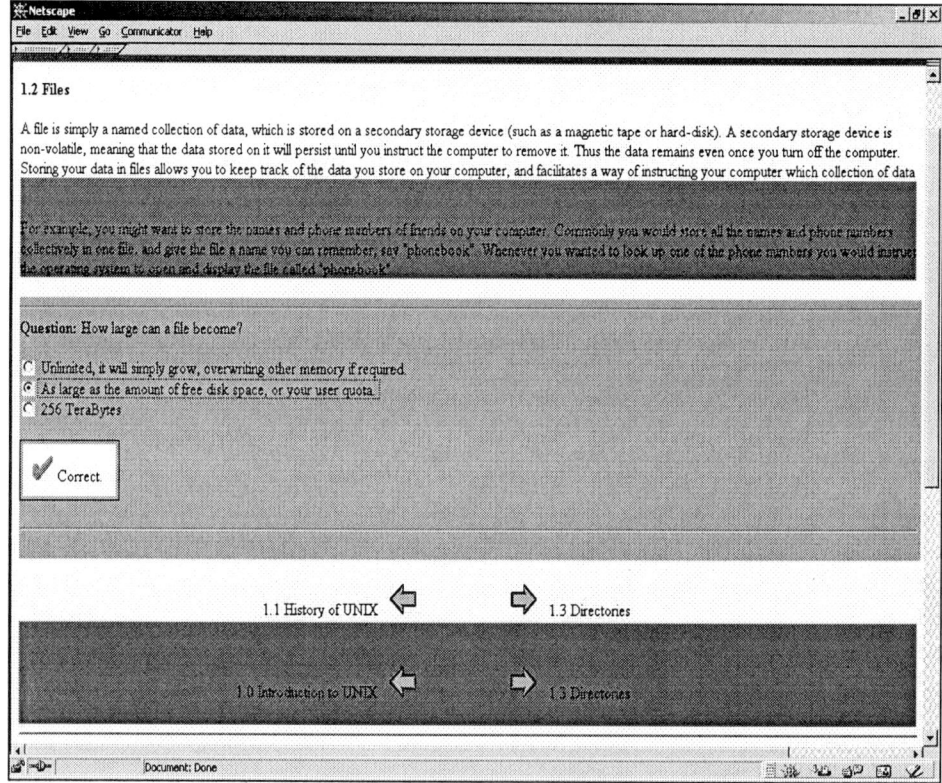

Fig. 2. This depicts the scenario where a user has activated the Show all view on the page from Fig. 1 and then clicked the provided hyperlinks to highlight the first, second and fourth adaptive sections. The first and fourth adaptive sections were excluded from the page hence are highlighted with a red background (dark grey). The second section was included and hence is highlighted with a green background (lighter grey).

4 Discussion and Conclusions

The current work extends the basic of notion of adaptive hypertext with support for *scrutability* so that the reader can determine how the document was customised for them. The current system comprises of an authoring tool to support the author of meta-hypertexts and a web interface to enable the reader to interact with their customised and scrutable hypertext. Basic explanations of the adaptivity are presented at the bottom of each page so that the user can identify which triggers caused the presentation of each adaptive element on the page. These also enable the user to see where optional material was omitted and the user model values causing this. This enables the user to scrutinise the detailed adaptation. In addition, there is support for seeing the global adaptation: the user can easily alter their profile and see the consequent hypertext pages.

This approach can be used for *what-if* experiments, enabling the user to see what the system would do if they answered user modelling questions differently. When a user does this, they can scrutinise the effect of the large grain-size.

It offers a coherent and elegant structure for the author of the adaptive, individualised hypertext material. The current trial of out system demonstrates interesting, useful, though modest adaptation and represents a foundation for continuing work in supporting and delivering scrutable, adaptive hypertext.

References

1. Corbett, A.T., Anderson, J.: Knowledge tracing: modeling the acquisition of procedural knowledge. User Modeling and User-Adapted Interaction. 4 (1995) 253—278
2. Crawford, K., Kay, J.: Metacognitive processes and learning with intelligent educational systems. In: Slezak, P., Caelli, T., Clark, R., Perspectives on Cognitive Science, Ablex (1993) 63-77
3. Fischer, G., Ackerman, D.: The importance of models in making complex systems comprehensible. In: Tauber, M.: Mental models and Human-computer Interaction 2. Elsevier (1991) 22—33
4. Höök, K., Karlgren, J., Waern, A., Dahlbeck, N., Jansson, C.G., Lemaire, B.: A glass box approach to adaptive hypermedia. User Modeling and User-Adapted Interaction 6:2-3 Kluwer (1996) 157—184
5. Paiva, A., Self, J., Hartley, R.: Externalising learner models. Proceedings of World Conference on Artificial Intelligence in Education. AACE, Washington (1995) 509—516
6. Self, J.: Bypassing the Intractable Problem of Student Modelling: Invited paper. Proceedings of the 1st International Conference on Intelligent Tutoring Systems. Montreal (1988) 18—24
7. Czarkowski, M.: An adaptive hypertext teaching system. Honours Thesis, Basser Dept of Computer Science, University of Sydney (1998)

AHA! Meets AHAM

Paul De Bra, Ad Aerts, David Smits, and Natalia Stash

Department of Computer Science
Eindhoven University of Technology
PO Box 513, NL 5600 MB Eindhoven
The Netherlands
debra@win.tue.nl

Abstract. After many years of hypertext research, the Dexter model was defined [7] to capture the features of most existing hypertext systems in a single, formal reference model. Likewise, the AHAM model [5] (based on Dexter) describes most features that are found in adaptive hypermedia systems (ahs). In the AHA! project funded by the NLnet Foundation we are extending the simple AHA system [4, 6] with the condition-action rules that were introduced in AHAM [8]. This results in a more versatile adaptation engine, with more intuitive and more powerful rules.

1 Introduction

In 1994 we started a course on Hypertext, consisting of lectures and a Web-based course text. From 1996 on the lectures were discontinued and the course text was augmented with *adaptive content and linking*. Our adaptive software later became the AHA! system [4,6], for **A**daptive **H**ypermedia **A**rchitecture. Also in 1996, Peter Brusilovsky published a survey article [2] on adaptive hypermedia systems (ahs). This article was updated in 2001 [3] to include more recent developments in this research field. The overview articles show (informally) which kinds of features are offered by the different systems. In 1999 we developed a reference model for adaptive hypermedia, called AHAM (Adaptive Hypermedia Application Model) [5]. Based on the formal Dexter model for hypermedia [7] AHAM provides a framework to express the functionality of any ahs. Hence, AHAM is not the model behind the AHA! system (as some people have asked us in the past) but rather the model behind almost every ahs. In [8] we studied the adaptation rules and the behavior of adaptive engines that can be expressed in AHAM. In this paper we describe our current efforts to bring the simple AHA! system closer to the powerful adaptation systems that AHAM suggests. This effort is part of a project, funded by the NLnet Foundation, to turn AHA! into a general-purpose (Web-based) ahs.

In Sect. 2 we briefly describe the overall architecture of the AHA! system. Section 3 discusses the new rule system and adaptive engine. Section 4 provides an outlook to the future of AHA!.

2 The AHA! System

According to Brusilovsky [2] there are two types of adaptation in ahs: *adaptive presentation* and *adaptive navigation support*. Each time the user visits a page a *user model* is updated. This user model is used to determine how the presentation of the "next" page should be adapted and which advice should be given to the user regarding the links to follow next. While some systems take sequences of pages into account, and possibly even the behavior of user groups, AHA! is one of the simpler systems that work on a page (access) by page basis. The main functions of AHA! are:

- For every user there is a user model that represents how the user relates to the Web-pages and to (higher-level) concepts. Each time a user visits a page a set of *generate rules* determines how the user model is updated. We describe these rules below.
- Each page contains (zero or more) fragments that are conditionally included in the presentation. The requirement rules for inclusion are also described below. The conditional inclusion of fragments is AHA!'s main *adaptive presentation* technique.
- For each page there is a similar requirement rule. It is used for *adaptive navigation support*. AHA! uses different colors for link anchors to indicate the "desirability" of the links. Depending on the choice of colors AHA! can be configured to use the *link hiding* technique (with black undesirable links) or the *link annotation* technique (with all links shown in visible, different colors).

The AHAM reference model proposes a rich user model, with for each page or higher level concept a set of attribute/value pairs, and with an adaptation model based on condition-action rules. The (old) AHA! system on the other hand, as described in [4, 6], has a very simple user model with for each page or concept a single numerical attribute (called *knowledge*), and with simple rules, mostly intended to describe the propagation of knowledge from pages to sections to chapters. In this paper we describe how the "new" AHA! system adopts user model and adaptation model elements introduced in the AHAM model. The result is a new AHA! that tries to preserve its initial simplicity while making the adaptation more versatile.

The "new" AHA! system uses multiple (user model) attributes per page or concept. The author of an application can choose attribute names that match what attributes are used for. It thus becomes possible to indicate e.g. *interest in* a certain concept as well as *knowledge about* a concept. Also, the attributes can have Boolean, numeric or string values.

For every page and fragment there is a *requirement* to decide whether links to the page should be shown as "desirable" or whether the fragment should be included in the presentation. The requirement is a Boolean expression in (user model) attribute values for concepts (or pages). An example, using the non-existent website on Belgian products we used in [6]:

```
beer.interest > 70 and chocolate.interest < 30
```

While browsing the site, visits to pages about beer contribute to the system's confidence that the user is interested in beer and not in chocolate. So a user who is interested in beer can be shown additional information that is hidden for chocolate lovers.

For every page or concept there is a set of *generate* rules. Each rule has a *condition* that is checked to see whether the associated *action* should be performed. (It is also possible to specify an *alternate action* to be performed when the condition is not satisfied.) Each rule is associated with an attribute of the page or concept, and the rule is "triggered" by an update to that attribute. For a page there are also rules that are triggered by an access to the page. (This is treated as an update to an `access` attribute).

The following rule expresses that when the user reads a page the "knowledge" about a concept increases by an amount that depends on a condition. Assume that the interest in beer should be high to understand everything on the page about "Duvel":

```
C:    beer.interest > 70
A:    duvel.knowledge := 100
AA:   duvel.knowledge := 35
```

As another example, the following rule, to be associated with the `interest` attribute of `beer`, expresses that if the user shows a low interest in chocolate, then any increase of the user's interest in beer will induce a small (namely 20% of that increase) decrease in interest for chocolate. If the user has already shown great interest in chocolate then reading about beer no longer affects that.

```
C:    chocolate.interest < 50
A:    chocolate.interest -= 20
```

There is no limit to the number of (condition-action) rules that can be associated with an attribute of a concept.

AHA! uses XML to represent the *generate* rules, but that syntax is too verbose to write down in this short paper. Furthermore, the actual syntax is irrelevant as we are also developing authoring tools that will hide the syntax from the author, and (mySQL) database support that will use XML only for import and export of rule sets.

3 The AHA! Adaptation Engine

When a user accesses a page the *generate* rules for (the `access` attribute of) that page are executed (as if `access` was changed from 0 to 100). AHA! distinguishes between two kinds of updates that can be defined in actions:

- *absolute*: a value, specified in the action, is assigned to an attribute of a page or concept. (symbol := used above)
- *relative*: the specified value is used as a percentage of the triggering update to be added to or subtracted from the attribute; relative updates only make sense for numerical attributes of course. (symbol += or -= used above)

The adaptation engine keeps track of which attributes of which pages or concepts are updated by rule actions, and "triggers" the execution of their associated rules. This process continues until there are no more rules to execute.

From research in active databases [1] we know that the rule execution process is not guaranteed to *terminate* and may also not be *confluent* (meaning it may generate different results depending on the order in which triggered rules are executed). In [8] we showed how such problems can be detected at authoring time.

4 Conclusions / Future Work

The "new" AHA! user model and adaptation engine greatly improve the versatility of AHA!. The extensions are based on the rule system presented in [8] for the AHAM reference model. In the future we want to bring AHA! even closer to AHAM through at least the following new features:
- links to concepts (not just pages), and a method to "select" the best page to present when following such a link;
- a way to express *generic* rules, so that rules don't need to be replicated for every page or concept they apply to.

Also, authoring tools for the concept structure and the adaptation rules will be extended with static analysis methods to warn authors of potential *termination* and *confluence* problems.

Acknowledgement

The development of the AHA! system is supported by a NLnet Foundation grant, through "Adaptive Hypermedia for All!" project (conveniently abbreviated to AHA!). More information about AHA! can be obtained at the Website http://aha.win.tue.nl/.

References

1. E. Baralis, and J. Widom. An algebraic approach to static analysis of active database rules. ACM Transactions on Database Systems, Vol. 25, nr. 3, pp. 269–332, 2000.
2. Brusilovsky, P. Methods and Techniques of Adaptive Hypermedia. User Modeling and User-Adapted Interaction, Vol. 4, pp. 1–19, Kluwer academic publishers, 1996.
3. Brusilovsky, P. Adaptive Hypermedia, User Modeling and User-Adapted Interaction, Vol. 11, nr. 1–2, pp. 87–110, Kluwer academic publishers, 2001.
4. De Bra, P., A. Aerts, G.J. Houben, and H. Wu. Making General-Purpose Adaptive Hypermedia Work. Proceedings of the AACE WebNet Conference, pp. 117–123, San Antonio, Texas, 2000.
5. De Bra, P., G.J. Houben, and H. Wu. AHAM: A Dexter-based Reference Model for Adaptive Hypermedia. Proceedings of the ACM Conference on Hypertext and Hypermedia, pp. 147–156, Darmstadt, Germany, 1999.
6. De Bra, P., and J.P. Ruiter. AHA! Adaptive Hypermedia for All. Proceedings of the AACE WebNet Conference, pp. 262–268, Orlando, Florida, 2001.
7. Halasz, F., and M. Schwartz. The Dexter Hypertext Reference Model. Communications of the ACM, Vol. 37, nr. 2, pp. 30–39, 1994.
8. Wu, H., E. De Kort, and P. De Bra. Design Issues for General-Purpose Adaptive Hypermedia Systems. Proceedings of the ACM Conference on Hypertext and Hypermedia, pp. 141–150, Århus, Denmark, 2001.

Adaptive Real Time Comment Generation for Sail Racing Scenarios

Andrea Esuli[1], Antonio Cisternino[1], Giuliano Pacini[2], and Maria Simi[1]

[1]Dipartimento di Informatica, Università di Pisa, Corso Italia 40, 56125 Pisa, Italy
{esuli, cisterni, simi}@di.unipi.it
[2]Accademia Navale di Livorno, Livorno, Italy
pacini@di.unipi.it

Abstract. We describe a comment generation subsystem developed as part of an expert authoring system for sail racing scenarios. The result of the expert system analysis is sent to a multimedia presentation subsystem composed of a 3D player and a speaker agent. Comments output by the text-to-speech component must be carefully generated so that they are concise, relevant, non repetitive and timely since they must be synchronized with the 3D animation. The comment generation process is adaptive with respect to the time available and to the user profile and preferences.

1 Introduction

As part of our work in developing intelligent tutoring systems for sail racing, we designed and implemented a system for the multimedia presentation of scenarios involving dynamic objects in general [1]. The architecture of the system, (see Fig. 1) was inspired by the simulated soccer system within the RoboCup initiative [2].
Each module is implemented as a program that interacts with other modules using a TCP connection and a text protocol.

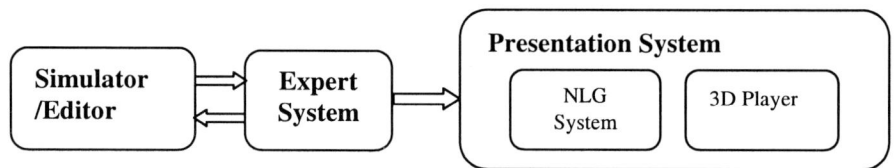

Fig. 1. The architecture of the expert authoring system

The authoring of sail scenarios is performed by means of a visual editor, working in close cooperation with a simulator of boats movements. The editor offers a number of high-level functionalities specific of the sail racing domain (such as *combining trajectories*); the simulator ensures that the dynamic scenarios comply with physical constraints. The simulation *history*, output of the *Simulation/Editor* module, consists of a stream of instantaneous snapshots describing the boats positions (bi-dimensional) and status (direction, rudder and sails).

The role of the *Expert System* module is to analyse and annotate with comments histories received by the editor, using knowledge about the racing rules. In some cases, in order to verify some conditions, the expert system needs to ask the simulator how a given hypothetical situation will possibly evolve. The expert system analysis results in a structured representation of all the facts worth commenting about, marked with their importance. The expert however is not in the position to do a detailed planning of the comment since it does not know about the rendering media, time constraints or user preferences.

The *presentation system* (see Fig. 2) consists in a 3D player that is responsible for showing the simulation and uttering the comments generated by the comment generation module. A Web browser with a VRML plug-in is used to render the virtual scene, under the control of a Java applet through the *External Authoring Interface*. The main control functions are written in Jscript. The Microsoft Agent technology is used to implement the animated character [3].

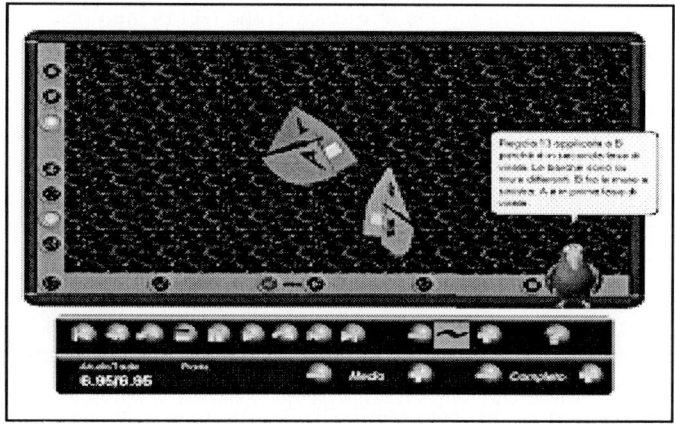

Fig. 2. Player interface

The comment generation sub-system needs to perform a complex natural language generation task in close cooperation with the visual rendering and the user. It is responsible for generating the most informative messages that can be pronounced in the available time and to pass control to the Microsoft Agent, who will output them using a text-to-speech component.

The rest of the paper will give more details about the strategy of adaptive comment generation implemented.

2 The Comment Generation Subsystem

The language generation task consists in producing meaningful natural language comments from *comment structures* provided by the expert system for each snapshot of the scenario. This process has to take into account temporal constraints imposed by the dynamics of the scene and other parameters such as the level of expertise of the users and their preferences, expressed by suitable controls in the interface.

As traditional in NL generation [4,5] this task is performed in two phases. First, a contents selection phase is performed in order to discard repetitions, select and organize the concepts to be communicated. In the second phase, concepts are rendered as natural language text [6]. This two phases however are not strictly sequential; in fact contents selection needs to be performed again, after text generation, when the time available does not allow completion of the generated comment. We regard this interplay of the contents selection and generation phases as one of the main characteristics of our approach.

2.1 Contents Selection

A comment is represented by a structure whose basic elements are *primitive facts*, represented as sentences composed of a subject (s), a predicate (p) and an object (o). Two parameters are associated to each primitive fact:
- the *importance*: a value rating the relevance of the fact in the present context;
- the *difficulty level*: specifying the language complexity class for which the fact is appropriate, ranging from a highly specialized language to an ordinary language.

Here is an example of primitive fact, represented in Jscript syntax:
`{s:"B", p:"is", o:"beyond herd to wind", i:400, d:[0,1]}`
where i is the importance value and d assigns difficulty levels to the fact.

Each comment structure is composed of a number of primitive facts related by predefined relations, namely:
- *Facts-Additional facts* (FA): additional facts are complements to the main facts
- *Facts-Explanations* (FS): explanation facts further describe main facts.
- *Cause-Effect* (CE): cause-effect relation between the two groups of facts.

The expert system produces a comment for each fired rule, thus the same primitive facts may appear in more than one comment. A pre-processing step takes care of collapsing such duplicate facts into one instance. As a consequence, facts belonging to different rules may become related.

The main task in contents selection is the selection based on the *richness level*, as selected by the user through the interface. This is based on a threshold value (similar to [7]), computed as the weighted sum of a static factor and a dynamic one. Primitive facts that have an importance level above the threshold pass the selection.

The *static factor* is a percentage, which depends on the richness of the comment, of the maximum importance value of the facts in the current snapshot. The *dynamic factor* is a percentage of the threshold value of the previous snapshot and it is used for allowing the completion of important comments at the expense of successive less important ones (Fig. 3). This aspect is strongly related to the extension strategy described next.

2.2 Comment Generation

In principle selected comments should be all presented but often this is impossible due to time constraints. The generation phase consists in a cycle where comments are progressively discarded until temporal constraints are satisfied. At each iteration two main steps are performed for comment generation:

- *Linearization*: the selected facts are ordered according to their relations in order to construct a plan of the comment sentence (*text design*).
- *Realization*: the natural language sentence is produced according to the previous linear structure (*text realization*).

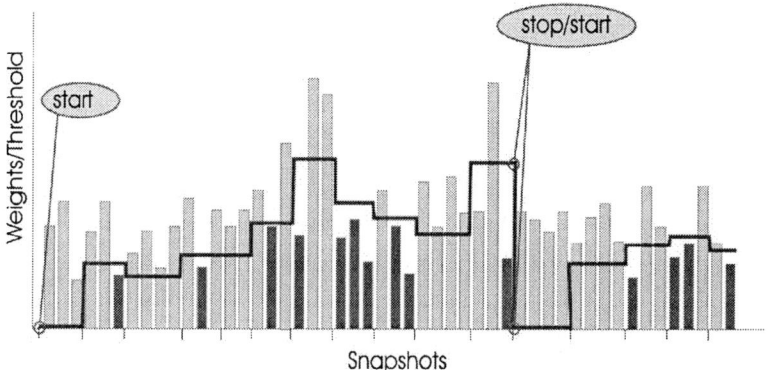

Fig. 3. Evolution of the threshold. Discarded comments are darker.

At the end of each iteration if the generated text comment can be output during the animation time (according to an experimental estimation) the cycle is terminated and the sentence is sent to the text-to-speech synthesizer of the Microsoft Agent. Otherwise an attempt is made to extend the comment to successive snapshots.

This *extension process* activates the selection phase on the next snapshot; if no comment remains after selection, this snapshot is marked as *silent* and the time available to pronounce the comment is extended with the animation time of this snapshot. If the time is still not sufficient, the function is called recursively on successive snapshots until the end of the planning window is reached.

If the necessary time cannot be found by this strategy, two alternatives remain:
- In case of a reproduction modality that we call *guided by the comment*, the commentator slows down the animation by increasing by a small percentage the animation time and repeats the extension cycle. No comment is discarded.
- If the reproduction modality is *fixed*, the commentator is forced to discard the least important comment in the current snapshot and the generation cycle is repeated.

The problem of real time comments has been tackled by RoCCo (RoboCup Commentator) in the context of simulated soccer [8]. Our approach to comment generation however is not based on text templates but on concept structures more similar to the ones used for example in the ILEX system [9].

References

1. Cisternino A., Del Cioppo E., Marotta P., Pacini G., Silenzi A., Simi M.: An expert authoring tool for dynamic scenarios, *Proc. of ED-MEDIA*, (2001)
2. Kitano, H., Asada, M., Osawa, E., Noda, I., Kuniyoshi, Y., Matsubara, H.: RoboCup: A Challenge Problem for AI, *AI Magazine*, Vol. 18, No. 1, (1997)

3. Microsoft Agent Software Development Kit, Microsoft Press, Redmond, (1999)
4. Cole, A., et al: Survey of the State of the Art in Human Language Tecnology, Kluwer, Dordrecht, (1996)
5. Wahlster: Intelligent Multimedia Interface Agents, Tutorial MICAI 2000, (1999)
6. Feiner S.K., McKeown K.R.: Generating Coordinated Multimedia Explana-tions, *Proceedings of the 6th IEEE Conference on A.I. Applications*, (1990)
7. Fraczak L., Lapalme G., Zock M.: Automatic generation of subway directions: salience gradation as a factor for determining message and form, *Proceedings.of the Ninth International Workshop on Language Generation*, Canada, (1998)
8. Voelz D., André E., Herzog G., Rist, T.: RoCCo: A RoboCup Soccer Commentator System, *Lecture Notes in Computer Science*, Vol 1604, (1999)
9. Oberlander J., O'Donnell M., Knott A., Mellish C.: Conversation in the museum: experiments in dynamic hypermedia with the intelligent labelling explorer, *New Review of Hypermedia and Multimedia*, Vol. 4, (1998) 11-32

A Web-Based Selling Agent That Maintains Customer Loyalty through Integrative Negotiation

Michael Grimsley[1] and Anthony Meehan[2]

[1] School of Computing & Management Science, Sheffield Hallam University, Pond Street,
Sheffield S1 1WB, UK
m.f.grimsley@shu.ac.uk
[2] Faculty of Mathematics & Computing, The Open University, Walton Hall, Milton Keynes
MK7 6AA, Buckinghamshire, UK
A.S.Meehan@open.ac.uk

Abstract. In many transactions, the seller's objective includes promoting customer loyalty in order to increase the likelihood of further transactions. Integrative bargaining styles foster positive relationships between parties. This short paper describes a protocol for a web-based selling agent that adopts an integrative selling style to identify alternative sales contracts that match customer priorities and hence promote customer satisfaction.

1 Introduction

Part of the value of many sales transactions is realised by securing repeated business. Thus, customer loyalty is an important outcome of any transaction. We describe a protocol for an adaptive web-based selling agent that is designed to engender loyalty in a customer by adopting a selling style that promotes confidence and trust. This is achieved through an integrative negotiation style using cues from the customer's interaction to infer customer priorities and respond positively to them.

Negotiation theory provides a framework within which to understand selling. A successful sale can be viewed as a contract negotiated between a vendor of goods or services and a prospective customer. An integrative bargaining style seeks an agreement that allows all parties to feel their priorities have been acknowledged and incorporated in the agreed deal. Integrative behaviour has a stabilising effect on relationships: parties enjoy the relationship and seek to help the relationship persist [1].

An important tactic in integrative negotiation is logrolling. This involves trading concessions on different issues, typically, when an issue is marginal to one party but significant to another. For a selling agent to engage in logrolling, it must infer the relative importance of issues from the earliest stages of an interaction with a new customer.

2 Selling Agent Protocol

A high-level description of an integrative protocol for a selling agent is as follows. During the sales dialogue, the selling agent infers the customer's priorities from the (short) sequence of contract proposals. The agent searches for alternatives that are most similar to those proposed by the customer but which maintain value for the vendor. The measure of similarity improves on conventional measures of similarity [2,3] by incorporating the inferred the priorities of the customer. The logrolling tactic is realised by selecting those similar alternative proposals that reflect the issue priorities of both vendor and purchaser.

To implement this protocol, we specify the following: a means to represent sales contracts for each agent; a metric which infers the relative importance of issues for a customer; a means of expressing relative issue importance as weights in a weighted similarity measure over pairs of alternative contracts; the construction of a set of alternatives that reflect the relative priorities of both vendor and customer.

An agent interprets alternative proposals on the basis of a set of issues or attributes, some public, some private [4]. An agent-centred representation of a sales contract is

$$c = (..., p_i, ..., q_j, ...); (p_i, q_j \in P^s). \quad (1)$$

P^s is the set of public (p_i) and private (q_j) issues for a selling agent s. (Note: we do not require agents to share representations.). Table 1 provides an example of a sequence of eight contract proposals over six issues. Issue *1* is conceded most reluctantly, issue *2* is conceded gradually from the outset, as perhaps is issue *5*, but in this case relatively larger concessions are made earlier on. Issues *4* and *6* seem to vary without any obvious intent. (Note: the issues are not necessarily independent of each other.)

Table 1. Example sequence of sales contract proposals from a customer.

Contract (*i*)	Issue (*p*)					
	1	*2*	*3*	*4*	*5*	*6*
1	700	610000	7900	10	300	40
2	600	940000	10000	100	200	30
3	700	1100000	10000	60	400	40
4	900	1250000	12000	200	1500	200
5	1500	1800000	25000	110	1400	240
6	1650	1980000	27500	121	1540	264
7	2400	1800000	43000	120	2700	300
8	18000	2330000	20200	1000	3300	20

Having found no work in the literature on assessing the relative importance of issues over such short temporal interaction sequences we have developed an empirical metric that scores issues for importance over a short sequence of multidimensional proposals.

The function, *Pen*, penalises relatively large early concessions and/or seemingly non-goal directed variation in the values taken by issue p over a sequence of k contract proposals:

$$Pen_{p,k} = \frac{a_k}{R_p} \max\left(|c_k(p) - c_i(p)|_{i=1}^{(k-1)} \right). \quad (2)$$

R_p is the known range of values for issue p. a_k is chosen to be decreasing over $1..k$ so as to penalise relatively early concessions.

The obvious cumulative penalty, *CPen*, for issue p after k proposals is simply,

$$CPen_{p,k} = \sum_{i=2}^{k} Pen_{p,i}. \quad (3)$$

There are many ways to express this measure of issue importance as a weight. We wish high penalties to map to low weights and so choose

$$w_p = 1 - \frac{CPen_{p,k} - \min(CPen_{i,k})_{i=1}^{p}}{\max(CPen_{i,k})_{i=1}^{p} - \min(CPen_{i,k})_{i=1}^{p}} \quad (4)$$

Given any two contracts, c_i, c_j, the similarity of these contracts for selling agent, s, may be given as

$$Sim^s(c_i, c_j) = F_{p \in P^s} \, w_p \, Sim_p^s(c_i(p), c_j(p)). \quad (5)$$

F is a function the choice of which is domain dependent. (The choice $F_{p \in P^s} = \Sigma_{p \in P^s}$ is common but assumes independence of the issues.) w_p is a weight associated with an issue, p, by the agent (see below) and may be normalised ($\Sigma_{p \in P} w_p = 1$). Sim_p is a specific similarity measure for issue, p [5]. In the context of sales contracts not all issues take values that are numeric. Hence, a fuzzy measure of similarity is appropriate [6,7]. Following [5] and [6], a fuzzy similarity function can be defined as

$$Sim_p^s(c_i, c_j) = Inf_{1 \le i \le n}(h_i(c_i(p)) \leftrightarrow h_i(c_j(p))). \quad (6)$$

where *Inf* is infimum and $h(c_i) \leftrightarrow h_i(c_j)$ is a fuzzy equivalence relation determined by the comparison function, h_i. There are many possible choices of h_i, examples include [7,3]

$$h(c_i) \leftrightarrow h(c_j) = 1 - |h(c_i) - h(c_j)| \quad (7)$$

and

$$h(c_i(p)) \leftrightarrow h(c_j(p)) = min(h(c_i(p))/h(c_j(p)), h(c_j(p))/h(c_i(p))). \quad (8)$$

Given the expressions above and a current contract proposal, c_k, from the customer, a set of alternative contracts can be generated which reflect both the vendor's and the customer's priorities.

$$L(c_k) = Sim^s(c_k, c_j) \cap Sim^c(c_k, c_j) \qquad (9)$$

$L(c_k)$ contains contracts whose strength of membership is given by fuzzy intersection [8]. Sim^c incorporates the vendor's estimate of the customer's relative priorities using expressions 2-4. The issues and weights for Sim^s may be elicited directly from the seller. (This is often a significant knowledge elicitation task and there may be significant difficulties if there are many highly correlated issues [9].)

The membership function of the set of 'logrolling' contracts in $L(c_k)$ reflects the issue priorities of both the selling agent and the customer. The selling agent can now select alternative proposals from $L(c_k)$, choosing those that have strong membership and at least maintain, and possibly increase, value to the vendor.

3 Conclusion

This paper has presented a protocol for an adaptive web-based selling agent. It has focused on using inferences about a customer's priority issues to help the selling agent find alternative sales contracts that are integrative and thus give the customer a sense that their priorities are acknowledged and responded to. This offers the prospect of enhanced customer confidence and loyalty.

References

1. Pruitt, D.G.: Negotiation Behaviour. Academic Press (1981)
2. Hahn, U., Ramscar, M.,: Similarity and Categorisation. Oxford University Press (2001)
3. Everitt, B.S., Landau, S., Leese, M.: Cluster Analysis. Arnold, London (2001) 35-53
4. Barker, R., Holloway, L.P., Meehan, A.: A negotiation model to support material selection in concurrent design. In *Proceedings of the 14th International Conference on Engineering Applications of AI and Expert Systems*. Monostori. L, Vancza, J. and Ali, M. eds. Lecture Notes in Artificial Intelligence 2070; Springer-Verlag, (2001) 697-707.
5. Sierra, C., Faratin, P., Jennings, N.R.: Deliberative Automated Negotiators Using Fuzzy Similarities. Proc EUSFLAT-ESTYLF Joint Conference on Fuzzy Logic, Palma de Mallorca, Spain, (1997) 155-158.
6. Valverde, L.: 1985 On the structure of F-indistinguishability. *Fuzzy Sets and Systems* 17:313-328 (cited in Sierra, et al 1997 above.)
7. Yao, Y.Y.: Qualitative similarity, Soft Computing in Industrial Applications, 4th Online World Conference on Soft Computing in Industrial Applications (WSC4), September 21-30 (1999) 339-348.
8. Zadeh, L.A.: Fuzzy Sets. Information and Control. 8 (1965) 338-353
9. Grimsley, M.F., Meehan, A.S.: Perceptual Scaling in Materials Selection for Concurrent Design. FLAIRS 2002, Pensacola Florida. AAAI Press, (2002)

Adaptive Content for Device Independent Multi-modal Browser Applications

Jennifer Healey, Rafah Hosn, and Stéphane H. Maes

Human Language Technologies Group
IBM T.J. Watson Research Center
Route 134, Yorktown Heights, NY 50198
{jahealey,rhosn,smaes}@us.ibm.com

Abstract. Adapting content appropriate to the device and modality of a user's preference becomes more important as users begin to expect universal access to information, whether they are on the phone, on a desktop or using a PDA. This paper outlines the design of a travel application authored using an XForms compliant language and deployed using a DOM-based MVC multi-modal browser. The travel application authored in a language of conversational gestures that can be transcoded into multiple synchronized views for access via a variety of devices.

1 Introduction

The next generation of human computer interaction will implement multiple forms of input and output. People will expect the information they need to be available to them where ever they are and from whatever device they are currently using. This paper describes a device independent application written using an XForms [9] based meta-language that is adaptively transcoded into multiple synchronized presentation languages (e.g. HTML, VXML and XHTML-MP etc.) using XSLT [10] rules. The XSLT transformation can adapt content and style to suit the mode of interaction and the restrictions of the device. The XForms application is served using a DOM-based MVC [1] multi-modal browser (MMBrowser) [4] with an added forms based dialog manager (FDM). The MMBrowser contains a controller module that acts as a hub to all modules inside the MMBrowser as well as a mediator between the devices, the application server and the FDM. This module is also responsible for device registration and synchronization. The added FDM is an adaptation of a previous dialog manager [7] developed for the DARPA Communicator competition [2] where XForms is now used for the data and interaction models, DOM level two events are now used for communication with the MMBrowser and VoiceXML is used as the speech input/output voice channel.

2 Multi-mode and Multi-channel

Computer systems are being developed that support a variety of modes of interaction including speech, keyboard, handwriting, gesture, facial expression, context and affect. These multiple modes of interaction can be used to facilitate both recognition [6] and communication [5, 11]. Often these modalities require specialized channels to allow access modalities such as cameras, microphones and sensors. A multi-modal multi-channel system faces the challenge of accepting information from any input method and delivering information through the appropriate output methods. In this paper, we show how a declarative language based on XForms [9] encodes user interaction as a set of conversational gestures [8] and binds these gestures to an XForms data model using XPath expressions. The interaction is presented to the user after being transformed by XSLT [10] rules adapted to the user and the device. The dialog manager insures that an appropriate sequence of inquiry and response gestures continues the conversation. The MMBrowser uses standard DOM events to synchronize modalities, allowing the user to switch modalities during a conversation so that voice, keyboard or mouse can be used interchangeably. The framework [3] derives its power by separating application content from its presentation and providing a controller that manages the interaction with the user while updating the application data following the model view controller programming paradigm. The framework also leverages evolving XML-based industry standards for modeling application content and representing user interaction as well as for communicating the results of user interaction among various components of the system.

3 Authoring Applications

There are three components to application authoring in this framework: the user interaction; the data model and the presentation. This section describes each of these components and the relationships between them.

3.1 User Interaction: Encoding Conversation

The multi-modal application is written in a simple, declarative language designed to encode conversation at the highest level consistent across modalities. A set of primitive conversational gestures including "dialog", "message", "input", "select" and "submit" is used to specify the behavior of the application. For example each **message** or **input** that the system uses to present or collect data is simply defined and can be bound to information the data model using XPath. To illustrate, the following is an excerpt from a travel application written for the system:

```
<dialog name="trip/air" action="submit">
 <message>
   Welcome <value name="trip/user/firstName"/>
   <value name="trip/user/lastName"/>!
 </message>
 <input name="arrivalCity">
```

```
    <grammar src="travel.gram"/>
    <caption> Where will you be flying to?</caption>
  </input> ...
  <submit target="http://localhost/DB"/>
</dialog>
```

This example shows a "Welcome" message gesture bound to the *firstName* and *lastName* data model instance nodes for output presentation and an "arrivalCity" input gesture bound to the arrivalCity data model instance node. The message uses full XPath expressions such as **"trip/user/firstName"** while the input constructs the path **"trip/air/arrivalCity"** from both the binding in the nearest dialog gesture **name="trip/air"** and the binding inside the input gesture **name="arrivalCity"**.

3.2 Data Model Specification

The data model is specified in XML and is distinct from the presentation and the controller. An example of a data model containing the passenger and air travel information could be specified as:

```
<?xml version="1.0"?>
<trip>
  <user>
    <firstName/>
    <lastName/>
    <password/>
  </user>
  <air>
    <departureCity/>
    <departureDate/>
    <arrivalCity/>
    <returnDate/>
  </air>
</trip>
```

Each of the slots in this model such as "firstName" and "departureCity" will be populated through interaction with the user. The dialog structure is flexible and allows users to fill multiple slots, in various order, in a single interaction. The dialog manager uses the data model to keep track of the conversation context to determine which slots have been filled with information from the user and which slots still need to be presented to complete the form.

3.3 Presentation Rules

Speech, text and gesture all serve as a means to the same end, but the methods are inherently different. In a visual presentation the application author might wish to have strict control over the spatial presentation of information, however in speech conversation the system should adapt to receive whatever information the user chooses to present and respond appropriately. In this application, the XSLT rules allow the author to specify the details of data presentation in a particular modality while the XForms language allows information to be collected from the user in a flexible order across modalities.

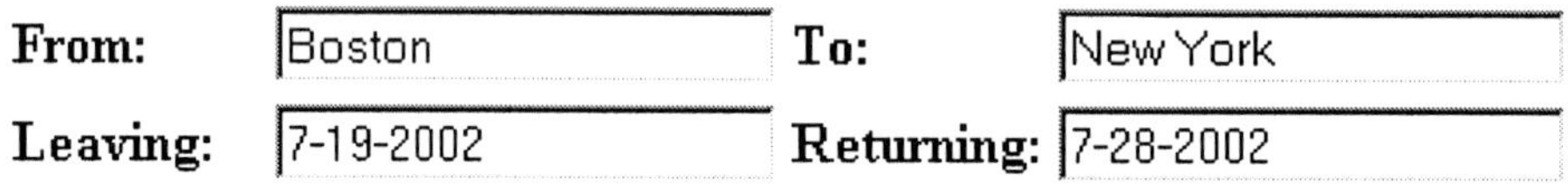

From: Boston   **To:** New York
Leaving: 7-19-2002   **Returning:** 7-28-2002

Fig. 1. An example of the synchronized text modality response synchronized to the voice input "I want to fly to New York on third Friday in July and return a week later on Monday"

For example the designer can exactly specify the exact order, font, size, color and placement of visual data by including special tags in XSLT rules for HTML:

```
<xsl:template match="dialog[@format_key='D2']">
  <p>I want the best round-trip travel:</p>
    <table><tr><td><b>From:</b></td>
      <td><xsl:apply-templates select="input[@select_key='I4']"/>
      </td><td><b>To:</b></td>
      <td><xsl:apply-templates select="input[@select_key='I5'"/>
      </td></tr> ...   </table> ...
</xsl:template>
```

In addition, individual users with special needs might use special XSLT rules to show larger fonts, bigger buttons or to allow selection input through gesture or alternative input devices.

Presentation customizations are entirely separate from the interaction logic layer and the data model. As a result, a visual presentation might show as output particularly placed "From:" and "To:" fields while the voice channel might say as output "Where would you like to go?." The separation of presentation from the underlying interaction logic also allows users the flexibility to express input in different ways through different modalities. For example in the presentation shown in Fig. 1, the "From" field precedes the "To" field, since visually the user might think of a right to left line describing the trip. However, the user can still verbally express the information in whatever order they prefer, e.g. "I want a flight to New York, leaving from Boston." Since the gestures are synchronized and bound to the same data model using XPath, when the user speaks this response the information will appear in the reverse order in the appropriate fields of the HTML display.

4 Discussion

This system separates data from presentation which allows ubiquitous adaptation of information to the mode and device of the user's preference. Multiple modalities can be used collectively to enhance user experience or modalities can be used independently to allow access through a greater variety of devices. Applications can be simply written using a declarative XForms language and additional sophistication can be added to presentation by creating specialized formatting using XSLT. A single application and data model are used to model the conversation synchronously across modalities. A dialog manager keeps track of the conversation so that information is presented at a level that best suits the user's modality, channel and context. This system allows content to be adapted to a variety of devices with different modes of access, allowing the user the greatest freedom of expression when available and the greatest access to information from the most convenient device.

References

1. S. Burbeck. Applications programming in smalltalk-at: How to use model-view-controller - mvc. http://st-www.cs.uiuc.edu/users/smarch/st-docs/mvc.html.
2. M. W. et al. Darpa communicator dialog travel planning systems: The june 2000 data collection. In *Proc. of Eurospeech '01*, 2001.
3. R. Hosn, T. Raman, and S. H. Maes. Single application model, multiple synchronized views. In *Proc. ICME '01*, Tokyo, Japan, 2001.
4. J. Keindienst01. A dom-based mvc multi-modal e-business. In *Proc. ICME '01*, Tokyo, Japan, 2001.
5. R. Lau, G. Flammia, C. Pao, and V. Zue. Webgalaxy – integrating spoken language and hypertext navigation. In *Proc. Eurospeech '97*, pages 883–886, Rhodes, Greece, 1997.
6. C. Neti, G. Potamianos, J. Luettin, I. Mathews, H. Glotin, and D. Vergyri. Large vocabulary audio-visual speech recognition - a summary of the johns hopkins summer 2000 workshop. In *Proc. IEEE workshop on Multi-media signal processing*, pages 619–624, Cannes, France, 2001.
7. K. A. Papineni, S. Roukos, and R. T. Ward. Frames based dialog management using forms. In *Proc. Eurospeech '99*, volume 3, pages 1411–1414, Budapest, Hungary, September 1997.
8. T. Raman and S. H. Maes. Multi-modal interaction in the age of the information appliance. In *Proc. ICME '02*, New York, July, 2000.
9. W3C. Xforms 1.0 working draft. http://www.w3.org/MarkUp/Forms, 2001.
10. W3C. Xslt. http://www.w3.org/TR/xslt, 2001.
11. V. Zue, S. Seneff, J. Polifroni, M. Phillips, C. Pao, D. Goodine, D. Goddeau, and J. Glass. PEGASUS: A spoken dialogue interface for on-line air travel planning. *Speech Communication*, 15:331–340, 1994.

Behavioral Sequences: A New Log-Coding Scheme for Effective Prediction of Web User Accesses

Rushed Kanawati[1] and Maria Malek[2]

[1] LIPN-CNRS UMR Q 7030, Av. J. B. Clément, F-93430 Villetaneuse
rushed.kanawati@lipn.univ-paris13.fr
[2] LAPI-EISTI, Av. du Parc, F-95011 Cergy
maria.malek@eisti.fr

Abstract. Mining web site logs for predicting user actions is a central issue in the field of adaptive web site development. In order to match the dynamic nature of today web sites we propose in this paper a new scheme for coding Web server log data into sessions of *behavioral sequences*. Following the proposed coding scheme the navigation sessions are coded as a sequence of hypothetical actions that may explain the transition from one page to another. The output of a prediction algorithm will now be an action that can be evaluated in the context of the current navigation in order to find pages that to be visited by the user.

1 Introduction

One hot topic in the field of adaptive web site development is the problem of mining usage log data in order to predict future user actions [1,3,5]. Web-user access prediction can be used for a variety of different applications such as: prefetching web pages [9] and recommending links and pages [4,7,8]. In almost all-existing approaches log data are pre-processed to form a set of *navigation sessions* [2,6]. A session is defined as a chronologically ordered sequence of Web pages visited by a given user. Most web user access approaches apply some sequence prediction algorithm on navigation sessions. By the very nature of used data, existing prediction systems can only predict access to pages that have been visited earlier by some users (e.g. pages that have been registered in the log file). This feature is a serious limitation of the usability of prediction systems for adapting today highly dynamic Web sites. In order to match the dynamic nature of web sites we propose in this paper a new scheme for coding log data into sessions *of behavioral sequences*. A behavioral sequence is defined as an ordered list of *elementary behaviors*. Each elementary behavior describes a visited Web page associated with a set of hypothetical actions that may explain how the user acts to reach the next visited page. Using this coding scheme the output of a prediction algorithm will consist on predicting the action to be made by the observed user. Actions can be evaluated in the context of the observed user navigation in order to find pages to be visited later by that user. Next, we describe briefly the concept of behavioral sequences.

2 Turning Log Data into Behavioral Sequences

For sake of clarity, we start by introducing some notations that are used later in this paper.

- **Web page (P).** A web page P is defined as a triple $P = <U, L, I>$. Where U is the page address (i.e. the page URL), L is the list of links contained in the page P, and I is some information record about the page (i.e. the record I may contain a description of the page content, the page author, etc). We denote by $L(P)$ (respectively $U(P)$ and $I(P)$) the U (respectively L and I) component of the page P.

- **Web site (S).** A web site, denoted S, is a set of n web pages. We write $S = \{P_i, 0<i<=n\}$.

- **Navigation (N).** A user navigation session in a site S denoted N, is a *sequence* of steps s_i. We write $N = [s_i]_{i=0..m}$ where m is the navigation length.

- **Step (s).** A step s is defined as a couple $s = <P_i \in S, SI>$ where P_i is a web page, and SI is some information structure about the step. The SI structure can contain entries about request result (i.e. successful access, page not found, etc), page visualization time, user satisfaction from the page, etc. The ith step in a navigation N_j is designated by $N_j[i] = s^j_i$. We use the notation $P(s^j_i)$ (respectively $I(s^j_i)$) to designate the page (respectively information) component of a step.

- **Transition (T).** We call a *transition* T^j_i a sequence of two pages visited sequentially in navigation N_j at steps i and $i+1$. Formally, we write $T^j_i = [P(s^j_i), P(s^j_{i+1})]$.

- **Navigation Base (NB).** We define a navigation base NB as a set of past navigation sessions that have occurred in the site S.

- **Navigation action template.** We define a navigation action template, denoted NAT_k, as a generator of *hypothesis* that can explain a transition T^j_i occurring in navigation N_j. The set of all used templates is denoted by NAT. The composition of the NAT set is *site-dependent*. Next, we give some examples of different templates based only on the definition of a hypermedia navigation process. The given list is far from being exhaustive and it should be taken just as a simple example of hypothesis we can generate to explain transitions in a navigation. The four examples are the following:
  1. NAT_1 : *Follow a link.* If page P_i contains a hypertext link that points to P_{i+1}, then one plausible hypothesis that can explain the transition from P_i to P_{i+1} is that the user has clicked that link. Two sub-types can be derived from NAT_1 type: *Follow a link with anchor A (NAT_{11})* and *Follow a link with rank X (NAT_{12})*.
  2. NAT_2. *Move backward.* If page P_{i+1} has already been visited in the same navigation then a plausible transition explanation would be that the user has

made a backward move. Once again, we can derive several sub-types of that action type such as moving backward n steps, moving up to the start, etc.
3. NAT_3. *Page Reload*. If page P_{i+1} is the same as P_i then one plausible explanation is that the user has reloaded the same page.
4. NAT_4. *Follow an URL*. A simple transition explanation is that the user has simply typed the address (i.e. the URL) of the page P_{i+1} after visiting page P_i.

The application of a template, NAT_i, on navigation N_j allows to generate for each transition T_i^j a set of *hypothetical* actions, defined by the template NAT_i that may explain the transition. Let A_i be the set of concrete actions from type NAT_i that can explain the transition T_i^j, we write: $A_i = Apply(N_j, NAT_i, T_i^j)$

The generated navigation action set can be the empty set. For example consider the web site illustrated in Fig. 1. Consider a navigation N_j in that site. N_j is composed of the following steps:

N_j = [<P1, SI1>, <P3, SI2>, <P4, SI3>, <P4, SI5>]

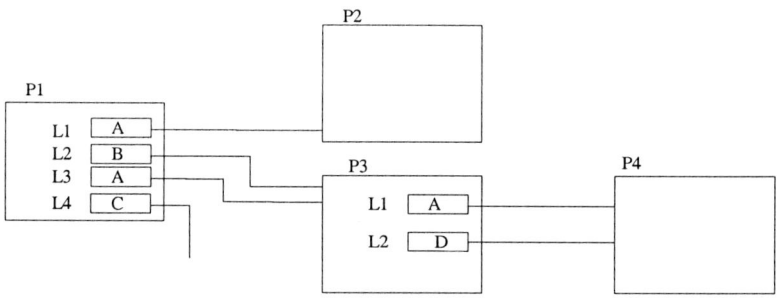

Fig. 1. Example of a simple Web site

The following table illustrates the result of applying the different templates defined above on each simple transition in the navigation N_j.

Table 1. Example of generated actions by applying navigation action templates

Transition	NAT_{11}	NAT_{12}	NAT_3	NAT_4
Nj[1,2]	follow link with anchor B follow link with anchor A	follow link 2 follow link 3	-	follow URL: P3
Nj[2,3]	follow link with anchor A follow link wit anchor D	follow link 1 follow link 2	-	follow URL P4
Nj[3,4]	-	-	Reload	follow URL P4

- **Action evaluation function (Eval).** We define the function of action evaluation as follows:

$$eval : A \times NB \times S \rightarrow \wp(S)$$

Where A is the set of all actions, NB is the navigation base and S is the web site. The evaluation of an action $a \in A$ is made in the context of a given navigation $N_i \in NB$ and on a given page $P_i \in S$. The result of the evaluation is either a set web page $\{P_x\} \subseteq S$ or the null (ϕ) value. For example consider the action A_x: *follow link with anchor equal to "A"* to be evaluated for each page in the navigation example given above (Fig. 1). Evaluation results are given in the following table.

Table 2. Evaluation of the action *follow link with anchor A* in the context of the example illustrated in Fig. 1.

Page	Evaluation result
P_1	$\{P_2, P_3\}$
P_2	ϕ
P_3	$\{P_4\}$
P_4	ϕ

- **Elementary behavior (EB).** Given a navigation N_j. With each step $s^j_i \in N_j$ we can associate an elementary behavior EB^j_i, defined as follows: $EB^j_i = <s^j_i, LA_i, CF_i>$ where:
  - LA_i is the set of all actions from all types that verify the following condition: $\forall a_j \in LA_i : eval\ (a_j, N_p, P(s^j_i)) = P(s^j_{i+1})$.
  - CF_i is a vector that represents the system confidence in each action listed in LA_i.

Using the concept of elementary behavior we can now represent a navigation session N_j as a sequence of elementary behaviors $N_j = [EB_i]_{i=0..N}$ where each EB_i represents the elementary behavior associated to the step s^j_i in N_j. Turning web access log into behavioral sequences requires modifying the Web server. The following algorithm is to be executed on each ongoing navigation: $N_o = [s_1, ..., s_m]$.

LA ←Φ;	// LA the list of actions
For each $NAT_i \in NAT$ do:	// Computing all actions of all types that
A = Apply(NAT_i, N_o, T_o^m)	// could explain the transition T_o^m
LA ← LA ∪ A	
N = |LA|	// N is the number of found actions
For i=0 to N do:	// Computing the default confidence in
CF[i]=1/N	// each action
EB = <S_m, LA, CF>	// Setting the elementary behavior of rank
N_o[m] = EB	// m in navigation No.

Applying a prediction algorithm on the obtained behavioral sequences allow getting as output an action or set of actions. These actions can be evaluated, using the *eval* function, in order to indicate pages to be visited by the user. An example of using this scheme is detailed in [4].

3 Conclusion

In this paper we have introduced a new scheme for coding web log data. The proposed scheme transforms log data into behavioral sequences. A behavioral sequence represents a sequence of pages visited by the user. Each page is associated with a set of hypothetical actions that can explain the user motivation to go from one page to another. The main advantage of this new coding scheme consist on allowing to apply sequence prediction algorithms to predict actions to be made by the user rather than pages to be visited by the user as the majority of existing systems do. This feature is essential for predicting user actions in dynamic web sites.

References

1. P. Brusilovsky, Methods and Techniques of Adaptive Hypermedia. In User Modelling and User-Adapted Interaction 6: 87-129, Kluwer academic publishers, 1996.
2. R. Cooley, B. Mobasher and J. Srivastava. Data Preparation for Mining World Wide Web Browsing Patterns. In Knowledge and Information Systems 1(1). pp. 5-32, 1999.
3. P. De Bra, Design Issues in Adaptive Web-Site Development. In Proceedings of the Second Workshop on Adaptive Systems and User Modelling on the World Wide Web, pp. 29-39, Toronto and Banff, Canada, 1999. (Editors P. Brusilovsky and P. De Bra), 1999.
4. M. Malek, R. Kanawati. COBRA: A CBR-Based Approach for Predicting Users Actions in a Web Site. In (D. Aha and I. Watson eds.) Proceedings of the 4th International Conference on Case-Based Reasoning (ICCBR 2001), (LANI 2080) Springer, Vancouver BC., Canada, July/August 2001. pp. 336-346.
5. A. Mobasher, R. Cooley and J. Srivastava. Creating Adaptive Web sites Through Usage-Based Clustering of URLs. In proceedings of the IEEE workshop on Knowledge and Data Engineering (KDEX'99), 1999.
6. J. Pitkow. In search of reliable usage data on the WWW. In Sixth International World Wide Web pages 451 463, Santa Clara ,CA, 1997.
7. M. Spiliopoulou, C. Pohle and L. C. Faulstich. Improving the Effectiveness of a Web Site with Web Usage Mining. In proceedings of KDD workshop WebKDD'99, San Diego, August 1999.
8. B. Trousse, M. Jaczynski, and R. Kanawati. Using User Behaviour Similarity for Recommendation Computation: The Broadway Approach. In H-J Bullinger and J. Ziegler, editors, proceedings of the HCI International (HCI'99), Munich. pp 85-89. Lawrence Erlbaum Associates, august 1999
9. I. Zukerman, David W. Albrecht, and E. Nicholson, Predicting users' requests on the WWW, Proceedings of the Seventh International Conference on User Modelling, 1999.

A Fuzzy-Based Approach to User Model Refinement in Adaptive Hypermedia Systems

Cveta Martinovska

Electric Engineering Faculty, Karpos II
1000 Skopje, Macedonia
cmma@mt.net.mk

Abstract. This paper presents an approach for refinement of the user model in hypermedia applications using fuzzy adaptation rules. The rules register relevant user browsing actions and this way change the strength of relationship between the user model attributes and the concepts of the knowledge domain. The process of fuzzy inference is formalized with fuzzy automaton. Using appropriate authoring tool fuzzy automata provides a method for detecting conflicts and inconsistency in the set of rules, in an automated fashion.

1 Introduction

Managing personalized views over the information spaces is the main problem in developing adaptive hypermedia systems. Models that represent relevant user aspects as goals, interests, cognitive abilities, decision styles or way of learning enable user oriented adaptivity. The system gathers the knowledge about the user through the initial interview and/or continuous monitoring of the user's browsing behavior.

Hypermedia systems offer freedom in the navigation through the hyperspace but more of the users prefer guided over unguided browsing. The user will lose the interest if the links he/she follows are meaningless, and needs to go back to the links related to the area of interest. In the hypermedia systems used in education the system has to keep track what the user has read in order to avoid presenting redundant information or pages that the user can not understand. There are several ways to overcome the navigation problems in adaptive systems like restructuring the link configuration according to the user models, changing the content of the nodes, supporting the user browsing by showing the links that are most suitable in certain state. An overview of methods and techniques for adaptive hypermedia systems can be found in [1].

In adaptive systems user model is usually independent from the domain knowledge. A discussion about modeling an application domain and user modeling in adaptive hypermedia systems and especially in Web-based systems is presented in [2]. The domain model is concerned with the content and structure of the information that has to be presented to the user. It deals with the link relationships between the concepts as well as with the decomposition of the concepts in a hierarchy of sub-concepts and atomic information like paragraphs of text, sounds, videos, and images. Part of the adaptive hypermedia systems is a mechanism that performs adaptation based on the user model and updates the user model. This mechanism might be in the form of adaptive rules as described in [3]. The if-then rules might be built in the adaptive hypermedia systems when they are not dependent on the domain or provided by the author of the hypermedia application when they are domain dependent.

Interactive systems for modeling user expectations, motives, abilities or interests have to deal with imprecise knowledge, because users prefer to express this type of information in terms of vague concepts. Several systems for user modeling applying uncertainty techniques are described in [4].

In this paper is proposed refinement of the user model with fuzzy adaptation rules. The formal description of the process is modeled with fuzzy automaton that maintains a dynamic characterization of user knowledge and interests through the process of browsing.

This paper is organized as following: Section 2 discusses the basic characteristics of the fuzzy-based user model and the format of the rules for its revising. Section 3 gives a formal definition of fuzzy automaton corresponding to the fuzzy adaptation rules. The concluding remarks and next research are presented in Section 4.

2 User Modeling and Rule-Based Adaptivity

In this section some relevant descriptions of the user model and the fuzzy adaptation rules are provided.

2.1 User Model

The adaptive system has to construct and maintain a matrix containing the concepts and their constitutional parts, and attributes like the information about the relevance of the concept for the user and whether the user is familiar with the concept.

The natural way to characterize the relationship between the attributes in the user model and concepts of the domain is using fuzzy linguistic labels. Fuzzy linguistic labels are obtained from the term set T (A) of the linguistic variable A [5]. For example, let A=interest then T(A)={very interested, quite interested, more or less interested, not interested,...} where the hedges very, quite and more or less are used to modify the meaning of the notion.

This paper is not concerned with the initialization of the user model. The user is asked to select linguistic value for domain concepts in the initial dialog or he/she is classified into some stereotypical category. In the following text the updating of an individual user model is discussed representing single user characteristics relevant for the knowledge domain.

2.2 Fuzzy Adaptation Rules

The user model is modified by fuzzy adaptation rules with the following general pattern: if x_1 is A_1 and x_2 is A_2 and ... and x_n is A_n or ... then y is B, where A_i and B are linguistic variables from the universes of discourse U and V respectively, x_i is an instance in the universe U corresponding to membership value $\mu_{Ai}(x_i)$, y is an instance in V with membership value $\mu_B(y)$.

Condition part of the rule might for example include external events like selection of certain links in the presented pages, access of some pages or checking the user model for the relevance of the concept. Action part might specify new values for the attributes in the user model or might activate other rules.

The operators *and, or, not* are defined as fuzzy operators. The author has to choose appropriate membership functions and operator definitions. For example, he/she must determine whether it is appropriate a single attribute to block the application of the rule giving the operator *and* meaning minimum of the membership values.

More than one rule can be activated with the execution of some events leading to conflict, which has to be signaled to the author, or the author might add a rule that is inconsistent with the rest of the rules. Analyzing the process of fuzzy inference using fuzzy automaton may help in detecting undesirable and ambiguous situations. That is, this representation can be used as a basis for an authoring tool, which will discover conflicting results or potential infinite loops.

3 Fuzzy Inference

The process of fuzzy inference is formalized with fuzzy automaton $FA=(I,S,O,f,\lambda)$ where I is a set of input linguistic variables, S is a set of automaton's internal states and O is a set of output linguistic variables. Transition function f is defined from $S \times I \times S$ to $\{0,1\}$ and output function λ is a function from $S \times I \times O$ to $\{0,1\}$, where

$f(s_i,i_p,s_j)=1$ if there is link from state s_i to s_j, and $f(s_i,i_p,s_j)=0$ in other cases, and $\lambda(s_i,i_p,o_p)=1$ if o_p is the output at state s_i when input is i_p and $\lambda(s_i,i_p,o_p)=0$ otherwise.

The fuzzy automaton has to be deterministic. That is, for a given input and current state there is only one next state and output. So, some constraints are imposed: function f has value 1 for exactly one next state s_j being in state s_i when the input is i_p, and λ has value 1 for only one output o_k being in state s_i when the input is i_p.

To obtain next states the automaton computes max-min operations from the current state and inputs. Let current input x has membership values $I=[\mu_{i1}(x),..., \mu_{ip}(x)]$ for every input linguistic variable i_k and S is the current state of the automaton distributed over several states, where the degree of activation of the states is defined with value in the interval [0,1]. The next state S' is computed as fuzzy composition

$$S'=S \circ max[min(\mu_{i1}(x),f(s_p,i_1,s_j)),...,min(\mu_{ip}(x),f(s_p,i_p,s_j))] \quad (1)$$

As an example, Figure 1 shows a fuzzy automaton which corresponds to the following fuzzy rules:

if in subdomain D12 user selection of links is low then
set the attribute value12 to not interested

State	input	output	next state
s_1	medium	more or less interested	s_2
s_1	low	not interested	s_3
s_2	medium	more or less interested	s_2
s_2	low	not interested	s_3
s_3	low	not interested	s_3
s_3	medium	more or less interested	s_2

Fig. 1. An example of fuzzy automaton based on fuzzy rules

*if in subdomain D21 user selection of links is medium then
set the attribute value21 to more or less interested*

The automaton has 3 internal states { s_1, s_2, s_3 }, two input variables {low, medium} and two output variables {not interested, more or less interested} and s_1 is the initial state. The membership functions for input and output variables are $\mu_{medium}(x)$, $\mu_{low}(x)$, $\mu_{not\ interested}(x)$ and $\mu_{more\ or\ less\ interested}(x)$. For example, $\mu_{low}(x)$ is a membership function mapping from number of selected links to a value in [0,1] describing to what degree x is a member in the set.

4 Conclusion

To customize the process of navigation through the hypermedia space user modeling component may have the possibility to register the relevant browsing events and to modify the user model to adequately reflect certain user interests, familiarity with the concepts, domain expertise and his/her cognitive abilities.

This report presents an approach for updating the user model using fuzzy adaptation rules formalized with fuzzy automaton. The set of rules that revise the user model are domain specific rather than built in the adaptive hypermedia application. Developing the user modeling component the author has to verify whether the set of rules satisfies his/her expectations and to detect the potential conflicts in the rule set.

For analyzing the set of fuzzy rules an authoring application will be needed that allows an author to express properties without having to be concerned with the methods and techniques of fuzzy inference.

References

1. Brusilovsky, P.: Methods and Techniques of Adaptive Hypermedia. UMUAI, Vol. 4. Kluwer academic publishers (1994) 21-45
2. De Bra, P.: Design Issues in Adaptive Web-Site Development. Proceedings of the 2nd Workshop on Adaptive Systems and User Modeling on the WWW (1999), 29-39 (Workshop proceedings http://wwwis.win.tue.nl/asum99/, TU/c CNS99/07)
3. Wu, H., De Bra, P., Aerts, A., Houben, G.J.: Adaptation Control in Adaptive Hypermedia Systems. Proceedings of the AH2000 Conference, LNCS Vol. 1892. Springer-Verlag, Berlin Heidelberg New York (2000) 250-259
4. Jameson,A.: Numerical Uncertainty Management in User and Student Modeling: An overview of Systems and Issues. UMUAI, Vol.5. Kluwer academic publishers (1996)
5. Zadeh, L.A.: Outline of a New Approach to the Analysis of Complex Systems and Decision processes. IEEE Transactions on Systems, Man, and Cybernetics, vol.smc-3,1,(1973) 28-44

Towards an Authoring Coach for Adaptive Web-Based Instruction

Judith Masthoff[1]

University of Brighton, UK
Judith.Masthoff@brighton.ac.uk

Abstract. A new approach to adaptive web-based instruction is outlined and advocated, which is based on models and principles that allow the course material to organize itself. This is particularly useful when course material originating from multiple authors is to be combined into a coherent whole.

1 Background

In previous research, an "artificial teacher" has been developed, which adapts instruction to the learner [1]. This artificial teacher needs an abstract description of the course material (often called metadata). Additionally, there needs to be sufficient variation in the course material to be able to reach a high level of adaptation. We are developing a system ('Authoring Coach') that coaches authors to provide both the metadata and the variation needed for the adaptation to be effective. It shall
- Provide an easy user-interface for entering course material and metadata.
- Stimulate authors to enter metadata by clarifying its purpose and consequences.
- Stimulate authors to provide variation by indicating the amount of adaptation possible with the current material and how this can be increased.
- Enable multiple authors to contribute without need for coordination. An essential aspect of the World Wide Web has been that is has organically grown: authors from around the world (without coordination) have contributed material. We use the same principle for the authoring of courseware.
- Generate personalized web-based lesson books from the material provided by the authors, which are easy to use, have a good narrative flow, and allow the artificial teacher to monitor and optimally support student learning.

2 Existing Systems

To model the teaching domain, both InterBook [2] and NetCoach [3] use concepts, which are organized in a network, with links reflecting different types of relationships between them. Concepts in InterBook are "elementary pieces of knowledge for the

---

[1] The author is supported by Nuffield grant NAL/00258/G.

given domain". All examples mentioned are noun phrases, like "production rule". In NetCoach concepts are "internal representations of pages", like "Chapter-2-1-2". In InterBook, the author provides an electronic textbook that is hierarchically organized (chapters, sections, etc). Each page has a set of *outcome concepts* and a set of *prerequisite concepts* associated with it (analogous to pre- and post-conditions in programming). These are used to support adaptive navigation and hyperlink annotation. NetCoach also uses prerequisites, but as relations between concepts. In MetaLinks [4], authors provide the hierarchical relationship between pages.

3 Proposed Authoring Coach

We will describe here a number of aspects of our Authoring Coach that are vital for supporting authoring by multiple authors, in a self-organizing way.

Use of action verbs in outcomes and prerequisites. The use of concepts to express outcomes, as in InterBook, is not enough to make the outcomes sufficiently precise and unambiguous. It can result in multiple pages in an electronic textbook that cover apparently the same outcome. In the pedagogical literature, outcomes are always described as containing an action verb, indicating what the student will be able to *do* [5]. We will express each outcome as a combination of an action verb with a concept. For instance, an outcome of a page will not be "search methods", but something like "explain search methods" or "implement search methods". This will allow authors to specify the content of a page more accurately.

Lists of recommended verbs exist, often classified into six levels of learning according to Bloom's taxonomy [5]. This allows the Authoring Coach to advice whether there is enough material at a suitable level. For example, in a third year module, the students should display higher levels of learning, like analysis and evaluation. The coach could give advice like "Please add pages that encourage critical thinking, using verbs like evaluate". The verbs will also inspire authors about which pages could still be added (comparable to the thematic links in MetaLinks). The Authoring Coach will coach the authors, by using requests like "Please write a page that covers outcome X", and "Please write a page that uses prerequisite X".

Generation of page titles, exercises, etc. Some aspects of the presentation of material can be *generated* automatically on the basis of underlying information, such as verbs and concepts (cf. [6]). A simple example relates to the generation of titles. Table 1 shows some example mappings between verbs and titles. Similarly exercises could also sometimes be generated. In both cases, an advantage of using generation is that it allows better support of narrative flow and consistency in terminology.

Table 1. Example mappings between verbs and titles

Verb	Title
implement CONCEPT	How to implement CONCEPT
advocate CONCEPT	Why use CONCEPT
explain CONCEPT	What are CONCEPT
compare CONCEPT1 CONCEPT2	How do CONCEPT1 and CONCEPT2 compare?

Generation of a hierarchy. In authoring tools like InterBook, MetaLinks, and NetCoach, authors explicitly provide the textbook hierarchy (like page1 has subsection page1-1). In contrast, Authoring Coach will *generate* the hierarchy on the basis of the concept network and the prerequisites and outcomes associated with pages (and some additional information, see below). The concept network provides information about which concepts are 'children' of which other concepts. Note that there are (at least) two different kinds of parent-child relationships: in AI, "Blind search" is a special case of "Search Methods" (an aggregation relationship), while "Criteria for evaluation" is a subtopic within "Search Methods" (a 'uses' relationship).

A concept will be included in the hierarchy if it has either (1) at least two children that are included in the hierarchy, (2) two pages that use it in their outcomes, or (3) one page that uses it in its outcome and one child that is included in the hierarchy. The included children of an included concept and the pages that use it in their outcomes will be shown as subsections or pages below that concept.

A concept can be a child of multiple other concepts. Additionally, a page can use multiple concepts in its outcomes. In those cases, the generated hierarchy may contain multiple instances of a concept (as section title) or page. This will allow the student to more easily find material, and to follow different paths through the course.

Making a custom book. Books can be generated that are tailored to individual needs. Authors, teachers and students can choose the outcomes to be covered by a book. The system will only include pages that are related to achieving those outcomes, either directly or indirectly (needed for prerequisite).

Dealing with alternatives. Different authors may have different views on how a specific outcome should be taught. So, different pages can exist with the same outcomes. We call these pages *alternatives*. As alternatives have the same outcomes, they will share the same generated titles (see above). The decision on which page out of a set of alternatives to include in the textbook can be postponed till the moment that the student (or artificial teacher) clicks on the title for the first time. Several strategies can be used. A page can be chosen on the basis of:

- Author: written by the same author as the previous page in the section (if exists), or by the same author as the last visited page. This may support narrative flow. Students (or teachers) may also provide an ordered list of their favorite authors.
- Its learning style. This would require the author to annotate learning style related characteristics of a page. Alternatively, deductions could be made based upon the page content, like use of images, formulas, words like "example".
- A quality measure. Experts could review (alternative) pages and indicate a quality rating. Students could also rate pages seen. Alternatively, deductions could be made based upon the time spend on the page (not very reliable), links clicks, and the students performance on exercises after having visited the page.
- Its prerequisites being most closely met. Different authors may have different views on the relative order in which outcomes need to be addressed. This can lead to pages sharing the same outcomes, but having a different set of prerequisites. When links are annotated, like in [7], the annotation should be the most favorable one, i.e., if there is a page with the outcome whose prerequisites have been met, then the "ready to be learned" indication ought to be given.

The student can select an alternative, via links available from the page.

Ordering siblings. Pages can have outcomes that use different verbs on the same concept. For instance, a page with outcome "implement loops", and another page with outcome "explain loops". We call such pages siblings. When generating the hierarchy, siblings are ordered in such a way that a page with outcome X will precede all siblings with prerequisite X. Within this constraint, different strategies can be used to support narrative flow.
- A page with outcome X is followed immediately (or as soon as possible) by a page with prerequisite X.
- A page is followed by another page by the same author.

The relative level of verbs in Bloom's taxonomy can also aid the ordering process. For instance, "explain" precedes "design", which in its turn precedes "evaluate".

4 Conclusions

This paper describes an alternative approach to authoring adaptive web-based instruction systems. Though this work is only in its starting phases, it is clear that the choice to generate hierarchies automatically poses interesting problems and opportunities. If we want web-based instruction systems to grow organically, while maintaining narrative flow and user guidance then this seems a way forward.

References

1. Masthoff, J. An agent-based interactive instruction system. Ph.D. thesis, Eindhoven University of technology. (1997)
2. Brusilovsky, P., Eklund, J., and Schwarz, E. Web-based education for all: A tool for developing adaptive courseware. Computer Networks and ISDN Systems, Proceedings of Seventh International World Wide Web Conference (1998) 291-300
3. Weber, G., Kuhl, H-C., Weibelzahl, S. Developing adaptive internet based courses with the authoring system NetCoach. Proceedings of the third workshop on adaptive hypertext and hypermedia, UM2001, TU/e Computing Science Report 01/11. (2001)
4. Murray, T. MetaLinks: Authoring and affordances for conceptual and narrative flow in adaptive hyperbooks. Submission to the International Journal of Artificial Intelligence in Education. As accessed on http://helios.hampshire.edu/~tjmCCS/cv.html December 2001.
5. Bloom, B.S. (Ed.). Taxonomy of educational objectives: Book 1 Cognitive domain. Longman, London (1979)
6. Reiter, E. and Dale, R. Building natural language generation systems. Cambridge university press (2000)
7. Brusilovsky, P., Schwarz, E., and Weber, G. ELM-ART: An intelligent tutoring system on World Wide Web. In C. Frasson, G. Gauthier, & A. Lesgold (Eds.): Third International Conference on Intelligent Tutoring Systems, ITS-96. Lecture Notes in Computer Science, Vol. 1086. Springer Verlag, Berlin (1996) 261-269

Generation of Personalized Web Courses Using RBAC

Susana Montero, Ignacio Aedo, and Paloma Díaz

Laboratorio DEI. Computer Science Department
Universidad Carlos III de Madrid
Avda. de la Universidad 30. 28911 Leganés, Spain
smontero@inf.uc3m.es, aedo@ia.uc3m.es, pdp@inf.uc3m.es

Abstract. Role-based access control policies model the users domain by means of complex structures where the roles assumed by the users are specialized into more concrete subroles which inherit properties and authorizations from their parents. In this paper, we describe how to combine these principles and adaptation to provide personalized access to the different types of users of a web-based course. We also present Courba, a platform that generates personalized web-based courses using XML to support the definition of access policies.

1 Introduction

In a hypermedia educational application, there are two candidates to be adapted to the user learning style: the browsing structure (*navigation adaptation*) and the content delivered to the user (*presentation adaptation*) [1]. In order to adapt the hyperdocument, course developers have to build a user model gathering relevant information about the user knowledge, learning style, goals and needs. In predictive statistical models, two approaches are applied for user modeling: content-based and collaborative- based learning [6]. Content-based learning uses an individual model based on the user's behavior whereas collaborative-based learning uses group based models on the assumption that users behave in a similar way than other users. In order to specify such group-based user models, we propose in this paper the use of Role Based Access Control (RBAC) policies.

2 Role Based Access Control Modeling

RBAC policies [3, 4] model users by means of roles which represent functions or responsibilities. To gather the complexities of most organizations, hierarchies of roles are defined as a DAG (Directed Acyclic Graph) [3], where general roles are specialized into more specific roles that inherit attributes and authorizations from their parents. Each role is granted permission to perform some operations. Finally, each user is assigned a number of roles, whether static or dynamically, so that during the application operation each user exercises the abilities specified for the role(s) she belongs to.

RBAC can be applied within the context of educational applications, as far as a number of roles with different access and manipulation abilities are identified (e.g. lecturers, students, course coordinator, etc.). Moreover, even though RBAC is oriented towards modeling security policies, it can be extended to support the adaptive access to the courseware, translating authorizations rules to access rules that will state the contents, navigation facilities and interface of each node for each existing role, using a collaborative-based personalization mechanism as explained in the next section. Such rules can be explicitly specified or derived for each role, depending on whether the system is an adapted or adaptive one.

3 A RBAC-Based Hypermedia Model to Specify Personalization

The RBAC model proposed for providing safe access to hypermedia applications in [2] has been extended in order to provide a rational framework to specify the personalized access policy of web applications in terms of a number of access rules. Such rules specify the access category of a subject for a given object and how the object will be presented (presentation specifications): *Access rule = (subject, object, access category, presentation specifications)*

Subjects are active entities that execute actions on the objects (e.g. retrieve a node, modify a link or create a new content). Two kinds of abstractions are identified as subjects: roles and teams. While a role is an organizational position or job function, a team is just a group of users established whether to represent collaborative group as in [5] or to simplify the administration tasks. Roles and teams support composition mechanisms to be able to deal with complex user structures.

Objects are passive entities that receive the effects of the actions executed by the subjects. Nodes and contents are considered as objects, and links which always resolve into a node or content, inherit the rules that apply to the elements making up their definition.

Access categories embody the access capabilities for a given hyperdocument or course. Four categories are considered: *No access*, *Browsing*, *Personalizing* and *Editing*.

4 Courba: A Platform to Generate Personalized Web-Based Courses

Courba is a platform devoted to create web-based courses that will be accessed following a RBAC policy. The current version does only deal with personalized courses where access rules are hard coded for the roles so that personalization of the course structure, contents and interface is supported.

4.1 Courba Architecture and Implementation

Courba is made up of a series of modules where structure, content and presentation features have been separated to make possible the personalization to different users roles in a web-based course (see Fig. 1).

The **Information Base** holds information on the course as well as on the users. First, there is a course DTD which defines a logical structure where a course has a number of roles, access rules and a set of pages. Each page can be a cover page, index, theory page

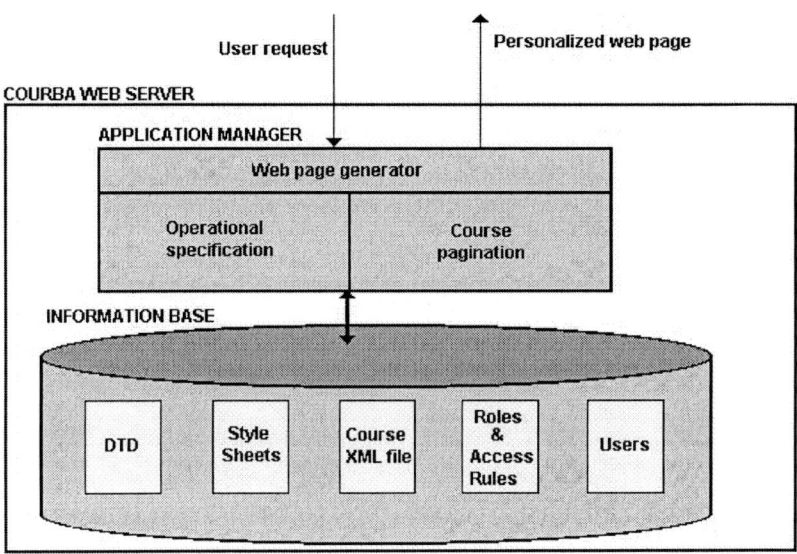

Fig. 1. Courba Architecture

or exercise. In turn, a index page has some contents and some operations which can be performed on that page (e.g. go to the parent page). The course contents are held in an XML document and the information about the presentation features (color, style and so on) is contained in separated style sheets. Finally, the roles as well as the assignment of their users are maintained in a separated file. When a user has to be included or removed from a course, only this latter users file is modified while the course DTD, XML document and style sheets remain unchanged.

The **Application Manager** is responsible for answering to the user's requests. Their tasks are to divide the XML document of the course into a series of pages (or nodes) taking into account the structure of the course represented in the DTD and to execute the manipulation operations that will be supported by the course. Current version of Courba supports the navigation operations where are established the target of each link according to the role of the user who is accessing the node. Access rules determine which operations will be available for each role. Finally, this module creates the web page corresponding to a users request taking into account the information about the page (structure, contents, interface and operations) as well as the user's role.

4.2 Personalized Access in a Courba Courseware

In order to create a personalized hypermedia courseware, developers have to create the XML document containing the course components, to specify which roles will be used in their course and which users hold that roles. Finally, they have to establish the access rules for the course components that will be nodes (that is, pages) and contents (that is, each information item - text, image, plug-in or operation-) included in a page.

The Courba platform has been tested in a course on Hypermedia Design. In the XML document has been included an index of topics, two different roles (the `novice` and the `expert` learner) and a set of access rules are specified to let build a dynamic personalized index. Figure 2 shows output created by Courba. In Fig. 2.A, it can be seen that a novice learner in this subject will have access to four topics. Once a learner has some experience (see Fig. 2.B), she is also given the opportunity of accessing sections about more specific problems and basics concepts are hidden. The targets of links Previous ("Anterior" in the figures), Parent ("Padre" in the figures) and Next ("Siguiente" in the figure) are calculated in runtime by the Courba Operational Specification module depending on the user's role.

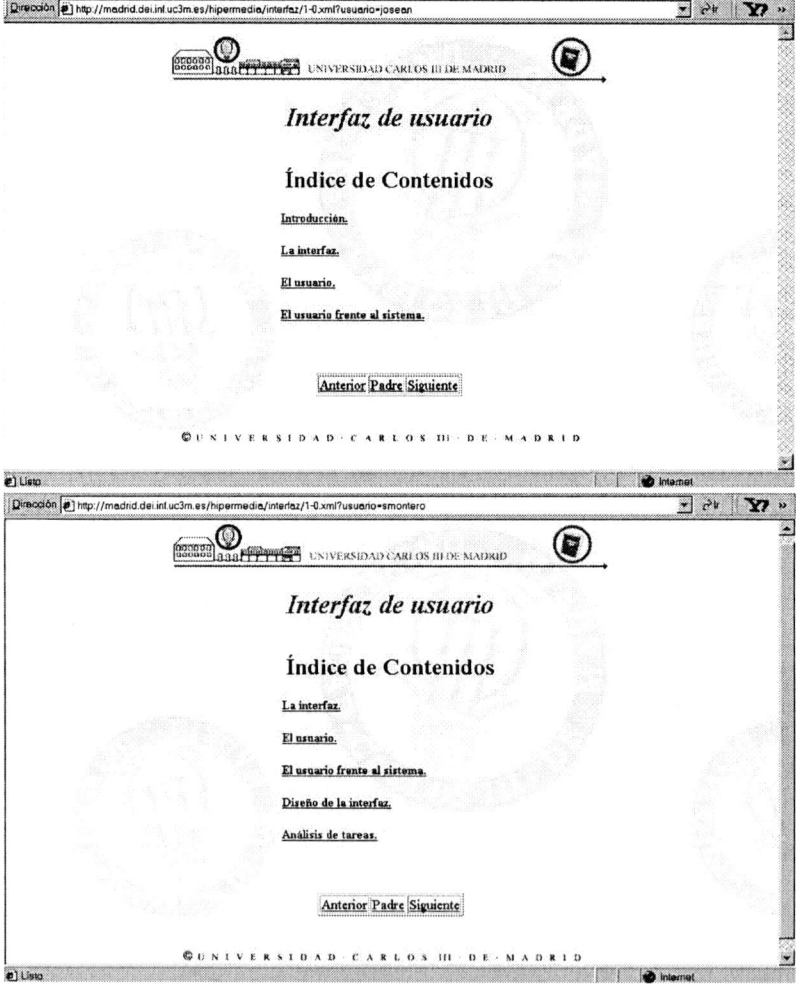

Fig. 2. Table of contents of the subject "User Interface" for a novice and an expert learner

5 Conclusions

In this paper, we have discussed how to combine the basic principles of adaptation for hypermedia applications with RBAC policies in order to support personalized access to a web-based courseware. With this purpose, a platform to support personalization in web courses, called Courba, based on a modular architecture has been proposed.

Acknowledgements

We'd like to thank Jose Ángel Cruz for his cooperation in the development of Courba. The RBAC model used in Courba is part of a project funded by "Dirección General de Investigación de la Comunidad Autónoma de Madrid y Fondo Social Europeo (07T/0012/2001)".

References

1. Brusilovsky, P. Adaptive hypermedia. *User Modeling and User-Adapted Interaction*, 11:87–110, 2001.
2. Díaz, P., Aedo, I. and Panetsos, F. Modelling security policies in hypermedia and web-based applications. In *Web Engineering: Managing diversity and complexity of web application development*, volume 2016 of *Lecture Notes in Computer Science*, pages 90–104. Murugesan, S. and Deshpande, Y. Eds. Springer, 2001.
3. Ferraiolo, D., Barkley, J. and Kuhn, R. A role-based access control model and reference implementation within a corporate intranet. *ACM Transactions on Information and System Security*, 2(1):34–64, 1999.
4. Shandu, R.S., Coyne, E.J., Feinstein, H.L. and Youman, C.E. Role-based access control: A multi-dimensional view. In *Proc. of the Tenth Annual Computer Security Applications Conference*, pages 54–62, Orlando, Florida, 1994.
5. Wang, W. Team-and-role-based organizational context and access control for cooperative hypermedia environments. In *Proc. of Hypertext'99*, pages 37–46, Darmstad.
6. Zukerman, I. and Albrecht, D.W. Predictive statistical models for user modeling. *User Modeling and User-Adapted Interaction*, 11:5–18, 2001.

An Automatic Rating Technique Based on XML Document

Hyeonjeong Mun[1], Sooho Ok[2], and Yongtae Woo[1]

[1] Changwon National University, Changwon Kyungnam 641-773, Republic of Korea,
{mun,ytwoo}@sarim.changwon.ac.kr
[2] Kosin University, Yeongdo-gu Pusan 606-701, Republic of Korea,
shok@kosin.ac.kr

Abstract. In this paper, we propose an automatic rating technique to collect the interest of users on the contents, such as e-books and electronic catalogs that are composed of XML documents, for developing a personalized recommender system. Our approach focuses on a method to collect implicit rating values for the elements in an XML document accessed by a user, when the content is converted into HTML format. In general, existing implicit rating techniques collect rating values after analyzing access logs in batch mode, however our method can collect the rating values in realtime. As a result of experimentation, we show that the implicit rating values collected by the proposed method are strongly correlated with explicit rating values.

1 Introduction

The main purpose of a recommender system is to provide personalized suggestions about the items in an E-commerce system. Therefore, a recommender system requires an intelligent user interface that can determine the interest of a user. The common solution is to use explicit ratings, where users tell what they think about a piece of information to the system, is well understood and fairly precise [1]. Even though the explicit rating technique can collect the exact interest about items from users, it can make troublesome overloads for them and deteriorate the efficiency of the recommendation if the rating information is insufficient or rating features had been changed.

Several implicit rating techniques have been studied to collect rating values automatically, where a rating is obtained by a method other than obtaining it directly from the user. Claypool has studied the correlation between various implicit ratings and the explicit rating for a single item, and the impact of implicit interest indicators on user privacy [2]. Morita has proposed an implicit rating technique to accumulate a user's preference for information based on user behavior monitoring by measuring the time spent for each article [3]. Nichols has sought to construct a comprehensive view of implicit feedback, with a focus on its use in information filtering systems. He has presented a list of potentially observable behaviors; adding purchase, assess, repeated use, refer, mark, glimpse, associate, and query to those mentioned above [4]. Oard and Kim have built upon work by Nichols by categorizing implicit ratings, dividing them into the following categories: Examination, where a user studies an item; Retention, where a user saves an item for later use; and Reference, where a user links all or part of an item into another item [5].

Recently, XML(eXtensible Markup Language), a data format for structured document interchange is promoted actively in various application areas such as e-books and electronic catalogs [6]. In this paper, we propose a new technique to collect users' interest automatically for a content based on the hierarchical structure among the elements in an XML document for personalized recommender system.

2   Implicit Ratings Using XML Hierarchical Structure

XML is way of marking up data, adding metadata, and separating structure from formatting and style. An XML document is composed of a hierarchical set of elements depending on the root element. When users access an XML document, which is converted into HTML using styles defined in the XSL script, instead of accessing XML documents directly.

We suggest a new method to collect rating values of the elements implicitly in an XML document accessed by a user when the document is converted into HTML document. Figure 1 shows a conceptual diagram of the proposed system.

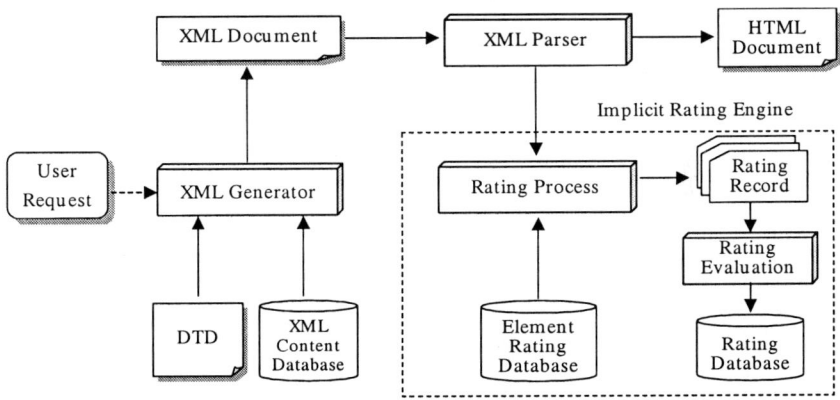

Fig. 1. The proposed implicit rating system based on XML document

Initially, all elements in an XML document can be assigned predefined rating value in accordance with their priority. For example, the elements related to purchasing intention such as price or ordering products are given higher value than such elements as product description or an image in an E-commerce system. Whenever a user accesses the XML document, The Implicit Rating Engine is activated to evaluate rating values related to that content. The Rating Process retrieves rating values of those elements in the Element Rating Database, and generates rating records for those elements. Afterwards, the Rating Evaluation calculates a rating value for the content, and saves the value into the Rating Database.

The total rating value for an XML document can be defined as an accumulated value multiplied level weight by rating value of each element accessed by the user. A level weight is assigned to each element in accordance with its level in the XML hierarchy. In our approach, we have defined a formula, R_c to evaluate total rating value for an XML document as follow:

$$R_c = \sum_{i \in V} w_i \cdot r_i,$$

where V is a set of elements of an XML document accessed by a user, w_i is a level weight, and r_i is a rating value assigned to each element. Therefore, R_c means that the total rating value for an XML document and a degree of interest on the specific content accessed by a user.

3 Experimental Results

We have performed an experiment with a total of 2,030 users from a recruiting site to verify the effectiveness of our approach. In the experiment, we have collected explicit rating grades from 1 through 5, implicit ratings with the proposed method, and reading time from the access logs on 326 XML documents. Correlations between the explicit ratings and the reading time, as well as the explicit ratings and the implicit ratings, have been calculated. Figure 2 shows the results of comparison with each method.

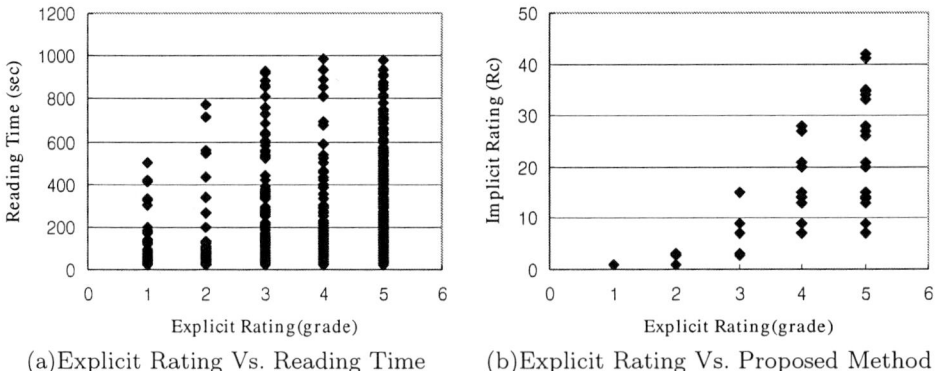

(a) Explicit Rating Vs. Reading Time   (b) Explicit Rating Vs. Proposed Method

Fig. 2. The results of experiment

Figure 2(a) shows the results of correlation between the explicit rating values and the reading time for the same set of contents. As the result of experiment, a correlation coefficient between the explicit rating values and the reading time was

0.41. The result shows weak correlation due to the difference in understanding the content among the users or network speed.

Figure 2(b) shows the results of correlation between the explicit rating values and the implicit ones collected with the proposed method. Correlation coefficients show a range from 0.75 to 0.83 depending on various rating values and weights. The implicit rating values collected with the proposed method, therefore, have shown strong correlation with explicit ones.

4 Conclusion

In this paper, we have proposed a new method to collect users' interests automatically for content in order to develop a personalized recommender system. Our approach focuses on collecting implicit rating values of the elements in an XML document accessed by a user. Our method can collect implicit rating values in realtime mode, while the existing implicit rating techniques collect rating values after analyzing access logs in batch mode. The result of our experiment shows that the implicit rating values collected with the proposed method has more strongly correlated with the explicit rating values than the correlations between the explicit ratings and the reading time. The proposed method can be thus expected to contribute more to the development of an efficient personalized recommender system as it collects users' interests automatically to substitute explicit ratings.

Acknowledgement

This work was supported by grant No. 2001-111-2 from the University fundamental research program of the Ministry of Information & Communication in Republic of Korea.

References

1. Konstant, J., Miller, B., Maltz, D., Herlocker, J., Gordong, L., Riedl, J.: GroupLens: Applying Collaborative Filtering to Usenet News. Communications of the ACM., 40(3) (1997) 77–87
2. Claypool, M., Brown, D., Le, P., Waseda, M.: Inferring User Interest. Technical Report WPI-CS-TR-01-97 (2001)
3. Morita, M., Shinoda, Y.: Information Filtering Based on User Behavior Analysis and Best Match Text Retrieval. Proceedings of the 17th Annual International ACM-SIGIR Conference on Research and Development in Information Retrieval (1994) 272–281
4. Nichols, D.: Implicit Rating and Filtering. Proceedings of the Fifth DELOS Workshop on Filtering and Collaborative Filtering (1997) 10–12
5. Oard, D., Kim, J.: Implicit Feedback for Recommender Systems. Proceedings of the AAAI Workshop on Recommender Systems (1998) 80–82
6. Abiteboul, S.: On views and XML. Proceedings of ACM Symposium on Principles of Database Systems (1999) 1–9

Using Effective Reading Speed to Integrate Adaptivity into Web-Based Learning

Muan Hong Ng[1], Wendy Hall[1], Pat Maier[2], and Ray Armstrong[3]

[1] Intelligence, Agents and Multimedia Research, University of Southampton,
SO17 1BJ Southampton, United Kingdom
{mhn99r,wh}@ecs.soton.ac.uk
[2] Center of Learning and Teaching, University of Southampton,
SO17 1BJ Southampton, United Kingdom
pjm@soton.ac.uk
[3] Rheumatology Unit, Mail Point 78, Southampton General Hospital,
SO16 6YD, Southampton, United Kingdom
rayarmstrong@btinternet.com

Abstract. It has always been difficult to determine to what extent a user has read a page especially in the area of educational adaptive hypermedia systems. We propose the use of an individual's effective reading speed to estimate how much of a page a user has read during their browsing activity. This method is currently used to apply history-based link annotation in a medical web-based learning application, JointZone. A validation test of this work has shown a positive result in approximating user's reading value when compared to conventional methods.

1 Introduction

A difficult problem faced by many adaptive hypermedia developers is to identify whether a page has been read. A generally unreliable solution is to use the viewing of a page as an indicator that the page has been read and understood (e.g. InterBook [2]). This method is obviously inefficient as the student might only be surfing through the pages without paying much attention to the content. In MANIC [11], the system assumes a high studied rating for a page if a user spends an optimal amount of time on it. This optimal time that is generated, based on the length of the content, is static for every user irrespective of their individual reading speed. However, Psychological research has shown that there are "astonishing differences in the rate of reading speed" among individuals [10]. It has also been found that two individuals reading at the same speed can have different rates of comprehension [5]. Motivation for this research comes from the users' unpredictable browsing behavior on the web, particularly the speed used in reading web pages. Research has shown that users frequently skim read the web pages instead of reading them in detail [4]. Studies have also shown that there is a general decline in the level of comprehension (especially in the recall of specific details) with faster reading as compared to reading at a normal speed [3, 7, 8]. Hence the reading speed, the time spent and the level of understanding on each page varies among individuals. The work in this paper captures this aspect of users' differences in reading speed and uses this to calculate how well they have read a web page based on the display time of the page.

2 Calculating the Effort Index

JointZone [13] is an interactive website for Rheumatology for both undergraduate medical students and practicing doctors. It contains approximately 80 documents, 750 images and 30 interactive case studies. The user model in JointZone contains an *effort index* (0-100%) for each page in the domain. This index is the system's estimation of the 'degree of effort spent' by a user on each page. The effort index is actually calculated by comparing the display time of a web page with an individual's optimal reading time. The optimal reading time for a page is identified for each user depending on the individual's reading rate, comprehension rate and prior knowledge of the domain. These user's characteristics are obtained when they use the system for the first time. Prior their first entry, a user will be asked to complete a knowledge test (10 multiple choice questions based on the general concept of the domain) to give a measurement of their prior knowledge (0-100%). Then each user has to take a 'reading speed test' where their reading rate is captured in number of words read per minute. The reading time is recorded through a start and stop button on the web page. This is followed by a comprehension test (six true or false questions on general ideas of the text) to give a score of their comprehension rate (0-100%). The combined measure of reading rate and comprehension gives the index of *effective reading speed* [6]. This index is commonly used in the commercial product for speed-reading courses [9, 12]. We have however, modified the equation by adding the factor of prior knowledge (see Equation 1).

$$\text{Effective reading speed} = \text{reading rate} \times \frac{1}{2} \left(\text{comprehension rate} + \text{prior knowledge} \right) \quad (1)$$

$$\text{Optimal reading time for a page} = \frac{\text{total number of words in the page}}{\text{Effective reading speed}} \quad (2)$$

$$\text{Effort Index Estimation, } G(x) = e^{\frac{-(x-\text{optimalTime})^2}{2\sigma^2}}, \text{ where } \sigma = 1.23 \quad (3)$$

During a browsing session the optimal reading time for any page in the domain is calculated in real time using Equation 2. The effort index on each page is then estimated using a Gaussian function (see Equation 3) by comparing the actual time spent on a page (x) with the optimal reading time. If 'x' approaches the optimal reading time, a high effort index is assumed. However, one problem still exists, as it is difficult to determine if a user has indeed read a page when it is displayed on the screen. To tackle this, a heuristic cutoff point is used to give a zero effort index to cases where display time falls below eight second or three times the optimal reading time. On the other hand, the use of individual optimal reading time enable us to skew the effort index based on a user's prior knowledge since a good student who skims a page will gain a higher effort index (with lower optimal reading time) as compared to a poor student who spent the same amount of time on the page.

3 Validation Test

A validation test was carried out to study the correlation between the effort index and the users' understanding of the content itself. Thirty subjects took part in the evaluation. Prior to the experiment, all users are instructed to complete a series of reading tests to capture their individual effective reading speed. The analysis for thirty users shows a mean effective reading speed of 116 word/min (sd = 58.74), mean prior knowledge of 30.67% (sd = 15.52) and mean comprehension rate of 63% (sd = 15.93). In the experiment, they were asked to read a page (length = 443 words) in the domain followed by a performance test to examine how much they understand the page. This test contains five multiple-choice questions, which asked users to recall some important aspects in the text (main factual type) [3]. All users spent an average of 3.19 minutes reading the page (sd = 1.12 minutes). The effort index for each user was estimated by the system using Equation 3. The score of the performance test was then compared with the effort index. The Pearson correlation test showed a significant correlation between the effort index and the performance test (r = 0.521, p = 0.003). The performance score was also compared with a separate calculation of effort index using a standard optimal reading time for all users (2.25 minute using the average on-screen reading rate of 200wpm). The Pearson correlation test shows a non-significant correlation of 0.056 (p = 0.767). Hence, we can conclude that each user has a different optimal reading time, which gives a relatively better approximation of the user's understanding of the domain.

Fig. 1. An example of the use of effort index in the history-based link annotation in a personalized site map

4 History-Based Link Annotation

The effort index is used as a basis to form the history-based link annotation [1] in the JointZone web-based medical learning. As shown in Fig. 1, this adaptive feature is applied on a personalised site map to provide feedback to the user on the system's assumption of his/her reading value for each page. This site map acts as a navigational support mechanism for the users and helps them to quickly gain an overview of the domain on pages they have read or not read.

5 Conclusions and Future Work

The individual effective reading speed used in calculating the effort index on web pages gives us a relatively good approximation in judging how well a page has been read. However, the cognitive issues in measuring the user's understanding have yet to be addressed in this work. Hence we cannot claim that the effort index completely represents a user's understanding of the text on the page. Nevertheless, the validation test showed that our method gives a comparatively more accurate approximation than existing methods. With this encouraging result, we will continue to expand the use of history-based link annotation with the effort index. We will also undertake a set of evaluations to specifically analyze this adaptive procedure within JointZone, to discover if this feature aids the user.

Acknowledgements

Arthritis Research Campaign, UK, educational project grant A0549.

References

1. Brusilovsky, P.: Adaptive Hypermedia. Journal on User Modeling and User Adapted Interaction, 11 (2001) 87-110
2. Brusilovsky, P., Eklund, J., and Schwarz, E.: Web-based Education For All: A Tool for Developing Adaptive Courseware. In: Proceedings of Seventh International World Wide Web Conference, 14-18 April, 30 (1-7) (1998) 291-300
3. Dyson, M. and Haselgrove, M.: The Effects of Reading Speed and Reading Patterns on Our Understanding of Text Read From Screen. Journal of Research in Reading 23 (2000) 210-223
4. Horton, W., Taylor, L., Ignacio, A and Hoft, N. L.: The Web page Design Cookbook. John Wiley, New York (1996)
5. Huey, E. B.: The Psychology and Pedagogy of Reading. The Macmillan Company (1908)
6. Jackson, M. D. and McClelland, J.L.: Processing Determinants of Reading Speed. Journal of Experimental Psychology: General 108 (1979) 151-181
7. McConkie, G., Rayner, K. and Wilson, S.: Experimental Manipulation of Reading Strategies. Journal of Educational Psychology 65 (1973) 1-8
8. Poulton, E. C.: Time for Reading and Memory. The British Journal of Psychology 49 (1958) 230-245
9. ReadingSoft.com found at http://www.readingsoft.com
10. Romanes, G. J.: Mental Evolution in Animals. Appleton & Co, New York (1885)
11. Stern, M. and Woolf, B. P.: Adaptive Content in an Online Lecture System. In: Proceedings of the International Conference on Adaptive Hypermedia and Adaptive Web-Based Systems, Trento Italy (2000)
12. TurboRead Speed Reading found at http://www.turboread.com
13. JointZone – A Study for Rheumatology found at http://www.iam.ecs.soton.ac.uk/users/mhn99r/learn/userlogin/index.jsp

A Non-invasive Cooperative Student Model

Teresa Roselli, Enrica Gentile, Paola Plantamura, Veronica Rossano,
and Vittorio Saponaro

Dipartimento di Informatica, Università degli Studi di Bari
Via Orabona, 4 - 70126 Bari, Italy
roselli@di.uniba.it

Abstract. A crucial issue in building a user-centered Intelligent Educational System is that of building and maintaining user models to enable the system to tailor its behavior to the needs of the given individual. Various student modeling techniques are described in the literature (overlay, perturbation, differential), that represent the student's knowledge in different ways. A common problem affecting these techniques is how to obtain the data needed to build the student model. Open models are one of the possible solutions but these have some drawbacks. In the present article we propose a new open model aiming to solve some of these, by minimizing the invasiveness of the requirement for student involvement in the self-assessment process, together with the sense of frustration such a requirement can arouse in students who are unable to assess themselves and are therefore ignored by the system.

1 Introduction

One of the essential aims of teaching-learning processes is to enable students to acquire the ability and knowledge needed to carry out successful problem solving in the relative domain. The method adopted by Intelligent Educational Systems is to induce the student to build a domain model, which is then compared with the system knowledge base [1]. Various student modeling techniques have been reported in the literature. These aim primarily to construct cognitive models of the learner's domain knowledge and can also include some meta-cognitive aspects [2], going beyond simple user modeling to build explanations of students' behavior not only by observing their actions but also by engaging them in various learning situations.

In the overlay model proposed by Carr and Goldstein [3], the student's knowledge is treated as a subset of the system knowledge base and the model is built by comparing the expert's and the student's responses. The system starts from the assumption that all differences between the two are to be attributed to student deficiencies in one or more abilities. The overlay model thus has the drawback that is not equipped to deal with any student knowledge or opinions differing from those of the expert. If the student adopts a problem-solving strategy that has not been included in the system, the tutor will intervene to correct the "error".

An alternative method is differential modeling, which compares the student's behavior, rather than his/her knowledge, with that of the expert in the same situation. However, the student's knowledge is still assumed to be a subset of the expert knowledge, so that the model is again incomplete.

A third method, the perturbation method thought up by Brown and Burton in 1978 [4], provides a similar student and expert model, in which differences between the student's and the system's behavior are represented as perturbations.

In any case, the problem arises of how to acquire the data needed to build the student model. A promising solution is offered by open student models. These require the student to take an active part in the construction of the model, with the aim of increasing the data obtained and hence the accuracy of the model. The fact of giving students the opportunity to inspect and discuss their knowledge makes it possible to cover wider cognitive aspects and make better forecasts of their future performance, because the process of discussion of the model gives them the chance to reflect on their understanding and experience of the domain, to revise and reconsider their ideas and thus become more aware. This reflection stimulates a better perception of the relationships and connections between different knowledge parts and encourages active participation in the learning process [5,6].

However, one of the side effects of student involvement in the assessment process is that students who are unable to make a self-assessment are ignored by the system. The resulting sense of frustration could affect their performance, although this does not, in fact, seem to occur, according to the experiments conducted by Beck [7]. However, the requirement for student involvement in management of their model may be too invasive if too many opinions on their knowledge level are called for. Many negative effects could result, such as distraction (while reflecting on acquired knowledge, the new notions proposed could be neglected) and a feeling of insecurity that could hinder the overall learning process.

The aim of the present work was to build a cooperative user-system student model that could solve some of the problems reported in the literature with such models. As regards the difficulty of the requirement for student involvement in the assessment process being too invasive, causing annoyance and distraction, the solution proposed is to merge the tutor's communication of the expert assessment with a request for optional self-assessment by the student. Another feature aims to minimize students' frustration if they are unable to carry out self-assessment and are therefore ignored by the system. Use is made of graduated negative feedback according to the student's estimated self-assessment ability.

2 The Weighted Cooperative Student Model

The student's calculation of his/her self-assessment ability is merged with the tutor's assessment, to obtain a combined (tutor-student) view. The differences are attributed variable weights according to the expert estimate of the student's self-assessment ability. Another feature of the model is the fact that students are not obliged to make a self-assessment. This prevents excessive invasiveness of the tutor, that might systematically distract and condition the student by obliging him/her to make continual judgments, is avoided [7].

After doing an exercise, the results are communicated and the option of making a self-assessment is given. If the pupil does not wish to do so, or agrees with the tutor's assessment, he/she can go straight on to the next phase. Instead, in the case of a different opinion, the process for conflict solving is activated and leads to an integrated assessment that merges the student's and tutor's assessments, by calculating the weighted mean of the two. The weights are calculated according to a confidence function. The whole process is illustrated in Figure 1.

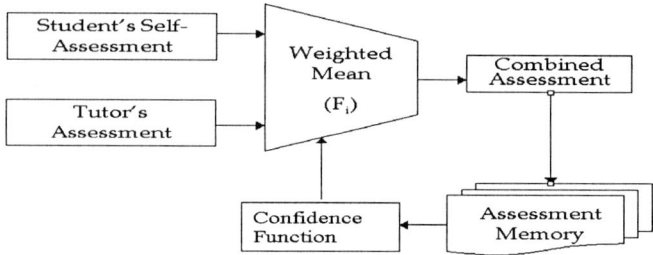

Fig. 1. Combined student-tutor assessment

Calculation of the combined assessment. The method for calculating the combined assessment is based on a series of confidence coefficients (F_i) that attribute the appropriate weights to the student's ($V_{student}$) and tutor's (V_{tutor}) opinions.

The starting confidence coefficient is $F_1 = 0.5$, while the combined assessment (V_{final}) is calculated by:

$$V_{final} = F_i \cdot V_{student} + (1-F_i) \cdot V_{tutor} \quad (1)$$

There are three main factors involved in the calculation of the new confidence coefficient: the previous coefficient, the student's mean self-assessment ability and the mean spread ratio between this and the tutor's assessment.

Self Assessment Mean Capability Ratio. The sum of the equation below is defined as the index of the student's mean self-assessment ability:

$$SAMCR = mean(V_{student} - V_{final})_i \quad (2)$$

where $i = (1...N)$ indicates the ith self-assessment made.

The domain of the SAMCR is [-2, 2]. At each step, this index represents the mean self-assessment error.

Mean Spread Ratio of Student Errors. The mean spread ratio of student errors is the sum:

$$MSRSE = mean \, |(V_{student} - V_{final})_i - SAMCR|_i \quad (3)$$

where $i = (1...N)$ indicates the ith self-assessment made.

This index gives an overall idea of how the student's errors are spread over the domain, i.e. how consistently the student correctly/incorrectly estimates, or over/underestimates his/her performance.

Confidence function. The confidence function (f) enables calculation of the confidence coefficients on the basis of the current SAMCR and MSRSE indexes, that keep track of the student's self-assessment ability, together with the current confidence coefficient F_i. At the ith step, the next confidence coefficient is calculated as follows:

$$F_{i+1} = f(SAMCR_i, MSRSE_i) \cdot F_i = k_i \cdot F_i \quad (4)$$

The lower the student's self-assessment ability, the lower the k_i value and the lower the tutor's confidence in the student. In addition, the student will receive suggestions aiming to improve his/her self-assessment ability.

If the combined assessment is positive the student receives positive feedback; if negative, the theoretical lesson for the ability in question is re-proposed and a new, remedial, exercise is set to improve his/her ability. Further self-assessment is avoided to prevent excessive invasiveness of the system.

3 Conclusions and Future Work

The student model described has been implemented in an intelligent hypermedial system, 'Frazionando', that targets primary school pupils. The knowledge domain includes the study of fractions and their main properties. A pilot test was carried out to verify the efficacy of the confidence function and confidence coefficients used by the system and, in general, the reliability of the collaborative student model. Twelve primary school students were selected on the basis of heterogeneous scholastic performance and level of maturity, as assessed by their teachers. Among the positive results obtained, the approach was judged useful and was particularly appreciated by typically introvert students who have greater difficulty in communicating learning problems to a human tutor. Another satisfactory result was that of reducing the sense of frustration the system could arouse in students with less ability to make self-assessment: thanks to the advice the system gave students about how to make their self-assessments, they felt involved as participants in the overall assessment process.

For future developments of the model, further experiments on a larger student sample must be made. We also aim to integrate the domain knowledge with data on the typical errors made by students and to set up strategies for increasing the powers of adaptation of the hypermedial system [8].

References

1. Roselli, T. : Artificial Intelligence can improve Hypermedial Instructional Technologies for Learning. ACM Computing Surveys, Vol. 27, No 4 (1985)
2. Paiva, A., Self, J., Hartley, R.: Externalising learner models. Proceedings of World Conference on Artificial Intelligence in Education. Washington DC. (1995) 509-516
3. Carr, B., Goldstein, I.: Overlays: a theory of modelling for computer aided instruction. (AI MEMO 406) Cambridge. MA: M.I.T.. AI Laboratory (1977)
4. Brown, S., Burton, R.B.: Diagnostic Models for procedural bugs in basic mathematical skills. Cognitive Science, 2 (1978)
5. Boud, D., Keogh, R., Walker, D.: What is reflection in learning. In Boud. Keogh.Walker eds. Reflection: turning experience into learning Kogan Page. London. (1996) 7-17
6. Dimitrova, V., Self, J., Brna, P.: Involving the learner in diagnosis – Potentials and problems. Computer Based Learning Unit, Leeds University, Leeds LS29JT, UK. (2000)
7. Beck, J., Stern, M., Woolf, B.P.: Cooperative Student Models. Computer Science Department, University of Massachusetts. Proceedings of the AIED. (1997) 127-134
8. Brusilovsky, P.: Adaptive Hypermedia. User Modeling and User-Adapted Interaction 11. (2001) 87-110

Category-Based Filtering in Recommender Systems for Improved Performance in Dynamic Domains

Mikael Sollenborn and Peter Funk

Mälardalen University
Department of Computer Science and Engineering
Västerås, Sweden
{mikael.sollenborn,peter.funk}@idt.mdh.se

Abstract. In Recommender systems, collaborative filtering is the most commonly used technique. Although often successful, collaborative filtering encounters the latency problem in domains where items are frequently added, as the users have to review new items before they can be recommended. In this paper a novel approach to reduce the latency problem is proposed, based on category-based filtering and user stereotypes.

1 Introduction

For personalization of web pages, Recommender systems are currently the most common approach. Based on the information filtering technique known as collaborative filtering [1,2], standard Recommender systems essentially function on a peer review basis. When making recommendations, users with similar preferences are identified, and their item ratings are used to propose items to one another.

In addition to collaborative filtering, personalized selections based on matching the user's previous selections with meta-data or content keywords for individual items - known as content-based filtering - is also very common.

Traditional Recommender systems often encounter the *latency* problem [3], i.e. new items cannot be used in collaborative recommendations before a substantial amount of users have evaluated it, as the recommendations rely on other users opinions. This problem is especially apparent in domains where new items are often added and old items quickly get out of date. Content-based filtering may be a solution, but runs the risk of only recommending items almost identical to the ones the user has appreciated before [3]. As noted in [4], the most obvious solution to the latency problem is to categorize the items in the system. In this paper we go one step further and propose that for quickly changing domains, Recommender systems solely based on categories may provide sufficient personalization.

2 Category-Based Filtering Approach

We refer to the personalization approach proposed in this paper as *category-based filtering*. Its main characteristic is that selection of information is based on category ratings instead of item ratings. To function, category-based filtering requires categorization of every item, either manually or by an automated process.

The selection of items is based partly on individual user models, and partly on collective user stereotypes. A *user model* represents the current knowledge about a user's reaction towards shown categories of items. The model consists of a preference matrix containing the number of times the user has seen items belonging to each category, and the frequency with which these items were clicked. A *user stereotype*, in contrast, consists of collective category preference information for a group of users, acquired through clustering. When the information in a user model is insufficient for deciding which items to select, the user stereotype assigned to the user is consulted to make assumptions about the user's expected behavior.

The focus on categories reduces the latency problem, as new items can be recommended as soon as the user's attitude towards the item's category is known. The method is thus especially suited for domains with a constant flow of new information (e.g. news, adverts), provided that efficient classification is possible.

2.1 Creation of User Stereotypes

User stereotypes are identified using offline hierarchical clustering of system users. The variables determining cluster membership are as many as there are categories in the system. Different values are assigned to the category attitudes negative, neutral, and positive, and the Manhattan distance metric is used to measure distance between clusters. Similar clusters are merged using the unweighted pair-group average method.

The chosen method of capturing collective interests in user stereotypes is to utilize what will be referred to as *appreciation nets*. Appreciation nets are graphs with nodes and directed edges, where edges represent a probabilistic relationship. In Fig. 1 an example of an appreciation net is given for four item categories. Here, the likelihood that a person who likes hunting is also interested in motor sports is 60%, and 30% in the opposite direction. Of the persons belonging to this population, 50% enjoy motor sports, but only 20% appreciates hunting, as indicated in the category nodes.

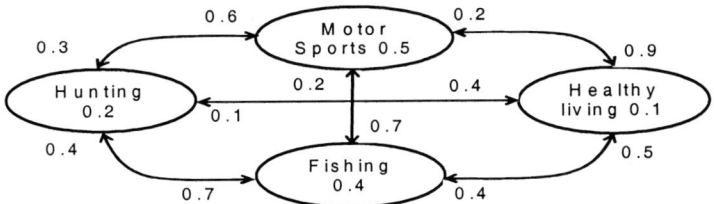

Fig. 1. An appreciation net with four item categories

A user stereotype consists of an appreciation net, with all nodes connected to every other node in both directions. When forming such a net, a joint distribution is made from the ranked category preferences of every user belonging to the cluster. For each category C the system stores the probability of a positive evaluation by any user belonging to the group, as node values in the appreciation net. Secondly, the probability of a user appreciating C in case the user likes D, P(C|D), is preserved for each category-to-category connection, stored as binary relationships between category nodes in the appreciation net.

2.2 Classification of New Users

A new user must be assigned a user stereotype before personalized items can be selected. Initially, the system doesn't know enough about the user to decide which stereotype is the most appropriate. Automatic classification is attempted by targeting the user with information corresponding to differential probability values in the user stereotypes appreciation nets. The goal is to determine which user stereotype resembles the new user the most. Initially, it is assumed that the biggest cluster is an appropriate starting point.

Category nodes in the appreciation net with high appreciation probabilities are sought for, with these values being as unique as possible compared to the equivalent category values in other clusters. The appropriateness of being chosen, F, is calculated for every category node C by comparing it to the corresponding category node C_i in every other user stereotype appreciation net, using

$$F = P(C) * \sum_i |P(C) - P(C_i)|. \quad (1)$$

The categories with highest F are chosen for stereotype identification, i.e. a number of items belonging to these categories will be shown to the user. After the user has responded, a stereotype determination is performed. The categories involved in the test are compared to the appreciation net in each user stereotype, putting emphasis on similar categories with high probability values. The dissimilarity D is calculated for every user stereotype, where Cui is category i in user model u, Csi is the corresponding category i in user stereotype s, and M is an empirically chosen modification rate (about 1.25), using

$$D = \sum_i |P(Cui) - P(Csi)| * (1 - P(Csi) \div M). \quad (2)$$

The user stereotype that most closely resembles the initial behavior of the user is now chosen for a second pick of categories using (1). The process continues until the collected information indicates that the user can be classified safely.

2.3 Selection of Personalized Items

Personalized information is divided into *appreciation-known* and *appreciation-assumed*. A new user is confronted with a lot of appreciation-assumed information, but as the user model stabilizes, appreciation-known information gradually replaces it.

Appreciation-known items are chosen only from categories the user has evaluated enough times to be reasonably sure about his/her attitude towards it. Information is selected by ranking the user preferences, picking items from categories that have been positively evaluated. In this process, the system tries to balance the number of shown items among the positive preferences, as well as sometimes picking sufficiently evaluated categories with a less positive ranking to allow for re-evaluation.

When appreciation-assumed items are to be selected, the system chooses a category node starting point in the appreciation net among the users positively ranked preferences, and examines all connected category nodes. The category to select information from is chosen randomly from a dynamically generated pie chart, where each category not among the user's positive preferences gets a slice size (choice probability) calculated using equation 3. W is the connection weight, C the number of selections of items belonging to this category, S the number of times shown to the user, and L how many of the last H items in the category that has been selected by the user. H is domain dependent; in our test evaluation the history length is ten items.

$$P = W * ((C + 1)/(S + 1) + (L+1)/H) \qquad (3)$$

Another form of appreciation-assumed selection, used in parallel with the method above, works similarly to the automatic classification process by picking items from categories in the appreciation net where the probability of a positive response is high.

The items selected by using each of these techniques are finally merged, and presented to the current user.

3 Conclusions

In this paper we have presented an approach to Recommender systems for application domains where items are frequently added. Provided that sufficient categorization is possible, category-based filtering enables handling the latency problem.

Initial evaluations are showing expected good results, and large-scale testing is currently ongoing.

References

1. Shardanad, U., Maes, P.: Social Information Filtering: Algorithms for Automating 'Word of Mouth'. Proceedings of the ACM Conference on Human Factors in Computing Systems, ACM Press (1995) 210-217
2. Konstan, J.A., Miller, B.N., Maltz, D., Herlocker, J.L., et. al.: GroupLens: Applying collaborative filtering to usenet news. Communications of the ACM 40 (1997) 3:77-87
3. Funakoshi, K., Ohguro, T.: A content-based collaborative recommender system with detailed use of evaluations. In Proceedings of 4th International Conference on Knowledge-Based Intelligent Engineering Systems and Allied Technologies, Volume 1 (2000) 253-256
4. Hayes, C., Cunningham, P., Smyth, B.: A Case-Based Reasoning View of Automated Collaborative Filtering. In Proceedings of 4th International Conference on Case-Based Reasoning, ICCBR2001 (2001) 243-248

Protecting the User from the Data:
Security and Privacy Aspects of Public Web Access

Adrian Spalka and Hanno Langweg

Department of Computer Science III, University of Bonn
Roemerstrasse 164, 53117 Bonn, Germany
adrian@cs.uni-bonn.de

Abstract. Observance of laws on the protection of minors is a serious problem at places with Internet access. We examine protection mechanisms in view of the Internet's open and dynamic nature and claim that those based on deterrence and restoration should be preferred to purely preventive ones. We then present a strategy adequate for secondary schools. The technical part relies on adaptable filter and logging components, which check and log requested web-pages. In a feed-back loop a human auditor provides more information to the system, thus increasing the effectiveness. On the other hand, separation of powers among auditors ensures the users' privacy.

1 Introduction

Schools use the Internet in the education of minors. But on the other hand, most of them worry about misuse of the Internet. From the viewpoint of a school that makes the Internet accessible to minors it is the users who need protection from harmful material on the Internet. This situation is a departure from traditional computer security paradigms and poses a range of new problems. We believe that measures to protect minors from content should be adaptable to a school's particular position.

As our empirical data reveal, at present left on their own schools with access to the Internet pursue mainly two extreme approaches. The restrictive one confines access to a small number of predetermined web sites. While suitable at elementary level schools the pupils of which have little or no media competence, it only hides the richness of information from older minors. The liberal approach allows unlimited access to the Internet. If harmful material is discovered on the school's computers, the affair is most often innocuously swept under the carpet.

We have focused our attention on secondary schools with two aims in mind. The Internet should be usable as an open environment and legal restrictions and the school's habits should be observed. Since preventive measures alone are inadequate for this purpose, we favour a self-responsible and controlled access to the Internet, depending on administrative, preventive and restorative methods. The result is a system with both increasing technical precision and reliability and of educational value. The system is implemented on a Microsoft Windows NT basis and the sources can be freely obtained upon request to the authors.

2 Internet Access at Schools and Existing User Protection Efforts

Today many secondary schools in highly developed countries possess PCs; many of them have the PCs connected in a local network and some operate an intranet. In the first place one can think of applying the well-known protection methods accredited in the industry, private and government institutions. Yet a look at the following list reveals that many of the conditions these methods rely on cannot be found at schools.

We can say of the pupils that they often have a competent understanding of computers, are sometimes driven by a temptation to go over limits and have no contractual obligations with the school. On the other hand we can say of many of the teachers that they often have only little knowledge of computers, teach different classes and that their acceptance of security measures degrades with increasing effort. We see that security ergonomics must play an important role in the overall design.

At first glance we have a traditional threat scenario. The protection units are data, programs and the hardware and they are all well known. Given that teachers are assumed to behave in concordance with the rules, pupils are the only potential intruders. The only protection goal is to protect data, programs and hardware from adventurous or malicious-minded pupils – a task, which can be solved almost with traditional means.

The situation changes drastically with the addition of Internet access. With this the environment becomes open and dynamic. We now have a reversal in the protection goal: it is the pupils who must be protected from the data. The problem is that there is no technical way of completely specifying and locating the harmful content.

That on the Internet there is as much material proper to minors as harmful to them is not new. Therefore, protection efforts are made at various levels. At the legal level national laws can be enforced within the perimeter of their validity. Though useful, the overall effectiveness of national legal measures is quite limited. As of yet international legal agreement among most countries has been reached only on the prohibition of child pornography – an essential but small part of harmful material.

Today's technical systems rely solely on two filtering approaches, i.e. purely preventive measures. The first one uses a web site's address (e.g., NetNanny or Cyber Patrol) and the second one a web page's rating-label (e.g., the W3C PICS standard) to determine if a requested page should be blocked or passed to the client.

3 A Comprehensive Protection System for Schools

Our approach is based on that the notion of protection of minors should not be confused with the protection of young people from the world just because there are dangers. Protection of minors is the protection from dangers in their education and development and it can be best done by teaching them how to cope with dangers. Our system as a whole is a combination of several types of measures: administrative, preventive and restorative. Its effectiveness depends on an implementation of all of them. It consists of four consecutive phases, which we subsequently describe in detail: establishment of a school policy, automatic technical blocking and logging of web accesses, semi-automatic post-processing, and sanctioning.

Phase I: The school's security policy. The first phase is the establishment of a written school law on the use of the Internet by pupils. It corresponds to a security policy in the traditional sense. For the teachers it must comprise explicit statements on their responsibilities, duties and prohibitions. They must accept it, approve of it and act accordingly. For the pupils, the law must also comprise explicit statements on their responsibilities and duties. Most important are the statements on the intended use of the Internet, the automatic logging activities, the post-processing activities of particular teachers to discover each improper use of the Internet and the types of sanctions that can be applied upon improper use. We have prepared a skeleton policy, which a school can adapt and extend according to its requirements.

Phase II: Automatic technical measures. Most schools have access to the Internet through one or more dial-up lines. We assume that all these lines are connected to a proxy, which our system can take control of. As a web server returns the requested data, we intercept and process it in the following order. If the returned item's web-address can be derived from an entry in our white-list, it is immediately passed to the client without any further action. If the returned item's web-address can be derived from an entry in the address-black-list of an enabled harmful category, the access is logged and blocked, ie the client is notified of an improper access attempt. If the returned item is a picture (GIF and JPEG at present) and its hash-value is found in our picture-black-list of an enabled harmful category, the access is also logged and blocked. Otherwise, the access is logged and the returned item is passed to the client.

The entries in the white-list are complete or partial web-addresses of content that is considered appropriate without objections. Lists and categories are managed by the school in phase III. We maintain two black-lists, one for addresses and one for hash-values of pictures. An entry in the address-black-list comprises an address as in the white-list and the categories it belongs to. We provide three classes: pornography, racism and violence. A school is free to add more categories at its discretion.

A log-entry comprises all data to view the returned web-item later in the same way as it was presented on the client's computer and to identify client and time of access.

Phase III: Semi-automatic post-processing. The logged data are assessed and evaluated. At first we use a classification program, which rates the logged web-content's degree of harmfulness with respect to existing categories. A list of weighted keywords is associated with each category. The categories and their lists can be changed by the school. The degree of possible harmfulness of a web-page is the weighted sum of the keywords' frequencies.

The next steps require manual intervention of two teachers. First, teacher *A* starts the determination-function in a browser. He is shown a list of the logged web-addresses and the computed rating in each category. He can order the list and can selectively display a web-page or scan them like in a slide-show. It is now at his discretion to decide if an access actually is a violation of the policy or not: If our guess is right, he can mark this page and any pictures on it as harmful with respect to the matching categories. The chosen part of the web-address and the pictures' hash-values are entered in black-lists. The page is marked for submission to identification. If our guess is wrong, the page's address can be entered in the white list.

From a purely functional perspective one teacher suffices to do both tasks: determination and identification. Possible objections with respect to the protection of both the teachers' and the pupils' privacy led us to a separation of duties, which guarantees the privacy of both parties.

Phase IV: Sanctioning. That decision is at the sole discretion of the school.

Advantages and disadvantages. Some drawbacks of our system are easily spotted. Its effectiveness decreases as the volume of logged data increases. It is possibly imprecise if not all logged data is scanned by a teacher and the system requires regular manual intervention of teachers, at least 1-2 hours per week.

On the other hand, it offers a number of benefits. Improper use of the Internet is detectable and the school has full discretion as regards determination of harmful content and the decision on when a pupil's behaviour should be counted as a violation. Lists and assessment of content increase over time in concordance with the school's policy and can be extended in co-operation with other schools. Our system uses ergonomic features; to the teachers it is like any other work on the Internet.

4 Conclusion

Schools have a legal obligation to protect pupils from harmful material on the Internet but little technical assistance in accomplishing it. Owing to the global extent of the Internet, legal regulations do not solve the problem in practice. We have examined existing products and arrived at the conclusion that preventive measures are useful and necessary but insufficient or inadequate for many reasons. Our approach gets its strength from a combination of administrative, preventive and restorative methods. It achieves the most important goals: it preserves the Internet's open nature, offers protection from known harmful content and teaches how to deal with the unknown part.

References

1. Frishberg, M.: *Protecting Kids, Here and There.* http://www.wired.com/news/politics/0,1283,36005,00.html, (2000)
2. Kobsa, A.: *User Modeling, Privacy and Security.* Invited talk held at the First International Conference on Adaptive Hypermedia and Adaptive Web-Based Systems, (2000)
3. Kobsa, A.: Tailoring Privacy to User's Needs. In: Bauer, M., Gmytrasiewicz, P., Vassileva, J. (Eds.). *User Modeling 2001.* 8th International Conference, UM 2001. Lecture Notes in Artificial Intelligence 2109, (2001)
4. Net Nanny Software: Net Nanny 4 Product Description. http://www.netnanny.com/, (2002)
5. SurfControl: *Cyber Patrol Web Filter.* http://www.surfcontrol.com/, (2002)
6. webwasher.com AG: *Statement on protection of minors.* http://www.webwasher.com/en/corporate/minors.htm, (2002)
7. World Wide Web Consortium.: *Platform for Internet Content Selection (PICS).* http://www.w3c.org/PICS, (1997)

Exploiting a Progressive Access Model to Information

Marlène Villanova-Oliver, Jérôme Gensel, and Hervé Martin

Laboratoire LSR – IMAG, BP 72, 38402 Saint Martin d'Hères cedex, France.
Tel.: (33) 4 76 82 72 80, Fax: (33) 4 76 82 72 87
{villanova,gensel,martin}@imag.fr

Abstract. We propose here to stratify the Information Space of a Web-based Information System (WIS) by decomposing it into personalized sub-Information Spaces. This stratification is described through a Progressive Access Model (PAM) written in UML. The PAM gives WIS users, first, access to some minimal and essential information, and then, allows them to navigate through larger and/or smaller personalized Information Spaces. Together with the PAM, we present a specific query language which allows to query a stratification and to format replies according to the different levels of details of the stratified user's Information Space.

1 Introduction

The appropriateness of information a WIS delivers to its users turns out to be an acute problem when designing such systems one ignores that 1) all users do *not* need the same information, 2) users do *not* need all the available information all the time. The first point often referred to as *adaptability* (see for instance [1]) can be addressed by distinguishing users profiles. Recent approaches [1] announce a new generation of web applications able to track down the behaviour of users and to dynamically adapt information to users rights, needs, characteristics and material configurations (WAP, browser, etc.), in terms of both content and presentation. The second point deals with the delivery of information and the fact that users may occasionally need *only* some parts of information. In order to protect users against a cognitive overload, we provide them with a gradual organization for progressively accessing information. In [3] we have defined two notions for organizing at a conceptual level the data of a WIS so that users are offered a personalized and progressive access. The data model of the WIS is stratified into different levels of detail which are exploited by progressive access mechanisms. Once stratified, a data model constitutes an Information Space in which a (group of) user(s) can navigate gradually from a level of detail to another. The stratification is described through an extensible Progressive Access Model (PAM), which has been implemented in KIWIS, a platform for the design and automatic deployment of WIS [4].

In this paper, we propose first a UML description of the PAM for object-oriented WIS. Then, we introduce a query language, called PAM QL, which allows to query a stratified Information Space. Not only query expressions can concern the stratification itself, but also levels of detail can be used in query expressions. The reply to a query, whether this latter explicitly refers to the stratification or not, is formatted according to the levels of detail defined by the stratification of the user's Information Space.

2 The Progressive Access Model

The Progressive Access Model (PAM) stratifies the Data Model of the application domain addressed by the WIS by introducing different levels of detail. In [3] we describe how the PAM is coupled with both the Data Model and a model of the users, called Generic User Model (GUM). The connections between these three models allow a WIS designer to define as many adapted stratified views on the data model as required for individuals or groups of users.

We give here a UML description of the PAM in the particular case of an object-oriented Data Model (*cf.* Fig. 1). The class *UserCategory* connects the PAM to the GUM. The class *MaskableEntity* (ME) corresponds to the set of information to be stratified. It specializes in two classes called *ClassDiagram* and *Class*, since the stratification can be performed at these different granularities. The class *Representation of Maskable Entity* (RoME) denotes the different representations available for a *ME* and which constitute its stratification. Each RoME of this set corresponds to a level of detail at which the *ME* is presented more or less completely. The sub-classes of RoME, called *RoME_DataModel* and *RoME_Class*, are respectively defined for the two sub-classes of *ME*. The association *structures* between the classes *UserCategory*, *ME* and *RoME* (or theirs sub-classes) is so that:
- 0 to *n* instance(s) of *RoME* can be linked to one couple of instances (*UserCategory*, *ME*). No (0) instance means no stratification: the user is given no progressive access to information, which is delivered in a whole. On the contrary, *n* instances of *RoME* offer to the user *n* levels of representation for this *ME*.
- 1 to *n* instance(s) of *UserCategory* can be linked to one couple of instances (*ME*, *RoME*), allowing several users to share the same stratification.
- one and only one instance of *ME* is linked to one couple of instances (*UserCategory*, *RoME*), meaning that the stratification is proper to one *ME*.

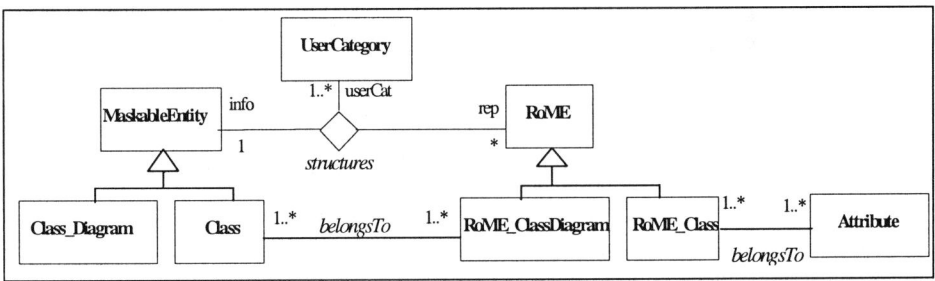

Fig 1. PAM extended description, fitting an object-oriented data model.

The class *RoME_DataModel* is linked to the class *Class* through the association *belongsTo*. Linking a set of instances of *Class* to one instance of *RoME_DataModel* means that these classes are accessible at the level of detail to which corresponds this instance of *RoME_DataModel*. The class *RoME_Class* is linked to the class *Attribute* through the association *belongsTo*. Linking a set of instances of *Attribute* to one instance of *RoME_Class* means that these attributes are accessible at the level of detail to which corresponds this instance of *RoME_Class*.

3 PAM QL: A Query Language for the PAM

Once the stratification has been created or modified by instantiating the PAM, the PAM Query Language, which is based on a OQL-like formalism [5] can be used *i)* for querying the stratification performed on an Information Space, *ii)* for querying the Data Model and getting reply formatted to the stratification (i.e. according to levels of detail). We give below examples of a *query on stratification* (left part) and of a query which includes stratification features used in the formatted reply (right part):

```
GIVE STRATIFICATION                   SELECT ME.information, …
FROM maskable_entity ME               FROM maskable_entity ME
[ FOR all_levels | level_interval     [WHERE expression]
= [min, max] ]                        [ FOR all_levels | level_interval
                                      = [min, max] ]
```

A query based on the GIVE STRATIFICATION element returns the different levels of the stratification defined for the maskable entity ME (by default, from level one to the current level). SELECT FROM queries (on the right part) search for the instances of ME, whose presentation is limited to the field(s) of the information associated with ME, and which respect the expression given in the optional clause WHERE. When ME is a schema, information concerns its classes, while when ME is a class, information concerns its attributes.

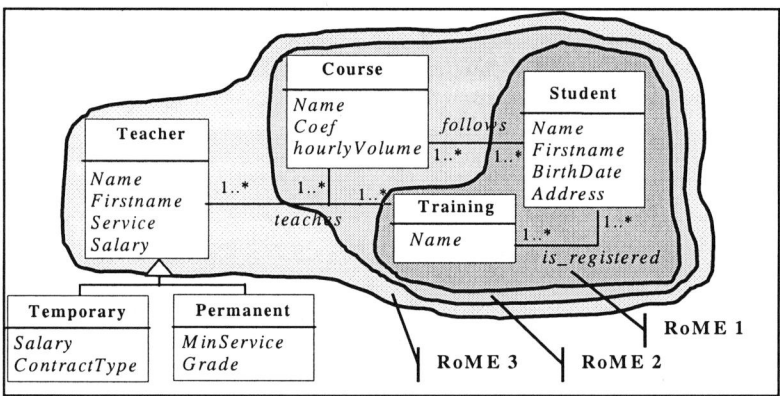

Fig. 2. Example of a stratified schema (3 RoME are defined).

If * is used in the SELECT, information corresponds to the RoME of the current level. In these two cases, the optional clause FOR allows either to expand the query to the whole stratification (i.e. all the levels are presented) or to limit the list of the presented levels to the given interval.

Some examples of such queries applied to the stratified Information Space of Fig. 2 are given in Table 1. Due to space limitation, we only present queries about the schema although a similar approach exists for stratified classes.

Table 1. Examples of PAM QL queries applied to the stratified Information Space of Fig. 2

CURRENT LEVEL	QUERY	RESULT
Schema RoME 3	GIVE STRATIFICATION FROM schema Training	Level 1 : class Training, class Student Level 2 : class Course Level 3 : class Teacher
Schema RoME 3	GIVE STRATIFICATION FROM schema Training FOR level_interval = [1, 2]	Level 1 : class Training, class Student Level 2 : class Course
Schema RoME 2	SELECT * FROM schema Training	All instances of classes Training, Student and Course are listed, which corresponds to RoME 2. Each class, if it is stratified, is represented at its lower level of detail

4 Conclusion

In this paper, we have presented a way to stratify the Information Space (data model) of a Web-based Information System (WIS) in order to provide users with a progressive access to information. This stratification is described by a Progressive Access Model (PAM) written in UML. Users of a WIS can access, first, essential information, through different levels of granularity, and then, more or less information, depending on their interest, time or material configuration, etc. We have also proposed PAM-QL a OQL-like query language which allows to query the WIS about the stratification performed on the Information Space, but also aims at formatting the data contained in a reply, according to the stratification (i.e. according to levels of detail).

Our research is now directed towards dynamic adaptability techniques in order to react more efficiently to end-users actions. The idea is to dynamically elaborate and modify both the stratification and the navigation schema of a WIS, learning from the user's behavior. The use of cookies technology to track information about users' sessions in order to automatically adapt information, coupled with some meta-rules of navigation, is one way we have started to explore.

References

1. Brusilovski P.: Methods and Techniques of Adaptive Hypermedia. User Modeling and User-Adapted Interaction, Vol. 4, Kluwer academic publishers (1996) 21-45
2. De Bra P.: Design Issues in Adaptive Hypermedia Application Development, 2nd Workshop on Adaptive Systems and User Modeling on the WWW, Proc. of WWW'99, (1999) 29-39
3. Villanova-Oliver M., Gensel J., Martin H.: Stratification of the Information Space in Web-based Information Systems, ECIS'02, Gdansk, Poland, June 6-8 (2002)
4. Villanova-Oliver M., Gensel J., Martin H., Erb C.: Design and Generation of Adaptable Web Information Systems with KIWIS, ICIT'02 : Coding & Computing. Session on Web & Hypermedia Systems, Las Vegas, NV, US, April 8-10 (2002)
5. Cluet S.: Designing OQL: Allowing Objects to be Queried, Information Systems. 23(5) (1998)

Adapting to Prior Knowledge of Learners

Stephan Weibelzahl and Gerhard Weber

Pedagogical University Freiburg, Germany
{weibelza,webergeh}@ph-freiburg.de

Abstract. Prior knowledge is an important factor that influences the interaction with a hypertext and the learning gain. Our authoring system NetCoach provides a way to assess the users' prior knowledge and to adapt the course in different ways. We describe how the adaptation mechanism assesses the user's knowledge with test items, infers the user's current learning state from this information, and finally adapts accordingly. An evaluation study with an adaptive HTML course demonstrates that this kind of adaptation might reduce the completion time, but retains the learning gain.

1 Online Learning Courses and Prior Knowledge

Online learning courses are used by people that differ widely in prior knowledge of the domain. Especially in further education and learning on demand settings some learners will have a background of parts of the course while others are complete beginners. However, regardless of the prior knowledge, everybody should have the same knowledge after course completion. On the one hand users might get bored if they have to work on topics that they are already familiar with. On the other hand they are probably not able to estimate whether they do really know everything on a topic of a course without having seen the chapters. Thus, letting users decide on their own whether they have enough knowledge or not might result in incomplete knowledge acquisition. Moreover, prior knowledge has an impact on the learning gain. When constructing a hypertext authors should considers the users' prior knowledge [3]. It might be useful to adapt the hypertext's structure [2] or to provide different advisements [4].

In any case such adaptations require the assessment of prior knowledge. The authoring system NetCoach [6] provides a mechanism both to assess the user's prior knowledge and to adapt the course accordingly.

2 Adaptation Mechanism

NetCoach is designed to enable authors to build adaptive online courses without programming. While authors generate the content by filling in templates and forms, the course functionality including user management, adaptation, communication facilities, and tutoring is provided by NetCoach.

Each NetCoach course implements several adaptive features, that require an adequate assessment of the prior knowledge. Based on this information NetCoach infers the user's knowledge about each chapter and decides how to adapt.

2.1 Assessment of Prior Knowledge

Similar to a book, a NetCoach course is structured hierarchically with chapters and subchapters. The knowledge about a subchapter or a set of subchapters is assessed in so called test groups, i.e., a set of test items. Three types of test items are evaluated on the fly automatically: multiple choice tests, forced choice tests, and gap filling tests. Authors may define the difficulty of the test items and a critical value of points that are required for completing the test. After the learner has completed the chapter the items are presented in small groups (e.g., two in a row). Users achieve points for correct answers and loose points for false answers until they reach a critical value.

In the beginning of a chapter that has subchapters with test groups a link to a pretest is offered. In this case a random selection of the test groups' difficult items is presented.

In summary, the test items of test groups in subchapters which are usually presented after the chapter are aggregated and now serve as pretest for the superordinated chapter.

2.2 Inference of Current Learning State

Each item is evaluated as if it was answered in the test group. The only exception is that the result is weighted (default is 1.5). Afterwards, the current learning state is updated, i.e, NetCoach computes on the fly whether a chapter is *solved*, *inferred*, *ready* or *not ready*. See Weber, Kuhl and Weibelzahl [6] for a detailed description of the overlay model and the different states of chapters used in NetCoach. Such an inference mechanism requires information about relations between chapters which is stored in a so called knowledge base. NetCoach supports the two concept relations *prerequisite* and *inference* [6].

In summary, the inference of a user's current learning state is done in two steps. First, the items of the pretest are evaluated and points weighted by an factor are assigned to test groups accordingly. Second, if a test group has been solved because the critical value has been reached, this chapter is assumed to be learned and other chapters might be inferred to be learned in correspondence with the knowledge base.

2.3 Adaptation Decision

Finally, the learning state is used for two types of adaptations: adaptive annotation and curriculum sequencing. First, links to other chapters are annotated according to the state of this chapter (e.g., a green bullet indicates that the chapter is *ready to be visited*).

Second, NetCoach suggests which page to visit next and thus guides users to chapters that are *ready* and that are required to complete the course. Chapters that are assumed to be learned are skipped. Thus, the pretests provide an easy way to guide users to those chapters that they should learn. Other adaptation techniques that use the same information would be possible (e.g., link hiding [1] or changing the adaptation method [5]), but are not implemented in NetCoach.

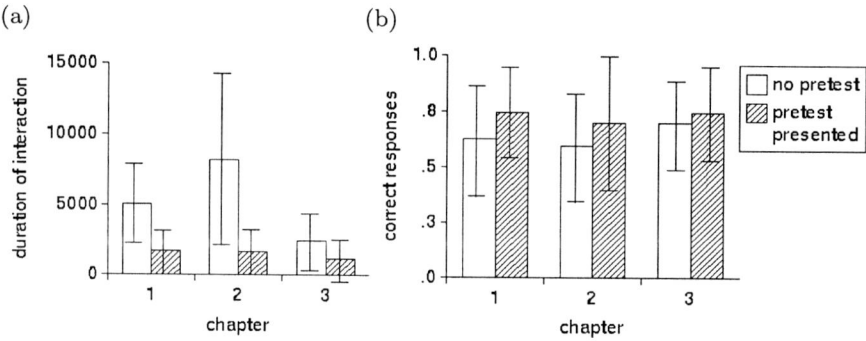

Fig. 1. (a) Duration of interaction (seconds). People who solved the pretest on one of the three chapters required less time to complete these chapters (including the time to complete the pretest). (b) Relative number of correct responses in the posttest. People who solved the pretest on one of the three chapters gave equally or more correct responses to test items in the post test. The standard deviations are indicated.

3 Evaluation

The pretest mechanism of NetCoach has been evaluated with the so called *HTML-Tutor*. This online course introduces to publishing on the web and programming HTML. We wanted to know whether the pretests can assess the prior knowledge correctly and how the learning gain is influenced by the adaptation.

We observed a total of 140 users who accessed the public course from all over the world. Two groups of users are distinguished: the first group (no pretest) ignored the pretest and completed the chapters as usual, while the second group (pretest presented) decided to answer the pretest. Consequently, most of them were advised to omit at least some subchapters. In the end of the course users completed a final test that included several test items on the pretest chapters. If the pretest assessment was successful the second group should know as much as the first group about the chapters, even though they did not read the contents.

We found that the pretest group completed the chapters much faster than the standard group. For all three pretest that have been included in this analysis the mean duration of interaction was lower (see Figure 1a). A 2-factor MANOVA yielded significant differences between these groups (see Table 1). However, the analysis of the posttest shows that the pretest group had at least as much knowledge on these chapters as the standard group. Their relative number of correct responses was even higher for chapter 1. The remaining chapters did not differ significantly (see Figure 1b).

In summary, the pretest group had at least as much knowledge about the chapters although they spent less time for browsing these chapters. Note that the users saved up to 80% of the interaction duration, but performed about 10% to 20% better in the posttest. Especially for learning on demand settings when people want to learn specific contents as efficiently as possible this could be an important benefit.

Table 1. (a) Statistical results of a 2-factor MANOVA (dependent variables duration and knowledge). (b) Statistical results of a 2-factor ANOVA (dependent variable duration). For each factor the F-value (F), the degrees of freedom (df $_{effect,\ error}$) and the statistical significance (α) are reported (sample size N=140).

(a)

factor	F	df	α
F1: presentation	15.84	2, 133	.000
F2: chapter	3.15	4, 268	.015
F1*F2	2.82	4, 268	.026

(b)

factor	F	df	α
F1: presentation	31.07	1, 134	.000
F2: chapter	6.56	2, 134	.002
F1*F2	5.54	2, 134	.005

4 Conclusion

NetCoach offers easy creation of pretests by summarizing items from test groups. The assumed state of each chapter is computed in dependence of the answers in the pretest and the relations between chapters. Our results suggest that the HTML-Tutor assesses the prior knowledge correctly. Despite the fact that people were adaptively guided to omit those chapters that are assumed to be learned, they were able to answer test items on the chapter's contents even better than the standard group. Thus, assessing knowledge with test items facilitates interesting adaptation opportunities. Adapting to prior knowledge is an important approach to increase the effectiveness and efficiency of learning courses and might even increase the users' satisfaction.

References

1. P. De Bra and L. Calvi. AHA! An open adaptive hypermedia architecture. *The New Review of Hypermedia and Multimedia*, 4:115–139, 1998.
2. S. McDonald and R. J. Stevenson. Effects of text structure and prior knowledge of the learner on navigation in hypertext. *Human Factors*, 40(1):18–27, 1998.
3. I. Park and M. J. Hannafin. Empirically-based guidelines for the design of interactive multimedia. *Educational Technology Research & Development*, 41(3):63–85, 1993.
4. E. C. Shin, D. L. Schallert, and W. C. Savenye. Effects of learner control, advisement, and prior knowledge on young students' learning in a hypertext environment. *Educational Technology Research & Development*, 42(1):33–46, 1994.
5. M. Specht. Empirical evaluation of adaptive annotation in hypermedia. In T. Ottmann and I. Tomek, editors, *Proceedings of the 10th World Conference on Educational Telecommunications, ED-MEDIA & ED-Telecom '98, Freiburg, Germany*, pages 1327–1332, Charlottesville, VA, 1998. AACE.
6. G. Weber, H.-C. Kuhl, and S. Weibelzahl. Developing adaptive internet based courses with the authoring system NetCoach. In S. Reich, M. Tzagarakis, and P. de Bra, editors, *Hypermedia: Openness, Structural Awareness, and Adaptivity*, pages 226–238, Berlin, 2001. Springer.

Monitoring Partial Updates in Web Pages Using Relational Learning

Seiji Yamada and Yuki Nakai

CISS, IGSSE, Tokyo Institute of Technology
4259 Nagatsuta, Midori, Yokohama, 226-8502, Japan
yamada@ymd.dis.titech.ac.jp

Abstract. This paper describes an automatic monitoring system that constantly checks partial updates in Web pages and notifies the user about them. While one of the most important advantages of the WWW is frequent updates of Web pages, we need to constantly check them out and this task may take much cognitive load. Unfortunately applications to automatically check such updates cannot deal with partial updates like updates in a particular cell of a table in a Web page. Hence we developed an automatic monitoring system that checks such partial updates. The user can give a system regions in which he/she wants to know the updates in a Web page as training examples, and the system is able to learn rules to identify the partial updates by relational learning. We implemented the system and some executed examples were presented.

1 Introduction

We currently obtain various information from the WWW and utilize them. While one of the most important advantages of the WWW is its constant updates of Web pages, we needs to frequently check the updates for acquiring the latest information and this task forces much cognitive load on us. Thus, a number of applications to automatically check and notify updates of Web pages have been developed[1,2]. Unfortunately almost all of them notify the suer about updates whenever any part of a Web page is updated, and most of such updates may not useful to him/her.

Consider a weather report Web page and a user who has a plan to go to a picnic on the next Sunday and is interested in the weather. He/she needs to frequently check the next Sunday's weather in the Web page. If a user employs a Web update checking application, it notifies him/her all of updates including other days' weather changes thought such notifications are meaningless. Thus *partial update* is defined as an update of a region in which a user is interested, not of any part of a Web page. We argue that this partial update monitoring is widely necessary in a lot of fields like stock market pages, the exchange rate pages, etc.

We developed an automatic monitoring system PUM (Partial Update Monitoring) that constantly checks partial updates in Web pages and notifies the user about them.

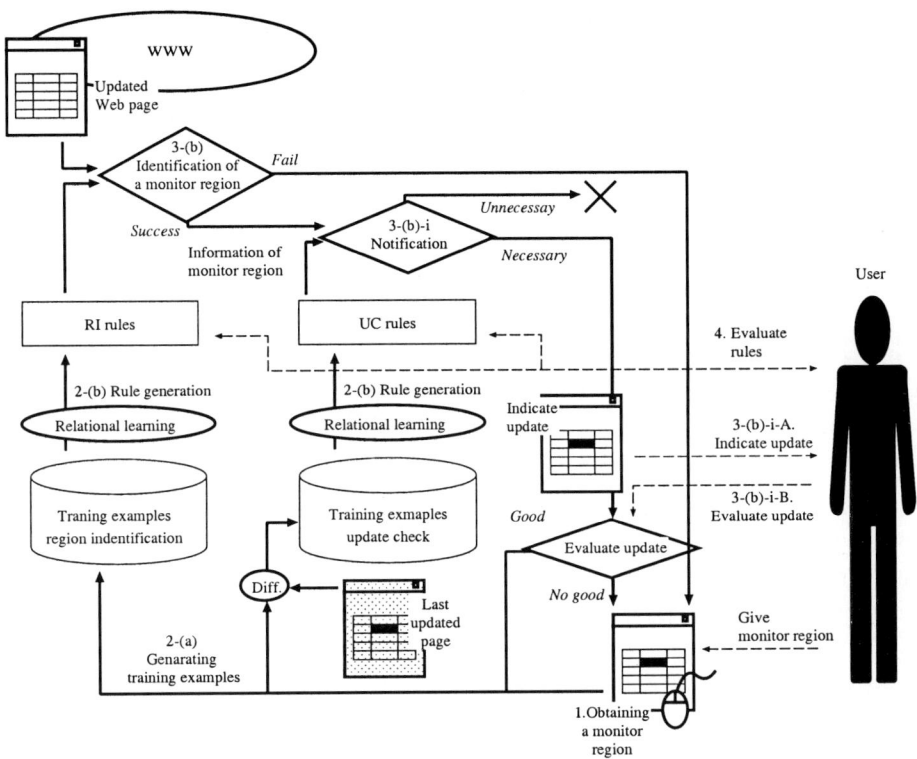

Fig. 1. System overview.

2 PUM: Partial Update Monitoring in a Web Page

2.1 System Overview

PUM is a system that identifies a region indicated by a user in a Web page, checks for partial updates in the region and notifies the user about the updates which he/she wants to know. Figure 1 shows overview of PUM, in which a dotted line indicates interaction between a user and PUM.

Figure 1 also stands for the procedure of PUM. First of all, PUM obtains a monitor region from a user. The user indicates a region in which he/she wants to know the update by mouse highlight operation on interface of PUM (Fig. 2). Next PUM extracts training examples for both of RI (region identification) and UC (update check) from a region indicated by a user.

Then a relational learning system automatically acquires two kinds of rules for region identification and update check. PUM utilizes RIPPER[3] as a relational learning system. RIPPER acquires rules to classify examples into two classes, and the learned rule is described with a symbolic representation.

After such rules are generated, PUM becomes able to identify a partial update and to determine whether it is one which a user wants to know or not. It does so

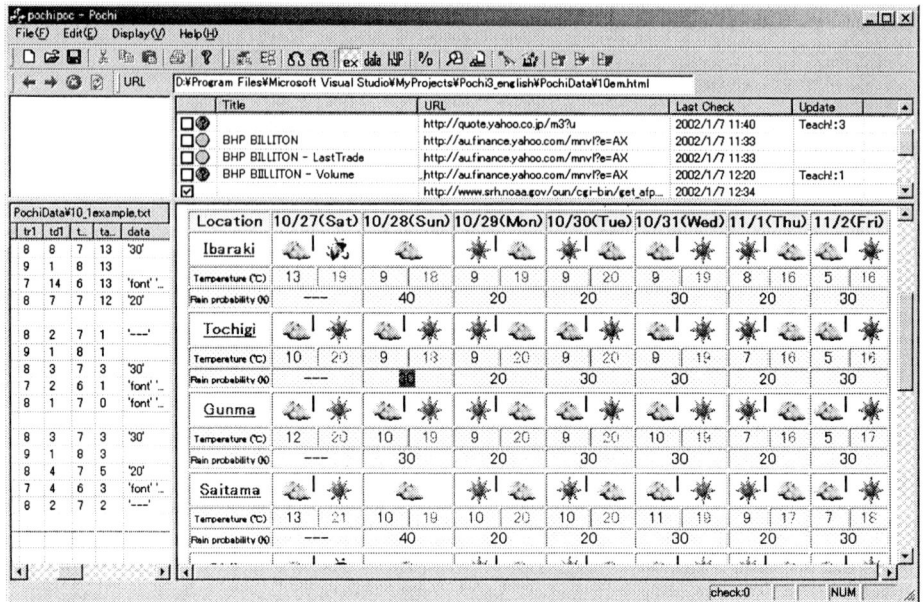

Fig. 2. Interface of PUM.

by using two kinds of rules (RI and UC). If PUM decides that an update is useful to a user, it notifies the user about the update. Otherwise, PUM indicates the updated Web page to a user and asks for his/her evaluation. PUM is implemented using Visual C++ and Ruby on Windows2000.

Figure 2 shows the interface of PUM. The window consists of three subwindows: a Web browser window, a URL window and a training example window. The Web browser window (lower right in Fig.2) shows a Web page in the same way as a Web browser and a user can easily indicate a region by highlighting it using the mouse. The URL window (upper in Fig.2) shows URLs of updated pages. The training example window (lower left in Fig.2) indicates a table of attributes and values of stored training examples.

2.2 Negative Examples for Region Identification

Since relational learning is a kind of inductive learning, negative examples play an important role to avoid over-generalization. Thus PUM automatically generates negative example for region identification to improve learning efficiency.

We consider the neighborhood of an indicated region as near miss examples. Hence PUM generates negative examples from four regions: left, right, upper and lower regions to an indicated region.

Table 1. RI rules.

Eval. No.	Class	Condition
1	Good	cIndex ~'10/14(Sun)', rNo ~'7'.
2	Good	rNo ~'7', cIndex ~'Sun'.

3 Executed Examples

A typically successful example for PUM is on updates in a weather report Web page shown in Fig.2. This page shows the weather forecast for the next seven days in a table that scrolls horizontally. In this example, a user wants PUM to notify of an update when the rain probability of Tochigi on Sunday (a highlighted cell in Fig.2) decreases to less than 40%. Thus PUM needs to learn RI rules to identify a cell indicating weather probability of Tochigi on Sunday and UC rules to check whether the value of weather probability is less than 40. PUM successfully was able to to extract the correct partial update after several evaluations by a user.

Table 1 shows the number of user's evaluations and learnt RI rules at that time. A rule consists of "Class" and "Condition", and if the update satisfies "Condition", it is classified into the "Class". $A\tilde{\ }B$ in "Condition" means a condition that B is included in an attribute A. An RI rule learnt from the first evaluation identified a cell which is in the 7th-row and has '10/14(Sun)' as a column index. This rule succeeded in identifying a region for four days; however it failed on the fifth day. This is because a target region included '10/21(Sun)' instead of '10/14(Sun)' by scrolling. Then, PUM required a second user's evaluation and learned a new rule shown in Table 1. This second rule identifies a correct cell using more general condition 'Sun' as a column index, not '10/14(Sun)'.

Additional successful examples were investigated in stock market, CD ranking, exchange rate Web pages, etc.

4 Conclusion

We proposed a monitoring system PUM that constantly checks partial updates in Web pages and notifies a user about them. The user can give a system regions for which he/she wants to know the updates in a Web page as training examples; the system can then learn rules to detect the partial updates by relational learning. We implemented our system and presented some executed examples.

References

1. Web Secretary. (http://homemade.hypermart.net/websec/)
2. Saeyor, S., Ishizuka, M.: WebBeholder: A revolution in tracking and viewing changes on the web by agent community. In: WebNet 1998. (1998)
3. Cohen, W.W.: Fast effective rule induction. In: Proceedings of the Twelfth International Conference on Machine Learning. (1995) 115–123

Adaptation in the Web-Based Logic-ITA

David Abraham and Kalina Yacef

School of Information Technologies, University of Sydney, Australia
dabraham@ug.it.usyd.edu.au, kalina@it.usyd.edu.au

Abstract. The Logic-ITA is an Intelligent Teaching Assistant system for the teaching/learning of propositional logic. The system is tailored to two different types of uses: for students, it is an autonomous Intelligent Tutoring System, whilst for teachers, it includes functionality to set up learning levels, adjust parameters for progressing through these levels, monitor the class' progress and collect data. This paper presents some characteristics of the Web-based version of the Logic-ITA. In particular, the web-based version allows a centralisation on the server of the student models, which contain all the users' individual information related to their learning. This means that all the adaptation features of the Logic Tutor are maintained, whilst providing (1) students with a large degree of flexibility in terms of when and where they choose to use the tool, and (2) teachers with the possibility to monitor accurately the results and statistics.

1 Introduction

The aim of the Logic-ITA is to enhance the adaptation of the teaching in the context of large classes. The ratio of one professor to several hundreds students necessarily mean that the teaching strategy will be broad- leaving many students to experience difficulties. Problem solving sessions (also called tutorial classes) help, but then again the ratio is 1 to 20, and with a different person than the professor. The Logic-ITA aims to be another teaching assistant, but one that interacts with all students at a detailed level. It does this by providing students with an intelligent tutoring system, which allows them to practice formal proofs, receive adaptive feedback and attempt personalised exercises. And while doing all of this, the Logic-ITA is able to report the student's progress back to the teacher and tutors. The disproportional ratio between teachers and students is broken down so the teacher can redirect his/her teaching style to the class level, address specific difficulties. The Logic-ITA also addresses the students' feeling of being 'lost in the mass' because recurrent difficulties and problems that are not resolved during the interaction with the system are brought to the teacher's attention.

As with any adaptive system, the availability of a user model is paramount. In a learning context, it is called a student model. The data collected from the student's interactions with the system is necessary for adapting the teaching, and also for providing feedback to the teaching team. However these models must be unique and easily accessed by the teacher to ensure that use of the adaptation features is maximized.

The Logic-ITA has been integrated in our Languages and Logic course, since 2001. We have now built a web-based version to help centralise the data while making it more convenient for students for students. This paper highlights the characteristics of the web-based Logic-ITA. The following section introduces the reader to the tool. Then Sect. 3 describes the main adaptation features and finally Sect. 4 explains the advantages of the web-based version.

2 Overview of the Logic-ITA

The Logic-ITA contains several tools: the Logic Tutor, the LT-Configurator, and the LT-Analyser. The general architecture is outlined below.

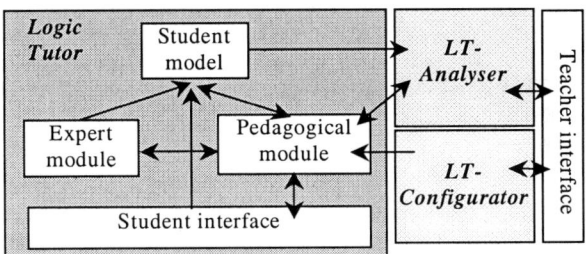

Fig. 1. General architecture of the Logic-ITA

The *Logic Tutor* is an Intelligent Tutoring System that allows students to practice formal proofs, whilst providing them with context-sensitive feedback and tailored exercises. A multimedia presentation of the Logic Tutor can be found at [1].

The system creates and maintains a Student model for each individual user. It records all the attempted exercises along with the mistakes, and stores the student's level, performances, and student information. The student is able at any time to browse through this data and compare his/her level and results with those of the class. We believe that allowing students to scrutinise their student model enhances their learning [4].

The Expert module contains the expertise of the system in propositional logic: it contains the rules of equivalence and laws of inference, and it is able to apply them validly. Proofs are not unique. Paths that the student follows to derive a conclusion from given premises can vary. What really matters is that each step is validly derived from the previous lines and that the conclusion is finally reached. The Expert module does not solve the exercise but is able to check the correctness of students' answers dynamically as well as producing proper feedback when errors occur. This feedback is provided using a bug library.

The Pedagogical module is the main module of the system. It contains the high-level rules for sequencing the exercise training objectives, using the student model data. It updates the student model, and then suggests exercises for the student to solve. However it allows the student to select other exercises or even to create a new one, thus leaving him/her in control of the learning.

The curriculum sequencing in the Logic Tutor is semi-dynamic. Through the *LT-Configurator*, the teacher defines students' learning levels and sketches the high-level sequencing of the progression through the levels. The finer grain of training objectives is decided on the fly with the data stored in the student model. The LT-Configurator is a super-version of the Logic Tutor. Configuration settings are stored in separate files.

Finally, the teacher can monitor the class's results, levels and problems through the *LT-Analyser*. These results are stored in a database and displayed graphically according to the criteria entered by the teacher. For example, the teacher may look at the performance results of the class on a particular exercise, or on all exercises involving a particular rule, or the distribution of levels among a given group of students, and so on.

The Logic Tutor and the LT-Configurator are written in Java, and use the Java Swing library for the user interface. The LT-Analyser uses Microsoft Access and Excel.

3 Student Model and Adaptation

The key to adaptation in any system is a user model, or student model in this learning context. For each user of the system, the student model maintains up-to-date information about the user that is relevant to the system: background, knowledge, level, preferences and so on. In the Logic Tutor, the student model contains the user id, user's preferences, level, history of exercises and respective performances, number of rules used correctly and incorrectly (broken down per rule), the number of mistakes made (broken down per type of mistake). Below we describe how the Logic-ITA uses this information to adapt to individual users.

Curriculum Sequencing. The educational material provided by the Logic Tutor consists of a large set of exercises and simple HTML tutorial pages. The system is able to choose exercises that are best suited to the student's needs by using the student model and the parameters set by the teacher in the LT-Configurator. High-level parameters define the difficulty of the exercise and class of rules that can be used. Within these constraints, the rules are given weights according to the student model data. The exercise obtaining the higher weight will be selected for the student. Exercises are indexed with the levels of difficulty and the rules they are likely to involve.

First, the system calculates the level of difficulty that the student should face. This is done using the previous performance results. At the end of each exercise, a performance is calculated. There are discrete numbers, ranging from 1(the student has solved the problem without making any mistake and using a minimal number of lines) to 5 (the student has not solved the exercise and made mistakes). They are used to assess how well the student is coping with the current level of difficulty. The range of exercises that are considered for this evaluation is determined by the teacher in the LT-Configurator.

Once this level is determined, rules are selected according to the student model. For example, if a student is at level 2 and has made repeated mistakes with, say, the

Modus Tollens and Addition rules, an exercise using these two rules is more likely to be selected next.

The student has the choice of either following or ignoring the suggestion made by the system. This is similar to the mechanism used in ELM-ART[2]. In this sense, it provides an adaptive learning support: the user is free to make a choice while still seeing an opinion of an intelligent system [3].

Tailoring of Interface. Students are able to make a number of small changes to the user interface. This allows the students to personalise their learning environment to what they are most comfortable with. These personalisations are stored in the student model.

Tailoring of the Human Teacher's Interventions. One of the goals of the Logic-ITA is to help the teacher adapt the content of lectures to the class' current state of learning, and attend to individuals' problems. The student's interactions results in adaptation of the system to the student. Here, there is an additional level of adaptation, which occurs at the teacher level: with the information provided, he/she is in a better position to adapt his/her teaching material at the class level as well as the individual level.

Using the LT-Analyser, the teacher can monitor the class' progress by querying a database containing users' information. Some examples of queries are (for the whole class, a subgroup or an individual):
- Which rule caused the most mistakes
- What were the 5 most common mistakes
- Which exercise caused the most mistakes
- What was the average number of mistake per student
- Trend in the number of mistakes in time, per rule and for all rules
- How many students are still at level 1?

Tested in 2001 at the class level, the LT-Analyser was found very helpful. It helped the teacher to re-direct the content of the lectures, address the common misconceptions and focus the revision lectures. In 2002 it is planned to use it at a problem solving session level and individual level.

Tailoring of Feedback and Hints. When the student makes a mistake, the system queries a bug library, which contains mistake patterns. Instead of giving a generic feedback, the patterns are instantiated to the current mistake: the explanations given to the student are contextualised with the current exercise and lines entered by the user. For instance, if the student uses the 'Simplification' rule before the 'Commutation' rule to deduce the right hand side of a conjunction, the mistake module will use the original formula to construct an explanation detailing how only the left hand side can be deduced by Simplification.

Similarly, when hints are available, the user reads them in the context of the current exercise. According to the evaluation survey, this feature contributes greatly to the feeling of being individually assisted.

When no patterns can be found for the current mistake, the feedback states the rule that has not been respected.

4 Why a Web-Based Version?

The original Logic Tutor was written as a Java application and so could easily be downloaded and run on a local computer. However, this type of usage would lead to a number of problems:
- The Intelligent Tutoring System will work to some extent, but not the Intelligent Teacher-Assistant System. The teacher side of the Logic-ITA will not have access to the student models – because they are stored locally on the students' computers. This means that a significant part of the Logic-ITA cannot be exploited.
- The ITS will work normally only if each user always use the same copy of the Logic Tutor. If a student downloads the Logic Tutor onto two different machines, or uses two different accounts, then there will be two different and incomplete student models representing the same student. Therefore each system will have an inaccurate model of the user, resulting in a slower progress in the curriculum, inadequate feedback, duplication of exercises for the student, and of course inaccuracy of the information provided to the student about his/her model.

Therefore we can see that to fully exploit the Logic-ITA, it is paramount that the student models be unique and stored on a location that is both known and accessible to the teacher side of the Logic-ITA.

Last year we released the Logic Tutor to the 450 students enrolled in our Languages and Logic course on a Unix central account. Students could only use it from their university undergraduate account and a script, run each night, collected the relevant information from their home directory (they knew this was happening, of course). Whilst this resolved the access of the student models, it was not very satisfactory, because it created time and geographical constraints for the students. Three weeks before the exams, we made the Logic Tutor fully available for download. Constraints were released for student use but of course we no longer had access to their student models.

Fortunately, WWW technology can provide a solution to this problem:
- centralised storage of student models on the server. Uniqueness of each student model is guaranteed and the teacher has immediately access to up-to-date information about the student's learning progress and difficulties.
- time and geographical flexibility for the students. Students can study when and from any computer they want, without carrying their student model with them or creating duplicates.
- easy update of the software and databases. New exercises, new configurations and software update are easier to manage.
- We have now completed the last stage of the implementation of the Logic-ITA and have a web-based version ready for use in 2002. Transforming the Logic Tutor java application into a java applet was not difficult. There are of course issues specific to the web-based version:
- download times: the Logic Tutor is packaged as a 400Kb compressed Java Archive (jar) file. This represents a significant download time: approximately 80 seconds with a 28800 bps line speed. However, once the file has downloaded, the program's response times are the same as the non-web version. Furthermore, after the first download, many browsers will place the file in cache. This means

that subsequent download times are comparable with the boot time of the original non-web-based Logic Tutor.
- security: accounts administration has been centralised to avoid users creating multiple student models. University students are given an account corresponding to their login, and external users need to request their user account.
- student models are kept private and cannot be accessed externally except by the relevant student. All requests for a student model are forced to go through a server program, which requires a valid user name and password pair before granting access.

5 Conclusion

The Logic-ITA is an Intelligent Teacher-Assistant System requiring centralised storage of the student models. We have tested a non-web-based version last year with 450 students enrolled in the Logic course. The user evaluation survey showed that, whilst the learning benefits of the Logic Tutor were appreciated, the students would have preferred the freedom of using it from both their Unix undergraduate accounts and home.

The web-based version of the Logic-ITA is now ready for use this year and will enable students to work from anywhere with Web access. It also enhances the adaptation features and accuracy of the data of the Logic Tutor by ensuring unique and centrally located student models.

References

1. Abraham, D., Crawford, L., Lesta, L., Merceron, A., Yacef, K. (2001) The Logic Tutor: A multimedia presentation, Interactive Multimedia Electronic Journal of Computer-Enhanced Learning, October 2001 issue (http://imej.wfu.edu/articles/2001/2/03/index.asp).
2. Brusilovsky, P., Schwarz, E., and Weber, G. (1996) ELM-ART: An intelligent tutoring system on World Wide Web. In C. Frasson, G. Gauthier, & A.Lesgold (Eds.), Third International Conference on Intelligent Tutoring Systems, ITS-96 (Lecture Notes in Computer Science, Vol. 1086), Berlin: Springer Verlag, pp. 261-269.
3. Brusilovsky, P. (2001) Adaptive Educational Hypermedia (Invited talk). In: Proceedings of Tenth International PEG conference, Tampere, Finland, June 23-26, 2001, pp. 8-12.
4. Kay, J. (2000). Invited keynote: Stereotypes, student models and scrutability. In the proceedings of Intelligent Tutoring Systems, pp19-30

Collaborative Radio Community

Paolo Avesani, Paolo Massa, Michele Nori, and Angelo Susi

ITC-IRST,
Via Sommarive 18 - Loc. Pantè, I-38050 Povo, Trento, Italy
{avesani,massa,nori,susi}@irst.itc.it

Abstract. Recommender systems have been usually designed to support a single user in a one-to-one relation between a human and a service provider. This paper presents a collaborative radio community where the system delivers a personalization service on the fly, on the basis of the group recommending, promoting a shift from the one-to-one approach to a one-to-group scenario where the goal is assisting people in forming communities.

Keywords: recommender systems, web radio, learning preferences, multicast streaming, virtual community.

1 Introduction

Usually, recommender systems have been designed to support a single user in a one-to-one relation between a human and a service provider. Although advices are generated on the basis of the opinions of other users, the system doesn't support a direct relation between two users that play the different roles of recommender and recommended. Moreover, current personalization systems distinguish between the recommendation step and the use step (i.e. listening in the case of music).

The new technological landscape concerning connectivity has been exploited to conceive user centered services as Smart Radio [6], where an entire radio channel is devoted to a single user to deliver a fully personalized program. Very often in the past this emphasis on personalization has penalized the advantages that could arise from the interaction of a community of users. More recently a new awareness is developing that considers helping people to help each other a new challenge for recommender systems [7]. In this perspective we promote a shift from a one-to-one approach to a one-to-group-of-many scenario where the goal is assisting people in forming communities.

At the technological level the "group-of-many" can be managed with a peer-group approach that is receiving growing attention as new protocols become available e.g. JXTA [5].

In this paper we present a collaborative radio community where, taking advantage of a low band multicast streaming, the system delivers a personalization service on the fly devoted to group recommending. The users are involved both as listeners and as recommenders. The live interaction allows the users to elicitate their disagreement on the radio program. A different preference can be formulated providing alternative order relation among the sountracks. This kind of preferences are closely related to the current theme of radio program: in this context, a theme plays the role of a potential new category of music that should inform the selection of the contents.

Learning how to summarize partial order relations associated to a given theme into a global preference model allows the detection of new kind of non standard categories of music, i.e. the theme. This feature extends our previous work on *CoCoA* [1] a Compilation Compiler Advisor based on case-based reasoning, that supports the detection of the genres of use (from which the name *CoCoA-Radio* comes).

In the following we describe how *CoCoA-Radio* works and show a brief overview of the learning issues that arise when a community of users has to be recommended.

2 The Application

CoCoA-Radio is a *thematic interactive community* radio. It streams continuously radio programs of a fixed number of MP3s (usually 20); every radio program is relative to a given theme. The radio program is the same for every user of the community and can be thought as an hits list for the current theme where the songs at the top level can be considered more representative of this theme. Users can interact with *CoCoA-Radio* using a web browser expressing their preferences related to what they think it is the hits list for the scheduled theme. In this way they play the main roles of authoring, recommending and listening.

Let us introduce the main concepts of the radio. A *theme* is just a mnemonic label that refers to a common target feeling about music or a perspective to look at the music; themes can range from traditional "pop" or "women rock" to more fuzzy and undefined "hands moving". A *playlist* is a user defined list of songs to be submitted to the radio. A *program* is the current list of songs that *CoCoA-Radio* is playing; it is relative to a theme and is a synthesis of the submitted playlists.

Let us now describe in details about how *CoCoA-Radio* works. It streams music programs for given themes continuously. The user can contribute to the radio program related to the next theme by submitting a playlist as a proposal. The system is in charge of summarizing a radio program taking into account the contributions of the users. The challenge is to schedule a radio program that best fits the scheduled theme and consequently best satisfies the listeners feeling.

It is important to stress that the goal of the radio is not to satisfy the user requests but the user expectation concerning the music for the current theme. We could argue that there are two mutual expectations. First, given a theme the users are constrained to submit playlists related to this theme. Second, the users can give their feedback, specifying the relative order of couples of songs in the syntesized program, when the program doesn't satisfy their expectation on the music related to the given theme.

It is a goal of the system to adaptively modify its schedule in order to satisfy the users' expectation and consequently to minimize the users' feedback.

With *CoCoA-Radio*, what can be seen as a minus (the fact that every user gets the same music) becomes a plus; infact users can benefit of the presence of other users because they are all together concurring to form the hit lists for a theme. In essence *CoCoA-Radio* is a *social* application because users have a common goal and they are supposed to work in a cooperative manner to achieve it. Moreover, in a certain way users exploit their reciprocal musical knowledge. Of course this means that there should be a minimum agreement among users; but this could be overcome by replicating channels and clustering users on them depending on their musical preferences; this poses another interesting challenge.

3 Multicast Streaming

Another advantage of streaming a single line of music for a community is the possible bandwidth saving. *CoCoA-Radio* is intended for (but not limited to!) Intranet LAN use and, for this reason, we used multicast IP to stream music. In this way, our streamer does not establish a connection with every client but sends a single stream of packets on the net in multicast; thus every machine that needs to play the music gets this packet. One can imagine the great bandwidth saving with, for example, 100 users! The protocol used for streaming is RTP[1] (short for Realtime Transport Protocol). It is an Internet protocol specifically designed for transmitting realtime data such as audio and video. Typically, RTP runs on top of the UDP protocol and so it allows multicast transmission.

4 Learning Issues

In the following we describe some interesting open learning issues in the radio domain. In general users refer to music using categories that don't belong to the standard taxonomy of music genres and genres of use are not stable during the time, so a possible goal is to recognize which tracks can be classified under a given theme and how much a track is representative for it. Moreover the synthesis of the program starting from a collection of submitted playlists is a satisfiability problem that usually does not have solution due to possible unsolvable conflicts between users' playlists; in the context of the radio community it could be reasonable to avoid this problem detecting the reliability of the users and assigning less priority to playlists submitted by the less reliable of them. Both these aspects are analyzed in the learning algorithm included in *CoCoA-Radio* described in the next section.

5 Radio Program Synthesis

The *CoCoA-Radio* domain can be described as a set of songs to be ordered called $S = \{s_1, \ldots, s_N\}$, a set of radio listeners called $U = \{u_1, \ldots, u_M\}$, a set of themes, i.e. music categories $C = \{c_1, \ldots, c_L\}$, and a *ranking function R* (possibly induced from a playlist P) that is proposed by a user u_i on a given theme c_j, $R_{u_i}^{c_j} : S \times S \to [0, 1]$, where $R_{u_i}^{c_j}(s_1, s_2) = 1$ is a strong recommendation that s_1 should be ranked above s_2, 0 the opposite; a value closed to $1/2$ is interpreted as an abstention from making recommendation.

Starting from the user preference functions R_{u_i} can be derived a *preference function* of the form: $PREF(s_1, s_2) = \sum_{i=1}^{M} w_{u_i} R_{u_i}(s_1, s_2)$ where w_{u_i} are weights assigned to each listener u_i, determining the reliability of the user u_i respect to the given music theme c. A learning algorithm [2–4] can be designed to update incrementally the weight values.

Learning is assumed to take place in a sequence of rounds. On each round, we assume the learning algorithm is provided with a set of S^t of songs to be ranked. A combined preference function $PREF^t$ is computed and than used to produce a total ordering function $\rho_{c_j}^t$ said *Program* of songs S^t. After producing $\rho_{c_j}^t$ the radio receives *feedback* from the listeners. The feedback at time t, F^t, is a set of assertions "song s_1 should be preferred to song s_2" so F^t is a set of pairs (s_1, s_2). The feedback allows to compute

---
[1] http://www.ietf.org/rfc/rfc1899.txt

the function $Loss(R, F)$ that describes the loss of a preference function R given by a user respect to the users' feedback. The loss is the major component in the incremental adequacy of the weights w_{u_i} given by the learning algorithm to every radio user during the learning procedure.

At the end of the procedure for each theme c_j we have an order for the instances in S called ρ_{c_j}. This order is a sequence of instances. It is possible to map it in the Radio domain calling it *Program*, a sequence of S elements.

The *CoCoA-Radio* interaction can be summarized in three phases: *An initial phase of playlists submission*, given the set of possible songs in the database and a theme, users can submit their own playlist (an ordered list of songs) related to the given theme; *A phase of synthesis of a program on the basis of the submitted playlists*; *A final phase of users' feedback acquisition*, users can give information about the synthesized order in terms of songs pairs $< s_1, s_2 >$; the program will be then recomputed on the basis of the received feedback.

6 Future Work

At the time of writing we have developed a first version of *CoCoA-Radio* using a J2EE software platform. The system has been deployed on a LAN with a few hundreds hosts and an archive of 6000 mp3 tracks.

Our primary goal in the short term is to test our architecture on the field with a restricted and controlled community of users, i.e. the researchers of our institute. We are interested in assessing on a real interactive environment both the technological and the collaborative architectures. The main focus of our experiment is the analysis of the learning curve at run time; our goal is to assess the relation between the feedback from users and the learning process. In this context, not only accuracy is important but also how fast is the convergence of the process.

A secondary goal is related to the acquisition of a meaningful dataset taking advantage of the contribution of the real users. This dataset could be exploited to evaluate alternative working hypothesis off line.

Currently, we have two the planned enhancements to extend the application: the first is the opportunity for the user to submit a proposal for the next theme, the second is the replication of the *CoCoA-Radio* with an added service of recommendation to help the user to choose what kind of channel to subscribe.

References

1. S. Aguzzoli, P. Avesani, and P. Massa. Compositional CBR via Collaborative Filtering. In *ICCBR'01 Workshop on CBR in Electronic Commerce*, Vancouver - Canada, 2001.
2. William W. Cohen, Robert E. Schapire, and Yoram Singer. Learning to Order Things. In Michael I. Jordan, Michael J. Kearns, and Sara A. Solla, editors, *Advances in Neural Information Processing Systems*, volume 10. The MIT Press, 1998.
3. Y. Freud, R. Iyer, R. Schapire, and Y. Singer. An Efficient Boosting Algorithm for Combining Preferences, 1998.
4. Y. Freund and R. Schapire. A Short Introduction to Boosting, 1999.
5. L. Gong. Project JXTA: A Technology Overview, 2001.
6. C. Hayes and P. Cunningham. Smart radio: Building music radio on the fly, 2000.
7. Loren Terveen and Will Hill. *HCI In The New Millenium*, chapter Beyond Recommender Systems: Helping People Help Each Other. Addison-Wesley, 2001.

Improving Interactivity in e-Learning Systems with Multi-agent Architecture

Ricardo Azambuja Silveira[1] and Rosa Maria Vicari[2]

[1] Universidade Federal do Rio Grande do Sul – UFRGS
Universidade Luterana do Brasil - ULBRA
`rsilv@inf.ufrgs.br`
[2] Universidade Federal do Rio Grande do Sul – UFRGS
`rosa@inf.ufrgs.br`

Abstract. Over the last years, many organizations started to use Distance Teaching tools as instruments in employees' qualification programs, creating what we may call *E-learning* or *Virtual Training* in Human Resources Development Programs. However, usually these organizations tend to use technological resources already available, and do not shape their technological platform into a pedagogical project. Recent advances in the field of Intelligent Teaching Systems have proposed the use of Artificial Intelligence through architectures based on agents' societies. Teaching systems based on Multi-Agent architectures make possible to support the development of more interactive and adaptable systems. The objective of the paper is to discuss the feasibility of implementing Distributed Intelligent Learning Environment – DILE based on the Multi-Agents Architecture approach, aiming at the achievement of human resources qualification through Virtual Training. Besides, we present a proposal of an architecture named JADE - Java Agent Framework for Distance Learning Environments.

1 Introduction

Computer Science, together with Psychology and Education, has been trying to refine teaching computational tools towards personalized self-learning. Every day, new approaches to the use of Computer and Education are bringing new perspectives to this area. The evolution of Computer and Education became computational teaching environments an excellent choice for Distance Learning, by bringing new vigor to this field of science.

The projects of E-learning must take into consideration that there are different classes of students: the *non-cooperative*, those who act in a passive way or even try to frustrate the program's objective; the *cooperative,* who follow orientations, but do not necessarily know where to go; and the *pro-active* students, who know very well their objective, and search for aid to relief the task burden. The teaching methodology employed in each case is different and there must have a clear concern by the technological environment on the profile of the student that will use the system. In order to reach this goal, cognitive student's modeling is required, and it must make a clear specification of him or hers.

The state of the art in the Intelligent Tutoring Systems and Intelligent Learning Environments fields points to the use of Agent Society-Based Architectures [4,5]. The fundamentals of the Multi-Agent systems have demonstrated to be very appropriate to design tutoring systems, since the teaching-learning problem could be handled as a cooperative approach. That is why the Intelligent Learning Environments, such as JADE, are a class of teaching instruments much more advanced in the pedagogical and organizational point of view, more adequate to the aims of Virtual Training in organizations.

2 The JADE Project

The *Java Agent framework for Distance learning Environments* – JADE project [5,6] proposes an infrastructure of project, development and implementation of Distribute Intelligent Learning Environments – DILE, based on the approach of Multi-Agents architecture towards Distance Education, for multiple domains. In this project we implemented different versions of Eletrotutor prototype. Eletrotutor is a teaching environment for Electrodynamics teaching, and in each version we refined JADE architecture.

The environment we proposed contains a special agent responsible for each teaching strategy developed, that is, for the domain knowledge retrieval over each point to be presented to the student, for the task of proposing exercises and evaluating proposals, examples and extra activities.

JADE architecture encompasses, therefore, a Multi-Agent environment composed of an agent responsible for the system general control (Student's Model), and a Communication Manager and other agents (Pedagogical Agents), which are responsible for tasks related to their teaching tactics, where each agent may have its tasks specified according to its goal. All actions of student's data accessing are taken by the Student's Model, thus when a pedagogical agent is required to update the student's historic, this agent sends to the Student Model data to be updated, as well as any other change in the student's state of teaching (see Fig. 1).

Communication between agents happens through a definition of a KQML-based message set, implemented through communication resources of JAVA language objects named RMI (Remote Method Invocation), used in the project [1].

The agent's architecture is designed as robust and standardized as possible and that enables reusing codes for different kinds of agents. The tasks performed in teaching are decomposed and performed individually or in groups of agents. How the task will be decomposed is defined by the content of messages exchanged between agents.

The cycle of agents' execution, shown in Fig. 2, consists of the following steps:
- New messages processing: the task is decomposed;
- Determination of which rules are suitable in the current situation: analysis of task and if necessary delegation of other agent(s) task;
- Execution of actions specified for such rules: task execution;
- Mental state update according to those rules: management of knowledge about the world;
- Planning: module that must develop plans that reach goals specified by agents intentions.

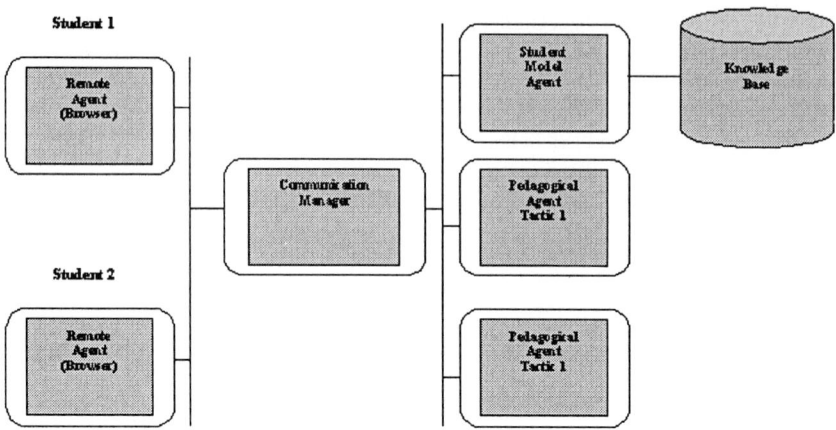

Fig. 1. System Architecture: The Architecture of JADE system is composed of a set of agents: (*Pedagogic Agent*) in charge of performing learning activities as examples, exercises, an others. One special agent (*Communication Agent*) performs communication management among the agents. There is an agent (*Student Model Agent*) responsible for student modeling and agents' coordination. The Browser component (*Remote Agent*) performs the student interface and the communication between the student and the system.

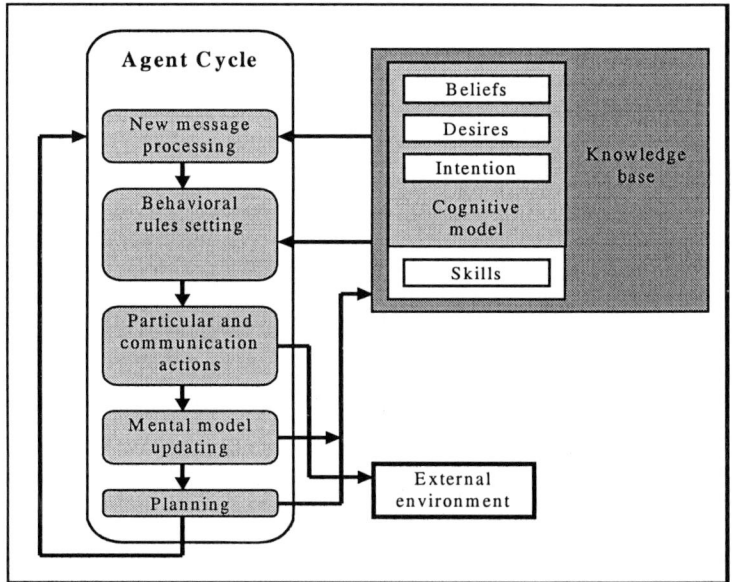

Fig. 2. The agents' cycle performs messages sending and receiving and specific task of the agent, according to the knowledge base. As the agent receives a new KQML message it processes the message according to its content, Appling the adequate behavioral rule. According to this rules the message-receiving event can trigger some message sending, mental model updating and some particular specific agent action.

2.1 The ELETROTUTOR Prototype

The Eletrotutor prototype was implemented as a test bed to evaluate JADE platform. It is an Electrodynamics client-server intelligent learning environment designed according to JADE architecture (available in http://www.inf.ufrgs.br/~rsilv)

Figures 3 and 4 show two snapshots of The Eletrotutor prototype:

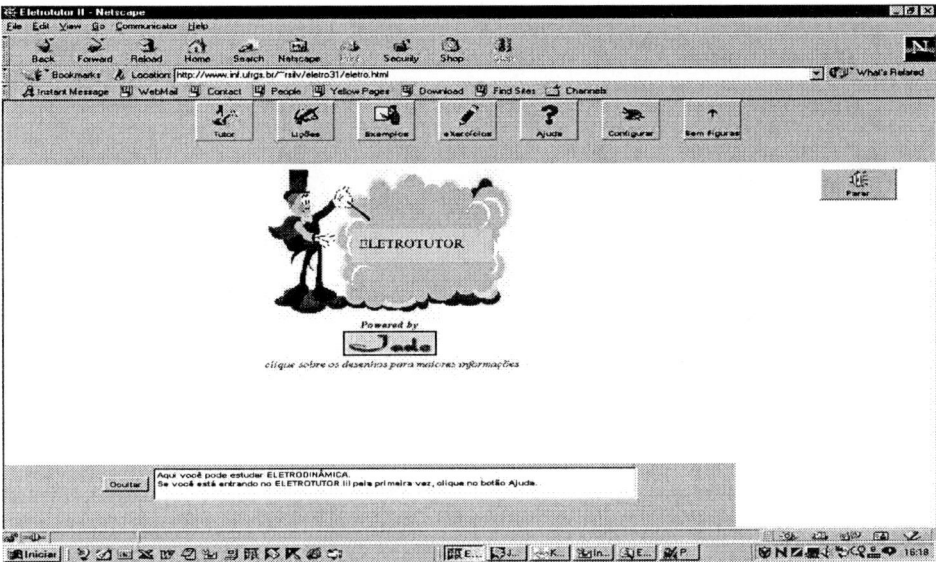

Fig. 3. Eletrotutor's snapshot 1 shows the main screen. The first button (*Tutor*) changes from the autonomous mode to the tutorial mode. The second (*Lições*) invokes the lessons menu. The third (*Exercícios*) invokes the exercises menu. The fourth (*Exemplos*) invokes the examples menu. The fifth (*Ajuda*) call the help system. The sixth (*Configurar*) seventh (*Sem* figures) and eighth (*parar*) change several interface configurations

The environment may be used in Tutorial, and Autonomous modes. In the first mode, the student has total control over the study session, and may perform any lesson, check any example or make any exercise. In the Tutorial mode, the system undertakes the session control, defining the sequence of lessons, examples, and exercises. For that end, the tutor makes use of a student's cognitive diagnostic, taken through the record of every action the student takes. Thus, teaching strategies observe the student's historic before taking the next actions. Teaching strategies are the sequence of contents, examples and exercises that will be proposed to the student.

3 Conclusions

Distance Education systems based on the Internet does not have any time or space constraint. Students can interact with the system anytime, anywhere. However, most of Distance Education systems based on the web are not intelligent or adaptable.

Researches have turned towards the use of adaptive www by using systems based on Intelligent Tutors and Intelligent Agents architectures. All these issues have in common a strong dependence on a sharp and robust student modeling. Through the student model it is possible to provide customized teaching tactics, which reflect the knowledge level of each student, his/her learning abilities and objectives. In this work we intended to bring some important contributions, refining the efficacy of learning environments and stressing the use of cooperative solving problem paradigm using Multi-agent architecture. Further work will integrate the JADE implementation of pedagogical agents with commercial or well-known academic learning environments or frameworks and improve some issues like Agent Communication and Negotiation.

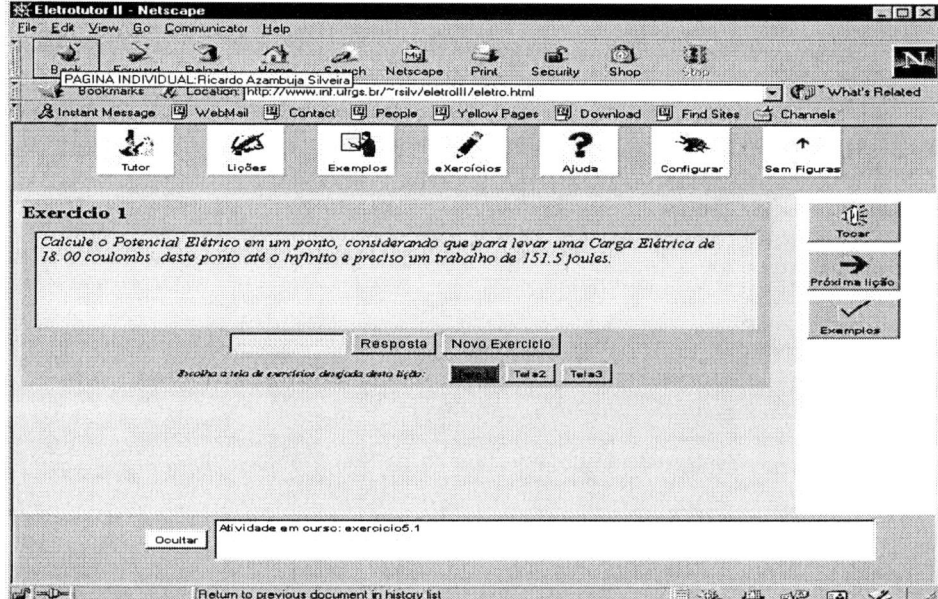

Fig. 4. Eletrotutor's snapshot 2 shows an exercise. The system presents as many exercises as the student want by clicking (*Novo Exercício*) button. This changes the instance of this kind of exercise. By clicking the buttons (*Tela1, Tela2, Tela3*) the student invokes different kinds of exercises for this lesson

References

1. BICA, Francine, Eletrotutor III: Uma abordagem multiagente para o Ensino a distância. Porto Alegre: CPGCC da UFRGS, 1999. Master Dissertation.
2. CHEIKES, B. A. GIA: An Agent Based Architecture for Intelligent Tutoring Systems. In: THE CIKM WORKSHOP ON INTELLIGENT INFORMATION AGENTS, 1995. Proceedings, 1995
3. MATHOFF, J.;VAN HOE, R. APEALL: A Multi-agent approach to interactive learning environments. In: EUROPEAN WORKSHOP ON MODELING AUTONOMOUS AGENTS MAAMAW, 6., 1994. Proceedings Berlin: Springer-Verlag, 1996.

4. SILVEIRA, Ricardo Azambuja. Modelagem Orientada a Agentes Aplicada a Ambientes Inteligentes Distribuídos de Ensino – JADE - *Java Agent framework for Distance learning Environments* Porto Alegre: PPGC da UFRGS, 2000. Doctoral Thesis.
5. SILVEIRA, Ricardo Azambuja, VICARI, Rosa Maria. JADE - Java Agents for Distance Education framework. In: DEC 2001, 2001, Austin. DEC 2001. CD-ROM, 2001

Adaptive Hypermedia Made Simple with HTML/XML Style Sheet Selectors

François Bry and Michael Kraus

Institute for Computer Science, University of Munich
http://www.pms.informatik.uni-muenchen.de/

Abstract. A simple extension is proposed for enhancing HTML and XML with adaptation. It consists in using the path selectors of style sheet languages such as CSS and XSLT for expressing content and navigation adaptation. The needed extensions to a path selector language are minimal, a few additional constructs suffice. The processor of the language can be kept almost unchanged, no new algorithms are needed. Furthermore, it is proposed to use XML for expressing user model data like browsing history, browsing environment (such as device, time, etc.), and application data (such as user performances on exercises).

1 Introduction

In existing systems, extending HTML and XML with simple adaptive hypermedia functionalities is done using a combination of cookies, ie client-side user identification, server-side scripting languages like PHP [6], and URIs. This has several drawbacks. Information about the user has to be stored and processed on the server. Due to the nature of the Web's HTTP protocol, this information is limited as compared to the information (possibly) available on the client side: For example, it is not possible to track navigation using the back and forward buttons, navigation in different windows, or navigation on more than one server. This prevents implementing non-trivial adaptive hypermedia systems.

In contrast, the approach outlined in this paper does not suffer from the above-mentioned drawbacks, as it works on the client side. In common adaptive hypermedia systems, the structure of the information, the information itself, and the way of information acquisition together form a user model [2]. This paper does not propose a specific user model, but a framework relying upon HTML and XML that allows a simple implementation of user models. The main advantage of this framework is to make adaptive hypermedia techniques available in the Web context at low cost, ie with minimal changes of the existing standards.

This framework is described in more detail in [3]. It has been proposed to the W3C Device Independence Working Group [4].

2 Browsing Context: A Data Structure for Expressing User Models

HTML and XML have no means to express a user model. Therefore, a data structure called *browsing context* is proposed [3], which allows a user model to be stored by the browser, ie on the client side, to be accessed through style sheets, and to be updated through Web applications using scripting languages like Javascript [5]. These features make the data structure "browsing context" convenient for an adaptive presentation of Web pages.

A browsing context consists of three components that can be distinguished according to data acquisition: *browsing history*, *browsing environment* and *application data*. "Browsing history" data are informations about the browsing actions performed by the user in the past such as visiting Web pages, traversing hyperlinks, opening and closing windows, etc. This information is automatically generated by the browser and it is updated each time the user performs a browsing action. "Browsing environment" data are informations about the device (hardware), browser (software), location, time, language, etc. Like browsing history data, this information is automatically generated and updated by the browser. "Application data" are informations specific to the Web application being browsed by the user. In the case of an electronic tutor system, this can be the user performances on exercises, like the numbers of correct answers.

Using style sheets and scripting languages in conjunction with a "browsing context" offers the possibility to easily implement an adaptive hypermedia system cf. [3]. For accessing the "browsing context" with style sheets and scripting languages in a convenient manner, it is preferable to store it in XML format, eg as proposed in [3]. Web browsers store an internal representation of the document currently being displayed, eg as a DOM [1] tree. This document is referred to in the following as *naked document* because it does not contain any browsing context information. In a similar way as this naked document is stored by the browser, a *browsing context document* [3] can also be stored by the browser. Both the "naked document" and the "browsing context document" can be considered as the two parts of one (virtual) *context enriched document* stored within the browser. The "context enriched document" takes over the role of the original "naked document" within the browser, ie style sheets are applied to the "context enriched document" instead of the "naked document", scripting languages have access to the DOM tree of the "context enriched document" instead of the DOM tree of the "naked document", etc. Thus, the "context enriched document" is a virtual document combining a "browsing context" (using which adaptation is expressed) with a standard HTML or XML document. Note that the materialization of this virtual document is not needed.

3 Implementing Adaptation Using Style Sheet Selectors

A simple extension to style sheet selectors makes it simple to implement adaptive hypermedia functionalities with HTML and XML. The path expression of a style sheet selector is not to be matched against the original "naked document" tree, but against the new *context enriched document tree*.

Typical Web style sheet languages like CSS and XSLT have constructs of two kinds: style rules and selectors. Style rules define certain presentation parameters for elements in the document tree (like fonts, colors and margins), and transformations of the document tree (like insertion and sorting of elements). Selectors are path expressions that determine which style rule is applied to which element in the document tree. Matching a path expression of a style sheet selector not against the original "naked document" tree, but against the *context enriched document tree* makes it possible to build path expressions that depend on the content and structure of both, the "naked document" and the "browsing context document". Note that if the path expression of a selector contains no parts referring to a browsing context, the semantics of a style rule remains unchanged. Examples are given in [3].

4 Possible Extensions

Updating Application Data using Scripting Languages. Using style sheet selectors to express content and navigation adaption is not sufficient for modeling certain complex aspects of adaptive hypermedia systems. Still missing is the possibility to store data in the "browsing context", which then could be used by style sheets as a source of adaptation. Scripting languages like Javascript can be used to achieve this. In a similar way as Javascript code contained in Web pages can change the ("naked") document tree, Javascript code contained in Web pages can change the content of a "browsing context"'s application data.

Modeling Locations. There are several different notions of location. (1) Locations can be informations about the country or region where the user is, like Germany or France. This information is available in desktop computer systems and does not change during a browsing session. (2) Locations can be informations about the geographical position of the user, expressed, eg as longitude and latitude. This information is available in mobile devices like cellular phones or PDAs with special positioning equipment, eg a GPS device. Geographical location information can change during a browsing session. (3) Locations can also be informations about *virtual locations* like home, car, office, meeting, etc. Informations about virtual locations can change during a browsing session. "Virtual locations" are represented neither in current computer devices, nor within current Web standards. All of these notions can be represented simultaneously as browsing environment data in a "browsing context".

5 Discussion and Concluding Remarks

The approach outlined here has both, advantages and limitations. First, the approach is quite simple. It introduces a wide range of adaptation features into existing HTML and XML standards at the cost of very limited extensions to these standards. The extensions to these standards are as follows: (1) Information like browsing history and browsing environment data, most of which is already stored by conventional browsers, is to be stored as a standardized "browsing context" in an internal XML representation like DOM. (2) The style sheet processor(s), eg those of CSS or XSLT, match the selector part of a style rule not against the original "naked document", but against the (virtual) "context enriched document" (consisting of the "naked document" enriched with a browsing context). The style sheet processor must recognize those selector components referring to the "naked document" and those referring to the browsing context. This is conveniently achieved using namespaces.

Apart from these, no further changes are needed, especially, no new algorithms are needed. Only the processing of style sheet rules is extended, the style sheet languages remain otherwise unchanged (because of the use of namespaces cf. [3] section 3). This ensures upward compatibility with already existing style sheets. Also, style sheets that make use of "browsing context" selectors are downwards compatible with non-browsing context enabled browsers. With such browsers the data can be accessed, only the adaptation features are missing. Upwards and downwards compatibilities are essential for extensions to existing Web standards. Thus, the approach proposed in this paper is a conservative extension of the already existing and well-established Web standards.

The approach outlined in this paper is not specific to CSS or XSLT. It relies only on path selectors, which play a central role in Web standards. The same approach can easily be applied to other or future style sheet languages or to other Web standards like XML query languages, as long as they build on path selectors. Note also that this approach is stable against the changes from XPath 1.0 to XPath 2.0, which have introduced a considerably more complex type system, a set of relational operators, and (certain kinds of) variables.

References

1. V. Apparao et al. Document Object Model (DOM) Level 1 Specification Version 1.0. W3C Recommendation, 1998. http://www.w3.org/TR/REC-DOM-Level-1 .
2. P. Brusilovsky. Methods and Techniques of Adaptive Hypermedia. User Modeling and User-Adapted Interaction, 6(2-3):87–129, 1996.
   http://www.contrib.andrew.cmu.edu/ plb/UMUAI.ps .
3. F. Bry and M. Kraus. Adaptive Hypermedia Made Simple Using HTML/XML Style Sheet Selectors. Technical report, Inst. for Computer Science, University of Munich, 2002. Full version of this paper. http://www.pms.informatik.uni-muenchen.de/publikationen/#PMS-FB-2002-1 .
4. F. Bry and M. Kraus. Style Sheets for Context Adaptation. W3C Workshop on Delivery Context, 2002. http://www.pms.informatik.uni-muenchen.de/publikationen/#PMS-FB-2002-3 .
5. Standard ECMA-262. ECMAScript Language Specification, 1999. ftp://ftp.ecma.ch/ecma-st/Ecma-262.pdf .
6. PHP - Hypertext Preprocessor. http://www.php.net/ .

A Framework for Educational Adaptive Hypermedia Applications

Félix Buendía and Paloma Díaz*

Escuela Universitaria de Informática. Universidad Politécnica de Valencia.
46022-Valencia (Spain)
fbuendia@disca.upv.es
*Departamento de Informática.Universidad Carlos III de Madrid
28911 Leganes (Spain)
pdp@inf.uc3m.es

Abstract. Hypermedia technology has a large spread in the instructional field, specially in Web-based educational environments. Adaptive hypermedia systems have been focused on such aspects as specifying user models to adapt the educational contents and the navigation structure providing learning paths. The work presented in this paper addresses a new aspect based on adapting the access to the didactic structures, that encapsulate educational contents and learning paths, to support useful educational adaptive applications. It is presented a framework to support the design process which is divided in two main parts: the first one is focused on instructional issues such as the organization of educational contents and the learning tasks to access them; and the second one is based on the translation of these instructional entities into hypermedia components, for which the Labyrinth hypermedia model is used.

1 Introduction

Hypermedia technology has a large spread in the instructional field, specially in Web-based educational environments. In this context, adaptive hypermedia systems (AHS) have been focused on adapting the educational contents and the links that provide learning paths but few attention has been paid to structural aspects dealing with didactic requirements of instructional applications. Indeed, most AHSs mainly focus on displaying sequences of contents in user adapted ways but they are not aware of a key aspect in instructional applications: the structures in which educational contents are organized to reach a specific learning goal or the activities that a student can perform on these structures. This approach is supported by the thesis of authors like Merrill 1 who suggests that adequate instruction would require multiple types of knowledge structures (KS) to be identified and made explicit to the learner. In 2 there is a proposal to use these KS entities and extend them, becoming *Didactic Structures* (DS) able to capture didactic relationships between the *Instructional Objects* (IO) used to transmit some piece of knowledge. Another important aspect to be considered with adaptation purposes is how learners access DS entities by means of *Instructional*

Tasks (IT). In this paper we define a framework to deal both with instructional design topics and, at the same time, with the design of computer-based applications. This framework is based on the proposal presented in 2 which considers a triple model: Domain, User and Adaptation. The remainder of the paper is organized as follows. Section 2 describes some related work. Current definition of the Domain and User model, and their translation to Labyrinth entities 4 are described in sect. 3. Section 4 goes deeper into the Adaptation model and, finally, section 5 presents some remarking conclusions.

2 Related Work

Adaptive technologies have been traditionally applied in Web-based education in two main areas: the adaptive presentation and the navigation support. The references to structural aspects are restricted to rigid proposals such as the 'curriculum sequencing' technology 5. It is used in 6 where the adaptive functionality is based on following the internal structure of the subject domain. A more advanced sequencing technique is found in DCG 7 which allows the dynamic adaptation of Web-based courses. The main idea of the DCG architecture is the explicit representation of the concept structure of the domain, separated from the teaching materials. Nevertheless, it is not involved in the adaptation of the access to the underlying structures.

Moreover, proposals to develop adaptive courseware such as Interbook 8 or Net-Coach 9 are mostly based on traditional course structures. For instance, Interbook is based on the 'electronic textbook' metaphor and a sequence of learning goals as the navigation guide but it does not include references to other internal structures that could guide the learning process. More advanced techniques of knowledge-based navigation support are described in KBNS 9 and in HyperTutor 11 but they do not consider structure-based adaptation.

3 Domain and User Model

According to 2 an adaptive application uses a Domain model, describing how the information content of the application is structured. In this case, it is based on a Didactic model defined in 2 to design instructional applications. This model provides static entities, the *Instructional Objects* (IO) and the *Didactic Structures* (DS), that embody didactic information used to teach a specific topic. The functional model entities are *Instructional Tasks* (IT) and *Learning Scenarios* (LS). Each DS has a set of IT entities that represent its interface and they are dependant on the structure type. For example, the instructor can define tasks such as *Access* or *Identify*. The first one consists of doing a trip around the hierarchy tree at a given level (e.g. Europe states). The *Identify* task requires a higher level because it involves setting up the relationship between two o more hierarchy concepts (e.g. the geographical situation of a state). The user must have a certain competency level (CL) before accessing an IT. An IT also returns a competency value when the task is finished. LS represent the terms and conditions that characterize the user learning. The adaptive functionality is focused on the kinds of structures the users will be able to work with and the tasks they will execute on these structures. In order to ease their management from a computer-based point of view, the Didactic model entities are specified using a Labyrinth notation. This translation is described as follows (see Fig. 1). An instructional application is assigned with an Instructional Hyperdocument whose student user set is initially empty. It contains a group of DSs which are assigned to Labyrinth nodes. Each of these nodes has an anchor list which locate the associated ITs. These anchors represent the DS interface and they are connected using links with User Hyperdocuments. Each DS has a set of IO entities which contain knowledge objects represented as Labyrinth contents.

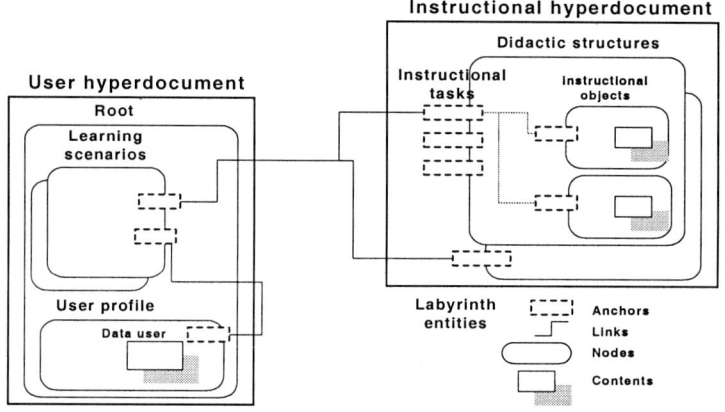

Fig. 1. Labyrinth representation of the Domain and User model entities.

4 Adaptation Model

Adaptation is based on the domain model (that is, DS and IT entities) and the user model (that is, LS and CL entities). With this purpose the instructor must provide an adaptation model consisting of rules enabling the user access to a DS given a certain CL. These rules can be further specified by means of weighted graphs or a similar notation (e.g. Petri nets) to represent the transitions between the different IT entities. In the current case, the ability to include event-based specifications for each component of a hypermedia application supported by Labyrinth [4] is used to specify the conditions that activate a new IT as the next example shows:

Event with condition *('LS_by_examples' node) AND ('Access_ task' completeTaskAttribute)* triggers action *[create_link_with ('Identify_task' node) in ('Europe_parts' node)]*

in which, a new link is set between a 'learning by examples' scenario and an *Identify* task if an *Access* task has been already completed. Several events can be defined in an analogous way and they can be assigned with different priority levels using the Labyrinth event value function. A given link is triggered (navigated) if it has a play event whose priority allows it to be scheduled by the adaptation engine.

5 Conclusions

This work presents a framework for designing educational hypermedia applications that intends to set a bridge between instructional and hypermedia aspects. On the one hand, it provides a model to specify Didactic Structures that eases the management and access to educational contents. A XML-based notation is being developed to help the instructor in such specification. On the other hand, the use of the Labyrinth hypermedia model permits the translation of the instructional entities to computer-based specifications. This feature will ease the implementation and validation of educational applications in hypermedia environments like the Web.

References

1. Merrill M. D., & ID2 Research Team. Instructional Transaction Theory: Instructional Design based on Knowledge Objects. Educational Technology, 36(3), 1996 pp. 30-37.
2. Buendía, F.; Diaz, P. Benlloch J.V;, A Framework for the Instructional Design of Multi-Structured Educational Applications, ED-MEDIA 2002, World Conference on Educational Multimedia, Hypermedia & Telecommunications, Denver, USA, 2002.
3. Wu, H., De Kort, E., De Bra, P.,Design Issues for General-Purpose Adaptive Hypermedia Systems. Proceedings of the ACM Conference on Hypertext and Hypermedia, , Aarhus, Denmark, August 2001, pp. 141-150.
4. P.Díaz, I. Aedo and F. Panetsos, Modeling the dynamic behavior of hypermedia applications. IEEE Transactions on Software Engineering vol 27 (6), June 2001, pp. 550-572.
5. Brusilovsky, P. Adaptive and Intelligent Technologies for Web-based Education. In C. Rollinger and C. Peylo (eds.), Special Issue on Intelligent Systems and Teleteaching, Künstliche Intelligenz, 4, 1999 pp.19-25.
6. Maria Grigoriadou, Kyparisia Papanikolaou, Harry Komilakis and George Magoulas INSPIRE: An INtelligent System for Personalized Instruction in a Remote Environment. Third Workshop on Adaptive Hypertext and Hypermedia, Sonthofen, Germany, July 13-17, 2001
7. J. Vassileva, Dynamic Courseware Generation on the WWW, Proceedings of the workshop 'Adaptive Systems and User Modeling on the World Wide Web', Sixth International Conference on User Modeling, Chia Laguna, Sardinia, 2-5 June 1997.
8. Brusilovsky, P., Eklund, J., and Schwarz, E. (1998) Web-based education for all: A tool for developing adaptive courseware. Computer Networks and ISDN Systems (Proceedings of Seventh International World Wide Web Conference, 14-18 April 1998,, pp.291-300.
9. Gerhard Weber, Hans-Christian Kuhl and Stephan Weibelzahl Developing Adaptive Internet Based Courses with the Authoring System NetCoach Third Workshop on Adaptive Hypertext and Hypermedia, Sonthofen, Germany, July 13-17, 2001
10. Eklund, J. and Sawers, J., Customising Web-based course delivery in WEST® with navigation support, in: Proceedings of WebNet'96, World Conference of the Web Society, San Francisco, CA, October 15–19, 1996, pp. 534-535.
11. Pérez, T., Lopistéguy, P., Gutiérrez, J., and Usandizaga, I. (1995b). HyperTutor: From hypermedia to intelligent adaptive hypermedia. In Maurer, H., ed., Proceedings of ED-MEDIA'95, World Conference on Educational Multimedia and Hypermedia. Graz, Austria: AACE. pp.529-534.

METIORE: A Publications Reference for the Adaptive Hypermedia Community

David Bueno[1], Ricardo Conejo[1], Cristina Carmona[1], and Amos A. David[2]

[1] Department of Languages and Computer Science, University of Málaga,
29071, Málaga, Spain.
{bueno,conejo,cristina}@lcc.uma.es
[2] LORIA, BP 239, 54506 Vandoeuvre, France
adavid@loria.fr

Abstract. The Web is one of the most powerful sources of information on any topic. However looking for scientific literature is a difficult task. Prior knowledge of link sites is necessary and if you are lucky they point to conferences proceedings available on-line. In fact the case the user is not able to make queries about the available documents and must check them one by one using general purpose search engines. In this paper we propose our system METIORE as a source of information for the Adaptive Hypermedia community. The idea is to put together all the publications on this research area and provide an adaptive tool to find papers or people working in the field. METIORE is a Personalized Information Retrieval system that keeps a user model based on objectives.

1 Introduction

The medium most used by the research community to find relevant work is the Web. The search engines such as Altavista or Google are improving their way of retrieving information. These engines index Web documents, but many of the scientific publications are in postcript or pdf formats which are not indexed by the engines. Also, because of the large quantity of Web pages they index, many of the results that can be obtained are not relevant. It is therefore necessary to provide information resources and associated tools where researchers can just find scientific contents without the usual noise introduced by typical search engines.

The idea of having a search engine exclusively for scientific information has already been developed. FermiVista [3] is an index of articles and prepublications available on the Web or FTP servers of Universities and Research Centers. It contains documents in the domain of mathematics, computer science and physics. Unfortunately this index has not been updated since 1998.

One of the best specific indexes is the CiteSeer [4]. It locates scientific articles on the web using search engines like AltaVista and allows for the extraction of information of the citations in publications. The main feature is the creation of an Autonomous Citation Indexing [5]. Even though this system can be applied to any field of research, it is specific for Computer Science literature.

In this paper we present the application of our Retrieval System METIORE oriented to the implementation of an index/search engine for the Adaptive Hypermedia (AH) publications. In Sect. 2 the generalities of METIORE will be presented. The adaptation to the Web to make the AH index is explained in Sect. 3. Finally the conclusions and future work are presented in Sect. 4.

2 METIORE

METIORE is the acronym of Multimedia coopErative InformaTIOn Retrieval SystEm. It is a multipurpose IRS that can be applied to different kinds of database. It has been used in three different areas. For the first area, METIORE_STREEMS is an IRS for managing multimedia information on trees authorized for reforestation by the European Union (EU). The project was sponsored under the EU project LEONARDO. For the second area, METIORE_LORIA is used for managing the database of publications of the computer science laboratory research center, LORIA, Nancy France. Some evaluations of METIORE have been done using this database [1]. In the third area, METIORE_REVUES is used for the access and analysis of a collection of journals called 'Relations Publiques Informations'.

The ability of METIORE to manage different types of data is in part due to the use of XML to import the different databases. From these sources it generates files with inverted lists and cluster information to provide a fast access. The core of METIORE is independent from the data; it only needs to know the parameters that will be used for the personalization. So if it is working with publications it may use author, title, keywords, etc. But if it is working with data on trees, the parameters may be height, altitude, scientific name, etc.

METIORE has a powerful search interface that allows the user to make simple or complex queries and also perform global analysis of the database. It is also possible to explore the database without knowing anything about its content. This last possibility is very useful as a starting point in the process of information retrieval. The following are examples of the types of query that can be processed using METIORE on the database of publications:
- Documents about Script languages published after 1998
- List of all authors with their number of publications
- Authors who have written with X and how many times (this shows people working together)
- Names of authors and keywords that they use
- The yearly frequency of the use of the keyword 'expert systems' (this provides a means of observing the evolution of a research topic in terms its frequency of use in publications)

The most relevant feature of METIORE is the personalization of the response. Our approach on personalization is based on the concept of objective. For us the objective is the expression of the user's information needs formulated in natural language. The objective is currently used to group the set of queries, concepts and decisions that the user makes on the system having his objective in mind. Our hypothesis is that grouping the user's interactions into objectives will help the user to find information in his history and help the system to build a specific model of the user from one or more sessions.

This concept is very important to us since we believe that every user has a minimum knowledge of his information needs before attempting to use an IRS. This knowledge can of course be improved with the use of the system and consequently the user's ability to express his information needs through the system's interaction. For us, the queries do not necessarily express all the information needs of the user but rather his approach towards solving the problem of his information needs.

For each user objective the system constructs a model. In order to give users a personalized response, after querying the system, they should evaluate some documents of the response. This provides the system with the user's preferences for this objective and thus help the user in future queries to have the most relevant solutions first. This is different from many retrieval systems that gives a list of solutions (for example 400 documents) that are sorted only according to the user's query. METIORE sorts the solutions using the query and the user model in order to select the best solutions that are presented at the top of the list.

Another interesting feature of METIORE is that the user has available his history of evaluated documents. This history is organized by objectives, for each of which the evaluated documents are sorted by their relevance to the user's objective. With the history the user can review his past solutions, modify his evaluations and also look for related documents.

3 METIORE on the Web

To make METIORE more accessible, it has been necessary to make it available on the Web. The best option has been to keep the core of METIORE to maintain all its functionality and used as a server. The user will have a web interface that is connected to a *Java Servlet* which will send transactions to the METIORE daemon through a socket connection. A specific protocol has been created for the communication between the applications. The main programming language of METIORE is *incrTcl*. Fig. 1 shows the architecture for METIORE on Web.

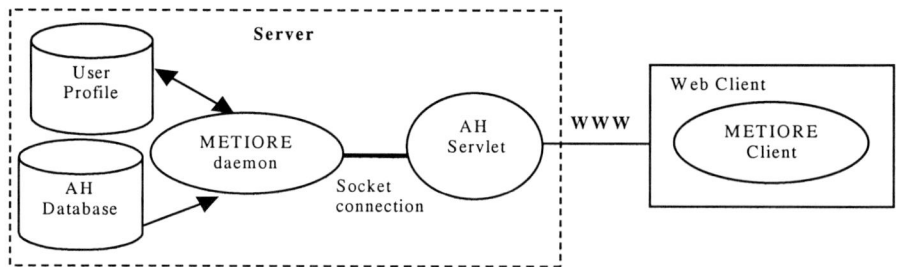

Fig. 1. The architecture to make METIORE accessible through Web

For Adaptive Hypermedia literature and in general for scientific publications on the Web we have designed a database that contains all the information needed to represent a publication (including its url). It also includes the information on authors and conferences/journals with links to their homepages. This makes METIORE_AH a source of data where papers, conferences, editorials and people can be easily found and contacted.

All the publications of the Adaptive Hypermedia Home Page [2] and related conferences are included in the database. We have realized that most of the papers don't have associated keywords. In order to obtain the keywords (more precisely the root of keywords) and have them as a source of information in queries, the full documents are treated in the following way: The paper is parsed using a stop words list and the porter algorithm [6]. Then the frequency of words is obtained and the most relevant are chosen to represent the article. A web page is also provided to let researchers include their publications in METIORE. When all these documents are inserted, it will be possible to use the characteristics of METIORE to obtain relevant publications for the users through the Web.

4 Conclusions and Future Work

In this paper we have presented the application of METIORE for managing the Adaptive Hypermedia publications on the Web. We hope to integrate some other functions that are available in similar systems such as CiteSeer. One of the functions is the processing of the references to have some kind of citation index, or to automatically include papers to the database. However, METIORE offers other possibilities that can't be found in other applications, like the complex data analysis, the objectives of retrieval that can be maintained in different sessions, or the active history to review relevant publications. Others features such as having the list of the most relevant articles or authors according to the interactions of users with METIORE will be available soon. With the data obtained through the user's interactions, new evaluations of METIORE will be made. Our objective is to apply METIORE to other areas of research after evaluating this application.

References

1. Bueno, D., & David, A. A. (2001). 'METIORE: A Personalized Information Retrieval System '. User Modeling 2001
2. De Bra, P. (1999) Adaptive Hypertext and Hypermedia [Web Page]. http://wwwis.win.tue.nl/ah/.
3. Fermigier, S. (1996) FermiVista [Web Page]. http://fermivista.math.jussieu.fr/.
4. Lawrence, S. (1997) CiteSeer Research Index [Web Page]. http://citeseer.nj.nec.com/.
5. Lawrence, S., Lee Giles, C., & Bollacker, K. 'Digital Libraries and Autonomous Citation Indexing'. IEEE Computer, 32(6), 67-71
6. Porter, M.F., (1980). 'An algorithm for suffix stripping', *Program*, **14** (3),130-137

User-Driven Adaptation of e-Documents

P. Carrara[1], D. Fogli[2], G. Fresta[3], and P. Mussio[2]

[1] Istituto per le Tecnologie Informatiche Multimediali del CNR, Milan, Italy
paola.carrara@itim.mi.cnr.it
[2] Dipartimento di Elettronica per l'Automazione, Università di Brescia, Brescia, Italy
{fogli,mussio}@ing.unibs.it
[3] Istituto di Scienza e Tecnologie dell'Informazione "A. Faedo" del CNR, Pisa, Italy
g.fresta@cnuce.cnr.it

Abstract. This paper proposes a new strategy for designing e-documents adaptable to user's aims and habits. This strategy is based on the creation of a cascade of interaction environments requiring the local adaptation of the e-documents. The strategy is supported by a recently introduced model of Human Computer Interaction, and made effective by the development of BANCO, an environment allowing Web modification by the users at the client side.

1 Introduction

The increasing diffusion of end-user computing based on the interaction with hypermedia systems and applications poses several new problems: the environment with which users are interacting is a new type of document, an *electronic document* (*e-document*), which evolves the traditional documentation styles, opening to their users new communication possibilities as well as creating new dangerous situations. E-documents are less persistent than traditional ones, because they only exist and are perceivable if an electronic machinery maintains them in existence. They can be managed and adapted more easily than paper ones; they can be active and reactive to users' requests; they appear to the users as a whole, but they can result from merging of different elements which may be distributed in different, geographically remote repositories. This paper reports on a strategy for designing e-documents adaptable to user's aims and habits [1], based on the user generation of a cascade of environments. The strategy is based on a recently introduced model of Human Computer Interaction [2] and has been made effective by the development of BANCO (Browsing Adaptive Network for Changing user Operativity) [3], a feasibility prototype for the Web, designed to explore the interaction with e-documents.

2 Bootstrapping Workshops for e-Documents Adaptation

In usual practice, designers develop the tools to manage e-documents focusing on the computational and management aspects and not on the solution of problems. This design approach forces end-users to translate their problems and solutions in computer oriented notations, generally not amenable to their reasoning, but often misleading. The approach we present reverses this situation: the designer has to produce an e-document in a form understandable by the users, prone to their habits and adaptable to the user situation. To this aim, it is important to distinguish the various kinds of users and their roles. In general, users belong to specific user communities, playing distinct roles: Figures 1 and 2, for example, show e-documents designed for an application aimed at monitoring glacier evolution. In Fig. 1 the intended user is a photo interpreter, while in Fig. 2 the e-document should be used by environmental agency clerks, to monitor the situation and prepare reports based on data analyzed and archived by other experts. These e-documents are called *application workshops:* they are devoted to end-users who perform a given task to obtain some final product.

The two e-documents of the figures are designed for two communities, whose notations share a common subset of symbols. These two communities may be considered members of the larger community of experts interested in glaciological data. However, they also use different tools to perform their tasks: a photo interpreter, for example, obtains the spectral characterization of the glacier areas, the clerk derives reports on the environmental situation. The use of two different application workshops lessens their cognitive load in choosing tools, avoids possible errors, mistakes and misunderstandings and makes the navigation in the workshop more simple and reliable. In our view, the creation of the application workshops has to be done by an expert in the management of environmental data, who knows notation and needs of both the communities, and is able to plan the documentation to be produced. This expert, here called 'the manager', needs a workshop to create new application workshops. This workshop, called *manager workshop*, is an instance of a different type of workshops, called *system workshops*, in which tools are available for creating a workshop for a community of users. System workshops can be recursively defined for experts who create the system workshops for managers.

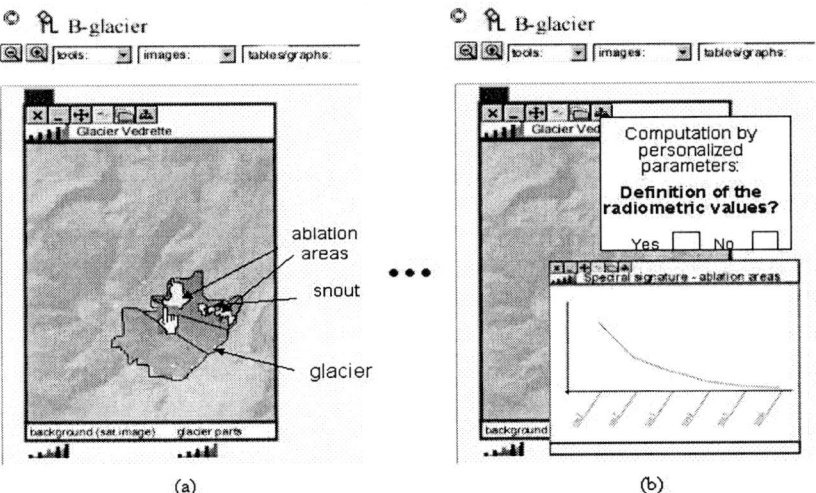

Fig. 1. Interaction with B-Glacier, the workshop for a photo-interpreter: 1a) the selection of an ablation area; 1b) the results of the computation fired by the previous selection.

In this way a cascade of system workshops can be created. At each level, an expert uses a system workshop to create the tools and notations for a more specialized expert, who will contribute in creating a final application workshop customized to specific end-users and type of task. On the whole, the approach defines workshops to support task achievement by a community of users. The number of levels between the top computer scientist workshop and the bottom application workshops and the number of the workshops at each level are determined by the work organization in the community.

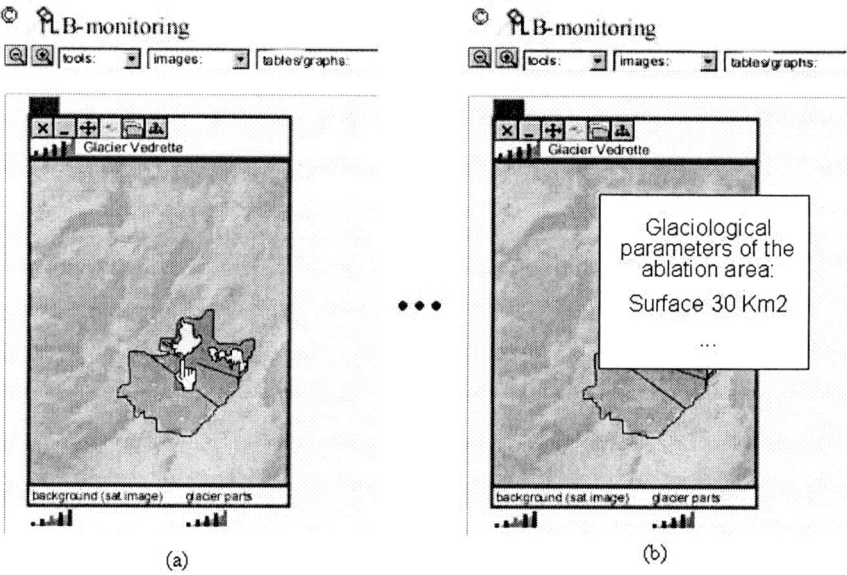

Fig. 2. Interaction with B-Monitoring, the workshop for a clerk: the selection of an ablation area (1a) in this context fires the simple retrieval of data relative to that area (1b).

3 A Model of the Human - e-Document Interaction Process

The strategy for designing workshops is supported by a model of human-e-document interaction [4], which informally evolves the PCL (Pictorial Computing Laboratory) model presented in [2] for WIMP (Windows, Icons, Menus, Pointers) environments [5]. In this approach, Human-Computer Interaction is modeled as a cyclic process in which the user and the interactive system communicate by materializing and interpreting a sequence of messages at successive time stamps, the user by cognitive criteria, the computer by programmed criteria [2]. Users interpret the whole images represented on the screen display, formed by text, graphs, pictures, icons, etc. by recognizing *characteristic structures* (CSs), i.e. sets of image pixels which they perceive as functional or perceptual units. The CS recognition results into the association of a meaning with a structure. Once interpreted the message, the user decides what to do next and manifests his/her intention by an activity performed operating on the input devices of the system. On the other hand, the system associates each graphical entity, which is in turn a set of pixels, i.e. a cs, with a program , and computes the response to user activity materializing the results on the screen, so that they can be perceived and interpreted by the user. In principle, this cycle is repeated until the user decides that the process has to be finished.

4 Workshop Implementation with BANCO

The tool by which the cascade of workshops can be implemented is BANCO [3]. It exploits a novel architecture on the Web, in which a user can locally customise his/her environment still maintaining the consistency of data and tools with those of the Web. On the user side, BANCO, enriched by a kernel of scripts and a library of customisation files, is accessed by a XML/SVG-complaint browser. The messages exchanged with the server are in eXtended Markup Language (XML), and convey also the specification necessary for their interpretation by the browser, in Scalable Vector Graphics (SVG) format [6]. SVG is used to specify the set of cs and their organization into the layout of the user interface as well as the links to computational tools. The programs representing the meaning of the css are written in Jscript. They materialise data according to customisation rules. Changing the library of rules they can be adapted to different user habits. The workshops are implemented by several instances of BANCO, each one specialized to its users and tasks through the definition of the set of its css, computational meanings and links between them, which are interpreted by a uniform mechanism.

BANCO is an e-document written not to be read, but able to transform other unreadable e-documents into a form readable by users of a specific community.

References

1. Brusilowsky, P.: Methods and techniques of adaptive hypermedia, User Modelling and User Adapted Interaction 6(2-3) (1996), 87-129
2. Bottoni, P., Costabile, M. F., Mussio, P.: Specification and Dialog Control of Visual Interaction, ACM TOPLAS 21(6) (1999) 1077-1136
3. Carrara, P., Fresta, G., Mussio, P.: SVG: More than a markup language for vector graphics, Euroweb 2001, Pisa (Italy), (2001), 245-257
4. Carrara, P., Fogli, D., Fresta, G., Mussio, P. (2002) Toward overcoming culture, skill and situation hurdles in human-computer interaction. appear on Journal Universal Access in Information Society
5. Dix, A., Finlay, J., Abowd, G., Beale, R.: Human Computer Interaction, Prentice Hall, London, (1998)
6. W3C: WWW Consortium, 2001. http://www.w3c.org/

Server Independent Personalization for Effective Searching in the World Wide Web *

Lillian N. Cassel[1], Ursula Wolz[2], and Robert E. Beck[3]

[1] Villanova University; Villanova, PA USA
lillian.cassel@villanova.edu
[2] The College of New Jersey; Trenton, NJ USA
wolz@tcnj.edu
[3] Villanova University; Villanova, PA USA
robert.beck@villanova.edu

1 Introduction

Effective Web searching involves two components: (1) a search tool must know about and characterize as many Web pages as possible and (2) it must match a user query to the most suitable resource. The essential problem addressed by personalization systems relates to the second component of Web searching. How can the information that a search service holds about resources available on the Web be matched to the diverse needs of the global user base? In this paper we introduce an alternative to the usual model for user personalization.

2 WHAT

The Web Host Access Tool (WHAT) project is a research effort aimed at improved access to relevant information on the Web for users at all levels of expertise in a highly personalized manner. We focus on effective presentation and management of search results to users after assisting in the construction of a search query. The expected effect of this project is to reply to a user search query with a set of resources that (1) has been obtained from a variety of Web search tools, (2) has been pre-evaluated for suitability to the user's request, and (3) has been formatted for effective presentation of the results to the user.

A fundamental premise is that the user wants control of the search and the search results, but the user should not be burdened with the details of obtaining the results. We posit the need for a highly individualized search context that includes knowledge of prior search experiences, general knowledge of search and search engines as well as explicit information provided by the user. The user should be sheltered from the details of formats, query construction rules, and search strategies of particular search services. In particular, if a user does repeated searches within a particular domain, the experience of those searches

---

* This work is partially funded by the United States National Science Foundation Awards EIA-0079770, EIA-0130798

should remain accessible and inform the new search. Ideally, the user's changing expectations within a search context (such as discussed by Vakkari and Hakala [9]) should drive the selection of results presented by the search tool. The burden for providing this history should be undertaken by the search system.

A distinguishing characteristic of our work is that the added functionality is provided by a program running entirely on the user's own local system, namely one under the user's control. Access to the system while traveling and while using other computers is expected and the mechanism is beyond the scope of this paper. This placement has implications for privacy, for ethical treatment of the user's requirements, and for system effectiveness and efficiency.

The major focus of our work is to aggregate search results from numerous sources, merge these results with what we know about our user's preferences and responses to prior searches, and present a view of the merged search results consistent with these preferences. We keep our personalization procedures independent of the actual structure of the knowledge representation used by the information source. Thus, our approach is not tied to any particular search environment and can be considered a generalization of the problem of personalization of search support.

As with a search through a general-purpose search engine, our user poses a query through query terms. Unlike users of a general search engine interface, the WHAT user is able to specify a context for the search. The context is defined by its title and a list of keywords that help to specify its meaning. The set of results is retrieved, based on both the query terms and the context keywords. The user is presented with an ordered list of results and selects those most relevant to the current interest. User feedback concerning the appropriateness of the results becomes part of the context definition and influences responses to future queries. Changing the context adapts the user's setting to the user's preferences and focus.

2.1 System Design: WHAT and the WHAT Observer

The Web Host Access Tools (WHAT) system, implemented in Java, includes a query constructor, a context manager (and database), and a response filter. Undergraduate research assistants have presented posters on iterations of the system since 1998. [1–3]

The query constructor interacts with the context manager and the user interface. From the context manager, the query constructor learns of terms that have previously been included in similar searches that can assist the current search. It combines the user search terms with weighted keywords associated with the context to form search strings to send to a set of search services. In collaboration with the user, the context manager accumulates and analyses prior search topics enhancing the search context. The response filter, in addition to eliminating duplicate results, examines prior results in this context for clues about user preferences. The response filter also captures user impressions about results and updates the context history for use in future searches. Current work builds on known techniques [4] for judging the relevance of a page to a search query to predict the user response.

While a number of projects are attempting to link a given query to a specialized search engine [8], WHAT has the advantage of an explicit specification of a context for the query. Specification of the search context gives important information for routing the search to specialized search engines, as well as filtering results that come from general search engines.

We seek to minimize the client's need to interact with a server, both for performance reasons and to protect the user's privacy. At the same time, we do not want to burden individual client systems with tasks better suited to a central facility. Tasks well suited to a server facility include recognition of changes at the search sites that require software updates, learning about new search tools and integrating them into the system, determining performance characteristics that affect choice of which tools to use for a given type of query, perhaps determining time-of-day factors for making a good choice of search tool. Gregg Davis at Villanova made initial steps in identifying types of seach engine failures that can easily be recognized and corrected in a client system and those better suited to intervention from a WHAT system server. [5]

2.2 WHAT Observer

System assessment requires evaluating the "goodness" of a response as impacted by the various systems we have implemented and plan to enhance. As we developed specific evaluation questions we saw the need for the WHAT Observer to be used exclusively as a research tool. [7] This continues the work of Hartson, et al [6] on remote interface evaluation, but extends it to allow the evaluation of the impact of underlying analysis systems (such as the context manager). The WHAT Observer allows us to selectively observe the interaction between the user and the WHAT system. Data are automatically stored in a server-based database. User surveys elicited through web forms can augment the database.

2.3 Goodness Metrics

Our initial "goodness" metric is determined by the order of query responses. We posit that in any search, the "best" responses should appear before "worse" responses in the presentation order. When a user initiates a query through WHAT, three ordered lists result that can be captured by the Observer: (1) The web search services return an ordering determined by their metric. (2) The WHAT context manager reorders the initial list and presents it to the user. (3) The user implicitly reorders the list when assigning "yes", "no", or "maybe" tags to some items and ignoring others. The tags create a tripartite grouping of the examined items. We presume in this analysis that examination is systematic and complete up to a point in the initial list. Items that are unexamined come after such a point and are consigned to the "no" group.

In a perfect response, the contents of each group would exactly match the groups assigned by the user. We can analyze the migration of items from WHAT's response list to the user groupings. Little migration suggests a "good" ordering. Note that there is no significance within the grouping. An item's position in the group is derived entirely from its position in the original list. An exact definition of "little migration" awaits analysis of our initial test results. Furthermore, it is dependent upon whether the user thought the search was "successful." Consequently, we anticipate that the degree of migration as a metric will not be fixed for all users, but will be dependent upon the user and the scenario in which the search occurred.

The migration metric also provides insight into the efficiency of personalization. A system that expends significant resources in time and space may not be cost-effective if there are only small improvements in minimizing migration.

3 Summary

The WHAT project, which builds on existing Web search tools, places resources oriented to user-specific services on the user's system. This allows specific personalization to an individual user and addresses the important issues of privacy and user trust. The resulting system includes an assessment component and early results indicate significant improvement over general Web search techniques.

References

1. Jonathan Anderson and Jason Dobies. The web host access tools (what) project. SIGCSE 2001 Charlotte, NC, 2001.
2. Brice Behringer, Mark Nikolsky, and Michael Sipper. A gui for web host access tools. Technical report, The College of New Jersey, Ewing, NJ, 1998.
3. Greg Bronevetsky. The brains of what: A data structure for internet searches. SIGCSE 99, New Orleans, LA page 378, 1999.
4. Chris Buckley, Gerald Salton, and James Allan. The effect of adding relevance information in a relevance feedback. In *Proceedings of the 17th ACM-SIGIR Conference on Research and development in information retrieval*, pages 292–300, 1994.
5. Greg R. Davis. Web host access tool updating protocol. Technical report, Villanova University Department of Computing Sciences, 1999. Independent Study Project under the direction of Dr. Lillian Cassel.
6. Rex Hartson, José C. Castillo, John Kelso, and Wayne C. Neale. Remote evaluation: the network as an extension of the usability laboratory. In *Conference proceedings on Human factors in computing systems*, pages 228–235, 1996.
7. Jared Klett. Web host access tools observer. SIGCSE 99, New Orleans, LA, page 379, 1999.
8. Atsushi Sugiura and Oren Etzioni. Query routing for web search engines: Architectures and experiments. In *Ninth International World Wide Web Conference (WWW9)*, Amsterdam, The Netherlands, May 2000.
9. Pertti Vakkari and Nanna Hakala. Changes in relevance criteria and problem stages in task performance. *Journal of Documentation*, 56(5):540–562, September 2000.

Preventing Misleading Presentations of XML Documents: Some Initial Proposals

Alison Cawsey, Euan Dempster, Diana Bental, Daniel Pacey, Howard Williams, Lachlan MacKinnon, and David Marwick

Department of Computing and Electrical Engineering,
Heriot-Watt University, Riccarton,
Edinburgh EH14 4AS, UK; Tel: +44 131 451 3410; Fax: +44 131 451 3431
alison@cee.hw.ac.uk

Abstract. It is now straightforward to develop a range of different stylesheets to present XML documents in different ways, for example to create personalised presentations. If the XML document is available on the World Wide Web, then (subject to copyright) anyone can create their own stylesheet to present that document in new ways. This has the potential to allow improved "added value" services, such as personalised news feeders. But the power of stylesheet languages such as XSLT means that the document may be substantially transformed, with sections deleted or re-ordered. This re-structuring may result in a misleading and even dangerous presentation. This paper presents some proposals for putting some control in the hands of document authors, to allow them to indicate allowable transformations, and to provide a limited validation mechanism to verify that a transformed document meets the requirements of the author.

1 Introduction

Anyone can create their own stylesheets to present XML documents that are available on the World Wide Web. It is straightforward in JavaScript, for example, to specify that a stylesheet at one location should be applied to an XML document taken from another location. This has great power - for example, it allows those providing information services to "pull in" material from different sites and present it in a way that suits their users. Similarly one can develop services to present material in the optimum manner for various display devices, or to meet the needs of users with disabilities. Abstracting services could display certain sections with the amount presented tuned to the readers' requirements.

Already there are a number of systems that use XML in personalisation. GUIDE 3 is an online tourist guide where a user profile is supplied by the tourist; SETA 1 is a web shopping assistant that personalises information on products. More personalised systems are reviewed in 2. Currently, the development of the resources and the personalisation services are typically managed by a single group, hosted on one server. But as more and more resources are designed in this way we will see new services emerging which use the data in the XML resources provided by others, but present this information in new ways. However, the power of stylesheet languages such as XSLT 5 mean that the document may be substantially transformed in the process of presenting it in these new ways. Sections may be omitted, re-ordered, or generally restructured. This may result in misleading or dangerous presentations, as important information is omitted, or re-ordering changes the document semantics. This problem is very familiar to the document summarisation community 6. Simple sentence extraction systems can result in confusing summaries, as the juxtaposition of two sentences originally taken from separate sections of a document results in incorrect interpretation.

This paper presents an initial analysis of this problem, and some limited proposals to enable authors of XML documents to specify just what transformations are allowable, and to provide a way of validating transformed documents. We start by looking at some possible problems that may arise in transforming documents, taking medical documents as our case study. We then suggest an annotation scheme that would allow authors to specify allowed transformations, avoiding the problems identified. Finally we consider how or whether that scheme may be enforced, and suggest the use of a simple validation service, where the transformed document can be validated against the annotations.

2 The Problem of Misleading Transformations

We have looked at a range of document types in order to determine some of the likely problems that may arise through transformation, and how an author could state constraints. Here we will focus on an example of a drug catalogue (available as a publicly accessible XML file). This catalogue might include name, price, side-effects and use of a range of drugs. Using stylesheets an intermediary provider could:

- Present just part of the catalogue – maybe just the drugs that relate to the user's condition.
- Omit part of the drug information (e.g., the side effects).
- Re-order the catalogue, perhaps putting relevant drugs at the top, or ordering by price.
- Combining the catalogue with another, perhaps adding the supplier name into the table.
- Include some side-effects of drugs, but only as space allowed.
- Add or omit disclaimers, or recommendations to consult professionals.

It should be clear that some of these transformations are inadvisable and potentially harmful, whereas others may play a useful role. As a result the provider of the catalogue may want to specify certain constraints on the transformation, such as:

- If a drug is included, then its side effects should always be listed as given.
- A disclaimer of liability should always be included.

There will be many other constraints of different forms. Suppose the catalogue also provided some information on the advantages and disadvantages of a drug. These could be omitted, but if the advantages are listed, so should the advantages. It may be further required to list the advantages and disadvantages in the order given. And there are cases where the juxtaposition of elements is significant. For example, adding in a paragraph into a paper might destroy its coherence.

From this analysis we suggest that authors may want to provide constraints of the following forms.
1. Element is required to be included.
2. The ordering within Element must be retained.
3. If Element1 is included, so must be Element2.
4. Element1 and Element2 must not be split.

In most cases general rules such as this applying to all drugs may suffice. But there may be special cases where the author may wish to supply additional constraints.
- If presenting DRUG-X, ensure that the additional information is included.

So we want to be able to describe whether rules apply to all elements of a given type (e.g., for all drug data always include any side-effects), or just to specific elements listed (e.g, for this drug, ensure the additional information is included).

3 A Proposed Annotation Scheme

Based on the discussion above, we need a way of specifying, for a given document or document type, which sections can be re-ordered, deleted, and which sections are dependent on others (so the inclusion of one demands the other). If every (significant) element in the document has an associated ID, then we can indicate these constraints using some simple statements based on describing relationships in groups of elements. We specify for groups whether the group is mandatory, must retain order, and whether elements can be split. The following two examples illustrate this scheme:

```
<group order="no" maysplit="no" mandatory="yes">
  <item required="yes">Image1<item>
  <item required="yes">Legend1<item>
</group>
```

Image1 and Legend1 are mandatory, but they can be re-ordered. Extra material cannot be inserted between them – perhaps that would destroy the connection between image and legend

```
<group order="yes" maysplit="no" mandatory="no">
  <item required="yes">advantages1<item>
  <item required="yes">disadvantages1<item>
</group>
```

The advantages and disadvantages are optional, but if the group is included then both items are required.

The above scheme allows rules to be applied to individual elements (through their IDs). However it is easy to expand this approach to allow rules that apply to all elements of a given type. We could simply supply default values for an element type (e.g., side-effect) which can be overridden in a specific case. This annotation scheme allows authors to indicate the transformations permitted, in a machine-processable format, but leaves open the problem of how to verify that these constraints are met. Although we cannot avoid malicious action, we can provide some simple tools that would allow a co-operative information provider to check that their transformed document meets the constraints requested by the source provider.

4 Validation

If the information provider is transforming the document into a completely different document type (as is indeed currently normal) then the problem is difficult - at best, if they retained the element IDs, we could use simple tree traversal to verify orderings, etc. However, things become a little easier if we assume that the presentation of the document will be done in two stages: transformation (into the same document type) and formatting (into formatting objects 5, or into XHTML). We will therefore look briefly at the specific problem of validating a transformed document against constraints, given that it is in the same document type as the original.

To a limited extent, we could merely ensure that the DTD or Schema is as "tight" as possible and require that the transformed document is a valid instance of this document type. Schemas (or DTDs) allow us to state ordering constraints and compulsory elements). But we also want to be able to specify rules-- IF there is an element matching this constraint THEN do this check. We also want to be able to assert constraints that just apply to one document instance, or one particular element (e.g., for THIS paragraph, don't omit the copyright). Such specific constraints are not easily handled within the document type.

What is needed is a schema language that allows you to flexibly specify rules -- IF there is an element matching this constraint THEN do this check. At first glance Schematron 7 seems to provide a solution. Schematron is a schema language based on such rules. It allows you to identify patterns in the document, and, if these patterns occur, check for the existence of some other element. An example rule is given below, which checks and reports on obligatory child elements for a drug element.

```
<pattern name="Drug checker">
  <rule context="drug">
    <assert test="side-effect"> Side effect is missing
    </assert>
    <report> Side effect is present </report>
    <assert test="@producer"> Producer attribute is missing
    </assert>
  </rule>
</pattern>
```

The above would apply to all drugs. We could specify more rules for more specific elements in a similar manner, with, for example, context=drug[@ID="d2"].

Schematron is very good for specifying fairly simple rules such as these, but more complex cases are harder to handle. We have also looked at using XSLT as the language for the validator, providing significantly more flexibility. We can specify templates that result in error messages being written out if constraints are violated:

```
<xsl:template match="drug">
 <xsl:choose>
  <xsl:when test= "side-effect"> OK </xsl:when>
  <xsl:otherwise> No side effect listed. </xsl:otherwise>
 </xsl:choose>
</xsl:template>
```

We have developed an XSLT stylesheet which validates documents against constraints expressed in the format indicated in the previous section. This could be used in an online validation service, allowing cooperative providers who use their resources to verify that transformed documents meet the source providers' constraints (perhaps adding some icon if it does).

5 Conclusion

We have presented an initial analysis of a likely problem with misleading presentations, if authors "lose control" of the styles applied to their document. We suggest a simple annotation scheme allowing authors to specify allowed transformations, and explore how simple validators could be written to check that constraints are obeyed. A simple validation procedure such as this cannot address the problem of malicious adaptation (which requires a social/legal solution), but allows information providers to describe some basic constraints on transformation, which can be checked by cooperative secondary providers.

Acknowledgements

This work has been funded by the Engineering and Physical Science Research Council, grant reference GR/N22229/01 Dynamic Information Presentation, and we gratefully acknowledge their support.

References

1. Ardissono, L. & Goy, A., Tailoring the interaction with users in electronic shops. in Kay, J., (ed), User Modelling: Proceedings of the Seventh International Conference, UM99, Springer, (1999).
2. D Bental, L MacKinnon, H Williams, D Marwick, D Pacey, E Dempster and A Cawsey, Dynamic Information Presentation through Web-based Personalisation and Adaptation - An Initial Review, In Joint Proccedings of HCI 2001 and IHM 2001, A Blandford, J Vanderdonckt and P Gray (Eds), pp 485-500, Springer, (2001).
3. Cheverst, K., Davies, N., Mitchell, K. & Smith, P., Providing tailored (context-aware) information to city visitors. in Brusilovsky, P., Stock, O. & Strapparava, C., (eds), Adaptive Hypermedia and Adaptive Web-Based Systems, 73 -85. Springer, (2000).
4. Extensible Stylesheet Language (XSL), Version 1.0, W3C Recommendation 15 October 2001, (2001), http://www.w3.org/TR/xsl/
5. Kay, M., XSLT 2nd Edition - Programmer's Reference, Wrox Press Ltd, Birmingham, UK, (2001).
6. Mani, I., & Maybury, M., (eds) Advances in Automatic Text Summarization, MIT Press, (1999).
7. Van der Vlist E., XML Content Management System Using XSLT, Schematron, and Ant, O'Reilly Open Source Convention, XTech 2001: Cutting Edge XML. (2001).

Adaptivity Conditions Evaluation for the User of Hypermedia Presentations Built with AHA!

Alessandra Cini [1] and José Valdeni de Lima [2]

[1] Fundação Universidade de Caxias do Sul, Rua Francisco Getúlio Vargas, 1133,
Caxias do Sul - RS, Brazil, Phone: + 55 (54) 218 2278
alessandra@malbanet.com.br
[2] Universidade Federal do Rio Grande do Sul, Av. Bento Gonçalves, 9500 - Bloco IV / 226,
Porto Alegre - RS, Brazil, Phone: +55 (51) 33 16 61 61
valdeni@inf.ufrgs.br

Abstract. The importance of adaptive hypermedia propelled the development of several authoring tools. Even though most tools are efficient for their designed task, they do not guarantee that the adaptivity is used in a high degree, in order to satisfy users with distinct goals, preferences, background and/or needs, as usual on the Web. In this paper we will present a system in development built to evaluate the adaptivity degree of presentations built into the AHA! authoring tool. The author, after build his presentation in AHA!, submits it to our system for evaluation. The results obtained from the evaluation can aid the author to know if the built presentation it is according to the proposed goals or the adaptivity degree should be increased.

1 Introduction

The importance of adaptive hypermedia area in recent years and the difficulties of adaptive presentations authoring propelled the development of several authoring tools for adaptive hypermedia.

The several authoring tools available, such as AHA! [1] (Adaptive Hypermedia Architecture), developed at Eindhoven University of Technology and InterBook [2], developed at Carnegie Mellon University, have countless resources to promote the adaptation and to facilitate the construction of a presentation.

The production of an adaptive presentation must consider the peculiarities of the content that is being approached and the user's individual goals, preferences, background and/or needs. Considering that most of the presentations are available via the Web, the user's profile can be quite distinct, requiring the presentations to have a high adaptivity degree to satisfy such users.

2 Importance of Adaptivity Degree Evaluation of a Presentation

The use of an authoring tool for adaptive hypermedia doesn't assure that a presentation is built with high adaptivity degree. As a consequence, presentations can be built with insufficient adaptive resources. If we consider the fact that, in a presentation, the author can define a display requirement for only one page and that this requirement can be fulfilled by accessing another single page, the adaptivity degree can be very low. Still, we cannot say that such presentation is not adaptive.

Starting from the perception of this limitation, we are building a system able to measure the presentation adaptivity degree. We did opt for evaluating presentations built in the AHA! system, because the current release of InterBook is only available for Apple Macintosh computers. Due to the differences in the presentations syntax, we didn't yet get to evaluate presentations built in any other authoring tool.

We believe that the larger the number of concepts participating in the adaptive process, the larger will be the adaptivity degree and the larger will be the amount of users that can use the presentation in a personalized way.

It is important that the user interacts with the presentation in an adaptable way, reporting as much as possible about what he already knows about each concept, updating or even correcting the values of his user model [3]. The larger the number of concepts which may be directly changed by the user, the more freedom will be available to adapt the presentation for real needs. Thus we believe we will have a presentation with a greater adaptivity degree.

The existence of an adaptive global navigational map helps the user to understand the overall hyperspace structure and his absolute position on it [4], which can make the navigation through the presentation more pleasant.

We believe the more fragments and conditional links a page of the presentation has, the more opportunities it has of being adapted to the user. It is not desirable that users with different needs and requirements receive a page in the same way.

3   AHA! Functions and the Authoring Process

The AHA! architecture is based in the elements defined in the AHAM reference model [5], that are: domain model, user model, adaptation model and adaptive engine.

The domain model describes the application domain in terms of fragments, page concepts and abstract concepts. A page concept is a concept represented by a page while an abstract concept is a concept that is not a page. Each page is a XML file that contains fragments of HTML text that are conditionally included, and with hypertext links that, in a similar way, can also be conditionally shown. The fragments are content parts presented in the pages [1].

The adaptive definitions the author inserts in an AHA! presentation are part of the user model and the adaptation model and include *value generation relationship rules for concepts* and *requirement relationship rules for concepts* [6]. The first ones indicate which other concepts are also updated when a given concept has its value updated in the user model, while the last ones indicate which conditions must be true so that a certain concept can be presented. These relationships rules are stored in two XML files named, respectively, *genlistfile* and *reqlistfile*. The conditional expressions are also part of the adaptation model and are presented directly in the XML pages of the presentation, indicating the desirability of fragments.

4 Characteristics and Operation of the Presentation Evaluation System

Our presentation evaluation system, developed in Java, analyzes XML pages of a presentation built in AHA! and generates some statistical information. The information is used to measure the adaptivity degree (high, medium or low) of a presentation from several points of view.

In this system, the presentation evaluation starts by reading the *properties* file of the presentation. In a presentation built in AHA!, the properties file contains basic information. For example, the physical name of the reqlistfile and genlistfile files and the physical name of the documentslistfile file which contains a list of all pages of the presentation.

An analysis of the reqlistfile and genlistfile files allow important information to be obtained which can be used to evaluate the adaptivity degree of a presentation. The following information is generated by the presentation evaluation system: total amount of course pages; amount and name of page concepts that update values in other concepts; amount and name of page concepts or menu items (separately) that have restrictions for their display; amount and name of page concepts (separately) that can have their values in the user model updated directly by the user; amount and name of the concepts that are restrictions for other concepts; amount and name of pages of the presentation that have fragments and/or links that are conditionally displayed; and amount and name of the menu items that are updated by rules.

From the obtained information, it is possible to measure several adaptivity aspects. The following ones are considered: a) the *adaptivity degree of the user model in the generation of updates* is measured by the percentile of pages that update other concepts in relation to the total pages of the presentation. When we have a very small amount of pages that update other concepts, it means that most of the pages don't influence the personalization of the presentation; b) the *adaptivity degree in restrictions of the adaptation model* is measured by the percentile of pages that have restriction for their presentation in relation to the total pages of the presentation. If few pages have display restrictions, the presentation tends to be very similar for users with different characteristics; c) the *user adaptable behavior degree in the presentation* is measured by the percentile of concepts which can be altered directly by the user and are used as requirements in restrictions for other concepts in relation to the total number of concepts which can be altered directly by the user; d) the *content adaptation degree in the pages* is measured by the percentile of pages that have conditional fragments in relation to the total of pages of the presentation. The larger the amount of pages with conditional fragments, the greater the possibility of the page to be adapted to each user; e) the *adaptive navigation degree in the pages* is measured by the percentile of pages that have conditional links in relation to the total pages of the presentation. The larger the amount of pages with conditional links, the greater the possibility of the page to be adapted to each user; f) the *existence of an adaptive navigational map* is another adaptivity aspect measured, which indicates if there exist menu items updated by rules. The information is presented with only Boolean values.

For the first five adaptivity aspects presented, if the percentile obtained is lower than 20% the adaptivity degree is considered low, if it is from 20% to 40% it is considered medium and if it is larger than 40% is considered high.

5 Conclusions and Future Work

The percentiles above defined to measure the adaptivity degree for each of the analyzed aspects were established by preliminary analyses. A form of evaluation of the results obtained with the system would be to build a presentation with two version with different adaptivity degrees, one classified by our system as a high degree and the other as a low adaptivity degree. The two presentations would use the same content pages, just the information of the reqlistfile and genlistfile files would be different, as well as the fragments and conditional links of the pages. Different user groups could use the two presentations and, later on, the groups would be evaluated to verify the satisfaction degree with the presentation and the amount of acquired information. This could confirm that presentations indicated by our system as having a high degree of adaptivity are really better.

Studies still need to be done to establish new tests that can be applied to the adaptive presentations built in AHA! to evaluate other adaptivity aspects, as support to multiple languages, media adaptation, etc.

References

1. De Bra, Paul; Aerts, Ad; Houben, Geert-Jan; Wu, Hongjing: Making General-Purpose Adaptive Hypermedia Work. Proceedings of the WebNet Conference. San Antonio, TX (2000) 117-123.
2. Brusilovsky, P., Eklund, J., and Schwarz, E.: Web-based education for all: A tool for developing adaptive courseware. Proceedings of Seventh International World Wide Web Conference. Brisbane, Australia (1998) 291-300.
3. De Bra, Paul; Ruiter, Jan-Peter: AHA! Adaptive Hypermedia for All. Proceedings of the WebNet Conference. Orlando, FL (2001) 262-268.
4. Brusilovsky, Peter: Methods and Techniques of Adaptive Hypermedia. Adaptive Hypertext and Hypermedia, Klumer Academic Publishers. The Netherlands (1998) 1-43.
5. De Bra, Paul; Aerts, Ad; Houben, Geert-Jan; WU, Hongjing: AHAM: A Dexter-based Reference Model for Adaptive Hypermedia. Proceedings of ACM Hypertext'99. Darmstadt, Germany (1999) 147-156.
6. Wu, Hongjing; Houben, Geert-Jan; De Bra, Paul: Supporting User Adaptation in Adaptive Hypermedia Applications. Proceedings InfWet2000. Rotterdam, the Netherlands (2000).

Development of Adaptive Web Sites with Usability and Accessibility Features

Marta Fernández de Arriba and José A. López Brugos

Computer Science Department. University of Oviedo, Viesques Campus, Gijón. Spain.
martafer@correo.uniovi.es, brugos@etsiig.uniovi.es

Abstract. This paper discusses a development system of Web sites adapted to the preferences of each user. A markup language (AWUML - Adaptive Web site Usable Markup Language) based on XML technology is defined for use in the specification of the page contents, which guarantees the fulfillment of usability and accessibility requirements. Each user visualizes his own version of the web site resulting from the application of his profile, as much in presentation aspects as in content topics. The separation of document contents from its presentation makes maintenance of the web site easier. The use of this system facilitates access to the network, independent of the disabilities or the technical equipment limitations of the end user.

1 Introduction

The way to achieve success and user loyalty consists in developing adaptive web sites that take into consideration their preferences, limitations and necessities.

Furthermore, most web sites present deficiencies in their orientation to a specific hardware/software configuration. This deficiency makes it difficult for some of the potential users to browse the web site, sometimes even blocking access to certain resources.

Another problem is that nowadays most of the developed web sites mix the content definition of the site with its presentation, thus the consequent increase in cost and effort in its maintenance (this is especially important due to the continuous updating that the web sites undergo).

In this paper, a development structure of web sites adapted to the needs of users while fulfilling usability and accessibility requirements is defined. Thus, the system architecture will be defined as well as a markup language(AWUML: Adaptive Web site Usable Markup Language) using XML technology [5].

2 Web Site Structure

A web site developed using the system defined in this paper is made up of a set of pages whose contents are defined in a series of XML files. The XML files follow the syntax specified for the AWUML markup language.

The web site relies on a user identification module to recover the user's preferences of presentation as well as of contents. These preferences are stored in the corresponding user profile.

Once identified, the user will receive the requested web site page in his browser, which is generated by applying (filtered according to the corresponding parameters of the profile of this user) the translation file to the contents using XSLT format [6]. The XSLT file is generated by the presentation filter according to the related parameters of the profile, as presented in Fig. 1.

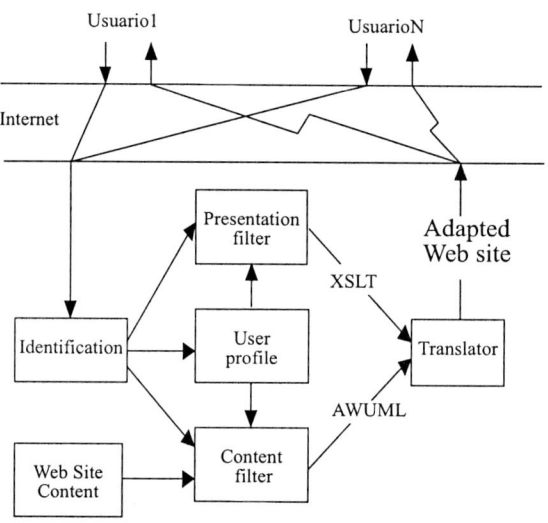

Fig. 1. Adaptive web site structure.

The presentation features selected by the user as well as the web site content preferences are stored in the user profile.

Each web site has a list of topics (using a hierarchical structure) related to the page information presented. Every page must belong to one of these topics. All content elements and links can belong to a subcategory of the main topic of the page (by default, they belong to the same topic as the page).

Each user sets up the preferred topics list to be shown to him in his profile. When selecting a topic, all parent topics are automatically selected. The user will also be able to indicate all the children at the time he selects a topic.

3 AWUML: Adaptive Web Site Usable Markup Language

The page contents of a web site developed using AWUML are presented in Fig. 2. The web site is made up of a set of pages written in XML following the AWUML syntax, forming a tree design, and beginning on a node root that is the home page.

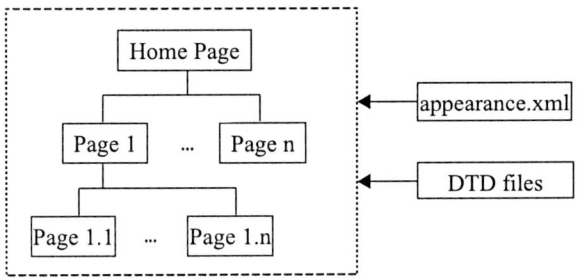

Fig. 2. Web Site Contents in AWUML.

All the web site pages must have an *'appearance.xml'* file that defines the common presentation features of all its pages.

The structure and the contents of the web site pages (using AWUML syntax) are defined in two DTD files (one for the home page and the other for the rest).

Each page of the web site developed using AWUML is an XML document that uses the syntax defined by the language according to the following structure:

1. Reference.
   The XML version is specified, as well as the DTD file associated to the page, the XML file that specifies the common aspect and the translation module.
2. Root element.
   Head. This includes the reference to the appearance file, the title of the page, the topic to which it belongs and the location within the web site.
   Sections. The different links are specified from the current page to the sections at an inferior level. In each section, a link, a description, the topic and a quick access key appear.
   Contents. A series of multimedia elements is specified. They define the contents of the page. Thus, textual contents, images, sounds and links can appear with their corresponding associated attributes.
   Returns. Links to the home page of the web site, to the previous page or to the beginning of the present page are specified.

4 Document Translations

From the specification of a web site written in AWUML, the server shall translate the corresponding XML pages using the style sheet *translate.xsl*.

The translated XML pages are obtained from the web site content pages applying them to a filter according to the content preferences stored in the profile of the user who requests the pages.

The translation file (*translate.xsl*) is generated online, as determined by the presentation preferences in the user profile. Therefore, a page will reach each end user adapted to his preferences and necessities as a result of his request, so that the same page of the web site could be shown in as many final versions as different user profiles exist.

5 Usability and Accessibility Requirements Achieved

The development of web sites using strictly AWUML language allows us to assure the fulfilment of a set of usability and accessibility requirements defined by the standards of the Web Accessibility Initiative [7], the recommendations published in Spain by AENOR (Spanish Agency for Standardisation and Certification)[1], heuristic usability [3] and usability designing guidelines [4] and [2].

Among the requirements achieved, the following should be emphasised:

- Provide equivalent alternatives to auditory and visual contents.
- Use style sheets to control layout and presentation.
- Identify the primary natural language of a document.
- Ensure user control of time-sensitive content changes.
- Design for device-independence and provide keyboard shortcuts to links.
- Provide clear navigation mechanisms.
- Ensure that documents are clear and simple.

6 Conclusions

In this paper, a system for the development of adaptive web sites is presented, considering usability and accessibility problems.

The definition of a complete markup language is presented, using the capacities provided by XML, which allows the development of web sites that fulfil accessibility and usability requirements, facilitating the development and maintenance of these sites (from the point of view of the contents of the pages as well as of their presentation). This separation of contents from presentation allows the generation of versions different from the final documents (even in different languages) that the user receives in his browser by merely generating a translation module (*translate.xsl*) on-line, based on the user profile.

The possibility of multimedia element configurations that are sent to the end client allows for the sending of optimized information through the network, either for adapting to the limitations or preferences of the user or to fulfill requirements of the client software (as in the case of WAP technology).

The use of this language allows the standardisation of the interfaces in the Network, enabling anyone's access to and use of its contents (including disabled people).

References

1. AENOR: UNE 139.802 EX (1998). URL: http://acceso2.uv.es/aenor/accengl.htm
2. Nielsen, J.: Usabilidad. Diseño de sitios Web, Ed. Prentice-Hall (2001)
3. Nielsen, J.: Heuristic Evaluation. URL:http://www.useit.com/papers/heuristic
4. Pearrow, M.: Web Site Usability HandBook, Ed. Charles River Media (2000)
5. W3C: Extensible Markup Language (XML) URL:http://www.w3.org/xml
6. W3C: XSL Transformations (XSLT). Version 1.0. W3C Recommendation 16 November 1999. URL:http://www.w3.org/TR/WD-xslt
7. W3C: Web Content Accessibility Guidelines 1.0. W3C Recommendation 5 May 1999. URL:http://www.w3.org/TR/WAI-WEBCONTENT/

An Adaptive e-Commerce System Definition

Francisco José García[1], Fabio Paternò[2], and Ana Belén Gil[1]

[1] Departamento de Informática y Automática – Facultad de Ciencias
University of Salamanca – Spain
{fgarcia, abg}@usal.es
[2] CNUCE - C.N.R.
Pisa – Italy
fabio.paterno@cnuce.cnr.it

Abstract. The emergence and growing popularity of electronic commerce and more specifically of catalogue-based sales, has made it a necessity to define flexible and adaptive e-commerce systems and architectures. Our work describes an e-commerce system that is suitable for small and medium enterprises, where several enterprises share a common e-commerce site, which automatically adapts its interface to offer end-users the products organised in electronic catalogues (e-catalogues). To be precise, in this paper we present the overall architecture of the e-commerce system, an architecture that is based on an agent-oriented technology. We also describe the actual state our system, which is called e-CoUSAL, and implements an adaptive agent in the server side of the architecture.

Keywords. Adaptive agent; E-commerce; Adaptivity in E-commerce; Adaptive interface; E-catalogue; XML.

1 Introduction

Inspired by the growing popularity of new technologies and owing to the increasing use of the Internet, several kinds of systems with worldwide scope have appeared recently. Perhaps the major application area of Internet development is precisely e-commerce. An especially popular e-commerce segment is the one based on product catalogues, also known as electronic catalogues or e-catalogues. An e-catalogue can be defined as the electronic presentation of information about the products and/or services of an organisation. While other applications can provide similar services, e-catalogues provide a range and effectiveness of service that exceeds the capability of any competing application, such as physical or CD catalogues. The interactive possibilities of e-catalogues eliminate physical storage and make continuous updating possible and efficient [1].

The entry of an enterprise into the e-commerce world involves strategic decisions [2] that are not cost and risk free, this is often an obstacle for the integration of an organisation into the virtual commerce community. The impediments are more important in small organizations or business, the so-called Small and Medium Enterprises (SME), in which the amount of investment in technology solutions cannot be very large.

In this work the overall e-CoUSAL architecture [3] is presented from an agent-based perspective, and we also describe the first prototype of this e-commerce system; it implements an adaptive agent in the server side of the architecture. Thus, the remainder of this paper is organised as follows: Section 2 explains the proposed agent-based e-commerce architecture with their components, Section 3 examines the adaptive components of this architecture that are actually implemented. Finally, Section 4 closes the paper, presenting our conclusions and some ideas on further work needed.

2 An Agent-Based e-Commerce Architecture

2.1 Components of the e-CoUSAL e-Commerce Architecture

In a schematic way, we show in Fig. 1 the major components of the proposed architecture. As we stated above, the main commercial policy is based on e-catalogue shopping, supported by two main components: the e-commerce web server and the visual catalogue-designer tool. The e-commerce server is the central element, which interconnects the different parts involved in a typical commerce environment but more dinamically. The e-catalogue is the element by means of which the end-user views the seller's information and interacts with it.

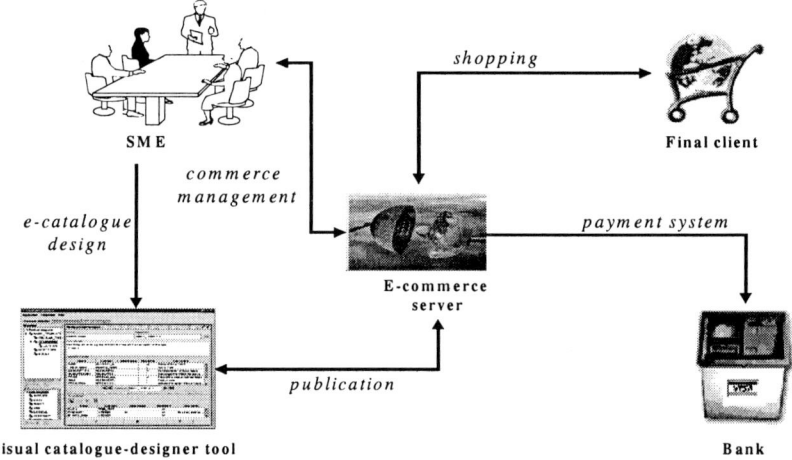

Fig. 1. Components of the e-CoUSAL e-commerce architecture

The SME becomes the main actor of its own virtual business approach as an active element within the commercial process. It is the responsible for the inclusion and management of its own contents in the e-commerce site through the use of a specialised software tool. The designer tool permits the definition, publication and update of an e-catalogue, and also the configuration of a web server architecture that allows end-users to have access to this e-catalogue.

The relationships between the SME and the e-commerce server, through the catalogue-designer tool and also through the server management services, represent a

B2B dimension in this e-commerce model. Moreover, the server has to provide the end-users with the commercial services needed for browsing the e-catalogue and for purchasing; these functionalities in the server site define a B2C dimension of this model. Thus, the overall architectural model defined above presents a B2B/B2C hybrid e-commerce model [2].

2.2 Agential View of the Defined Architecture

In a multi-agent e-commerce environment it is necessary to organise agents into different categories, depending on their functionality and competencies. Several different forms of agents for e-business systems are distinguished in [5].

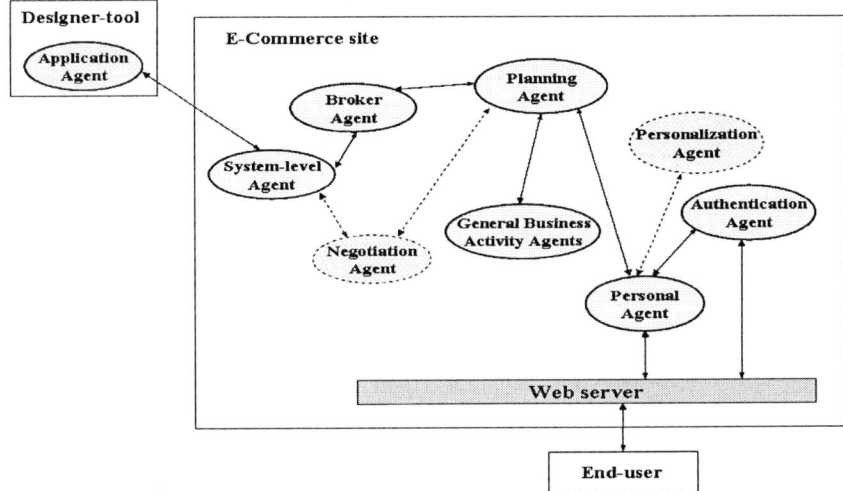

Fig. 2. Agents in e-CoUSAL architecture: ovals represent agents and arrows represent communication between them or between external entities, as end-users. Bold shapes or lines mean that the agent is actually completely or partially implemented; dotted shapes or lines mean future development in our architecture.

According to this classification, we have identified the agents and relationships needed to support our e-commerce architecture proposal, in Fig. 2. We present the agent-based architecture in coarse granularity and in high abstraction levels, because we are defining the architectural layer of the system, relating the agents to the main components presented in Fig. 1.

The *application agent* is the visual designer tool used by a SME to create e-catalogues.

The *broker agent* is in charge of receiving the e-catalogues, expressed in XML format, validating and storing information in the proper internal database. The tool sends these catalogues through the *system-level agent*.

The *negotiation agent* is still in its first stages of development. This kind of agent will receive the business components of each SME in the same way that the broker agent receives the e-catalogues. This property will allow SMEs personalize their business policies (discount, payments and so on) through these components.

General business activity agents are a set of agents that manage the typical e-commerce services of the site: shopping-cart management, selling certificates...

The *authentication agent* is a security agent type that is in charge of identifying the end-user, which makes it possible to adapt its interfaces to the user's shopping tastes.

The *personal agent* is the responsible of customising the interaction with the user into the e-catalogues and therefore it is implemented as an adaptive agent.

Finally, a *planning agent* is needed. The presence of heterogeneous problems to be faced and the fact that many tasks could be carried out at the same time invite to design the multi-agent architecture outlined above. Its responsibilities include publishing the e-catalogues that are sent by the SME, managing the e-catalogues database, accepting the orders of the e-commerce service agents, and giving to the personal agent the proper data to generate customised information pages.

3 Personalizing Capabilities in e-Commerce Server Site

The e-commerce site offers its clients efficient access and shopping management for the different products that are published in the server. Customizing capabilities of the site are very important to tailor all the kind of customrer preferences and they are actually supported by the personal agent. Concretely, the implementation of this personal agent is based on an adaptive agent-pattern derived from the adaptive agent model proposed in [4], including a meta-level layer that gives each agent the ability to take appropriate decisions about control or adapt the specific attributes of the system over time to new circumstances. The user interacts with the e-commerce server that presents the customized pages to offer relevant information to the client. The hypermedia pages that represent the e-catalogues are generated on the fly, getting the contents from the e-catalogues that were sent by the SMEs, which is the knowledge layer.

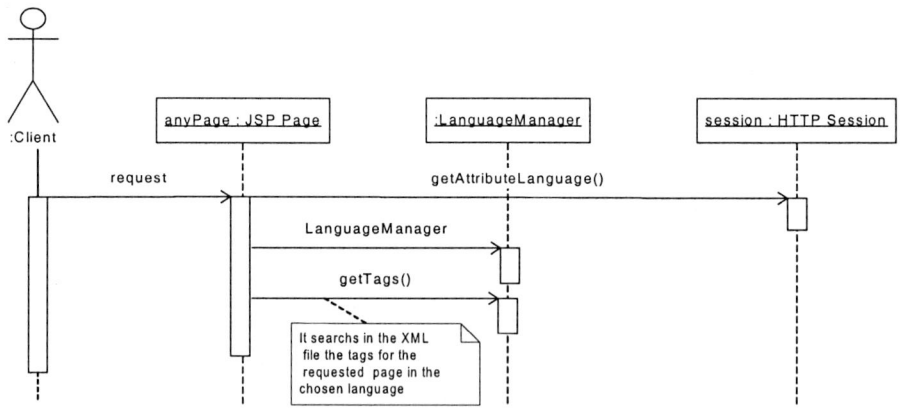

Fig. 3. DTD of the idiomatic XML file

Other interesting part of this adaptive process is the internalisation capability of the server site. In this system there are not pre-compiled pages because all of them are generated to support the chosen language by the end-user. To perform the dynamic generation of the language-independent pages there exists a database where the elements that have language dependencies are stored. This mechanism is XML-based.

The idiomatic XML-file is hierarchically organised, and it has as many nodes as languages supported by the e-commerce site. Each language includes the contents shown by the system, these contents are classified by the elements that use them (JSP pages in this case). Each JSP page has an object, called **LanguageManager**, which is in charge of extracting the necessary elements for the requested page from the XML file. The selected elements are expressed in the same language as the language of the session. This scenario is depicted in Fig. 3.

4 Conclusions and Further Work

As it's defined in [6], adaptable systems are systems that allow one to modify some of their parameters and then adapt their behaviour accordingly. If the system adapts to the user automatically it is called adaptive. According to this definition, in this paper we have introduced an adaptive system for e-commerce proposal, a system that is especially suitable for SME, called e-CoUSAL, an agent-based architecture for the e-commerce system, and two main components are identified: a visual catalogue-designer tool to generate e-catalogues and an e-commerce server site that stores the generated catalogues.

Various types of adaptation can be supported by a system. Currently the server site implements an adaptive agent that performs the interaction with the user, adapting the content, the presentation and the navigation properties of the dynamically generated information-pages from the e-catalogues stored in the server.

Further work is needed to implement the whole architecture, in which there are two more adaptive agents: the negotiation agent and the customisation one. The definition and implementation of these two agents are very important to achieve a flexible and adaptive e-commerce system, because we have now an adaptive system in the interface area, but with the new agents we will have customisation profiles that allow a more usable and flexible system for the end-user, and, on the other side, the enterprises.

References

1. Baron, J. P., Shaw, M. J., Bailey, A. D. Jr.: Web-based E-catalog Systems in B2B Procurement. Communications of the ACM, 43(5):93-100. (2000)
2. García, F. J.: A B2B/B2C Hybrid E-Commerce Model. Submitted to SIGecom Exchanges, Newsletter of the ACM Special Interest Group on E-commerce. (2001).
3. García, F. J., Moreno, Mª N., Hernández, J. A.: e-CoUSAL: An E-Commerce Architecture for Small and Medium Enterprises. In *Advances in Business Solutions*. Catedral. (In Press). (2002)
4. Guessoum, Z., Quenault, M., Durand, R.: An Adaptive Agent Model. In *Proceedings of AIB'S*. (York, March 20-24, 2001). (2001)
5. Papazoglou, M. P.: Agent-Oriented Technology in Support of E-Business. Communications of the ACM, 44(4):71-77. (2001)
6. Paterno, F., Mancini, C.: Designing Web User Interfaces Adaptable to Different Types of Use. In *Proceedings of Museums and the Web*. (New Orleans, LA, USA). (1999)

Web Site Personalization Using User Profile Information

Mohit Goel[1] and Sudeshna Sarkar[2]

[1] Indian Navy, INSMA, Headquarters Western Naval Command,
Mumbai, India 400001
goelmohitin@yahoo.co.in
[2] Dept. Of Computer Science Engineering, IIT, Kharagpur
West Bengal, India 721302
sudeshna@cse.iitkgp.ernet.in

Abstract. In this paper we discuss a technique for web site personalization. Connectivity analysis has been shown to be useful in identifying high quality web pages within a topic or domain specific graph of hyper linked documents. We have implemented a system that creates a view of a subset of a web site most relevant to a given user. This sort of personalization is useful for filtering a useful subset of a site so that the user gets a low volume of quality information. The essence of our approach is to augment a previous connectivity analysis with content analysis. We present an agent which assists the user when he browses and distills a personalized sub graph of the website based on his user profile.

1 Introduction

The Web is full of information and resources [1]. In this project we present a personal agent that assists a user when he browses. Adaptive web pages help the user in finding relevant information by tailoring their content and layout specific to the visiting user.

Another motivation to develop such a system is for users with poor Internet connectivity. Search engines often return top-level home pages, which do not have much of content, and invariably a user needs to browse deeper to extract the relevant information. Take the case of a school in rural India where Internet access can only me made feasible through dial-up connection restricted to one or two hours in a day, and the number of computers available are limited. In such scenarios, online browsing is not feasible, and yet we will like to make available to the teachers and students of such schools the power of the Internet. We can use our system to transmit offline requests from the users to such sites, and build a system where a limited view of the site can be packaged and sent to the user in off-line mode. Our approach is unique as it attempts for *'on the fly'* personalization which is different for each user. We model a Web site as a graph. Each node of the graph as an individual URL and the links embedded in the HTML are the edges between the nodes.

2 Motivation of Our Work

The motivation for this algorithm stems from the fact that a user may like to have a condensed or wrapped up view of the site or a collection of documents depending upon the constraints or limitations he is dealing with. A typical constraint may be on the bandwidth of Internet connection a user has. People who have poor Internet connectivity often find online browsing of documents impractical due to slow downloads and frequent dropping of connections. Many a times they have a window of good connectivity available to them, which is not sufficient for online browsing. In these cases, which are very relevant to rural areas of India, we can download the sites on the client and view them offline. In this case a user may give her profile or a query and she expects the result to be downloaded on her disk, which is connected. The problem with a condensed user view of the site is that we get too many broken links and the site is not navigable using the hyper links.

In our algorithm we take care of this problem explicitly and connect the sub graph using a backward breadth first traversal. Another scenario is when a user desires ease of navigation and he still wants the freedom to surf all the pages, which are there in the site. This requires a slightly different adaptation where the good links are highlighted or annotated and uninteresting links are maintained as in the original graph.

3 System Architecture

The algorithm computes two scores for each document: a *hub* score and an *authority* score. Documents that have high authority scores are expected to have relevant content, whereas documents with high hub scores are expected to contain *links* to relevant content. We wish to get the high content pages and for that we need nodes with good authority score. For reaching these nodes we need to traverse the sub graph through the nodes with high hub score, which act as good junctions in the sub graph.

The algorithm works in two distinct phases. Phase 1 of the algorithm is termed as preprocess which generates the profile of the web site or the document collection. The algorithm first parses HTML to text but maintains information regarding various Meta tags so as to enable us to give weights to HEAD, TITLE etc. For each node in the site we store the pointer to the TFIDF value, which is a vector representation in our system. Hub and Authority scores are calculated using a simplified version of *Kleinberg's* algorithm [4] for finding hubs and authorities.

We define a good node based on four heuristics. We define a *good hub score* and check the hub score of each node against this score and in case it is more than the *good hub score,* it is considered as a good node irrespective of the fact whether the node itself does not contain relevant information for the user. The heuristic is that good hubs in any case act as focal points for navigation and in general improve the ease of browsing for a given website.

Similarly we define a *good similarity measure* and check the cosine similarity [8] score of user profile with each node in a site and in case the similarity is more than this measure, it is obvious that this particular node is very relevant to the user's interest and is therefore included as a good node.

Our system identifies the relevant content pages in a site. The system then attempts to connect these pages together with the home page to make available to the user. The problem is that the pages selected thus may not be all connected from the home page. Sometimes, it happens that even if a page is reachable from the home page, its depth is very high. The system first identifies non-reachable nodes, and then attempts to find a set of hub pages that are each ancestors of a set of these unreachable pages. By including these extra pages we make all the pages reachable. In case where we do not find appropriate link pages, we separately display these pages. We plan to use unsupervised clustering to group these unreachable pages.

4 Experimental Results

One of our experimental sites was http://www.Bharat-rakshak.com. This site is an unofficial website for Indian Armed Forces. The front page of the site is broken into sections corresponding to the main organization of the site: Indian Navy, Indian Army, Indian Air Force, Indian Space, Indian Missiles, Famous battles, Recruitment information and general information etc. For this experimentation we assumed that a user is interested in Indian Navy and in past has shown a keen interest in the Navy section of the site. This is represented as a directory, which consists these files. Once the system is executed, a user profile is generated using the various files in this directory and a similar profile vector is generated for each node of the site.

Observation on Pages Selected as Good Nodes. The majority of the pages given high ranking were from the sub graph, which contained nodes dealing with Navy. All the starting nodes of various arms were also selected as they had many outgoing links giving them a higher hub score. A lot of pages from the 'Missile' and ' Air Force' section were also selected. On closer scrutiny it was found that these pages had related information and matching keywords with the 'Navy' pages such as information on Naval version of missiles, about maritime patrolling by Air Force (A joint operation carried out by Navy and Air Force) etc.

Observation on Pages Not Selected as Good Nodes. The pages, which were not selected as Good Nodes, were found mostly from the unrelated pages and pages having more images and less content (Although some of these pages were dealing with Navy). This was primarily due to low cosine similarity of user profile with these pages.

5 Conclusion

We have developed a system that adapts a website based on the user profile. We also carried out experimentation on various websites with different user profiles and found the results in conformance to most of our heuristics about deciding a good node for the user. This agent can be run at the user's machine, the web server or at the proxy server based on the requirement and connection bandwidth, web server load etc. The client side implementation of our system can be integrated with a dial up connection where a user gives an initial set of query words and the search is further refined using an auxiliary set of query words (User Profile in this case). This filtering will get us a subset of the original website or domain which then be connected as explained in previous chapters and a coherent browsable personalized sub graph can be either mailed or send via normal HTTP protocol to the user.

At present the system displays all the nodes in a frame and also when shortcuts are generated. The system can also be further enhanced using supervised and unsupervised clustering methods, which can cluster the results displayed in the adaptive frame.

Using machine-learning algorithms for automatically processing web server logs and generating user profiles can further augment the system. At present we feed the user profile explicitly by giving a collection of documents. This user profile can be generated by the system by data mining on web logs for the server side implementation of this system.

References

1. Etzioni, O., Perkowitz, M., Adaptive Web Sites: an AI Challenge, In Proceedings of the Fifteenth International Joint Conference on Artificial Intelligence, 1997.
2. Etzioni, O., Perkowitz, M., Adaptive Web Sites: Automatically Synthesizing Web Pages, AAI, 1998.
3. Lieberman, H. (1995). Letizia: An agent that assists web browsing. In International Joint Conference of Artificial Intelligence, Montreal, Aug.1995.
4. Kleinberg, J. 1998. 'Authoritative sources in a hyper linked environment.' Proc. Of 9th ACM-CIAM Symposium on Discrete Algorithms.
5. Kramer, Joseph et al. 'A User-Centered Design Approach to Personalization'. CACM. August 2000. Vol. 43 No. 8. pp. 45-48. ACM: 2000.
6. Balabanovic, M., Shaham, Y.. *1995,* Learning Information Retrieval Agents: Experiments with Automated Web Browsing. Proceedings of the AAAI Spring Symposium Series on Information Gathering from Heterogeneous, Distributed Environments: 13-18.
7. Porter, M.F. (1980) An algorithm for suffix stripping. Program; Automated Library, and Information Systems, 14(3), 130-137.
8. Salton, G. (1992). The state of retrieval system evaluation. Information processing & Management,8(4): 441.

Who Do You Want to Be Today?
Web Personae for Personalised Information Access

J.P. McGowan, Nicholas Kushmerick, and Barry Smyth

Smart Media Institute, Department of Computer Science, University College Dublin
{jp.mcgowan,nick,barry.smyth}@ucd.ie

Abstract. Personalised context sensitivity is the Holy Grail of web information retrieval. As a first step towards this goal, we present the Web Personae personalised search and browsing system. We use well-known information retrieval techniques to develop and track user models. Web Personae differ from previous approaches in that we model users with multiple profiles, each corresponding to a distinct topic or domain. Such functionality is essential in heterogeneous environments such as the Web. We introduce Web Personae, describe an algorithm for learning such models from browsing data, and discuss applications and evaluation methods.

1 Introduction

Despite recent advances in Web information retrieval technologies (e.g. [1,2]), Web search services will find it increasingly difficult to return relevant and valuable results unless they deploy mechanisms for delivering personalised context-sensitive results. As a step towards this goal, we introduce Web Personae, a simple method for developing web user models, and describe several applications that use Web Personae to deliver personalised context-sensitive search results.

Web Personae are designed to address a long standing issue in personalised information filtering: people often have multiple information needs, and attempting to model a user with a single monolithic profile can lead to poor retrieval accuracy. Consider the following scenario. Michelle has a variety of interests: she is a medical doctor, and enjoys golf, plays computer games, and regularly visits the theatre. Given a list of Michelle's favourite web pages or other aspects of her browsing history that reflect these interests, a Web Personae system should automatically discover that Michelle can be modelled by distinct personae such as Golf, Games, Theatre and Medical. Furthermore, given these models and a sample of her current browsing behaviour, the Web Personae system should recognise which persona is currently active, and personalise her information access. For example, if Michelle browses on pages with words such as 'green' and 'tee', then the Web Personae system should recognise that her active topic is Golf.

Web Personae enable a variety of personalised information access applications. First, as a user surfs, several kinds of adaptive hypertext applications could dynamically transform the HTML of web pages. The most obvious application is web page recommendation: based on recent pages, we can recommend either links on the current page, or new pages entirely. For example, if a user is interested in Golf, then, when they visit a generic sports site, the application could highlight links specifically relevant to golf. Similarly, if the user then goes to a search engine, it would be possible to highlight the results returned for their query that more closely match their personal needs – based on their estimated web persona. A more sophisticated method would involve a full re-ranking of the results based on the current persona, so that relevant results are ranked higher. For example, the application could apply a modified version of the PageRank [1] or HITS [2] topology-based algorithms that weights pages according the similarity to the current persona, before calculating the topology-based ordering. Finally, another application is query expansion based on high-weight terms in the current persona. These applications demonstrate a variety of ways in which Web Personae can deliver customised context-sensitive information access. Several of these have been implemented.

2 Web Personae Construction and Recognition

The three main components of the Web Personae system are the Constructor, which learns the personae, the Recogniser, which estimates which persona is currently active, and the Application, which uses this to provide personalised context-sensitive hypertext adaptation.

Personae Construction
The Constructor component uses hierarchical clustering techniques over web page content. This content is initially provided in the form of a list of frequently visited pages, browsing history, or bookmarks. Given these URLs for a given user, the Constructor clusters the web pages using the standard TF-IDF cosine similarity metric. In order to automatically discover a user's distinct personae, the clustering process is halted when the ratio of intra-cluster similarity to inter-cluster similarity has reached a maximum. The clusters learned by this process are assumed to represent the user's several Web Personae. Below we describe some experiments we intend to run to evaluate this assumption. As well as this offline functionality, the Constructor has a greedy, incremental mode in which the personae are modified to track preference changes. However, due to noise and transient browsing behaviour we have found that this online mode poses several thorny user-interface challenges.

Personae Recognition
Once the personae have been identified in the offline stage, we must utilise these when the user is online. An essential design requirement is that the user should not have to explicitly indicate which persona is currently active; the system should be able to infer the current persona based on user actions. Furthermore, this inference must be made rapidly as the user surfs from page to page.

The Recogniser component uses a simple and efficient similarity estimate. We convert the centroids of the personae clusters and the current pages into term vectors that captures only the word frequencies, without taking IDF into account. We then select the Web Persona that has the largest cosine similarity with the current document. This gives us a quick persona recognition system, which has worked well in preliminary experiments.

3 Related Work

Document clustering has mainly been used in information retrieval for improving the effectiveness and efficiency of the retrieval process. We utilise automatic clustering to reveal different domains of user interest. The documents are represented in a vector space [3], then we use hierarchical agglomerative techniques to produce a cluster tree. Web document clustering has been extensively researched in recent years [4,5,6,7]. Applications range from bookmark organising to recommendation systems.

Many systems have been developed which assist web browsing. Letizia [8] learns the interests of a user by observing their browsing behaviour - it can then recommend links to follow - i.e. it models the browsing process, rather than explicitly modelling the user, as our system does. WebWatcher [9] takes some user interests as an initial input, then updates these interests based on pages they visit. The system then recommends pages, based on these interests and the previous browsing behaviour of other users with similar interests.

Various systems have been developed which utilise user models for personalisation. WebMate [6] is an agent that assists browsing and searching. It represents different domains of user interest using multiple term vectors - it updates these incrementally when users give positive feedback for visited pages. However, it does not cluster the vectors to produce a 'persona' as in our system. WebACE [5] constructs a customised user profile by recording information about the documents the user browses. It then clusters these documents, using novel clustering techniques, and uses these to generate queries to search for similar documents.

Personal View Agent [10] tracks, learns and manages user interests. Beginning with a fixed palette of categories, the system follows the user, detecting their domains of interest. This 'personal view' takes the form of a tree and corresponds closely to our notion of web personae. This view can be updated - i.e. it can adapt to changing user interests using a 'personal view maintainer', which can split and merge categories in the personal view.

4 Applications and Evaluation

We have introduced the notion of Web Personae, discussed how they enable personalised context-sensitive information access, and described how they can be automatically learned and recognised from browsing behaviour using standard information retrieval techniques.

We are currently conducting an empirical evaluation of the learning and recognition components. Preliminary tests indicate good performance but we are currently designing more sophisticated evaluations. One experiment involves looking at logs for servers that provide a local search facility. Using a user's accesses to the server obtained from the web logs, we build their personae. We then look at click-through data from local searches run by that user to estimate how effective the Web Personae system would have been at re-ranking these search results.

We have built some applications for the system, such as the search result reorderer (see Fig. 1), and are currently building more, such as the page recommender service and web query expansion service discussed earlier. Our main application will be a personalised search service, based on both result-persona similarity, and the more sophisticated system that does a full re-ranking based on link analysis techniques. (*Acknowledgements:* This research was funded in part by grant N00014-00-1-0021 from the US Office of Naval Research.)

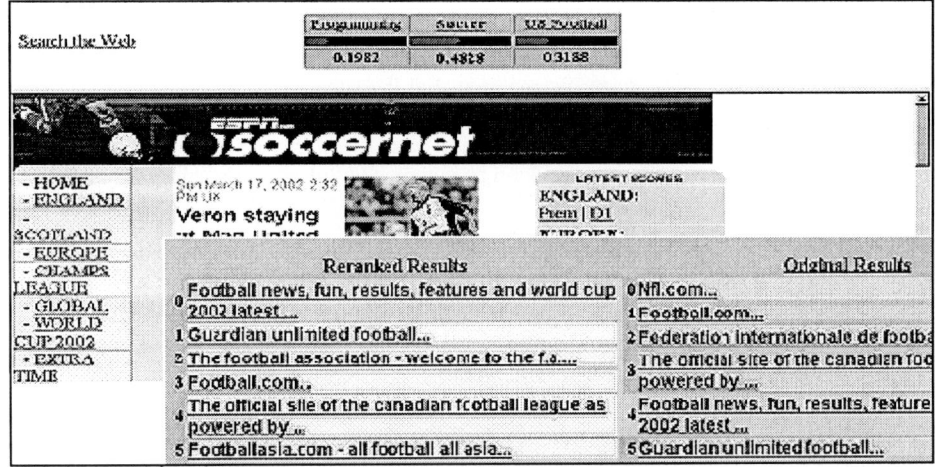

Fig. 1. Search Reorderer Application - background window indicates active persona, foreground shows result of reranking based on this active persona. Details and a demonstration of the system are online at http://www.smi.ucd.ie/WebPersonae.

References

1. S. Brin and L. Page. The anatomy of a large-scale hypertextual web search engine. In *Proc. 7th International World Wide Web Conference*, 1998.
2. D. Gibson, J. Kleinberg & P. Raghavan. Inferring Web communities from link topology. In *Proc. ACM Conf. Hypertext & Hypermedia*, 1998.
3. G. Salton & M. McGill. Introduction to Modern Information Retrieval. McGraw-Hill, 1983
4. D. Cutting, D. Karger, J .Pederson, J.Tukey. Scatter/Gather: A Cluster-Based Approach to Browsing Large Document Collections. In *Proc. SIGIR*, 1992.
5. E. Han, *et al*. WebACE: A web agent for document categorization and exploration. In *Proc. 2nd Int. Conf. on Autonomous Agents*, 1998
6. L. Chen, K.Sycara. WebMate: A personal agent for browsing and searching. In *Proc. 2nd Int. Conf. on Autonomous Agents*, 1998
7. Y. Maarek, I. Ben Shaul. Automatically Organising Bookmarks per Contents. In *Proc. WWW5*, 1996.
8. H.Lieberman. Letizia: An agent that assists web browsing. In *Proc. IJCAI-95*, Montreal, Canada
9. T. Joachims, D. Freitag & T. Mitchell. WebWatcher: A tour guide for the World Wide Web, In *Proc. IJCAI-97*, Nagoya, Japan
10. Chien Chin Chen, Meng Cheng Chen, Yeali Sun. A Web Document Personalisation User Model and System. In Proc. User Modelling, 2001.

Adaptive Navigation Path Previewing for Learning on the Web

Akihiro Kashihara, Shinobu Hasegawa, and Jun'ichi Toyoda

The Institute of Scientific and Industrial Research, Osaka University,
8-1, Mihogaoka, Ibaraki, Osaka 567-0047,
kasihara@ai.sanken.osaka-u.ac.jp
http://www.ai.sanken.osaka-u.ac.jp/thome2/kasihara/index-e.html

Abstract. The main issue addressed in this paper is how to help learners plan a navigation path in existing web-based learning resources, which is an important process of self-directed learning in hyperspace. Our approach to this issue is to provide learners with the adaptive preview of a sequence of web pages as navigation path. Following the idea of path previewing, we have developed an assistant system. The system displays an overview of a web page selected by learners from a hyperspace map, by extracting information from the HTML document file related to the navigation path-planning context. It also enables learners to transform a sequence of previewed pages into a navigation path plan.

1 Introduction

Existing web-based learning resources provide learners with hyperspace where they can navigate through the web pages in a self-directed way to learn domain concepts/knowledge. The self-directed navigation involves making a sequence of the pages navigated, which is called navigation path [2]. It also involves constructing knowledge from the contents embedded in the navigated pages, which would enhance learning [4].

On the other hand, learners often fail in making a navigation path [4]. The self-directed learning in hyperspace requires them to comprehend the contents of web pages they have visited, and concurrently to monitor their own navigation process such as planning the navigation path to be followed, which can be viewed as meta-cognitive activities in self-directed learning [1,2,3]. Navigation monitoring holds the key to success in self-directed learning. However, it is difficult to maintain navigation monitoring since the learners would focus on comprehending the contents of the visited pages [2].

This paper proposes navigation path planning with adaptive previewing of the navigation path. The key point of this idea is to provide learners with an adaptive preview of a sequence of web pages. The path previewing enables them to plan the navigation path in a learner-centered way before navigating the web pages.

We have developed an assistant system, which consists of path previewer, page previewer, and hyperspace map [3]. The page previewer extracts information attached to some HTML tags in a web page, which learners select in the hyperspace map, from the HTML document. The information to be extracted depends on the topic on which the learners focus in planning the navigation path. The path previewer makes a sequence of previewed pages, and displays it as navigation path preview. These facilities help learners plan which page to visit without visiting real web pages in hyperspace.

2 Navigation Path Planning

Self-directed learning with navigation path planning is done in two spaces, which are the space for planning the navigation path based on a learning goal and hyperspace for executing the plan. In the path planning space, learners preview web pages, and plan which page to visit and the sequence of pages to be visited so that the learning goal can be achieved. In the hyperspace, they are expected to navigate web pages according to the path planned. The path planning and navigation are repeated during learning in hyperspace.

Figure 1 shows a user interface of the assistant system where learners can preview a navigation path in a learner-centered way. The system is composed of spatial map, page previewer, and path previewer. The spatial map represents the hyperspace of a web-based learning resource selected by learners as a network of nodes corresponding to web pages. It is automatically generated and displayed in the map window when they select the learning resource. Nodes in the spatial map are tagged with page titles indicated by title tags in the HTML document files.

By double-clicking any node in the spatial map, learners can have an overview of the web page corresponding to the clicked node in the page preview window, which is generated by the page previewer. Assuming that such information is located within representative HTML tags such as *Title*, *Headings*, etc., the page previewer can extract words, sentences, images or links indicated by these tags [3].

When the learners decide the starting point of the navigation path, they can trigger the path previewer, which changes the page preview window into the path preview window. The path previewer constructs a sequence of previewed pages starting with the current page, which represents a navigation path. The path preview window has a link list, which includes anchors of the links the current page contains. Selecting any one from the list, they can have an overview of the page, to which the selected link points, next to the preview of the current page, and then put the previewed page into the sequence, making a navigation path. The page preview is adapted to the context of planning the navigation path. The page preview generation consists of the following two processes:

(1) Identifying the topic on which learners focus in planning, and
(2) Identifying information to be previewed according to the focal topic.

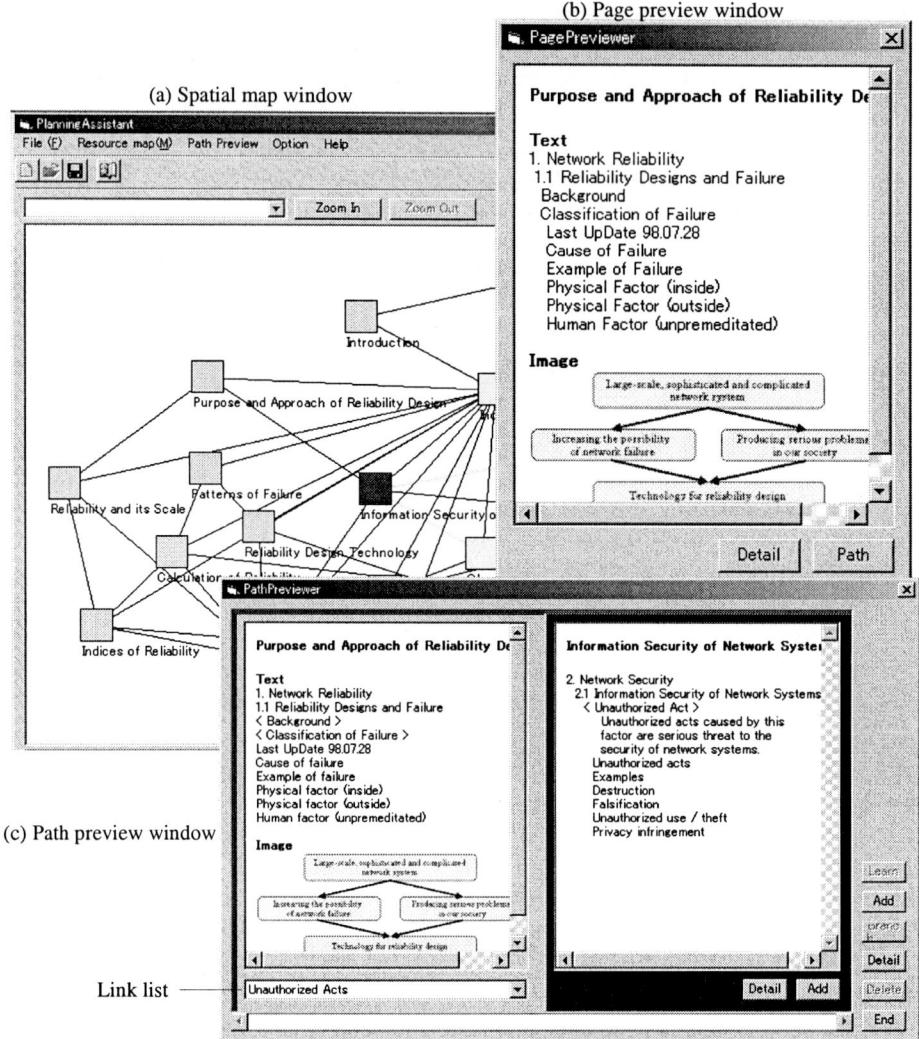

Fig. 1. User Interface for Navigation Path Planning.

The path previewer first identifies the focal topic from keywords included in the anchor that learners select from the link list of the current page for previewing the next page. Next, by using the *Heading* tags of the HTML document of the page to which the selected anchor points, the page previewer divides the document into sections, which are indicated by the tags. Among these sections, it identifies a section whose *Heading* tags include the focal topic, as the section to be previewed. If no *Heading* tag includes the focal topic, it finds in which section keywords representing the focal topic appear most frequently and selects this as the section to be previewed.

The page previewer next extracts information to be previewed to generate the adaptive page preview. It first extracts not only information attached to the *Heading* tag of the identified section, but also information attached to *Title* tags, and the ancestor/ descendant *Heading* tags. This enables the page preview to preserve the hierarchical structure of topics embedded in the page. The page previewer then extracts key information from the identified section, that is attached to the representative HTML tags, such as *FontSize/Color/Face, Img*, and *A href* tags.

Let us illustrate this with a simple example. In this example, a learner whose learning goal is to explore factors reducing the reliability of computer networks first tries to plan a navigation path for achieving the goal from the web page *Purpose and Approach of Reliability Design*. The starting page in the navigation path is generated as shown in Fig. 1(b). Next, he/she selects the anchor *Unauthorized Acts* from the link list in the path previewer to have a page preview of the web page *Information Security of Network Systems*, to which the anchor points. In this case, he/she seems to focus on unauthorized acts. The path previewer accordingly identifies the focal topic with *Unauthorized Acts*, and then generates the adaptive preview of the page as shown in Fig. 1 (c), which includes proper information for the focal topic.

3 Conclusions

This paper has described navigation path planning system with an adaptive previewing function of the navigation path in a hyperspace of web-based learning resources. The distinction between navigation path planning and navigation allows learners to raise their awareness of monitoring their navigation process, and to focus on comprehending the contents of the learning resources in hyperspace. Since the navigation path planned also gives learners an overview of the contents to be learned before navigating the hyperspace, their learning can be improved.

References

1. Cunninghan, D.J., Duffy, T.M., and Knuth, R.A. The Textbook of the Future, in McKnight, C., Dillon, A., and Richardson, J. (eds): HYPERTEXT A Psychological Perspective (1993), Ellis HorwoodLimited, 19-49.
2. Hammond, N. Learning with Hypertext: Problems, Principles and Prospects, in McKnight, C., Dillon, A., and Richardson, J. (eds): HYPERTEXT A Psychological Perspective (1993), Ellis HorwoodLimited, 51-69.
3. Suzuki, R., Hasegawa, S., Kashihara, A., and Toyoda, J. A Navigation Path Planning Assistant for Web-based Learning, Proc. of World Conference on Educational Multimedia, Hypermedia & Telecommunications (2001), 851-1856.
4. Thuering, M., Hannemann, J., and Haake, J.M. Hypermedia and Cognition: Designing for Comprehension. Communication of the ACM, 38, 8 (1995), ACM Press, 57-66.

A Case-Based Recommender System Using Implicit Rating Techniques

Youngji Kim[1], Sooho Ok[2], and Yongtae Woo[1]

[1] Changwon National University, Changwon Kyungnam 641-773, Republic of Korea,
{yjkim@cdcs,ytwoo@sarim}.changwon.ac.kr
[2] Kosin University, Yeongdo-gu Pusan 606-701, Republic of Korea,
shok@kosin.ac.kr

Abstract. We propose a new case-based recommender system using implicit rating information. We present intra-attribute and inter-attribute weight derived from past interests of a user stored in the access logs, and a new similarity function to estimate similarities between new items set and the user profile. To verify the efficiency of our system, we have performed experimental comparisons between the proposed model and the collaborative filtering technique by mean absolute error(MAE) and receiver operating characteristic(ROC). The results show that the proposed model is more efficient than the traditional collaborative filtering technique.

1 Introduction

A recommender system is an automated information filtering system to recommend personalized items that are identified by user's preferences. There are several approaches to develop a recommender system using collaborative filtering(CF), content-based, and case-based reasoning techniques. First, CF predicts a user's preference based on the similarity between the rating pattern of the user and other users, but it has several problems such as early rater, sparsity, and gray sheep. Content-based method uses information about the item itself to make suggestions, but the method does not account for community endorsements [1]. Some researchers have exploited hybrid CF and content-based recommendation models to complement the disadvantages of the both [2]. On the other hand, case-based reasoning technique regards items in which a user is interested as the cases and recommends the most similar cases compared to the past historical interests when a new case presents to a user [3]. Individual item preferences can be supplied explicitly by users or collected implicitly by analyzing access logs. Recently, several implicit rating techniques have been proposed to collect information automatically from the user's behavior patterns in the access logs and to predict an individual preferences [4].

In this paper, we propose a personalized recommender system based on case-based reasoning approach using implicit rating technique. We present a new implicit rating method based on intra-attribute and inter-attribute weights derived from past preferences of a user stored in the access logs. The proposed system has been tested using the access logs of the users in a recruiting site. The results show that the proposed system is more efficient than the typical CF technique in [2].

2 The Proposed Recommender System

Conceptual Architecture. In a traditional case-based reasoning system, when a new problem appears, the system retrieves the most similar case(s), reuses the case(s) to solve the problem, revises the proposed solution if necessary, and retains the new solution as a part of a new case [5]. We have adopted the principles of case-based reasoning for our system. In order to recommend new items to a user, the system suggests the recommendation of the most similar ones using the past preference information stored in the user profile, and the result of the recommendation is updated in the user profile for learning the new case. Figure 1 shows the conceptual diagram of the proposed system.

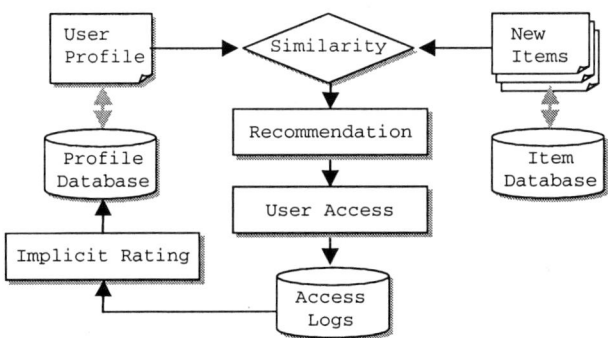

Fig. 1. Conceptual diagram of the proposed system

User Profile and Implicit Rating. We define a user profile as $P = \{u, A, W, D\}$, where u is the personal information about the user; A is a set of attributes of an item; W is a set of intra-attribute weights; and D is a set of inter-attributes weights among attributes. The weights W and D are automatically computed by analyzing each user's access logs.

Intra-attribute Weight. We assume that an item has n attributes $A_1, A_2, \cdots, A_n$, and each attribute A_i has m attribute values $a_{i1}, a_{i2}, \cdots, a_{im}$. Let $W_i = \{w_{i1}, w_{i2}, \cdots, w_{im}\}$ be the intra-attribute weight corresponding to an attribute $A_i, i = 1, 2, \cdots, n$. We define intra-attribute weight w_{ij} corresponding to a_{ij} by

$$w_{ij} = \frac{k_{ij}}{\sum_{p=1}^{m} k_{ip}}, \ i = 1, 2, \cdots, n, \ j = 1, 2, \cdots, m, \quad (1)$$

where k_{ij} is the access count to a_{ij} of the user.

Inter-attribute Weight. Inter-attribute weight is a set of statistical coefficients $D = \{d_1, d_2, \cdots, d_n\}$ corresponding to A. Let x_{ij} be the probability of access to a_{ij} among $a_{i1}, a_{i2}, \cdots, a_{im}$, then inter-attribute weight d_i of A_i is defined as follows:

$$d_i = \left| y_i - \frac{1}{m}\sum_{j=1}^{m} x_{ij} \right|, \ y_i = \max_{1 \leq j \leq m}(x_{ij}), \ i = 1, 2, \cdots, n \qquad (2)$$

For example, a user looking for a job position in a recruiting site. Here, we have assumed that the major factors to select a job are the academic major, job type, and location attributes. If intra-attribute weights in the user profile are given as follows: major={database:0.8, network:0.2}, job type={professor:0.6, researcher:0.3, Post-Doc.:0.1}, and location={Seoul:0.2, Daejeon:0.3, Pusan:0.5} by equation 1. Thus, the inter-attribute weights will be 0.30, 0.27, and 0.17 respectively by equation 2. In case of d_i equals to zero, the attribute is ignored. Therefore, we can ensure that the major attribute is the most important one for the user in this case.

Similarity Computation and Recommendation. When new items are presented to the system, the similarity between the new items and each user's preferences is evaluated by calculating intra-attribute and inter-attribute weights for each user's profile. The results of the recommendation are presented in the similarity order. A new item set I contains explicit information about the specific field, and is defined as $I = \{A'\}$, where A' is a set of attributes as such attribute $A'_i = \{a'_{i1}, a'_{i2}, \cdots, a'_{ik}\}$, and they have k attribute values. The domains of attributes in user profile are the same as the domains of attribute A'_i in new item set correspondingly. We define a new similarity function between a user profile P and a new item set I as follows:

$$Similarity(P, I) = \sum_{i=1}^{n}(f(a_{ij}, a'_{ij}) \times d_i \times W_i), \qquad (3)$$

where $f(a_{ij}, a'_{ij})$ is a filtering function which returns to 1 if a_{ij} and a'_{ij} match one another.

In the above example, three new job positions as job1 = <major: database, job type: researcher, location: Seoul>, job2 = <major: network, job type: professor, location: Pusan>, and job3 = <major: algorithm, job type: professor, location: Pusan> are presented. Then, the similarities between the user profile and three new jobs are evaluated as follows: job1: 0.355, job2: 0.307, and job3: 0.247. Therefore, the system recommends these jobs as job1, job2, and job3 in order to the user.

3 Experimental Results

To verify the effectiveness of the proposed system, we have tested the users of a recruiting site using mean absolute error(MAE) and receiver operating characteristic(ROC) [6]. MAE and ROC are commonly used to measure the statistical

Table 1. Experimental results

	MAE	ROC-sensitivity	ROC-specificity	ROC-accuracy	ROC-error rate
CF	0.923	0.667	0.210	0.701	0.299
Proposed	0.818	0.900	0.424	0.809	0.191

accuracy and decision-support one of recommendations respectively. First of all, we have gathered the explicit preferences grade from 1 through 5 for 1,030 contents and 824 users. We have then collected 14,263 implicit ratings from the access logs for them. In the experiment, 1,484 recommendations have been used as test set by the proposed method and CF algorithm in [2]. In general, the lower values of MAE, ROC specificity and ROC error rate, or the higher values of ROC sensitivity and ROC accuracy means the better results of recommendation. Table 1 shows the comparisons of the MAE and ROC(by sensitivity, specificity, accuracy, and error rate) values between the proposed method and CF. Experimental results show that the proposed method is more efficient than CF one.

4 Conclusion

In this paper, we proposed a personalized recommender system to recommend specific items to a user based on case-based reasoning approach using implicit ratings. We presented two weights, intra-attribute and inter-attribute weight, related to attributes of items. These weights are evaluated implicitly from access logs of each user. A new similarity function using those coefficients have proposed to estimate similarities between new item set and the user profile. MAE and ROC values in the experimental results show that the proposed system makes more efficient recommendation than traditional CF technique.

Acknowledgement

This work was supported by grant No. 2001-111-2 from the University fundamental research program of the Ministry of Information & Communication in Republic of Korea.

References

1. Popescul, A., Unger, L., Pennock, D., Lawrence, S.: Probabilistic Models for Unified Collaborative and Content-Based Recommendation in Sparse-Data Environments. Proceedings of the Seventeens Conference on Uncertainty in Artificial Intelligence(UAI-2001), Morgan Kaufmann, San Francisco (2001) 437–444
2. Claypool, M., Gokhale, A., Miranda, T., Murnikov, P., Netes, D., Sartin, M.: Combining Content-Based and Collaborative Filters in an Online Newspaper. Proceedings of ACM SIGIR Workshop on Recommender Systems, August 19 (1999)

3. Bradley, K., Rafter, R., Smyth, B.: Case-based user profiling for content personalisation. Proceedings of the International Conference on Adaptive Hypermedia and Adaptive Web-based Systems, Trento, Italy, August (2000) 62–72
4. Oard, D., Kim, J.: Implicit Feedback for Recommender Systems. Proceeding of AAA Wrokshop on Recommender Systems, Wisconsin, USA, July (1998) 81–83
5. Watson, I.: Applying Case-based Reasoning: Techniques for Enterprise Systems. Morgan Kaufmann Publishers, Inc. (1997)
6. Good, N., Schafer, B., Konstan, J., Borchers, A., Sarwar, B., Herlocker, J., Riedle, J.: Combining Collaborative Filtering with Personal Agents for Better Recommendations, Proceedings of the AAAI conference. (1999) 439–446

IMAP - Intelligent Multimedia Authoring Tools for Electronic Publishing*

Sarit Kraus[1], Alexander Kröner[2], and Lea Tsaban[1]

[1] Department of Mathematics and Computer Science
Bar-Ilan University, Ramat-Gan, 52900, Israel
{sarit,lea}@macs.biu.ac.il
[2] German Research Center for Artificial Intelligence (DFKI) GmbH
Stuhlsatzenhausweg 3, 66123 Saarbrücken, Germany
kroener@dfki.de

Abstract. IMAP provides software tools that support the authoring of electronic presentation by helping the author in multimedia content selection and layout design. IMAP consists of a Content Manager and a Layout Manager. In this paper we present the usage of IMAP tools for the authoring of on-line newspapers. The content selection is based both on the author's specifications and the user's interests, where the interrelations between objects play an important role in the evaluation of the set of objects. Layout management relies on a set of layout requirements taken from a layout profile and an author-defined style sheet. As was demonstrated in our experiments, integrating of both techniques yields interesting newspapers, whose layout can be customized by the reader.

1 Introduction

The long-term goal that we address in IMAP is the development of software tools for content and layout management that will simplify and accelerate the creation of electronic presentation by automating the complex, time-consuming tasks of multimedia content selection and layout design. In this contribution, we focus on the authoring of personalized online newspapers.

Personalization of presentations has become a main issue in recent years (e.g., [1, 2]). Part of this research focuses on electronic access to news (e.g., [5]). However, most of these works focus on identifying the user's fields of interest, i.e. the construction of a *user profile*. Then the articles are scored using the user profile and the highest scored documents are included in the newspaper. We focus on the interest of the user in the overall newspaper while enabling the author to influence the content of the newspaper via constraints, and maintaining the satisfaction of the user.

An appropriate layout for the personalized content selection should reflect the user's personal interests as well. From the manifold approaches to automated

---

* This research was supported by a Grant from the G.I.F., the German-Israeli Foundation for Scientific Research and Development.

layout (e.g., [8, 4, 9]), we chose constraint techniques, which had already turned out to be a valuable means for creating Web pages (cf. [3, 6]). We show how to extend such an approach so that the layout reflects constraints imposed by the given browsing environment, and may further be customized by the user according to his preferences.

2 Content Management

The input of the Content Management (CM) system includes: (i) A set of candidate documents for the newspaper. (ii) A set of constraints on the selection of documents provided by the *author* (editor) of the newspaper, e.g., "At least a certain percent/number of the documents should be from a certain subject and sub subject." (iii) A *reader profile*: The profile of preferences of the reader. (iv) A number K: The number of documents the newspaper should include. The output of the CM is a list of K documents for the newspaper, ranked according to the level of the reader's interest.

The evaluation of a set of documents depends on the estimation of the agent's interest in the documents and the measure of the satisfaction of the set of documents of the author's constraints. We score each document according to the reader profile, using the correlation between the two. The similarity between a reader profile and a document profile is calculated by referring to the keywords that appear both in the reader's profile and the document's profile (see [7]). Given a set of K documents, and a set of constraints we compute the satisfaction measure of each of the constraints by the documents. The score assigned to a constraint increases as the set of chosen documents comes closer to fully satisfying the constraint. We use the following function to predict the reader's satisfaction from a set of documents: $Eval(constraints, K\ documents) = Par \cdot \sum_i w_i + (1 - Par) \cdot \sum_j c_j \cdot v_j$ where: (i) Par is a number between 0 and 1, indicating the level of importance we give to the reader's preferences. This parameter is determined by the author. (ii) i goes through the K documents in the set considered for the newspaper. (iii) w_i is the normalized relevancy measure of the i'th document according to the reader profile. (iv) j goes through all the constraints. (v) c_j is the weight of the j'th constraint (vi) v_j is in the interval $[0, 1]$, according to the level of satisfaction of the j'th constraint.

We asked 31 readers to use the software we developed, with 1225 documents we downloaded from CNN (see *http://www.cnn.com/*). We built reader profiles for the readers by explicitly asking about their interests. By checking the similarity between each pair of readers we verified that the readers were not too similar. Each reader received three different newspapers, one with no constraints, and the other two with two different sets of constraints.

The first set: (i) At least 1 document from the subject "World" and the sub subject "Middle East" should appear. Importance: 6 (ii) No more than 20% of the documents will be from each subject. Importance: 6 (iii) Each document that appears will not be lower than a relevancy of 0.004. Importance: 1 (i) At least one document from each subject shall appear. Importance: 10

The second set: (i) At least 1 document from the subject "World" and the sub subject "Middle East" should appear. Importance: 10 (ii) At least 10% of the documents should be from the subject "US" and the sub subject "News". Importance: 8 (iii) The documents that appear will not be lower than a relevancy of 0.004. Importance: 1 (iv) The documents that appear will not exceed a similarity of 0.7. Importance: 10

For each newspaper, we asked the readers to give each document a score from 1 to 5, where: 1 means "not interesting at all" and 5 means "very interesting". We also asked the reader to answer the following questions about the newspaper in the same manner: (i) How interesting did you find the newspaper? (ii) How varied did you find the newspaper? (iii) How good did you find the newspaper? (according to the way the reader defines "a good newspaper").

The answers of the readers show that the first set of constraints is better than the second set. Our results show that with respect to all the measurements, the first set of constraints is significantly better than the second set and also better than the "empty" set. We also checked which portion of the documents received a score higher than 3 from the reader, i.e. "interesting" or "very interesting". We found that the documents of the newspaper with the good set of constraints received significantly higher scores than the documents of the other two newspapers. Significance was tested using the *one-tailed paired t-test* with $p = 0.05$.

3 Layout Management

The Layout Management (LM) aims at achieving a layout for the selected content, which meets a set of layout requirements imposed by an author-defined style sheet as well as by a *layout profile*, which describes the reader's technical requirements and preferences.

In IMAP, layout is created by the *DesignComposer* (DC), which computes layout for a given XML file, a layout profile and a style sheet (for details, see *http://www.dfki.de/~kroener/DC.htm* and [6]). This software is embedded in a *layout server*, which provides the reader with a portal to the documents selected by the CM. The server uses the DC to create layout in two steps: first, the layout of the portal page is created. Then, when a user tries to access one of the offered documents, a layout for the requested document is created on-the-fly before delivery. If the creation fails, e.g., because of exceeding the generation time bound, the non-optimized XML file (which is in IMAP an XHTML file) is provided as fall-back solution.

The layout profile is created by a so-called *Client Analyzer* (CA), which is implemented as an applet that is submitted by the layout server to the client side. In the first place, the applet collects layout-related data, such as the browser window's dimension, the installed fonts, and the display's DPI. Furthermore, the CA enables the reader to communicate with the layout server and thus to customize layout. Therefore it provides a GUI, which enables several kinds of interaction.

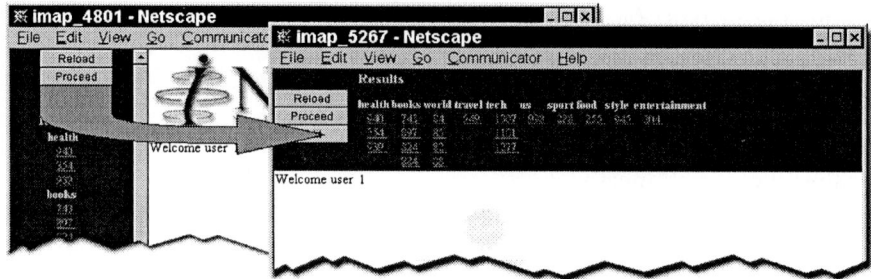

Fig. 1. Two layout alternatives of the portal page; the layout profile is identical

First of all, the reader may submit his profile to the server. In that case, the layout server decides using thresholds (e.g., about changes in the window dimension) if the changes in the current profile require a re-generation of layout. Furthermore, the reader may request a layout alternative. Such a request affects that the server evokes the DC again with the current layout, which in turn starts searching for a new layout for the last requested document (see Fig. 1). The CA allows the reader also to edit parameters included in his profile, which have been prepared by the author of the applied style sheet for customization. This way, the reader may modify style aspects (e.g., colors and font sizes) and/or the content selected for layout, just depending on which modifications the author has granted.

References

1. L. Ardissono, L. Console, and I. Torre: *On the application of personalization techniques to news servers on the WWW.* In Proc. AI*IA 99, 2000.
2. P. Baumgartner and A. Blohm: *Automated deduction techniques for the management of personalized documents.* In Proc. of MKM 2001.
3. A. Borning, R. Lin, and K. Marriott: *Constraint-Based Document Layout for the Web.* In Multimedia Systems **8.3** (2000), 177–189.
4. S. Feiner: *A Grid-based Approach to Automating Display Layout.* In Proc. of the Graphics Interface 1988, 192–197, Morgan Kaufmann, Los Altos, CA.
5. T. Kamba, H. Sakagami, and Y. Koseki: *ANATOGONOMY: a personalized newspaper on the World Wide Web.* In International J. of HC Studies, **46**, 1997, 789–803.
6. A. Kröner: *Adaptive Layout of Dynamic Web Pages.* In DISKI - Dissertationen zur künstlichen Intelligenz **248**, infix (2001), ISBN 3-89838-248-6
7. L. Tsaban: *Intelligent Multimedia Authoring Tools For Electronic Publishing.* Master thesis, Bar-Ilan University, Ramat-Gan, 2001.
8. L. Weitzman and K. Wittenburg: *Automatic Generation of Multimedia Documents Using Relational Grammars.* In Proc. of the ACM Multimedia 1994, 443–451, CA.
9. W.H. Graf: *Constraint-Based Graphical Layout of Multimodal Presentations.* In M.T. Maybury and W. Wahlster, Readings in Intelligent User Interfaces, 1997.

A Hybrid Recommender System Combining Collaborative Filtering with Neural Network

Meehee Lee[1], Pyungseok Choi[2], and Yongtae Woo[2]

[1] Changshin College, Masan Kyungnam 630-764, Republic of Korea,
mihil@csc.ac.kr
[2] Changwon National University, Changwon Kyungnam 641-773, Republic of Korea,
{choips,ytwoo}@sarim.changwon.ac.kr

Abstract. We propose a new recommender system which combines collaborative filtering(CF) with Self-Organizing Map(SOM) neural network. First, all users are segmented by demographic characteristics and users in each segment are clustered according to the preference of items using the SOM neural network. To recommend items to a user, CF algorithm is then applied on the cluster where the user belongs. As a result of experimentation for well-known movies, we show that the proposed system satisfies the predictability of CF algorithm in GroupLens. Also, our system improves the scalability and the performance of the traditional CF technique.

1 Introduction

A recommender system in E-commerce means information filtering process to supply personalized information by predicting user's preferences to specific items. The CF technique is widely used to suggest new items or to predict the utility of a certain item for a particular user based on the user's previous likings and the opinions of other like minded users [1]. The CF technique, however, suffers from some limitations such as early rater problem, sparsity, and gray sheep [2]. For the most part these limitations are related to the scalability and efficiency of the k-NN approach. Essentially, k-NN requires that the neighborhood formation phase be performed as an online process, and for very large data sets this may lead to unacceptable latency for providing recommendations [3]. In neighborhood-based CF systems, the time complexity can be very time consuming with millions of users and items in the database and potentially make the whole process unsuitable for realtime recommendation generation [1].

Recently, to improve the scalability of the CF algorithms and the quality of the recommendations for the consumers, a hybrid model that combines CF with other techniques has been studied. PTango has been combined content-based prediction and CF for an online newspaper by basing a prediction on a weighted average of the content-based prediction and the collaborative prediction [4]. Good et. al have shown that CF can be used to combine personal IF agents with the community opinion of the users to obtain better recommendations than those of agents or the users themselves [5]. O'Connor has proposed a model combining clustering algorithm with CF to separate the set of items based on users' rating data to predict independently within each partition [6].

In this paper, we propose a hybrid recommender system, which combines CF with the SOM neural network to improve the scalability and performance of the traditional CF technique. We, first analyze user's demographic characteristics to segment users, and then cluster them according to preference of items using the SOM neural network. In order to recommend items for a user, we determine a cluster in advance where the features are similar to the user. A CF algorithm is then applied to the users who belong to the cluster in order to predict user's preference for items.

2 A Collaborative Filtering Combining with SOM

2.1 Motivation

The preference of contents such as movies or music shows differences among users depending on their taste. Also, the preference may be distinguished based on the demographic characteristics such as sex, age, and academic career. However, the CF technique utilizes the user's preference for items, it is quite difficult to consider the demographic characteristics. Moreover, as the tastes of other similar users are considered in CF, it is not easy to reflect the features of the item itself.

The CF algorithm requires a large amount of computation that grows with both the number of users and items because the pearson correlation coefficients are calculated for the whole users. Therefore, a more sophisticated technique is required to improve these problems.

2.2 The Proposed Hybrid Model

User Segmentation and Clustering. Demographic characteristics can be used to identify the types of users that like a certain item. User segmentation is a classification process in accordance with their demographic characteristics for all users. Clustering is a learning process which groups users in each segment based on the preference of items using the SOM neural network.

The SOM is an unsupervised learning model adequate to clustering, and allows easier computations to the multidimensional data. Also, the SOM is little affected from the size of data [7].

Applying Collaborative Filtering upon Cluster. The users in a cluster have common demographic characteristics and similar preference for items. In order to predict the preference for a user, CF algorithm is applied on the cluster to which the user belongs. Therefore, our approach can reduce the computations on the cluster which had been evidently decreased the size of the data. Figure 1 shows the conceptual diagram of the proposed hybrid recommender system.

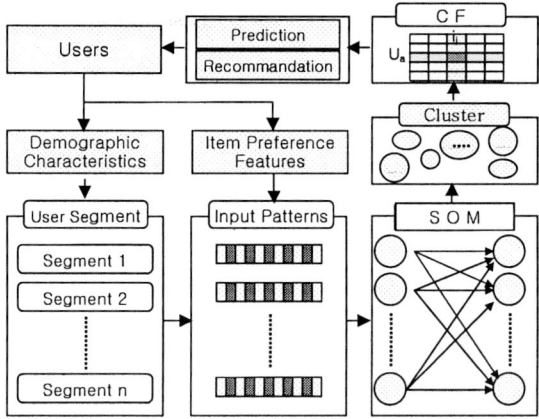

Fig. 1. The Proposed Hybrid Model

3 Experimental Analysis

To verify the efficiency of the proposed model, we have tested for 54 well-known movies and 174 users. We have gathered 5,331 rating values for the preference of movie from 1 through 5 by the users explicitly. First, all users are segmented by sex or age. Then, the users in each segment are clustered according to the preference of genres using the SOM. To simplify the learning process, we have used input patterns for the SOM as the preference values of genre, and generated two clusters to each segment. The preference values of genre for a user are derived from the average rating values of movies. The genres of movies had been categorized into action, drama, comedy, fiction and thriller. Thus, each cluster contains a set of users whose preferred genres are similar in the segment determined by sex or age. Although the test set of movies were selected in a restricted area, the preference of the movies are clearly distinguished by sex or age.

To recommend movies to a user, the CF algorithm is then applied on the cluster where the user belongs. As a result of experimentation, we show that the proposed system satisfies the predictability of the CF algorithm in GroupLens. MAE (Mean Absolute Error) value was compared to the proposed method and a traditional CF algorithm. Figure 2 shows that our approach is a little better than that of the traditional CF algorithm. Also, we could ensure that the computation time of the proposed method was enhanced than that of the traditional CF algorithm in GroupLens system.

4 Conclusion

In this paper, we have proposed a new hybrid recommender system that combines the SOM and the collaborative filtering technique. This model has composed of neighborhood generation and prediction generation. In neighborhood generation,

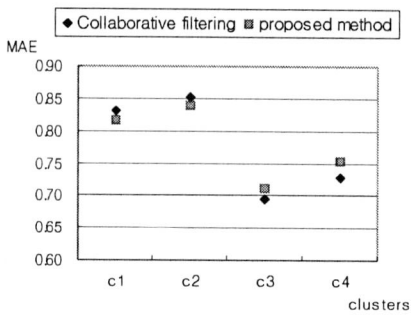 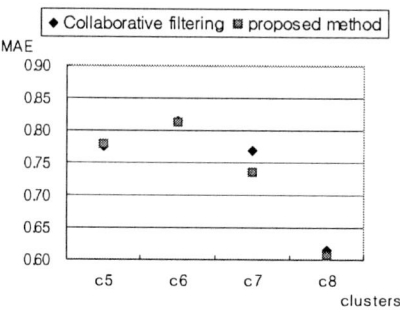

(a) CF vs Proposed Method(by sex) (b) CF vs Proposed Method(by age)

Fig. 2. The results of experiment

all users were segmented by their demographic characteristics such as sex or age. Then, clusters were generated using the SOM which learns the preference of items in each segment. In prediction generation, the CF algorithm was applied to a certain cluster including the user, and the results were recommended to the user.

The system has tested on the movies data set to verify the efficiency of the proposed technique. Experimental results show that the proposed system yields a little better predictability than the traditional CF-based system. Also, our system can reduces a large amount of the computation time to calculate correlation coefficients. In conclusion, we can expect that our system improves the scalability and the performance of the traditional CF technique.

References

1. Sarwar, B., Karypis, G., Konstan, J., Riedl, J.: Item-based Collaborative Filtering Recommendation Algorithms. Proceedings of the 10th International World Wide Web Conference(WWW10), Hong Kong, May (2000)
2. Sarwar, B., Karypis, G., Konstan, J., Riedl, J.: Analysis of recommendation algorithms for e-commerce. Proceedings of ACM Conference on E-Commerce (2000) 158–167
3. Mobasher, B., Dai, H., Luo, T., Nakagawa, M.: Improving the Effectiveness of Collaborative Filtering on Anonymous Web Usage Data. Proceedings of the IJCAI2001 Workshop on Intelligent Techniques for Web Personalization(ITWP01), August (2001)
4. Claypool, M., Gokhale, A., Miranda, T., Murnikov, P., Netes, D., Sartin, M.: Combining Content-Based and Collaborative Filters in an Online Newspaper. ACM SIGIR Workshop on Recommender Systems, Berkeley, CA. (1999)
5. Good, N., Schafer, B., Konstan, J., Borchers, A., Sarwar, B., Herloker, J., Riedl, J.: Combining Collaborative Filtering With Personal Agents for Better Recommendations. Proceedings of the AAAI conference. (1999) 439–446
6. O'Connor, M., Herlocker, J.: Clustering items for Collaborative Filtering. ACM SIGIR Workshop on Recommender Systems, Berkeley, CA. (1999)
7. Kohonen, T.: The Self-Organizing Map. Proceedings of the IEEE, (1990) 1564-1479

An Adaptive Cooperative Web Authoring Environment

Ana María Martínez-Enríquez[1], Dominique Decouchant[2],
Alberto L. Morán[2,4], and Jesus Favela[3]

[1] Depto de Ingeniería Eléctrica, CINVESTAV-IPN, D.F., México
`ammartin@mail.cinvestav.mx`
[2] Laboratoire "Logiciels, Systèmes, Réseaux", Grenoble, France
`Dominique.Decouchant@imag.fr, Alberto.Moran@imag.fr`
[3] Ciencias de la Computación, CICESE, Ensenada, B.C., México
[4] Facultad de Ciencias UABC, Ensenada, B.C., México
`favela@cicese.mx`

Abstract. Using AllianceWeb, authors distributed around the world can cooperate producing large documents in a consistent and concerted way. In this paper, we highlight the main aspects of the group awareness function that allows each author to diffuse his contribution to other co-authors, and to control the way by which other contributions are integrated into his environment. In order to support this function, essential to every groupware application, we have designed a self-adaptive cooperative interaction environment, parametrized by user preferences. Thus, the characteristics of an adaptive group awareness agent are defined.

Keywords: Cooperative and distributed authoring, World Wide Web, group awareness agent, GAA, adaptive cooperation interface.

1 Introduction

World Wide Web technology enables users distributed over the Internet to access a growing amount of information. However, this information is stored and managed on Web servers, and users only remain consumers of information. In this way of operation, Web servers only reply to requests of client applications.

In spite of the existence of several interactive browser/editor tools, the information located on WWW servers is usually updated manually by the site manager: documents are prepared in a private editing environment and then pushed into the public space on a server. At the same time, many current trends in Web publishing research focus on providing elaborate functions to access documents and publishing them on a remote site.

2 Cooperative Editing

The cooperative production of documents is the result of the coordination between different authors to carry on the activities needed for the joint production of documents. Then, co-authors will use cooperative editing tools to enhance their effectiveness, to enforce consistency, to control the validity of contributions, and finally to ensure the quality of the commonly produced work.

The PIÑAS (Platform for Interaction, Naming And Storage) middleware [2], used to develop the AllianceWeb cooperative authoring system [1], aims to determine the specific requirements and the dedicated techniques to support Web cooperative authoring environments.

It supports cooperative authoring based on document fragmentation, and so introduces several interesting distributed features: author identification, document and resource naming, document replication, consistency of the concurrent (distributed) production, and an ad-hoc distributed document storage system.

3 Adaptive and Deductive Group Awareness Function

Group awareness is a key feature of a cooperative application. Cooperative authoring applications developed on top of PIÑAS allows each user 1) to diffuse his contribution to other users, and 2) to control the integration of other contributions into his working environment.

AllianceWeb uses a PIÑAS asynchronous notification mechanism that allows the user to be notified of other coauthor editing actions. Currently, the group awareness function allows each user to configure the notification level (automatic updating or attentive/unattended reading) for each fragment he is consulting.

Considering the object space manipulated by the co-authors, and the set of actions applied on the object space, the goal is to define a flexible, deductive and adaptive cooperative group awareness environment. By these terms we mean:

Deductive - The system is able to analyze the cooperative working actions of each user and to determine user objectives.

Adaptive - Taking into account each user's goals, and with respect to their individual preferences, it guides and dynamically adapts user environments.

In order to avoid the need for users to manage their cooperative environments and to allow them to cooperatively work more efficiently, our system is defined as an autonomous agent (see section 3.1) that manages the group awareness environment (e.g. What are the suited tools to highlight in the user environment to make him more efficient in the cooperation process? On what user activities is it judicious to concentrate interaction or group awareness tools? etc).

3.1 A Group Awareness Agent

The goal of the Group Awareness Agent (GAA) is to determine the manipulated entities and the executed cooperative actions, to modify the presentation of this information on the user's screen. It is important to notice that this presentation is constrained by the user preferences applied using presentation filters.

Periodically the agent re-evaluates and updates the set of manipulated objects. This periodic re-evaluation is performed in parallel with the actions applied by the user. This re-evaluation is completed both by statistic measures of the manipulated object space and by the analysis of the concurrent interactions (**concerned users, manipulated objects and action frequency**).

The GAA is guided by **user preferences** (figure organization, formats, presentation, tool interfaces, etc) and **user roles** on the shared fragments.

For instance, let us consider the cooperative environment of user Jean, who mainly acts as a reviewer on most of the shared document.

```
If author (document) = x
If role (x) = ''reader''
If frequency ("reader") > 0.5
If annotationTool (x) ≠ ''installed''
Then
    InstallInEnvironment (x) ← annotationTool
EndIf
```

Thus, the action components of the agent trigger specific cooperation actions (annotation tool) in the environment of user Jean ("reader").

The system announces to all users the degree of availability of everyone in the global cooperation process. Then, each user may decide whether or not to change his interest or his restrictions to avoid conflicts.

3.2 The Object and Action Spaces

In order to define a deductive and adaptive agent to support the group awareness function, it is required to identify the manipulated objects, and the actions performed on these objects.

The documents - Single entities as well as object compositions to support information partitioning and sharing.

Some Special Objects - Cooperative tools may be present in the user environment: an electronic white board, a multimedia teleconferencing tool, etc.

Objects for Group Awareness Support - These tools allow them to consult the state variables (current work, availability, interests, available interaction tools, etc) of other user environments and build or update his own interface.

Actions Applied on Documents - Among the observable actions, we can identify: document creation, renaming or removing, addition, modification or deletion of a document resource, document fragmentation, among others.

Document Editing Actions - The observable action list (GAA input information) is not restricted, and includes events explicitly or implicitly generated by editing, resource managing, and cooperative activities management.

Each running instance of the AllianceWeb application is composed of two separated active parts: the browser/editor and the assistant (see Fig. 1).

The browser/editor goal is to manage user interactions: document displaying interpretation of user editing commands. All editing commands generate modification actions only for the local document copies. Eventually, they generate some asynchronous remote requests that are delegated to the assistant.

The AllianceWeb assistant constitutes the interface with the servers. It takes in charge all communication failures, and thus it periodically tries to recontact all temporarily unreachable servers. It works in autonomous mode.

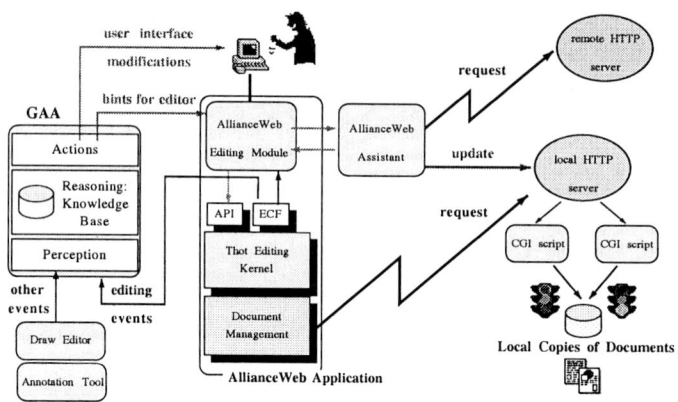

Fig. 1. AllianceWeb and the Group Awareness Agent (GAA)

4 Conclusion

AllianceWeb allows several authors distributed over the Internet to produce shared Web documents in a concerted and consistent way; to achieve this we have created a seamless production/consultation space where co-authors cooperatively produce shared documentation. At the same time, all users doing Web navigation can consult the documents whose versions are automatically updated.

The group awareness function allows each user to be aware of the production of others and allows them not only to adjust their contribution, but also to influence or to guide other user contributions.

We presented the first principles of a group awareness agent (GAA) that allows the automatic adaptation of each user's interaction environment, taking into account their preferences and their actions in the shared object space.

Acknowledgements. This work is supported by ECOS and ANUIES organizations (project M98M01), by CONACyT projects (29729-A and 33067-A), by CNRS-CONACyT cooperation projects (9018 / E130-505 and 10395 / E130-706), and by SEP-SESIC and UABC (grant P/PROMEP: UABC-2000-08), with the scholarship UABC-125 provided to the third author.

References

1. D. Decouchant, A. M. Martínez et E. Martínez, "Documents for Web Cooperative Authoring", *In Proc. CRIWG'99, 5th CYTED-RITOS International Workshop on Groupware*, IEEE Computer Society, Cancun, Mexico, 15-18 September 1999.
2. D. Decouchant, J. Favela and A. M. Martínez-Enríquez, "PIÑAS: A Middleware for Web Distributed Cooperative Authoring", *In Proc. of the 2001 Symposium on Applications and the Internet (SAINT'2001)*, IEEE Computer Society and IPJ Information Processing Society of Japan, San Diego, California (USA), pp. 187-194, 8-12 January 2001.

Adapting Learner Evaluation by Plans

Alke Martens and Adelinde M. Uhrmacher

University of Rostock, Department of Computer Science,
18051 Rostock, Germany
{martens, lin}@informatik.uni-rostock.de

Abstract. State of the art intelligent tutoring systems (ITS) provide ample opportunity for adaptability. Typically, they adapt single pages and contents to the learner's knowledge level and evaluate the learner based on his past and current behavior. However, to decide whether a learner behaves in a coherent manner, the learning system requires some means for anticipating the learner's goals and intentions. Thus, not only the structure of the tutoring process, but also the evaluation strategy should be adaptive. The ITS PLAIT reasons about and evaluates the learner's behavior according to a plan adapted for that purpose. To facilitate the adaptation, the plan is structured into a three-layered hierarchy. The topmost layer reflects the teaching objectives suggested by pedagogy and the psychology of learning; the middle one embeds domain-dependent refinement. The third layer represents the steps the learner has taken and should optimally take.

1 Introduction

In a case-based intelligent tutoring system (ITS), the learner should not only acquire knowledge about facts and how to apply them, but also knowledge about learning behavior, and how to proceed in the context of a given training case. The process of acting and interacting becomes part of the learning. To decide whether a learner behaves in a coherent manner, the learning system has to anticipate the learner's goals and intentions. The tutoring system PLAIT (Planning Agents in Intelligent Tutoring) adopts an approach to that effect in a case- and web-based context. Based on techniques of hierarchical planning, plan recognition, and agents, it tries to draw conclusions about the learner's intentions. A similar has been successfully employed in human-computer interaction, e.g. in the system Collagen [1]. In PLAIT, the learner's choice of sequence of steps is monitored and continuously evaluated. Reflected in a user model, this information is used to adapt a flexible tutoring process during runtime and to provide context-sensitive help and explanation. The final evaluation offers hints and advice to the learner, according to his progress in the training domain, and indicates possible fundamental learning gaps.

2 PLAIT - Reasoning and Intelligent Tutoring

PLAIT [6] is an extension of the case- and web-based ITS "Docs 'N Drugs - The Virtual Policlinic" [2], which is used at the University of Ulm as a constitutive part of the medical curriculum. The system is implemented as a classical ITS, described in, e.g., [3]. The extension PLAIT proposes to enrich the system with planning facilities, a plan library, and mechanisms for plan recognition. As described in, e.g. [1], we assume that learner and intelligent tutor collaborate in the learning environment. Thus, we have modeled them as two separated agents. This allows mimicking the concurrent activities and the role of learner and tutor within a training scenario. The idea to embed planning agents in the system is based on the approach to perceive "plans as complex mental attitudes", as described in [5]. PLAIT works with an adaptive flexible tutoring process. Series of interrelated steps lead from the initial page to the last page. Internally, each page consists of a set of page elements and a set of possible next steps that the learner could pursue. Page elements and steps are equipped with pre- and post-conditions and a required experience level of the learner. The subset of page elements and next steps, which is actually displayed is adapted to the learner's profile and history in current and past training cases. The interrelated steps and pages form paths in the training cases; they are called the tutoring process.

Reasoning about the learner's progress in the training case can happen in different ways. Whereas reasoning about interaction elements and checkpoints seems straightforward, reasoning about the learning process is more difficult. At every state in the tutoring process, the learner's actual choice of next step can be evaluated differently. Either the chosen step could be the correct next step, foreseen as optimal by the author. Or, the next step might be unnecessary, i.e. not optimal but not totally wrong either, and would likely not immediately affect the training case's development. Or, the chosen step could be definitely wrong. In that case, the immediate effects differ depending on the step's importance and content; only cumulative effects might prove critical. In addition, it has to be taken into account that a learner might choose a series of steps that are wrong with respect to the training case's goals, but that are intrinsically coherent with respect to his current mental strategy and knowledge. Thus, a chosen step can be correct, given the facts the learner has acquired so far. Even if it is wrong in the case's overall context, it would be logically coherent with the former steps the learner chose. Moreover, it could open an avenue to a series of interrelated steps, all of which are wrong with respect to the original purpose of the case. These steps have to be evaluated and supported differently compared to "simply" wrong or unnecessary steps. Reasoning about the learner's understanding of the required behavior in the training case is achieved by comparing a pre-defined optimal path in the training case to the path the learner actually has chosen. The assumption is that the learner follows a certain strategy, which the tutoring system perceives as the learner's mental plan. The learner agent observes the learner's activities and reports them as a sequence of steps to the tutor agent. The evaluation of the learner's choices takes place in consideration of his former

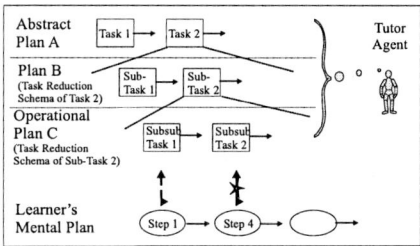

Fig. 1. The hierarchy of plans in PLAIT [6]

decisions, i.e. the learner's background knowledge and the sequence of steps he has chosen becomes part of the reasoning [5].

2.1 A Three Layered Planner and Adapting Plans

The Hierarchical Task Network (HTN) in PLAIT is realized as a three layered plan (Fig. 1). A goal in the HTN planner is a high level operator that shall be achieved. Associated with every high level operator is a set of skeleton plans, called operator reduction schemata, each of which can alternatively be used to achieve the high level goal.

The abstract plan A at the topmost layer contains high level tasks that reflect skills the learner should acquire, independent of the training domain. A skill is part of a pedagogical strategy which the author of the training case defines, for example according to [4]. Thus, a skill might be "knowledge of specific facts", "analysis of relationships", etc. [4]. The high level tasks will be reduced into subtasks by predefined task reduction schemata. Sub-tasks at plan level B are constructed by a set of context dependent learning sub-goals that are domain dependent. For example in the medical domain, sub-tasks are "order the correct examination before conducting a surgery", "choose the correct diagnosis", etc. Tasks in plan B denote macro steps within the training domain. A further task reduction leads to the operational plan C. Each of the sub-tasks at plan level B will be reduced to operational subsub-tasks, which finally correspond to concrete actions the author expected the user to apply. Those actions might be e.g. choose "anamnesis" or order "X-ray of left arm". The tutor agent compares the operational plan C with the sequence of steps reported by the learner agent. For a more detailed description see [6]. If the learner starts a training case, the learner agent generates a tutoring process, which is adapted to the learner's profile. The learner's history monitors the steps chosen in the current training case. It allows conclusions about the learner's actual state of knowledge. The learner starts the training case with the first page, and a set of next step choices, both adapted to his abilities. The learner makes his first choice of next step. Each of the steps he chooses is reported to the tutor, which compares the steps with the suggested subsub-tasks in plan C. If the learner chooses a step that is not part of the optimal plan C, the tutor uses plan recognition. It queries the plan library whether it contains a new sub-plan at the operational level C that is a task reduction schema for the task in plan B and is consistent with the steps the learner took so far. If such a new task reduction schema exists, the tutor will skip the actual plan and embed the new sub-plan as plan C. The new sub-plan will then be used as new reference plan. If no such plan is available in the plan library, re-planning can be initiated. In some situations, the tutor agent will offer the learner help, i.e. a plan repair strategy, to lead him back to the proper path. The learner has the option to ignore this offer and continue following his own ideas. The tutor agent will mark the subsub-task at layer C as not fulfilled. The higher layers of the current plan indicate whether the learner lacks certain skills, e.g. in applying knowledge in a certain situation. This information will be part of the final evaluation. At the end of the training case, in addition to the objective which the learner has finally achieved, the effort required to adapt the plan, and the number and type of mistakes, are used as indicator for the learner's success. From the bottom to the top of the hierarchy, plans are used for evaluation.

3 Conclusion

The system PLAIT extends the functionality of the web- and case-based ITS "Docs 'N Drugs". It is aimed at supporting a "more intelligent" evaluation of the learner's progress. Moreover, the mechanisms contained in PLAIT will help the training cases' author to develop training cases in a structured manner based on pedagogical theories. PLAIT employs two agents. The tutor agent uses a three-layer HTN plan, techniques of plan recognition, and plan repair. The three layers of the hierarchical plan reflect learning skills (based on learning theory), learning sub-goals, and concrete operational sub tasks. The tutor agent compares the learner's actions as reported by the learner agent to the lowest plan layer. It adapts the plans of the plan hierarchy according to the learner's activity. Thereby, it tries to trace, interpret, and anticipate the mental plan of the learner. Based on the goals and the pedagogical strategies at the topmost layer, conclusions about the learner's skills are derived.

References

1. Lesh, N., Rich, C., Sidner, C.L.: Using Plan Recognition in Human-Computer-Collaboration. Technical Report No. 98-14, IBM Watson Research Center (1998)
2. Docs 'N Drugs - Die Virtuelle Poliklinik http://www.docs-n-drugs.de (2000)
3. Martens, A., Bernauer, J., Illmann, T., Seitz, A.: Docs 'n Drugs - The Virtual Polyclinic. In:American Medical Informatics Conference, Washington USA (2001)
4. Bloom, B.S.: Taxonomy of Educational Objectives, Handbook I: Cognitive Domain. David McKay Company, Inc, New York (1956), Reprint 1971
5. Pollack, M.E.: Plans as Complex Mental Attitudes. In: Cohen, P.R., Morgan, J., Pollack, M.E. (eds): Intentions in Communication, MIT Press (1990)
6. Martens, A., Uhrmacher, A.M.: Adaptive Tutor Processes and Mental Plans. Accepted for: Intelligent Tutoring Systems ITS, Biaritz, France (2002)

WETAS: A Web-Based Authoring System for Constraint-Based ITS

Brent Martin and Antonija Mitrovic

ICTG, Department of Computer Science, University of Canterbury
Private Bag 4800, Christchurch, New Zealand

Abstract. Constraint-Based Modelling (CBM) is a student modelling technique for Intelligent Tutoring Systems (ITS) that is rapidly maturing. We have implemented several tutors using CBM, and demonstrated their suitability to, in particular, open-ended domains. It is easier to build tutors in some domains (e.g. open-ended) using CBM than other common approaches. We present WETAS (Web-Enabled Tutor Authoring System), a tutoring engine that facilitates the rapid implementation of ITS in new domains. We describe the architecture of WETAS, and give examples of two domains we have implemented.

1 Introduction

Constraint-Based Modelling (CBM) [5] is an effective approach that simplifies the building of domain and student models. We have used CBM to develop SQL-Tutor [3], an ITS for teaching the SQL database language. SQL-Tutor tailors instructional sessions in three ways: by presenting feedback when students submit their answers, by controlling problem difficulty, and by providing scaffolding information. Students have shown significant gains in learning after as little as two hours of exposure to this system [4].

While CBM reduces the effort of building domain models for ITS, the task of building an ITS is nevertheless still large. To reduce the authoring effort, we have developed WETAS, a web-based tutoring engine that performs all of the common functions of text-based tutors. To demonstrate the flexibility of WETAS, we have re-implemented SQL-Tutor, and developed a new Language Builder ITS (LBITS). Although these domains share the property of being text-based, they have very different problem/solution structures.

2 Constraint-Based Modelling

CBM [5] is a relatively new approach to domain and student modelling, based on the theory of learning from performance errors [6]. It models the domain as a set of state constraints, where each constraint represents a declarative concept that must be learned and internalised before the student can achieve mastery of the domain. Constraints represent restrictions on solution *states,* and take the form:

```
If     <relevance condition> is true for the student's
       solution,
THEN   <satisfaction condition> must also be true
```

The relevance condition of each constraint is used to test whether the student's solution is in a pedagogically significant state. If so, the satisfaction condition is checked. If it succeeds, no action is taken; if it fails, the student has made a mistake, and appropriate feedback is given. Ohlsson does not impose any restrictions upon how constraints are encoded and/or implemented. We have used a pattern-matching representation designed for this purpose [2]. For example, the following constraint from the SQL domain checks that names used in the 'WHERE' clause are valid names from the database:

```
(147
'You have used some names in the WHERE clause that are not
from this database.'
   (match SS WHERE (?* (^name ?n) ?*))        ; relevance cond

   (or      (test SS (^valid-table (?n ?t)))         ;
satisfaction
        (test SS (^attribute-p (?n ?a ?t))))   ; condition
'WHERE')
```

3 Architecture

WETAS is a web-based tutoring engine that provides all of the domain-independent functions for text-based ITS. It is implemented as a web server, written in Allegro Common Lisp, and using the Allegroserve Web server (see www.franz.com). WETAS supports students learning multiple domains at the same time; there is no limit to the number of domains it may accommodate. Students interact through a standard web browser such as Netscape or Internet Explorer. Figure 1 shows a screen from SQL-Tutor implemented in WETAS. The interface has four main components: the problem selection window (top), which presents the text of the problem, the solution window (middle), which accepts the students input, the scaffolding window (bottom), which provides general help about the domain, and the feedback window (right), which presents system feedback in response to the student's input.

WETAS performs as much of the implementation as possible, in a generic fashion. In particular, it provides the following functions: problem selection, answer evaluation, student modelling, feedback, and the user interface. The author need only provide the domain-dependent components, namely the structure of the domain (e.g. any curriculum subsets), the domain model (in the form of constraints), the problem/solution set, the scaffolding information (if any), and, possibly, an input parser, if any specific pre-processing of the input is necessary.

WETAS provides both the infrastructure (e.g. student interface) and the 'intelligent' parts of the ITS, namely the pedagogical module and the domain model interpreter. The former makes decisions, based on the student model, on what problem to present to the student next, and what feedback they should be given. The latter evaluates the student's answers, by comparing them to the domain model, and uses this information to update the student model.

Problems are selected by determining the difficulty of each candidate exercise with respect to the student. When the problems are authored, the system compares them to the domain model to determine their *structural complexity*, which is based on the

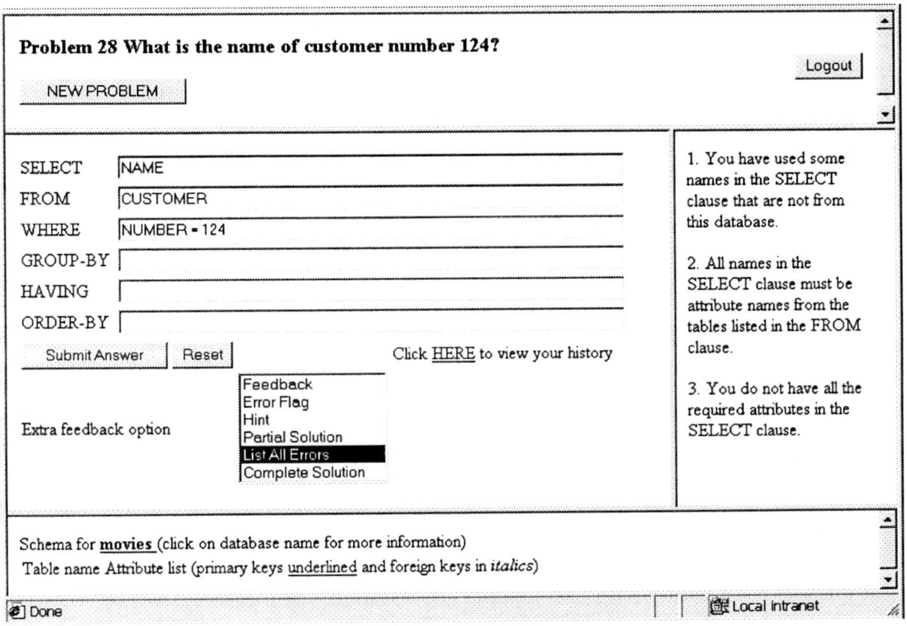

Fig. 1. WETAS Interface

number and complexity of the constraints that are relevant to them. When a new problem is to be selected, each candidate is compared to the student model, and the difficulty is increased by a constant amount for each constraint the student currently doesn't know, and by a different constant for each constraint that has never been relevant. Thus, the difficulty of each problem differs according to each student's strengths and weaknesses. The system then chooses the one with a difficulty that is closest to the student's current ability rating.

4 Example Domains

WETAS has been implemented in prototype form, and used to build two tutors, to explore its capabilities and evaluate its effectiveness in reducing the ITS building effort. These two implementations are now described.

SQL-Tutor. SQL-Tutor [3] teaches the SQL database query language to second and third year students at the University of Canterbury, using Constraint-Based Modelling. Students are given a textual representation of a database query that they must perform, and a set of input fields (one per SQL clause) where they must write an appropriate query. This system was implemented in 1998 as a standalone tutor, in 1999 as a Web-enabled tutor, and has been re-implemented in WETAS. The general design and interface of WETAS borrows heavily from the original SQL-Tutor. We had no problems implementing SQL-Tutor in WETAS.

Language Builder ITS (LBITS). Language Builder is an existing paper-based teaching aid that is currently being converted to a computer system. It teaches basic English language skills to elementary and secondary school students, by presenting them with a series of 'puzzles', such as crosswords, synonyms, rhyming words, and plurals. We created an ITS from Language Builder (LBITS) by adding a domain model so that feedback could be expanded from a simple right/wrong answer to more detailed information about what is wrong, such as that the meaning of their answer didn't match the meaning of the clue, or they have got the letters 'i' and 'e' reversed. These rules were inferred from a school spelling resource book [1]. We generated the problem set automatically from a vocabulary list in [1]. The constraints were authored in just five hours, and the problem set was created in around two days. LBITS contains 315 constraints and 222 puzzles.

We have so far implemented a subset of the Language Builder puzzles, all of which share the common format of a set of clues, each requiring one or more single-word answers. The system has been evaluated at a New Zealand elementary school, where the children found the system easy to use, and felt they had learned a lot. An analysis of constraint failures supported this latter statement: a plot of the average failure rate for each constraint versus the number of times it was relevant gave a 'power curve', indicating the constraints were being learned.

5 Conclusions

Constraint-Based Modelling (CBM) is an effective approach that simplifies the building of domain and student models for some domains, particularly open-ended ones. We have developed a prototype authoring system called WETAS for CBM tutors, which we intend to use to develop additional tutors for further research into CBM, and for release into classrooms. We have reimplemented SQL-Tutor using WETAS, and built a new tutor, LBITS. WETAS draws upon the strengths of CBM, plus research carried out to date in practical implementations of CBM. It appears to be a promising tool for the rapid development of new tutors, and a useful step towards the large-scale deployment of Intelligent Tutoring Systems.

Acknowledgement. This research is supported by the University of Canterbury, grant U6430.

References

1. Clutterbuck, P. M. (1990). The art of teaching spelling: a ready reference and classroom active resource for Australian primary schools. Melbourne, Longman Australia Pty Ltd.
2. Martin, B. and Mitrovic, A. (2000). Tailoring Feedback by Correcting Student Answers. In G. Gauthier, C. F., K VanLehn (Ed.), *Proceedings of the Fifth International Conference on Intelligent Tutoring Systems*, Montreal, Springer, pp. 383-392.
3. Mitrovic, A. (1998). Experiences in Implementing Constraint-Based Modeling in SQL-Tutor. In, *Proceedings of the ITS'98*, pp. 414-423.
4. Mitrovic, A. and Ohlsson, S. (1999). Evaluation of a Constraint-Based Tutor for a Database Language. *International Journal of Artificial Intelligence in Education* 10, pp. 238-256.
5. Ohlsson, S. (1994). Constraint-Based Student Modeling. In *Student Modeling: The Key to Individualized Knowledge-Based Instruction*, Springer-Verlag, pp. 167-189.
6. Ohlsson, S. (1996). Learning from Performance Errors. *Psychological Veview* 3(2), pp. 241-262.

Open-Ended Adaptive System for Facilitating Knowledge Construction in Web-Based Exploratory Learning

Hiroyuki Mitsuhara, Youji Ochi, and Yoneo Yano

Dept. of Information Science and Intelligent Systems, Faculty of Engineering, Tokushima University, 2-1 Minamijosanjima, Tokushima, Japan
{mituhara, ochi, yano}@is.tokushima-u.ac.jp

Abstract. A typical learning method using the Internet is exploratory learning, where learners construct knowledge through exploring the web autonomously. A problem with web-based exploratory learning is insufficient hyperlinks. An open-ended adaptive system has been developed that facilitates knowledge construction in web-based exploratory learning by avoiding the impasse.

1 Introduction

Rapid spread of the Internet enables us to learn with informative web pages that exist all over the world. A typical learning method using the Internet is exploratory learning, where learners construct knowledge through exploring the web on the basis of their own needs, goals, or interests. In web-based exploratory learning, the learners frequently reach a learning impasse caused by insufficient hyperlinks. If a page is not complete with sufficient hyperlinks to make up for learners' lack of knowledge, the learners will not be able to understand the page. Thus insufficient hyperlinks lead the learners to the impasse.

Search engines, which can supply suitable hyperlinks (pages), help escape from the impasse but occasionally return meaningless hyperlinks. Adaptive web-based learning systems, which alter the hypertext contents/structure to learners' characteristics, can avoid the impasse. The existent adaptive web-based learning systems do not fulfill learners' expectations that the open web (i.e. arbitrary web pages) will be adapted. Almost all such systems limit the adaptation to the closed web (i.e. web pages inside one server). Recently, this limitation has become a major focus in the domain of adaptive hypermedia [1].

The goal of this study is to develop an open-ended adaptive system for facilitating knowledge construction in web-based exploratory learning. Key factors for such a system are the open web, adaptive hyperlink addition, and zero-input learner modeling. The open web containing numerous pages is indispensable in fulfilling learners' expectations. The adaptive hyperlink addition avoids the impasse by enabling learners to refer to well-structured knowledge seamlessly from the open web. A zero-input learner modeling is needed in order not to interrupt learners' exploration activity. ITMS (Individualized Teaching Material System), a complete system with all the key factors, has been developed.

Similar systems have appeared up to the present. AHA expands exploration scope by adapting hyperlinks that connect with the open web [2]. KBS-Hypertext actualizes extensible learning environment by integrating the open web with independent courseware [3]. These systems can be classified as the system that utilizes the open web from the closed web. However, ITMS is in the opposite classification.

2 ITMS

ITMS, which has a simple system composition (Fig. 1), can apply to diverse domains of teaching. Basically, learners can use this system on a web browser without plug-in software.

2.1 System Composition

The closed web: The closed web consists of knowledge components (KC for short) created by teachers. KC is a fraction divided from educational web pages and can be combined with KCs stored in distributed servers. Although heterogeneous KCs may trigger off an incoherence that lowers learning effectiveness [5], these can conversely enhance learners' ability to select correct knowledge and associate new knowledge with already acquired knowledge.
Hyperlink addition engine: This engine first fetches a page requested by learners from the open web. Secondly, it extracts the related knowledge from the page by means of keyword matching. Thirdly, it combines corresponding KCs using hierarchical stretch-text [4]. Additionally, this engine modifies original hyperlinks on the page in order that the learners' requests are always sent to ITMS.
Learner model: ITMS builds a learner model that represents knowledge states, 'acquired', 'unstable', and 'forgot'.
Adaptation engine: This engine adapts the combined KCs on the basis of knowledge states. The adaptation techniques used are adaptive link annotation and adaptive link sorting (from the taxonomy in [1]).

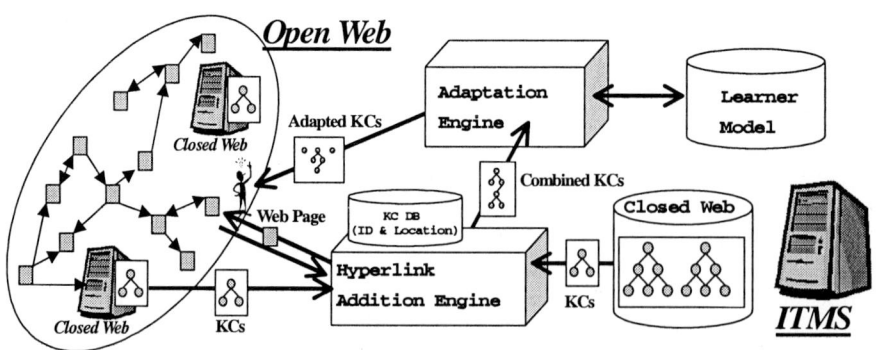

Fig. 1. System Composition

2.2 Learner Modeling

ITMS adopts zero-input learner modeling that estimates knowledge states from a learner's actions to KC. It differs from existing modeling methods, which generally consider that learners with understanding of the upper knowledge understand its lower knowledge already. Our modeling method is based on the following hypotheses.
- *The lower knowledge is difficult for learners to notice and easy to forget.*
- *They notice knowledge from the caption of the knowledge.*
- *When they notice forgotten knowledge, they refer to that knowledge and acquire it.*
- *Even if they notice knowledge they have acquired, they do not refer to it.*
- *The state of knowledge that they did not notice deteriorates to 'forgot'*

In this paper, T represents the number of times that they do not notice knowledge sequentially, T_f ($T_f >= 2$ and natural numbers) represents the threshold for estimating a knowledge state to be 'forgot'. When they notice knowledge, $T=0$ is performed for the knowledge. In the contrary case, $T=T+1$ is performed.

ITMS estimates the knowledge state by comparing T and T_f, and updates T_f by observing whether a learner refers to the knowledge in the 'forgot' state. Referring to such knowledge may indicate that the estimate was correct and the knowledge had already been forgotten before he/she noticed it; therefore $T_f=T_f -1$ is performed. Conversely, not referring to such knowledge may indicate that the estimate was incorrect and the knowledge will keep acquired for a while; therefore $T_f=T_f +1$ is performed. Low value T_f indicates that the knowledge is easy to forget. High value T_f indicates that the knowledge is difficult to forget. Learners' continuous exploration will bring T_f closer to the true tendency of forgetting.

2.3 Adaptation

The adaptation in ITMS facilitates equalizing knowledge construction by making learners notice the knowledge in the 'forgot' state. This adaptation also facilitates our zero-input learner modeling. Specific adaptation methods are to transfer such knowledge from the initial layer to the top layer (i.e. adaptive link sorting) and to highlight the caption of such knowledge with icons (i.e. adaptive link annotation). Knowledge with low value T_f is frequently adapted. Conversely, knowledge with high value T_f is infrequently adapted. Figure 2 shows an actual example of the adaptation.

3 Summary

Learners may increasingly be inclined to construct knowledge in web-based exploratory learning. This paper has outlined an open-ended adaptive system, which facilitates such knowledge construction by avoiding the learning impasse caused by insufficient hyperlinks.

This research has many remaining discussing points. One future topic of interest may be proving the reliability of zero-input leaner modeling through a large-scale experiment.

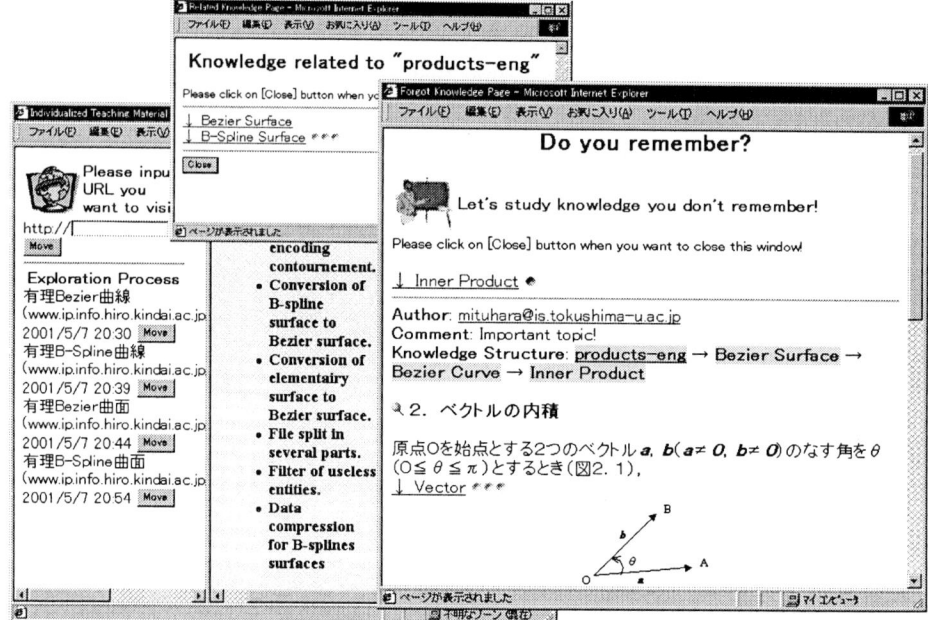

Fig. 2. An actual example of the adaptation in ITMS: Here, a learner visits the page of 'CAD products' (on the left). Words of 'Bezier surface' and 'B-Spline surface' appear on the page. ITMS extracts the KCs concerning Bezier surface and B-Spline surface as related knowledge and combines these KCs into a new page (on the top center). The KC of the 'Inner Product', which is the lower knowledge of Bezier and B-Spline surface, is shown on another new page (on the right). This occurs because the state of the KC is 'forgot'. In this way, the adaptation encourages the learner to notice the knowledge in the 'forgot' state and enables the learner to directly refer to such knowledge. Each KC sketches its own linear knowledge structure, which functions as a path indicator.

References

1. Brusilovsky, P.: Adaptive Hypermedia, *User Models and User-Adapted Interaction 11*, pp87-110 (2001).
2. De Bra, P., and Calvi, L.: AHA! An open Adaptive Hypermedia Architecture, *The New Review of Hypermedia and Multimedia, vol. 4*, pp. 115-139 (1998).
3. Henze, H. and Nejdl, W.: Extensible Adaptive Hypermedia Courseware: Integrating Different Courses and Web Material, *Proc. of AH2000*, pp.109-120 (2000).
4. Hook, K., Karlgren, J., Waern, A., Dahlback, N., Jason, C.G., Karlgren, K., and Lemaire, B.: A glass Box Approach to Adaptive Hypermedia, *User Models and User-Adapted Interaction 6(2-3)*, pp.157-184 (1996).
5. Seeberg, C., Steinacker, A., and Steinmetz, R.: Coherence in Modularly Composed Adaptive Learning Documents, *Proc. of AH2000*, pp.375-379 (2000).

Adapting Web Interfaces by WHAT

Wilfred Ng and Jerry Yau

Department of Computer Science
The Hong Kong University of Science and Technology, Hong Kong
{wilfred,csjerry}@cs.ust.hk

Abstract. We have previously presented a Java database application, called WHAT, which is developed to analyse the users' navigation behaviour. Herein, we discuss our on-going work, which makes use of the output results from WHAT to develop an enhanced interface for a commercial web site. The adapted interface provides the additional frames of popular trails and pages, which help reduce the navigation problem and facilitate better web topology adaptation.

1 Introduction

Web usage mining is the process of extracting interesting patterns in web server logs [1,2,6], which is related to the objectives of our WHAT system developed earlier on [4,5]. WHAT (Web Hypertext Associated Trail) system is a Java-based application developed for analysing web log data and mining web association rules as shown in the architecture given in Fig. 1 (see [5] for details). WHAT is implemented on top of an Oracle 8i server, which stores and manages the pre-processed web log data. We also use Thin JDBC Driver and TCP/IP-based network. The essential idea is that when users interact with a web site, data recording their behaviour is stored in the corresponding web server logs. By analysing such log data, web designers/developers can have a better understanding in the user navigation behaviour on their web sites.

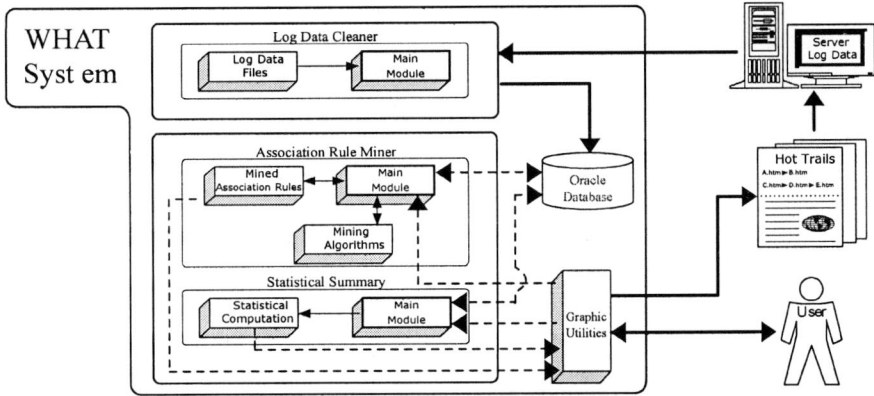

Fig. 1. The Architecture of WHAT Mining System

2 The Methodology of WHAT System

The underlying principle of WHAT in analysing web log data is classified into the following two areas: (1) To produce general statistical reports concerning web log data, such as frequency counts of requested pages and their temporal information, and (2) To mine the web association rules by using the modified Depth First Search (DFS) algorithm and Incremental Step (IS) algorithm developed in [1], and then to present the corresponding reports in appropriate visualisation tools. For the generation of statistical summary, users can impose queries to WHAT concerning analyses on a web site such as 'What are the total/average numbers of hits received per day?', 'What are the total/average numbers of pages viewed per day?', and so on. The web topology is modelled as a hypertext as proposed by [1]. A web server log file contains information that characterises user accesses to the server, including the user identifications (or their IP addresses), the URL of the requested page and the timestamp of the access. A user navigation session can be reconstructed as a sequence of page requests such that no two consecutive requests are separated by more than 25 minutes proposed in [2].

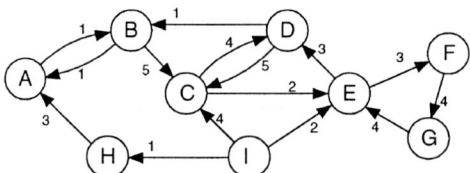

Fig. 2. A Weighted Directed Graph

We view a web site as a hypertext system. With the user navigation sessions reconstructed, a weighted directed graph $G = (N, E)$ can be built as follows: each node of N corresponds to a visited page and each arc of E corresponds to a traversed link. Figure 2 presents a weight directed graph which models the navigation data embedded into a web site. Since the model concerns only a collection of sessions, the concept of individual session will be lost. Therefore, the resulting weighted graph is intended to represent the navigation information of a group of users. Our aim is to mine trails of these users in the manner of mass customisation. To capture the user's preferences among the available links in a page, the concept of a web association rule can be used to describe 'when a user browses the hypertext system he or she will traverse the trail with a certain probability'. A web association rule is expressed as $(A_1 \rightarrow A_2) \wedge \cdots \wedge (A_{n-1} \rightarrow A_n)$ where $A_1, \ldots, A_n \in N$ and $(A_i, A_{i+1}) \in E$ with $i = 1, \ldots, (n-1)$, meaning that when a user traverses the hypertext system, there is a certain confidence that he or she will follow the trail $(A_1, \ldots, A_n)$. Confidence C_r in the rule is defined as the product of the confidences of all the corresponding components as the equation given below:

$$C_r = \prod_{i=1}^{n-1} C(A_i \rightarrow A_{i+1}) \text{ where } C(A,B) = |(A,B)| \Big/ \sum_{\{x|(A,x)\in E)\}} |(A,x)| \qquad (1)$$

In the graph shown in Fig. 2, $C_{(B \to C \to D)} = 5/(5+1) \times 4/(2+4) = 0.55$. Support S_r represents the average of times the links of the rule were traversed over the average of times all the links of the graph were traversed. It is defined by the following equation: (Rules with support greater than 1 consist of links traversed more than the average.)

$$S_r = \left(\sum_{i=1}^{n-1} |(A_i, A_{i+1})| \bigg/ (n-1) \right) \bigg/ \left(\sum_{\{i | (x_i, x_{i+1}) \in E\}} |(x_i, x_{i+1})| \bigg/ |E| \right) \qquad (2)$$

In the example of Fig. 3, $S_{(B \to C \to D)} = [(5+4)/2]/[43/15] = 1.57$. We adopt the modified DFS algorithm and the IS algorithm proposed in [1] for mining all the trails in the graph with support and confidence above specified thresholds.

3 Integrating WHAT with a Real Web Site

We demonstrate that WHAT adapts a commercial web site with respect to the server web log and contributes to enhance the web interface. The web log files (74.8 MB) is downloaded from [7]. The output results from WHAT, which provide the information of a sequence of most popular trails and pages, are then fed into the web interface as shown in Fig. 4. The raw web log data in the file is cleaned, transformed and stored in Oracle database server by the cleaning module of WHAT. Note those entries generated by inline images are filtered out. Figure 3a presents some of the samples rules mined with the DFS Algorithm under specified parameters of confidence, support and rule lengths. Figure 3b presents the sample result of Requested Page Summary of the ten most frequently requested pages (see [5] for details of the other services).

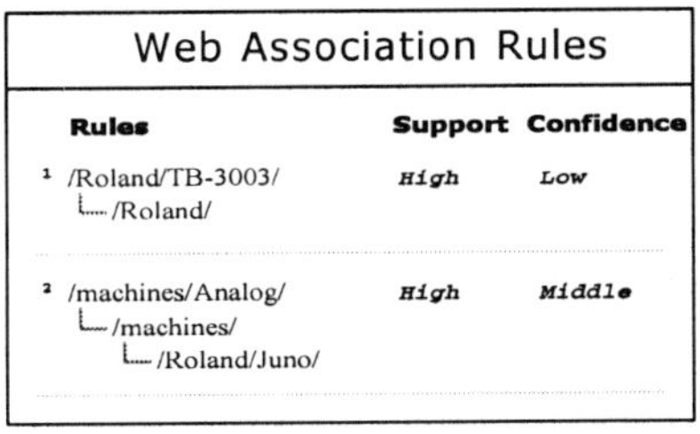

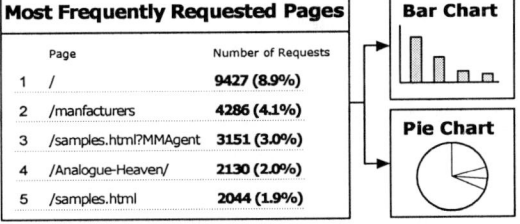

Fig. 3a. Sample Association Rules Identified

Fig. 3b. Screen Shots of Most Frequently Requested Page Summary

The interface of Hyperreal (in www.hyperreal.org/music/machines) is enhanced by providing two additional frames given in Fig. 4: the first one is the frame of 'hot trails', shown on the top of left-hand side, and the second one is the frame of the most popular pages, shown on the bottom of the left-hand side. These frames are built upon the output results from WHAT as already discussed in Sect. 2. The 'Hot Trails' frame consists of the top 10 most popular trails defined by the association rules. We set the confidence and support thresholds to be 0.5 and 1.0 in WHAT. The pages along a trail can be collapsed into a 'trail folder' whenever necessary, and all the trail folders are listed in the descending order of the support values. A visitor is able to click on the hot trails, once opening the folder, to navigate the site following the trail suggestion, or to go to any one of the most popular pages listed in the lower frame. In Fig. 4 we can see the top 10 pages, which are the most frequently requested ones. We may provide in this frame other popular objects such as the most popular downloaded files, or other most popular items depending on the related business objectives.

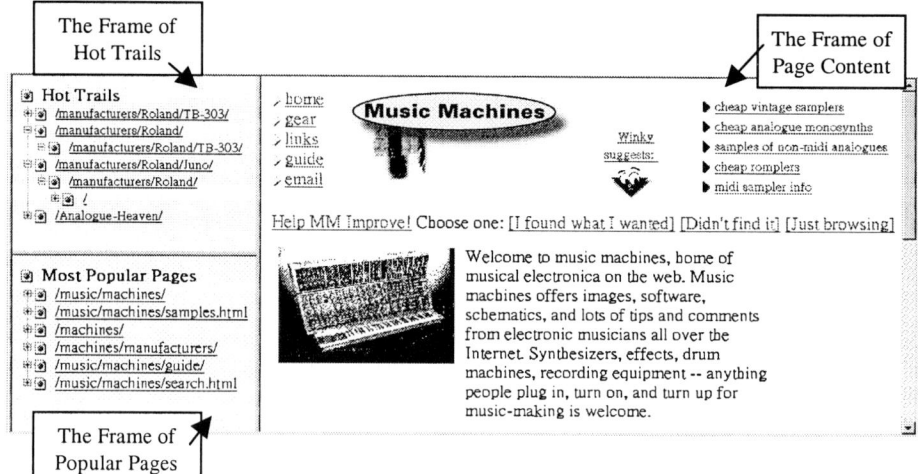

Fig. 4. An Enhanced Interface of Hyperreal

4 Conclusions

This paper describes an integrated system WHAT, which is developed to mine web association rules and to generate important statistics for web server log data on a real web site. The underlying principle of this system is based on the formal web hypertext model, which views the topology of a web site as a hypertext graph. Using the output result of WHAT we develop an enhanced web interface, which provides a useful guide for user navigating a complex web site and can be used to achieve the business objectives such as placing advertisements along the most popular trails.

Acknowledgements

This work is supported by the Hong Kong Polytechnic University Grant POLYU5095/00E and the Hong Kong University of Science and Technology Area-Of-Excellence-IT Grant.

References

1. Borges J. and Levene M. *Mining Association Rules in Hypertext Databases.* Proc. of the 4th Int. Conf. on Knowledge Discovery and Data Mining, pp. 149-153, 1998.
2. Catledge L. D. and Pitkow J. E. *Characterizing Browsing Strategies in the World Wide Web.* Computer Networks and ISDN Systems, 27(6), pp. 1065-1073, 1995.
3. Ng W. *Evaluating the Client Side Approach and the Server Side Approach to the WWW and DBMS Integration.* Proc. of the 9th Int. Database Conf., pp. 72-82, 1999.
4. Ng W. *Implementing WHAT to Support Web Usage Management.* Proc. of the International Conference on Internet Computing IC'2001, USA, pp. 35-40, 2001.
5. Ng W. and Chan C. *WHAT: A Web Hypertext Associated Trail Mining System.* Proc. of the 9th IFIP 2.6 Working Conf. on Database Semantics, pp. 205-220, 2001.
6. Ng W. *Capturing the Semantics of Web Log Data by Navigation Matrices.* Proc. of the 9th IFIP 2.6 Working Conf. on Database Semantics, pp. 169-183, 2001.
7. *Raw Web Log Files from Hyperreal.* http://www.cs.washington.edu/research/adaptive/download.htm, 2001.

Considering Sensing-Intuitive Dimension to Exposition-Exemplification in Adaptive Sequencing

Pedro Paredes and Pilar Rodriguez

Escuela Técnica Superior de Informática, U. A. M., Cantoblanco, 28049 Madrid, España
{Pedro.Paredes, Pilar.Rodriguez}@ii.uam.es

Abstract. This paper shows a way of using sensing-intuitive dimension of learning styles of students in order to improve the efficiency of adaptive learning systems. Firstly, it introduces the procedure of extracting information about sensing-intuitive students from the Felder-Soloman ILS questionnaire. Then, it presents a mechanism of application of sensing-intuitive dimension to exposition-exemplification sequencing. The example used to explain the adaptation effects is taken from a chess course developed with TANGOW, Task-based Adaptive learNer Guidance On the Web.

1 Motivation

The theory of learning styles states that people have different approaches to learning and studying [1]. We all have learning preferences that enable us to learn more effectively. Adapting the course to the learning style of the student changes the point of view of the learning process from teacher's perspective to learner's perspective. In this sense, it is necessary to mention the experience of Arthur [2]. It is one of the first systems which incorporates learning styles as a significant feature to their student models.

There are a large number of learning styles models: The Myers-Briggs Type Indicator (MBTI) derived from the theory of psychologist Carl Jung [3]; Kolb's Learning Style Model classifies students depending on how they perceive and process information [4]; Herrmann Brain Dominance Instrument (HBDI) is based on four different task-specialized quadrants of the brain [5]. Felder-Silverman Learning Style Model categorizes an individual's preferred learning style along a sliding scale of five dimensions [6,7]. One of them is called the *sensing-intuitive* dimension.

Sensing learners prefer learning first concrete and practical information oriented toward facts and procedures while intuitive learners prefer conceptual and innovative information oriented toward theories and meanings. In this paper we propose an adaptation procedure for moderate and strong sensing-intuitive learners, as detected by means of the Felder-Soloman ILS questionnaire. In our approach, adaptation lies in presenting examples before expositions to sensing learners and quite the opposite to intuitive learners. In doing so, it makes use of this adaptation in TANGOW [8,9].

2 Extracting Information about Sensing-Intuitive Students

Based on the Felder-Silverman classification, Felder and Soloman have built a questionnaire called ILS, *Index of Learning Styles* [10]. The aim of ILS questionnaire is to determine the learning style preferred by each student. ILS questionnaire is still under construction and nowadays it is formed by 44 questions with two possibly answers; *a* or *b*. These questions are divided into four groups, with eleven questions each, corresponding to four categories in Felder and Silverman's classification.

To take measurements of student's preferences in a given dimension, we have to subtract the answers relating to one extreme to the other one of the same dimension. Therefore, someone could be sensing-intuitive in a scale of odd values between 1 and 11. For example, if a student chose four of the answers classified as sensing and seven of the answers classified as intuitive, then it is intuitive with a score of 7-4=3.

Felder and Soloman [10] interpret the results in sections. If you obtain a score of 1 or 3 you have a mild preference but you are well balanced. Otherwise, if your score is 5 or 7, you have a moderate preference and will learn more easily in teaching systems which favor that dimension. Finally, if you score 9 or 11, you could have difficulty learning in a system which does not support that preference.

We have chosen the Felder-Silverman model among the existing learning style models because its ILS Questionnaire gives us the possibility of linking directly its results to automatic adaptive environments. Thanks to the distribution of the ILS Questionnaire in four different dimensions with two extremes we can build user models corresponding to each of these four dimensions.

3 Adapting Exposition-Exemplification Sequencing

Felder [7] claims that the goal of the teacher is to strengthen those learning styles that students do not prefer. This procedure should improve the global learning capability of the students. It is a long-term objective and the aim is that students perceive and process information in all the ways. However in a Web based learning environment we try to attain a short-term goal: an easiest and most effective learning process through adaptation of learning courses to individual learning styles.

In this environment, we propose to make use of the ILS results to adapt the exposition-exemplification sequencing in a Web-based learning environment. The procedure is as follows: firstly the student fills out the questionnaire; then the score obtained points out the sensing-intuitive preference of the student: mild, moderate or extreme; finally we use that preference to adapt the exposition-exemplification sequencing in case of moderate and extreme sensing-intuitive learners.

We have implemented the described adaptation procedure on TANGOW, Task-based Adaptive learNer Guidance On the Web [8,9]. In TANGOW a course is described in terms of Teaching Tasks and rules. Knowledge is represented by means of TTs that need to be achieved. TTs may be exposition tasks (E), practical or examples (e).

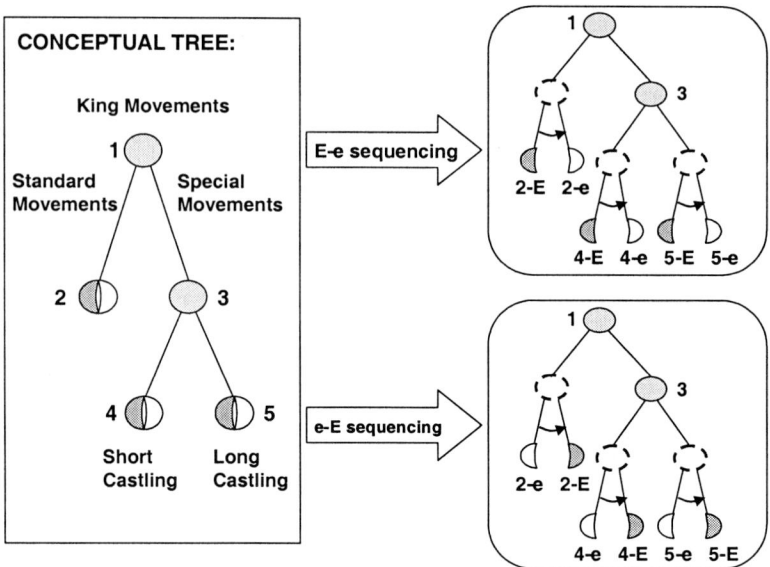

Fig. 1. Exposition-exemplification sequencing in sensing (lower) and intuitive (upper) students in a piece of chess course about king movements.

Exposition TTs can have an example associated. Designers establish the default order, that is, the order of the tasks and, consequently, the order of the task types (examples first or exposition first). Our approach is to dynamically modify that last order according to the learning style. If the student obtains a score of 1 or 3 his/her preference to one or the other style is balanced and we apply the default order. On the contrary if the student scores 5 or more than 5, the order of exposition-example tasks will be in harmony with his/her learning preference.

In Fig.1 it is presented a conceptual tree with three E-e nodes. Nodes 2, 4, and 5 are E-e nodes; this means that student could see exposition before example (E-e) or vice versa (e-E). This tree shows the King standard and special movements (short and long castling). On the right side two different trees are presented showing the runtime sequencing based on sensing-intuitive adaptation. The lower tree with e-E nodes corresponds to moderate and extreme sensing students. The upper tree with E-e nodes will be presented to moderate and extreme intuitive students. The default sequencing is suitable for students with a mild preference and we assume that it is a common practice to expose firstly and provide examples later (E-e sequencing).

4 Conclusions and Future Work

This paper suggests the application of the results of the ILS questionnaire to adapt the sensing-intuitive dimension to the exposition-exemplification sequencing. We assume that a strong relationship between examples and their related theoretical expositions exists with independence of the conceptual representation. This relationship is more powerful than any other sequencing consideration, and can eventually be combined with other dimensions. In this sense, we are exploring the adaptation effects of combining the *sensing-intuitive* with other dimensions [11].

In addition to sequential-global and sensing-intuitive dimensions, at present our research examines the incorporation of other learning style dimensions, according to the ILS, to the general model. It involves the study of possible conflicts between adaptive actions based on different learning style dimensions and the resolution of these conflicts by establishing a priority of some dimensions against others.

Acknowledgments

The Spanish Interdepartmental Commission of Science and Technology (CICYT) has sponsored this paper, project number TEL1999-0181 and project number TIC2001-0685-C02-01.

References

1. Dunn, K., Dunn, R.: Teaching students through their individual learning styles. Reston, VA.: National Council of Principles (1978)
2. Gilbert, J. E., Han, C. Y.: Adapting instruction in search of 'a significant difference'. Journal of Network and Computer Applications, 22 (1999).
3. Briggs Myers, I., McCaulley, M.: Manual: A Guide to the Development and Use of the Myers-Briggs Type Indicator. Consulting Psychologist Press (1985)
4. Kolb, D.: Experiential learning: Experience as the source of learning and development. Englewood Cliffs, NJ: Prentice-Hall (1984)
5. Herrmann, N.: The Creative Brain. Lake Lure, NC, Brain Books (1990)
6. Felder, R. M., Silverman, L. K.: Learning Styles and Teaching Styles in Engineering Education. Engr. Education, 78 (7) (1988) 674-681
7. Felder, R. M.: Reaching the Second Tier: Learning and Teaching Styles in College Science Education. J. Coll. Sci. Teaching, 23 (5) (1993) 286-290
8. Carro, R.M., Pulido, E., Rodríguez, P.: Task-based Adaptive learNer Guidance on the Web. Proc of the 2nd Workshop on AS and UM on the WWW. CS Report 99-07, Eidenhoven University of Technology (1999) 49-57
9. Carro, R.M., Pulido, E., Rodríguez, P.: TANGOW: a Model for Internet Based Learning. IJCEELLL, 11 (1-2) (2001).
10. Felder, R. M., Soloman, B. A.: Learning Styles and Strategies. December (2001) on-line at: http://www2.ncsu.edu/unity/lockers/users/f/felder/public/ILSdir/styles.htm
11. Paredes, P., Rodríguez, P.; Tratamiento de los casos secuenciales-globales moderados y extremos en un sistema de enseñanza adaptativa. Submitted to IPO2002, December (2001)

PlanEdit: An Adaptive Problem Solving Tool for Design

M.A. Redondo[1], C. Bravo[1], M. Ortega[1], and M.F. Verdejo[2]

[1] Dpto. de Informática
Universidad de Castilla – La Mancha
Paseo de la Universidad, 4. 13071 – Ciudad Real. Spain
{mredondo,cbravo,mortega}@inf-cr.uclm.es
[2] Dpto. de Lenguajes y Sistemas Informáticos
Universidad Nacional de Educación a Distancia
Ciudad Universitaria, s/n. 28040 – Madrid. Spain
felisa@lsi.uned.es

Abstract. Experimental learning environments based on simulation usually require monitoring and adaptation to the actions the user carries out. In this work we present the monitoring and adaptive features of PlanEdit, a tool for learning integral automation methods in buildings and housing by design and simulation.

1 Introduction

Design and simulation environments for learning should provide students with mechanisms to enhance effective learning. For that purpose, it is convenient to interactively monitor the learner while he/she is solving a problem [1].

This work describes the monitoring and adaptability features of PlanEdit, an evolution of the DomoSim environment [2], to learn the design of the automation of buildings and housing. The environment included a knowledge-based editor to plan the design of a model satisfying a set of requirements and a simulation program to test the behavior of the model built.

The domain where a pressing need arises and where our investigation is applied is the learning of the design of automated control facilities in buildings and housing, also called Domotics. In this kind of training, the realization of practical experiments is especially important. However, the material necessary to carry out these assignments is usually expensive and in many cases is not adequately provided. This problem gets worse with the difficulty to bring the student closer to real situations, to replicate accidents and to simulate those chaotic situations, which may happen in the real world; Domotics designs aim to cope with those troublesome situations too.

In order to soften this problem by means of the use of technology, we have developed a distributed environment with support for distance learning of domotics design: DomoSim-TPC [3]. It includes setting, realization, tracking, tasks analysis and storage of collaborative learning activities. PlanEdit is one of the tools included in this environment and it approaches learning from a individual perspective. This is a supporting tool for the design of models that should satisfy a specification. The design is approached in two steps, first a plan is built, and then a refinement of the plan is carried out. A plan is specified as a partially ordered set of generic actions for the construction of a model. We will now describe the characteristics considered in the student model, the monitoring of the work carried out and how the system adapts to the user.

2 Student Model

The user model consists of entities with information about the following categories:
- The student's profile that defines the student's role in the system. This profile stores restrictions and obligations on the type of actions that the student should carry out.
- The user's interaction with the editor in order to plan the design.
- The sequence of actions that the student dynamically specifies in his/her search of a solution to a problem. Additionally, the time dedicated to the elaboration and the mistakes made in this process are considered. This way, each element in this sequence is defined by a unique identifier, the moment the action is planned, the mistake associated to it (if there is one) and the action preceding the current action. This is, `<item>::= <id> <time> <action> <prevAct> | <id> <time> <action> <error> <prevAct>`, where, `<action>::= <kind> <area> <section> <element>`, and `<error>::= ACTION | SEQUENCE | DUPLICATE | NON_OBLIGATORY`

3 Tutoring Module

The main objective of tracing the student's resolution strategy is to determine if he/she is close to a good solution. In many cases, there is not a unique solution. The *Optimal Plan of Design* (OPD) represents the set of possible solutions for a particular problem. If he/she moves away from what the experts consider a good solution, the system will display warnings offering help and reinforcement with the purpose of communicating the student the mistakes he/she is making and driving him/her towards a better solution. This circumstance can make the student reflect in search of an explanation and the correction of the mistake. This way, hopefully, meta-learning situations are promoted.

Figure 1 shows a schema which summarizes the mechanism used for monitoring and guiding the learner's work. The beginning is the *General Plan of Design* (GPD) for a generic kind of problem. In this plan there is a sequence of elements following this schema `<action>:<type>:<requirements>:<influences>`.

The system can modify the GPD according to the specification of the parameters that characterize the problem. As a result, the OPD is obtained for the proposed problem. This constitutes a resolution schema with some flexibility in the tasks to carry out. Additionally, the teacher sets up a help level that will display the kind of messages that the system will provide in order to warn the student or to prevent the mistakes that the solution proposed by the student can produce. Therefore, the generated and displayed help messages will be a consequence of an inference process starting from the OPD, the help level and the design proposed by the student.

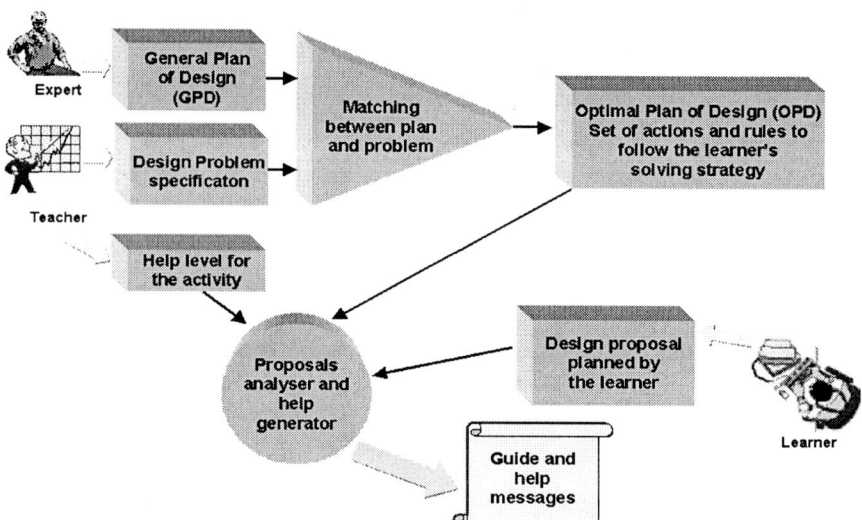

Fig. 1. Components involved in the mechanism of tracing and monitoring the construction procedure of the solution to a design problem.

In order to increase the controlled flexibility of the OPDs, a set of rules can be defined. These rules define the form in which a strategy can be changed and the possible side effects of the changes. We consider three sources of information that can cause a variation in the structure of the resolution of design problems:

i) The characteristics of the problem
The design problems with similarities in their solutions can be classified into categories. For each category a general strategy of resolution is defined: the GPD.

Nevertheless, a particular problem will be identified by a set of parameters. In some cases these are fixed and in others, variable. These parameters may condition the solution and allow adapting the construction mechanism to each student. To every parameter we associate a rule of the type IF <condition> THEN <modifyAction>. This rule can modify the design actions and their structure. This is, the adaptation depends on the domain.

ii) Design actions
The design strategy is defined according to a series of actions with a high level of abstraction. Among these certain dependences are established. The order the student establishes when approaching each generic action defines his/her resolution strategy. When reaching a state of the design at which different alternatives to continue are offered, the student chooses one of them and discards the rest. He/she may choose a non-obligatory option, but the fact of selecting it will imply the obligatory realization of other actions. Therefore, the learner's decision will cause an adaptation of the OPD depending on the alternative chosen.

iii) Help level
When the teacher proposes an activity in which a problem should be solved, he/she specifies the help level. This level makes the use of scaffolding [4] possible, defining the degree of difficulty of the problem and the level of help that the system offers to the student. This will reinforce the intrinsic structure of the process of problem solving in which the new knowledge is built through a successive process of elaboration and integration.

The help level influences PlanEdit in two ways: the messages that will be displayed in order to guide the learner during their work; and the set of possible actions that will be shown to the student. The learner has to choose the most appropriate action in each moment from them.

4 Conclusions

PlanEdit considers several aspects of the users, such as their procedural strategy to solve a problem as a history trace of the path followed and their behavior as to interaction with the system. With all this information, the tool adjusts the current alternatives at each stage in the resolution process (generation and adaptation of nodes). This adjustment shapes up the presence of reinforcing help and the concealing/prohibition of alternatives to guide the learner around the resolution process (adaptation of the path).

In our proposal, the path the learner outlines has to match one of the plans. However, the outstanding characteristic of our tool in contrast to hypermedia systems is that the learner does not follow a content-based path. Rather, he/she builds a path as a plan or a solution strategy to a proposed problem. The system adapts to the characteristics of the solution the students propose, trying to guide them so that they can achieve their objective.

Our proposal is applicable to any domain where the resolution of design problems in a structured way is approached. This resolution can be specified in terms of the design actions to build a model. These actions can be inferred from the user interaction.

References

1. Verdejo, M.F., (1992). A Framework for Instructional Planning and Discourse Modeling in Intelligent Tutoring Systems. In E. Costa (ed.), New Directions for Intelligent Tutoring Systems. Springer Verlag: Berlin, pp. 147-170.
2. Bravo, J., Ortega, M., & Verdejo, M.F., (1999). Planning in Distance Simulation Environments. Full Paper in Communications and Networking in Education COMNED'99. Aulanko, Hämeenlinna, Finlandia.
3. Bravo, C., Redondo, M.A., Bravo, J., & Ortega, M., (2000). DOMOSIM-COL: A Simulation Collaborative Environment for the Learning of Domotic Design. Reviewed Paper. Inroads - The SIGCSE Bulletin of ACM, vol. 32 (2), pp.65-67.
4. Rosson, M.B., & Carroll, J.M., (1996). Scaffolded Examples for Learning Object-Oriented Design. Communications of ACM, vol. 39, num. 4.

Dynamic Generation of Interactive Dialogs Based on Intelligent Agents

Martín González Rodríguez, Benjamin López Pérez, María del Puerto Paule Ruíz, and Juan Ramón Pérez Pérez

Laboratory of Object Oriented Technologies (OOTLab – HCI Area) – Department of Computing Science, University of Oviedo, Asturies, Spain
{martin, benja, paule, jrpp}@lsi.uniovi.es

Abstract. The design of the lexical and syntactical levels of the user interface of any web based system is commonly based on general human-computer interaction principles targeted to match the interaction requirements of the so-called typical user, an abstract generalization of each user of an application. However the identification of such typical user at the web design stage seems to be an impossible task, considering the dynamic nature of the web, where the user interface of a popular web systems can be used by thousands of different users everyday. In order to avoid this problem, we have designed GADEA, an intelligent user interface management system able to detect different kinds of users by mean of distributed data gathering agents. The information obtained by those agents is used to design interactive dialogues at execution time, which are adapted to the specific cognitive, perceptive and motor characteristics of the current user.

1 Introduction

Traditional design of user centred interfaces is based on the identification and definition of the target audience of the application under development. Some design guidelines include the identification and understanding of the target audience as the most important steps to start designing a product [1, pp. 13; 2]. The idea is that once the target audience has been understood an interface that effectively satisfies their needs can be designed.

However, the quest for the typical user is opposite to the individuality and diversity that makes up some much of our identity. If the design of the interaction mechanisms of an application aims to make interfaces accessible and appealing to all users, it shouldn't rely on an abstract generalisation [2]. In the design of applications targeted to a wide range of users it is almost impossible to determine the typical user without falling in serious misconceptions. For example, we should ask ourselves whether its is possible to describe the typical user of Microsoft Office or not. Another interesting question without a clear answer is whether it is possible or not to identify the typical user of generic web portals visited by thousands of user everyday such as for example Lycos, Terra or MSN. For some authors such as Schneiderman [3], the answer to those questions is definitely 'no' as 'there is no average user'. For him, 'either compromises must be made or multiple versions of a system must be created' in order to satisfy the specific interaction needs of every single user.

Following this design principle we have developed the GADEA User Interface Manager Expert System (UIMES) for the development of automatic generic adaptive user interfaces. The tools provided by this system allow programmers to create multiple versions of the user interface of an application dynamically. Each version of the user interface is created and adapted dynamically in order to satisfy the interaction requirements of the current user of the application. The design of each version will depend on the specific state of the cognitive, perceptive and motor system of the mentioned current user.

Current version of this UIMES has been entirely written in Java, so it can use as an alternate User Interface Manager System (UIMS) for platforms such as Windows, Linux or Macintosh. The internal design of this development framework also includes the generation of dynamically adapted user interfaces in the web engineering and adaptive hypermedia environments.

2 Overview of GADEA

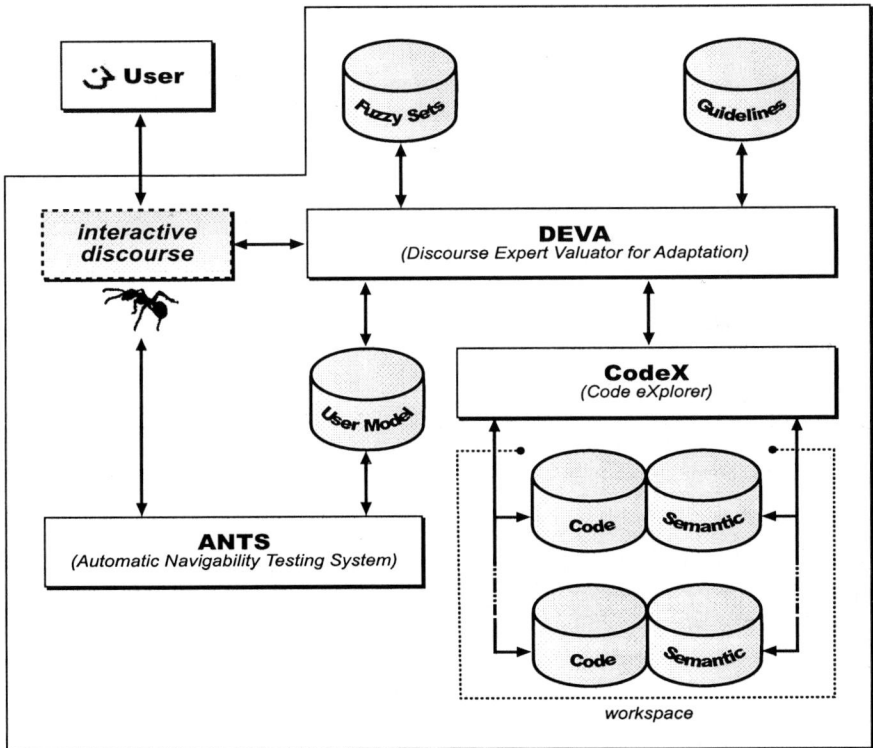

Fig. 1. GADEA's main components

The internal architecture of GADEA relies on three independent components specially designed to cope with the problems derived of the three most important features of the system. Those features are the separation of the client application's user interface from its functionality, the creation of a single tailored interactive dialog for each user of an application and the constant update of each user model. The components that address each problem are CodeX, DEVA and ANTS respectively (see Fig. 1).

The CodeX (Code eXplorer) module represents the interface between GADEA and the client applications of this UIMES. This module must convert the user interaction requests into calls to specific methods inside the application's domain workspace. To reach this objective, this module automatically inspects the binary code of every client application at execution time, looking for any user process defined by the programmers during the design time. CodeX consider a 'user process' as those methods designed to satisfy a specific user's interaction request and will represent them as options or commands in the respective application user interface. This module is also in charge update every single piece information displayed by the user interface, keeping track of possible changes in the value of public variables and data structures associated to the interface by the application at both execution and design time. All this information is obtained automatically inspecting the client application's code by mean of the structural reflection mechanism of the Java platform also included as part of the servlet specification.

The interactive dialogs established to interact with the user inside the scope of ever 'user process' are created from the data that the application needs to perform a certain task (provided by the user) or by the information that must be displayed as the result of a user data request.

The current version of our prototype supports four kinds of data primitives used to create an interactive dialog with the user. Those data primitives are strings, integers, real and dates. Each of those primitives is encapsulated inside a JavaBean component [4], which can be configured by mean of their own set of properties. Depending on the kind of data required by the situation and kind of user process (input or output process) the programmer must select and configure the appropriate primitive data component, inserting it in an 'interactive dialog object'. The primitive data components can be grouped together creating semantic meaningful blocks called 'chunks'. Semantically the chunks represent groups of related data elements that must be perceived as a conceptual unit by the user. Internally, every chunk contains primitive data components as well as other chunks, allowing the creation a hierarchy of chunks.

The information collected by CodeX is sent periodically to DEVA (Dialog Expert Valuator for Adaptation) which represent the agent software in charge of the simulation of the behaviour of human expert in Human-Computer Interaction (HCI). This module converts the application's and user's interaction requests into adaptive interactive dialogs. Based on the general knowledge and guidelines provided by the HCI discipline as well as by specific knowledge stored about the current user model of the client application, DEVA uses its fuzzy inference engine to evaluate, to select and to adapt the best interactive dialog available for the current user. The dynamic creation of the user tailored interactive dialog will depend on the current user's cognitive, perceptive and motor skills, which might fluctuate over the time.

Finally, the ANTS module will be the agent responsible for keeping the information about the users of any client application of GADEA updated. This component makes use of different kinds of automatic remote agents designed to observe the user behaviour in any of the interactive dialogs designed by DEVA. Those agents obtain crucial information about the specific user's skills, which is stored in specific distributed user model.

3 Conclusions

The automatic code exploring system provided by GADEA allows an easy adaptation of the low-level aspects of a user interface with little or almost no programming effort. The approach adopted by CodeX in the design interactive dialogs in terms of data primitive components instead in terms of static-based widgets allows designers to focus their effort in the design of the high level interaction mechanisms (metaphors) of their applications saving up time and resources.

The information captured by ANTS in every interactive dialog allows DEVA to adapt the user interface to the current state of the user's cognitive, perceptive and motor system, which tends to fluctuate over time.

The use of an expert system (DEVA) to take every decision concerning with the interaction style and techniques to be applied, guarantees a strong user interface homogeneity in every application. As there isn't any ambiguous natural language-based HCI guideline to be interpreted by a human designer, this approach eradicates troubles with consistency, which it is present in many computer platforms.

Currently, we are working on the design of a low-level adaptive Internet browser based entirely on GADEA's technology, able to be used with the same utility by sighted and blind users, as well as users with different degrees of physical disability.

References

1. Apple Computer Inc; (1992) Macintosh Human Interface Guidelines. Adison-Wesley Publishing Company. ISBN 0-201-62216-562216.
2. Reynolds, C.; (1997) A Critical Examination of Separable User Interface Management Systems: Constructs for Individualisation. ACM SIGCHI. 29(3).
3. Schneiderman, B.; (1987) Designing the user Interface. Reading, MA: Addison-Wesley.
4. Sun Microsystems (1996). The JavaBeans 1.0 API specification. http://www.sun.con/beans.

A Simple Architecture for Adaptive Hypertext

Oreste Signore

CNR-CNUCE, Area della Ricerca di Pisa - San Cataldo, via Moruzzi, 1 - 56124 Pisa
oreste.signore@cnuce.cnr.it

Abstract. We describe a general, flexible architecture based on web standards (W3C Recommendations) where users access data through the mediation of intelligent agents. Architecture is based on simple but effective document and user models, with weighted and semantic tagging of both documents and links. User's profile and preferences affect the agents' behaviour, so that actions can occur on the server as well at the browser side. Profile and preferences accompany the URL reference, avoiding dependence from any central site.

1 Introduction

The Web is a Universal Information Space, and it is easily seen that there is need for *adaptive* and *intelligent* systems. User needs in accessing information have been widely addressed by researchers ([1,2]), and some possible solutions, like *information filtering*, *user profiling* and *two-level hypertext* seem to give good results with a fairly low overhead and complexity ([3,4,5,6]). An architecture where users access data through the mediation of *intelligent software agents* can be a first step towards the Semantic Web [7]. In this framework, a basic role is played by XML, as the basis for the exchange of structured information. However, we should carefully consider the effect of deep structuring and tagging. In the following, we will describe ABWR (Adaptive Browsing of Web Resources), a general, flexible and web standards compliant architecture where an intelligent software agent performs information filtering based upon users' profiles and preferences.

2 Architecture of ABWR

The architecture has been driven by some basic principles, namely *simplicity* (evident in both the underlying principles and the architecture), *no centralization* (as architectures relying on some central site would be in contrast with the ideas that lead to the development of the web, as described in [8]), *light tagging* (to emphasize the semantic categories, more than the specific role played by the single, atomic information item), *weighted and semantically tagged links* (to screen out useless links and suggest appropriate interaction paradigms).

ABWR mainly relies on modules able to perform document *filtering* and *personalization*. Some specific modules check the user behaviour during navigation. The architecture aims to reduce the centrality of the agent, split in two equivalent components: the *ServerAgent* and the *ClientAgent*. Generally speaking, ClientAgent plays an active role when user behaviour is not stable or the server is unable to perform actions. The agent gets appropriate directives from the user *Preferences*. To *avoid any centralization* and have a *generally valid profile*, the browser, when asking the server for data, sends current profile and preferences.

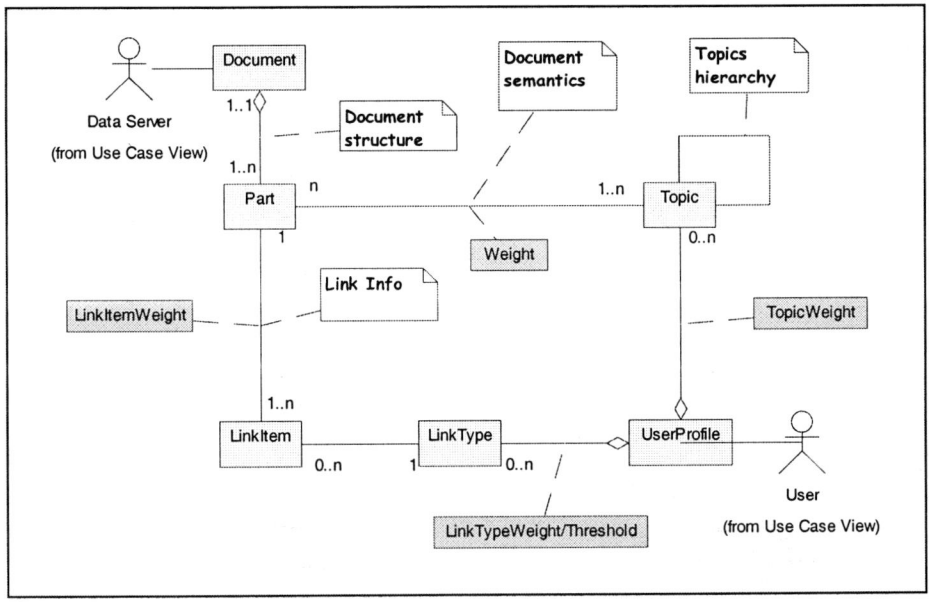

Fig. 1. User, link and document model

The ABWR architecture (Fig. 1) is based on an abstract representation of *documents* and *user*, based on Document model, Link taxonomy and model, User model, Preferences. They can easily be described according to the RDF syntax ([9]).

Semantic model of documents. Traditional documents are often organized in parts (sections, paragraphs, etc.). XML documents, where every field is recognizable and appropriately tagged, have more complex structures. However, we must clearly distinguish between *structural* and *semantic* information. Assigning semantics to the document as a whole can just accommodate for very simple and flat documents. In the majority of cases, we need a finer granularity level, with semantics attached to specific parts of documents.

A relevant issue is to consider that users should be able to match their topics of interest even if they are not experts in the field. Too specific topics would affect the user/system communication. This approach leads to the definition of a limited and rough general set of semantic categories (like Art, Economy, Politics, Music, Sport, Literature, Science) that can be shared by a wide variety of users, and can be used to define a user profile and to *semantically characterize* both various parts of the documents[1] and links. Topics identifying concepts belonging to this predefined set of cognitive categories in the semantic model can be tied to the document as a whole, or to a document part. We have also to specify a *weight*, stating the relevance in the document context. Every Topic is modelled as an element of a hierarchy of Topics, so building a thesaurus, even if limited to a few terms and of reduced depth.

Link taxonomy and model. Links are an essential component of hypertext, allowing the navigation on the web, and can implement the abstraction mechanism needed to move from the data space to the concept space[2]. In the data space, documents are connected by *extensional* links; in the concept space, associations among concepts implement *intensional* links among documents ([3,4,5]). Semantic qualification of links is equivalent to explicitly identify the meaning of the link in the document and the role of involved resources. The *reason* why the link has been inserted in the document, that is the nature of association (geographical, explicative, etc.), can be addressed as link *semanticType*. To define a profile independently from the context, it is useful to select a limited number of semantic types (Location, Time, Person, Linguistic resource, etc.) It is worthwhile to note that different types of links, and therefore of the referred resource, can suggest different, and specialized, *interaction paradigm* (time, map, classification, etc.). This can have a terrific effect on the potential association mechanism: two documents can be linked through an intensional link existing in the concept space, without having any extensional link specified in the document ([10]). The semantic model of links should be appropriately mapped onto the W3C Xlink Recommendation ([11]).

User Model. As a first approximation level, user model is defined in terms of a profile. User profile is essentially dynamic. In our approach, the user profile specification is tightly related to the semantic model of documents and links: user profile is defined in terms of *semantic categories*, *link types* and *link roles*. For each of them, the user profile will specify a degree of interest, assigning a weight. In addition, for each topic or link type, a *threshold* value is defined.

Preferences. Several factors can affect filtering and personalization of documents. Among them, *device characteristics*, *abilities* and *behaviour* (accounting for dynamic aspects of the profile). Preferences act as directives to the agent, specifying, among other properties, where manipulation should be performed (server or client side), if the profile should be considered stable, the intended behaviour when user profile topic is at a different detail level respect to document assigned topic.

A sample implementation. A prototype has been implemented[3]. There is an extensive use of W3C Recommendations ([12]). Up to now, it has been tested on a very limited document base.

---

[1] In this paper, we will generically refer to 'documents' irrespective the sites will provide just a set of (somehow indexed and searchable) 'pages', or dynamically access Information Retrieval Systems, or produce 'documents' from a traditional database.
[2] The concept space is a simplified version of Semantic Web architecture's ontology level.
[3] Thanks are deserved to A. Cristofaro, who implemented a first version of the prototype.

3 Conclusion and Future Developments

Considering the difficulties that arise from the large amount of documents available on the Web, and the growing interest in the semantic web research area, we proposed a simple and hopefully effective approach, which resulted in a system architecture and an operating prototype.

The relevant features are simplicity of architecture, flexibility of document, link and user models, independence from centralized resources, intelligent software agent operating on the server or the browser, depending on user's willingness or server capabilities, openness to further enhancements, adherence to W3C Recommendations and trends, like Semantic Web.

We are considering several future developments, like supporting a set of filtering algorithms, more sophisticated user profile, automatic assignment of topics to documents, full support of new W3C Recommendations.

References

1. http://wwwis.win.tue.nl/ah/
2. http://ah2000.itc.it/
3. Signore O.: Issues on Hypertext Design, DEXA'95 - Database and Expert Systems Application, Proceedings of the International Conference in London, United Kingdom 4-8 September 1995, Lecture Notes in Computer Science, N. 978, Springer Verlag, ISBN 3-540-60303-4, pp. 283-292
4. Signore O.: Modelling Links in Hypertext/Hypermedia, in Multimedia Computing and Museums, Selected papers from the Third International Conference on Hypermedia and Interactivity in Museums (ICHIM'95 - MCN'95), October 9-13, San Diego, California (USA), ISBN 1-88-5626-11-8, pp. 198-216
5. Signore O.: Exploiting Navigation Capabilities in Hypertext/Hypermedia, Proceedings of HICSS '96, Maui Hawaii, 3-6 January 1996
6. Brusilovsky P.: Adaptive Hypermedia, User Modeling and User-Adapted Interaction 11: 87-110, 2001, on-line at:http://umuai.informatik.uni-essen.de/brusilovsky-umuai-2001.pdf
7. http://www.semanticweb.org/
8. Berners-Lee T.: Weaving the Web: The Original Design and Ultimate Destiny of the World Wide Web by Its Inventor, Harper San Francisco (1999), ISBN 0-06-251587-X
9. Lassila O., Swick R.: Resource Description Framework (RDF) Model and Syntax Specification, W3C Recommendation 22 February 1999, http://www.w3.org/TR/REC-rdf-syntax
10. Signore O., Bartoli R., Fresta G., Loffredo M.: Implementing the Cognitive Layer of a Hypermedia, Museum Interactive Multimedia 1997: Cultural Heritage Systems Design and Interfaces – Selected papers from ICHIM 97 the Fourth International Conference on Hypermedia and InterActivity in Museums, Paris, France, 3-5 September, 1997, (Edited by David Bearman and Jennifer Trant) Archives & Museum Informatics (1997), p. 15-22, ISBN 1-885626-14-2
11. XML Linking Language (XLink), W3C Working Draft 21 February 2000 http://www.w3.org/TR/xlink/
12. http://www.w3.org/TR/

Adaptive Learning Environment for Teaching and Learning in WINDS

Marcus Specht, Milos Kravcik, Roland Klemke, Leonid Pesin, and Rüdiger Hüttenhain

Fraunhofer Institute for Applied Information Technology FIT
53754 Sankt Augustin, Germany
{specht, kravcik, klemke, pesin, huettenhain}@fit.fraunhofer.de

Abstract. This paper introduces one approach to e-Learning describing the Adaptive Learning Environment (ALE). The system provides a new methodological approach to design education on the web. ALE will be used to build a large knowledge base supporting Architecture and Civil Engineering Design Courses and to experiment a comprehensive Virtual University of Architecture and Engineering Design in the project WINDS. Here we outline the system architecture and present its learning environment. The system combines classical structuring of learning materials based on reusable learning objects with an alternative structure - the course index.

1 Introduction

Web-based Intelligent Design and Tutoring System (WINDS) [1] is an ongoing European project[1] with the objective to implement a learning environment integrating an intelligent tutoring system, a computer instruction management system and a set of cooperative tools. We have developed the current version of the system and our project partners prepare on-line courses that should be used from autumn 2002 at 21 universities.

ALE produces individualized courseware for the students depending on their current state of knowledge, their preferences and learning styles. The author specifies the metadata according to which various adaptation methods can be applied. In this way, the system can adapt the sequence of learning objects according to the chosen learning strategy. As a difference to earlier adaptive learning management systems ALE also integrates the possibilities of using user modeling methods and data mining for building expertise networks and supporting human resources management and knowledge management for organizations. High quality expert and co-learner finding algorithms can build on detailed user and learner models from ALE.

This paper describes the system architecture, presents the adaptive learning environment, and outlines future perspectives.

---

[1] Web based intelligent design system (WINDS) is EU funded project in the 5th framework of the IST programme # IST-1999-10253.

2 Learning Objects and Roles

In ALE authors can create reusable and sharable learning objects and specify for them metadata and relationships according to standard specifications like LOM [2] and DCMI [3]. Learning objects are built of content blocks. Every content block has a pedagogical role what gives additional possibilities for reusing and even recompiling dynamic learning elements from content blocks of different pages. By taking into account the pedagogical role of each content block also pedagogical patterns for learning elements can be identified.

Additionally all learning objects in a course unit are linked dynamically by the underlying index defined by the course authors. The index reflects a common understanding of the domain and the subject matter. The index terms are described by a term name, a description, synonyms, and relations to other terms. A learning object can be viewed with highlighted index terms. This allows giving the learner different approaches for working through the learning materials.

A user of the WINDS system can have one or more of the following roles assigned: *student*, *author* (teacher), *tutor*, and *administrator*. Each role has access to one special environment [4,5]. Additionally each user has a workspace to store and exchange documents with colleagues. Synchronous and asynchronous collaboration facilities are available too.

3 Adaptive Learning Environment

The WINDS learning environment is designed to support various learning strategies. Paragraphs contain materials for expository (explanatory) education. Exploratory (discovery) learning is encouraged not only by hyperlinks but also by index terms and their interconnection with learning objects and external documents. Collaboration facilities promotion of constructivist learning approaches.

The presented content can be adapted to the current knowledge level of the student on the base of the *User Model* and the structure of learning objects. The user model contains for each user all his or her educational events, called *user episodes*. These episodes include events of different types:
- all the user's actions with the learning objects
- all evaluations of completed tests made by the system
- teacher's reviews of homework submitted by the student
- self assessment and self estimation of learners

Based on all these data the system can infer conclusions about the user's knowledge and goals. These are stored in the user model as well. Thus the user model always reflects the current state of the user's progress. The information is available both for the teacher to control the student's study process and for the system to adapt the course presentation and navigation for the student. The learning environment in WINDS consists of the following parts.

3.1 Learning Object Display

The main part of the screen is occupied by the content of the current learning object. Its complete path in the course tree is displayed together with navigation buttons to support orientation and navigation in the course. A learning element can be displayed with or without emphasized index terms hyper-linked with their explanations. Content blocks in learning elements may be represented by texts, images, hyperlinks, multimedia, or special formats (e.g. Word, PDF, PPT). Some of these content blocks can be displayed as icons activating additional window possibly with a note or more detailed information.

3.2 Annotated Course Structure

In another frame of the WINDS learning environment the course structure overview is displayed. It supports student's orientation in the course and helps to choose suitable learning objects for the next study providing annotations for the learning objects.

The states of the learning objects in WINDS can be considered from several points of view or in several dimensions. The system distinguishes three of them: *interaction history*, *tested knowledge*, and *user's readiness*. Additionally some other characteristics can be defined depending on the followed objectives, e.g. current task or context. Interaction history and tested knowledge can be expressed by quantitative information defining the extent of the seen learning object or the tested knowledge, user's readiness is nominal information and depends on the prerequisites specified by the author and on the interaction history of the user.

To represent various states or dimensions of an information space various visual emphasis techniques can be used. Some studies (e. g. [6]) of visual perception recommend the following visual attributes for different kind of information:
- Nominal information: texture, color (hue), position
- Quantitative information: length, position

Currently the system uses icon annotations. Other applicable annotation techniques include hiding and presentation without hyperlinks. These can be also student's options.

3.3 Course Index

With each learning object corresponding index terms are displayed that provide a means to interrelate heterogeneous course contents and to find individualised paths through the learning materials. The WINDS course index component maintains the index terms together with their respective descriptions, synonyms, relations between terms, their occurrences in the course materials as well as in external documents. The student can access all this information about a specific term by choosing it in the *Index* frame. The index component can retrieve and highlight occurrences of index terms within the course materials as well as within registered external documents (such as web sites).

3.4 External Documents

External documents relevant to the course domain explain in more detail some specific issues or provide up-to-date information like specialized portals do. Such external documents serve also as resources for homework and projects. These materials can go into more details than the course or give alternative views of the domain. In the *Documents* frame the student can choose an external document related to the current learning object and view this document either with or without emphasized index terms.

3.5 Feedback and Recommendation Area

In the feedback and recommendation area the students can see their progress. Additionally several recommendation strategies will be implemented which guide learners in the course (prerequisite warnings, next step recommendations), learning style support (learning material preferences, learning activity selections) and cooperation initialisation (co-learner finding, expert finding and tutor support).

4 Conclusions and Further Research

This paper presented the current state of the ALE system, especially its learning environment providing adaptive courseware. The learning objects can be delivered in a variety of ways. The indexing system and the connection of the learning objects allows for personalized coaching of students. We plan to extend the coaching functionality by pedagogical agents. Different tutorial and navigation support strategies will be implemented that allow the teacher to adjust the adaptive method to the concrete target group and pedagogical framework. Open exploration of contents will be supported on a level of index terms that where already explored by a learner. In more strictly focused training settings the systems will keep the student close to the default path of a curriculum based on the teacher's specifications.

References

1. WINDS project: http://www.winds-university.org
2. LTSC IEEE Draft Standard for Learning Object Metadata, IEEE P1484.12/ D6.1 (2001)
3. Dublin Core Metadata Initiative (DCMI), http://dublincore.org/documents, DCMI
4. Specht, M., Kravcik, M., Pesin, L., Klemke, R.: Integrated Authoring Environment for Web Based Courses in WINDS. Proceedings of ICL2001, Villach, Austria (2001)
5. Specht, M., Kravcik, M., Pesin, L., Klemke, R.: Authoring Adaptive Educational Hypermedia in WINDS. Proceedings of ABIS2001, Dortmund, Germany (2001)
6. Bertin, J.: Semiologie Graphique. Paris: Editions de l'Ecole des Hautes Etudes en Sciences (1967/1999)

Adaptation through Interaction Modelling in Educational Hypermedia

Elio Toppano

Dipartimento di Matematica e Informatica
Università di Udine, Via delle Scienze 206, Loc. Rizzi, 33100 Udine, Italia

Abstract. The poster describes MMforTED, an adaptive educational hypermedia system supporting the acquisition of several conceptualisations that can be used for reasoning about technical artefacts from different perspectives. Adaptation is performed by a next button that leads the learner to the best page to be read next (direct guidance). The decision which page is best is taken by analysing the properties of the course of interaction of the student up to a given time and selecting the next page on the base of the affordances of potential interaction it offers.

1 Introduction

Adaptive hypermedia are becoming increasingly popular as web-based educational systems [1,2,3]. This poster describes a cognitive tool called MMforTED - an acronym for MultiModelling for Technical Education - that has been developed to foster the acquisition of several conceptualisations that can be used to represent and inquiry about technical artefacts from different perspectives. The system enables users to browse through a network of HTML pages illustrating descriptions of several devices together with prototypical questions, ontologies and exercises supporting the analysis and comprehension of a device structure and functioning. MMforTED has been designed to be usable for diverse learning goals and thematic threads, so we do not impose a single overarching perspective or global narrative structure to the material. As shown by the experimental activity performed with students of various ages and levels of proficiency, the lack of guidance produces disorientation and cognitive overload especially in novice learners. To tackle this problem we have introduced adaptivity through *direct guidance* [4]. Direct guidance implies that the system informs the student which of the links on the current page will drive him or her to the 'best' page in the hyper space. The best page is decided on the basis of some characteristics of the user and on the base of the user's behaviour as it will be explained in the following sections.

2 Adaptation through Interaction Modelling

The approach we followed to implement direct guidance is inspired to a recent proposal made by Akhras and Self [5]: instead of modelling what the student knows we focus on the course of interaction and on the process of learning. More specifically, we assume that a student using the MMforTED system passes through a series of situations <(S1, t1); (S2, t2); ...,(Sn,tn) >, specifying a *course of interaction*, via a sequence of events/actions (e.g. by activating hyperlinks). There are six different types of situations S depending on the educational role of the pages that constitute the hyperspace: situations showing a model of an artefact, representing assumptions lying behind a model, providing the ontology used to build a model, presenting exercises, questions, or relations between two models of the same artefacts. Each situation type has a content represented by the specific instructional material it contains and affords to a learner a specific pattern of interaction. The same situation type can be visited by the student several times during a course of interaction. What must be stressed is that the content of a situation is seen more as a resource that can be utilised, accessed, etc. rather than a target knowledge that must be acquired.

When the student has reached situation (Sn,tn) there are several events (e1, e2, .. , ek) that could possibly follow. Each event choice extends the course of interaction in a specific way. The aim of the adaptation mechanism is to select and suggest the event that will optimise the learning opportunity for the student. There are basically two ways for doing that. The first way is to select a situation (Sn+1, t+1) that affords to the learner a *pattern of interaction* with desired properties. For example, the mechanism can try to reduce the cognitive overload of a novice student by selecting 'simple' instructional material according to some criterion as discussed in the next section. The second way is to select a situation that affords to the learner a course of interaction <(S1, t1); .. ;(Sn+1,t+1)> that exhibits particular *regularities* which are considered conducive to learning. In both cases, the adaptation mechanism tries to provide profitable spaces of interaction to the learner based on some model of the affordances of potential situations. This is a different focus to the traditional student model that would be evaluating what a student has learned up to a given point.

2.1 Selecting Simple Models

A model simplification can be made by changing its conceptual content, the symbolic representation or both these components. We use conceptual schemes to specify the content of a model that is the *types* of entities, relations and properties (i.e. attributes with associated domains of values) that have been used to build the model. Plex structures are, instead, employed to externalise models [6]. A plex structure is a kind of diagrammatic representation that is formed by interconnecting elements with N attaching points called 'napes' by means of tie points. The conceptual schema associated to a model gives the elements of the plex structure a semantic content.

In order to assess the 'simplicity' of a model we have introduced some metrics that can be used to characterise internal features of a description. Internal features are those that can be measured by examining a system description (the plex structure) on its own separate from its environment. The metrics for internal features are [7]:
- *Size*: the number of occurrences of napes and tie points used to represent the model by a plex structure;
- *Density of connectivity*: the ratio of the total occurrences of tie points to the total number of napes. Density of connectivity increases as we add more connections among napes;

- *Ontological variety*: the total number of concept classes included in the conceptual schema associated to a model;
- *Concept density*: for a concept type Ci, it is the ratio of the number of total instances of Ci to the total number of instances of all concepts used in the model.

Lower counts of these metrics imply 'simpler'. Metrics are used to adapt the amount of information presented by a model to the learner in order to try to prevent overloading and possibilities of distraction.

2.2 Enforcing Regularities of the Courses of Interaction

Three properties of the courses of interaction are currently monitored to perform direct guidance namely cumulativeness, constructiveness and self-regulatedness. See [5] for a formal definition of these properties. We are interested in applying these properties to conceptualisations. *Cumulativeness* refers to the property that a course of interaction exhibits when a conceptualisation (i.e. a conceptual schema) experienced by the learner in a situation is in some way revisited in a later situation of the course of interaction. *Constructiveness* refers to the property that a course of interaction exhibits when a conceptualisation experienced by the learner in one situation is in some way related to a new conceptualisation that the learner accesses in a later situation. *Self-regulatedness* refers to the property that a course of interaction exhibits when a learner's action performed in a situation is in some way evaluated by the learner in another situation of the course of interaction and this evaluation is taken into consideration to guide the next learner's actions or change the effects (e.g. interpretation, understanding) of previous actions.

2.3 The Decision Making Approach

The above properties and metrics can be combined in various ways. For example, it is possible to enforce cumulativeness with respect to a conceptualisation in order to keep the course of interaction on the same conceptual basis of the models visited up to a certain time and further minimise the amount of information to be presented to the learner by decreasing the size or the density of connectivity of the proposed model with respect to the currently focused one. Suppose, for example, that the learner is visiting a page representing an artifact X from a structural perspective. The system may suggest to visit a linked page describing another artifact Y that is represented under the same perspective - and thus using the same conceptual schema - but using a lower number of instances of the concepts types included in the schema. In this way, the student can gain *knowledge transferability* by seeing multiple manifestations of the same conceptualisation. Alternatively, it is possible to enforce constructiveness. The system may suggest, for example, to visit a page representing the same artifact X under a different perspective (e.g. a behavioral model) together with a page illustrating codesignation relations between the two models. Codesignation relations allow to integrate the two perspectives - the structural and the behavioral one - by showing which elements of a model are connected to which elements of the other model. In this way the student can gain *cognitive flexibility* by being exposed to multiple interpretations (perspectives) of the same device. These decisions are taken according to a set of *rules* that consider the learner's profile (e.g. show simplified material to novice learners and more complex details to advanced learners) and the properties and characteristics of the past student's interaction with the MMforTED system as they are inferred from the server access log.

Given a set of requirements (e.g. enforce cumulativeness, minimise the amount of information) the decision mechanism is able to analyse - by accessing metaknowledge about educational material - the characteristics of the models accessible from the current position in the information space and to order the available alternatives on the base of their appropriateness with respect to the desired properties. Informally, requirements induce a preference ordering on possible choices and this, in turn, determines the next page to be suggested to the learner. The decision making mechanism, which is a modification of the algorithm used in the TAMS system [8], embodies a hill climbing search process in the space of available alternative choices.

3 Conclusions

The instructional system we present in the poster performs direct guidance by selecting material that affords to the learner a pattern of interaction or a course of interaction with desired properties. This approach is in line with constructivistic learning. Adaptation benefits from hierarchical organisation of domain conceptual knowledge that enables to select material by performing smooth transitions from coarse (abstract) material to fine grained detailed material and vice versa. The adaptive version of MMforTED is still at its prototypical stage and no formal user assessment have yet been carried out.

References

1. Murray, T.: MetaLinks: Authoring and Affordances for Conceptual and Narrative Flow in Adaptive Hyperbooks. JAIED, Vol. 13, (2002) to appear
2. De Bra, P., Calvi, L.: AHA: a Generic Adaptive Hypermedia System. In: Proc. of the 2nd Workshop on Adaptive Hypertext and Hypermedia, Hypertext '98, Pittsburgh (1998), http://www.contrib.andrew.cmu.edu/~plb/HT98_workshop/DeBra.html
3. Brusilovsky, P.: Adaptive and Intelligent Technologies for Web-based Education. In: Rollingen, C. and Peylo, C. (eds.) Kunstliche Intelligens, Special Issue on Intelligent Systems and Teleteaching, Vol. 4, (1999) 19-25
4. De Bra, P.: Design Issues in Adaptive Web-Site Development. In: Proc. of the 2nd Workshop on Adaptive Systems and User Modeling on the WWW (1999), http://wwwis.win.tue.nl/asum99/debra/debra.html
5. Akhras, F.N., Self, J.A.: System Intelligence in Constructivistic Learning. JAIED, Vol. 11, (2000), 344-376
6. Feder,J.: Plex Languages. Inform. Sci., Vol. 3, (1971), 225-241
7. Toppano, E.: Using Graph Transformations to Support Multilevel Reasoning in Engineering Design. Machine Graphics & Vision, Vol. 8 (3), (1999), 395-425
8. Toppano, E.: Rational Model Selection in Large Engineering Knowledge Bases. Applied Artificial Intelligence, Vol. 10 (3), (1996), 191-224

The Hybrid Model for Adaptive Educational Hypermedia

Mohamed Ramzy Zakaria[1], Adam Moore[2], Helen Ashman[1], Craig Stewart[3], and Tim Brailsford[1]

[1] School of Information Technology and Computer Science
University of Nottingham, Nottingham, NG8 1BB, UK
{mrz,helen.ashman,tim.brailsford}@nottingham.ac.uk
[2] School of Civil Engineering
University of Nottingham, Nottingham, NG8 1BB, UK
adam.moore@nottingham.ac.uk
[3] School of Life and Environmental Sciences
University of Nottingham, Nottingham, NG8 1BB, UK
craig.stewart@nottingham.ac.uk

Abstract. Web-based distance learning is becoming increasingly prevalent as the Internet permeates every aspect of our culture, and many educational content management systems are now in use on the web. However, learners' experiences of these systems are almost invariably static, with information being delivered regardless of their background or knowledge. Due to variation between learners', it is suggested that these web-based distance-learning systems would benefit from the capability of adapting their content to meet individual needs. To effectively implement this adaptation of educational material, we require a user model that supplies the system with information about the learners using the system, such as their backgrounds, knowledge, interests and learning styles. This paper focuses on presenting a user model that combines the advantages of two techniques (overlay and stereotyping) in a way that provides the system with the ability to deliver information that is fully informed by the requirements of individual users.

1 Introduction

The brave new era of the information age has ramifications for all disciplines, at the most fundamental of levels. From education, to commerce and music, the Internet impinges on every field where data and knowledge are currency. Arising out of this worldwide network of communications comes the globalisation of information - in which hypermedia tools are at the forefront enabling direct user access to information [1]. As the amount of information on the web continues its exponential increase, the number of users with different goals and interests also expands. It therefore becomes increasingly important that the information available be adapted to suit each user's individual knowledge and aspirations.

For example, in traditional web-based educational hypermedia systems, the contents are generally static, in so far as once written, their contents cannot be changed without external intervention. This provides a uniform learning experience to all learners, regardless of their needs and requirements. One example of such a system is WebCT [2]. This is a hypermedia educational system developed in 1995 at the University of British Columbia. It is an environment for authoring and delivering educational materials over the web. WebCT presents a static and inflexible pedagogic experience, without any kind of adaptation at the user level. Hence a web application, such as those delivered via WebCT, which are designed with a particular class of users in mind, may not suit those even marginally different from the original target audience [3].

In response to this clear need, adaptive hypermedia systems have been created such as AHA [4] and CHEOPS[5]. They build a model of the goals, interests, preference and knowledge of their users; so that they may present them with the information they need in a timely and appropriate manner [1].

This paper describes a hybrid user model, which is cooperative [6], (i.e. it collaborates with users in gathering information, as they are required to supply the system with some personal information, e.g. their occupation and preferences). This model also involves users in the user modelling process, as the contents of topics or courses are adapted according to their knowledge level about the topic they study. The hybrid model described below has the benefit that it should suit any adaptive educational hypermedia system, and we suggest that it is likely to provide a powerful addition to any technology-based learning programme.

2 The Hybrid Model

2.1 Architecture

The hybrid model combines the use of two major techniques that are prevalent within the user modelling community. The first of these is the *overlay model,* perhaps currently the most widely used technique of user modelling. This is used to measure the knowledge level of users in any given topic or domain. A user's knowledge according to this model is considered to be an overlay of the total knowledge representing that domain. This knowledge level is represented in the form of "Concept-Value" pairs [7,8].

The second model is the stereotype; this technique assumes that knowledge is customised for specific groups, with each user being assigned to one and only one group at any given time. Thus, users who share the same background or knowledge should be assigned to the same group. Users cannot change from one group (or class) to another until they trigger the specific conditions of the new group [9,10].

Aspects of each of these models are utilised by the hybrid model as follows:

1. *Overlay technique*: the overlay measures the knowledge level of each learner within certain subject domains. This knowledge level might represent the score achieved in the system assessment at the end of each lesson, although any other pa-

rameters the system authors may choose may also be used. For example, the score achieved in self-assessment quizzes is a widely used and well-accepted metric of the comprehension of information.
2. *Level stereotype*: level stereotypes mainly depend on the knowledge level of users. For example, they may simply be defined as Beginner, Intermediate and Advanced, but any classes may be used as appropriate to each system. According to the users knowledge level they will be assigned to a single class of the level stereotype within any given domain they of study. For example, a user studying biomechanics might be assigned simultaneously to the novice class in biology and to the advanced class in mathematics. Classes in the level stereotype are concerned with providing assistance that is appropriate, and adapting the contents of the lesson to suit the learner. Each class may define an article or set of articles, links to external documents, or to lessons in other courses. For example, if a user belongs to one of the advanced classes he may be provided with advanced articles or links to help the user to find more about the topic or domain he studies. Level stereotypes not only adapt the contents to suite a user's level, but they also facilitate learning by identifying domain weaknesses in the topic under study.
3. *Category stereotype*: the hybrid model has been designed for systems that simultaneously run multiple courses for different levels of users. For example, the system may be running courses for first year undergraduate as well as postgraduate users.

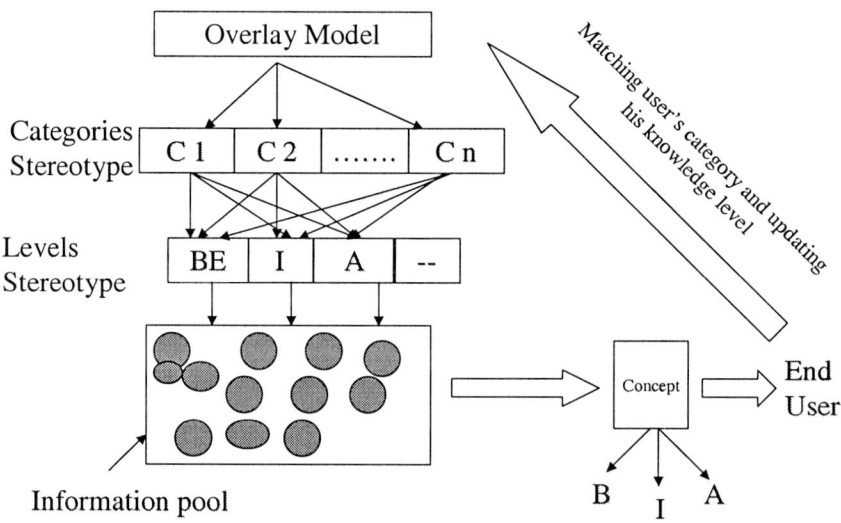

Fig. 1. The components of the hybrid model. An overlay model combines with a category and level stereotype to retrieve appropriate content from the information pool to convey concepts to the user. The user interacts with the system to inform and update the user model. BE – Beginner, B – Basic, I – Intermediate, A – Advanced

For this reason the users need to be categorised, as the knowledge level of undergraduate users in a certain stereotype level of a certain domain may not be the same as that of postgraduate users in the same stereotype level of the same domain. For example, consider two users, one of them a first year undergraduate and the second one a studying for a higher degree. Both of these students are classified in the intermediate level stereotype for the biology domain. Both of them are in the same level stereotype, but the intermediate level of postgraduates will be much more advanced than that of first year undergraduates. The categories stereotype helps the system to distinguish between different users in the same level stereotype, and to provide each of them the appropriate adaptation and help.

There is one other important aspect of this hybrid model - the information pool. This is categorised by the domain model, and consists of a pool of articles, links, and other items that encapsulate the resources of an adaptive system. The information pool is likely to differ in both form and content from one system to another.

The overlay technique, level stereotype and category stereotype combine to pick from the information pool the most convenient articles and links that suit each user's level, knowledge and background. Thus, according to a user's knowledge level and category, the most appropriate materials will be chosen from the information pool. Figure 1 shows the hybrid model's components, comprising of two stereotypes and one overlay, to provide the maximum flexibility and to have the capability to serve a wide range of users.

2.2 Mechanism

When a user logs on to the system for the first time, he/she will be given an initial knowledge level value according to an estimate of prior knowledge about the subject under study. That recommends the user to a certain level stereotype, and the category is determined according to any parameters that the system authors may choose such as user's occupation. Each time a user passes from one lesson to another the knowledge level for that user is updated according to the score in the system assessment (as well as other parameters the system's authors may choose). According to the user's new knowledge level, the class assigned according to the level stereotype might be changed or might be the same (i.e. if the user still has the same knowledge level). The adaptation of the contents and the supporting articles are available according to the class of the user in the level stereotype as well as the category. The steps involved in adaptation are illustrated in Fig. 2.

3 Implementation of the Hybrid Model in a Hypermedia Learning Environment

The hybrid model is currently being integrated into an adaptive educational hypermedia system called WHURLE (Web-based Hierarchal Universal Reactive Learning

Environment), [11,12,13] an XML-based integrated learning environment. In WHURLE the content consists of atomic chunks, each of which consists of the smallest conceptually self-contained unit of information that the author can envisage. The domain of WHURLE content is contained within the melange, which consists of all

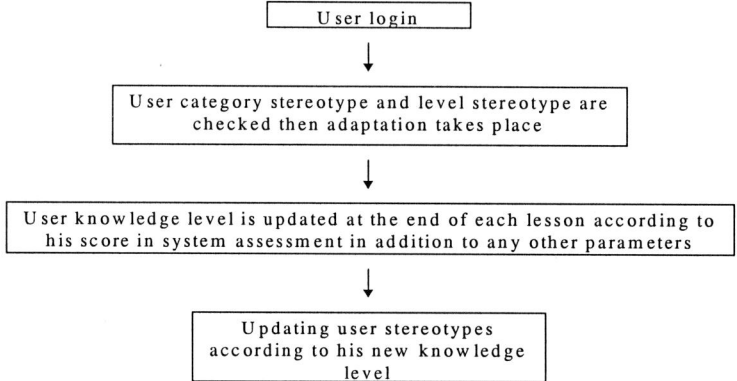

Fig. 2. The hybrid model mechanism to adapt materials to users. Once the user logs in, the system either adapts its material according to the existing user model, or creates a new one. At the end of each lesson, the user model is updated.

the available chunks in any single installation. In WHURLE conditional transclusion [14] is used to construct virtual documents, which contain one or more of these chunks. The hybrid model is integrated into WHURLE as the filter for the lesson plan. This filter generates an adapted virtual document dependant upon both the adaptation rules within the lesson plan and user profile. WHURLE lesson plans represent the information pool of the hybrid model [11, 12, 13].

4 Conclusion

The hybrid model is a user model that gathers together the most commonly used techniques of user-modelling for adaptive hypertext. This utilises the advantages of each of these techniques in a way to provide a full understanding for the user's needs and requirements on several different levels. Using this technique we have implemented adaptation within WHURLE to allow students to see pages of information containing one or more chunks in a manner relevant to their skills, knowledge and learning styles, following rules set by the author of the lesson that they are viewing. Using this model we hope that the WHURLE system will provide a strong pedagogic framework for a variety of web-based learning scenarios.

Acknowledgements

We wish to thank Peter Murray-Rust, Peter Davies, and Ban Seng Choo for many useful discussions, and colleagues in the WTG, VSB and IBiS for their support and encouragement. Craig Stewart is a research associate funded by the Hong Kong University Grants Committee.

References

1. Brusilovsky, P. (1996). *"Methods and techniques of adaptive hypermedia"*. User modeling and user-adapted interaction, 6(2-3), pp. 87-129.
2. Beshears, Fred. "WebCT overview". http://socrates.berkeley.edu:7521/articles/webct/WebCT-Presentation
3. Eklund,J; Brusilovsky,P; Schwarz,E.(1997). *"Adaptive Textbooks on the World WideWeb"*, Proceedings of AUSWEB97, the third Australian conference on the world wide web, Queensland, Australia, July 5-9, 1997, Southern Cross University press, pp. 186-192 .http://ausweb.scu.edu.au/proceedings/eklund/paper.html.
4. De Bra,P;Calvi,L.(1998).*"AHA Adaptive Hypermedia Architecture"*.NRHM journal, V.4, pp 115 - 139
5. Ferrandino,S; Negro,A;Scarano,V.(1997).*"CHEOPS :Adaptive Hypermedia on the World Wide Web"*. Proceedings of the European Workshop on Interactive Distributed Multimedia Systems and Telecommunicazion Services (IDMS '97).
6. Kay, J. 1995,*"The UM toolkit for cooperative user models"*. User Models and User Adapted Interaction 4(3), 149-196.
7. Valley,K. (1997). *"Learning Styles and Courseware Design"*. Association of Learning Technology Journal, 5(2), p42-51
8. Carr,B; Goldstein, I. (1977). *"Overlays, a theory of modelling for computer aided instruction"*. A technical report. AI memo 406, MIT, Cambridge, MA.
9. Rich, E. (1983). *"Users are individuals: individualizing user models"*, Journal of man-machine studies vol.18, 199-214.
10. Benaki,E; Karkalestsis,V; Spyropoulos,C. (1997). *"User modelling in WWW: the UMIE prototype"*. Proceedings of sixth international conference on user modelling, Chia Laguna, Sardinia, 2-5 June1997 http://www.contrib.andrew.cmu.edu/~plb/UM97_workshop/Benaki/Benaki.html
11. Brailsford, TJ ; Moore, A ; Stewart, CD ; Zakaria, MR ; Choo, BS ; Davies, PMC.(2001). *"Towards a framework for effective web-based distributed learning"*. WWW10 proceedings, HongKong.
12. Moore,A; Brailsford,T.J, Stewart, C.D. (2001). *"Personally tailored teaching in WHURLE using conditional transclusion"*. The twelfth ACM conference on hypertext and hypermedia. August 14-13, 2001, Denmark.
13. Brailsford,T; Stewart,C; Zakaria,M; Moore,A.(2002)."Autonavigation, Links and Narrative in an Adaptive Web-Based Integrated Learning Environment". Proceedings of www2002, Hawaii, USA.
14. Nelson, T.H. (1995). "The Heart of Connection: hypermedia unified by transclusion". Communications of the ACM.

Navigation Modelling in Adaptive Hypermedia*

Peter Dolog and Mária Bieliková

Department of Computer Science and Engineering
Slovak University of Technology
Ilkovičova 3, 812 19 Bratislava, Slovakia,
{dolog, bielikova}@dcs.elf.stuba.sk,
http://www.dcs.elf.stuba.sk/\char126{dologp,bielik}

Abstract. In this paper we reflect the need for modelling in a systematic production of adaptive hypermedia applications. Proposed approach is based on the Unified Modelling Language (UML). State diagrams are used to model possible paths through hypertext. The user model expressed by a class diagram determines structural and behavioural features, which are used for specification of adaptations in states and transitions contained in state diagrams.

1 Introduction

One of the main goals of any adaptive hypermedia application is to increase user efficiency measured either in the time spent searching for information or the amount of information absorbed by the user. Another important issue is to aid developers of such systems which are going to be more and more complex. The increased complexity of hypermedia applications raises the need to employ modelling in hypermedia development process.

The modelling of a hypermedia is extensively studied only in past two decades. Models help us understand developed system by simplifying some of details. Adaptation of navigation, together with a user model, should be addressed in hypermedia application modelling. The goal of this paper is to present an approach to modelling adaptive navigation. The Unified Modelling Language, namely state diagrams together with sequence and class diagrams are employed for these purposes.

2 Process of Adaptive Navigation Modelling

A navigation model represents possible paths through information chunks and their contextual grouping. To develop such navigation model, an analytical model of information structure and user roles should exist.

Basic modelling technique for navigation modelling in our approach is a state diagram, which enables to model dynamic character of navigation. We proposed

---

* This work was partially supported by Slovak Science Grant Agency, grant No. G1/7611/20.

five basic steps of navigation modelling process: identifying basic interaction scheme, identifying states, identifying transitions, identifying events, and mapping the user model elements to the state diagram. These steps can be performed in parallel and in iterations. Moreover, proposed approach can be used at several levels of abstraction (of a hypermedia system).

Adaptive navigation strongly depends on a user modelling. The user model incorporates various characteristics of users. Hypermedia application usage data are also represented in the user model. In our approach a user is modelled by a class diagram similarly to [12]. The user model is derived from user roles. Structure of the user model follows the well known Adaptive Hypermedia Application Model (AHAM) [6]. The user model should at least contain a class, which represents the level of user knowledge. Other classes (user preferences, goals, interests, knowledge, background, hyperspace experience, etc.) can be incorporated when it is needed [9]. The user model contains operations for reading the current state of user characteristics and for updating user characteristics. Environment or context data [2] are carried during mapping to navigation model likewise data in the user model.

I. Identifying basic interaction scheme. The first step in navigation modelling is basic interaction scheme modelling. This is intended to identify a sequence of interactions between main system roles. The UML sequence diagram is used for these purposes.

II. Identifying states. States in a navigation model fulfil the role of information chunks [8]. They can be grouped into superstates. The states are created from an information model. There are two possibilities of mapping: (1) a superstate mapped to a class with substates mapped to class attributes, and (2) a superstate mapped to a class instance with substates mapped to class instance attributes.

Parallel substates are mapped to attributes of a class or its instances, which are presented simultaneously. Attributes, which do not need to be presented simultaneously are grouped into ordinary substates. The classes, which are aggregates of another class are mapped to parallel or ordinary substates of that class' state. In addition, these substates are determined by the cardinality of the aggregation relationship. Specialised classes are mapped to ordinary substates. Special information chunks derived from several attributes and/or classes or special states needed for purposes of navigation can also be considered. States can be extended with a history. The history indicates that a user can start his browsing where he finished when exited system last time.

III. Identifying transitions. A transition represents an active interconnection between information chunks. Association relationships from information model are transformed to transitions. When it is needed, additional transitions can be incorporated into the model. The `fork` and `join` pseudostates, and `SyncState` are intended to model a synchronisation of parallel states. The first two are intended for splitting or joining transitions. The latter is for synchronizing substates of parallel regions.

A condition can be assigned to the transition. A transition can also be conditionally forked; i.e. the transition can end in several states. Transition can also have associated time event for modelling sequential hypermedia timing. A transition can also have associated side effect actions, which together with transition conditions are very important for adaptation modelling.

IV. Identifying events. Events raise transitions in a state machine. Events can be directly mapped to presentation elements, which have associated actions. They are mediators between navigation model and presentation model of actions. Events can be joined to a generalisation/specialisation tree. An event can be mapped to more than one transition.

V. Mapping user model elements to state diagram. The adaptive behaviour is modelled by an introduction of features of user model classes into state diagrams. Accessible attributes of user model classes are mapped to guards conditions. They are tested for specific values, which have to be satisfied when transition is raised. Operations are mapped to actions of transitions. They are used for upgrading the user model state or for specific operations with the user model and/or information chunks. Operations for retrieving current user model state can also be used in guard conditions. Guard conditions of transition specify local rules of adaptation. Global rules of adaptation, can be specified as guards of internal transitions, parts of entry, exit or do actions, and conditions of superstates.

3 Modelling of Techniques for Adaptive Hypermedia

Several efficient techniques for adaptive hypermedia were proposed [3]. We selected some of these techniques for presentation of capabilities of the proposed approach. The examples cover both link-level and content-level adaptation.

Figure 1 depicts part of an adaptive navigation model, which was created according to the approach proposed in this paper. The example figures the model of a lecture on functional programming (FP). This lecture consists of four topics: **Functional Programming, Programming Schemes, Examples of Linear Lists Processing** and **Examples of Non-Linear Lists Processing**. The aim of such lecture is to exercise programming of basic list processing functions in the Common Lisp language. First, some introduction is needed. This is carried out by **Introduction to FP, Computation in FP**, and **Introduction to LISP** fragments. Next, the introduction to Programming schemes (**Programming Schemes** state) is performed. It is represented by **Introduction** substate and simple categories of **Linear Lists Processing** and **Non-Linear Lists Processing**.

Adaptation rules are involved in transition labels or as internal transitions of states. Events handle user interaction or internal system events. Conditions and actions are taken from the user model.

Conditional text is modelled by *Entry* internal transition of a state. It is followed by a condition, which determines whether the fragment is displayed or not. In Fig. 1, conditional text is represented by the **Introduction to LISP**

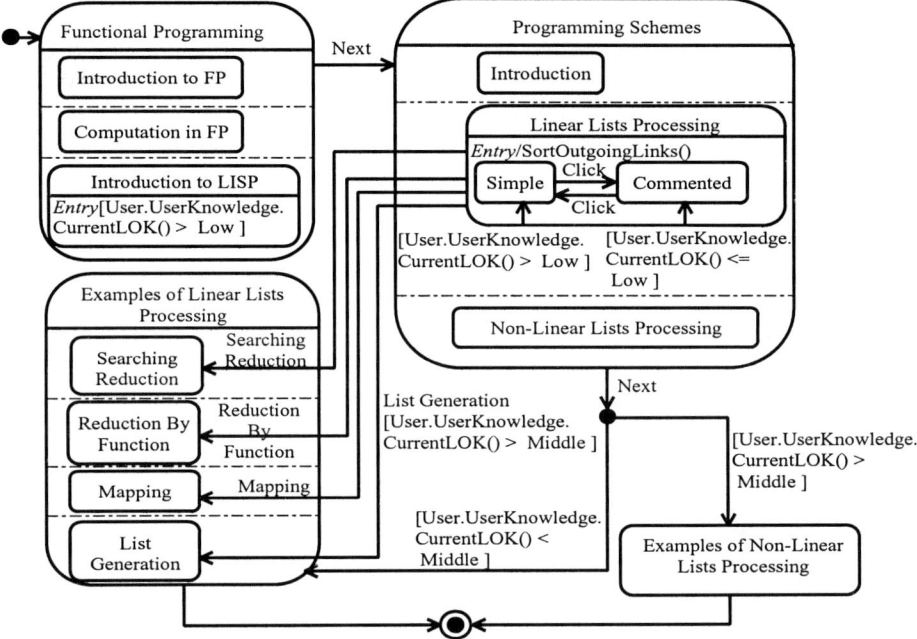

Fig. 1. A part of an adaptive navigation model.

state. There is the condition, which examines the level of current user knowledge. The fragment is displayed only if the level of knowledge is greater than `Low`.

Stretchtext can be modelled by two approaches. The first is to represent stretched and unstretched text as two *different alternative states* with transition between them. The transition has associated `Click` event. The second approach is to model stretchtext with *two parallel states*, where one state is conditionally constrained. It means that the state, which is conditionally constrained is presented only if the condition is satisfied. Condition is mostly based on a history (usage data). In Fig. 1, stretchtext is represented in the `Linear List Processing` state containing `Simple` and `Commented` version of introduction. The text is displayed unstretched if current user level of knowledge is greater than `Low`. Otherwise, `Commented` version is displayed. These two alternatives can be switched by clicking (`Click` event).

Commented text is modelled similarly. The difference between commented text and stretchtext is that stretchtext can be clicked and thus unstretched.

Alternative pages or fragments are modelled by conditional transition split. The decision symbol (junction) represents modelling element for alternation. Another possibility is to employ the diamond symbol. In Fig. 1, there are two alternatives when the next event occurs. If current level of user knowledge is less than `Middle` only the `Examples of Linear Lists Processing` state is displayed.

Otherwise, **Examples of Non-Linear Lists Processing** as more challenging task is provided by adaptive hypermedia application.

Direct guidance can be modelled by assigning the **next** or **back** event to particular transition. Another approach is to use directly state diagram as a guide, which is interpreted and displayed as a map and the current position and allowed links are sufficiently indicated (for example like marking in petri nets).

Hiding of a link is modelled by guard condition of a transition. When the condition is not satisfied, link is not enabled (not displayed). The transition in Fig. 1 labelled by **List Generation** event is an example of such a link. The link is displayed (transition is allowed) only if current user level of knowledge is greater than **Middle**.

Link sorting is an operation. It is obviously performed when a user reached particular fragment, where the links have to be sorted. Such operation can be modelled as the **Entry** action of particular state. Figure 1 depicts **Linear List Processing** state, which represents such fragment. The **SortOutgoingLinks()** action is invoked when the user reached this state.

The state/transition diagram can be used also as a model of *adaptive map*. Special manipulation function can be provided, which interprets meta-model and rules of states, and according to them displays particular part of the model to the user.

4   Related Work and Conclusions

In this paper we described an approach to adaptive hypermedia modelling. Application of a state/transition diagram modelling technique is the first advantage of the proposed approach. A hypermedia application reacts to user actions. Thus, it seems that state-transition diagrams are more natural for modelling navigation than structural techniques such as in OOHDM [14], UHDM [12] or WebML [4] (for a review of others, see for example [7]).

Provided guidelines for user modelling and the integration of a user model and navigation model is another advantage. User modelling is supported by UHDM [12], WebML [4] and W2000 [1] but independently from navigation. According to [10] the adaptation specification can be involved as slice or slice relationship condition. But slices and their relationships do not satisfactorily deal with interactions. The authors do not explicitly discuss relationships between user model and presentation or application model. In [13] the graph formalism is employed for modelling paths. Adaptation is specified as text composition templates with linguistic rules.

HMBS/M [5] and χTrellis [11] are based on behavioural techniques. However, the former only allows to map states to class instances. Both approaches do not emphasize on adaptation and user modelling.

Our approach can be used for modelling known techniques of adaptive navigation and presentation. Our further research is oriented to extension of proposed approach to support implementation modelling.

References

1. Luciano Baresi, Franca Garzotto, and Paolo Paolini. Extending UML for modeling web applications. In *Proc. of 34th Anual Hawaii International Conference on System Sciences (HICSS'34)*, Maui, Hawai, January 2001. IEEE Press.
2. Mária Bieliková. Adaptive presentation of evolving information using XML. In T. Okamoto, R. Hartley, Kinshuk, and J.P. Klus, editors, *Proc. of IEEE International Conference of Advanced Learning Technologies (ICALT'2001)*, pages 193–196, Madison, USA, August 2001. IEEE Press.
3. Peter Brusilovsky. Methods and techniques of adaptive hypermedia. *User Modeling and User-Adapted Interaction*, 6(2-3):87–129, 1996.
4. Stefano Ceri, Piero Fraternali, and Aldo Bongio. Web Modeling Language (WebML): a modeling language for designing web sites. *Computer Networks and ISDN Systems*, 33(1–6):137–157, June 2000.
5. Marcia Regina de Carvalho, Maria Cristina Ferreira de Oliveira, and Paulo Cesar Masiero. HMBS/M - an object oriented method for hypermedia design. In *Proc. of Brazilian Symposium on Multimedia and Hypermedia Systems (SBMIDIA'99)*, pages 43–62, Goiânia, June 1999.
6. Paul De Bra, Geert-Jan Houben, and Hongjing Wu. AHAM: A dexter-based reference model for adaptive hypermedia. In K. Tochtermann, J. Westbomke, U.K. Wiil, and J. Leggett, editors, *Proc. of ACM Conference on Hypertext and Hypermedia*, pages 147–156, Darmstadt, Germany, February 1999.
7. Peter Dolog. Modelling in hypermedia development, August 2001. Technical Report (A Written Part of PhD Examination). Department of Computer Science and Engineering, Slovak University of Technology.
8. Peter Dolog and Mária Bieliková. Modelling browsing semantics in hypertexts using UML. In J. Zendulka, editor, *Proc. of ISM'2001 - Information Systems Modelling*, pages 181–188, Hradec nad Moravicí, Czech Republic, May 2001.
9. Peter Dolog and Mária Bieliková. Hypermedia modelling using UML. In *Proc. of ISM'2002 - Information Systems Modelling*, Rožnov pod Radhoštěm, Czech Republic, April 2002.
10. Flavius Frasincar, Geert Jan Houben, and Richard Vdovjak. A RMM-based methodology for hypermedia presentation design. In A. Caplinskas and J. Eder, editors, *Proc. of ADBIS 2001 - Advances in Databases and Information Systems*, pages 323–337, Vilnius, Lithuania, September 2001. Springer, LNCS 2151.
11. Richard Furuta and P. David Stotts. A formally-defined hypertextual basis for integrating task and information, 1994. Tech. Report TAMU-HRL 94-007.
12. Nora Koch. Software engineering for adaptive hypermedia systems? In Paul De Bra, editor, *Proc. of Third Workshop on Adaptive Hypertext and Hypermedia, 8th International Conference on User Modeling*, July 2001.
13. Daniela Petrelli, Daniele Baggio, and Giovanni Pezzulo. Adaptive hypertext design environments: Putting principles into practise. In *Proc. of International Conference on Adaptive Hypermedia and Adaptive Web-Based Systems (AH'2000)*, pages 202–213, Trento, Italy, August 2000. Springer, LNCS 1892.
14. Daniel Schwabe and Gustavo Rossi. An object-oriented approach to web-based application design. *Theory and Practise of Object Systems (TAPOS), Special Issue on the Internet*, 4(4):207–225, October 1998.

An Adaptive Agent Model for e-Commerce Architecture

Ana B. Gil[1], Francisco García[1], and Zahia Guessoum[2]

[1] University of Salamanca, Dept. Informática y Automática
Facultad de Ciencias, Plaza de la Merced s/n, 37008, Spain
{abg, fgarcia}@usal.es
[2] LIP6, UPMC 4 Place Jussieu, Case 169, 75252 Paris Cedex 05
Zahia.Guessoum@lip6.fr

Abstract. For building easily e-commerce applications, adaptive agent models are useful. These systems therefore should be equipped with the ability to improve their performances themselves, working over the basis of building a model with the goals, preferences and knowledge of each individual user in the environment. This paper presents a new architecture to support sales in Web stores centered on business based on product catalogs. The main goal of this architecture is focused on endowing capability of adaptivity in several ways: contents, navigation and presentation, while analyzing the different ways to develop the adaptivity in e-commerce.

Keywords: Adaptive Agents, E-commerce, Negotiation, User Model.

1 Introduction

The Internet, a network of computer networks that have no central control or organization, is changing the way people think about and do business. The basis of competition and wealth creation in the e-commerce is not only a good use of information, quality, re-engineering process, speed, effective decision-making, empowerment or other countless management techniques popular today. It is also the flexibility and adaptability when working on business. Lots of customers with different expertise and interest access to the online marketplaces, therefore they may need support to explore the catalogs and to select the products for purchase making the best choice.

In recent years, researchers from different fields have pushed toward greater flexibility and intelligent adaptation in their systems. The development of intelligent adaptive agents has been rapidly evolving in many fields of science. Such agents should have the capability of dynamically adapting their parameters; improve their knowledge base or operation methods in order to accomplish a set of tasks. These agents should therefore be equipped with the ability to self-improve their performance, applying the principles and concepts of this kind of learning in real-world contexts.

The purpose of this paper is to present a new architecture to support sales in Web stores centered on business based on e-catalogs. The paper is organized as follows: Section 2 explains the proposed agent-based e-commerce architecture and examines the components of this architecture that are actually implemented and some work plans for be added. Finally, Section 3 closes the paper, presenting our conclusions and some ideas on further work needed.

2 An Adaptive Agent Model for e-Commerce

Online marketplaces are an opportunity and a threat to retail merchants. They offer traditional merchants an additional channel to advertise and sell products to consumers thus potentially increasing sales. They provide the hope and the promise of the global perfect market. A commerce model typically includes activities such as advertising, searching, negotiating, ordering, delivering, paying, using, and servicing [2].

EC is one of the most important applications for Agent Technologies [1]. Agents are not limited to simple information gathering tasks, but they are increasingly becoming involved in the more complex process of actual trading: making purchases and deals. Therefore *Multi-Agent System* (MAS) have to be endowed with adaptive behavior because the environment in this kind of scope is complex and dynamic.

2.1 Adaptive Agent Model

An *adaptive* agent can be defined as an agent with the ability to strengthen rules, which "work" best, and the ability to discover new plausible and possibly "better" rules applying several techniques. To build a generic adaptive agent model and following the tradition of explicating and separating representation of control in meta-level architecture, Guessoum [4] proposes a meta-behavior in the agent architecture. This meta-behavior gives each agent the ability to make appropriate decisions about control or to adapt its behaviors over time to new circumstances. It provides the agent with a self-control mechanism to dynamically schedule its behaviors in accordance with its internal state and its world state.

A standard adaptive agent model has two main components: (i) a behavior and (ii) a meta-behavior. Behavior and meta-behavior are both based on two kinds of elements: actions and conditions, and they have both a decisional system. Actions, conditions and decisional system are the minimal structure for each kind of behavior.

The meta-behavior allows to dynamically updating the set of rules describing the agent behaviors relies on data about the agent itself, its environment, and the decision system used by the behavior and the way to modify it too. So the meta-behavior provides two kinds of adaptation, (i) structural adaptation, adapting the structure of the agent to the evolution of his environment and (ii) behavioral adaptation, adapting the decision-making process of the agent to the evolution of its environment.

The main feature provided is that these two kinds of adaptation can be combined to have at same time agents that adapt their structure and their behavior.

2.2 An Adaptive Approach for e-CoUSAL

Our group is interested in the definition of e-commerce models that allow the entry of the Small and Medium Enterprises (SMEs) into the virtual commerce bandwagon. The model here presented it is based on an architecture for product catalog-based e-commerce architecture, which we call e-CoUSAL [3]. This is an architecture based on two main components: a visual catalog-designer tool and an e-commerce web server.

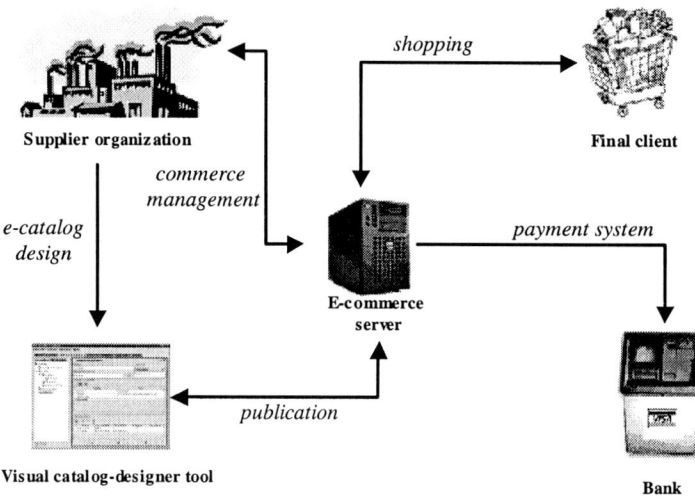

Fig. 1. General structure of the proposed architecture

The first one, the authoring tool is used by the enterprise to generate and manage the e-catalog that presents its business in the e-commerce site. The e-catalog will be published in the e-commerce web server automatically. Then, the e-commerce site needs to adapt itself to show the correct interfaces and the actual information to its end-users through its e-commerce services.

The e-commerce site supports a catalog-based policy; this means that this kind of system diverges quite far from classic on-line information systems. While a hyperspace of information items still constitutes a major part of these systems, browsing this hyperspace is not a major activity, but only a by-product of the major activity (such as shopping for goods). In fact, the better these systems work, the less browsing should be required. Adaptive characteristics are particularly interesting here. In this section we introduce the different components that comprise the proposed architecture and propose the future work to make it adaptive.

2.2.1 The e-CoUSAL e-Commerce Architecture

e-CoUSAL is an e-commerce architecture especially directed to SMEs, where the amount of investment in technology solutions cannot be very large. Therefore two main objectives are considered to develop this model: *flexibility* in the business environment and that the business property should be able to maintain its electronic business in *self-sufficient* way.

As we can see in Fig. 1, the central element is the e-commerce server, which interconnects the different parts involved in the commercial environment. The SME is responsible for the inclusion, across a specialized software tool (as described explained in next section), of the e-catalog that introduces the offers into dynamically generated web pages in the server where a client could find and buy the commodity.

2.2.2 The Visual Catalog-Designer Tool

The practical use of this tool is subordinated to being part and link vehicle of an e-commerce oriented architecture while introducing a general platform that makes possible an e-catalog based business strategy over the Internet. In this way, enterprises can create their own e-catalogs using this tool, and then they can offer their goods for sale through the e-commerce architecture.

A symbiotic relationship arises from this tool and the e-commerce site where the e-catalogs are published. The server imposes a minimum set of criteria for product and catalog. On the other hand, the tool offers the server all the necessary information for the publication of the organization contents. This information exchanged is the logical definition of the products that will be published, their conceptual organization in an e-catalog, and the precise visualization format. For this information interchange the markup language XML is used due to its flexibility for modeling, its document semantic validation capability, and the separation between the data and their visualization format.

This tool has customizing capabilities in its interface. The most important one is its language independence through locate messages defined in external XML files so it can be extended easily to any language.

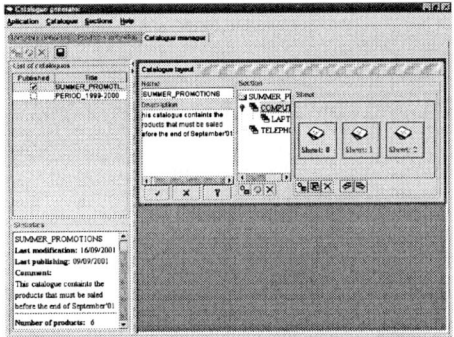 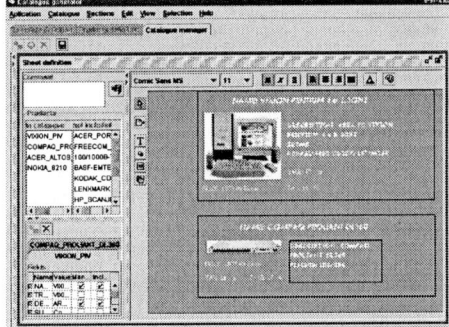

Fig.2. Catalog layout   **Fig.3.** Catalog sheet definition

The working process with this tool is structured around the work-view concept, which reduces the amount of information that is shown to the user of the tool, thus avoiding an unnecessary information overload. The main work-views defined in the presented visual design tool are as follows: the template definition view, the product view, and the catalog manager view.

The *template definition view* consists of *the data template* and *the product template*. The data template could be defined as the mechanism that allows defining the data format of one field for product description then helping the user to define the contents in a more effective way. On the other hand, a product template serves as a model for the later definition of precise products into e-catalogs.

All the functionality for precise products is gathered in the *product work-view*. While templates make our work easier, the products are the conceptual definition of each element that appears in the e-catalog.

The *catalog manager view* presents the grouping of the products in e-catalogs for their later publication and maintenance in the server. When an e-catalog is defined there is a separation between its conceptual definition and its visualization in the server. This characteristic directs the e-catalog composition process as can be seen in Figures 2 and 3.

Another non-functional view is introduced to guarantee the consistency among the other work-views. This is the repository view.

2.2.3 Application of Adaptive Agents to e-CoSUSAL

The adaptive agent model explained in previous section is our ground basis to be implemented in the actual e-CoUSAL architecture prototype, where specialized adaptive agents have to be designed to carry on the activities of the front-end of the Web store. For this purpose, we aim to implement with the multiagent platform DIMA tool, founded on open and modular agent architecture.

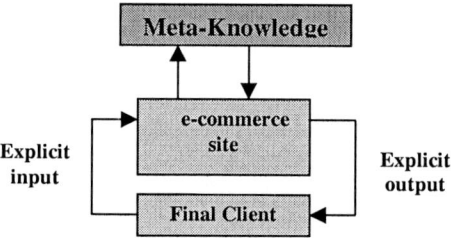

Fig. 4. e-commerce adaptive agent model

The *requirements* for the adaptation system architecture can occur at three levels: presentation, information and navigation. These three faces are combined and connected to conform the proposal architecture.

The user in order to the level of expertise and interest needs an agent that assists him with the navigating the web site (*Navigation*). The main goal is to endow *business-object* to the architecture, therefore *negotiation processes* reinforced with adaptive user interfaces (*Presentation*) for making offers in way of discount stockbrokers (*Information*) to the final client will be another task.

Therefore, it's necessary monitoring the interactions on the client-side taking into account the system customer is working on (kind of medium, downloading time, content attributes) also while agents analyzing web logs, determining similarity between documents and searching for making recommendations and learning about users. At this point there are twofold ways of learning, (i) about a concrete user, and (ii) to learn from patterns of use. For modeling this information and combined all the users aspects, dynamic user modeling techniques are necessary.

The adaptive model we propose for e-commerce (see Fig. 4), interacts with the final client due to negotiation techniques helped with the e-commerce site client interface, adapting in according to the inputs. So this structure allows agents to register the users interests and personalized pages to offer relevant information to the client. Negotiation will locate the mutually preferred deals. User's preferences are expressed to the agent that performs negotiation. On this way a flexible virtual business adapts its strategy and the site where is hosted.

3 Conclusions and Future Work

This paper has shown a brief look into Adaptive Systems and how have a real importance in e-commerce because of adaptive models are more suitable for building solutions for real-life applications, therefore this framework is a great promise for the further advancement in this ground.

We have presented an adaptive multiagent model for e-commerce that could serve as starting point for creating an e-commerce site. We plan to implement the presented model with the profiled adaptive architecture with DIMA that offers to build the adaptive structure and experiment with several adaptation mechanisms. The adaptation is mainly across the negotiation agent that will allow the SME personalize their business policies (discount, payments and so on) and also the customization one to adapt the interaction to the both principal actors, the end-user and also the SME-user.

References

1. Gil, A. B., García, F. J., Guessoum, Z. "Adaptive Agents for E-commerce Applications". In New Methods and Tools Supporting E-Commerce – Proceedings of the ZOCO Meeting. Catedral, Salamanca. 2002.
2. J. Eriksson, N. Finne and S. Jason. SICS MarketSpace, an Agent-Based Market Infrastructure. Agent Mediated Electronic Commerce. Noriega, P., Sierra, C.(Ed.). Lecture Notes in Computer Science. VOL. 1571. Springer-Verlag, pp 41-53. 1999.
3. J. García, Mª N. Moreno and J. A. Hernández. E-CoUSAL: An e-commerce architecture for small and medium enterprises. In Advances in Business Solutions. Ed. Catedral. (In press). 2002.
4. Z. Guessoum, M. Quenault and R. Durand. An Adaptive Agent Model. Proc. AIB'S, York, 2001.

Personalized Adaptation to Device Characteristics

Eelco Herder and Betsy van Dijk

Department of Computer Science
University of Twente
{e.herder, e.m.a.g.vandijk}@cs.utwente.nl

Abstract. Device characteristics, such as screen size and means of interaction, and the context in which a device is used, seriously affect the user's mental representation of an information environment and its intended use. We hypothesize that user characteristics are valuable resources for determining which information is of interest in specific situations. Our project goal is to design mechanisms for adapting navigation support to device characteristics and its context of use, thereby considering that user goals and the resulting expected navigation behavior might be subject to change.

1 Introduction

Mobile access to information is becoming more and more important. A handheld device equipped with a browser and a wireless connection provides an opportunity to connect to the Internet at any time from anywhere [2]. As we know, handheld devices are smaller than desktop devices, in order to 'fit into your pocket' more easily. This has its consequences for screen size and interaction mechanisms. Although screen resolution and input devices can be improved, interaction mechanisms for handheld devices will remain limited because of their size. Advanced adaptive presentation and adaptive navigation support techniques are said to be indispensable for making a small-screen interface more usable [1].

Hypertext systems have the ability to produce complex, richly interconnected and cross-referenced bodies of information. Because of their non-linearity, users frequently experience cognitive overload and disorientation [11]. Various navigation aids have been developed in order to provide the context needed to prevent this problem. Adaptive hypermedia systems build a model of the goals, preferences and knowledge of each individual user, and use this model throughout the interaction in order to adapt to the user's needs [1]. It has been demonstrated that navigation suggestions based on user goals as well as on navigation behavior of previous users have a positive effect on users' spatial and temporal awareness [6]. Sorting, hiding and annotating links as well as map adaptation are some example methods that may help users to find their paths in hyperspace.

It is expected that mobile Internet users primarily want to extract particular bits of information relevant to a current task. Navigation therefore requires strong support for this goal-directed activity [2]. Several systems have been developed that summarize 'regular' web pages in order to display them conveniently on a small-screen handheld device. Some of them (e.g. [2]) also provide specialized navigation facilities such as alternative link sorting schemes. Unfortunately, these systems merely make use of content information, although user characteristics are a valuable resource for determining which information may be of interest.

In contrast to handheld interfaces, virtual (three-dimensional) worlds are typically used for exploration and entertainment [3]. Although the environment still needs to offer goal-directed navigation aids, it is likely that users also will want to look around for related information they might be interested in. Ideally, such an interface should posses challenging navigation aids, should invite exploration and should be *fun* to use. Enhanced perceived fun will most likely lead to increased time spent in a virtual world [5], which is interesting from an e-commerce point of view [3].

When providing information through such different interfaces as handheld devices, virtual worlds and regular web pages – which all serve different user goals – adaptation to the environment is an important issue. This environment does not only consist of the device being used, but also of the context of use (e.g. waiting at a bus stop) [1]. Our research is aimed at determining what navigation support is needed in different situations and how user characteristics can be used for selecting the areas of interest. For this purpose, we will consider three different interfaces which all present the same information environment:
- a handheld device interface (which is typically used in a goal-directed way)
- a virtual world (which is typically used in an explorative way)

  a 'regular' web page (which is a mix of both ends of the spectrum)

For each of these interfaces, mechanisms will be developed for adapting navigation support to the richness of interaction means provided, its – possibly varying – context of use and the resulting user needs, which might be subject to change as well.

2 Adapting Navigation Aids to Device Characteristics

While navigating a hypermedia document, people use environmental cues and artificial aids such as site maps so that they can achieve their goals without getting lost. Their navigation behavior can be categorized as either goal-directed or explorative. Though mutually exclusive, these activities may become connected: exploration may result in goal-directed search activities, but the opposite direction is likely as well. These two navigation types call for different types of navigation assistance [3].

Handheld interfaces most likely invite a goal-directed kind of use – not only because of the limited interaction mechanisms of such devices, but also because of the situations in which they are used. Interfaces that are rich in interaction means, such as virtual worlds, invite mainly explorative behavior.

Online information can be accessed using such an increasing variety of equipment from almost any place. It is desirable to make use of the same information source for representation on different devices; duplicate effort could seriously tax human and machine resources [2] and, even worse, may lead to inconsistency. As stated before, navigation support should be adapted to the device characteristics and the context in which it is used.

Equally important to selecting the *right* navigation suggestions, is the *number* of suggestions that should be given to the user. An overwhelming amount of information will cause the user to have to spend considerable time scanning through, whereas too little information might not provide sufficient cues. It is obvious that the ideal number of navigation suggestions is highly dependent on the device characteristics and the context of use; users with small screens are reported to follow links less frequently than those provided with larger screens [2].

As suggested in the introduction, there is not one approach for selecting navigation aids that fits all users. When user characteristics are taken into account in the process of adapting navigation support to handheld devices, this might improve the effectiveness of such small screen interfaces [2].

Alternatively, the same user characteristics can be used for creating a virtual world that invites exploration by means of visually attractive navigation aids and embodied agents that support the users' explorative behavior, leading them to those places they are interested in [3]. Such a virtual world might be modeled after the real world (e.g. cities, buildings); it might as well be symbolic, with a topology that is based on non-geographical relations between information nodes.

3 A Pragmatic, User-Centered Approach

Past research has generally been overly technology-oriented, forgetting that the original goal was to deal with usability problems [13]. In our project *PALS Anywhere*[1] we try to overcome this problem by separating research into a cognitive track and a technological track, carried out in parallel by researchers from both disciplines.

Cognitive theory is needed for distinguishing the environmental factors that affect human cognitive task performance. There is no such comprehensive theory, so we will have to develop limited or practical theories on the influence of accepted features of cognition on navigation behavior [10], in order to obtain a foundation for the mechanisms to be incorporated in our models. The applicability of the cognitive theories and the functionality of the resulting system will be validated by usability tests.

Since there is not one single approach that is most suitable for modeling both user and environment [7], it is important to know *what* knowledge such models should express and *how* this knowledge can be obtained, before a proper choice can be made. Observations of user behavior, for example, are commonly represented as statistical data. However, it might be desirable to propagate this primary knowledge to higher-level assumptions that apply to more than one specific device or interface. Such conceptual data is typically represented by explicit, logic-based formalisms, which have strong inferential capacities [12]. Statistical models, on the other hand, are more apt

---

[1] PALS stands for Personal Assistant for onLine Services; the project is supported by the Dutch Innovative Research Program IOP-MMI. Our research partners are TNO Human Factors and the University of Utrecht, faculty of Mathematics and Computer Science.

to deal with uncertainty and the incremental acquisition of observational data [14]. At present, the only motivation for preferring a particular modeling technique is its observed success [14]. Since we aspire to find generic formalisms based on practical empirical theories, we intend to build our models of both user and environment incrementally and eclectically.

The models will be implemented in an agent-based framework that is able to reason about the interface, the user and environmental characteristics. This framework will provide the core functionality of a collaborating personal assistant [8] that learns about its users and helps them to reach their goals, either solicited or on its own initiative.

Hypermedia documents can be seen as a collection of nodes (separate chunks of information) that are richly interconnected. This structure facilitates capturing its contents and its structure in simple but powerful formalisms, such as adjacency matrices and directed graphs. These representations enable assessment of navigational patterns [9]. With the joint features of these formalisms and user modeling techniques an overlay can be derived that contains only those connections that are relevant to the user. Naturally, in the information model the various relation categories should be categorized. An obvious solution is the use of typed links, such as *analogy*, *abstraction* and *simultaneity* [4].

This overlay is not primarily meant to be shown to the user, but merely as a starting point for the navigation assistance design. Each connection category can be translated into an appropriate structuring element, for instance annotated hyperlinks and contextual menus on web pages or topological layout and landmarks in virtual worlds.

4 Research Goals

Device characteristics – such as screen size, interface design and means of interaction – and the context in which these devices are used, have their impact on the user's mental representation of an information environment. In our project we want to determine how spatial and temporal abilities are affected and what navigation aids can help users to find the information they need. An important consideration is the expected navigation behavior an interface should support, which is either goal-directed, explorative or a mix of both.

We hypothesize that adaptive hypermedia techniques are an important means for adapting an interface to the device and the situation in which it is used. Our research goal is to model user, device and context of use – the 'Trinity of Context' – in order to adapt navigation support to the continuously varying user needs.

A clever selection of navigation aids will offer the user more freedom in navigation. On tiny screens, omitting all items that are not of interest leaves more space for relevant navigation support. Analogously, virtual worlds will become more surveyable; tailored landmarks and personalized assistance in wayfinding prevent the user from getting lost.

We will evaluate our theories on three existing devices, significantly different in intended use, representation and richness of interaction means. Notwithstanding technological improvements, devices will remain different on these factors, because of the contexts of use for which they are designed. Therefore we expect the outcomes of our research will not only be of immediate use, but also be useful in designing navigation aids of novel interfaces.

References

1. Brusilovsky, P.: Adaptive Hypermedia. *User Modeling and User-Adapted Interaction 11*. Kluwer Academic Publishers, The Netherlands, 2001, pp. 87-110
2. Buyukkokten, O., Garcia-Molina, H., Paepcke, A., Winograd, T.: Power Browser: Efficient Web Browsing for PDAs. *CHI 2000 Conference Proceedings*. ACM, New York, 2000, pp. 430-437
3. Van Dijk, B., Op den Akker, R., Nijholt, A., Zwiers, J.: Navigation Assistance in Virtual Worlds. *Proceedings 2001 Informing Science Conference*. Krakow, 2001
4. Greer, J.E., Philip, T.: Guided Navigation Through Hyperspace. *Proceedings of the workshop "Intelligent Educational Systems on the World Wide Web"*. 8th World Conference of the AIED Society, Kobe, 1997, pp. 18-22
5. Hassenzahl, M., Platz, A., Burmester, M., Lehner, K.: Hedonic and Ergonomic Quality Aspects Determine a Software's Appeal. *CHI 2000 Conference Proceedings*. ACM, New York, 2000, pp. 430-437
6. Kaplan, C., Fenwick, J., Chen, J.: Adaptive Hypertext Navigation Based On User Goals and Context. *User Modeling and User-Adapted Interaction 3*. Kluwer Academic Publishers, The Netherlands, 1993, pp. 193-220
7. Kobsa, A.: Generic User Modeling Systems. *User Modeling and User-Adapted Interaction 11*. Kluwer Academic Publishers, The Netherlands, 2001, pp. 49-63
8. Maes, P.: Agents that Reduce Work and Information Overload. *Communications of the ACM 37, no. 7*. ACM, New York, 1994, pp. 31-40
9. McEneaney, J.E.: Graphic and numerical methods to assess navigation in hypertext. *International Journal of Human-Computer Studies 55*. Academic Press, London, 2001, pp. 761-786
10. Neerincx, M., Lindenberg, J., Rypkema, J., Van Besouw, S.: A practical cognitive theory of Web-navigation: Explaining age-related performance differences. *Position Paper CHI 2000 Workshop Basic Research Symposium*. ACM, The Hague, 2000
11. Park, J., Kim, J.: Effects of Contextual Navigation Aids on Browsing Diverse Web Systems. *CHI 2000 Conference Proceedings*. ACM, New York, 2000, pp. 257-271
12. Pohl, W., Nick, A.: Machine Learning and Knowledge Representation in the LaboUr Approach to User Modeling. *Proceedings of the 7th International Conference on User Modeling*. Banff, Canada, 1999, pp. 197-188
13. Schneider-Hufschmidt, M., Kuehme, T.: *Adaptive User Interfaces: principles and practice*. Elsevier Science, Amsterdam, 1993
14. Zukerman, I., Albrecht, D.W.: Predictive Statistical Models for User Modeling. *User Modeling and User-Adapted Interaction 11*. Kluwer Academic Publishers, The Netherlands, 2001, pp. 5-18

Users Modeling for Adaptive Call Centers

Ilaria Torre

Department of Computer Sciences – University of Torino
Corso Svizzera 185 - 10149 Torino (Italy)
`ilatorre@di.unito.it`

Abstract. The project described in this paper applies the principles of adaptivity to a "traditional" Call Center in order to support the Operator in the interaction with the Customer. The system uses the models of both the Customer and the Operator and builds up the stepwise answer through an adaptive workflow.

1 Introduction

The term Call Center can be used with several meanings. In this context, a Call Center is a system which manages the phone calls some human agents (operators) receive from the users (typically, the customers of a company) or perform toward them. For more precision, the first type of calls are defined as inbound calls and the second ones as outbound calls. A classic example of the former are the calls for solving a problem or getting information, while an example of the latter are the promotional calls.

The operators can play different roles and have different levels of autonomy, but the important thing is that they are human, with a voice and a *heart*. Many studies are demonstrating that lots of people prefer a *cool* contact on the other side of the line, instead of the *cold* contextual helps, mailing systems, automatic answerers, SMS, WAP and so on. As a matter of fact, the companies have been increasing the implementations of CTI (Computer Telephony Integration) solutions which are able to integrate all these channels and manage all the messages in a single workflow, where the human agent has a central role.

But besides the advantages of supporting customers with *hearty* agents and higher flexibility, such a solution represents a problem for the companies as it implies high costs of work, costs of training, frequent turnover, no standard answers, no control of the interactions, etc. The project described in this paper aims at finding out an intelligent solution for such a matter, in order to exploit the advantages of both the human and the software agents and minimize the disadvantages. As it will be shown, the idea is that of using adaptivity to manage the workflow of the answering process.

To achieve that, the Call Center System can be seen as a Three Tier Adaptive System where the function of the web server is performed by the operator: (s)he is an alive interface[1] between the customers and the system (the company). But to represent an interface, the work of the operator has to be mechanized, becoming similar to a

---

[1] An interesting example of human to human helping system, integrated in an automatic help-desk, is in [1].

software agent's work and, therefore, yielding the same benefits: interchangeability of the operators, low costs of training, standard and correct answers and sharing of knowledge about the users. But it is not enough, adding adaptivity to the workflow, other benefits can be gained: efficient routing of the calls to the most appropriate operators, adaptation of the system to the level of expertise of the operator and above all ability of the operator to adapt to the users even at their first interaction.

Given the importance of the matter, many CRM[2] vendors have been developing solutions to manage the workflow of the answering process, but no one customizes the screen views that the support systems show to the operators in the answering workflow, combining together the profiles of the customer and of the operator.

2 How the System Works: The Adaptive Work Flow

Starting from the moment the customer dials up and provides her/his identification code, or does not provide any code, as a prospect, to the moment the phone call ends, the whole process is structured as an adaptive workflow (see the figure below which presents a simplified *Use Case* of an inbound call), managed by two agents:

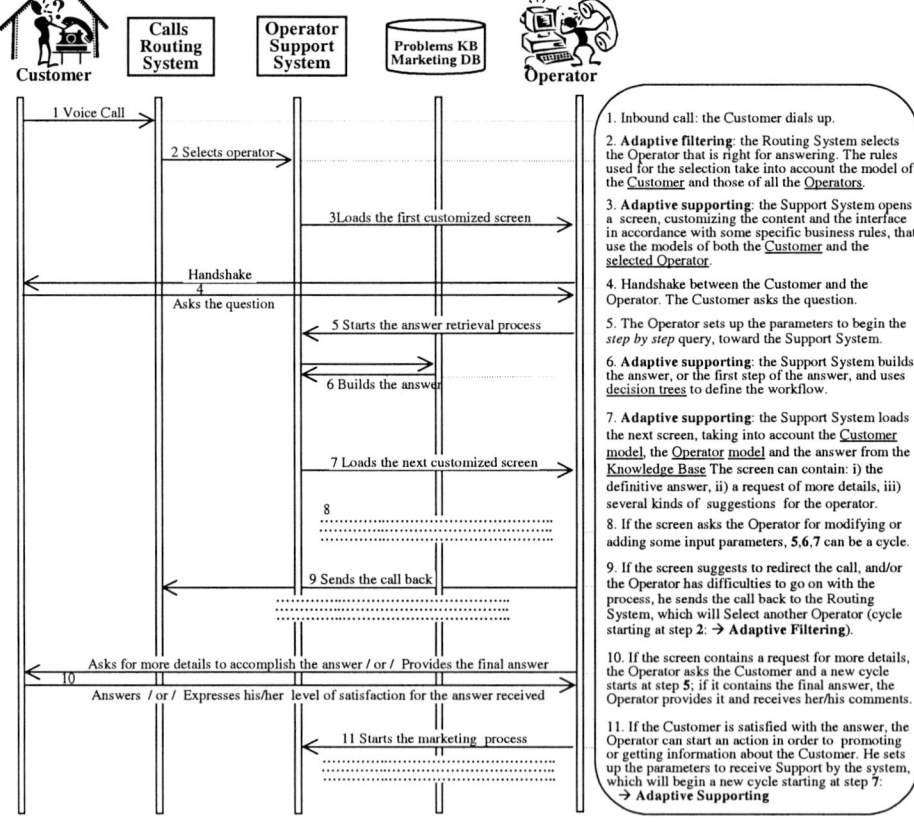

- the "Call Routing System" RS, is activated as soon as the customer dials up and is responsible for routing the calls to the most suitable operator: *adaptive filtering,*
- the "Operator Support System" SS, is involved in a more complex activity, that is the adaptive support of the operator in building the answer or in making a marketing proposition. This task is complex as it sums up together three jobs: i) support for problem solving ii) adaptation of the support to the characteristics of the user iii) adaptation of the support to the characteristics of the operator.

Finally, the component, called "Problems Knowledge Base and Marketing Data Base", represents a whole of different kinds of knowledge bases that the SS uses to support the operator in the process, in particular they contain:

- the rules that define the workflow of the interaction with the customer, build the stepwise answers and generate the screens for the operator,
- the object of the rules, namely, the knowledge regarding the solutions of technical problems, information on services and commercial propositions.

3 *Users* Modeling and Adaptation

Among the components described above, the users modeling knowledge has not been mentioned. It would have reduced the readabilities of the schema, requiring at least two new flows for almost all the actual flows of the schema. Indeed, the actions performed by each agent are preceded by: i) reasoning on the customer's model and on the models of all the operators, for the routing agent and ii) reasoning on the models of the customer and of the selected operator, for the supporting agent.

The definition of the features (of the *customer* and of the *operator*), necessary for *users* modeling, covers an important part of the project. It has been performed following the approach in [3], which provides a methodology for identifying the important user modeling dimensions (UMD) for a given system. Such a method starts from the hypothesis that the choice of the UMD depends, on the one hand, on the adaptive goals and tasks of the system, and, on the other, on the domain features. Goals and features, once decomposed in a sort of tree functional analysis, become the axes of a matrix which allows us to determine, at each point of intersection, the UMD that are essential for performing the adaptation. For example, given the goal's cascade of "improving the image of the company"→"satisfying customers"→"solving problems" →"choosing the right operator for the calling customer", etc., and the domain features "inbound call"→"technical call", etc., the features of the *customer* that have to be considered are: "customer status (open calls, churn probability, new account, etc.), "customer commercial value", "service level required (time of answer, time of solution, etc.)", etc. and the features of the *operator* that have to be taken into account are: expertise, domain knowledge, speed, previous interaction with that customer, status (free of calls and messages, with calls in queue, etc), etc.

Following such a methodology all the necessary features of the users have been identified, and organized in the respective models.

- The *Customer User Model* is distributed and divided in four parts: i) the first one contains the descriptive features. The data come from the operational systems[3] (trading and banking systems, call center, etc.) and are loaded in the DataWareHouse every night ii) a second part contains some synthetic data calculated on the basis of the previous data (e.g. risk level, commercial value, expertise, satisfaction, etc.), iii) a third part contains a ranking of the operators sorted in accordance with the degree of match with the customer's model. This sorting allows the RS to switch the calls very rapidly to the most suitable operator, iv) the fourth part consists of a daily table with the relevant actions of the day (pendent calls, request of services, etc.).
- The *Operator User Model* is divided in four parts too: i) descriptive data ii) synthetic predictive data concerning expertise, skill, domain knowledge, speed of answer, commercial and communicative ability, etc. iii) extended predictive data, regarding the domain knowledge, iv) status (free, with calls in queue, etc.)

The adaptation is performed by the RS and the SS, using different techniques. The RS selects the operator firing some rules like: "if the customer has no pendent calls and there are no successful closed calls in the day, then select the first operator in the rank of the customer's model and check her/his status". The rank is calculated as a weighed scoring. For example a high probability of churn of the customer requires that the call is routed toward operators with high expertise, domain knowledge and commercial ability: this is obtained as a weighted combination of such features in the count for the rank.

As regards the SS, it uses decision trees (see [4]) to identify, step by step, the best node toward the solution and compose the customized screen for the operator. For any answer, that the operator receives from the customer, the decision tree produces the next screen to support the operator. A typical screen contains a central frame with the answer from the knowledge base or with a new question the operator has to ask the customer in order to refine her/his problem, a set of dynamic list boxes the operator has to select communicating the system the questions/answers provided by the customer, a bar with the progress of the answer process, a customized tool bar with helps and facilities (more ore less descriptive, according with the operator's model), information about the customer and advices on how to manage her/him, according with the customer's model (commercial value, risk level, domain knowledge, etc.).

As a conclusion, the project puts together technologies from different fields, trying to unify them under the common feature of adaptivity. To reduce the complexity deriving from this, in the first phase, the system will rely on a given Call Center System - Genesys -, integrating the functions of adaptive routing and adaptive workflow.

---

[2] The CRM (Customer Relationship Management) area is very wide as it covers all the fields and applications related to the management of the customer (marketing automation systems, personalization agents, ecommerce, olap, erp and contact systems. Some of the vendors that manage, inside their enterprise product or with specific modules, the answering workflow process are: Siebel, e.Piphany, Pivotal, Remedy, Genesys, etc. (see [2] for an overview).

[3] The project aims at being general, but it actually concerns the Call Center of a Bank.

References

1. Greer, J., McCalla, G., Cooke, J., Collins, J., Kumar, V., Bishop, A., Vassileva: J.The Intelligent HelpDesk: Supporting Peer Help in a University Course. In Proc. ITS'98. LNCS 1452, Springer-Verlag, Berlin (1998) 494-503
2. International Journal of Call Centre Management, http://www.winthrop-publications.co.uk
3. I. Torre: A modular approach for user modelling. In Adaptive Hypermedia and Adaptive Web-Based Systems 2000. LNCS 1892, Springer-Verlag (2000) 414-420
4. M. Stolze, M. Ströbel: Utility-Based Decision Tree Optimization: A Framework for Adaptive Interviewing. In Proc. User Modelling 01. LNCS, Springer-Verlag (2001) 105-116

The Exploratory of Personal Assistants

Lim Tek Yong and Tang Enya Kong

School of Computer Science
University Science Malaysia
11700 Minden, Penang, Malaysia
604-6577888 ext 3002
{tylim, enyakong}@cs.usm.my

Abstract. This paper presents a perspective of using personal assistants in personalized systems, particularly in both understanding the user model and generating appropriate adaptation and response. The paper discusses the use of a personal assistant as a data input source and the expected stereotypes based on mind-sets. This is the framework of exploring a user-centered design approach to building up the intelligent personalized system.

1 Introduction

"Users using the web are only one click away from a competitor." This is the common phrase used to encourage customer relationship management on the Internet. In electronic commerce, the development of relationships with remote users is vital to maintaining customer loyalty. Computers are now acting as an agent to attract and retain users. Therefore, information technologies have transformed into relationship technology. Thanks to the advances in technology, dynamic pages can be created on the fly. Web sites have taken the steps by delivering tailored products and services on the web in order to establish, maintain and extend a customer base. They will create stable long-term relationships with repeat customers in the long run. A lot of personalization systems are being proposed by researchers and companies to cater web pages to the needs of the current users (Brusilovsky, 2001). However, some data collection is not appropriate to be used to model the user profile precisely (Kobsa, Koenemann and Pohl, 2001). Besides that, quite a number of reported researches are not supported by empirical experimentation (Chin, 2001). So, one might not able to justify whether the proposed personalized system is usable and efficient. Therefore, this paper will look into how a personalized system uses a personal assistant as a data input in the next section.

2 Personal Assistant

The acquisition task is the first step in identifying the data input for personalized systems (Kobsa, Koenemann and Pohl, 2001). There are three types of data input for personalized systems, namely data about users' characteristics, data about users' computer usage and data about users' hardware, software and physical environment.

However, the paradox of an active user and the task orientation of users should be taken into account as the users visit a site. The user should not be exposed to a lengthy registration procedures or initial interviews (e.g. in a short survey format). Therefore, some researchers suggested quizzes as entertainment and offering incentives such as free merchandise. The other possible alternative is using a dialog system integrated with current personalized systems. The area of user modeling for dialogues has recently seen a welcome and increasing use of empirical methods (Zukerman and Litman, 2001). We proposed using a personal assistant to extend the dialogue system on an electronic shopping web site.

Why are personal assistants important in the user modeling? There are two important reasons. The first reason is that the "human figure" communicating with users captures their attention and makes them alert to messages delivered to them (Reategui and Campbell, 2001). A flower shop reported an increase in sales of up to three -times after a personal assistant, who helps the user to buy flowers and bouquets, was implemented on the Internet. Perhaps personalized information is more acceptable and salient if a personal assistant instead of a system-like interface presents it. A combination of a personal assistant and an information intensive site can build customer trust and acceptance (Urban, Sultan and Qualls, 1999). Besides that, several experiments using the "wizard of oz" method have proven that users benefit from the personal assistant during their online shopping session. However, most of them were using a pre-recorded session of interaction (McBreen, Shade, Jack and Wyard, 2000), using pre-defined questions to ask the personal assistant (Urban, Sultan and Qualls, 1999) and a real human as the assistant on the web (Aberg and Shahmehri, 2001). The users were having limited options of exploring the personal assistant's capabilities.

The second reason is because the personal assistant would allow users to develop a social relationship and allow a new way of data acquisitions for the user model. De Angeli, Johnson and Coventry (2001) have found that users would treat the personal assistant as a new relationship. Their research has shown some understanding of social rules driving the interaction between a user and a chatterbot. One of the most important processes in the formation and maintenance of a relationship is that of self-disclosure (the act of revealing private and personal information to others). It is a clear sign of trust and commitment to the relationship. In human-relationship and in Internet Chat Rooms, self-disclosure is intended to be a mutual process (refer to Example 1). Both parties are required to exchange intimate and personal details as well as feelings with each other.

Example 1. A typical self-disclosure in Internet chat room.
A: Hello
B: Hi there!
A: a/s/l please.
B: 25 f Malaysia. how about u?
A: me 26 m Singapore.
B: What are u looking 4?
A: looking 4 new friendship.
...

However, most chatterbots only simulate conversation without utilizing any knowledge about the users and their actual behavior during the online session. Secondly, they are not able to serve as a medium for customer advice if they are not able to interpret the individual dialog situation and allow goal-directed strategies to be pursued. Therefore, some exploration needed to be carried out to determine the real-time of user chatting with a personal assistant while searching the online shopping website. Besides that, we need to know how far the self-disclosure can be used as data input for a personalized system.

In order to explore the effect of a personal assistant, we are using the fixed stereotypes as the first step for representation references rather than having none. Ralph's (2000) preliminary study has shown that chatterbots with a sophisticated repertoire of conversational skills will fail to be more than entertaining, if the personal assistant does not treat a user as an individual having specific needs, preferences, etc. Therefore, an understanding of different user types will be beneficial to help developing an acceptable and believable personal assistant. Moe (2001) has identified four types of visitors on the Internet. They are

1. Directed-purchase visits. This user is ready to purchase right away.
2. Search and deliberation visits. This user is researching the information and eventually intends to buy.
3. Hedonic-browsing visits. This user is doing electronic window-shopping, that is shopping for pleasure or recreation.
4. Knowledge-building visits. This user is engaged in exploration to know more about the marketplace – a pursuit that may affect long-term shopping.

In the old-times, experienced sales people learned to distinguish between shoppers based on their in-store behavior. Sales people are more helpful when shoppers appear to be very focused in looking for a specific product. However, they are more likely to ignore shoppers who are merely just "window-shopping". In an electronic world, some reports argued that the behavior of users would be changed since most electronic marketplaces provide a more convenient way for goal-directed users to search for a product (Wind and Mahajan, 2001; De Kare-Silver, 2000). Now, the question is "Would the personal assistant be more helpful for users who are goal-directed, and be more sociable for users with exploratory behavior or vice-versa?" A user-centered design can be used to refine basic assumptions and the whole personalized system can be easily redesigned if needed (Petrelli, Angeli and Convertino, 1999). The reason is that their study pointed out some unpredicted situations and confirmed some working hypotheses.

3 Mind-Set

The concept of mind-set was originally suggested by Wurtzberg motivational psychologists (Kulpe, 1904, cited in Gollwitzer, 1996). A mind-set refers to a "specific cognitive orientation", imbued with distinct and unique features and can be of different types. Each mind-set is associated with different thought contents and different modes of information processing (Heckhausen & Gollwitzer, 1987). A mind-set can divided in two types: goal-directed mind-sets and experiential mind-sets.

Goal-oriented mind-sets consist of both deliberative and implemental mind-sets. A deliberative mind-set refers to a cognitive orientation where the consumer is intent on collecting and processing information, and is common in the problem-identification, information search, and decision-making stages of consumer behavior. On the other hand, an implemental mind-set refers to an action-focused, cognitive orientation that occurs after the decision has been made, and serves to facilitate smooth action execution for goal attainment.

An exploratory mind-set refers to a consumer's cognitive orientation to encounter new experiences and to satisfy his or her curiosity. On the other hand, experiential mind-set is the hedonic mind-set where the individual de-emphasizes cognitions, and focuses instead on the sensory elements of experience.

Security and privacy infrastructures should be used that both protect user data against possible attacks and allow users to remain highly anonymous with respect to the personalized system while still enjoying personalization. One of the suggested approaches is to provide comprehensive and intelligible advance notice to users about all the data that is to be collected, processed and transferred. As a result, this will increase users' trust in the application and is mandated by virtually all privacy laws. Furthermore, users can personalize ("opt-in") the processing of their data in voluntary consent.

4 Ongoing Work

This paper presents a perspective of using a personal assistant in personalized systems, particularly in both understanding the user model and generating appropriate adaptation and response. The research question is
1. What types of data input can be collected from first-time visitors, returning visitors, infrequent and frequent user needs when using a personal assistant?
2. What types of adaptation are needed for personal assistants when encountering first-time visitors, returning visitors, infrequent and frequent user needs?

At present, Moe (2001) proposed a typology of shopping strategies based on the user's click-stream in a website. Her result showed that each user can be classified into the four mind-set categories based on a series of click-streams. Our research is to investigate the user interaction, based on mind-set, with the personal assistant when visiting/shopping on a website. The first step is to identify the data input that can be used as a proper indication of the type of users. We are planning to build a prototype to simulate the personal assistant on a shopping website. Then we will perform online focus group sessions to collect the experiment data. The second step is to identify types of adaptation that are needed to support all these users. In this stage, we will prepare adaptation materials that are suitable for each type of users. Then we will perform a quantitative study online to collect the experiment data.

Therefore, our research is focused to comprehend users' acceptance of and reactions to the introduction of human characteristics in user interfaces. Defining the users' characteristics that may affect their acceptance of personal assistants and helping predict their behavior during the interaction is a major challenge. Before such adaptation can be designed and models can be developed, researchers must first understand the underlying interaction patterns of the users, and how to identify different types of behavior. This paper is a first step in that direction.

To conclude, creativity can support the different styles of presenting information to users. For example, a portal can create a simple style if the users are goal-directed searchers. They can create a more elaborate and artistic style if the users are experiential surfers. Therefore, a personalized system with personal assistant has to be intelligent enough to support all these users.

References

1. Aberg, J. and Shahmehri, N. (2001) An Empirical Study of Human Web Assistants: Implications for User Support in Web Information Systems. *Proceedings of SIGCHI '01* Seatle, WA, USA.
2. Brusilovsky, P. (2001) Adaptive Hypermedia. *Journal of User Modeling and User-Adapted Interaction,* 11, 87-110.
3. Chin, D.N. (2001) Empirical Evaluation of User Models and User-Adapted Systems. *Journal of User Modeling and User-Adapted Interaction,* 11, 181-194.
4. De Angeli, A, Johnson, G.I. and Coventry, L. (2001) The unfriendly user: exploring social reactions to chatterbots. In M.G. Helander, H.M. Kalid, T. Ming Po (Eds). Proceedings of the *International Conference oh Affective Human Factor Design*, Asean Academic Press, pp. 467-474.
5. De Angeli, A., Lynch, P. and Johnson G. (2001) Personifying the e-market: A framework for social agents. *Proceedings of Interact 2001 Conference on Human-Computer Interaction*, Tokyo, Japan, July 9-13, 2001.
6. De Kare-Silver, M. (2000) *E-Shock 2000 The electronic shopping revolution: strategies for retailers and manufacturers.* Macmillan Press Ltd, London.
7. Gollwitzer, P.M. (1996) "the Volitional Benefits of Planning." In Gollwitzer, P.M. and Bargh, J. A. (eds), *The Psychology of Action: Linking Cognition and Motivation to Behavior* (pp. 287-312) New York: Guilford Press.
8. Heckhausen, H. and Gollwitzer, P.M. (1987). "Thought Contents and Cognitive Functioning in Motivational versus Volitional States of Mind." *Motivation and Emotion*, 11, 101-120.
9. Kobsa, A., Koenemann, J. and Pohl, W. (2001) Personalized Hypermedia Presentation Techniques for Improving Online Customer Relationship. *The Knowledge Engineering Review* 16(2), 111-155.
10. McBreen, H., Shade, P., Jack, M. and Wyard, P. (2000) Experimental Assessment of the Effectiveness of Synthetic Personae for Multi-Modal E-Retail Applications. *Proceedings of Agents 2000* Barcelona Spain.
11. Moe, W.W. (2001) Buying, Searching or Browsing: Differentiating between Online Shoppers Using In-Store Navigational Clickstream. *Journal of Consumer Psychology* (forthcoming)
12. Petrelli, D., De Angeli, A. and Convertino (1999) A User-Centered Approach to User Modeling. *Proceedings of the Seventh International Conference,UM'99*, 255-264
13. Reategui, E. and Campbell, J.A. (2001) The role of personified Agents in Recommendation Delivery. *Proceedings of 2001 ACM SIGIR Workshop on Recommender Systems*, New Orleans, LA, USA.
14. Urban, G. L., Sultan, F. and Qualls, W. (1999) Design and Evaluation of A Trust Based Advisor on the Internet. MIT http://ebusiness.mit.edu/research/papers/Urban.pdf
15. Wahlster, W. (2001) Virtual Sales Agents for Electronic Commerce. *ACAI 2001* Prague.
16. Wind, J. and Mahajan, V. (2001) *Digital Marketing: Global Strategies From the World's Leading Experts*, John Wiley & Sons, Inc., New York.
17. Zukerman, I and Litman, D. (2001) Natural Language Processing and User Modeling: Synergies and Limitations. *Journal of User Modeling and User-Adapted Interaction,* 11, 129-158.

Author Index

Aaronson, J. 1
Abrahão, S.A. 358
Abraham, D. 456
Aedo, I. 317, 419
Aerts, A. 388
Ardissono, L. 14
Arjona, J.L. 24
Armstrong, R. 428
Aroyo, L. 122
Arruabarrena, R. 363
Ashman, H. 580
Avesani, P. 462

Bailey, C. 36
Bajuelos, a.A.L. 90
Barbosa, S.D.J. 274
Barra, M. 47
Baudisch, P. 58
Beck, R.E. 488
Behrendt, W. 368
Bental, D. 492
Berka, T. 368
Beschoren, K. 338
Bieliková, M. 586
Bontcheva, K. 69
Boticario, J.G. 143
Brailsford, T. 580
Bra, P. De 388
Bravo, C. 560
Breda, A.M. 90
Brueckner, L. 58
Bruen, C. 100
Brunstein, A. 372
Bry, F. 472
Buendía, F. 476
Bueno, D. 376, 480

Calvi, L. 79
Carmona, C. 376, 480
Carrara, P. 484
Carro, R.M. 90
Casanova, M.A. 274
Cassel, L.N. 488
Castillo, G. 90
Cawsey, A. 492

Chen, G.-L. 164
Chen, J. 164
Choi, P. 531
Cini, A. 497
Cisternino, A. 392
Coelho, T.A.S. 274
Coffey, J.W. 380
Conejo, R. 376, 480
Conlan, O. 100
Console, L. 112
Corchuelo, R. 24
Correa, J.S. 338
Cotter, P. 328
Cristea, A. 79, 122
Czarkowski, M. 384

David, A.A. 480
Decouchant, D. 535
Dempster, E. 492
Díaz, P. 317, 419, 476
Dijk, B. van 598
Dolog, P. 586

Esuli, A. 392

Favela, J. 535
Fernández de Arriba, M. 501
Fogli, D. 484
Fons, J. 358
Frasincar, F. 133
Fresta, G. 484
Funk, P. 436

Gams, E. 368
García-Cabrera, L. 284
García, E. 317
García, F. 592
García, F.J. 505
Gargan, M. 100
Gaudioso, E. 143
Gensel, J. 444
Gentile, E. 432
Gil, A.B. 505, 592
Gioria, S. 112
Goel, M. 510
González, J. 264

González, M. 358
González Rodríguez, M. 564
Gouli, E. 153
Goy, A. 14
Grigoriadou, M. 153
Grimsley, M. 397
Guessoum, Z. 592
Gutiérrez, J. 363
Gu, X.-D. 164
Guzman, E. 376

Hall, W. 36, 428
Hasegawa, S. 518
Healey, J. 401
Henze, N. 174
Herder, E. 598
Hosn, R. 401
Houben, G.-J. 133
Hübscher, R. 184
Hüttenhain, R. 572

Jameson, A. 193

Kanawati, R. 406
Kashihara, A. 518
Kay, J. 203, 384
Kim, Y. 522
Klemke, R. 572
Koch, N. 213
Kong, T.E. 608
Koychev, I. 223
Kraus, M. 472
Kraus, S. 527
Kravcik, M. 572
Krems, J.F. 372
Kröner, A. 527
Kukulenz, D. 233
Kummerfeld, B. 203
Kurhila, J. 242
Kushmerick, N. 514

Langweg, H. 440
Lauder, P. 203
Lee, M. 531
Lieberman, H. 2, 253
Liu, H. 2, 253
López Brugos, J.A. 501
López-Cuadrado, J. 363
López Pérez, B. 564
Lombardi, I. 112

Lucena, C.J.P. de 274

Ma, W.-Y. 164
Macías, M. 264
MacKinnon, L. 492
Madeira, M. 338
Maes, S.H. 401
Maglio, P. 47
Maier, P. 428
Malek, M. 406
Martens, A. 539
Martin, B. 296, 543
Martínez-Enríquez, A.M. 535
Martin, H. 444
Martinovska, C. 411
Martins, L.C. 274
Marwick, D. 492
Massa, P. 462
Masthoff, J. 415
McGowan, J.P. 514
Medina-Medina, N. 284
Meehan, A. 397
Miettinen, M. 242
Millard, D.E. 36
Mitrovic, A. 296, 543
Mitsuhara, H. 547
Mizzaro, S. 306
Montero, S. 419
Moore, A. 580
Morán, A.L. 535
Mun, H. 424
Mussio, P. 484

Nakai, Y. 452
Naumann, A. 372
Negro, A. 47
Nejdl, W. 174
Ng, M.H. 428
Ng, W. 551
Nokelainen, P. 242
Nori, M. 462

Ochi, Y. 547
Ok, S. 424, 522
Oliveira, J.P.M. de 338
Ortega, M. 560

Pacey, D. 492
Pacini, G. 392
Papanikolaou, K. 153
Paredes, P. 556

Parets-Llorca, J. 284
Pastor, O. 358
Paternò, F. 505
Paule Ruíz, M.P 564
Pérez Pérez, J.R. 564
Pérez, T.A. 363
Pesin, L. 572
Petrone, G. 14
Plantamura, P. 432
Puntambekar, S. 184

Redondo, M.A. 560
Reich, S. 368
Rodriguez, P. 556
Rodríguez-Fortiz, M.J. 284
Roselli, T. 432
Rossano, V. 432
Ruiz, A. 24

Sánchez, F. 264
Saponaro, V. 432
Sarkar, S. 510
Scarano, V. 47
Schwarzkopf, E. 193
Segnan, M. 14
Selker, T. 253
Sicilia, M.-Á. 317
Signore, O. 568
Silveira, R.A. 466
Simi, M. 392
Smits, D. 388
Smyth, B. 328, 514
Sollenborn, M. 436
Souto, M.A.M. 338
Spalka, A. 440
Specht, M. 572
Stash, N. 388
Stewart, C. 580
Sunderam, A.V. 348
Surano, V. 112

Susi, A. 462

Tasso, C. 306
Tirri, H. 242
Toppano, E. 576
Torasso, P. 14
Toro, M. 24
Torre, I. 112, 603
Toyoda, J. 518
Tsaban, L. 527

Uhrmacher, A.M. 539

Vadillo, J.A. 363
Valdeni de Lima, J. 497
Verdejo, M.F. 560
Verdin, R. 338
Vicari, R.M. 338, 466
Villanova-Oliver, M. 444

Wade, V. 100
Wahlster, W. 12
Wainer, R. 338
Waniek, J. 372
Warpechowski, M. 338
Weal, M.J. 36
Weber, G. 448
Weibelzahl, S. 448
Williams, H. 492
Wirsing, M. 213
Wolz, U. 488
Woo, Y. 424, 522, 531

Yacef, K. 456
Yamada, S. 452
Yano, Y. 547
Yau, J. 551
Yong, L.T. 608

Zakaria, M.R. 580
Zanella, R. 338

Lecture Notes in Computer Science

For information about Vols. 1–2266
please contact your bookseller or Springer-Verlag

Vol. 2267: M. Cerioli, G. Reggio (Eds.), Recent Trends in Algebraic Development Techniques. Proceedings, 2001. X, 345 pages. 2001.

Vol. 2268: E.F. Deprettere, J. Teich, S. Vassiliadis (Eds.), Embedded Processor Design Challenges. VIII, 327 pages. 2002.

Vol. 2269: S. Diehl (Ed.), Software Visualization. Proceedings, 2001. VIII, 405 pages. 2002.

Vol. 2270: M. Pflanz, On-line Error Detection and Fast Recover Techniques for Dependable Embedded Processors. XII, 126 pages. 2002.

Vol. 2271: B. Preneel (Ed.), Topics in Cryptology – CT-RSA 2002. Proceedings, 2002. X, 311 pages. 2002.

Vol. 2272: D. Bert, J.P. Bowen, M.C. Henson, K. Robinson (Eds.), ZB 2002: Formal Specification and Development in Z and B. Proceedings, 2002. XII, 535 pages. 2002.

Vol. 2273: A.R. Coden, E.W. Brown, S. Srinivasan (Eds.), Information Retrieval Techniques for Speech Applications. XI, 109 pages. 2002.

Vol. 2274: D. Naccache, P. Paillier (Eds.), Public Key Cryptography. Proceedings, 2002. XI, 385 pages. 2002.

Vol. 2275: N.R. Pal, M. Sugeno (Eds.), Advances in Soft Computing – AFSS 2002. Proceedings, 2002. XVI, 536 pages. 2002. (Subseries LNAI).

Vol. 2276: A. Gelbukh (Ed.), Computational Linguistics and Intelligent Text Processing. Proceedings, 2002. XIII, 444 pages. 2002.

Vol. 2277: P. Callaghan, Z. Luo, J. McKinna, R. Pollack (Eds.), Types for Proofs and Programs. Proceedings, 2000. VIII, 243 pages. 2002.

Vol. 2278: J.A. Foster, E. Lutton, J. Miller, C. Ryan, A.G.B. Tettamanzi (Eds.), Genetic Programming. Proceedings, 2002. XI, 337 pages. 2002.

Vol. 2279: S. Cagnoni, J. Gottlieb, E. Hart, M. Middendorf, G.R. Raidl (Eds.), Applications of Evolutionary Computing. Proceedings, 2002. XIII, 344 pages. 2002.

Vol. 2280: J.P. Katoen, P. Stevens (Eds.), Tools and Algorithms for the Construction and Analysis of Systems. Proceedings, 2002. XIII, 482 pages. 2002.

Vol. 2281: S. Arikawa, A. Shinohara (Eds.), Progress in Discovery Science. XIV, 684 pages. 2002. (Subseries LNAI).

Vol. 2282: D. Ursino, Extraction and Exploitation of Intensional Knowledge from Heterogeneous Information Sources. XXVI, 289 pages. 2002.

Vol. 2283: T. Nipkow, L.C. Paulson, M. Wenzel, Isabelle/HOL. XIII, 218 pages. 2002.

Vol. 2284: T. Eiter, K.-D. Schewe (Eds.), Foundations of Information and Knowledge Systems. Proceedings, 2002. X, 289 pages. 2002.

Vol. 2285: H. Alt, A. Ferreira (Eds.), STACS 2002. Proceedings, 2002. XIV, 660 pages. 2002.

Vol. 2286: S. Rajsbaum (Ed.), LATIN 2002: Theoretical Informatics. Proceedings, 2002. XIII, 630 pages. 2002.

Vol. 2287: C.S. Jensen, K.G. Jeffery, J. Pokorny, Saltenis, E. Bertino, K. Böhm, M. Jarke (Eds.), Advances in Database Technology – EDBT 2002. Proceedings, 2002. XVI, 776 pages. 2002.

Vol. 2288: K. Kim (Ed.), Information Security and Cryptology – ICISC 2001. Proceedings, 2001. XIII, 457 pages. 2002.

Vol. 2289: C.J. Tomlin, M.R. Greenstreet (Eds.), Hybrid Systems: Computation and Control. Proceedings, 2002. XIII, 480 pages. 2002.

Vol. 2290: F. van der Linden (Ed.), Software Product-Family Engineering. Proceedings, 2001. X, 417 pages. 2002.

Vol. 2291: F. Crestani, M. Girolami, C.J. van Rijsbergen (Eds.), Advances in Information Retrieval. Proceedings, 2002. XIII, 363 pages. 2002.

Vol. 2292: G.B. Khosrovshahi, A. Shokoufandeh, A. Shokrollahi (Eds.), Theoretical Aspects of Computer Science. IX, 221 pages. 2002.

Vol. 2293: J. Renz, Qualitative Spatial Reasoning with Topological Information. XVI, 207 pages. 2002. (Subseries LNAI).

Vol. 2294: A. Cortesi (Ed.), Verification, Model Checking, and Abstract Interpretation. Proceedings, 2002. VIII, 331 pages. 2002.

Vol. 2295: W. Kuich, G. Rozenberg, A. Salomaa (Eds.), Developments in Language Theory. Proceedings, 2001. IX, 389 pages. 2002.

Vol. 2296: B. Dunin-Kęplicz, E. Nawarecki (Eds.), From Theory to Practice in Multi-Agent Systems. Proceedings, 2001. IX, 341 pages. 2002. (Subseries LNAI).

Vol. 2297: R. Backhouse, R. Crole, J. Gibbons (Eds.), Algebraic and Coalgebraic Methods in the Mathematics of Program Construction. Proceedings, 2000. XIV, 387 pages. 2002.

Vol. 2298: I. Wachsmuth, T. Sowa (Eds.), Gesture and Language in Human-Computer Interaction. Proceedings, 2001. XI, 323 pages. 2002. (Subseries LNAI).

Vol. 2299: H. Schmeck, T. Ungerer, L. Wolf (Eds.), Trends in Network and Pervasive Computing – ARCS 2002. Proceedings, 2002. XIV, 287 pages. 2002.

Vol. 2300: W. Brauer, H. Ehrig, J. Karhumäki, A. Salomaa (Eds.), Formal and Natural Computing. XXXVI, 431 pages. 2002.

Vol. 2301: A. Braquelaire, J.-O. Lachaud, A. Vialard (Eds.), Discrete Geometry for Computer Imagery. Proceedings, 2002. XI, 439 pages. 2002.

Vol. 2302: C. Schulte, Programming Constraint Services. XII, 176 pages. 2002. (Subseries LNAI).

Vol. 2303: M. Nielsen, U. Engberg (Eds.), Foundations of Software Science and Computation Structures. Proceedings, 2002. XIII, 435 pages. 2002.

Vol. 2304: R.N. Horspool (Ed.), Compiler Construction. Proceedings, 2002. XI, 343 pages. 2002.

Vol. 2305: D. Le Métayer (Ed.), Programming Languages and Systems. Proceedings, 2002. XII, 331 pages. 2002.

Vol. 2306: R.-D. Kutsche, H. Weber (Eds.), Fundamental Approaches to Software Engineering. Proceedings, 2002. XIII, 341 pages. 2002.

Vol. 2307: C. Zhang, S. Zhang, Association Rule Mining. XII, 238 pages. 2002. (Subseries LNAI).

Vol. 2308: I.P. Vlahavas, C.D. Spyropoulos (Eds.), Methods and Applications of Artificial Intelligence. Proceedings, 2002. XIV, 514 pages. 2002. (Subseries LNAI).

Vol. 2309: A. Armando (Ed.), Frontiers of Combining Systems. Proceedings, 2002. VIII, 255 pages. 2002. (Subseries LNAI).

Vol. 2310: P. Collet, C. Fonlupt, J.-K. Hao, E. Lutton, M. Schoenauer (Eds.), Artificial Evolution. Proceedings, 2001. XI, 375 pages. 2002.

Vol. 2311: D. Bustard, W. Liu, R. Sterritt (Eds.), SoftWare 2002: Computing in an Imperfect World. Proceedings, 2002. XI, 359 pages. 2002.

Vol. 2312: T. Arts, M. Mohnen (Eds.), Implementation of Functional Languages. Proceedings, 2001. VII, 187 pages. 2002.

Vol. 2313: C.A. Coello Coello, A. de Albornoz, L.E. Sucar, O.Cairó Battistutti (Eds.), MICAI 2002: Advances in Artificial Intelligence. Proceedings, 2002. XIII, 548 pages. 2002. (Subseries LNAI).

Vol. 2314: S.-K. Chang, Z. Chen, S.-Y. Lee (Eds.), Recent Advances in Visual Information Systems. Proceedings, 2002. XI, 323 pages. 2002.

Vol. 2315: F. Arhab, C. Talcott (Eds.), Coordination Models and Languages. Proceedings, 2002. XI, 406 pages. 2002.

Vol. 2316: J. Domingo-Ferrer (Ed.), Inference Control in Statistical Databases. VIII, 231 pages. 2002.

Vol. 2317: M. Hegarty, B. Meyer, N. Hari Narayanan (Eds.), Diagrammatic Representation and Inference. Proceedings, 2002. XIV, 362 pages. 2002. (Subseries LNAI).

Vol. 2318: D. Bošnački, S. Leue (Eds.), Model Checking Software. Proceedings, 2002. X, 259 pages. 2002.

Vol. 2319: C. Gacek (Ed.), Software Reuse: Methods, Techniques, and Tools. Proceedings, 2002. XI, 353 pages. 2002.

Vol.2320: T. Sander (Ed.), Security and Privacy in Digital Rights Management. Proceedings, 2001. X, 245 pages. 2002.

Vol. 2322: V. Mařík, O. Štěpánková, H. Krautwurmová, M. Luck (Eds.), Multi-Agent Systems and Applications II. Proceedings, 2001. XII, 377 pages. 2002. (Subseries LNAI).

Vol. 2323: À. Frohner (Ed.), Object-Oriented Technology. Proceedings, 2001. IX, 225 pages. 2002.

Vol. 2324: T. Field, P.G. Harrison, J. Bradley, U. Harder (Eds.), Computer Performance Evaluation. Proceedings, 2002. XI, 349 pages. 2002.

Vol 2326: D. Grigoras, A. Nicolau, B. Toursel, B. Folliot (Eds.), Advanced Environments, Tools, and Applications for Cluster Computing. Proceedings, 2001. XIII, 321 pages. 2002.

Vol. 2327: H.P. Zima, K. Joe, M. Sato, Y. Seo, M. Shimasaki (Eds.), High Performance Computing. Proceedings, 2002. XV, 564 pages. 2002.

Vol. 2329: P.M.A. Sloot, C.J.K. Tan, J.J. Dongarra, A.G. Hoekstra (Eds.), Computational Science – ICCS 2002. Proceedings, Part I. XLI, 1095 pages. 2002.

Vol. 2330: P.M.A. Sloot, C.J.K. Tan, J.J. Dongarra, A.G. Hoekstra (Eds.), Computational Science – ICCS 2002. Proceedings, Part II. XLI, 1115 pages. 2002.

Vol. 2331: P.M.A. Sloot, C.J.K. Tan, J.J. Dongarra, A.G. Hoekstra (Eds.), Computational Science – ICCS 2002. Proceedings, Part III. XLI, 1227 pages. 2002.

Vol. 2332: L. Knudsen (Ed.), Advances in Cryptology – EUROCRYPT 2002. Proceedings, 2002. XII, 547 pages. 2002.

Vol. 2334: G. Carle, M. Zitterbart (Eds.), Protocols for High Speed Networks. Proceedings, 2002. X, 267 pages. 2002.

Vol. 2335: M. Butler, L. Petre, K. Sere (Eds.), Integrated Formal Methods. Proceedings, 2002. X, 401 pages. 2002.

Vol. 2336: M.-S. Chen, P.S. Yu, B. Liu (Eds.), Advances in Knowledge Discovery and Data Mining. Proceedings, 2002. XIII, 568 pages. 2002. (Subseries LNAI).

Vol. 2337: W.J. Cook, A.S. Schulz (Eds.), Integer Programming and Combinatorial Optimization. Proceedings, 2002. XI, 487 pages. 2002.

Vol. 2338: R. Cohen, B. Spencer (Eds.), Advances in Artificial Intelligence. Proceedings, 2002. X, 197 pages. 2002. (Subseries LNAI).

Vol. 2345: E. Gregori, M. Conti, A.T. Campbell, G. Omidyar, M. Zukerman (Eds.), NETWORKING 2002. Proceedings, 2002. XXVI, 1256 pages. 2002.

Vol. 2347: P. De Bra, P. Brusilovsky, R. Conejo (Eds.), Adaptive Hypermedia and Adaptive Web-Based Systems. Proceedings, 2002. XV, 615 pages. 2002.

Vol. 2350: A. Heyden, G. Sparr, M. Nielsen, P. Johansen (Eds.), Computer Vision – ECCV 2002. Proceedings, Part I. XXVIII, 817 pages. 2002.

Vol. 2351: A. Heyden, G. Sparr, M. Nielsen, P. Johansen (Eds.), Computer Vision – ECCV 2002. Proceedings, Part II. XXVIII, 903 pages. 2002.

Vol. 2352: A. Heyden, G. Sparr, M. Nielsen, P. Johansen (Eds.), Computer Vision – ECCV 2002. Proceedings, Part III. XXVIII, 919 pages. 2002.

Vol. 2353: A. Heyden, G. Sparr, M. Nielsen, P. Johansen (Eds.), Computer Vision – ECCV 2002. Proceedings, Part IV. XXVIII, 841 pages. 2002.

Vol. 2359: M. Tistarelli, J. Bigun, A.K. Jain (Eds.), Biometric Authentication. Proceedings, 2002. XII, 373 pages. 2002.